ANT COLONY OPTIMIZATION - METHODS AND APPLICATIONS

Edited by **Avi Ostfeld**

Ant Colony Optimization - Methods and Applications
Edited by Avi Ostfeld

Published by InTech

Janeza Trdine 9, 51000 Rijeka, Croatia

Publishing Process Manager Iva Lipovic

Technical Editor Teodora Smiljanic

Cover Designer InTech Design Team

Additional hard copies can be obtained from orders@intechopen.com

Ant Colony Optimization - Methods and Applications, Edited by Avi Ostfeld
p. cm.
ISBN 978-953-307-157-2

For EU product safety concerns:
IN TECH d.o.o., Prolaz Marije Krucifikse Kozulić 3, 51000 Rijeka, Croatia,
info@intechopen.com or visit our website at intechopen.com.

Meet the editor

Avi Ostfeld, D.Sc., P.E., D.WRE (www.technion.ac.il/~avi/avi.htm) is an Associate Professor at the Faculty of Civil and Environmental Engineering at the Technion – Israel Institute of Technology, and the Editor in Chief of the Journal of Water Resources Planning and Management Division, ASCE. Dr. Ostfeld was a Senior Engineer and Project Manager at TAHAL – Consulting Engineers Ltd. in Tel – Aviv from 1997 to 2000; a Research Associate at the Department of Civil Engineering, the University of Arizona, Tucson, AZ, from 1996 to 1997; and a Research Associate at the Technion Water Research Institute from 1994 to 1996. During 2008/2009 he spent sabbaticals as Visiting Professor at the University of Illinois at Urbana Champaign and at the University of Kyoto. Dr. Ostfeld research activities are in the fields of water resources systems, hydrology, and in particular in the area of water distribution systems optimization using evolutionary computation: water distribution systems security, optimal design and operation of water distribution systems, and integrating water quality and reliability into water distribution systems management and control.

Contents

Preface

Invented by Marco Dorigo in 1992, Ant Colony Optimization (ACO) is a meta-heuristic stochastic combinatorial computational discipline inspired by the behavior of ant colonies which belong to a family of meta-heuristic stochastic methodologies such as simulated annealing, Tabu search and genetic algorithms. It is an iterative method in which populations of ants act as agents that construct bundles of candidate solutions, where the entire bundle construction process is probabilistically guided by heuristic imitation of ants' behavior, tailor-made to the characteristics of a given problem. Since its invention ACO was successfully applied to a broad range of NP hard problems such as the traveling salesman problem (TSP) or the quadratic assignment problem (QAP), and is increasingly gaining interest for solving real life engineering and scientific problems.

This book covers state of the art methods and applications of ant colony optimization algorithms. It incorporates twenty chapters divided into two parts: methods (nine chapters) and applications (eleven chapters). New methods, such as multi colony ant algorithms based upon a new pheromone arithmetic crossover and a repulsive operator, as well as a diversity of engineering and science applications from transportation, water resources, electrical and computer science disciplines are presented. The following is a list of the chapter's titles and authors, and a brief description of their contents.

Acknowledgements

I wish to express my deep gratitude to all the contributing authors for taking the time and efforts to prepare their comprehensive chapters, and to acknowledge Ms. Iva Lipovic, InTech Publishing Process Manager, for her remarkable, kind and professional assistance throughout the entire preparation process of this book.

Avi Ostfeld
Haifa,
Israel

Part 1

Methods

1

Multi-Colony Ant Algorithm

Enxiu Chen[1] and Xiyu Liu[2]
[1]*School of Business Administration, Shandong Institute of Commerce and Technology, Jinan, Shandong;*
[2]*School of Management & Economics, Shandong Normal University, Jinan, Shandong, China*

1. Introduction

The first ant colony optimization (ACO) called ant system was inspired through studying of the behavior of ants in 1991 by Macro Dorigo and co-workers [1]. An ant colony is highly organized, in which one interacting with others through pheromone in perfect harmony. Optimization problems can be solved through simulating ant's behaviors. Since the first ant system algorithm was proposed, there is a lot of development in ACO. In ant colony system algorithm, local pheromone is used for ants to search optimum result. However, high magnitude of computing is its deficiency and sometimes it is inefficient. Thomas Stützle et al. introduced MAX-MIN Ant System (MMAS) [2] in 2000. It is one of the best algorithms of ACO. It limits total pheromone in every trip or sub-union to avoid local convergence. However, the limitation of pheromone slows down convergence rate in MMAS.

In optimization algorithm, it is well known that when local optimum solution is searched out or ants arrive at stagnating state, algorithm may be no longer searching the global best optimum value. According to our limited knowledge, only Jun Ouyang et al [3] proposed an improved ant colony system algorithm for multi-colony ant systems. In their algorithms, when ants arrived at local optimum solution, pheromone will be decreased in order to make algorithm escaping from the local optimum solution.

When ants arrived at local optimum solution, or at stagnating state, it would not converge at the global best optimum solution. In this paper, a modified algorithm, multi-colony ant system based on a pheromone arithmetic crossover and a repulsive operator, is proposed to avoid such stagnating state. In this algorithm, firstly several colonies of ant system are created, and then they perform iterating and updating their pheromone arrays respectively until one ant colony system reaches its local optimum solution. Every ant colony system owns its pheromone array and parameters and records its local optimum solution. Furthermore, once a ant colony system arrives at its local optimum solution, it updates its local optimum solution and sends this solution to global best-found center. Thirdly, when an old ant colony system is chosen according to elimination rules, it will be destroyed and reinitialized through application of the pheromone arithmetic crossover and the repulsive operator based on several global best-so-far optimum solutions. The whole algorithm implements iterations until global best optimum solution is searched out. The following sections will introduce some concepts and rules of this multi-colony ant system.

This paper is organized as follows. Section II briefly explains the basic ACO algorithm and its main variant MMAS we use as a basis for multi-colony ant algorithm. In Section III we describe detailed how to use both the pheromone crossover and the repulsive operator to reinitialize a stagnated colony in our multi-colony ant algorithm. A parallel asynchronous algorithm process is also presented. Experimental results from the multi-colony ant algorithm are presented in Section IV along with a comparative performance analysis involving other existing approaches. Finally, Section V provides some concluding remarks.

2. Basic ant colony optimization algorithm

The principle of ant colony system algorithm is that a special chemical trail (pheromone) is left on the ground during their trips, which guides the other ants towards the target solution. More pheromone is left when more ants go through the trip, which improved the probability of other's ants choosing this trip. Furthermore, this chemical trail (pheromone) has a decreasing action over time because of evaporation of trail. In addition, the quantity left by ants depends on the number of ants using this trail.
Fig.1 presents a decision-making process of ants choosing their trips. When ants meet at their decision-making point *A*, some choose one side and some choose other side randomly. Suppose these ants are crawling at the same speed, those choosing short side arrive at decision-making point *B* more quickly than those choosing long side. The ants choosing by chance the short side are the first to reach the nest. The short side receives, therefore, pheromone earlier than the long one and this fact increases the probability that further ants select it rather than the long one. As a result, the quantity of pheromone is left with higher speed in short side than long side because more ants choose short side than long side. The number of broken line in Fig. 1 is direct ratio to the number of ant approximately. Artificial ant colony system is made from the principle of ant colony system for solving kinds of optimization problems. Pheromone is the key of the decision-making of ants.

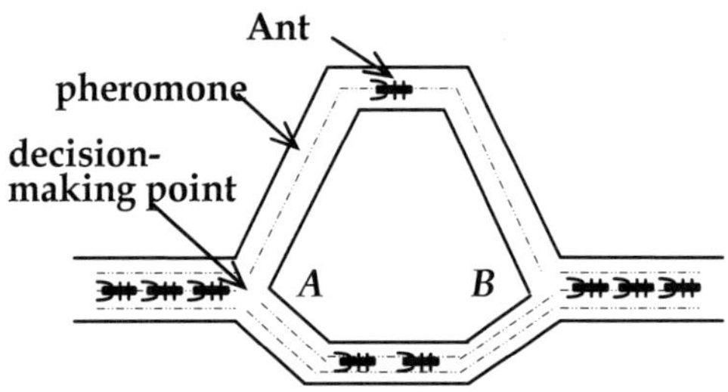

Fig. 1. A decision-making process of ants choosing their trips according to pheromone.

ACO was initially applied to the traveling salesman problem (TSP) [4][5]. The TSP is a classical optimization problem, and is one of a class of NP-Problem. This article also uses the TSP as an example application. Given a set of N towns, the TSP can be stated as the problem of finding a minimal length closed tour that visits each town once. Each city is a decision-making point of artificial ants.
Define (i,j) is an edge of city i and city j. Each edge (i,j) is assigned a value (length) d_{ij}, which is the distance between cities i and j. The general MMAX [2] for the TSP is described as following:

2.1 Pheromone updating rule

Ants leave their pheromone on edges at their every traveling when ants complete its one iteration. The sum pheromone of one edge is defined as following

$$\tau_{ij}(t+1) = \Delta\tau_{ij} + (1-\rho)\tau_{ij}(t) \quad (1)$$

$\rho \in (0,1)$, $1-\rho$ is persistence rate of previous pheromone. ρ is defined as evaporation rate of pheromone.

In MMAS, only the best ant updates the pheromone trails and that the value of the pheromone is bound. Therefore, the pheromone updating rule is given by

$$\tau_{ij}(t+1) = [\Delta\tau_{ij}^{best} + (1-\rho)\tau_{ij}(t)]_{\tau_{\min}}^{\tau_{\max}} \quad (2)$$

where τ_{max} and τ_{min} are respectively the upper and lower bounds imposed on the pheromone; and $\Delta\tau_{ij}^{best}$ is:

$$\Delta\tau_{ij}^{best} = \begin{cases} 1/L_{best} & \text{if}(i,j) \text{ belongs to the best tour,} \\ 0 & \text{otherwise} \end{cases} \quad (3)$$

where L_{best} is solution cost of either the iteration-best or the best-so-far or a combination of both [2].

2.2 Ants moving rule

Ants move from one city to another city according to probability. Firstly, cities accessed must be placed in taboo table. Define a set of cities never accessed of the kth ant as $allowed_k$. Secondly, define a visible degree η_{ij}, $\eta_{ij} = 1/d_{ij}$. The probability of the kth ant choosing city is given by

$$p_{ij}^{k}(t) = \begin{cases} \dfrac{[\tau_{ij}(t)]^{\alpha}[\eta_{ij}]^{\beta}}{\sum\limits_{k \in allowed_k} [\tau_{ik}(t)]^{\alpha}[\eta_{ik}]^{\beta}} & j \in allowed_k \\ 0 & \text{else} \end{cases} \quad (4)$$

where a and β are important parameters which determine the relative influence of the trail pheromone and the heuristic information.

In this article, the pseudo-random proportional rule given in equation (5) is adopted as in ACO [4] and modified MMAS [6].

$$j = \begin{cases} \arg \max\limits_{k \in allowed_k} \{\tau_{ik}(t)[\eta_{ik}]^{\beta}\} & \text{if } p \le p_0 \\ J & \text{else} \end{cases} \quad (5)$$

where p is a random number uniformly distributed in [0,1]. Thus, the best possible move, as indicated by the pheromone trail and the heuristic information, is made with probability $0 \le p_0 < 1$ (exploitation); with probability $1-p_0$ a move is made based on the random variable J with distribution given by equation (4) (biased exploration).

2.3 Pheromone trail Initialization

At the beginning of a run, we set $\tau_{max} = 1/((1-\rho)C_{nn})$, $\tau_{min} = \tau_{max}/2N$, and the initial pheromone values $\tau_{ij}(0) = \tau_{max}$, where C_{nn} is the length of a tour generated by the nearest-neighbor heuristic and N is the total number of cities.

2.4 Stopping rule

There are many conditions for ants to stop their traveling, such as number limitation of iteration, CPU time limitation or the best solution.

From above describing, we can get detail procedure of MMAS. MMAS is one of the most studied ACO algorithms and the most successful variants [5].

3. Multi-colony ant system based on a pheromone arithmetic crossover and a repulsive operator

3.1 Concept

1. **Multi-Colony Ant System Initiating.** Every ant colony system owns its pheromone array and parameters α, β and ρ. In particular, every colony may possess its own arithmetic policy. For example, all colonies use different ACO algorithms respectively. Some use basic Ant System. Some use elitist Ant System, ACS, MMAS, or rank-based version of Ant System etc. The others maybe use hyper-cube framework for ACO.

Every ant colony system begins to iterate and update its pheromone array respectively until it reaches its local optimum solution. It uses its own search policy. Then it sends this local optimum solution to the global best-found center. The global best-found center keeps the global top M solutions, which are searched thus far by all colonies of ant system. The global best-found center also holds parameters α, β and ρ for every solution. These parameters are equal to the colony parameters while the colony finds this solution. Usually M is larger than the number of colonies.

2. **Old Ant Colony being Eliminated Rule.** We destroy one of the old colonies according to following rules:

   a. A colony who owns the smallest local optimum solution among all colonies.
   b. A colony who owns the largest generations since its last local optimum solution was found.
   c. A colony that has lost diversity. In general, there are supposed to be at least two types of diversity [7] in ACO: (i) diversity in finding tours, and (ii) diversity in depositing pheromone.

3. **New Ant Colony Creating by Pheromone Crossover.** Firstly, we select m ($m \ll M$) solutions from M global best-so-far optimums in the global best-found center randomly. Secondly, we deliberately initialize the pheromone trails of this new colony to $\rho(t)$ which starts with $\rho(t)=\tau max(t)=1/((1-\rho)\cdot L_{best}(t))$, achieving in this way a higher exploration of solutions at the start of algorithm and a higher exploitation near the top m global optimum solutions at the end of algorithm. Where $L_{best}(t)$ is the best-so-far solution cost of all colonies in current t time. Then these trails are modified using arithmetic crossover by

$$\tau_{ij} = \rho(t) + \sum_{k=1}^{m} c_k \text{rand}_k()\Delta\tau_{ij}^k \quad (6)$$

where $\Delta\tau_{ij}^k = 1/L_{best}^k$ in which edge (i,j) is on the kth global-best solution and L_{best}^k denotes the kth global-best solution cost in the m chosen solutions; $rand_k()$ is a random function uniformly distributed in the range [0,1]; c_k is the weight of $\Delta\tau_{ij}^k$ and $\sum_{k=1}^{m} c_k = 2$ because the mathematical expectation of $rand_k()$ equals $1/2$. Last, the parameters α, β and ρ are set using arithmetic crossover by:

$$\alpha = \sum_{k=1}^{m} c_k \text{rand}_k()\alpha_k \text{ , } \beta = \sum_{k=1}^{m} c_k \text{rand}_k()\beta_k \text{ , } \rho = \sum_{k=1}^{m} c_k \text{rand}_k()\rho_k \tag{7}$$

where α_k, β_k and ρ_k belong to the kth global-best solution in the m chosen solutions.
After these operations, the colony starts its iterating and updating its local pheromone anew.
4. **Repulsive Operator.** As Shepherd and Sheepdog algorithm [8], we introduce the attractive and repulsive ACO in trying to decrease the probability of premature convergence further. We define the attraction phase merely as the basic ACO algorithm. In this phase the good solutions function like "attractors". In the colony of this phase, the ants will then be attracted to the solution space near good solutions. However, the new colony which was just now reinitialized using pheromone arithmetic crossover maybe are redrawn to the same best-so-far local optimum solution again which was found only a moment ago. As a result, that wastes an amount of computational resource. Therefore, we define the second phase repulsion, by subtracting the term $\Delta\tau_{ij}^{best}$ in association with the best-so-far solution in the pheromone-update formula when we reinitialize a new colony. Then the equation (6) will become as:

$$\tau_{ij} = \rho(t) + \sum_{k=1}^{m} c_k \text{rand}_k()\Delta\tau_{ij}^{k} - c_{best}\Delta\tau_{ij}^{best} \tag{8}$$

where $\Delta\tau_{ij}^{best} = 1 / L_{best}$ in which edge (i,j) is on the best-so-far solution, L_{best} denotes the best-so-far solution cost, c_{best} is the weight of $\Delta\tau_{ij}^{best}$, and the other coefficients are the same as in the equation (6). In that phase the best-so-far solution functions like "a repeller" so that the ants can move away from the vicinity of the best-so-far solution.
We identify our implementation of this model based on a pheromone crossover and a repulsive operator with the acronym MCA.

3.2 Parallel asynchronous algorithm design for multi-colony ant algorithms

As in [9], we propose a parallel asynchronous algorithm process for our multi-colony ant algorithm in order to make efficient use of all available processors in a heterogeneous cluster or heterogeneous computing environments. Our process design follows a master/slave paradigm. The master processor holds a global best-found center, sends colony initialization parameters to the slave processors and performs all decision-making processes such as the global best-found center updates and sorts, convergence checks. It does not perform any ant colony algorithm iteration. However, the slave processors repeatedly execute ant colony algorithm iteration using the parameters assigned to them. The tasks performed by the master and the slave processors are as follows:

- Master processor

1. Initializes all colonies' parameters and sends them to the slave processors;
2. Owns a global best-found center which keeps the global top M solutions and their parameters;
3. Receives local optimum solution and parameters from the slave processors and updates its global best-found center;
4. Evaluate the effectiveness of ant colonies in the slave processors;
5. Initializes a set of new colony's parameters by using both a pheromone crossover and a repulsive operator based on multi-optimum for the worst ant colony;

6. Chooses one of the worst ant colonies to kill and sends the new colony parameters and kill command to the slave processor who owns the killed colony;
7. Checks convergence.

- Slave processor

1. Receives a set of colony's parameters from the master processor;
2. Initializes an ant colony and starts iteration;
3. Sends its local optimum solution and parameters to the master processor;
4. Receives kill command and parameters from the master processor, and then use these parameters to reinitialize and start iteration according to the equation (8).

Once the master processor has performed the initialization step, the initialization parameters are sent to the slave processors to execute ant colony algorithm iteration. Because the contents of communication between the master processor and the slave processors only are some parameters and sub-optimum solutions, the ratio of communication time between the master and the slaves to the computation time of the processors of this system is relatively small. The communication can be achieved using a point-to-point communication scheme implemented with the Message Passing Interface (MPI). Only after obtaining its local optimum solution, the slave processor sets message to the master processor (Fig. 2). During this period, the slave processor continues its iteration until it gets kill command from the master processor. Then the slave processor will initialize a new ant colony and reiterate.

To make the most use of the heterogeneity of the band of communication between the master processor and the slave processors, we can select some slave processors the band between which and the master processor is very straightway. We never kill them but only send the global best-so-far optimum solution to them in order to speed up their local pheromone arrays update and convergence.

A pseudo-code of a parallel asynchronous MCA algorithm is present as follow:

- Master processor

```
Initialize Optimization
    Initialize parameters of all colonies
    Send them to the slave processors;
Perform Main-Loop
    Receive local optimum solution
        and parameters from the slave processors
    Update the global best-found center
    Check convergence
    If (eliminating rule met) then
        Find the worst colony
        Send kill command and a set of new parameters to it
Report Results
```

- Slave processor

```
Receive Initialize parameters from the master processor
Initialize a new local ant colony
Perform Optimization
    For k = 1, number of iterations
      For i = 1, number of ants
        Construct a new solution
```

If (kill command and a set of new parameters received) then
Goto initialize a new local ant colony;
Endfor
Modify its local pheromone array
Send its local optimum solution and parameters to the master processor
Endfor
End

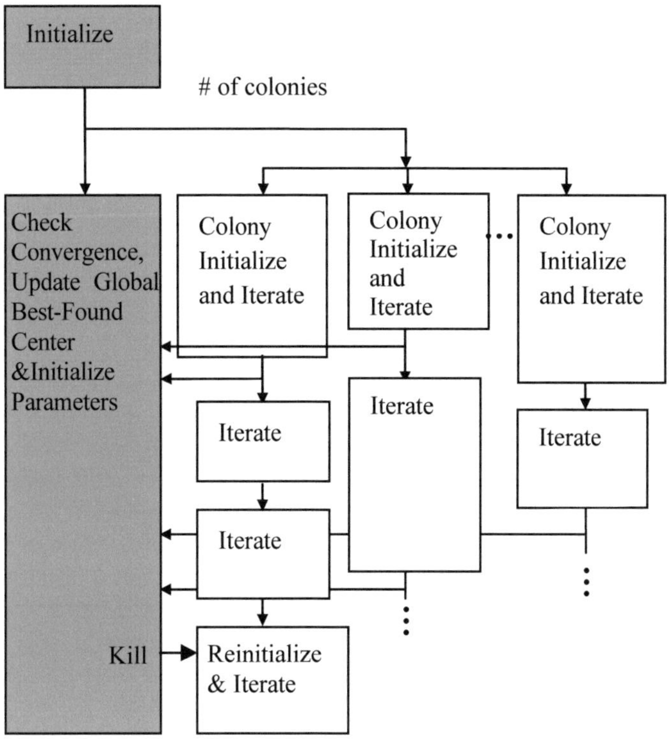

Fig. 2. Block diagram for parallel asynchronous algorithm. Grey boxes indicate activities on the master processor.

4. Experiment results

4.1 Parallel independent runs & Sequential algorithm

In this parallel model, *k* copies of the same sequential MMAS algorithm are simultaneously and independently executed using different random seeds. The final result is the best solution among all the obtained ones. Using parallel independent runs is appealing as basically no communication overhead is involved and nearly no additional implementation effort is necessary. We identify the implementation of this model with the acronym PIR. Max Manfrin et al [10] find that PIR owns the better performance than any other parallel model.

In order to have a reference algorithm for comparison, we also test the equivalent sequential MMAS algorithm. It runs for the same overall generations as a parallel algorithm (*k*-times the generations of a parallel algorithm). We identify the implementation of this model with the acronym SEQ.

4.2 Experimental setup

For this experiment, we use MAX-MIN Ant System as a basic algorithm for our parallel implementation. We remain the occasional pheromone re-initializations applied in the MMAS described in [2], and a best-so-far pheromone update. Our implementation of MMAS is based on the publicly available ACOTSP code [11]. Our version also includes a 3-opt local search, uses the mean 0.05-branching factor and *don't look bits* for the outer loop optimization, and sets q_0=0.95.

We tested our algorithms on the Euclidian 2D TSP PCB442 from the TSPLIB [12]. The smallest tour length for this instance is known to be 50778. As parameter setting we use α=1, β=2 and ρ=0.1 for PIR and SEQ; and $\alpha \in [0.8,1.2]$, $\beta \in [2,5]$, $\rho \in [0.05,0.15]$ for MCA. Computational experiments are performed with k=8 colonies of 25 ants over T=200 generations for PIR and MCA, but 25 ants and T=1600 for SEQ, i.e. the total number of evaluated solutions is 40000 (=25*8*200=25*1600). We select m=4 best solutions, c_k=2/4=0.5 and c_{best}=0.1 in the pheromone arithmetic crossover and the repulsive operator for MCA. All given results are averaged over 1000 runs. As far as eliminated rules in MCA, we adopt rule (b). If a colony had run more than 10 generations (2000 evaluations) for PCB442 since its local optimum solution was updated, we think it had arrived at the stagnating state.

4.3 Experimental result

The Fig. 3 shows cumulative run-time distribution that certain levels of solution quality are obtained depending on the number so far evaluated solutions. There is a rapid decrease in tour length early in the search in the SEQ algorithm because it runs more generations than SEQ and MCA in the same evaluations. After this, the improvement flattened out for a short while before making another smaller dip. Finally, the SEQ algorithm decreases at a much slower pace quickly and tends to stagnate prematurely. Although, the tour length decreases more slowly in PIR and MCA than in SEQ early in the search, after about 6600 evaluations SEQ and MCA all give better results than PIR in average. Moreover, for every level of solutions MAC gives the better performance than PIR. Conclusively, SEQ has great risk of getting stuck on a local optimum; however, the MCA is able to escape local optima because of the repulsive operator and the pheromone crossover.

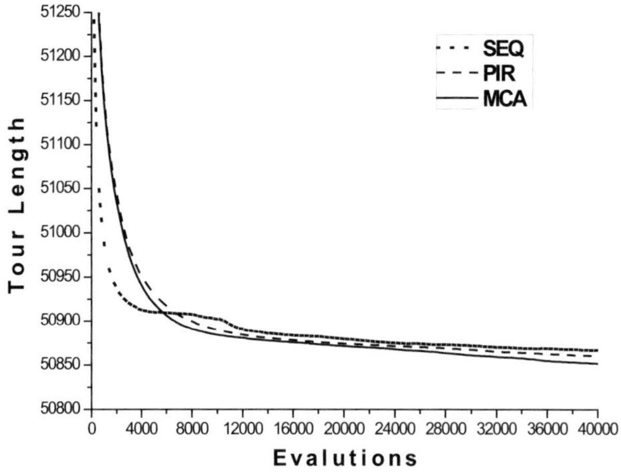

Fig. 3. The cumulative run-time distribution is given for PVB442

5. Conclusion

In this paper, an improved ant colony system, multi-colony ant algorithm, is presented. The main aim of this method is to increase the ant colonies' capability of escaping stagnating state. For this reason, a new concept of multiple ant colonies has been presented. It creates a new colony of ants to iterate, which is accomplished through application of the pheromone arithmetic crossover and the repulsive operator based on multi-optimum when meeting at the stagnating state of the iteration or local optimum solution. At the same time, the main parameters α, β and ρ of algorithm are self-adaptive. In this paper, a parallel asynchronous algorithm process is also presented.

From above exploring, it is obvious that the proposed multi-colony ant algorithm is an effective facility for optimization problems. The result of experiment has shown that the proposed multi-colony ant algorithm is a precise method for TSP. The speed of multi-colony ant algorithm's convergence is faster than that of the parallel independent runs (PIR).

At the present time, our parallel code only allows for one computer. In future versions, we will implement MPI-based program on a computer cluster.

6. Acknowledgment

Research is also supported by the Natural Science Foundation of China (No.60873058, No.60743010), the Natural Science Foundation of Shandong Province (No. Z2007G03), and the Science and Technology Project of Shandong Education Bureau. This research is also carried out under the PhD foundation of Shandong Institute of Commerce and Technology, China.

7. References

[1] M. Dorigo, V. Maniezzo, and A. Colorni, "Positive Feedback as a Search Strategy", *Technical Report 91-016*, Dipartimento di Elettronica, Politecnico di Milano, Milan, Italy,1991.

[2] T. Stützle and H. H. Hoos, "MAX-MIN Ant System", *Future Generation Computer systems*, 16(8), pp. 889-914, 2000.

[3] J. Ouyang and G. R. Yan, "A multi-group ant colony system algorithm for TSP", *Proceedings of the Third International Conference on Machine Learning and Cybernetics*, pp. 117-121, 2004.

[4] M. Dorigo and L. M. Gambardella, "Ant Colony System: A cooperative learning approach to the traveling salesman problem", *IEEE Transactions on evolutionary computation*, 1(1), pp. 53-66, April 1997.

[5] M. Dorigo, B. Birattari, and T. Stuzle, "Ant Colony Optimization: Artificial Ants as a Computational Intelligence Technique", *IEEE Computational Intelligence Magazine*, 1(4), pp. 28-39, 2006.

[6] T. Stützle. "Local Search Algorithms for Combinatorial Problems: Analysis, Improvements, and New", Applications, vol. 220 of DISKI. Sankt Augustin, Germany, Infix, 1999.

[7] Y. Nakamichi and T. Arita, "Diversity Control in Ant Colony Optimization", *Artificial Life and Robotics*, 7(4), pp. 198-204, 2004.

[8] D. Robilliard and C. Fonlupt, "A Shepherd and a Sheepdog to Guide Evolutionary Computation", *Artificial Evolution*, pp. 277-291, 1999.

[9] B. Koh, A. George, R. Haftka, and B. Fregly , "Parallel Asynchronous Particle Swarm Optimization", *International Journal for Numerical Methods in Engineering*, 67(4), pp. 578-595, 2006.

[10] M. Manfrin, M. Birattari, T. Stützle, and M. Dorigo, "Parallel ant colony optimization for the traveling salesman problem", *IRIDIA – Technical Report Series*, TR/ IRIDIA/2006-007, March 2006.

[11] T.Stützle. ACOTSP.V1.0.tar.gz http://iridia.ulb.ac.be/~mdorigo/ACO/aco-code/public-software.html, 2006.

[12] G. Reinelt. TSPLIB95 http://www.iwr.uni-heidelberg.de/groups/comopt/software/TSPLIB95/index.html, 2008.

2

Continuous Dynamic Optimization

Walid Tfaili
Université Paris Est Créteil Val-de-Marne (LISSI E.A. 3956)
France

1. Introduction

In this chapter we introduce a new ant colony algorithm aimed at continuous and dynamic problems. To deal with the changes in the dynamic problems, the diversification in the ant population is maintained by attributing to every ant a repulsive electrostatic charge, that allows to keep ants at some distance from each other. The algorithm is based on a continuous ant colony algorithm that uses a weighted continuous Gaussian distribution, instead of the discrete distribution, used to solve discrete problems. Experimental results and comparisons with two competing methods available in the literature show best performances of our new algorithm called CANDO on a set of multimodal dynamic continuous test functions.
To find the shortest way between the colony and a source of food, ants adopt a particular collective organization technique (see figure 1). The first algorithm inspired from ant colonies, called ACO (refer to Dorigo & Gambardella (1997), Dorigo & Gambardella (2002)), was proposed as a multi-agent approach to solve hard combinatorial optimization problems. It was applied to discrete problems like the traveling salesman, routing and communication problems.

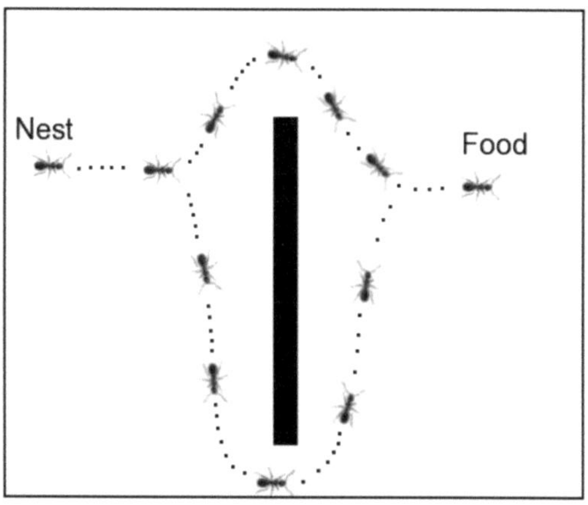

(a) When the foraging starts, the probability that ants take the short or the long path to the food source is 50%.

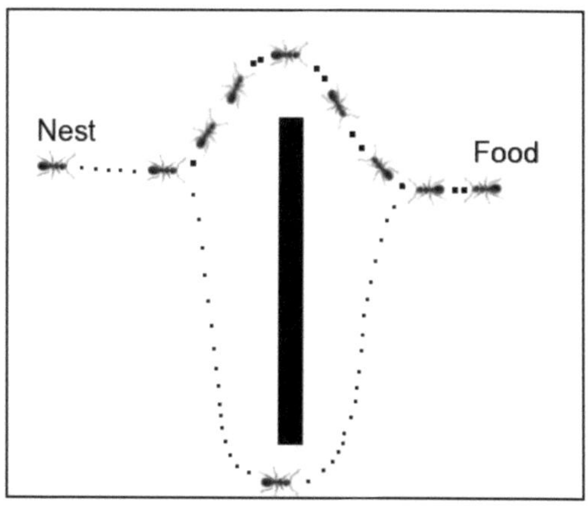

(b) The ants that arrive by the short path return earlier. Therefore, the probability to take again the short path is higher.

Fig. 1. An example illustrating the capability of ant colonies of finding the shortest path, in the case there are only two paths of different lengths between the nest and the food source.

Some ant colony techniques aimed at dynamic optimization have been described in the literature. In particular, Johann Dréo and Patrick Siarry introduced in Dréo & Siarry (2004); Tfaili et al. (2007) the DHCIAC (Dynamic Hybrid Continuous Interacting Ant Colony) algorithm, which is a multi-agent algorithm, based on the exploitation of two communication channels. This algorithm uses the ant colony method for global search, and the Nelder & Mead dynamic simplex method for local search. However, a lot of research is still needed to obtain a general purpose tool.

We introduce in this chapter a new dynamic optimization method, based on the original ACO. A repulsive charge is assigned to every ant in order to maintain diversification inside the population. To adapt ACO to the continuous case, we make use of continuous probability distributions.

We will recall in section 2 the biological background that justifies the use of metaheuristics, and more precisely those inspired from nature, for solving dynamic problems. In section 3 some techniques encountered in the literature to solve dynamic problems are exposed. The principle of ant colony optimization is resumed in section 4. We describe our new method in section 5. Experimental results are reported in section 6. We conclude the chapter in section 7.

2. Biological background

In the late 80's, a new research domain in distributed artificial intelligence has emerged, called swarm intelligence. It concerns the study of the utility of mimicking social insects for conceiving new algorithms.

In fact, the ability to produce complex structures and find solutions for non trivial problems (sorting, optimal search, task repartition ...), using simple agents having neither a global view of their environment nor a centralized control or a global strategy, has intrigued researchers. Many concepts have then been defined, like auto-organization and emergence. Computer science has used the concepts of auto-organization and emergence, found in social insects societies, to define what we call swarm intelligence.

The application of these metaphors related to swarm intelligence to the design of methods and algorithms shows many advantages:

- flexibility in dynamic landscapes,
- better performance than with isolated agents,
- more reliable system (the loss of an agent does not alter the whole system),
- simple modeling of an agent.

Nevertheless certain problems appear:

- difficulty to anticipate a problem solution with an emerged intelligence,
- formulation problem, and convergence problem,
- necessity of using a high number of agents, which induces conflict risks,
- possible oscillating or blocking behaviors,
- no intentional local cooperation, which means that there is no voluntary cooperative behaviors (in case of emergence).

One of the major advantages of algorithms inspired from nature, such as the ant colony algorithm, is flexibility in dynamic environments. Nevertheless few works deal with applications of ant colony algorithms to dynamic continuous problems (see figure 2). In the next section, we will briefly expose some techniques found in the literature.

3. Some techniques aimed at dynamic optimization

Evolutionary algorithms were largely applied to the dynamic landscapes, in the discrete case. Jürgen Branke (refer to Branke (2001), Branke (2003)) classifies the dynamic methods found in the literature as follows:

1. The reactive methods (refer to Grefenstette & Ramsey (1992), Tinos & de Carvalho (2004)), which react to changes (i.e. by triggering the diversity). The general idea of these methods is to do an external action when a change occurs. The goal of this action is to increase the diversity. In general the reactive methods based on populations loose their diversity when the solution converges to the optimum, thus inducing a problem when the optimum changes. By increasing the diversity the search process may be regenerated.
2. The methods that maintain the diversity (refer to Cobb & Grefenstette (1993), Nanayakkara et al. (1999)). These methods maintain the diversity in the population, hoping that, when the objective function changes, the distribution of individuals within the search space permits to find quickly the new optimum (see Garrett & Walker (2002) and Simões & Costa (2001)).
3. The methods that keep in memory "old" optima. These methods keep in memory the evolution of different optima, to use them later. These methods are specially effective when the evolution is periodic (refer to Bendtsen & Krink (2002), Trojanowski & Michalewicz (2000) and Bendtsen (2001)).
4. The methods that use a group of sub-populations distributed on different optima (refer to Oppacher & Wineberg (1999), Cedeno & Vemuri (1997) and Ursem (2000)), thus increasing the probability to find new optima.

Michael Guntsch and Martin Middendorf solved in Guntsch & Middendorf (2002a) two dynamic discrete combinatorial problems, the dynamic traveling salesman problem (TSP), and the dynamic quadratic assignment problem, with a modified ant colony algorithm. The main idea consists in transferring the whole set of solutions found in an iteration to the next iteration, then calculating the pheromone quantity needed for the next iteration.
The same authors proposed in Guntsch & Middendorf (2002b) a modification of the way in which the pheromone is updated, to permit keeping a track of good solutions until a certain time limit, then to explicitly eliminate their influence from the pheromone matrix. The method was tested on a dynamic TSP.
In Guntsch & Middendorf (2001), Michael Guntsch and Martin Middendorf proposed three strategies; the first approach allows a local re-initialization at a same value of the pheromone matrix, when a change is detected. The second approach consists in calculating the value of the matrix according to the distance between the cities (this method was applied to the dynamic TSP, where a city can be removed or added). The third approach uses the value of the pheromone at each city.
The last three strategies were modified in Guntsch et al. (2001), by introducing an elitist concept: the best ants are only allowed to change the pheromone at each iteration, and when a change is detected. The previous good solutions are not forgotten, but modified as best as possible, so that they can become new reasonable solutions.
Daniel Merkle and Martin Middendorf studied in Merkle & Middendorf (2002) the dynamics of ACO, then proposed a deterministic model, based on the expected average behavior of ants. Their work highlights how the behavior of the ants is influenced by the characteristics of the pheromone matrix, which explains the complex dynamic behavior. Various tests were carried

out on a permutation problem. But the authors did not deal with really dynamic problems. In section 5 we will present a new ant colony algorithm aimed at dynamic continuous optimization.

4. From nature to discrete optimization

Artificial ants coming from the nest pass through different paths until all paths are visited (figure 1). Pheromones have equal value initially. When coming back from the food source, ants deposit pheromone. The pheromone values are updated following the equation:

$$\tau_i = \tau_i + \frac{Q}{l_i}$$

with Q a constant and l_i the length of the path, which means that the new pheromone value is inversely proportional to the path length. A single trajectory from the nest to the food source

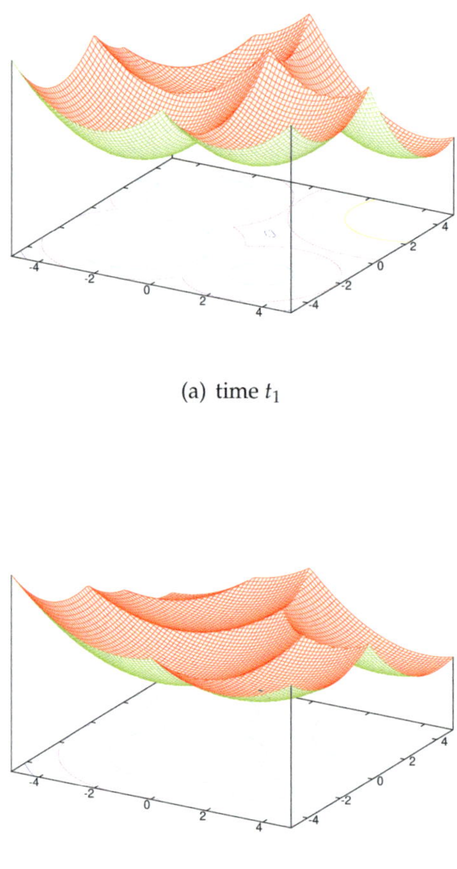

(a) time t_1

(b) time $t_2 > t_1$

Fig. 2. Plotting of a dynamic test function representing local optima that change over time.

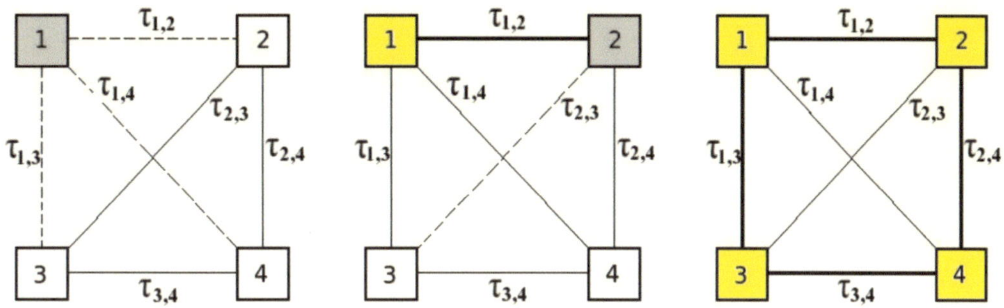

(a) At the beginning. (b) Choosing a path. (c) A complete path.

Fig. 3. An example showing the construction of the solution for a TSP problem with four cities.

is a complete construction of a solution. The process is iterated. The choice of a path is done following the probability :

$$P_{e_i} = \frac{\tau_i}{\sum_{i=1}^{n} \tau_i}$$

Let us consider an example (figure 3); an ant will choose its path according to three probabilities :

$$P_{e_1} = \frac{\tau_1}{\tau_1 + \tau_2 + \tau_3} \qquad P_{e_2} = \frac{\tau_2}{\tau_1 + \tau_2 + \tau_3} \qquad P_{e_3} = \frac{\tau_3}{\tau_1 + \tau_2 + \tau_3}$$

If we suppose that $l_1 < l_2 < l_3$, then $\tau_1 > \tau_2 > \tau_3$, which implies that $P_{e_1} > P_{e_2} > P_{e_3}$. The chosen path will be e_1. To prevent the pheromone value from increasing infinitely and to decrease the importance of some solutions, the pheromone values are decreased (evaporated) with time following the equation:

$$\tau_i = \tau_i.(1-\rho) \qquad \text{with} \quad \rho \in [0,1]$$

where ρ is a pheromone regulation parameter; by consequence this parameter will influence the convergence speed towards a single solution.
Ant colony algorithms were initially dedicated to discrete problems (the number of variables is finite), in this case we can define a set of solution components; the optimal solution for a given problem will be an organized set of those components. We consider the Traveling Salesman Problem "TSP" : the salesman has to visit all the N cities and must not visit a city more than once, the goal is to find the shortest path. In practice, the TSP can be represented by a connected graph (a graph where nodes are interconnected). Nodes represent the N cities with $i = \{1,...,N\}$ and N the total number of nodes. A path between two nodes (i.e. N_i and N_j) is denoted by e_{ij}. So a solution construction consists in choosing a starting node (city), adding to the current partial solution a new node according to a certain probability and repeating the process until the components number is equal to N. In discrete problems, solutions are not known in advance, which means that pheromones cannot be attributed to a complete solution, but to solution components.

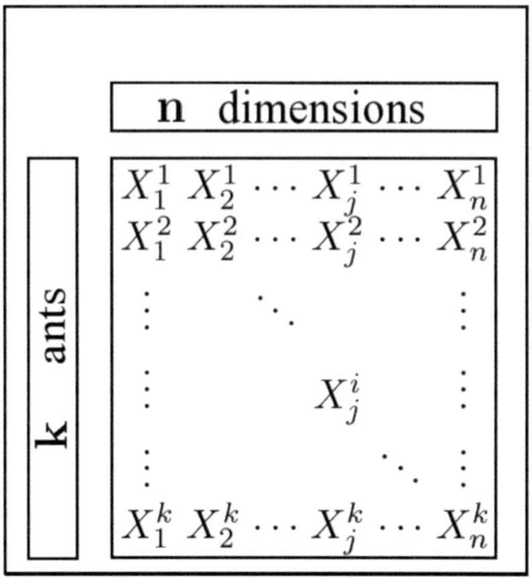

Fig. 4. Every ant constructs a complete solution which includes n dimensions.

5. CANDO: charged ants for continuous dynamic optimization

For problems with discrete variables, problem components are finite, therefore the pheromone values can be attributed directly to solution components. A deterministic solution to a discrete problem exists, even if its search may be expensive in calculation time. But for continuous problems, pheromone values cannot be attributed directly to solution components. The approach that we use is a diversification keeping technique (refer to Tim Blackwell in Blackwell (2003)), that consists in attributing to each ant an electrostatic charge, $a_i = \sum_{l=1;l\neq i}^{k} a_{il}$

$$a_{il} = \begin{cases} \dfrac{Q_i Q_l}{|x_i - x_l|^3}(x_i - x_l) & \text{if } R_c \leq |x_i - x_l| \leq R_p \\[2ex] \dfrac{Q_i Q_l}{{R_c}^2 |x_i - x_l|}(x_i - x_l) & \text{if } |x_i - x_l| < R_c \\[2ex] 0 & \text{if } R_p < |x_i - x_l| \end{cases}$$

where Q_i and Q_l are the initial charges of ants i and l respectively, $|x_i - x_l|$ is the Euclidean distance, R_p and R_c are the "perception" and the "core" radius respectively (see figure **??**). The perception radius is attributed to every ant, while the core radius is the perception radius of the best found ant in the current iteration. These charge values can be positive or negative. Our artificial ants are dispersed within the search space (see figure **??**), the values of charges change during the algorithm execution, in function of the quality of the best found solution.
The adaptation to the continuous domain that we use was introduced by Krzysztof Socha Socha (2004). The algorithm iterates over a finite and constant ant population of k individuals, where every ant represents a solution or a variable X^i, with $i = \{1,...,n\}$, for a n dimensional problem. The set of ants can be presented as follows (see figure 4) :
k is the ants number and n is the problem dimension. At the beginning, the population individuals are equipped with random solutions. This corresponds to the pheromone

initialization used for discrete problems. At each iteration, the new found solutions are added to the population and the worst solutions are removed in equal number; this corresponds to the pheromone update (deposit / evaporation) in the classical discrete case, the final goal is to bias the search towards the best solutions.
The construction of a solution is done by components like in the original ACO algorithm. For a single dimension (for example dimension *j*), an ant *i* chooses only one value (the jth value of the vector $< X_1^i, X_2^i, \ldots, X_j^i, \ldots, X_n^i >$). Every ant has a repulsive charge value, and a weighted Gaussian distribution. The choice of a single ant for a given dimension is done as follows: an ant chooses one of the Gaussian distributions according to its perception radius following the probability :

$$p_j^i = \frac{w_j^i}{\sum_{l=1}^{k} w_l^i}$$

Once a single Gaussian distribution is chosen, the ant *i* generates a random value according to the distribution:

$$G(X_j^i) = \frac{1}{\sigma_j \sqrt{2\pi}} \cdot e^{-\frac{(x-\mu_j)^2}{2.\sigma_j^2}}$$

where μ and σ are the mean and the standard deviation vectors respectively. For a problem with *n* dimensions, the solution construction is done by dimension, which means that every solution component represents exactly one dimension. While the algorithm proceeds on a dimension, other dimensions are left apart.
The final algorithm is presented in Algorithm 1:

Algorithm 1 Continuous charged ant colony algorithm

While stop criteria are not met **do**
  For 1 to *m* ants do
    Calculate the a_i value for the ant *i*
    Ant movement based on the charges values of neighbors
    $s^0 = \phi$
    Repeat for each of *n* dimensions
      Choose a single distribution $G(X_j^i)$ only among neighbors according to p_j^i
      Choose randomly the X_j^i value using the chosen $G(X_j^i)$
      $s^i = s^i \bigcup \{X_j^i\}$
    End
    Update ant charge based on the best found solution
    Update the weight (pheromone) based on the best found solution
  End
  Choose the best solution among the *m* ants
  Choose the best solution among current and old solutions
End while

6. Experimental results

	CANDO	eACO	DHCIAC
AbPoP	4.27(4.02)	4.34(4.15)	**4.09(3.86)**
AbVP	11.54(5.2)	12.03(5.45)	**9.73(3.49)**
APhL	**0.29(4.07)**	0.39(4.1)	0.38(4.18)
OVP	**1.78(8.09)**	1.84(9.11)	1.97(9.14)
OPoL	12.3(0.37)	13.61(0.42)	**10.62(0.14)**
AVP	**4.77E-005(0)**	5.43E-005(0)	6.54E-005(0)
APoL	2.87(2.24)	2.91(2.4)	**2.42(2.05)**

Table 1. Comparison of the error and, in brackets, the standard deviation related to the value for CANDO, eACO and DHCIAC (best results are in bold).

	CANDO	eACO	DHCIAC
AbPoP	0.043(4.29)	0.06(4.50)	**0.04(3.99)**
AbVP	-0.29(2.98)	-0.37(3.01)	**-0.21(2.54)**
APhL	**-3.04(1.56)**	-3.37(1.9)	-3.29(1.7)
OVP	**24.01(43.14)**	28.8(47.9)	31.49(52.76)
OPoL	-98.01(55.43)	-98.9(56.2)	**-92.95(50.1)**
AVP	**-17(19.6)**	-17.39(19.7)	-18(21.34)
APoL	-7.02(3.13)	-7.19(3.25)	**-5.8(2.96)**

Table 2. Comparison of the error and, in brackets, the standard deviation related to the position X1 value for CANDO, eACO and DHCIAC (best results are in bold).

Tests (figures 5, 6 and 7) were performed using the Open Metaheuristic project platform (see Dréo et al. (2007) and Dréo et al. (2005) for more information). We used a set of dynamic continuous test functions that we introduced in Dréo et al. (2007). Adding electrostatic charges to the ants has enhanced the found solution on the totality of the dynamic test functions (see tables 1, 2 and 3). We tested the competing algorithm eACO on the same dynamic functions to make a comparison with our approach. Our algorithm outperformed the classical algorithm eACO. This is due mainly to the continuous diversification in the search space over time. Ant electrostatic charges prevent ants from crowding around the found solutions thus preventing

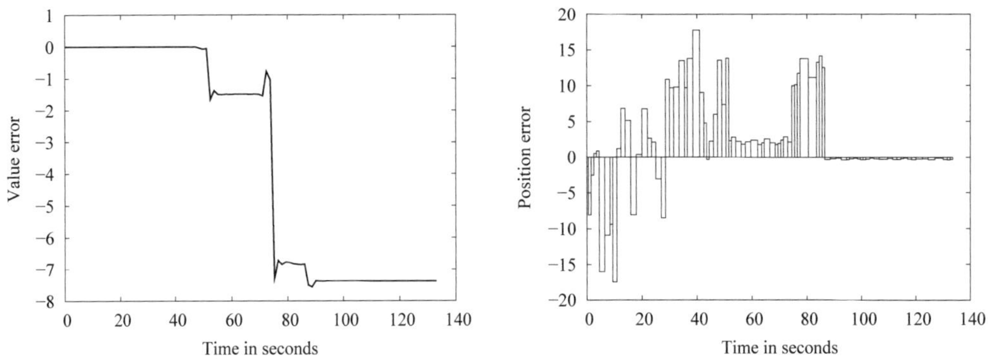

Fig. 5. Value and position errors results on the dynamic function AbPoP (*All but Position Periodic*), based on the static Morrison function.

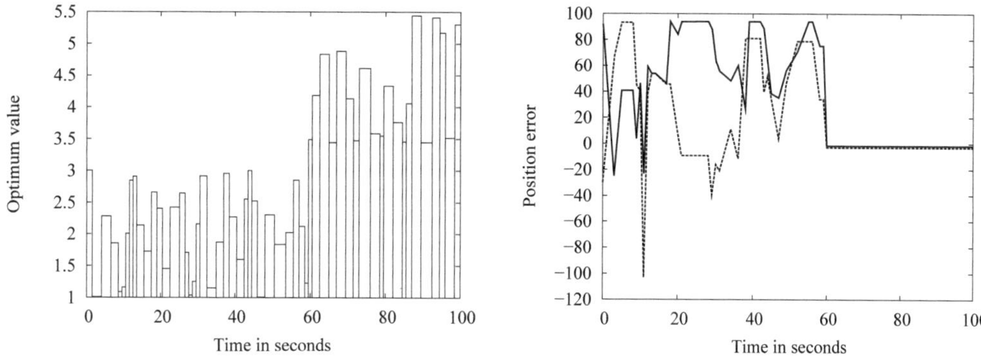

Fig. 6. Optimum value and position error results on the dynamic function AbVP (*All but Value Periodic*), based on the static Martin-Gady function.

	CANDO	eACO	DHCIAC
AbPoP	-0.91(2.74)	-0.97(2.81)	**-0.8(2.56)**
AbVP	-0.36(2.69)	-0.39(2.64)	**-0.27(2.62)**
APhL	**-3.02(1.51)**	-3.24(1.63)	-3.18(1.79)
OVP	**13.7(28.4)**	14.02(30.05)	15.55(31.36)
OPoL	-98.1(43.06)	-98.9(45)	**-97.91(40.16)**
AVP	**-16.5(18.3)**	-18.84(21.3)	-18.79(20.15)
APoL	-6.7(3.05)	-7.04(3.27)	**-5.9(2.88)**

Table 3. Comparison of the error and, in brackets, the standard deviation related to the position X2 value for CANDO, eACO and DHCIAC (best results are in bold).

from a premature convergence. We also notice that CANDO shows better performance than DHCIAC on the functions having many optima, due to the fact that charged ants form groups around different optima, which permits a better tracking of the changing optima, while DHCIAC converges more quickly on the dynamic functions with single optimum, due to the local search (through the Nelder-Mead simplex method). We notice that CANDO unlike

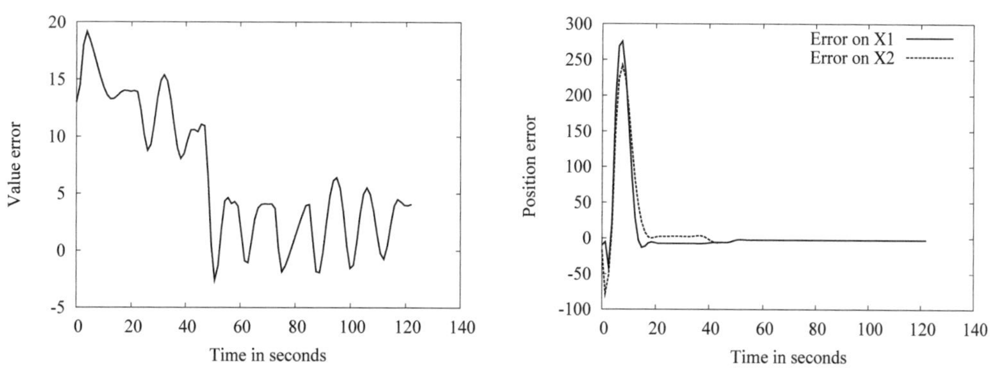

Fig. 7. Value and position errors results on the dynamic function OVP (*Optimum Value Periodic*), based on the static Morrison function.

DHCIAC does not use communication between ants and constructs the solution iteratively, which is the essence of the ant colony algorithms.

7. Conclusion

We presented in this chapter a new ant colony algorithm aimed at solving dynamic continuous optimization problems. Very few works were performed until now to adapt the ant colony algorithms to dynamic problems, and most of them concern only the discrete case. To deal with dynamic problems, we chose to keep ants simple and reactive, the final solution being obtained only through a collective work. The new algorithm consists in attributing to every ant a repulsive electrostatic charge, that is a function of the quality of the found solution. The adaptation of the ant colony algorithm to the handling of continuous problems is done by replacing the discrete probability distribution by a continuous one. This approach is interesting because it is very close to the original ACO. Experimental results on a set of dynamic continuous test functions proved the effectiveness of our new approach.

8. References

Bendtsen, C. N. (2001). *Optimization of Non-Stationary Problems with Evolutionary Algorithms and Dynamic Memory*, PhD thesis, University of Aarhus, Department of Computer Science Ny Munkegade 8000 Aarhus C.

Bendtsen, C. N. & Krink, T. (2002). Dynamic Memory Model for Non-Stationary Optimization, *Congress on Evolutionary Computation*, IEEE, pp. 145–150.
URL: *http://www.evalife.dk/publications/CNB*$_C$*EC2002*$_D$*ynamic*$_m$*emory.pdf*

Blackwell, T. M. (2003). Particle Swarms and Population Diversity I: Analysis, *in* J. Branke (ed.), *GECCO Workshop on Evolutionary Algorithms for Dynamic Optimization Problems*, pp. 9–13.

Branke, J. (2001). Evolutionary Approaches to Dynamic Environments - updated survey, *GECCO Workshop on Evolutionary Algorithms for Dynamic Optimization Problems*.
URL: *http://www.aifb.uni-karlsruhe.de/TILDEjbr/EvoDOP/Papers/gecco-dyn2001.pdf*

Branke, J. (2003). Evolutionary Approaches to Dynamic Optimization Problems: Introduction and Recent Trends, *in* J. Branke (ed.), *GECCO Workshop on Evolutionary Algorithms for Dynamic Optimization Problems*.
URL: *http://www.ubka.uni-karlsruhe.de/cgi-bin/psview?document=2003*

Cedeno, W. & Vemuri, V. R. (1997). On the Use of Niching for Dynamic Landscapes, International Conference on Evolutionary Computation, *IEEE.*

Cobb, H. G. & Grefenstette, J. J. (1993). Genetic Algorithms for Tracking Changing Environments, International Conference on Genetic Algorithms, *Morgan Kaufmann, pp. 523–530.*
URL: ftp://ftp.aic.nrl.navy.mil/pub/papers/1993/AIC-93-004.ps

Dorigo, M. & Gambardella, L. M. (1997). Ant Colony System: A Cooperative Learning Approach to the Traveling Salesman Problem, IEEE Transactions on Evolutionary Computation *1(1): 53–66.*

Dorigo, M. & Gambardella, L. M. (2002). Guest editorial special on ant colony optimization, IEEE Transactions on evolutionary computation *6(4): 317–319.*

Dréo, J., Aumasson, J. P., Tfaili, W. & Siarry, P. (2007). Adaptive learning search, a new tool to help comprehending metaheuristics, International Journal on Artificial Intelligence Tools *16(3): 483–505.*

Dréo, J., Pétrowski, A., Siarry, P. & Taillard, E. (2005). Metaheuristics for Hard Optimization,

Methods and Case Studies, *Springer.*

Dréo, J. & Siarry, P. (2004). Dynamic Optimization Through Continuous Interacting Ant Colony, in *M. Dorigo & al. (eds),* ANTS 2004, *LNCS 3172, pp. 422–423.*

Garrett, S. M. & Walker, J. H. (2002). Genetic Algorithms: Combining Evolutionary and 'Non'-Evolutionary Methods in Tracking Dynamic global optima, Genetic and Evolutionary Computation Conference, *Morgan Kaufmann, pp. 359–374.*

Grefenstette, J. J. & Ramsey, C. L. (1992). An Approach to Anytime Learning, in *D. Sleeman & P. Edwards (eds),* International conference on Machine Learning, *Morgan Kaufmann, pp. 189–195.*
URL: ftp://ftp.aic.nrl.navy.mil/pub/papers/1992/AIC-92-003.ps.Z

Guntsch, M. & Middendorf, M. (2001). Pheromone Modification Strategies for Ant Algorithms Applied to Dynamic TSP., EvoWorkshop, *pp. 213–222.*
URL: http://link.springer.de/link/service/series/0558/bibs/2037/20370213.htm

Guntsch, M. & Middendorf, M. (2002a). Applying Population Based ACO to Dynamic Optimization Problems, Third International Workshop ANTS, *Springer Verlag, LNCS 2463, pp. 111–122.*

Guntsch, M. & Middendorf, M. (2002b). A Population Based Approach for ACO, 2nd European Workshop on Evolutionary Computation in Combinatorial Optimization, *Springer Verlag, LNCS 2279, pp. 72–81.*

Guntsch, M., Middendorf, M. & Schmeck, H. (2001). An Ant Colony Optimization Approach to Dynamic TSP, in *L. Spector, E. D. Goodman, A. Wu, W. B. L. andHans Michael Voigt, M. Gen, S. Sen, M. Dorigo, S. Pezeshk, M. H. Garzon & E. Burke (eds),* Proceedings of the Genetic and Evolutionary Computation Conference (GECCO-2001), *Morgan Kaufmann, San Francisco, California, USA, pp. 860–867.*

Merkle, D. & Middendorf, M. (2002). Studies on the Dynamics of Ant Colony Optimization Algorithms, the Genetic and Evolutionary Computation Conference, *(GECCO), New York, pp. 105–112.*

Nanayakkara, T., Watanabe, K. & Izumi, K. (1999). Evolving in Dynamic Environments Through Adaptive Chaotic Mutation, Third International Symposium on Artificial Life and Robotics, *Vol. 2, pp. 520–523.*
URL: http://www.bme.jhu.edu/ thrish/publications/Arob981.ps

Oppacher, F. & Wineberg, M. (1999). The Shifting Balance Genetic Algorithm: Improving the GA in a Dynamic Environment, Genetic and Evolutionary Computation Conference (GECCO), *Vol. 1, Morgan Kaufmann, San Francisco, pp. 504–510.*
URL: http://snowhite.cis.uoguelph.ca/ wineberg/publications/gecco99.pdf

Simões, A. & Costa, E. (2001). Using biological inspiration to deal with dynamic environments, Proceedings of the Seventh International Conference on Soft Computing (MENDEL01), *Brno, Czech Republic.*

Socha, K. (2004). ACO for Continuous and Mixed-Variable Optimization, in *M. Dorigo & al. (eds),* ANTS 2004, *LNCS 3172, pp. 25–36.*

Tfaili, W., Dréo, J. & Siarry, P. (2007). Fitting of an ant colony approach to dynamic optimization through a new set of test functions, International Journal of Computational Intelligence Research 3*(3): 205–218.*

Tinos, R. & de Carvalho, A. (2004). A genetic algorithm with gene dependent mutation probability for non-stationary optimization problems, Congress on Evolutionary Computation, *Vol. 2.*

Trojanowski, K. & Michalewicz, Z. (2000). Evolutionary Optimization in Non-Stationary Environments, Journal of Computer Science and Technology 1*(2): 93–124.*

URL: http://journal.info.unlp.edu.ar/journal/journal2/papers/Mica.zip

Ursem, R. K. (2000). Multinational GA Optimization Techniques in Dynamic Environments, in *D. Whitley, D. Goldberg, E. Cantu-Paz, L. Spector, I. Parmee & H.-G. Beyer (eds),* Genetic and Evolutionary Computation Conference, *Morgan Kaufmann, pp. 19–26.*

3

An AND-OR Fuzzy Neural Network

Jianghua Sui
Mechanical Engineering College, Dalian Ocean University, Dalian 116023, P. R. China

1. Introduction

Fuzzy neural network combines the theories of fuzzy logical and neural network, including learning, association, identification, self-adaptation and fuzzy information process. The logic neurons have received much concern all the time as the important components of neural networks. From the models designing to the algorithms studying, there are many achievements. Glorennec[1]proposed a general artificial neuron to realize Lukasiewicz logical operate. Yager[2] employed a group of OWA fuzzy Aggregation operators to form OWA neuron. Pedrycz and Rocha [3] proposed aggregation neurons and referential neurons by integrating fuzzy logic and neural network and discuss the relation about the ultimate network structure and practical problem; Pedrycz i.e. [4],[5],[6] constructed a knowledge-based network by AND, OR neurons to solve classified problem and pattern recognition. Bailey i.e. [7] extended the single hidden layer to two hidden layers for improve complex modeling problems. Pedrycz and Reformat designed fuzzy neural network constructed by AND, OR neurons to modeling the house price in Boston [8].

We consider this multi-input-single-output (MISO) fuzzy logic-driven control system based on Pedrycz. Pedrycz[8] transformed T norm and S norm into product and probability operators, formed a continuous and smooth function to be optimized by GA and BP. But there is no exactly symbolic expression for every node, because of the uncertain structure. In this paper, the AND-OR FNN is firstly named as AND-OR fuzzy neural network, The in-degree and out-degree for neuron and the connectivity for layer are defined in order to educe the symbolic expression of every layer directly employing Zadeh operators, formed a continuous and rough function. The equivalence is proved between the architecture of AND-OR FNN and the fuzzy weighted Mamdani inference in order to utilize the AND-OR FNN to auto-extract fuzzy rules. The piecewise optimization of AND-OR FNN consists two phases, first the blueprint of network is reduced by GA and PA; the second phase, the parameters are refined by ACS (Ant Colony System). Finally this approach is applied to design AND-OR FNN ship controller. Simulating results show the performance is much better than ordinary fuzzy controller.

2. Fuzzy neurons and topology of AND-OR FNN

2.1 Logic-driven AND, OR fuzzy neurons

The AND and OR fuzzy neurons were two fundamental classes of logic-driven fuzzy neurons. The basic formulas governed the functioning of these elements are constructed with the aid of T norm and S norm (see Fig. 1, Fig. 2).Some definitions of the double fuzzy neurons show their inherent capability of reducing the input space.

Definition 1. Let $X=[x_1,x_2......x_n]$ be input variables $W=[w_1,w_2,......w_n]$ be adjustable connections (weights) confined to the unit interval. Then,

$$y=\overset{n}{\underset{i=1}{T}}(w_i S x_i) \tag{1}$$

is the AND fuzzy neuron, which completes a T norm and S norm composition operators like Fig.1.

Definition 2. Let $X=[x_1,x_2......x_n]$ be input variables, $W=[w_1,w_2,......w_n]$ be adjustable connections (weights) confined to the unit interval. Then,

$$y=\overset{n}{\underset{i=1}{S}}(w_i T x_i) \tag{2}$$

is the OR fuzzy neuron, which completes an S norm and T norm composition operators like Fig.2.

AND and OR neurons both are the mapping $[0,1]^n \rightarrow [0,1]$,the neuron expression is shown by Zadeh operators as Eq.(3)(4).

$$y=\overset{n}{\underset{i=1}{\wedge}}(w_i \vee x_i) \tag{3}$$

$$y=\overset{n}{\underset{i=1}{\vee}}(w_i \wedge x_i) \tag{4}$$

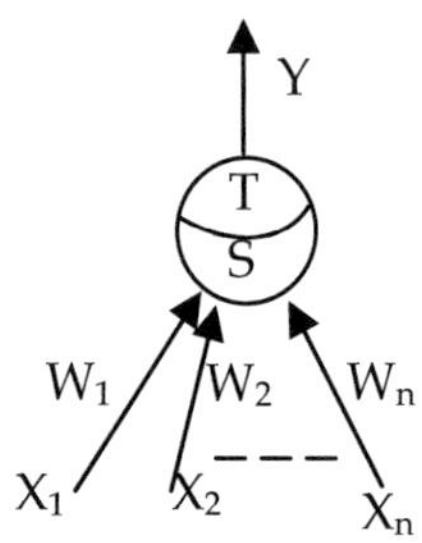

Fig. 1. AND neuron

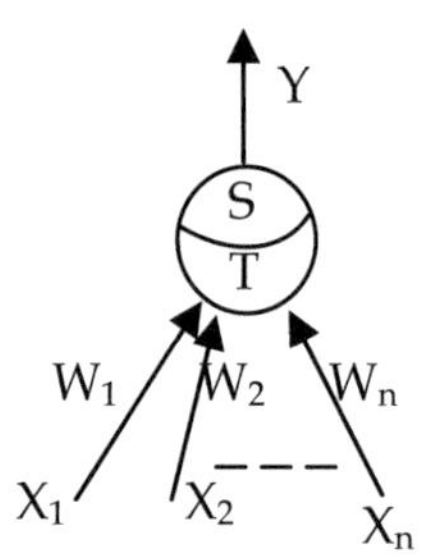

Fig. 2. OR neuron

Owing to the special compositions of neurons, for binary inputs and connections the neurons functional is equal to the standard gates in digital circuit shown in Table 1, 2. For AND neuron, the closer to 0 the connection w_i, the more important to the output the corresponding input x_i is. For OR neuron, the closer to 0 connection w_i, the more important to the output the corresponding input x_i is. Thus the values of connections become the criterion to eliminate the irrelevant input variables to reduce input space.

<table>
<tr><th>x_1</th><th>x_2</th><th>w_1</th><th>w_2</th><th>y</th></tr>
<tr><td>0</td><td>0</td><td rowspan="4">0</td><td rowspan="4">0</td><td>0</td></tr>
<tr><td>0</td><td>1</td><td>0</td></tr>
<tr><td>1</td><td>0</td><td>0</td></tr>
<tr><td>1</td><td>1</td><td>1</td></tr>
<tr><td>0</td><td>0</td><td rowspan="4">0</td><td rowspan="4">1</td><td rowspan="4">x_1</td></tr>
<tr><td>0</td><td>1</td></tr>
<tr><td>1</td><td>0</td></tr>
<tr><td>1</td><td>1</td></tr>
<tr><td>0</td><td>0</td><td rowspan="4">1</td><td rowspan="4">0</td><td rowspan="4">x_2</td></tr>
<tr><td>0</td><td>1</td></tr>
<tr><td>1</td><td>0</td></tr>
<tr><td>1</td><td>1</td></tr>
<tr><td>0</td><td>0</td><td rowspan="4">1</td><td rowspan="4">1</td><td>1</td></tr>
<tr><td>0</td><td>1</td><td>1</td></tr>
<tr><td>1</td><td>0</td><td>1</td></tr>
<tr><td>1</td><td>1</td><td>1</td></tr>
</table>

Table 1. AND neuron and AND gate

<table>
<tr><th>x_1</th><th>x_2</th><th>w_1</th><th>w_2</th><th>y</th></tr>
<tr><td>0</td><td>0</td><td rowspan="4">0</td><td rowspan="4">0</td><td>0</td></tr>
<tr><td>0</td><td>1</td><td>0</td></tr>
<tr><td>1</td><td>0</td><td>0</td></tr>
<tr><td>1</td><td>1</td><td>0</td></tr>
<tr><td>0</td><td>0</td><td rowspan="4">0</td><td rowspan="4">1</td><td rowspan="4">x_2</td></tr>
<tr><td>0</td><td>1</td></tr>
<tr><td>1</td><td>0</td></tr>
<tr><td>1</td><td>1</td></tr>
<tr><td>0</td><td>0</td><td rowspan="4">1</td><td rowspan="4">0</td><td rowspan="4">x_1</td></tr>
<tr><td>0</td><td>1</td></tr>
<tr><td>1</td><td>0</td></tr>
<tr><td>1</td><td>1</td></tr>
<tr><td>0</td><td>0</td><td rowspan="4">1</td><td rowspan="4">1</td><td>0</td></tr>
<tr><td>0</td><td>1</td><td>1</td></tr>
<tr><td>1</td><td>0</td><td>1</td></tr>
<tr><td>1</td><td>1</td><td>1</td></tr>
</table>

Table 2. OR neuron and OR gate

2.1 Several notations about AND,OR neuron

Definition 3. Let w_i be the connection value, x_i be the ith input variable. Then,

$$RD(x_i) = w_i \in [0,1] \quad (5)$$

is the relevant degree between the input x_i and the neuron's output. For AND neuron, if $RD(x_i) = 0$, then x_i is more important feature to the output; if $RD(x_i) = 1$, then x_i is more irrelevant feature to the output, it can be cancelled. For OR neuron, vice versa. Thus the RDV or RDM is the vector or matrix made up of connections, respectively , which becomes the threshold to obstacle some irrelevant input variables, also lead to reduce the input space.
Definition 4. In-degree is from directed graph in graph theory; the neural network is one of directed graph. The in-degree of the ith neuron $d^+(neuron_i)$ is the number of input variables, then the in-degree of the ith AND neuron $d^+(AND_i)$ is shown the number of his input variables; the in-degree of the jth OR neuron $d^+(OR_j)$ is shown the number of his input variables.
Definition 5. The out-degree of neuron $d^-(neuron_i)$ is the number of output variables, then the out-degree of the ith AND neuron $d^-(AND_i)$ is the number of his output variable; the out-degree of the jth OR neuron $d^-(OR_j)$ is shown the number of his output variables.

2.2 The architecture of AND-OR FNN

This feed-forward AND-OR FNN consists of five layers (Fig.3. MISO case), i.e. the input layer, fuzzification layer, double hidden layers (one consists of AND neurons, the other consists of OR neurons) and the defuzzification output layer, which corresponding to the four parts (fuzzy generator, fuzzy inference, rule base and fuzzy eliminator) of FLS (Fuzzy Logic System) respectively. Here the fuzzy inference and the fuzzy rule base are integrated into the double hidden layers. The inference mechanism behaves as the inference function of the hidden neurons. Thus the rule base can be auto-generated by training AND-OR FNN in virtue of input-output data.
Both W and V are connection matrixes, also imply relevant degree matrix (RDM) like introduce above. Vector H is the membership of consequents. The number of neurons in every layer is n , $n \times t$, m , s and 1 respectively (t is the number of fuzzy partitions.).

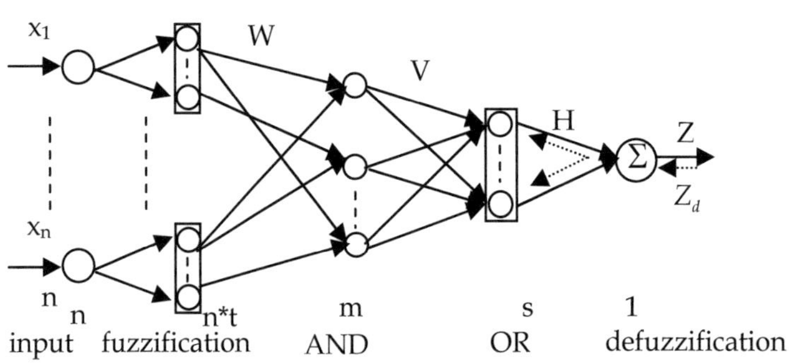

Fig. 3. The architecture of AND-OR FNN

Definition 6. The layer connectivity is the maximum in-degree of every neuron in this layer, including double hidden layer,

$$\begin{aligned} Con(AND) &= \max(d^{+}(AND_i)) \\ Con(OR) &= \max(d^{+}(OR_j)) \end{aligned} \tag{6}$$

where AND_i is the ith AND neuron, $d^{+}(AND_i)$ be the in-degree of the ith neuron. OR_j is the ith OR neuron, $d^{+}(OR_j)$ be the in-degree of the ith neuron.
Note: $Con(AND) \le n$ (n is the number of input variables). $Con(OR) \le m$ (m is the number of AND neurons).

2.3 The exact expression of every node in AND-OR FNN

According to the above definitions and the physical structure background, the AND-OR FNN model is derived as Fig. 3. The functions of the nodes in each layer are described as followers.
Layer 1 (input layer): For every node i in this layer, the input and the output are related by

7)

where O_i^1 denotes the output of ith neuron in layer 1, $i = 1,2,\cdots,n$. Here the signal only transfers to the next layer without processing.
Layer 2 (duzzification layer): In this layer, each neuron represents the membership function of linguistic variable. The most commonly used membership functions are shape of Bell and Gaussian. In this paper, Gaussian is adopted as membership function. The linguistic value (small ,$\cdots$, very large) A_j are used. The function is shown as.

$$O_{ij}^2 = \mu_{A_j}(x_i) = e^{\frac{-(x_i - m_{ij})^2}{\sigma^2}} \tag{8}$$

where $i = 1,2,\ldots n, j = 1,2,\ldots t$, m_{ij} and σ is the modal and spread of the jth fuzzy partition from the ith input variable.
Layer 3 (AND hidden layer): This layer is composed of AND neurons, Based on above definitions, the function is like.

$$\begin{aligned} O_k^3 &= \mathop{T}_{p_1=1}^{d^{+}(AND_k)} (wSO^2) \\ &= \mathop{\wedge}_{p_1=1}^{d^{+}(AND_k)} (w_{rk} \vee \mu_{A_{ij}}(x_i)) \end{aligned} \tag{9}$$

where $k = 1,2,\cdots,t^n$ $j = 1,2,\cdots,t$ $i = 1,2,\cdots,n$ $r = (i-1)\times t + j$, $d^{+}(AND_k)$ is the in-degree of the kth AND neuron. t^n is the total of AND neurons in this layer.
Note: when p_1 is fixed and $d^{+}(AND_i) \ge 2$, q must be different. That means the input of the same AND neuron O^2 must be from the different x_i
Layer 4 (OR hidden layer): This layer is composed of OR neurons, Based on above definitions, the function is like.

$$
\begin{aligned}
O_l^4 &= \mathop{S}_{p_2=1}^{d^+(OR_l)} (vTO^3) \\
&= \mathop{\vee}_{p_2=1}^{d^+(OR_l)} (v_{l,k} \wedge O_k^3)
\end{aligned}
\tag{10}
$$

where $k=1,2,\cdots,t''$, $l=1,2,\cdots,s$ $d^+(OR_l)$ is the in-degree of the lth OR neuron. s is the total of OR neuron.

Layer 5 (defuzzification layer): There is only one node in this layer, but includes forward compute and backward training. Center-of-gravity method is adopted for former compute as follows.

$$
z = O^5 = \frac{\sum O_l^4 h_{l,1}}{\sum O_l^4} \tag{11}
$$

where $l=1,2,\cdots,s$, H is the membership function of consequents. The latter is only imported to train data for optimization next. There is no conflict because the double directions are time-sharing. The function is like eq.(8)

$$
O^5 = \mu_{B_l}(z_d) = e^{\frac{-(z_d - m_j)^2}{\sigma^2}} \tag{12}
$$

3. Functional equivalent between fuzzy weighted Mamdani Inference and AND-OR FNN

This section demonstrates the functional equivalence between AND-OR FNN and fuzzy weighted Mamdani inference system, though these two models are motivated from different origins (AND-OR FNN is from physiology and fuzzy inference systems from cognitive science), thus auto-extracting the rule base by training AND-OR FNN. The functional equivalent under minor restrictions is illustrated

3.1 Fuzzy weighted Mamdani inference

The fuzzy weighted Mamdani inference system [9] utilizes local weight and global weight to avoid a serious shortcoming in that all propositions in the antecedent part are assumed to have equal importance, and that a number of rules executed in an inference path leading to a specified goal or the same rule employed in various inference paths leading to distinct final goals may have relative degrees of importance. Assume the number of the fuzzy IF-THEN rules with consequent $y\ is\ B_l$, then fuzzy rules can be represented as:

$$
\begin{aligned}
&Rule: if\ x_1 \text{ is } A_{1j} \text{and} \\
&\qquad\vdots \\
&\text{and } x_i\ is\ A_{ij} \text{ and} \\
&\qquad\vdots \\
&\text{and } x_n\ is\ A_{nj} \text{ then } y\ is\ B_l
\end{aligned}
\tag{13}
$$

where $x_1,\cdots,x_n$ are the input variables, y is the output, A_{ij} and B_i are the fuzzy sets of input and output, respectively. w_{ij} is local weights of the antecedent part; $v_1,\cdots,v_s$ is the class of global weight for every rules. $i=1,2,\cdots,n$, $j=1,2,\cdots,t$, $l=1,2,\cdots,s$, t is the total of antecedent fuzzy sets; s is the total of consequent fuzzy sets. The same B_i is collected to form s complex rules as follows:

$$
\begin{aligned}
Rule1: & \textit{if } x_1 \text{ is } A_{1i'} \text{and}\cdots \\
& \text{and } x_n \textit{ is } A_{ni''} \text{ then } y \textit{ is } B_1 \\
& or\cdots or \\
& \textit{if } x_1 \text{ is } A_{1j'} \text{ and}\cdots \\
& \text{and } x_n \textit{ is } A_{nj''} \text{ then } y \textit{ is } B_1 \\
& \vdots \\
RuleS: & \textit{if } x_1 \text{ is } A_{1k'} \text{and}\cdots \\
& \text{and } x_n \textit{ is } A_{nk''} \text{ then } y \textit{ is } B_s \\
& or\cdots or \\
& \textit{if } x_1 \text{ is } A_{nl'} \text{ and}\cdots \\
& \text{and } x_n \textit{ is } A_{nl''} \text{ then } y \textit{ is } B_s
\end{aligned}
\tag{14}
$$

where $i',i'',j',j'',k',k'',l',l'' \in [1,t]$

On the view of general fuzzy inference, to a single rule, the firing strength (or weight) of *ith* rule is usually obtained by min or multiplication operator, to the complex rule, the firing strength is the union λ_i, which is like:

$$
\begin{aligned}
\lambda_l &= \mathop{\vee}_{p_2=1}^{\Delta_l} (\mu_{A_{1i'}\times\cdots\times A_{ni''}}(x_1,\cdots,x_n), \\
&\qquad \cdots,\mu_{A_{1j'}\times\cdots\times A_{nj''}}(x_1,\cdots,x_n)) \\
&= \mathop{\vee}_{p_2=1}^{\Delta_l} \begin{pmatrix} \mathop{\wedge}_{p_1=1}^{\Psi_1}\left(\mu_{A_{1i'}}(x_1),\cdots,\mu_{A_{ni''}}(x_n)\right), \\ \cdots,\mathop{\wedge}_{p_1=1}^{\Psi_{n\times t}}\left(\mu_{A_{1j'}}(x_1),\cdots,\mu_{A_{nj''}}(x_n)\right) \end{pmatrix}
\end{aligned}
\tag{15}
$$

where Δ is the number of the same consequent B_l, Ψ the number of antecedent parts in this rule.

On the view of fuzzy weighted Mamdani inference, local weight and global weight are considered by a mode of $<\vee,\wedge>$ as follows:

$$
\lambda_l = \mathop{\vee}_{p_2=1}^{\Delta_l} \begin{pmatrix} v_1 \wedge \left(\mathop{\wedge}_{p_1=1}^{\Psi_1}\left(w_{1i'} \vee \mu_{A_{1i'}}(x_1),\cdots,w_{ni''} \vee \mu_{A_{ni''}}(x_n)\right)\right), \\ \cdots,v_{\Delta_l} \wedge \left(\mathop{\wedge}_{p_1=1}^{\Psi_{n\times t}}\left(w_{1j'} \vee \mu_{A_{1j'}}(x_1),\cdots,w_{nj'} \vee \mu_{A_{nj''}}(x_n)\right)\right) \end{pmatrix}
\tag{16}
$$

In general, center-of-gravity method is adopted for defuzzification as follows.

$$
Y = \frac{\sum_{l=1}^{s} \lambda_l \mu_{B_l}(y)}{\sum_{l=1}^{s} \lambda_l}
\tag{17}
$$

3.2 Functional equivalence and its implication

From (11) and (17), it is obvious that the functional equivalence between an AND-OR FNN and a fuzzy weighted Mamdani inference can be established if the following is true.

1. The number of AND neurons is equal to the number of fuzzy IF-THEN rules.
2. The number of OR neurons is equal to the number of fuzzy complex IF-THEN rules.
3. The T-norm and S-norm used to compute each rule's firing strength is min and max, respectively.
4. Both the AND-OR FNN and the fuzzy inference system under consideration use the same center-of-gravity method to derive their overall outputs.

Under these conditions, when $RDM(w_{ij})=0$, $RDM(v_{ij})=1$, AND-OR FNN is completely connected, which is shown that every part of antecedent is the same important to the output, $\Psi_k = n$, $\Delta_l = n \times t$ and equal to the general fuzzy inference. But it falls short of the practice. When $w_i \in [0,1]$, $v_i \in [0,1]$, every part of antecedent has different important degree to the output and every rules has different important degree to the final output.

4. Optimization for the AND-OR FNN

In general, gradient-based optimization is often chosen for ANN, Pedrycz [8] has proved that the output of AND neuron and its derivative are heavily affected by the increasing values of "n". Meanwhile, the final output of AND-OR FNN is not a smooth function. Obviously gradient-based optimization is not preferred, A far more comprehensive optimization policy is proposed, which is a hybrid learning methodology comprising of three fundamental techniques, namely genetic optimization, pruning algorithm and ant colony system.

4.1 Structure optimization

The key part is structure design to solve the problem using network, AND-OR FNN could be over parameterized, and in this case, they produce an over trained net, which leads to worse generalization capacity. That is the reason why, in order to eliminate unnecessary weights or parameters. There are no certain methods to solve the structure optimization. In this paper, GA (Genetic Algorithm) and PA (Pruning Algorithm) are adopted to optimize the structure for avoiding local optimization and reducing the connections.

4.1.1 GA optimization

GA (Genetic Algorithm) is a very effective method to solving the structure optimization problem because of the superiority of robust, random, global and parallel process[10]. Structure optimization is transferred to the species evolution by GA to obtain the optimal solution.

4.1.1.1 Structure code mode

Parameters encoding is the first phase of GA optimization. Parameters are often transformed to unsigned binary. Here the structure parameters of two hidden layers are considered on focus by double matrixes as follows:

$$\begin{aligned} RDM(AND) &= \left[w_{i,j}^{and} \right]_{m\times(n\times t)} \\ RDM(OR) &= \left[v_{i,j}^{or} \right]_{s\times m} \end{aligned} \tag{18}$$

where i,j, m,n,t and s is the same like before. Lining up the two matrixes to a binary string as initial population represents the structure status, which is exactly satisfied to GA. In the initialization, $RDM(w_{ij})=0$ and $RDM(v_{ij})=1$ are set, the status of AND-OR FNN is completely connected. The authoritative opinion from experts can be put into initial population as seeds to reach the best initialization.

4.1.1.2 Objective Function

Proceeding with the numeric data, we carry the genetic optimization of the network. The parameters of the GA used were chosen experimentally. The fitness function maximized by the GA is expressed in the form of the sum of squared errors between target values (data) and outputs of network. This fitness has to be minimized (it stands in contrast with the classic way of using fitness functions in GA whose values are maximized; if necessary a simple transformation of taking the reciprocal of the fitness, $1/fitness$, brings in line with the way of maximizing the fitness)

$$fitness=\frac{1}{(\sum(z_d-z)^2)} \tag{19}$$

4.1.2 Pruning algorithm

The pruning of the network is a process consisting of removing unnecessary parameters and nodes during the training process of the network without losing its generalization capacity [11]. The best architecture has been sought using GA in conjunction with pruning algorithms. There are three situations as follow:

1. For AND neuron, if the connection is equal to zero, this means that the corresponding input impacts the output of this neuron, the connection can be pruned away if its value is one. For the OR neuron a reverse situation occurs: the connection equal to one implies that the specific input is essential and affects the output of the neuron. The connection can be pruned away if its value is zero.
2. For $RDM(AND)$, the number of zero in every line is shown as the in-degree of this AND neuron, the node can be pruned away if all one in the line. For $RDM(OR)$, the number of one in every line is shown as the in-degree of this OR neuron, the node can be pruned away if all zero in the line.
3. For $RDM(AND)$, if there are the same line in the matrix, that means the node is redundant, can be pruned away. For $RDM(OR)$, that means the node is conflict each other, need be pruned away.

4.2 Ant Colony Optimization as parametric refinement

As well known, most neural networks are trained using Bp algorithm, whose main drawbacks are easily getting stuck in local minim and needing longer training time. And it also requires the output function is smooth, $\vee,\wedge$ operators can't satisfy at all. ACO (Ant colony optimization) algorithm [12] was adopted to optimize the connection value of AND-OR FNN here. This algorithm is a member of ant colony algorithms family, in swarm intelligence methods, and it constitutes some metaheuristic optimizations. Initially proposed by Marco Dorigo in 1992 in his PhD thesis, the first algorithm was aiming to search for an optimal path in a graph, based on the behavior of ants seeking a path between their colony and a source of food. The original idea has since diversified to solve a wider class of numerical problems, and as a result, several problems have emerged, drawing on various aspects of the behavior of ants.The main features are high-precision solution, fast search speed, convergence to global optimum and greedy heuristic search. The basic idea is: assuming that there are m parameters consist of the connections from GA and PA. First, all the parameters are sequenced and set to N randomly values in [0, 1], and for the parameter $p_i \ (1 \le i \le m)$, compose a set, denoted as I_{p_i}. And then the number of ants is set to h, they start from the random connection to search the optimal solution, choosing next connection from every set I_{p_i} according to the amount of pheromones as follows:

$$Prob(\tau_j^k(I_{p_i})) = \frac{\tau_j(I_{p_i})}{\sum_{g=1}^{N} \tau_g(I_{p_i})} \tag{20}$$

where $\tau_j(I_{p_i})$ is shown the amount pheromones of the jth connection $p_j(I_{p_i})$.

When an ant finishes choosing the connection in all the sets, it arrives at the food source, and returns its nest through the paths just gone by it, and then adjust the amount of pheromones corresponding to the chosen connection as follow rules.

$$\begin{aligned} &\tau_j(I_{p_i})(t+m) = \rho\tau_j(I_{p_i})(t) + \Delta\tau_j(I_{p_i}) \\ &\Delta\tau_j(I_{p_i}) = \sum_{k=1}^{h} \Delta\tau_j^k(I_{p_i}) \end{aligned} \tag{21}$$

where $\rho(0 \le \rho \le 1)$ is shown the evaporating of pheromone, $\Delta\tau_j^k(I_{p_i})$ is the kth ant leave pheromones on the jth connection in set I_{p_i}. It is described as follows:

$$\Delta\tau_j^k(I_{p_i}) = \begin{cases} Q / e^k & \text{if } p_j(I_{p_i}) \text{ is selected} \\ 0 & \textit{otherwise} \end{cases} \tag{22}$$

where Q is the constant to adjust factor. $e^k = |z_d - z|$ is shown the network output error with a group of connection value, which is selected by the kth ant. Obviously the less the error is, the more the increment of the corresponding amount of pheromone is.

Finally, until all the ants find the best optimal solution for the connections value.

5. Application to ship control

According to the principle of manual steering, it makes full use of the advantages of fuzzy logic and neural network. An AND-OR FNN controller is presented to adapt the change of navigation environment and get the information of ship maneuverability automatically. The structure and parameters of AND-OR FNN controller are learned by GA, PA and ACO. Fuzzy rules can be auto-obtained from a group of sample data, which is generated by a fuzzy control system. Fig.4 shows a block diagram of the AND-OR FNN autopilot. Test results show that an effect method has been provided for the improvement of ship steering control.

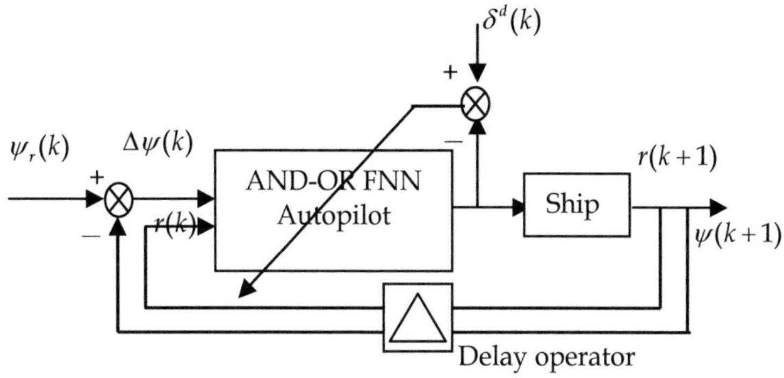

Fig. 4. AND-OR FNN autopilot for ship course-keeping

Double input variable of AND-OR FNN ship controller are heading error $\Delta\psi = \psi_k(k) - \psi(k)$ and yaw rate $\gamma(k) = \frac{d\psi}{dt}$. The control action generated by the autopilot is the command rudder angle $\delta(k)$. The range of values (universe of discourse) for a given autopilot inputs and output are $(-20^{\circ}, 20^{\circ})$ and $(-2.5^{\circ}/\sec, 2.5^{\circ}/\sec)$, respectively. It is usually required that the rudder should move from 35° port to 35° starboard within 30s.

5.1 The source of the experimental data set

In order to obtain integrated and exact training data, a fuzzy control system for a tanker is simulated with nonlinear Nomoto model as controlling plant. The input gains of a fuzzy controller (K=0.16sec^{-1}, T=100sec). The fuzzy controller includes double inputs, the error in the ship heading ($\Delta\psi(k)$) and the change in that error ($\gamma(k)$). Every input variable is fuzzied into 11 triangular membership functions; thus form 121 pieces of rules. The output of the fuzzy controller is the rudder input (δ). We want the tanker heading to track the reference input heading ψ_r. We assume the tanker as a continuous time system controlled by the fuzzy controller, which is implemented on a digital computer with a sampling interval of T=0.1sec. From manipulated index standpoints, it satisfied the index of 15000tdw tanker [13], a fuzzy closed-loop controlling system is designed with fuzzy rule base from experience. The positive direction angle is defined that the rudder angle goes around toward right. Center-of-gravity is adopted as defuzzification methods.

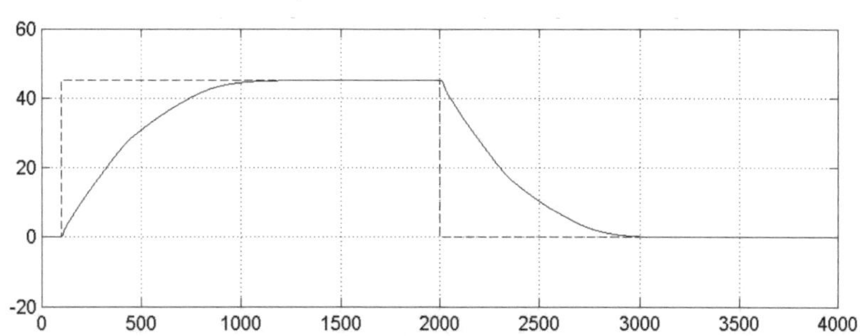

Fig. 5. Ship heading (solid) and desired ship heading (dashed)

The reference input heading ψ_r is increased 45 degree every 2000sec, rapidly. The digital simulation is completed to closed-loop with the sampling periods h=10sec, the sampling state variable $\Delta\psi$, γ and controlled variable δ , the ship heading and desired ship heading is like Fig. 5 and we obtain the change of rudder angle results utilizing conventional fuzzy control as Fig. 6.and the data sequence is $\{\Delta\psi(k),\gamma(k),\delta(k),k=1,2,...\}$.

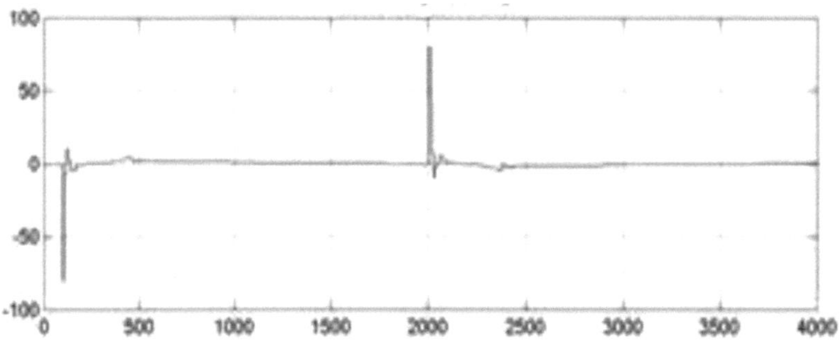

Fig. 6. Rudder angle in the conventional fuzzy control

5.2 The structure design and simulation result

In this section, an AND-OR FNN ship controller is constructed successfully. Firstly, $\Delta\psi(k)$ and $\gamma(k)$ are double input variable; $\delta(k)$ is the output variable, which are all fuzzied into 3 Gaussian membership functions with 0.5 overlap degree, thus there are 9 pieces of rules. According to analysis before, there are 9 AND neurons and 3 OR neurons in AND-OR FNN. Initialize structure parameters with all connections to form the structure string that is $RDM(w_i)=0$, $RDM(v_i)=1$. The input-output data is from $\{\Delta\psi(k),\gamma(k),\delta(k),k=1,2,...\}$ to train and test. .The structure and parameters are optimized by GA PA and ACO, some parameters is chosen experimentally, which is including population size=100, crossover rate=0.7, Mutation rate=0.01 and selection process is tournament, and the parameters of ACO are $m=19$, $p_i\in[0,1]$, $N=30$, $\rho=0.65$, $h=30$, $Q=10$ .The ultimate better structure result is transformed into the AND-OR FNN like Fig. 7. It is obviously that there are 5 AND neurons and 3 OR neurons left, that is, 5 pieces of fuzzy rules and 3 complex rules. The ultimate better performance result is compared with fuzzy control system. Test data set is

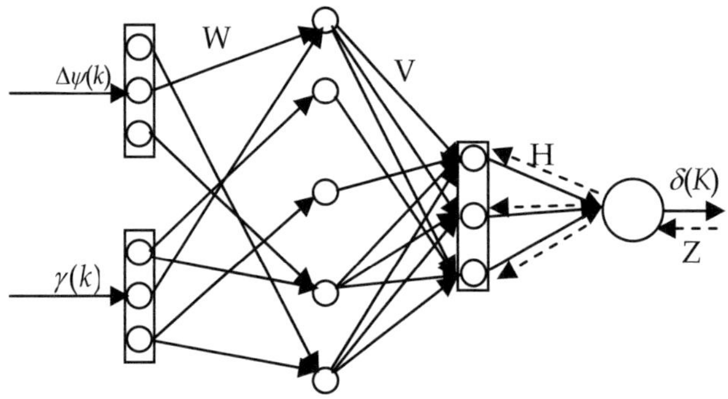

Fig. 7. The AND-OR FNN ship controller structure

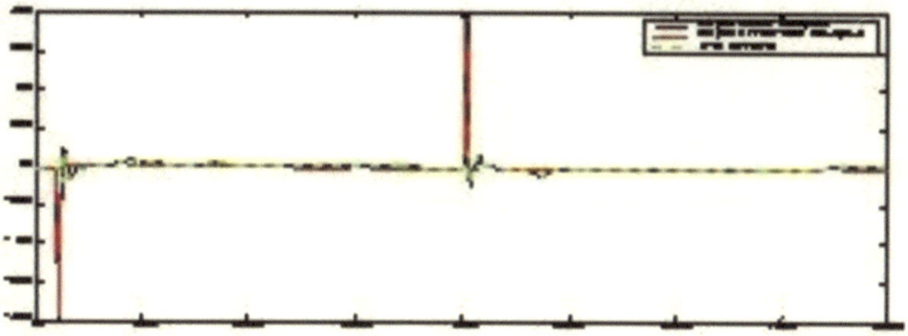

Fig. 8. The performance index compared

form the different part with training data in the same sequence introduce above. Fig. 8 shows the error comparison between test results and objective data. The simulation result illustrated the effectiveness of proposed method.

5. Conclusion

In this paper, we have proposed a novel AND-OR FNN and a piecewise optimization approach, the symbol expressions of every node in the AND-OR FNN are educed in detail, the input space is reduced by special inner structure of AND and OR. The equivalence is proved to the fuzzy weighted Mamdani inference. The fuzzy rule base auto-extracted is equal to optimize the architecture of AND-OR FNN. This novel approach has been validated using AND-OR FNN ship controller design. The simulation results illustrate the approach is practicable, simple and effective and the performance is much better than ordinary fuzzy controller.

6. Acknowledgements

This paper is supported by the Doctoral Foundation of Education Committees (2003151005) and Ministry of Communication of P. R. China (200332922505)

7. References

[1] Pierre Yves G.: Neuro-Fuzzy Logic [A].In: Proc. IEEE-FUZZ[C]. New Orleans:[s.n.], (1996).512-518.

[2] Yager R.: OWA neurons: Anew class of fuzzy neurons [A]. In: Proc. IEEE-FUZZ [c].San Diego:[s.n.],(1992).2316-2340.

[3] Pedrcy. W. and Rocha. A F.: Fuzzy-set based models of neurons and knowledge-based networks. IEEE.Trans. on Fuzzy System,1(4)(1993)254-266

[4] Hirota K, Pedrycz W.: Knowledge-based networks in classification problems. Journal, Fuzzy Sets and Systems, 59(3) (1993) 271-279

[5] Pedrycz W and Nicolino J.Pizzi.: Fuzzy adaptive logic networks Proceeding of NAFIPS 2002 June (2002) 500 -505

[6] Pedrycz W and Succi.G.: Genectic granular classifiers in modeling software quality. The journal of Systems and software, 75(2005)277-285

[7] Bailey S A, Chen Ye hwa.: ATwo Layer Network using the OR/AND Neuron [A]. In: proc. IEEE-FUZZ [C].Anchorage:[s.n.],(1998).1566-1571.

[8] Pedrycz W. Reformat M.: "Genetically optimized logic models" Fuzzy Sets and Systems 150(2) (2005)351-371
[9] Yeung D.S and Tsang E.C.C.: Weighted fuzzy production rules. Fuzzy sets and systems 88(1997)299-313
[10] Shuiling Zeng, Luanjiao Song and Weihong Xu.: Neural network structure optimization based on genetic algorithm. Journal of Jishou University Vol.26 No3 (2005)118-120
[11] Rosa Maria Garcia-Gimeno, Cesar Hervas-Martinez and Maria Isabel de Siloniz.: Improving artificial neural networks with a pruning methodology and genetic algorithms for their application in microbial growth prediction in food. International Journal of food Microbiology, 72(2002)19-30
[12] Haibin Duan.: Ant colony algorithm: theory and applications, science press (2005)390-397
[13] Guoxun Yang.: Study on ship motion hybrid intelligent control and its interacting simulation based on virtual reality. PhD Thesis. Dalian: Dalian Maritime University,(2002)

4

Some Issues of ACO Algorithm Convergence

Lorenzo Carvelli[1] and Giovanni Sebastiani[1,2]
[1]*Mathematics department, Sapienza Università di Roma*
[2]*Istituto per le Applicazioni del Calcolo "Mauro Picone", CNR*
Italy

1. Introduction

The study of the convergence of ACO algorithms, or more in general of stochastic algorithms for solving combinatorial optimization problems is very important. In fact, it can provide information that can be useful in practice when applying such algorithms. This information can be of different kinds.

The most basic question of interest is about algorithm capability of solving the problem of interest. Given the stochastic nature of the kind of algorithms considered, this question can be properly formulated in terms of the "failure" probability, i.e. the probability that after the current iteration the algorithm has not yet found the solution. We are of course interested in ACO algorithms whose failure probability converges to zero. Another kind of convergence, that is stronger than simply having the failure probability to converge to zero, is when the whole ACO colony approaches, as time goes to infinity, a set of individuals all corresponding to one of the problem solutions. In addition to algorithm's effectiveness, other natural questions arise. In fact, the user is interested in the quantification of the time used by the algorithm to solve the problem. Since this time is random, the quantification will involve its expected value, its variance and ideally its distribution. Let us now go back to the failure probability. There are often situations where, by applying ACO algorithms, or more in general stochastic algorithms, to solve combinatorial optimization problems, the failure probability goes to zero too slowly. In those situations, one could ask the question if, instead of running the ACO algorithm for a certain time, it would be more convenient to stop it after another time T, smaller than the former, and to start it again from the beginning, and so on, until the original time is reached. In the case of a positive answer to this question, one could also study the problem of finding an optimal value for the time T.

In this chapter, we will illustrate some relevant known theoretical results on the former issues. Furthermore, we will provide some results on a our ingoing research on the last issue. Beside this, some numerical simulation results will also be introduced and discussed.

2. Algorithm's convergence

By definition, the failure probability is a non-increasing function of the number of iterations. The effectiveness of the algorithm can then be translated into the convergence to zero of the failure probability. Although this kind of convergence requirement is very basic, it is not always fullfilled. Therefore, theoretical studies on this kind of convergence are well motivated. Knowing in advance that the failure probability is decreasing to zero makes the user confident

that waiting long enough time, there are very good chances that the algorithm will solve the problem.
Let $X^i(t)$, $t = 1,2,\ldots$ be the stochastic process modeling the configuration assumed by the i-th of the A ants of the colony. Let X^* denote the optimal set for the function f to be maximized (or minimized).
We can distinguish two kinds of convergence:

convergence in value: when it holds

$$p_v(t) := P\left(\bigcap_{i=1}^{A}\bigcap_{k=1}^{t}\left\{X^i(k) \notin X^*\right\}\right) \to 0;$$

convergence in model: if for some $x^* \in X^*$ we have

$$p_m(x^*,t) := P\left(\bigcap_{i=1}^{A}\left\{X^i(t) = x^*\right\}\right) \to 1.$$

The convergence in value is important. This property tells us something about the way in which the algorithm is exploring the configuration space X. It is strongly connected to the strict positivity of the conditional probability to visit at the end of any iteration one point of X^* given that we are not currently in X^*. However, the convergence in model is stronger than the one in value. In the former, the probabilistic model itself evolves towards one that generates only optimal solutions. Not all algorithms converging in value are also converging in model. For example, this is the case for the algorithm that explores the configuration space in a uniform and independent way, known as Random Search (RS). In fact, we have $p_v(t) = \left(1 - \frac{|X^*|}{|X|}\right)^{At} \to 0$, while it holds $p_m(x^*,t) = \left(\frac{1}{|X|}\right)^{A}$.
In the following, we will only cope with the case where the ACO algorithm does not use the visibility matrix η_{ij}. In this case, the configuration of each ant of the colony is built by a path over the construction graph [Gutjahr (2000)]:

$$p(j|s^p) = \frac{\tau_{ij}^{\alpha}}{\sum\limits_{j \in N(s^p)} \tau_{ij}^{\alpha}} \quad \forall j \in N(s^p), \tag{1}$$

where (i,j) is the arc by which we continue the partial path s^p, τ_{ij} is its current pheromone value, and α is a positive parameter.
By simply imposing some constraints on the pheromone matrix, it is possible to have an ACO algorithm that converges in value. Indeed, for an ACO algorithm with $0 < \tau_{min} \le \tau_{ij} \le \tau_{max}$, given any $\epsilon > 0$, we have that, for t large enough it holds

$$p_v(t) \le \epsilon,$$

that is, by definition,

$$\lim_{t \to \infty} p_v(t) = 0.$$

In fact, because of the bounds on the pheromone matrix, every choice made by the rule in Eq. (1) has a probability larger or equal to

$$p_{min} = \frac{\tau_{min}^{\alpha}}{(D_{max} - 1)\tau_{max}^{\alpha} + \tau_{min}^{\alpha}} > 0$$

where D_{max}, is the maximum value of the degree of the nodes of the construction graph. It then follows that any configuration of the whole space X, including an optimal one x^*, can be visited at any iteration with a probability larger or equal than $\hat{p} = (p_{min})^{L_{max}} > 0$, where $L_{max} = max_{x \in X} L(x)$, and $L(x)$ is the length of the path by which we have built the configuration x. From this, it follows that

$$p_v(t) \leq (1 - \hat{p})^{At}, \tag{2}$$

i.e. there is convergence in value.
Different kinds of ACO algorithms are such that suitable bounds on the pheromone matrix values hold. Among them, the Max Min Ant System (MMAS), where lower and upper bounds on the pheromone matrix values are imposed explicitly when updating recursively them along iterations

$$\tau_{ij}(t+1) = \min\{\tau_{max}, \max\{(1-\rho)\tau_{ij}(t) + \rho 1\{(i,j) \in x_b(t)\}/L(x_b(t)), \tau_{min}\}\},$$

where $0 < \rho < 1$, and $1(\cdot)$ is the indicator function [Stützle & Hoos (1997)], [Stützle & Hoos (2000)]. We notice that the pheromone is reinforced only on arcs belonging to one configuration $x_b(t)$, e.g. the best one (w.r.t. the objective function f) that we have visited so far, i.e. $x_b(t) = \arg \max_{i=1,\ldots,A,\, k=1,\ldots,t} f(x^i(k))$. We could use another kind of update where no bounds on the pheromone are explicitely imposed:

$$\tau_{ij}(t+1) = (1-\rho)\tau_{ij}(t) + \rho 1\{(i,j) \in x_b(t)\}/L(x_b(t)).$$

In this case, after t iterations, the pheromone values are bounded from above by

$$(1-\rho)^t \tau_0 + \rho \sum_{i=1}^{t} (1-\rho)^{t-i} / L_{min}.$$

The above quantity is bounded from above by $\tau_0 + 1/L_{min}$, where $L_{min} = min_{x \in X} L(x)$. In this case, we do not have in general any guarantee that also a lower bound holds. However, not having a lower bound sometimes can be a positive condition. In fact, as seen above, when we have both lower and upper bounds, convergence in value holds. When a lower bound holds, we cannot have convergence in model because at any iteration we have a lower bound for the conditional probability of reaching any configuration given any other. We will see now that if we impose the weaker condition that the lower bound of the pheromone matrix at time t, $\tau_{min}(t)$ (it always exists since there is a finite number of edges) goes to zero slowly enough, convergence in value still holds. This is stated by the following theorem [Dorigo & Stutzle (2004)].

Theorem 1. *Given an ACO algorithm with pheromone values having constant upper bound τ_{max} and lower bound $\tau_{min}(t)$*

$$\tau_{min}(t) = \Omega\left(\frac{1}{\ln(t+1)}\right),$$

then we have

$$p_v(t) \to 0.$$

In fact, similarly to Eq. (2), one can prove that

$$p_v(t) \leq \prod_{k=1}^{t}\left(1-(p_{min}(k))^{L_{max}}\right)^{A},$$

where

$$p_{min}(t) = \frac{\tau_{min}^{\alpha}(t)}{(D_{max}-1)\tau_{max}^{\alpha}+\tau_{min}^{\alpha}(t)} \geq \frac{\tau_{min}^{\alpha}(t)}{D_{max}\tau_{max}^{\alpha}}.$$

This implies that

$$p_v(t) \leq \prod_{k=1}^{t}\left(1-\left(\frac{\tau_{min}^{\alpha}(k)}{D_{max}\tau_{max}^{\alpha}}\right)^{L_{max}}\right)^{A} = \prod_{k=1}^{t}\left(1-K(\tau_{min}(k))^{\alpha Lmax}\right)^{A}. \quad (3)$$

Now, we prove that the infinite product on the final expression of Eq. (3) converges to zero. By the following lemma, it is sufficient to show that

$$\sum_{t=1}^{\infty}(\tau_{min}(t))^{\alpha L_{max}} \to +\infty.$$

Lemma 1. *Let $\{a_n\}_{n\in IN}$ be a sequence of real numbers converging to zero such that $0 \leq a_n < 1$, $\forall n$. Then, it follows that $\sum_n a_n \to +\infty \Rightarrow \prod_n (1-a_n)^k \to 0$, $\forall k \geq 1$.*

Since $\tau_{min}(t) = \Omega\left(\frac{1}{\ln(t+1)}\right)$, then the terms of the series $\sum_{t=1}^{\infty}(\tau_{min}(t))^{\alpha L_{max}}$ are asymptotically bounded from below by $\left(\frac{C}{\ln(t+1)}\right)^{\alpha L_{max}}$. Then, this series is diverging because $\sum_{t=1}^{\infty}\left(\frac{C}{\ln(t+1)}\right)^{\alpha L_{max}}$ is infinite. Finally, we have

$$\lim_{t\to\infty} p_v(t) = 0.$$

We will see now, that the variant of the MMAS algorithm such that τ_{max} is constant and $\tau_{min}(t) = \Omega\left(\frac{1}{\ln(t+1)}\right)$ converges in model. First, it is easy to see that, conditionally to the event $\{X_b(0) = x^* \in X^*\}$, the pheromone values of arcs that do not belong to x^* tends deterministically to zero [Dorigo & Stutzle (2004)]. In fact, $\forall t > 0$ we have $p(X_b(t) = x^*|X_b(0) = x^*) = 1$, and for any $(i,j) \notin x^*$, $\tau_{ij}(t) = \max\{\tau_{min}(t), (1-\rho)^t\tau_{ij}(0)\} \to 0$. Similarly, for any $(i,j) \in x^*$, $\tau_{ij}(t) \to 1/L(x^*)$.
We recall that $p_m(x^*,t)$ denotes the probability that each ant will build x^* at iteration t. A lower-bound for $p(x^*,t)$ is

$$\begin{aligned} p_m(x^*,t) &\geq p(X_b(\lfloor t/2\rfloor) = x^*)\cdot p\left(\bigcap_{i=1}^{A}\{X^i(t) = x^*\}|X_b(\lfloor t/2\rfloor) = x^*\right) \\ &= p(X_b(\lfloor t/2\rfloor) = x^*)\cdot[p(X^1(t) = x^*|X_b(\lfloor t/2\rfloor) = x^*)]^A. \end{aligned}$$

The last passage is justified because, conditionally to the event $\{X_b(\lfloor t/2\rfloor) = x^*\}$ the pheromone evolution after time $\lfloor t/2\rfloor$ will be deterministic and the A ants will evolve identically and independently from each other. Furthermore, it holds

$$
\begin{aligned}
p_m(x^*,t) &\geq p(X_b(\lfloor t/2 \rfloor) = x^*) \cdot \left[p(X^1(t - \lfloor t/2 \rfloor) = x^* | X_b(0) = x^*) \right]^A \\
&\geq p(X_b(\lfloor t/2 \rfloor) = x^*) \cdot \left(\frac{\min_{(i,j)\in x^*}(\tau_{ij}(t - \lfloor t/2 \rfloor))^\alpha}{\min_{(i,j)\in x^*}(\tau_{ij}(t - \lfloor t/2 \rfloor))^\alpha + \sum_{(i,h)\notin x^*}(\tau_{ih}(t - \lfloor t/2 \rfloor))^\alpha} \right)^{AL_{max}},
\end{aligned}
$$

where $(i,j) \in x^*$. We notice that

$$
\begin{aligned}
&\lim_{t\to\infty} \frac{\min_{(i,j)\in x^*}(\tau_{ij}(t - \lfloor \frac{t}{2} \rfloor))^\alpha}{\min_{(i,j)\in x^*}(\tau_{ij}(t - \lfloor \frac{t}{2} \rfloor))^\alpha + \sum_{(i,h)\notin x^*}(\tau_{ih}(t - \lfloor \frac{t}{2} \rfloor))^\alpha} \\
= &\lim_{t\to\infty} \frac{\min_{(i,j)\in x^*}(\tau_{ij}(t))^\alpha}{\min_{(i,j)\in x^*}(\tau_{ij}(t))^\alpha + \sum_{(i,h)\notin x^*}(\tau_{ih}(t))^\alpha} \\
= &\frac{1}{1 + \sum_{(i,h)\notin x^*} \frac{\lim_{t\to\infty}(\tau_{ih}(t))^\alpha}{\min_{(i,j)\in x^*} \lim_{t\to\infty}(\tau_{ij}(t))^\alpha}} = 1,
\end{aligned}
$$

where we used the fact that $\lim_{t\to\infty} (\tau_{ij}(t))^\alpha > 0$ when $(i,j) \in x^*$. Since we also have that

$$
\lim_{t\to\infty} p(X_b(\lfloor t/2 \rfloor) = x^*) = \lim_{t\to\infty} p(X_b(t) = x^*) = 1,
$$

it finally follows that $\lim_{t\to\infty} p_m(x^*,t) = 1$, that is we have convergence in model.

3. Expected time to convergence

For combinatorial optimization problems, exaustive search can provide problem solution in a finite time, although this time grows tremendously with problem size. Therefore, it is natural to study the expected time needed for an algorithm to solve the problem as function of problem dimension. This problem can be studied for some classes of ACO algorithms, by using discrete time Markov chains on a countably infinite state space. We will describe now some general results which can be used to provide upper bounds for the expected time needed by a certain class of ACO algorithms to find an optimal solution [Gutjahr & Sebastiani (2008)]. To show their utility, we will also apply them to the MMAS algorithm [Gutjahr & Sebastiani (2008)]. The class of ACO algorithms involved are those such that the recursive rule for the pheromone only depends on the best-so-far-solution $x_b(t)$. This is the case for the MMAS algorithm. We also assume that, $x_b(t)$ is changed only when there is a strict increase of the objective function: $x_b(t+1) \neq x_b(t) \Leftrightarrow f(x_b(t+1)) > f(x_b(t))$.

Definition 1. *For any objective function $f(\cdot)$, we assume that the elements $f_1, ..., f_M$ of the finite set $\{f(x)|x \in X\}$ are ordered such that $f_1 < f_2 < ... < f_M$. We also define*

$$
L_j = \{x \in S \,|\, f(x) = f_j\},
$$

i.e. the level set *of index j, with $j = 1, ..., M$. The number M of level sets may vary from 1, in the case of a constant function, up to $|X|$ when there are no points in X with the same value of f.*

We notice, that if at time m we have that $x_b(m) \in L_j$ for some $j \in \{1, ..., M-1\}$, then $x_b(m')$ will be equal to $x_b(m)$ for $m' = m+1, ..., \bar{m}-1$ up to iteration $\bar{m}$ in which a solution with a

value of f higher than $x(m)$, so that $x_b(\bar{m}) \in L_k$ with $k > j$. Hence, at iteration m', the point $x_b(m')$ is identical to the one of the last time or it belongs to L_k with $k > j$. This means that transitions between $x_b(t) \in L_j$ and $x_b(t+1) \in L_k$ are allowed only if $k > j$.
Let us consider the homogeneous Markov process $X^t = (X_b(t), \tau(t))$, where τ denotes the pheromone matrix. Since the real numbers are approximated on a computer by a subset of the set $\mathcal{Q}$ of the rational numbers, it is not restrictive in practice to assume that this process takes values in the set $X \times \mathcal{Q}^{|A|}$. This last set can be partitoned as

$$X \times \mathcal{Q}^{|A|} = \bigcup_{k=1}^{M} L_k \times \mathcal{Q}^{|A|} = \bigcup_{k=1}^{M} (L_k \times \mathcal{Q}^{|A|}) = \bigcup_{k=1}^{M} Y_k,$$

where $Y_k = L_k \times \mathcal{Q}^{|A|}$. Analogously as before, transitions between $Y(t) \in Y_j$ and $Y(t+1) \in Y_k$ are allowed only if $k > j$.
We can now introduce two lemmas [Gutjahr & Sebastiani (2008)].

Lemma 2. *Let $X^0, X^1, \ldots$ be a homogeneous Markov process on a countably infinite state space Y, with partition $Y_1, \ldots, Y_M$ each of which is also countably infinite, such that, $\forall k \neq j$, we have*

$$p(X^{t+1} = y | X^t = x) > 0, \; \forall y \in Y_k, \; \forall x \in Y_j \; \Leftrightarrow \; k > j,$$

and let $E[T_{x \to Y_M}]$ be the expected time to reach the set Y_M, that corresponds to the optimal set, starting from $x \notin Y_M$, that is

$$E[T_{x \to Y_M}] := \sum_{t=1}^{\infty} t p(X^t \in Y_M, X^s \notin Y_M, 1 \leq s \leq t-1 | X^0 = x).$$

Then, for $x \in Y_j$ and $j = 1, \ldots, M-1$, it follows that

$$E[T_{x \to Y_M}] \leq E[T_{x \to \bar{Y}_j}] + \sum_{k=j+1}^{M-1} \sum_{l=1}^{\infty} E[T_{x_{l,k} \to Y_M}] p(x \to x_{l,k}),$$

where $\bigcup_{l=1}^{\infty} \{x_{l,k}\} = Y_k$,

$$E[T_{x \to \bar{Y}_j}] := \sum_{t=1}^{\infty} t p(X^t \notin Y_j, X^s \in Y_j, 1 \leq s \leq t-1 | X^0 = x),$$

$$p(x \to x_{l,k}) := \sum_{t=1}^{\infty} p(X^t = x_{l,k}, X^s \in Y_j, 1 \leq s \leq t-1 | X^0 = x).$$

Lemma 3. *Under the same hypothesis of the last lemma, it follows that the expected value of the time T_M to reach the set Y_M, that is*

$$E[T_M] := \sum_{t=1}^{\infty} t p(X^t \in Y_M, X^s \notin Y_M, 0 \leq s \leq t-1),$$

is bounded from above by

$$E[T_M] \leq \sum_{j=1}^{M-1} p(X^0 \in Y_j) \sum_{k=j}^{M-1} \sup_{y \in Y_k} \{E[T_{y \to \bar{Y}_k}]\} \leq \sum_{k=1}^{M-1} \sup_{y \in Y_k} \{E[T_{y \to \bar{Y}_k}]\}.$$

We will now apply the last lemma to the MMAS algorithm [Gutjahr & Sebastiani (2008)]. It fullfills the hypothesis of this lemma. In fact, because of the pheromone bounds, transitions between different $x_b(t)$ at any two consecutive times have a strictly positive probability iff the index of the set Y_j increases. To this aim, we first show a useful property of the algorithm MMAS. If $x_b(0) = y \in L_k$ and $\tau_{max} < 1$, then exists a deterministic time t^*, independent from the initial pheromone, such that, for any time $t > t^*$ where $x_b(t)$ is unchanged, the pheromone $\tau(t)$ is constant and equal to $\tau(t^*) = \tau^*(y)$, where $\tau^*_{ij}(y) = \tau_{max}$ for any arc (i,j) belongs to y, and $\tau^*_{ij}(y) = \tau_{min}$ otherwise. The time t^* is given by $t^* = \max\{t_1, t_2\}$, where

$$t_1 = \left\lceil \frac{\log \tau_{min} - \log \tau_{max}}{\log(1-\rho)} \right\rceil,$$

and

$$t_2 = \left\lceil \frac{\log(1-\tau_{max}) - \log(1-\tau_{min})}{\log(1-\rho)} \right\rceil.$$

Based on this property, it is possible to prove the following lemma.

Lemma 4. *For the algorithms MMAS and for $\tau_{max} < 1$ we have that*

$$\sup_{y \in Y_k} \{E[T_{y \to \bar{Y}_k}]\} \le t^* + 1/\bar{p}_k,$$

where $\bar{p}_k$ it is the smallest probability to get out from Y_k after the pheromone became constant

$$\bar{p}_k := \inf_{y \in L_k} p(X^1 \notin Y_k | X^0 = (y, \tau^*(y))),$$

where $1 \le k < M$.

Finally, using the last two lemmas, we have that the expected value of T_M to reach the set Y_M is bounded from above

$$E[T_M] \le \sum_{k=1}^{M-1} (t^*_k + 1/\bar{p}_k) = \sum_{k=1}^{M-1} t^*_k + \sum_{k=1}^{M-1} 1/\bar{p}_k.$$

The last lemma has been used to provide upper bounds of T_M for the MMAS when used to optimized some simple pseudo-boolean functions [Gutjahr & Sebastiani (2008)]. These bounds provided information useful to choose among different alternatives for the parameter ρ as function of the length of the boolean strings.

In another work, a theoretical study was performed on the time of convergence of two variants of the MMAS algorithms when maximizing some pseudo-Boolean functions [Neumann et al. (2009)]. The study is asymptotical with respect to the number of binary variables. The two algorithms differ to each other only because of the updating of the best-so-far solution, depending whether the function value is either increased or not decreased. Moreover, some lower bounds for the expected time to convergence are provided.

4. Restarting the algorithm

Let X_t be the stochastic process describing a given algorithm to find an optimal point of a function f (w.l.g. we deal with the case of maximization). We consider now a new algorithm which consists of the former one restarted from beginning every T iterations. Let $\tilde{X}_t$ be the process that describes the new algorithm. Before of providing some results on the expected time to convergence, we introduce two examples. In particular, in the first example, due to the sub-exponential decay to zero of the failure probability $p_v(t)$, the algorithm with restart is successful. Instead, in the second example the failure probability goes to zero at exponential rate or even faster. Then, the restart is not convenient.

Example 1. If $p_v(t) = \frac{c}{t^\alpha}$, then, for any t sufficiently long, there exists $T < t$ such that the failure probability $p_v(t)$ of the algorithm after t iterations is larger than $p_v(T)^{\lfloor \frac{t}{T} \rfloor}$, that is the failure probability of the algorithm restarted $\lfloor \frac{t}{T} \rfloor$ times with restart time equal to T. To this aim, it will be sufficient to prove that

$$p_v(t) > p_v(T)^{\left(\frac{t}{T}-1\right)}.$$

To show this, we compute the derivate of $p_v(T)^{\frac{1}{T}}$:

$$\begin{aligned} \frac{d}{dT}\left(p_v(T)^{\frac{1}{T}}\right) &= \left(\frac{c}{T^\alpha}\right)^{\frac{1}{T}}\left[-\frac{1}{T^2}\ln\left(\frac{c}{T^\alpha}\right)+\frac{1}{T}\left(-\alpha\frac{cT^\alpha}{T^{\alpha+1}c}\right)\right] \\ &= -\left(\frac{c}{T^\alpha}\right)^{\frac{1}{T}}\frac{1}{T^2}\left(\ln\left(\frac{c}{T^\alpha}\right)+\alpha\right). \end{aligned}$$

This derivate vanishes when $\ln\left(\frac{c}{T^\alpha}\right)+\alpha = 0$ and hence for $T = ec^{\frac{1}{\alpha}}$. Of course we will choose a restart time equal to $\bar{T} = \left\lceil ec^{\frac{1}{\alpha}} \right\rceil = \beta ec^{\frac{1}{\alpha}}$, where $\beta \geq 1$. After having calculated $p_v(\bar{T}) = \frac{1}{(\beta e)^\alpha}$, we consider $p_v(\bar{T})^{t/\bar{T}-1}$:

$$p_v(T)^{t/\bar{T}-1} = \left(\frac{1}{(\beta e)^\alpha}\right)^{t/\beta e\sqrt[\alpha]{c}-1} < \frac{c}{t^\alpha} = p_v(t),$$

where the last inequality is true for t sufficiently great. Therefore, in this case there is an advantage to consider the process with restart.

Example 2. An example for which we have instead $p_v(T)^{\lfloor \frac{t}{T} \rfloor} \geq p_v(t)\ \forall T \leq t$ is when $p_v(t) = c^{t^\alpha}$ with $c < 1$ and $\alpha \geq 1$. In this case, it holds

$$p_v(T)^{\lfloor \frac{t}{T} \rfloor} \geq p_v(T)^{\frac{t}{T}} = c^{T^{\alpha-1}t} \geq c^{t^\alpha} = p_v(t)\ \ \forall\, T \leq t.$$

We will now study the restart algorithm in terms of the expected value of the first hitting time T_C of the process $\tilde{X}_t$ into the optimal set X^* of the function f. If each state of X^* is "absorbent" (i.e. $P(X_t \in X^* \mid X_s \in X^*) = 1$ for any s, t such that $s < t$), then it is easy to see that the expected value of T_C is

$$E[T_C] = \sum_{k=1}^{\infty} P(X_k \notin X^*).$$

In fact, for any non-negative random variable X it's possible to write

$$E[X] = \int_0^\infty P(X > t)\, dt.$$

In our case, the random variable T_C is discrete and the integral in the above equation will be replaced by a series whose generic term is $P(T_C > t)$. We remark that the event $T_C > t$ is equal to the event $X_t \notin X^*$. In fact if the first hitting time will be greater than t, then $X_t \notin X^*$. Viceversa, since the points in X^* are absorbent, if $X_t \notin X^*$, then X_s for $s < t$ does not belong to X^* and therefore the first hitting time will be greater than t.
Let T_R first hitting time of $\tilde{X}_t$ into X^*, which can written as

$$E[T_R] = \sum_{k=1}^{\infty} P(X_T \notin X^*)^{\lfloor \frac{k-1}{T} \rfloor} P(X_{k-\lfloor \frac{k-1}{T} \rfloor T} \notin X^*).$$

In general, we notice that a necessary condition for $E[T_C]$ to be finite is that $P(X_t \in X^*)$ is infinitesimal. Instead, the expected value of T_R is always finite because

$$E[T_R] \leq \sum_{k=1}^{\infty} P(X_T \notin X^*)^{\frac{k-1}{T}-1},$$

and the series is convergent. Below, there is an example of a case where $P(X_t \in X^*)$ is not going to zero as t goes to infinity. Let us focus now on the algorithm known as (1+1)EA with single flip proposed for maximizing pseudo-boolean functions [Gutjahr & Sebastiani (2008)]. This algorithm, consists at each iteration first of the flip of a single component, randomly chosen. Then, the proposed flip is accepted if it corresponds to a non-decrease of f. For this algorithm, the probability $P(X_k \notin X^*)$ has a positive lower-bound in the case when there are more than one local maximum of the objective function f. With local maximum we mean the existence of a point $\bar{x}$ and a set $R(\bar{x})$ containing it such that

$$f(\bar{x}) \geq f(x) \qquad \forall x \in R(\bar{x}), \qquad\qquad f(\bar{x}) > f(x) \qquad \forall x \in \partial R(\bar{x}),$$

where $\partial R(\bar{x})$ is the border of the set $R(\bar{x})$. This algorithm can be modeled through a Markov chain such that $P(X_{t+1} = y \mid X_t = x) > 0$ if and only if $f(y) \geq f(x)$. We consider a function f with at least two local maxima and only one global maximum. If the initial probability to be in the interior $\bar{R}$ of one of the regions not corresponding to the global maximum is positive then

$$P(X_k \notin X^*) \geq P(X_k \notin X^* \mid X_0 \in \bar{R})\, P(X_0 \in \bar{R}) > 0.$$

In the last inequality we have exploited the fact that $P(X_k \notin X^* \mid X_0 \in \bar{R}) = 1$. In fact, the considered algorithm only allows transitions towards points at Hamming distance equal to 1 and with values of the objective not decreased. Therefore, if the initial point belongs to the region $\bar{R}$, it will never go outside it. Since the generic term of the series that gives $E[T_C]$ is not infinitesimal, the series diverges and $E[T_C] = \infty$.
A sufficient condition to have $E[T_R] < E[T_C]$ is obviuosly

$$P(X_T \notin X^*)^{\lfloor \frac{k-1}{T} \rfloor} P(X_{k-\lfloor \frac{k-1}{T} \rfloor T} \notin X^*) < P(X_k \notin X^*). \tag{4}$$

for any $t > T$. We notice that, the above condition becomes an identity for $t \leq T$. In the following, we provide different kinds of sufficient conditions for Eq. (4), that therefore also imply $E[T_R] < E[T_C]$.

Proposition 1. *Let $\{X_t\}_{t \in IN}$ be a process such that it exists $T > 0$ and for $t > T$ it holds $P(X_{t+1} \notin X^* \mid X_t \notin X^*) > P(X_T \notin X^*)^{\frac{1}{T}}$, where each point of X^* is an absorbent state for the process X_t,* *then*

$$E[T_R] < E[T_C].$$

Proof.

$$\begin{aligned} P(X_t \notin X^*) &= P(X_t \notin X^* \mid X_{t-1} \notin X^*) P(X_{t-1} \notin X^*) \\ &> P(X_T \notin X^*)^{\frac{1}{T}} P(X_{t-1} \notin X^*) \\ &> \left(P(X_T \notin X^*)^{\frac{1}{T}}\right)^{\lfloor \frac{t-1}{T} \rfloor T} P(X_{t-\lfloor \frac{t-1}{T} \rfloor T} \notin X^*). \end{aligned}$$

Hence, we have

$$P(X_t \notin X^*) > P(X_{t-\lfloor \frac{t-1}{T} \rfloor T} \notin X^*) P(X_T \notin X^*)^{\lfloor \frac{t-1}{T} \rfloor},$$

that is (4). □

Proposition 2. *Let $\{X_t\}_{t \in IN}$ be a process such that it exists $T > 0$ for which it holds*

$$\frac{P(X_{t+1} \notin X^*)}{P(X_t \notin X^*)} > \frac{P(X_{t+1-\lfloor \frac{t-1}{T} \rfloor T} \notin X^*)}{P(X_{t-\lfloor \frac{t-1}{T} \rfloor T} \notin X^*)} \qquad \forall t > T, t \neq mT \quad \forall m \in \mathbb{N} \tag{5}$$

$$\frac{P(X_{mT+1} \notin X^*)}{P(X_{mT} \notin X^*)} > P(X_1 \notin X^*), \tag{6}$$

where each point of X^* is an absorbent state for the process X_t,
then

$$E[T_R] < E[T_C].$$

Proof. To obtain the thesis, it is sufficient to show that

$$P(X_T \notin X^*)^{\lfloor \frac{t-1}{T} \rfloor} P(X_{t-\lfloor \frac{t-1}{T} \rfloor T} \notin X^*) < P(X_t \notin X^*) \qquad \forall t > T. \tag{7}$$

We proceed by induction on t distinguishing two cases: the first one where $\lfloor \frac{t}{T} \rfloor = \left\lfloor \frac{t-1}{T} \right\rfloor$ and the second where $\lfloor \frac{t}{T} \rfloor = \left\lfloor \frac{t-1}{T} \right\rfloor + 1$. The inequality (7) it's true for $t = T+1$ because it is a particular case of inequality (6). We assume the inequality (7) to be true for t and we show that it is true also for $t+1$. We analyze first the case where $\lfloor \frac{t}{T} \rfloor = \left\lfloor \frac{t-1}{T} \right\rfloor$. We have

$$\begin{aligned} P(X_T \notin X^*)^{\lfloor \frac{t}{T} \rfloor} P(X_{t+1-\lfloor \frac{t}{T} \rfloor T} \notin X^*) &= P(X_T \notin X^*)^{\lfloor \frac{t-1}{T} \rfloor} \frac{P(X_{t+1-\lfloor \frac{t}{T} \rfloor T} \notin X^*)}{P(X_{t-\lfloor \frac{t}{T} \rfloor T} \notin X^*)} P(X_{t-\lfloor \frac{t}{T} \rfloor T} \notin X^*) \\ &< P(X_t \notin X^*) \frac{P(X_{t+1-\lfloor \frac{t}{T} \rfloor T} \notin X^*)}{P(X_{t-\lfloor \frac{t}{T} \rfloor T} \notin X^*)} \leq P(X_{t+1} \notin X^*). \end{aligned}$$

In the case where $\lfloor \frac{t}{T} \rfloor = \left\lfloor \frac{t-1}{T} \right\rfloor + 1$ we have

$$\begin{aligned} P(X_T \notin X^*)^{\lfloor \frac{t}{T} \rfloor} P(X_{t+1-\lfloor \frac{t}{T} \rfloor T} \notin X^*) &= P(X_T \notin X^*) P(X_T \notin X^*)^{\lfloor \frac{t-1}{T} \rfloor} P(X_{t+1-\lfloor \frac{t}{T} \rfloor T} \notin X^*) \\ &= P(X_T \notin X^*) P(X_T \notin X^*)^{m-1} P(X_1 \notin X^*) \\ &< P(X_{mT} \notin X^*) P(X_1 \notin X^*) \\ &< P(X_{mT+1} \notin X^*) = P(X_{t+1} \notin X^*). \end{aligned}$$

For the last inequalities we have used that in the considered case $t = mT$ with $m \in N$. □

We remark that, since X^* is absorbent for the chain $\{X_t\}_{t\in IN}$ then $\{X_{t+1} \notin X^*\} \subset \{X_t \notin X^*\}$ so that $\{X_{t+1} \notin X^*\} \cap \{X_t \notin X^*\} = \{X_{t+1} \notin X^*\}$. Hence, the left handside of Eq. (5) is equal to $P(X_{t+1} \notin X^* \mid X_t \notin X^*)$, and similarly for the right handside and for Eq. (6).

Proposition 3. *Let $\{X_t\}_{t\in IN}$ be a process such that it exists $T > 0$ for which it holds*

$$\forall m \qquad P(X_1 \notin X^*)P(X_T \notin X^*)^m < P(X_{(m+1)T} \notin X^*),$$

where each point of X^* is an absorbent state for the process X_t, then

$$P(X_T \notin X^*)^{[\frac{t-1}{T}]}P(X_{t-[\frac{t-1}{T}]T} \notin X^*) < P(X_t \notin X^*).$$

Proof. Let us consider the function $\forall t \to m(t) \mid t \in \{m(t)T + 1, \ldots, (m(t) + 1)T\}$. Then, we have

$$\begin{aligned} P(X_T \notin X^*)^{\lfloor\frac{t-1}{T}\rfloor}P(X_{t-\lfloor\frac{t-1}{T}\rfloor T} \notin X^*) &= P(X_T \notin X^*)^{m(t)}P(X_{t-\lfloor\frac{t-1}{T}\rfloor T} \notin X^*) \\ &\leq P(X_T \notin X^*)^{m(t)}P(X_1 \notin X^*) < P(X_{(m(t)+1)T} \notin X^*) \\ &\leq P(X_t \notin X^*). \end{aligned}$$

The last inequality follows from the non-increasing property of $P(X_t \notin X^*)$. □

We will illustrate now a simulation study where restarting an ACO algorithm is successful. We want to maximize the following pseudo-Boolean function

$$f(x) = \left|\sum_{i=1}^{N} x_i - \frac{N-1}{2}\right|, \tag{8}$$

with respect to all binary strings of length N. In Fig. 1, the function considered is plotted as function of the number of 1s in the case of $N = 20$.

This function has two local maxima but only one of them is a global maximum. The ACO algorithm considered is the MMAS. The presence of the pheromone bounds τ_{min} and $\tau_{\max}$ ensures convergence in value of the MMAS algorithm. However, if the algorithm visits a configuration with few 1s it takes a very long time in average to move towards the global maximum. Therefore, we expect that in this case the restart will be successfull.
By using as construction graph, the chain graph [Gutjahr (2000)], and by setting the initial values of the pheromone matrix equal to 0.5, the pheromone matrix coincides with the matrix of the probability of transitions [Gutjahr & Sebastiani (2008)]. The initial string was chosen uniformly in the state space $\{0,1\}^N$. The algorithms were implemented in Matlab. The values of the MMAS parameters were $\rho = 0.01$, $\tau_{min} = 0.3$, $\tau_{max} = 0.7$. We used one thousands runs of the algorithm each with 20000 iterations. Based on these simulations, we estimated the failure probability.
As suggested by Example 1, to find a good value of the restart time, we have computed the power $1/t$ of the estimated failure probability and then we have minimized it. In Fig. 2, the function $\hat{p}_v(t)^{\frac{1}{t}}$ is plotted. A minimum of this function is clearly visible at iteration 2900 ca.

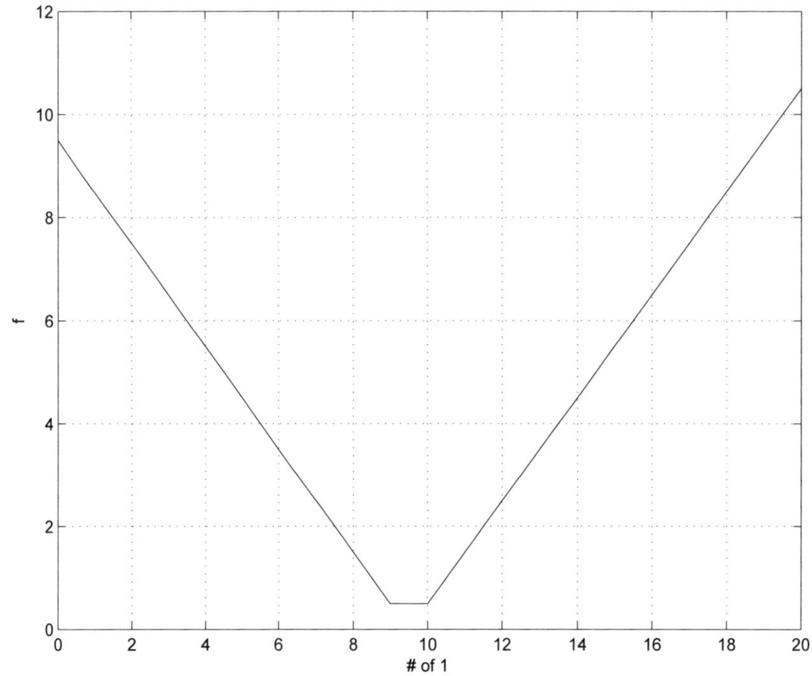

Fig. 1. The plot of the considered pseudo-Boolean function versus the number of 1*s* of the binary string

Finally, in Fig. 3 we show the estimated failure probability $\hat{p}_v(t)$ for the MMAS algorithm with chain graph to maximize the pseudo-binary function of Fig. 1 with $N = 20$ (continuous line). On the same figure, the failure probability of the restart algorithm with $T = 2900$ ca. is plotted (dashed line). As seen in the last figure, there is a clear advantage to use the restart MMAS algorithm when compared to the standard MMAS.

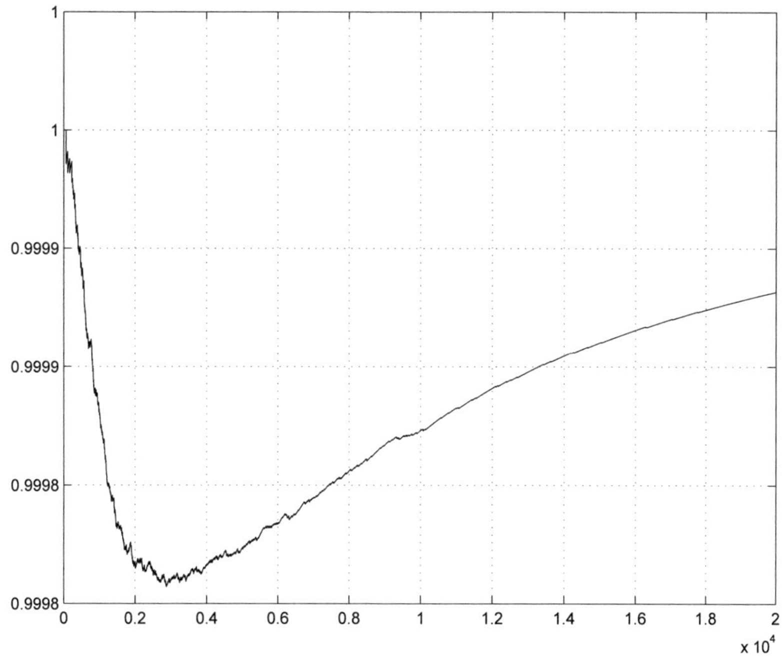

Fig. 2. The estimated failure probability raised to the power $1/t$

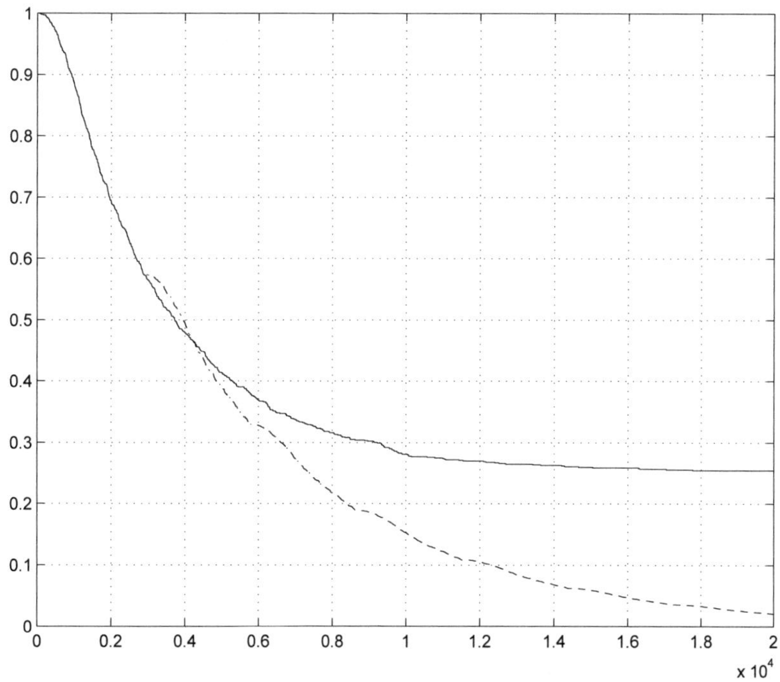

Fig. 3. The estimated failure probability for the standard MMAS (continuous line) and the restarted MMAS (dashed line)

5. References

Dorigo M., and Stutzle T. *Ant Colony Optimization* MIT Press, 2004.

Gutjahr W.J., "A graph–based ant system and its convergence", *Fut. Gener. Comput. Sys.* Vol. 16, pp. 873-888, 2000.

Gutjhar W.J., Sebastiani G. "Runtime Analysis of Ant Colony Optimization with Best-So-Far Reinforcement" *Meth. Comput. Appl. Prob.* Vol. 10, pp. 409-433, 2008.

Neumann F., Sudholt D., and Witt C. "Analysis of different MMAS ACO algorithms on unimodal functions and plateaus" *Swarm Intelligence* Vol. 3, pp. 35-68, 2009.

Stützle T., and Hoos H.H. "The MAX-MIN Ant System and local search for the travelling salesman problem" in Proc. ICEC '97 Int. Conf. on Evolutionary Computation (Baeck T., Michalewicz Z., and Yao X., eds) pp. 309-314 1997.

Stützle T., and Hoos H.H. "MAX-MIN Ant System" *Fut. Gener. Comput. Sys.* Vol. 16 pp. 889-914 2000.

5

On Ant Colony Optimization Algorithms for Multiobjective Problems

Jaqueline S. Angelo and Helio J.C. Barbosa
Laboratório Nacional de Computação Científica LNCC/MCT
Brasil

1. Introduction

Many practically relevant problems have several objectives to be maximized or minimized, taking us into the area of Multiple Objective Optimization (MOO).
In multi-objective optimization several conflicting objectives have to be simultaneously optimized. Therefore, there is usually no single solution which would give the best values for all the objective functions considered by the decision maker.
Instead, in a typical MOO problem, there is a set of alternatives that are superior to the remainder when all the objectives are considered. This set of so-called non-dominated solutions is known as the Pareto optimum set, and provides many options for the decision-maker. Usually only one of these solutions is to be chosen.
Due to the availability of and familiarity with single-objective optimizers, it is still common to combine all objectives into a single quantity to be optimized. Classical methods are usually based on reducing the multi-objective problem to a single objective one by combining (usually linearly) the objectives into one. It must be noted here that the (possibly conflicting) objectives are also non commensurable (cost, weight, speed, etc.), which makes it difficult to combine them into a single measure.
As a result, those classical techniques have serious drawbacks (Coello et al., 2002); as they require *a priori* information about the problem (weights or thresholds), which are usually not available, and many runs are needed in order to obtain different solutions, since only one solution is obtained in each run.
However, nowadays it is becoming clear that multi-objective problems can be successfully dealt with by employing a population based stochastic technique able to produce an approximation of the true set of non-dominated solutions in a single run.
Due to the increasing complexity of the problems being tackled today, those methods are often based on nature-inspired metaheuristics such as evolutionary algorithms, particle swarm optimization, artificial immune systems, and ant colony optimization (ACO) (Gandibleux et al., 2004; Silberholz & Golden, 2009).
Due to the good results obtained by ACO algorithms in a wide range of single-objective problems (Dorigo & Stützle, 2004) it is not surprising that several algorithms based on ACO have been proposed to solve multiple-objective problems.
ACO is a constructive search technique to solve difficult combinatorial optimization problems, which is inspired by the behaviour of real ants. While walking, ants deposit pheromone on the ground marking a path that may be followed by other members of the colony. Shorter

paths, as they accumulate pheromone faster than the longer ones, have a higher probability of being used by other ants, which again reinforce the pheromone on that path.
Artificial ants probabilistically build solutions considering: a pheromone trail (matrix τ), that encodes a "memory" about the search process, and is updated by the ants; and a heuristic information (matrix η), that represents *a priori* information about the problem instance to be solved.
In recent reviews (García-Martínez et al., 2007; Angus & Woodward, 2009; López-Ibáñez & Stützle, 2010) several multi-objective ACO (MOACO) algorithms were described for combinatorial optimization problems. The first paper proposed a taxonomy for MOACO algorithms, focused on an empirical analysis of the algorithms when solving the Bi-objective Traveling Salesman Problem, classifying them according to the use of one or several pheromone trails, and one or several heuristic informations. They also categorised the algorithms as Pareto-based, when the algorithm returns a set of non-dominated solutions (the Pareto set) or non-Pareto based, when it returns a single solution as output. The second review proposed a new taxonomy expanding the previous classification based on different features of the MOACO algorithms while the last one developed a technique for automatically configuring MOACO algorithms, presenting other algorithmic components that were not considered in previous works.
The objective of this chapter is to provide a comprehensive view of the use of ant colony optimization techniques in the realm of multiple-objective problems. The taxonomies proposed in (García-Martínez et al., 2007; Angus & Woodward, 2009; López-Ibáñez & Stützle, 2010) are considered in order to provide a global view of the current MOACO algorithms and their algorithmic components. This chapter also extends these taxonomies by including other MOACO algorithms that were not previously discussed on those papers.
This chapter presents in more detail some representative MOACO algorithms, indicating how well-known single objective ACO algorithms can be extended in order to tackle multiple objectives. The problem of comparing the quality of the solutions generated by MOACO algorithms is also discussed by considering different performance metrics and an empirical attainment function.

2. Multiple objective optimization problem

In a single-objective optimization problem one is trying to find a single solution, called optimal solution, that minimizes or maximizes an specified objective function subject to given constraints. On the other hand, multi-objective optimization problems consider several objectives that have to be simultaneously optimized.
With no loss of generality, the minimization case will be considered and the MOO problem reads

$$\begin{array}{l}\text{minimize } \mathbf{f}(\mathbf{x}) = [f_1(\mathbf{x}), f_2(\mathbf{x}), ..., f_k(\mathbf{x})] \\ \text{subject to } \mathbf{x} = (x_1, x_2, ..., x_n) \in \mathcal{S}\end{array} \tag{1}$$

where $\mathcal{S}$ is the *feasible region (set)*, $\mathbf{f}(\mathbf{x})$ is an objective vector with $k(\geq 2)$ objective functions to be minimized and $\mathbf{x}$ is a decision vector, which is a feasible solution if $\mathbf{x} \in \mathcal{S}$. The image of the feasible set, denoted by $\mathcal{Z}(=\mathbf{f}(\mathcal{S}))$, is known as the *feasible objective region (set)*. The elements of $\mathcal{Z}$ are the objective (function) vectors denoted by $\mathbf{f}(\mathbf{x})$ or $\mathbf{z} = (z_1, z_2, ..., z_k)^T$, where $z_i = f_i(\mathbf{x})$ for all $i = 1, ..., k$ are objective values.
The space, of which the feasible set $\mathcal{S}$ is a subset, is called the *decision space* and the space from which the objective values are taken is called the *objective space*.

If the objective functions are not conflicting, then a solution can be found where every objective function attains its optimum. However, in MOO frequently those objectives are conflicting (i.e, the improvement of one objective leads to another objective degradation) and possible non-commensurable (i.e., in different units). In such case, there is usually no single optimal solution, but a set of alternatives that outperform the remainder when all objectives are considered. Such solutions are called non-dominated solutions, the Pareto optimal set.
In MOO, usually only one of the solutions in the Pareto set is to be chosen. In this way, the decision maker (DM) plays an important role when choosing a single solution that better satisfies his or her preferences.
Different approaches are considered in the literature when the preference of the DM are used to guide the search (Miettinen, 1999).

- No Preference Articulation: the preferences of the DM are not taken into consideration. The problem can be solved by a simple method and the solution obtained is presented to the DM which will accept or reject it.
- A Priori Preference Articulation: known as preference-based, the hopes and opinions of the DM are taken into consideration before the solution process. Those methods require that the DM knows beforehand the priority of each objective.
- A Posteriori Preference Articulation: no preferences of the DM are considered. After the Pareto set has been generated, the DM chooses a solution from this set of alternatives.
- Interactive Preference Articulation: the DM preferences are continuously used during the search process and are adjusted as the search continues.

When the multiobjective optimization problem is converted into a simplistic single objective problem, the DM is invoked before the optimization step. In this case, the DM must have a thorough knowledge of the priority of each objective. Alternatively, the problem can be treated as a true multiobjective problem, invoking the DM either after the optimization process or in continuous interaction during the search process (Branke et al., 2008).

2.1 Pareto optimality

The definition of optimality for multi-objective problems is based on the Pareto optimality concept. Pareto dominance can be used to evaluate the relation between two candidate solutions in MOO (Tan et al., 2005). Without loss of generality, for a minimization problem, a decision vector $\mathbf{x} \in \mathcal{S}$ dominates another decision vector $\mathbf{x}' \in \mathcal{S}$ ($\mathbf{x} \prec \mathbf{x}'$) if and only if

$$f_i(\mathbf{x}) \leq f_i(\mathbf{x}') \quad \forall i \in \{1,...,k\} \quad \text{and} \quad \exists j \in \{1,...,k\} : f_j(\mathbf{x}) < f_j(\mathbf{x}') \tag{2}$$

A decision vector $\mathbf{x}^* \in \mathcal{S}$ is said to be Pareto-optimal when there is no other $\mathbf{x} \in \mathcal{S}$ that dominates $\mathbf{x}^*$. An objective vector $\mathbf{z}^* \in \mathcal{Z}$ is said to be Pareto-optimal when there is no other $\mathbf{z} \in \mathcal{Z}$ that dominates $\mathbf{z}^*$. The set of non-dominated solutions is called the *Pareto set* and the corresponding set of objective vectors is called the *Pareto front*. Therefore, the Pareto set is the best collection of solutions to the problem.
Figure 1 illustrates a decision space $\mathcal{S} \subset \mathbb{R}^3$ and an objective space $\mathcal{Z} \subset \mathbb{R}^2$. The bold line contains all the Pareto objective vectors, the Pareto front (Ehrgott, 2005).

3. Performance assessment

In multi-objective optimization, performance analysis is a difficult task, since one is trying to find a good approximation for a set: the Pareto front. Performance metrics are then needed

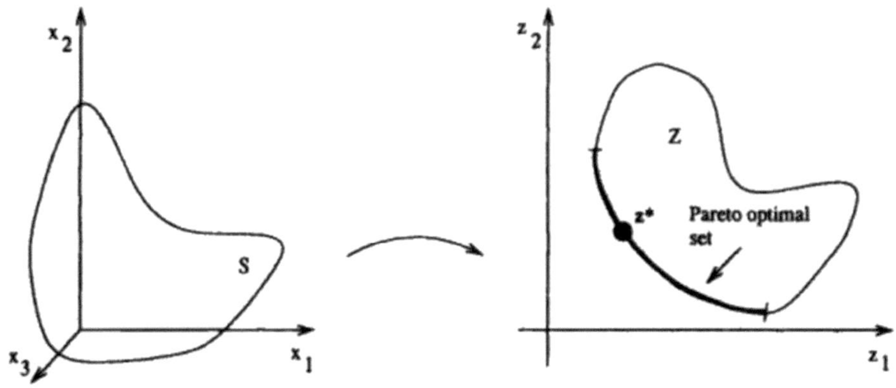

Fig. 1. Decision and objective spaces, and the Pareto front for a minimization problem with two objectives and three decision variables.

to assist the identification of the best non-dominated solution set whenever the results are difficult to interpret visually. However, the assessment problem itself is a multi-objective problem, since various aspects should be considered and no single metric encompasses them all.

Zitzler *et al* (Zitzler et al., 2000) suggest three main criteria that should be taken into account when assessing the quality of the non-dominated solutions set:

- The distance between the resulting non-dominated set and the true Pareto front should be minimized.
- A good (in most cases uniform) distribution of the obtained solutions is desirable.
- The size of the non-dominated front should be maximized, i.e., for each objective, a wide range of distinct solutions should be presented.

Many quality measures, or performance metrics, for comparing non-dominated solutions sets have been proposed. These quality measures can be classified into two categories (López-Ibáñez, 2004): unary measures, which associate a quality value to a Pareto set, using the Pareto optimal set as a reference; and binary measures, which compares two different Pareto sets.

The unary measures are defined in the case when the optimal Pareto set is known. Usually the Pareto optimal set is not known, so its necessary to calculate a pseudo-optimal Pareto set as a reference set, which is an approximation of the true Pareto optimal set.

The following topics describe some performance metrics, where ER, ONVG and $\mathcal{S}$ metrics are unary measures while $\mathcal{C}$ is a binary measure (Zitzler et al., 2000; Knowles & Corne, 2002; Li et al., 2007):

Error ratio (ER). The ER metric is defined as

$$Er(Z) = \frac{\sum_{i=1}^{n} e_i}{n}$$

where n is the number of vectors in the approximation set Z. Using Z^* as a reference set, which could be the Pareto front, $e_i = 0$ when i-th vector is in Z^*, and 1 otherwise. The ER metric measures the proportion of non-true Pareto vectors in Z. Lower values of the error ratio represent better non-dominated sets.

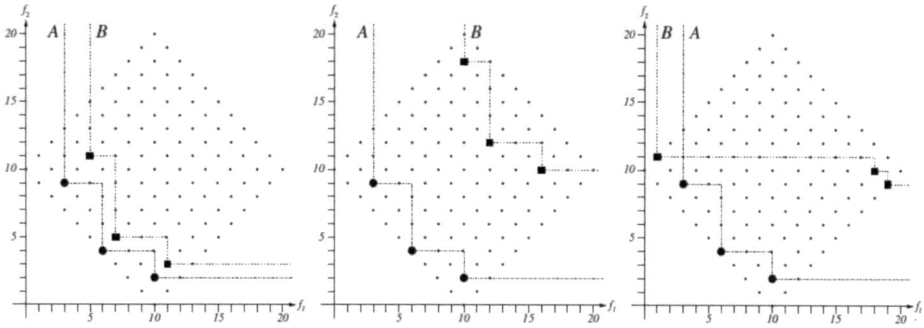

Fig. 2. The two figures on the left side indicate that the approximate set A dominates the approximate set B, but in one case the two sets are much closer than in the other case. On the right side, A and B cannot be compared, but it is clear that A gives more useful solutions than B.

Overall Non-dominated Vector Generation (ONVG). The ONVG metric is defined as $|Z|$, where Z represents a set of solutions. It measures the number of distinct non-dominated solutions obtained.

The $\mathcal{S}$ metric. The $\mathcal{S}$ metric measures the hypervolume of a multi-dimensional region covered by the set A and a reference point. It computes the size of the region dominated by A. A convenient reference point is needed so as not to induce misleading results.

The $\mathcal{C}$ metric. The $\mathcal{C}$ metric compares a pair of non-dominated sets by computing the fraction of each set that is covered by the other. $\mathcal{C}$ maps the ordered pair (A,B) into the interval $[0,1]$:

$$\mathcal{C}(A,B) = \frac{|b \in B, \exists a \in A : a \preceq b|}{|B|}$$

The value $\mathcal{C}(A,B) = 1$ means that all solutions in B are dominated by or equal to solutions in A. The opposite $\mathcal{C}(A,B) = 0$ means that none of the solutions in B are covered by the set A. It is important to note that $\mathcal{C}(A,B)$ and $\mathcal{C}(B,A)$ have to be considered, since $\mathcal{C}(A,B)$ is not necessarily equal to $1 - \mathcal{C}(B,A)$.

The performance metrics are not easy to define and it is probably not possible to establish a single metric that satisfies all users preferences in a satisfactory way, since each one of them measures different aspects of the non-dominated set found. Besides, depending on the solution's distribution over the Pareto set, some performance metrics could not adequately express the quality of the analysed set (Knowles, 2005). Figure 2 (Knowles et al., 2006) illustrates three examples of sets in the objective space and the difficulties in assessing how much better one set is over another.
Another way to measure the quality of the Pareto set is to analyse the results by means of a graphical representation (López-Ibáñez et al., 2009) based on the empirical attainment function (EAF) (Fonseca et al., 2001).
The attainment function gives the probability that an arbitrary point in the objective space is attained by (dominated by or equal to) the outcome of a single run of a particular algorithm. In practice, this function is not known, but it can be estimated collecting the outcome data from several independent runs of an algorithm.

The EAFs of two algorithms can be compared by computing the difference of the EAF values for each point in the objective space. Differences in favor of one algorithm indicate that those points are more likely to be attained by that algorithm than by its competitor, and, hence, that the performance of that algorithm is better (in that region of the objective space) than the performance of its competitor.
One can find a more detailed description of attainment functions in (Fonseca et al., 2001; Knowles et al., 2006)

4. Ant colony approach

The Ant Colony Optimization (ACO) is a metaheuristic inspired by the behaviour of real ants. Ants and other insects that live in a colony, like bees, termites and wasps, can be seen as distributed systems, that in spite of the simplicity of each individual, present a high level of social organization when observed together. Some examples of ant colony's capabilities found in (Dorigo et al., 1999) are: division of labor and task allocation, cemetery organization and brood sorting, cooperative transport and finding the shortest path between two or more locations (often between a food source and a nest).
The first ACO algorithm developed was initially applied to the Traveling Salesman Problem (Dorigo, 1992). The algorithm was based on the ant colony capability to find the shortest path between a food source and a nest. The algorithm uses artificial ants that cooperate on finding solutions to the problem through communication mediated by artificial pheromone trails.
While moving on the graph associated with the problem, artificial ants deposit pheromone on the edges traversed marking a path that may be followed by other members of the colony, which then reinforce the pheromone on that path. With this stigmergetic (Dorigo et al., 2000) communication, ants have their activities coordinated. This self-organizing behaviour results in a self-reinforcing process that leads to the formation of a path marked by high pheromone concentration, while paths that are less used tend to have a diminishing pheromone level due to evaporation.
This concept can be applied to any combinatorial optimization problem for which a constructive heuristic can be defined. The process of constructing solutions can be regarded as a walk on a construction graph where each edge of the graph represent a possible step the ant can take. ACO algorithms are essentially constructive, as ants generate solutions by adding solution components, corresponding to the edges chosen, to an initially empty solution until the solution is complete.
The ants movement is guided by (i) a *heuristic information* (η) that represents *a priori* information about the problem instance to be solved and by (ii) a *pheromone trail* (τ) that encodes a memory about the ant colony search process which is continuously updated by the ants. In many cases η is the cost of adding the component (associated with the given graph edge) to the solution under construction. These values are used by the ant's heuristic rule to make probabilistic decisions on the next node to be visited (or next edge to be used). When all ants have generated their solutions, the pheromone trail is updated considering the quality of the corresponding candidate solutions: reinforcing components of good solutions (positive feedback) and applying a certain level of pheromone evaporation in all edges.
The ACO algorithms were initially used to solve combinatorial optimization problems, inspired by the path marking behaviour, and later applied to many other problems. Also, other ant colony capabilities have inspired computer scientists to use ACO on different types of applications. A survey of ACO algorithms and applications can be found in (Dorigo et al., 2006).

In the multi-objective case García-Martínez *et al* (García-Martínez et al., 2007) proposed a taxonomy of the multi-objective ACO (MOACO) algorithms according to two different criteria: (i) the use of only one or several pheromone trails; and (ii) the use of only one or several matrices of heuristic information. In this classification some of them are Pareto-based, when they return a set of non-dominated solutions (an approximation to the Pareto set), while others, that are not Pareto-based, return a single solution as output.
The pseudo-code for a standard ACO metaheuristic in multiobjective optimization is given by Algorithm 1.

Algorithm 1: MultiobjectiveACO

```
Set parameters;
Initialize pheromone trails τ ;
Initialize heuristic matrix η ;
Initialize Pareto set P as empty;
while termination criteria not met do
    ConstructAntSolution();
    ApplyLocalSearch()    (optional);
    UpdateParetoSet();
    UpdateGlobalPheromone();
Return the Pareto set P
```

In the routine *ConstructAntSolution()*, from a given initial point, ants start walking according to the decision policy of choosing the next node to be visited. This movement is guided by the pheromone trail and the heuristic information associated with the problem instance. After constructing a complete path (feasible solution), it is possible to apply a local search procedure in order to improve the solution obtained. When all ants have generated their solutions, the Pareto set is updated in the procedure *UpdateParetoSet()*, keeping all non-dominated solutions generated up to this point. Then the pheromone trails are updated in *UpdateGlobalPheromone()*, considering the quality of the candidate solutions generated as well as a certain level of pheromone evaporation. Each algorithm presents different ways to choose the nodes and to update the pheromone trails.

4.1 ACO for constrained problems

A multiobjective optimization problem consists in a set of solutions $\mathcal{S}$, a set of objective functions **f** which assigns for each objective a value $f_k(s)$ to each candidate solution $s \in \mathcal{S}$, and a set of constraints Ω that must be satisfied.
Considering the Traveling Salesman Problem the only constraint is that all cities must be visited only once. In this case, the search space is restricted to permutations of the list of cities $(1,2,...,N)$.
An ACO algorithm deals with this constraint by equipping each ant with a memory that keeps track of the cities already visited during the tour construction. Thus, their choices are limited to the cities that have not been visited yet. However, for other problems such a simple procedure may not be available. When the constraints cannot be satisfied during the solution construction, other constraint handling techniques must be adopted.
Several techniques have been proposed in the literature in order to tackle constrained optimization problems which can be classified as *direct* (feasible or interior), when only feasible elements are considered, or as *indirect* (exterior), when both feasible and infeasible elements are used during the search process (Fonseca et al., 2007).

An MOACO algorithm that makes use of an indirect technique is the MOAQ algorithm (Mariano & Morales, 1999). The problem to be solved is the design of an irrigation water network. Basically, the optimization problem consists in minimizing the cost of the network and maximizing the profit, subject to ten different constrains. Constraint handling is performed by penalizing the solutions which violate such constraints.

4.2 Algorithmic components for MOACO

In the literature one can find various alternatives for the implementation of ACO algorithms for solving multiobjective combinatorial problems. They usually differ from each other with respect to the single objective ACO algorithms they were based on (such as AS, ACS and $\mathcal{MM}$AS), as well as due to variations in their algorithmic components.
In the following, we present some of the algorithmic components that were already examined, experimentally or comparatively, in the literature (García-Martínez et al., 2007; Angus & Woodward, 2009; López-Ibáñez & Stützle, 2010) concerning MOACO algorithms.

Multiple Colonies. In a multiple colony approach, a number of ants are set to constitute a colony. Each colony independently construct solutions considering its own pheromone and heuristic information, specializing its search on particular areas of the Pareto front. The colonies can cooperate with each other by: (i) exchanging solutions (information), using a shared archive of non-dominated solutions in order to identify dominated ones; or (ii) sharing solutions for updating the pheromone information, so that solutions generated by a certain colony affect the pheromone information of other colonies.

Pheromone and Heuristic Information. There are two standard models to define the pheromone/heuristic information: using one (*single*) or various (*multiple*) matrices . When multiple matrices are utilized, usually each matrix corresponds to one objective. With respect to the pheromone information, each matrix may contain different values depending on the implementation strategy applied. If a single pheromone matrix is used, the construction step is done similarly to single objective ACO algorithms. In this case, the pheromone information associated with each objective should be combined, so as to reduce the multiple objectives into a single one. The same is applied to the heuristic information.

Pheromone and Heuristic Aggregation. Whenever multiple matrices are used, they must be aggregated, using some form of aggregation procedure. In all of these cases, weights are needed to adjust the influence of each objective. Different techniques for setting the weights may lead to different search behaviour. For the MOACO algorithms, one can find in the literature three methods to aggregate the pheromone/heuristic matrices: (i) *the weighted sum*, where matrices are aggregated by a weighted sum ($\sum_{k=1}^{K} \lambda_k \tau_{ij}^k$), with K being the number of objectives; (ii) *the weighted product*, where matrices are aggregated by a weighted product ($\prod_{k=1}^{K} (\tau_{ij}^k)^{\lambda_k}$); and (iii) *random*, where at each construction step a randomly objective is selected to be optimized. Whenever weights are used for aggregating multiple matrices two strategies can be used for setting the weights, which are: (a) *dynamically*, where the objectives are combined dynamically so that different objectives can be emphasized at different times during the solution construction process, or ants can use specific weights to combine the matrices; and (b) *fixed*, where the weights are set a priori and each objective has the same importance during the entire algorithm run.

Component	Values
Colony	Single, Multiple
Pheromone matrix	Single, Multiple
Heuristic matrix	Single, Multiple
Aggregation	Weighted product, Weighted sum, Random
Weight setting	Dynamic, Fixed
Pheromone update	Non-dominated, Best-of-objective, Elite, All
Pareto archive	Offline, Online, No-archive

Table 1. MOACO algorithmic components and values

Pheromone Update. This algorithmic component can be implemented in many different ways. When only one matrix is used it is common to perform the update as in the single objective ACO algorithms, such as, selecting the iteration-best or the best-so-far (*elite solution*) solution to update the pheromone matrix. This same procedure can be applied when multiple matrices are used. In this case, one can select a set of iteration-best or best-so-far solutions to update the pheromone matrices, with respect to each objective (*best-of-objectives solutions*). Another way to update the pheromone matrices is to collect and store the non-dominated solutions in a external set. Only the solutions in the non-dominated set (*non-dominated solutions*) are allowed to update the pheromone. In this case, the individuals can update a specific pheromone matrix or many (or all) pheromone matrices. In other cases, all ants are allowed to update the pheromone matrices (*all solutions*).

Pareto Archive. For the Pareto-based MOACO algorithms, the Pareto set must be stored and updated during the algorithm execution. In many cases, the solution in the Pareto set is used to update the pheromone information. This algorithm component indicates how this set is stored and used during the algorithm run. In the MOACO literature, one can find two ways to do it. The first one is *offline storage*: the non-dominated solutions are stored in a external set and these solutions are not used for future solution construction. The Pareto set is used to update the pheromone information, and at the end of the execution, this set is returned as the final solution. The second one is *online storage*: the solutions in the Pareto set are connected to the pheromone update procedure. Each time the Pareto set is improved, the pheromone update procedure is guided by the improved set. This technique allows the pheromone matrix or matrices to reflect the state of the non-dominated set at any time. There are cases where the Pareto set is not used to update the pheromone information but it is used as a final solution.

As a reference guide to the MOACO taxonomy, Table 1 lists the algorithmic components of the MOACO algorithms that were discussed previously.

5. MOACO Algorithms

A large number of MOACO algorithms were developed during the last few years. This section presents different MOACO algorithms proposed in the literature. The main characteristics of the algorithms will be reviewed and some of them will be compared with the mono-objective ACO algorithm which they were based on.
The taxonomy proposed is based on the algorithmic components listed in the previous section, which follows the taxonomy proposed in (García-Martínez et al., 2007; Angus & Woodward, 2009; López-Ibáñez & Stützle, 2010).

Algorithm	[τ]	[η]	Colony	Agg./Weight	τ update	P. archive
MOAQ (Mariano & Morales, 1999)	1	k	multiple	w.p-w.s/-	ND	off
COMPETants (Doerner et al., 2001)	k	k	multiple	w.s./fix.	BoO	none
BicriterionAnt (Iredi et al., 2001)	k	k	single	w.p./dyn.	ND	off
SACO (Vincent et al., 2002)	1	1	single	-/-	E	none
MACS (Barán & Schaerer, 2003)	1	k	single	w.p./dyn.	ND	on
MONACO (Cardoso et al., 2003)	k	1	single	w.p./dyn.	all	off
P-ACO (Doerner et al., 2004)	k	k	single	w.s./dyn.	BoO	off
M3AS (Pinto & Barán, 2005)	1	k	single	w.p./fix.	ND	off
MOA (Gardel et al., 2005)	1	1	single	w.p./dyn.	ND	off
MAS (Paciello et al., 2006)	1	k	single	w.p. /dyn.	ND	off
MOACSA (Yagmahan & Yenisey, 2010)	1	1	single	w.p./dyn.	E	none

Table 2. Taxonomy of MOACO algorithms based on the algorithmic components listed.

Table 2 lists the MOACO algorithms that will be presented in the forthcoming subsections.

5.1 Ant system (AS) vs. multiobjective ant system (MAS)

The Ant System was the first ACO algorithm developed (Dorigo, 1992; Dorigo & Caro, 1999). The AS algorithm consists in two main phases: the ant's solution construction and the pheromone update.

The pheromone values τ_{ij} associated with arcs, are initially set to a given value τ_0, and the heuristic information $\eta_{ij} = 1/d_{ij}$ is inversely proportional to the distance between city i and j, in the case of the Traveling Salesman Problem.

At each iteration, each of the m ants in the colony constructs its solution according to the following probability of moving from city i to city j:

$$p_{ij}^{h} = \frac{[\tau_{ij}]^{\alpha}[\eta_{ij}]^{\beta}}{\sum_{l \in \mathcal{N}_i^h}[\tau_{il}]^{\alpha}[\eta_{il}]^{\beta}} \quad \text{if } j \in \mathcal{N}_i^h \text{, and 0 otherwise} \tag{3}$$

where α and β are two parameters that weigh the relative importance of the pheromone trail and the heuristic information, and $\mathcal{N}_i^h$ is the feasible neighbourhood of ant h in city i.

When all m ants have built a solution, the pheromone trail is evaporated according to

$$\tau_{ij} \leftarrow (1-\rho)\tau_{ij} \tag{4}$$

where $\rho \in (0,1]$ is the pheromone evaporation rate.

After the evaporation process, the ants increment the pheromone trail matrix

$$\tau_{ij} \leftarrow \tau_{ij} + \sum_{h=1}^{m} \Delta\tau_{ij}^{h} \tag{5}$$

with

$$\Delta\tau_{ij}^{h} = \begin{cases} 1/f(s_h), & \text{if arc } (i,j) \text{ belongs to the tour built by the } h\text{-th ant;} \\ 0, & \text{otherwise;} \end{cases} \tag{6}$$

where, $\Delta\tau_{ij}^{h}$ is the amount of pheromone deposit by ant h, on the arcs it has visited, which is proportional to the solution s_h (tour length) built by the ant.

When the termination criteria is achieved, the algorithm returns only one solution, which contains the best tour.

The AS with multiple objectives was initially proposed by Paciello and his colleges (Paciello et al., 2006). The algorithm was tested in three different combinatorial problems, the Quadratic Assignement Problem (QAP), the Traveling Salesman Problem (TSP) and the Vehicle Routing Problem with Time Windows (VRPTW).

The heuristic informations η_{ij}^{0} and η_{ij}^{1} are set for each objective in the same way as in AS, namely, inversely proportional to the cost of adding the arc (i,j) to the solution under construction. Only one pheromone matrix is used.

In the MAS algorithm, the next node j to be visited is selected according to the following probability

$$p_{ij}^{h} = \frac{\tau_{ij}[\eta_{ij}^{0}]^{\lambda\beta}[\eta_{ij}^{1}]^{(1-\lambda)\beta}}{\sum_{l\in\mathcal{N}_i^h}\tau_{il}[\eta_{il}^{0}]^{\lambda\beta}[\eta_{il}^{1}]^{(1-\lambda)\beta}} \quad \text{if } j \in \mathcal{N}_i^h, \text{ and 0 otherwise} \tag{7}$$

To force the ants to search in different regions of the search space, λ is calculated for each ant $h \in \{1,...,m\}$ as $\lambda_h = (h-1)/(m-1)$. Thus, in the extreme cases, the ant m with $\lambda = 1$ considers only the first objective whereas ant 1 with $\lambda = 0$ considers only the second objective. After the ants construct their solutions, the Pareto set is updated. The non-dominated solutions in the current iteration are added to the Pareto set, and those that are dominated are excluded. The pheromone trail update is performed only by ants that generate non-dominated solutions, i.e, solutions that are in the Pareto set. The rule for pheromone evaporation and deposit is applied to each solution s_p of the current Pareto set, as follows

$$\tau_{ij} \leftarrow (1-\rho)\tau_{ij} + \rho\Delta\tau \tag{8}$$

where ρ is the evaporation rate and $\Delta\tau$ is given by

$$\Delta\tau = \frac{1}{\sum_{k=1}^{K} f^{k}(s_p)} \tag{9}$$

A new procedure, named convergence control, is included in the MAS algorithm in order to avoid premature convergence to local optimal and a stagnation behaviour. The procedure consists in reinitializing the pheromone matrix if, for a given number of iterations, no improvement is reached, i.e, when no non-dominated solutions are found.

The MAS algorithm returns a set of non-dominated solutions, which contains the best values found during the run.

5.2 Ant colony system (ACS) vs. multiobjective ant colony system (MACS)

The Ant Colony System (ACS) (Dorigo & Gambardella, 1997a;b) is an extension of the Ant System. The ACS introduces three main changes in the AS algorithm: a local pheromone update is performed each time an ant uses an arc (i,j); a more aggressive action choice rule is used, called *pseudorandom proportional* rule; and the global pheromone update is applied at the end of each iteration by only one ant, which can be either the iteration-best or the best-so-far.

The action choice rule performed by each ant to choose the next node to be visited is applied according to the pseudorandom proportional rule, given by

$$j = \begin{cases} \arg\max_{j \in \mathcal{N}_i^h} \{\tau_{ij}[\eta_{ij}]^{\beta}\}, & \text{if } q \leq q_0 \\ \hat{j}, & \text{otherwise;} \end{cases} \tag{10}$$

where q is a random variable in $[0,1]$, $q_0 \in [0,1]$ is a parameter chosen by the user, β defines the relative importance of the objectives, and $\hat{j}$ is a random value obtained according to equation (3) (with $\alpha = 1$).
This algorithm implements a local pheromone update, performed every time an ant moves from one node to another, as follows:

$$\tau_{ij} \leftarrow (1-\varphi)\tau_{ij} + \varphi\tau_0 \tag{11}$$

where $\varphi \in (0,1)$ is the pheromone decay coefficient, and $\tau_0 = 1/f(s_{nn})$ is the initial value of the pheromone matrix, with n being the number of cities and $f(s_{nn})$ the length of a nearest-neighbor tour.
The global pheromone update is performed at the end of each iteration only by the best ant (the best-so-far or iteration-best ant), according to the following expression

$$\tau_{ij} \leftarrow (1-\rho)\tau_{ij} + \rho\Delta\tau_{ij}^{best} \tag{12}$$

where, $\Delta\tau_{ij}^{best} = 1/f(s_{best})$ is the amount of pheromone deposit by the ant that generates the best solution.
The multiobjective version of ACS algorithm was developed by Barán and Schaerer (Barán & Schaerer, 2003), to solve a vehicle routing problem with time windows. The MACS algorithm uses a single pheromone matrix τ and two heuristic matrices, η_{ij}^0 and η_{ij}^1. The next node to be visited follows the same transition rule of ACS, but adapted to the multiobjective problem as follows:

$$j = \begin{cases} \arg\max_{j \in \mathcal{N}_i^h} \{\tau_{ij}[\eta_{ij}^0]^{\lambda\beta}[\eta_{ij}^1]^{(1-\lambda)\beta}\}, & \text{if } q \leq q_0 \\ \hat{i}, & \text{otherwise;} \end{cases} \tag{13}$$

where q, q_0 and β are parameters as defined previously, λ is computed for each ant h as $\lambda = h/m$, with m being the total number of ants, and $\hat{i}$ is a city selected according to the following probability:

$$p_{ij}^h = \frac{\tau_{ij}[\eta_{ij}^0]^{\lambda\beta}[\eta_{ij}^1]^{(1-\lambda)\beta}}{\sum_{l \in \mathcal{N}_i^h} \tau_{il}[\eta_{il}^0]^{\lambda\beta}[\eta_{il}^1]^{(1-\lambda)\beta}} \quad \text{if } j \in \mathcal{N}_i^h \text{ and, 0 otherwise} \tag{14}$$

The local pheromone update is given by

$$\tau_{ij} \leftarrow (1-\rho)\tau_{ij} + \rho\tau_0 \tag{15}$$

Initially τ_0 is calculated by taking the average cost of solutions in each objective function $f^1(s_h)$ and $f^2(s_h)$, as:

$$\tau_0 = \frac{1}{n.\overline{f^1(s_h)}.\overline{f^2(s_h)}} \tag{16}$$

where n is calculated as an average number of nodes.
After the construction of solutions, each one is compared to the Pareto set. Each non-dominated solution is included in the Pareto set and the dominated ones are excluded.

At the end of each iteration, τ_0 is calculated according to the previous equation, but taking the average cost of the solutions in the Pareto set. If $\tau_0' > \tau_0$, then the pheromone trails are reinitialized to the new value, otherwise, the global pheromone update is performed with each solution s_p of the current Pareto set, as follows:

$$\tau_{ij} \leftarrow (1-\rho)\tau_{ij} + \frac{\rho}{f^1(s_p)f^2(s_p)} \tag{17}$$

The MACS algorithm returns the set of non-dominated solutions found.

5.3 Ant-Q vs. multiple objective Ant-Q (MOAQ)

The Ant-Q algorithm was based on a distributed reinforcement learning technique and was first applied to the design of irrigation networks. This algorithm was proposed by Gambardella and Dorigo (Gambardella & Dorigo, 1995) before ACS. They differ from each other only in the definition of the term τ_0 (Dorigo & Stützle, 2004), which in Ant-Q is set to

$$\tau_0 = \gamma \max_{j \in \mathcal{N}_i^h} \{\tau_{ij}\} \tag{18}$$

where γ is a parameter and the maximum is taken over the set of pheromone trails on the feasible neighbourhood of ant h in node i.

The multiple objective version of Ant-Q (MOAQ) proposed by Mariano and Morales (Mariano & Morales, 1999), implements a family/colony of agents to perform the optimization of each objective. Each colony is assigned to optimize one objective considering the solutions found for the other objectives. The MOAQ also implements a reward and penalty policy. A reward is given to the non-dominated solutions while the solutions which violate the constraints are penalized.

The MOAQ uses one pheromone trail and two heuristic matrices, one for each objective. One colony, say *colony-1*, optimizes the first objective, where the state transition rule, given by

$$j = \begin{cases} \arg\max_{j \in \mathcal{N}_i^h} \{\tau_{ij} + \eta_{ij}\}, & \text{if } t \geq t_s \\ p_{ij} = \frac{\tau_{ij} + \eta_{ij}}{\sum_{l \in \mathcal{N}_i^h} \tau_{il} + \eta_{il}}, & \text{otherwise;} \end{cases} \tag{19}$$

is related to the heuristic information associated to the first objective. This same process is applied to the second colony with respect to the second objective, where the state transition rule is given as follows

$$j' = \begin{cases} \arg\max_{j \in \mathcal{N}_i^h} \{[\tau_{ij}]^\alpha [\eta_{ij}]^\beta\}, & \text{if } t \geq t_s \\ p'_{ij} = \frac{[\tau_{ij}]^\alpha [\eta_{ij}]^\beta}{\sum_{l \in \mathcal{N}_i^h} [\tau_{il}]^\alpha [\eta_{il}]^\beta}, & \text{otherwise;} \end{cases} \tag{20}$$

where t and t_s are two variables.

The learning Q-values, which can be seen as pheromone information, are calculated using the following update rule:

$$\tau_{ij} \leftarrow (1-\alpha)\tau_{ij} + \alpha[r_{ij} + \gamma \max \tau_{pz}] \tag{21}$$

where α is the learning step, γ is the discount factor, r_{ij} is the reward given to the best solution found in each iteration and $\max \tau_{pz}$ is the maximum pheromone value in the next algorithm step.

Finally, MOAQ returns a set of non-dominated solutions as a final result. When a solution found violates any constraint, the algorithm applies a penalty to its components on the Q values.

5.4 $\mathcal{MAX} - \mathcal{MIN}$ Ant systems ($\mathcal{MM}$AS) vs. multiobjective $\mathcal{MM}$AS (M3AS)

$\mathcal{MAX} - \mathcal{MIN}$ Ant System ($\mathcal{MM}$AS), developed by Stützle and Hoos (Stützle, 1997; Stützle & Hoos, 2000) is considered one of the best performing extension of Ant System. In order to achieve a strong exploitation of the search process the $\mathcal{MM}$AS allows only the best solutions to add pheromone during the pheromone trail update procedure. Also, it imposes bounds on the pheromone trail values in order to avoid premature convergence.

The selection rule is the same as that used in AS, by applying equation (3) to choose the next node to be visited. After all ants construct their solutions, the pheromone matrix is updated by applying the AS evaporation equation (4), followed by the deposit of pheromone given by

$$\tau_{ij} \leftarrow \tau_{ij} + \Delta\tau_{ij}^{best} \tag{22}$$

where, $\Delta\tau_{ij}^{best} = 1/f(s_{best})$ is the amount of pheromone deposit by the ant that generates the best solution (s_{best}), which may be the best-so-far (s_{bs}) or the iteration-best (s_{ib}).

In order to avoid search stagnation, the pheromone trails are limited by lower and upper values τ_{min} and τ_{max} such that $\tau_{min} \leq \tau_{ij} \leq \tau_{max}, \forall i,j$. Additionally, the initial pheromone trails are set to the upper pheromone trail limits, so that the initial search phase promotes a higher exploration of the search space.

The $\mathcal{MM}AS$ occasionally reinitializes the pheromone trail matrix, so as to increase the exploration of edges that have small probability of being chosen, and also to avoid stagnation.

The $\mathcal{MM}$AS version with multiple objectives was proposed by Pinto and Báran (Pinto & Barán, 2005), to solve a Multicast Traffic Engineering problem. The M3AS algorithm uses one pheromone matrix and as many heuristic matrices as the number of objectives $\eta_{ij}^k = 1/d_{ij}^k$, with K being the number of objectives.

The probability of assigning the arc (i,j) is given by

$$p_{ij}^h = \frac{[\tau_{ij}]^\alpha \prod_{k=1}^K [\eta_{ij}^k]^{\lambda^k}}{\sum_{l \in \mathcal{N}_i^h} [\tau_{il}]^\alpha \prod_{k=1}^K [\eta_{il}^k]^{\lambda^k}} \quad \text{if } j \in \mathcal{N}_i^h \text{, and 0 otherwise} \tag{23}$$

where the parameters λ^k determine the relative influence of the heuristics information.

When all ants construct their solutions the pheromone evaporation is applied using equation (4) followed by the deposit of pheromone as follows

$$\tau_{ij}^k \leftarrow \tau_{ij}^k + \Delta\tau_{ij}^k \tag{24}$$

where $\Delta\tau_{ij}^k = 1/\sum_{k=1}^K f^k(s_p)$. The ants which are allowed to update the pheromone matrix are the ones that generated non-dominated solutions.

In the end of the algorithm execution, M3AS returns the set of non-dominated solutions found.

5.5 Omicron ACO (OA) vs. multiobjective omicron ACO (MOA)

The Omicron ACO (OA) algorithm proposed by Gómez and Barán (Gómez & Barán, 2005) is inspired by $\mathcal{MM}$AS. In OA, a constant pheromone matrix τ^0 is defined, with $\tau_{ij}^0 = 1, \forall i,j$. OA is a population based algorithm where a population of individuals is maintained which contains the best solutions found so far.

The first population of individuals is initialized using τ^0. Each ant of the colony constructs a complete tour using (3). At the end of the iteration, every time a new individual generates a

solution better than the worst individual and different from the others in the population, this new one replaces the worst one.
After the maximum number of iterations is reached, the pheromone matrix is updated using the solution in the population set, as follows

$$\tau_{ij} \leftarrow \tau_{ij} + \frac{O}{m} \tag{25}$$

where O (from *Omicron*) and m (number of individuals) are given values. The algorithm returns the best solution found.
The multiobjective version of the Omicron ACO (MOA) algorithm was proposed by Gardel and colleagues (Gardel et al., 2005) under the name of *Eletric Omicron*. The MOA was first applied to the Reactive Power Compensation Problem in a multiobjective context. In MOA the pheromone trails are initially set as in OA (that is, $\tau^0_{ij} = 1$) and the two heuristic matrices η^0_{ij} and η^1_{ij} associated with each objective are linearly combined to define the visibility

$$\eta_{ij} = \omega_1 \eta^0_{ij} + \omega_2 \eta^1_{ij} \tag{26}$$

where ω_1 and ω_2 are weight values (with $\omega_1 + \omega_2 = 1$) which are are dynamically changed at each iteration of the algorithm.
The artificial ants construct the solutions by using equation (3), with η_{ij} defined by equation (26). An external set is used to save the non-dominated solutions. At the end of the iteration, the pheromone trails are updated, using equation (25) only in the solutions contained in the Pareto set.

5.6 Ant algorithm for bi-criterion optimization (BicriterionAnt)

Iredi and co-workers (Iredi et al., 2001) proposed two ACO methods to solve the Single Machine Total Tardiness Problem (SMTTP) with changeover costs,considering two objectives. The difference between the algorithms is the use of one or several ant colonies. In this section we describe the so-called BicriterionAnt algorithm, which uses only one colony of ants. It uses two pheromone trail matrices τ and τ' and two heuristic information matrices η and η', one for each objective.
In every iteration, each of the m ants generates a solution to the problem using the following probability to select the next job j:

$$p^h_{ij} = \frac{\tau^{\lambda\alpha}_{ij} {\tau'}^{(1-\lambda)\alpha}_{ij} \eta^{\lambda\beta}_{ij} {\eta'}^{(1-\lambda)\beta}_{ij}}{\sum_{l \in \mathcal{N}^h_i} \tau^{\lambda\alpha}_{il} {\tau'}^{(1-\lambda)\alpha}_{il} \eta^{\lambda\beta}_{il} {\eta'}^{(1-\lambda)\beta}_{il}} \quad \text{if } j \in \mathcal{N}^h_i, \text{ and 0 otherwise} \tag{27}$$

where α and β are parameters that weight the relative importance of the pheromone trail and the heuristic information, η and η' are heuristic values associated with edge a_{ij} according to each objective, and $\mathcal{N}^h_i$ is the current feasible neighbourhood of ant h. In order to make the ants search in different regions of the Pareto front, λ is calculated for each ant $h \in \{1,...,m\}$, as:

$$\lambda_h = \frac{(h-1)}{(m-1)}$$

Thus, in the extreme cases, ant m, with $\lambda = 1$, considers only the first objective whereas ant 1, with $\lambda = 0$, considers only the second objective.

Once all ants generate their solutions, the pheromone trails are evaporated according to

$$\tau_{ij} \leftarrow (1-\rho)\tau_{ij} \ , \ \tau'_{ij} \leftarrow (1-\rho)\tau'_{ij}$$

where $\rho \in (0,1]$ is the evaporation rate.
The pheromone update process is performed only by the ants in the current non-dominated set. Each ant updates both matrices as follows:

$$\tau_{ij} \leftarrow \tau_{ij} + 1/l \ , \ \tau'_{ij} \leftarrow \tau'_{ij} + 1/l$$

where l is the number of ants that are allowed to do the updating in the current iteration.

5.7 Multiobjective network ACO (MONACO)

The MONACO algorithm was proposed in (Cardoso et al., 2003), to solve a dynamic problem, the optimization of the message traffic in a network. Hence, in the following, we present an adaptation of the original algorithm to solve static problems, where the policy of the network does not change during the algorithm's steps, as done in (García-Martínez et al., 2007).
This algorithm uses one heuristic information $\eta_{ij} = \sum_{k=1}^{K} d_{ij}^{k}$ and several pheromone matrices τ^k, one for each objective, where K is the number of objectives. Each ant, considered as a message, chooses the next node on the web according to the following probability:

$$p_{ij}^{h} = \frac{\eta_{ij}^{\beta} \prod_{k=1}^{K} [\tau_{ij}^{k}]^{\alpha_k}}{\sum_{l \in \mathcal{N}_i^h} \eta_{il}^{\beta} \prod_{k=1}^{K} [\tau_{il}^{k}]^{\alpha_k}} \tag{28}$$

if $j \in \mathcal{N}_i^h$, and 0 otherwise.
The α_k and β parameters weigh the relative importance of the pheromone matrices and the heuristic information, respectively. By the end of each iteration, the ants that built a solution update the pheromone trail matrices in the following way:

$$\tau_{ij}^{k} = (1-\rho_k)\tau_{ij}^{k} + \Delta\tau_{ij}^{k} \tag{29}$$

where

$$\Delta\tau_{ij}^{k} = \frac{Q}{f^k(s_h)} \tag{30}$$

with ρ_k being the pheromone evaporation rate for each objective k, Q is a constant related to the amount of pheromone laid by the ants, and s_h is the solution built by the ant h. In this adaptation of MONACO, the non-dominated solutions, that form the Pareto set, are stored in an external archive.

5.8 COMPETants

Doerner, Hartl and Reimann (Doerner et al., 2001) developed the COMPETants to solve a multiobjective transportation problem.
The basic idea behind COMPETants is the use of two populations with different priority rules. In COMPETants the population size is not fixed but undergoes adaptation during the algorithm execution. The ants utilize their own pheromone and heuristic information. However, some ants of each population which generate the best solutions, called *spies*, use not only their own information (pheromone and heuristic) but also the foreign information.

Decision rule for the ants is given by the following equation

$$p_{ij}^{h} = \frac{[\tau_{ij}]^{\alpha}[\eta_{ij}]^{\beta}}{\sum_{l \in \mathcal{N}_i^h}[\tau_{il}]^{\alpha}[\eta_{il}]^{\beta}}, \quad \text{if } j \in \mathcal{N}_i^h, \text{ and 0 otherwise} \tag{31}$$

noticing that each colony targets its own pheromone and heuristic information. For the spy ants, the decision rule is given by

$$p_{ij}^{h} = \frac{[0.5\tau_{ij}^{0} + 0.5\tau_{ij}^{1}]^{\alpha}[\eta_{ij}]^{\beta}}{\sum_{l \in \mathcal{N}_i^h}[0.5\tau_{il}^{0} + 0.5\tau_{il}^{1}]^{\alpha}[\eta_{il}]^{\beta}} \quad \text{if } j \in \mathcal{N}_i^h, \text{ and 0 otherwise} \tag{32}$$

where, in this new rule, the spies combine the information of both pheromone trails.
When all ants have constructed their solutions, the pheromone update rule is performed only by a number of best ants, ranked according to the solution quality. The update rule is as follows:

$$\tau_{ij} = \rho\tau_{ij} + \sum_{\lambda=1}^{\Lambda} \Delta\tau_{ij}^{\lambda} \tag{33}$$

where Λ represents the best ants of the population, and the constant $\Delta\tau_{ij}^{\lambda}$ is represented as

$$\Delta\tau_{ij}^{\lambda} = \begin{cases} 1 - \frac{\lambda-1}{\Lambda}, & \lambda \in [1,\Lambda], \quad \text{if } j \in \mathcal{N}_i^h \\ 0, & \text{otherwise;} \end{cases} \tag{34}$$

The algorithm returns the best solution found.

5.9 SACO

T'kindt *et al* (Vincent et al., 2002) proposed the SACO algorithm to solve a 2-machine bicriteria flowshop scheduling problem.
The SACO algorithm uses only one pheromone information and one heuristic information. This algorithm was developed to solve a lexicographical problem, where only one best solution is returned at the end of the algorithm execution.
Each ant constructs a feasible solution using the pheromone information, which can be done in two different modes: (i) by an intensification mode, where an ant chooses, as the most suitable job, the one with the highest value of τ_{ij}; or (ii) by a diversification mode, where an ant uses a random-proportional rule to select the most suitable job. A parameter p_0 was created for selecting the probability of being in one of these two modes, which is given by $p_0 = log(n)/log(N)$, where n is the iteration number, with $n \in [1,N]$. When an ant has built a complete solution, a local search procedure is applied.
The pheromone evaporation is performed on every edge and the pheromone update is done only by the best solution found at each iteration, as follows:

$$\tau_{ij} \leftarrow \begin{cases} \tau_{ij} + \frac{1}{f(s)}, & \text{if arc } (i,j) \in s_{best} \\ (1-\rho)\tau_{ij}, & \text{otherwise;} \end{cases} \tag{35}$$

where s_{best} is the best objective function value found and ρ is the evaporation rate.

5.10 Pareto Ant Colony Optimization (P-ACO)

Doerner *et al* in (Doerner et al., 2004) proposed a Pareto ant colony optimization algorithm to solve the multiobjective portfolio selection problem. It is based on ACS, but the global pheromone update is performed by two specific ants, the best and the second-best ant.
P-ACO uses as many pheromone matrices as the number of objectives k, and only one heuristic information. The decision transition rule is based on ACS with k pheromone matrices

$$j = \begin{cases} \arg\max_{j \in \mathcal{N}_i^h} \{\sum_{k=1}^{K} [p_k \tau_{ij}^k]^\alpha \eta_{ij}^\beta\}, & \text{if } q \leq q_0 \\ \hat{i}, & \text{otherwise;} \end{cases} \tag{36}$$

where p_k are determined randomly for each ant and $\hat{i}$ is a node selected according to:

$$p_{ij}^h = \frac{\sum_{k=1}^{K} [p_k \tau_{ij}^k]^\alpha \eta_{ij}^\beta}{\sum_{l \in \mathcal{N}_i^h} (\sum_{k=1}^{K} [p_k \tau_{il}^k]^\alpha \eta_{il}^\beta)} \quad \text{if } j \in \mathcal{N}_i^h, \text{ and 0 otherwise} \tag{37}$$

A local pheromone update is performed every time an ant traverses an edge (i,j), by applying the following equation, considering each pheromone matrix:

$$\tau_{ij}^k = (1-\rho)\tau_{ij}^k + \rho\tau_0 \tag{38}$$

where τ_0 is the initial pheromone value and ρ is the evaporation rate.
The global pheromone update is done only by the best and the second-best ants. The update rule for each objective k is given by:

$$\tau_{ij}^k = (1-\rho)\tau_{ij}^k + \rho\Delta\tau_{ij}^k \tag{39}$$

with $\Delta\tau_{ij}^k$ being an increasing quantity related to the best and second-best solutions according to objective k, which is represented as

$$\Delta\tau_{ij}^k = \begin{cases} 10 & \text{if arc } (i,j) \in s_{best} \\ 5 & \text{if arc } (i,j) \in s_{second-best} \\ 0 & \text{otherwise;} \end{cases} \tag{40}$$

During the algorithm run, the non-dominated solutions are stored in a external set and are returned as a final solution.

5.11 Multiobjective ant colony system algorithm (MOACSA)

Yagmahan and Yenisey proposed a multi-objective ant colony system procedure, based on ACS, for a flow shop scheduling problem (Yagmahan & Yenisey, 2010).
The MOACSA uses one pheromone matrix and one heuristic information. At the initialization step, the initial pheromone value is calculated by

$$\tau_0 = \frac{1}{n[f^0(s_h) + f^1(s_h)]} \tag{41}$$

where n is the number of jobs and s_h is the solution built by ant h, which is calculated considering each objective.
In the construction process the ant h in job i selects the job j by applying equation (10) (with $\alpha \geq 1$) as a state transition rule. Each time an ant selects a job, it applies a local pheromone update

$$\tau_{ij} = (1 - \xi)\tau_{ij} + \xi\tau_0 \tag{42}$$

where $\xi \in (0,1)$ is the local pheromone evaporation parameter.
The global update rule is performed only by ants that generates the best solutions, as follows

$$\tau_{ij} = (1 - \rho)\tau_{ij} + \rho\Delta\tau_{ij} \tag{43}$$

where $\Delta\tau_{ij}$ is the amount of pheromone deposit by ant h which generate the best solution in the current iteration.

6. Conclusions

This chapter reviewed the application of ant colony optimization algorithms to multiple objective problems. The extension of well known single objective ACO algorithms to tackle MOO problems has been presented. In addition, the algorithmic components that play a relevant role in MOACO algorithm design and performance have been discussed. Several algorithms from the literature which are representative of the many ways such components can be implemented have been presented. It is expected that this chapter provides the readers with a comprehensive view of the use of ACO algorithms to solve MOO problems and helps them in designing new ACO techniques for their particular applications.

7. Acknowledgments

The authors thank the support from the brazilian agencies CNPq (308317/2009-2 and 141519/2010-0) and FAPERJ (E-26/ 102.825/2008).

8. References

Angus, D. & Woodward, C. (2009). Multiple objective ant colony optimisation, *Swarm Intelligence* 3(1): 69–85.

Barán, B. & Schaerer, M. (2003). A multiobjective ant colony system for vehicle routing problem with time windows, *Proceedings of the 21st IASTED International Conference*, pp. 97–102.

Branke, J., Deb, K., Miettinen, K. & Slowiński, R. (eds) (2008). *Multiobjective Optimization: Interactive and Evolutionary Approaches (Lecture Notes in Computer Science)*, Springer.

Cardoso, P., Jesus, M. & Márquez, A. (2003). Monaco - multi-objective network optimisation based on an ACO, *In Proceedings of Encuentros de Geometria Computacional*.

Coello, C. A. C., Veldhuizen, D. A. V. & Lamont, G. B. (2002). *Evolutionary algorithms for solving Multi-Objective Problems*, Kluwer.

Doerner, K. F., Hartl, R. F. & Reimann, M. (2001). Are COMPETants more competent for problem solving? - the case of a routing and scheduling problem, *Proceedings of the Genetic and Evolutionary Computation Conference (GECCO-2001)*, Morgan Kaufmann, San Francisco, California, USA, p. 802.

Doerner, K., Gutjahr, W. J., Hartl, R. F., Strauss, C. & Stummer, C. (2004). Pareto ant colony optimization: A metaheuristic approach to multiobjective portfolio selection, *Kluwer Academic Publishers, Annals of Operations Research* (131): 79–99.

Dorigo, M. (1992). *Optimization, Learning and Natural Algorithms*, PhD thesis, Dipartimento di Elettronica, Politecnico di Milano, Milan, Italy.

Dorigo, M., Bonabeau, E. & Theraulaz, G. (1999). *Swarm intelligence: from natural to artificial systems*, Oxford University Press, Inc., New York, NY.

Dorigo, M., Bonabeau, E. & Theraulaz, G. (2000). Ant algorithms and stigmergy, *Future Gener. Comput. Syst.* 16(9): 851–871.

Dorigo, M. & Caro, G. D. (1999). Ant Colony Optimization: A new meta-heuristic, *in* P. J. Angeline, Z. Michalewicz, M. Schoenauer, X. Yao & A. Zalzala (eds), *IEEE Congress on Evolutionary Computation – CEC'99*, IEEE Press, Piscataway, NJ, pp. 1470–1477.

Dorigo, M. & Gambardella, L. M. (1997a). Ant colonies for the traveling salesman problem, *BioSystems* 43: 73–81.

Dorigo, M. & Gambardella, L. M. (1997b). Ant Colony System: A cooperative learning approach to the traveling salesman problem, *IEEE Transactions on Evolutionary Computation* 1(1): 53–66.

Dorigo, M. & Stützle, T. (2004). *Ant Colony Optimization*, The MIT Press, Cambridge, Massachusetts.

Dorigo, M., Stützle, T. & Birattari, M. (2006). Ant colony optimization - artificial ants as a computational intelligence technique, *IEEE Computational Intelligence Magazine* .

Ehrgott, M. (2005). *Multicriteria Optimization*, Lecture Notes in Economics and Mathematical Systems, Springer-Verlag.

Fonseca, L. G., Capriles, P. V. S. Z., Barbosa, H. J. C. & Lemonge, A. C. C. (2007). A stochastic rank-based ant system for discrete structural optimization, *Proceedings of the 2007 IEEE Swarm Intelligence Symposium (SIS 2007)*, pp. 68–75.

Fonseca, V. G., Fonseca, C. M. & Hall, A. O. (2001). Inferential performance assessment of stochastic optimisers and the attainment function, *EMO '01: Proceedings of the First International Conference on Evolutionary Multi-Criterion Optimization*, Springer-Verlag, London, UK, pp. 213–225.

Gambardella, L. M. & Dorigo, M. (1995). Ant-q: A reinforcement learning approach to the traveling salesman problem, *Twelfth International Conference on Machine Learning*, Morgan Kaufmann, pp. 252–260.

Gandibleux, X., Sevaux, M., Sörensen, K. & T'Kindt, V. (eds) (2004). *Metaheuristics for Multiobjective Optimisation*, Vol. 535, springer-verlag edn, Lecture Notes in Economics and Mathematical Systems.

García-Martínez, C., Cordón, O. & Herrera, F. (2007). A taxonomy and an empirical analysis of multiple objective ant colony optimization algorithms for the bi-criteria TSP, *European Journal of Operational Research* 180: 116–148.

Gardel, P., Estigarribia, H., Fernández, U. & Barán, B. (2005). Aplicación del Ómicron aco al problema de compensación de potencia reactiva en un contexto multiobjetivo, *Congreso Argentino de Ciencias de la Computación - CACIC2005*, Concordia Argentina.

Gómez, O. & Barán, B. (2005). Omicron aco. a new ant colony optimization algorithm, *CLEI Electronic Journal* 8(1).

Iredi, S., Merkle, D. & Middendorf, M. (2001). Bi-criterion optimization with multi colony ant algorithms, *Lecture Notes in Computer Science (LNCS)* 1993: 359–372.

Knowles, J. (2005). A summary-attainment-surface plotting method for visualizing the performance of stochastic multiobjective optimizers, *ISDA '05: Proceedings of the 5th International Conference on Intelligent Systems Design and Applications*, IEEE Computer Society, Washington, DC, USA, pp. 552–557.

Knowles, J. & Corne, D. (2002). On metrics for comparing non-dominated sets. In Congress on Evolutionary Computation (CEC 2002).

Knowles, J., Thiele, L. & Zitzler, E. (2006). A Tutorial on the Performance Assessment of Stochastic Multiobjective Optimizers, *TIK Report 214*, Computer Engineering and Networks Laboratory (TIK), ETH Zurich.

Li, X., Branke, J. & Kirley, M. (2007). On performance metrics and particle swarm methods for dynamic multiobjective optimization problems, *IEEE Congress on Evolutionary Computation*, Vol. 25-28, pp. 576–583.

López-Ibáñez, M. (2004). *Multi-objective ant colony optimization*, Master's thesis, Darmstadt University of Technology.

López-Ibáñez, M., Paquete, L. & Stützle, T. (2009). Exploratory analysis of stochastic local search algorithms in biobjective optimization, pp. 209–233.

López-Ibáñez, M. & Stützle, T. (2010). Automatic configuration of multi-objective ant colony optimization algorithms, pp. 95–106.

Mariano, C. E. & Morales, E. (1999). MOAQ an ant-Q algorithm for multiple objective optimization problems, *GECCO-99*, Vol. 1, Morgan Kaufmann, Orlando, Florida, USA, pp. 894–901.

Miettinen, K. (1999). *Nonlinear Multiobjective Optimization*, Kluwer Academic, Norwell, Massachusetts.

Paciello, J., Martínez, H., Lezcano, C. & Barán, B. (2006). Algoritmos de optimizacin multi-objetivos basados en colonias de hormigas, *XXXII Latin-American Conference on Informatics 2006 - CLEI2006*.

Pinto, D. & Barán, B. (2005). Solving multiobjective multicast routing problem with a new ant colony optimization approach, *LANC '05: Proceedings of the 3rd international IFIP/ACM Latin American conference on Networking*, ACM, New York, NY, USA, pp. 11–19.

Silberholz, J. & Golden, B. (2009). *Handbook of Metaheuristics*, Springer-Verlag, chapter Comparison of Metaheuristics.

Stützle, T. (1997). $\mathcal{MAX} - \mathcal{MIN}$ ant system for quadratic assignment problems, *Technical Report AIDA-97-04*, FG Intellektik, FB Informatik, TU Darmstadt, Germany.

Stützle, T. & Hoos, H. H. (2000). $\mathcal{MAX} - \mathcal{MIN}$ ant system, *Future Generation Computer Systems Journal* 16(8): 889–914.

Tan, K., Khor, E. & Lee, T. (2005). *Multiobjective Evolutionary Algorithms and Applications*, Springer.

Vincent, T., Monmarche, N., Tercinet, F. & Laugt, D. (2002). An ant colony optimization algorithm to solve a 2-machine bicriteria flowshop scheduling problem, *European Journal of Operational Research* 142(2): 250–257.

Yagmahan, B. & Yenisey, M. M. (2010). A multi-objective ant colony system algorithm for flow shop scheduling problem, *Expert Syst. Appl.* 37(2): 1361–1368.

Zitzler, E., Deb, K. & Thiele, L. (2000). Comparison of multiobjective evolutionary algorithms: Empirical results, *Evolutionary Computation* 8(2): 173–195.

6

Automatic Construction of Programs Using Dynamic Ant Programming

Shinichi Shirakawa, Shintaro Ogino, and Tomoharu Nagao
Yokohama National University
Japan

1. Introduction

Automatic programming is the research field of generating computer programs automatically. Genetic programming (GP) (Koza, 1992; 1994) is a typical example of automatic programming, which was proposed by Koza. GP evolves computer programs with tree structure based on genetic algorithm (GA). GP has, however, the problem of bloating (Langdon & Poli, 1998; Poli, 2003), the growth of the average size of an individual in the population. This chapter introduces a new method for automatic programming using ant colony optimization (ACO) (Dorigo et al., 1999; Dorigo & Stutzle, 2004). ACO is a technique for solving combinatorial optimization problems. ACO algorithm is inspired by the behavior of the ants.

Several automatic programming techniques using ACO were investigated (Engelbrecht, 2006). Typical examples are ant programming (AP) (Roux & Fonlupt, 2000), ant colony programming (ACP) (Boryczka & Czech, 2002), AntTAG (Abbass et al., 2002) and generalized ant programming (GAP) (Keber & Schuster, 2002). AP is similar to Probabilistic Incremental Program Evolution (PIPE) (Salustowicz & Schmidhuber, 1997), and it was used to solve the symbolic regression problems. PIPE generates successive populations from a probabilistic prototype tree. ACP was used to solve the symbolic regression problems with two different versions that are the expression approach and the program approach. AntTAG and GAP are grammar-based work.

The method proposed in this chapter is named dynamic ant programming (DAP). DAP is based on ACO and generates desired programs using the dynamically changing pheromone table. The nodes (terminal and nonterminal) are selected using the value of the pheromone table. The higher the rate of pheromone, the higher is the probability that it can be chosen. The unnecessary node in DAP is deleted according to pheromone value. Therefore, the average size of programs tends to be small, and it is possible to search desired programs effectively. In order to verify the effectiveness, we applied the proposed method to the symbolic regression problem that is widely used as a test problem for GP systems. We compare the performance of DAP to GP and show the effectiveness of DAP. In order to investigate the influence of several parameters, we compare experimental results obtained using different settings.

This chapter consists of five sections. Section 2 is an overview of some related works. Section 3 describes DAP. Several experiments are shown in Section 4. Section 5 is devoted to the conclusions and the discussion of future works.

2. Related works

2.1 Genetic programming

GP is a method of automatic programming, which was introduced by Koza (Koza, 1992; 1994). It evolves computer programs with tree structure, and searches a desired program using GA. A population (a set of programs) will evolve by repeatedly selecting the fitter programs, combining them, and producing new programs. In GP, individuals in the population are computer programs. These programs are usually represented as trees. This tree-form representation is a useful way of representing LISP expression (also known as S-expression). The internal nodes represent the functions (non-terminal) and the leaves are the terminal nodes. GP has the problem of bloating (Langdon & Poli, 1998; Poli, 2003) potentially, the growth of the average size of an individual in the population. The general GP method can be roughly described as follows:

1. Random generation of programs (trees);
2. Evaluation of programs (fitness measure);
3. Application of genetic operations to individuals: crossover, mutation;
4. Selection of individuals;
5. Go to step 2 until some termination criterion is satisfied.

2.2 Ant colony optimization

ACO (Dorigo et al., 1999; Dorigo & Stutzle, 2004) is a technique for solving combinatorial optimization problems, and it was introduced in the early 1990's. ACO algorithm is inspired by the behavior of real ants. It has been applied to many combinatorial optimization problems, e.g. Traveling Salesman Problems (TSP) (Dorigo et al., 1996; Stutzle & Hoos, 2000), network routing problems (Schoonderwoerd et al., 1996; Caro & Dorigo, 1998), graph coloring problems (Costa & Hertz, 1997), and so on. The first ACO algorithm, called ant system (AS) Dorigo et al. (1996), was proposed by Dorigo et al. and applied to the TSP. Figure 1 shows the AS algorithm.
An ant located at city i selects an edge between city i and city j by using the probabilities:

$$p_{ij}^{k}(t) = \begin{cases} \frac{[\tau_{ij}(t)]^{\alpha} \cdot [\eta_{ij}]^{\beta}}{\sum_{l \in N_i^k(t)} [\tau_{il}(t)]^{\alpha} \cdot [\eta_{il}]^{\beta}} & \text{if } j \in N_i^k(t) \\ 0 & \text{if } j \notin N_i^k(t) \end{cases} \quad (1)$$

```
definition m: the number of ants
Initialize
repeat
  for k = 1 to m do
    repeat
      From current node i, select next node j with probability as defined in Equation (1);
    until full path has been constructed;
  end
  Update pheromone using Equation (3);
until stopping condition is true;
```

Fig. 1. Ant system (AS) algorithm

where $\tau_{ij}(t)$ is the amount of pheromone trail on edge (i, j) at time t, a heuristic value η_{ij} equals to $1/d_{ij}$, where d_{ij} is the distance between city i and j, α and β are parameters which control the relative weight of the pheromone trail and the heuristic value respectively, where N_i^k is the set of cities which remains to be visited. After every ant completes a tour, pheromone is deposited:

$$\Delta\tau_{ij}^k(t) = \begin{cases} \frac{Q}{L_k} & \text{if } (i,j) \in T_k \\ 0 & \text{otherwise} \end{cases} \tag{2}$$

where Q is a constant; L^k is the length of the tour generated by ant k; T_k is the tour generated by ant k. The amount of pheromone is updated according to the rule:

$$\tau_{ij}(t+1) = (1-\rho)\tau_{ij}(t) + \sum_{k=1}^{m} \Delta\tau_{ij}^k(t) \tag{3}$$

where m is the number of ants and $\rho (0 < \rho < 1)$ is a parameter called evaporation rate. These processes are repeated a predefined $t_{\max}$ number of times.

In addition to finding very good solutions to 'static' problems, the ACO algorithm is also effective in 'dynamic' problems (Guntsch & Middendorf, 2001; Guntsch et al., 2001; Caro & Dorigo, 1998; Schoonderwoerd et al., 1996). The ACO algorithm maintains portions of solution as the pheromone trails, which can be especially useful when the problem is dynamically changing (Bonabeau et al., 2000).

Several extended and improved versions of the original AS algorithm were introduced. For instance, ant colony system (ACS) (Dorigo & Gambardella, 1997), elitist ant system (EAS) (Dorigo et al., 1996), rank-based ant system (RAS) (Bullnheimer et al., 1999), and MAX-MIN ant system (MMAS) (Stutzle & Hoos, 1997; 2000). One of the most successful ACO variants is MMAS. MMAS limits the possible range of pheromone trail values to the interval $[\tau_{\min}, \tau_{\max}]$. Additional difference is that only the best ant may reinforce pheromones, and initial pheromones are set to the maximum allowed value. The pheromone update rule in MMAS is:

$$\tau_{ij}(t+1) = (1-\rho)\tau_{ij}(t) + \Delta\tau_{ij}^{best}(t) \tag{4}$$

where $\Delta\tau_{ij}^{best}(t)$ is calculated on the basis of either the global-best path or the iteration-best path.

2.3 Ant colony optimization for automatic programming

Several automatic programming techniques based on ACO were investigated (Engelbrecht, 2006). AP (Roux & Fonlupt, 2000) appears to be the earliest attempt at using ACO to automatic programming. It is similar to PIPE (Salustowicz & Schmidhuber, 1997), and it was used to solve symbolic regression problems. PIPE generates successive populations from a probabilistic prototype tree. AntTAG (Abbass et al., 2002) and GAP (Keber & Schuster, 2002) are grammar-based works. AntTAG is an ACO algorithm which constructs programs using tree-adjunct grammar (TAG). GAP system uses context-free grammar.

The most related work to our proposed method is ACP (Boryczka & Czech, 2002). ACP was used for solving the symbolic regression problems with two different versions that are the expression approach and the program approach. The expression approach constructs an expression in prefix notation, while the program approach constructs an

```
definition m: the number of ants
Initialize
repeat
  for k = 1 to m do
    repeat
      From current node i, select next node j with probability as defined in Equation (5);
    until full path has been constructed (Ant completely has reached terminal);
  end
  Update pheromone using Equation (7);
  Deletion of nodes;
  Insertion of nodes;
until stopping condition is true;
```

Fig. 2. Dynamic ant programming (DAP) algorithm

expression from a sequence of assignment instructions. Both approaches base on the ACS (Dorigo & Gambardella, 1997). In expression approach, the components of graph $G = (N, E)$ have the following meaning: N is the set of nodes, where each node represents either a terminal symbol (i.e. a constant or variable) or a non-terminal symbol (i.e. an arithmetic operator or function). Each link in E represents a branch of the expression tree. The tabu list is not used, since the multiple occurrences of a node in the expression are not prohibited.

3. Dynamic ant programming

DAP is a novel automatic programming method using ACO. GP has the problem of bloating, potentially the growth of the average size of an individual in the population. In the conventional method, ACP, the number of nodes is fixed beforehand, and the tabu list is not used. Therefore, it tends to select the same node repeatedly and has the multiple occurrence of the same expression in one program.

The unnecessary node in DAP is deleted according to pheromone value. The size of the pheromone table in DAP changes dynamically in each iteration, and the number of nodes is variable. Therefore, the average size of programs tends to be small, and it is possible to search desired programs effectively. The tabu list is used in DAP; thus, it is possible to generate various programs. Figure 2 shows the DAP algorithm.

3.1 Construction of tree structure

First, the ant starts at *start node* (*start node* is an initial node for ants). The ant chooses the next node using pheromone values. The ant never selects a nonterminal node which was already selected (i.e. the tabu list is used), whereas terminal node can be visited by the ants repeatedly. If the selected node is a terminal node, the search is finished. The higher the rate of pheromone, the higher the probability that it can be chosen. The ant located in node i selects only the number of argument of node i using the pheromone value in the subsequent nodes. Therefore, the pheromone table size in DAP is:

- column size
  total number of nodes (terminal and nonterminal).
- row size
  total number of arguments + 1 (*start node*).

	Arg No.	x	1.0	+	$*$	sin
Start	–			1		
+	1	2				
	2					3
$*$	1	5				
	2		6			
sin	1				4	

Table 1. Example of pheromone table in DAP

Table 1 shows an example of the pheromone table, and Figure 3 illustrates how to construct tree structure using the pheromone table. The ant visits the sequence of nodes $\{\text{Start} \to + \to x \to \sin \to * \to x \to 1.0\}$ and constructs a numerical formula '$x + \sin(x * 1.0)$'.
The probability of ant k located in node i moving to node j through argument u at time t is:

$$p^k_{i_u j}(t) = \begin{cases} \frac{\tau_{i_u j}(t)}{\sum_{l \in N^k_i(t)} \tau_{i_u l}(t)} & \text{if } j \in N^k_i(t) \\ 0 & \text{if } j \notin N^k_i(t) \end{cases} \quad (5)$$

where $\tau_{i_u j}(t)$ is the amount of pheromone trail on edge (i_u, j) at time t; $N^k_i(t)$ is the set of nodes that remains to be visited.

3.2 Pheromone update

The pheromone update rules in DAP is similar to MMAS (Stutzle & Hoos, 2000). To avoid stagnation of search, a possible range of pheromone value is limited to an interval $[\tau_{\min}, \tau_{\max}]$. The parameters $\tau_{\min}$ and $\tau_{\max}$ are determined in advance. After each program (individual) is evaluated, the pheromone table is updated according to:

$$\Delta\tau^{\text{best}}_{ij}(t) = \begin{cases} f^{\text{ib}} & \text{if}(i,j) \in T_{\text{ib}} \\ 0 & \text{otherwise} \end{cases} \quad (6)$$

where f^{ib} is a fitness of iteration-best ant and T_{ib} is the tour (program) generated by iteration-best ant. The amount of pheromone is updated according to the rule:

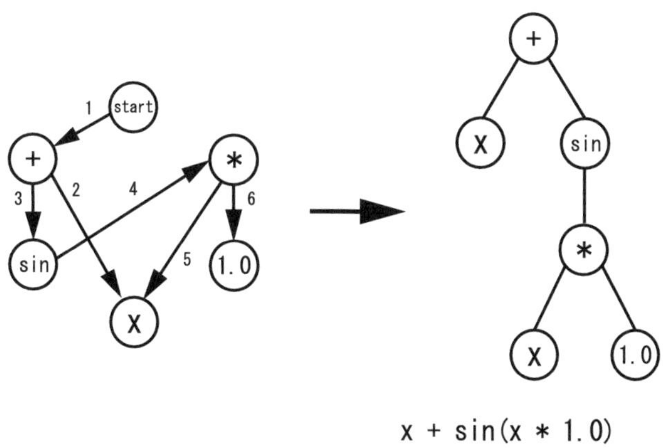

Fig. 3. An example of constructing tree structure in DAP. The ant visits the sequence of nodes $\{\text{Start} \to + \to x \to \sin \to * \to x \to 1.0\}$ and constructs a numerical formula '$x + \sin(x * 1.0)$'

Terminal or function	Arg No.	x	1.0	$+$	$*$	sin
Start	-			τ_{min}		
$+$	1			τ_{min}		
	2			τ_{min}		
$*$	1			τ_{min}		
	2			τ_{min}		
sin	1			τ_{min}		

Table 2. An example of deletion of node. The node '+' is deleted in this case

$$\tau_{ij}(t+1) = (1-\rho)\tau_{ij}(t) + \Delta\tau_{ij}^{\text{best}}(t) \tag{7}$$

where $\rho(0 < \rho < 1)$ is a parameter called evaporation rate. Initial pheromones are set to the maximum allowed value (τ_{max}).

3.3 Deletion and insertion of nodes

Deletion and insertion of nodes are performed after pheromone update in each iteration. So, the pheromone table changes dynamically in DAP. Table 2 illustrates an example of the deletion of node, and Table 3 illustrates an example of the insertion of node.

- Deletion of node
  If all pheromone values to the node j are minimum values τ_{min} (if all $\tau_{lj} = \tau_{min}, l = \{1,...,n\}$), the node j is deleted, where n is the number of row size of pheromone table).
- Insertion of node
  The probability of inserting node in iteration i equals to:

$$p(i) = \frac{\frac{1}{m}\sum_{k=1}^{m} L_i^k}{N_i} \tag{8}$$

  where L^k is the number of nodes generated by ant k; N_i is total number of nodes (column size of pheromone table); and m is the number of ants. The type of node inserted is decided randomly. The pheromone value of an inserted node is set to τ_{ins}.

Although the search space (i.e. the pheromone table of DAP) is dynamically changing, the ants find good solution using portions of solutions, which are pheromone trail values.

Terminal or function	Arg No.	x	1.0	$+$	$*$	sin	sin
Start	-						τ_{ins}
$+$	1						τ_{ins}
	2						τ_{ins}
$*$	1						τ_{ins}
	2						τ_{ins}
sin	1						τ_{ins}
sin	1	τ_{ins}	τ_{ins}	τ_{ins}	τ_{ins}	τ_{ins}	τ_{ins}

Table 3. An example of insertion of node. The node 'sin' is inserted in this case

4. Experiments and results

In this section several experiments with DAP and GP are performed. We use the well-known test problem, namely, the symbolic regression.

4.1 Symbolic regression

Symbolic regression is widely used as a test problem for GP systems. The problem is to search for a function that fits sampled data points. The functions used in these experiments are:

$$f_1(x) = x^4 + x^3 + x^2 + x \tag{9}$$

$$f_2(x) = \sin(x) + x^2 + 1 \tag{10}$$

$$f_3(x) = \sin(x^3 + x) \tag{11}$$

The set of sampled data points for these problems was generated using (for the variable x) 20 uniformly chosen values in the interval [-1, 1]. We use the mean error on the sampled data points as a fitness function, which is defined as:

$$\text{fitness} = \frac{1}{1 + \sum_{i=1}^{n} |C_{\text{correct}_i} - C_{\text{estimate}_i}|} \tag{12}$$

where C_{correct_i} is the correct value for the sampled data point i; C_{estimate_i} is the value returned by the generated program for the sampled data point i; and n is the size of the sampled data points. The range of this fitness function is $[0.0, 1.0]$. A higher numerical value indicates better performance. The common parameters between the two methods (DAP and GP) are identical. The individual parameters of DAP and GP are given in Table 4 and Table 5 respectively.

4.2 Experimental results

Results are given for 100 different runs with the same parameter set. Table 6 shows the success rate of 100 trials at the final generation. The success rate is computed as:

$$\text{Success rate} = \frac{\text{Number of successful runs}}{\text{Total number of runs}} \tag{13}$$

According to the result, DAP obtains a better solution than GP for all test problems.
Figure 4 (a) shows the comparison of the success rate between DAP and GP for $f_1(x)$, with the learning has been pursued on. We can see that DAP reaches 98% success rate in $f_1(x)$, while the success rate of GP is 69% after 1000 generations. Figure 4 (b) shows the average number of nodes of DAP and GP for $f_1(x)$. The average number of nodes in GP expands in the evolutionary process. After 1000 generations, the average number of nodes in GP is more than 100 nodes. So, the tree structural programs of GP bloat. However, DAP keeps the average number of nodes between 10 and 20 in this experiment. It shows that DAP is more efficient than GP.
The results for $f_2(x)$ and $f_3(x)$ are shown in Figure 5 (a), (b) and 6 (a), (b). For both test problems, DAP has better results than GP, with a smaller average number of nodes.
Figure 7 is the relationship between the average number of column size of pheromone table in DAP (total number of nodes) and the number of generations. The size of pheromone table in DAP changes dynamically. The size is 20-28 for $f_1(x)$, 18-25 for $f_2(x)$, and 8-14 for $f_3(x)$. It also shows that the size of the pheromone table does not bloat.

Parameter	Value
Terminal set	The variable x and the constant 1.0
Function set	$F = \{+, -, *, /, \sin\}$
The number of generations	1000
Population size	50
ρ	0.50
τ_{max}	1.0
τ_{min}	0.01
τ_{ins}	τ_{max} (= 1.0)

Table 4. The parameters of DAP algorithm for symbolic regression problems

Parameter	Value
Terminal set	The variable x and the constant 1.0
Function set	$F = \{+, -, *, /, \sin\}$
The number of generations	1000
Population size	50
Crossover probability	1.0
Mutation probability	0.9 (for individual)
Selection	Tournament selection
Tournament size	2

Table 5. The parameters of GP algorithm for symbolic regression problems

Incidentally, GP has a tendency to create redundant programs. In this experiment, GP does not have a factor for restraining the redundancy. On the other hand, DAP has a function for deletion of nodes. Therefore, the comparison between DAP and GP would not be fair. Figure 8 shows the comparison of the fitness between DAP and GP for $f_1(x)$. In terms of fitness value, the performance of DAP and GP is comparable. However, GP cannot find an accurate solution, while DAP has a higher success rate.

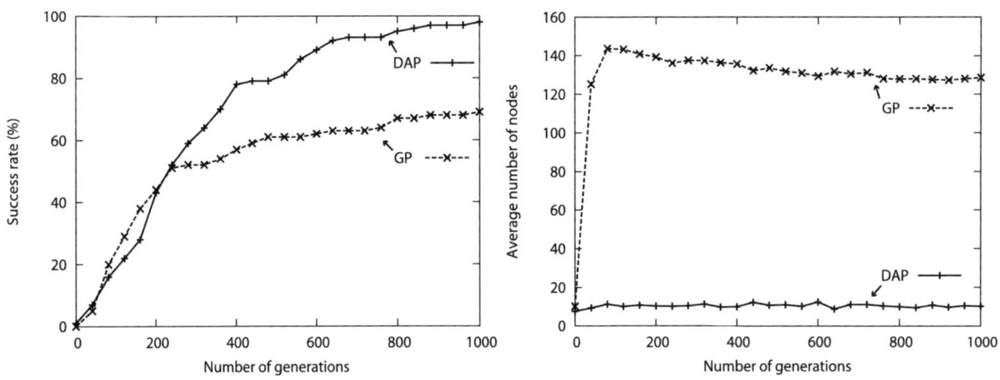

(a) Success rate (b) Average number of nodes

Fig. 4. The comparison of the success rate and the average number of nodes between DAP and GP for $f_1(x)$, with the learning has been pursued on

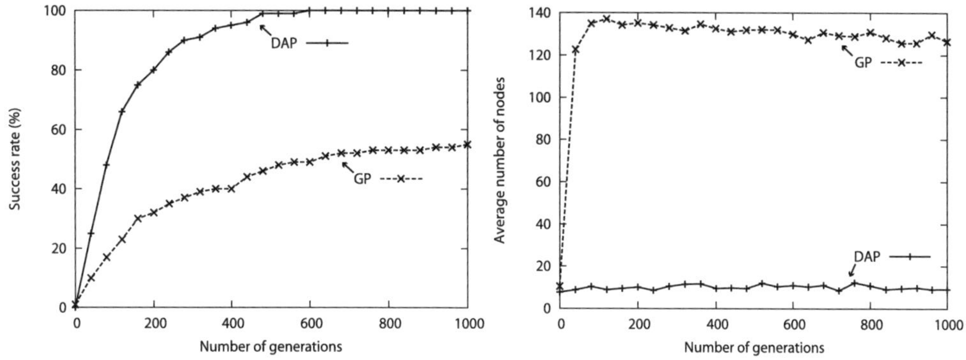

(a) Success rate (b) Average number of nodes

Fig. 5. The comparison of the success rate and the average number of nodes between DAP and GP for $f_2(x)$, with the learning has been pursued on

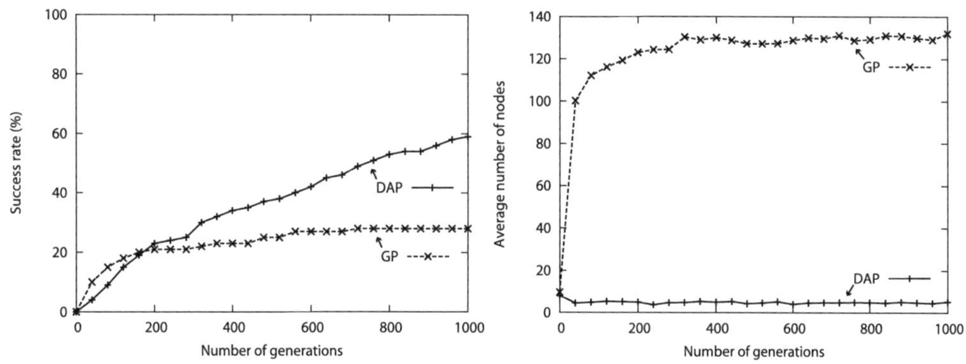

(a) Success rate (b) Average number of nodes

Fig. 6. The comparison of the success rate and the average number of nodes between DAP and GP for $f_3(x)$, with the learning has been pursued on

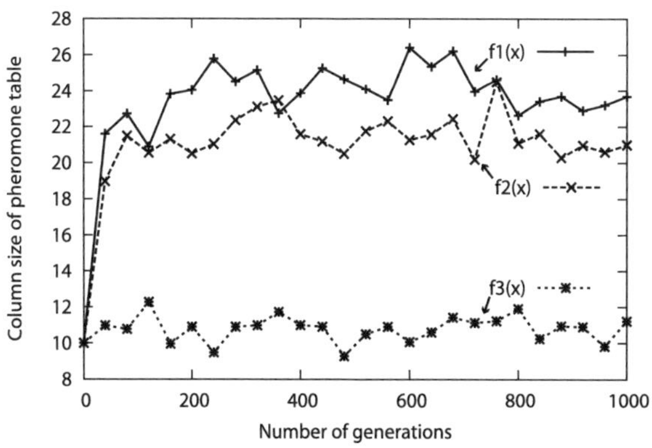

Fig. 7. The curves show the relationship between the number of column size of the pheromone table in DAP (total number of nodes) and the number of generations. Each curve is an average over 100 runs

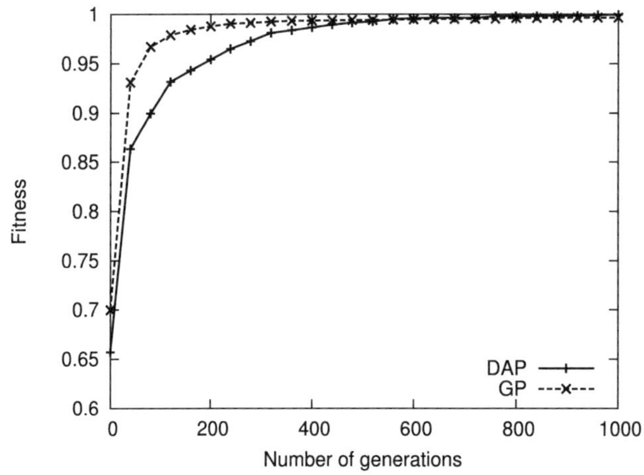

Fig. 8. The comparison of the fitness between DAP and GP for $f_1(x)$. Each curve is an average over 100 runs

	DAP (%)	GP (%)
$f_1(x)$	98	69
$f_2(x)$	100	55
$f_3(x)$	59	28

Table 6. Success rate of DAP and GP at final generation

4.3 Pheromone evaporation rate ρ

To examine the influence of the values of the pheromone evaporation rate ρ, we compare the experimental results obtained using different settings of ρ. The pheromone evaporation rate ρ is varied between 0.10 and 0.90. Results are given for 100 different runs with the same parameter set and using $f_1(x)$ as a test problem.

Table 7 shows the success rate of 100 trials at the final generation. Figure 9 showa the transitions of the success rate for $f_1(x)$ when different values have been set for the parameter ρ. In Table 7, it can be observed that better solutions are found when using higher values of ρ=0.50-0.70. This is due to the fact that the pheromone trail values decrease faster when the values of ρ are higher; hence, the size of the pheromone table tends to be small. Figure 10 shows the relationship between the average number of column size of pheromone table in DAP (total number of nodes) and the number of generations. The size of the pheromone table is small (about 10-25) when using the higher values of ρ, while the size is large (about 30-50) using the lower values of ρ. If ρ is low, it is difficult for the pheromone trail values to reach minimum value (τ_{min}).

4.4 Parameter of τ_{ins}

In order to investigate the influence of the values of τ_{ins}, we compare the experimental results obtained using different settings of τ_{ins}. τ_{ins} is the pheromone value of an inserted node, and it varies between 0.20 and 1.00. Results are given for 100 different runs with the same parameter

ρ	0.10	0.30	0.40	0.50	0.60	0.70	0.90
Success rate (%)	45	92	96	98	99	98	93

Table 7. Success rate of DAP at final generation

set using $f_1(x)$ as a test problem. The parameter of the pheromone evaporation rate ρ used is 0.50 in this experiment.

Table 8 shows the success rate of 100 trials at the final generation. The transitions of the success rate for $f_1(x)$ are shown in Figure 11. In Table 8, the success rate reaches 100% using τ_{ins}=0.80, 0.60, 0.40. In Figure 11, earlier convergence has been obtained when using a lower value of τ_{ins}. When the value of τ_{ins} is low, the inserted node has little chance to be visited, and the node will be deleted soon. Therefore, we can consider the value of τ_{ins} to be related to diversity. Figure 12 shows the transitions of the total number of nodes. The size of the pheromone table is between 20 and 30 for all parameter of τ_{ins}. There is little relationship between the size of pheromone table and the parameter of τ_{ins} although the size of pheromone table is dynamically changing.

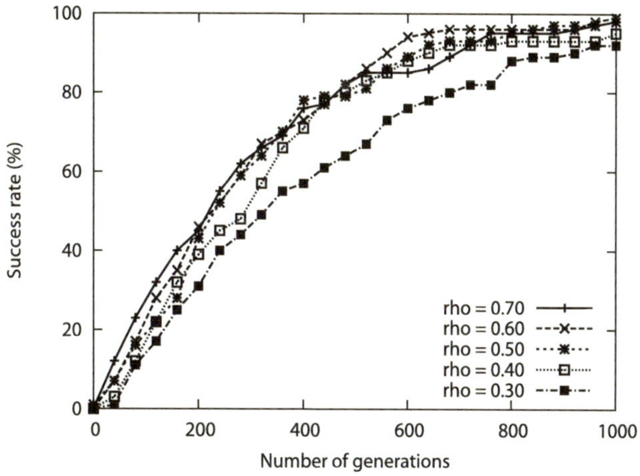

Fig. 9. The transitions of the success rate for $f_1(x)$ ($\rho = 0.30, 0.40, 0.50, 0.60, 0.70$)

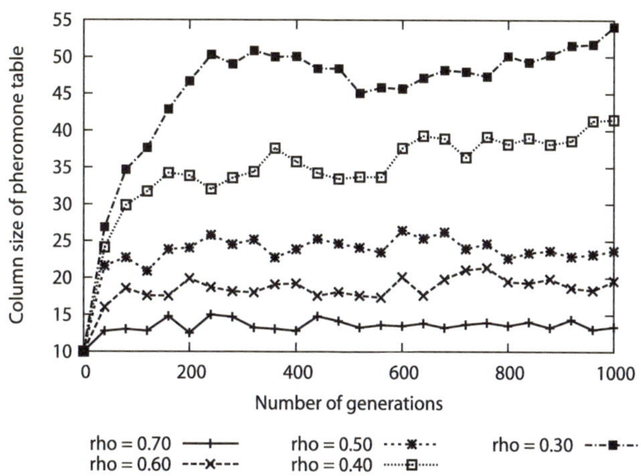

Fig. 10. The curves show the relationship between the number of column size of the pheromone table (total number of nodes) and the number of generations. Each curve is an average over 100 runs

τ_{ins}	1.00	0.80	0.60	0.40	0.20
Success rate (%)	98	100	100	100	99

Table 8. Success rate of DAP at final generation

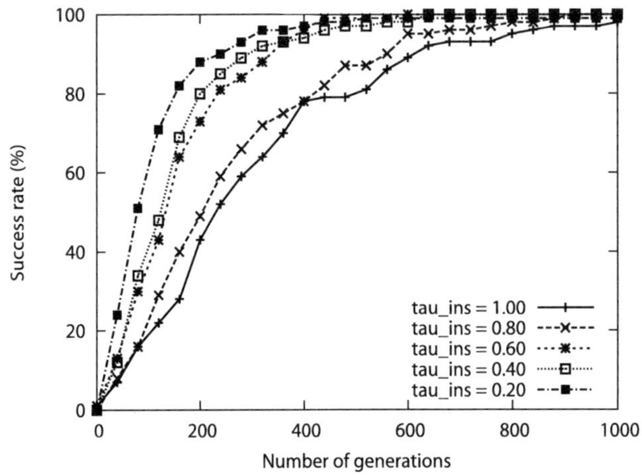

Fig. 11. The transitions of the success rate for $f_1(x)$ ($\tau_{ins} = 1.00, 0.80, 0.60, 0.40, 0.20$)

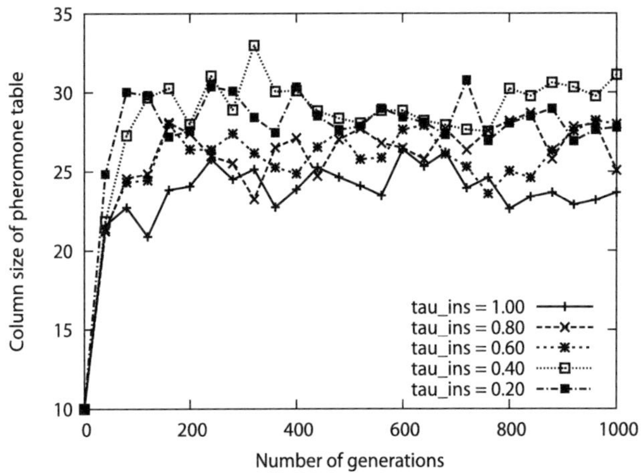

Fig. 12. The curves show the relationship between the number of column size of the pheromone table (total number of nodes) and the number of generations. Each curve is an average over 100 runs ($\tau_{ins} = 1.00, 0.80, 0.60, 0.40, 0.20$)

5. Conclusions

A novel automatic programming method based on ACO, which is DAP has been proposed in this chapter. We tested the performance of DAP against GP using the symbolic regression problems. In all test cases, DAP performed better than GP, and the search space of DAP was more compact. The size of the pheromone table of DAP is maintained at 10-30, while the tree size of GP bloats. From these tests, we can say that DAP has an advantage against GP. We also investigated the influence of the parameters of DAP. The parameter of ρ relates to the total number of nodes, and the parameter τ_{ins} relates to diversity.

In order to clarify the effectiveness of DAP, more experiments have to be run on a variety of test problems. In future works we plan to extend tests to other problems. We applied DAP to the construction of tree structural programs automatically in this work. In recent years other structures have been investigated in GP (e.g. linear structure (Brameier & Banzhaf, 2001), graph structure (Miller & Smith, 2006; Mabu et al., 2007; Shirakawa & Nagao, 2009)). We plan to apply DAP to construct other structures automatically as well.

6. References

Abbass, H., Hoai, N. & McKay, R. (2002). AntTAG: A new method to compose computer programs using colonies of ants, *Proceedings of the 2002 IEEE Congress on Evolutionary Computation (CEC '02)*, Honolulu, HI, USA, pp. 1654–1659.

Bonabeau, E., Dorigo, M. & Theraulaz, G. (2000). Inspiration for optimization from social insect behavior, *Nature* 406: 39–42.

Boryczka, M. & Czech, Z. J. (2002). Solving approximation problems by ant colony programming, *Late Breaking Papers at the Genetic and Evolutionary Computation Conference 2002 (GECCO '02)*, New York, pp. 39–46.

Brameier, M. & Banzhaf, W. (2001). A comparison of linear genetic programming and neural networks in medical data mining, *IEEE Transactions on Evolutionary Computation* 5(1): 17–26.

Bullnheimer, B., Hartl, R. F. & Strauss, C. (1999). A new rank based version of the ant system: A computational study, *Central European Journal for Operations Research and Economics* 7(1): 25–38.

Caro, G. D. & Dorigo, M. (1998). Antnet: Distributed stigmergetic control for communications networks, *Journal of Artificial Intelligence Research* 9: 317–365.

Costa, D. & Hertz, A. (1997). Ants can colour graphs, *Journal of the Operational Research Society* 48: 295–305.

Dorigo, M., Caro, G. D. & Gambardella, L. M. (1999). Ant algorithm for discrete optimization, *Artificial Life* 5(2): 137–172.

Dorigo, M. & Gambardella, L. M. (1997). Ant colony system: A cooperative learning approach to the traveling salesman problem, *IEEE Transactions on Evolutionary Computation* 1(1): 53–66.

Dorigo, M., Maniezzo, V. & Colorni, A. (1996). Ant system: Optimization by a colony of cooperating agents, *IEEE Transactions on Systems, Man, and Cybernetics -Part B* 26(1): 29–41.

Dorigo, M. & Stutzle, T. (2004). *Ant Colony Optimization*, MIT Press, Cambridge, MA.

Engelbrecht, A. P. (2006). *Fundamentals of Computational Swarm Intelligence*, John Wiley & Sons, New York.

Guntsch, M. & Middendorf, M. (2001). Pheromone modification strategies for ant algorithms applied to dynamic tsp, *Proceedings of the EvoWorkshops on Applications of Evolutionary Computing*, Vol. 2037 of *LNCS*, Springer, London, pp. 213–222.

Guntsch, M., Middendorf, M. & Schmeck, H. (2001). An ant colony optimization approach to dynamic TSP, *Proceedings of the Genetic and Evolutionary Computation Conference 2001 (GECCO '01)*, San Francisco, pp. 860–867.

Keber, C. & Schuster, M. G. (2002). Option valuation with generalized ant programming, *Proceedings of the Genetic and Evolutionary Computation Conference 2002 (GECCO '02)*, New York, pp. 74–81.

Koza, J. R. (1992). *Genetic Programming: On the Programming of Computers by Means of Natural*

Selection, MIT Press, Cambridge, MA.

Koza, J. R. (1994). *Genetic Programming II: Automatic Discovery of Reusable Programs*, MIT Press, Cambridge, MA.

Langdon, W. B. & Poli, R. (1998). Genetic programming bloat with dynamic fitness, *Proceedings of the First European Workshop on Genetic Programming (EuroGP '98)*, Vol. 1391 of *LNCS*, Springer, Paris, France, pp. 96–112.

Mabu, S., Hirasawa, K. & Hu, J. (2007). A graph-based evolutionary algorithm: Genetic network programming (gnp) and its extension using reinforcement learning, *Evolutionary Computation* 15(3): 369–398.

Miller, J. F. & Smith, S. L. (2006). Redundancy and computational efficiency in cartesian genetic programming, *IEEE Transactions on Evolutionary Computation* 10(2): 167–174.

Poli, R. (2003). A simple but theoretically-motivated method to control bloat in genetic programming, *Proceedings of the 6th European Conference on Genetic Programming (EuroGP '03)*, Vol. 2610 of *LNCS*, Springer, Essex, UK, pp. 204–217.

Roux, O. & Fonlupt, C. (2000). Ant programming: Or how to use ants for automatic programming, *in* M. D. et al. (ed.), *Proceedings of ANTS '00*, Brussels, Belgium, pp. 121–129.

Salustowicz, R. P. & Schmidhuber, J. (1997). Probabilistic incremental program evolution, *Evolutionary Computation* 5(2): 123–141.

Schoonderwoerd, R., Holland, O. E., Bruten, J. L. & Rothkrantz, L. J. M. (1996). Ant-based load balancing in telecommunications networks, *Adaptive Behavior* 5(2): 169–207.

Shirakawa, S. & Nagao, T. (2009). Graph structured program evolution: Evolution of loop structures, *in* R. L. Riolo, U.-M. O'Reilly & T. McConaghy (eds), *Genetic Programming Theory and Practice VII*, Springer, pp. 177–194.

Stutzle, T. & Hoos, H. (1997). The MAX-MIN ant system and local search for the traveling salesman problem, *Proceedings of the IEEE International Conference on Evolutionary Computation (ICEC '97)*, IEEE Press, Indianapolis, IN, USA, pp. 308–313.

Stutzle, T. & Hoos, H. (2000). MAX-MIN ant system, *Future Generation Computer Systems* 16(8): 889–914.

7

A Hybrid ACO-GA on Sports Competition Scheduling

Huang Guangdong and Wang Qun
School of Information Technology,
China University of Geosciences (Beijing), Beijing, 100083
China

1. Introduction

During the past 20 years sports competition scheduling (SCS) has received a great deal of attention in the operations research literature. The existed researches on SCS mainly focus on league scheduling and round-robin tournament play including American Football, baseball, chess, cricket, dressage, ice hockey, tennis and even the Olympic Games. Some of the applications use highly problem-specific approaches, others use more general techniques such as goal programming, simulated annealing, subcost-guided search, integer programming, tabu search and local search and so on. Graph theory was used by de Werra to develop schedules with desirable properties, such as the minimum number of breaks in the sequences of home and away games. Schreuder constructed a timetable for the Dutch professional soccer leagues that minimizes the number of schedule breaks. Russell and Leung developed a schedule for the Texas Baseball League that satisfied stadium availability and various timing restrictions with the objective of minimizing travel costs. Nemhauser and Trick created a schedule for the Atlantic Coast Conference men' s basketball season, taking into consideration numerous conflicting requirements and preferences.Most of problems of sports competition scheduling are NP-complete. The computationally burdensome presentation of SCS makes the use of heuristic approaches appropriate.

Swarm Intelligence (SI) is a property exhibited by some mobile systems such as social insect colonies and other animal societies that have collective behavior. Individuals of those systems such as ants, termites an wasps are not generally considered to be individually intelligent however they do exhibit a degree of intelligence, as a group, by interacting with each other and with their environment. Those systems generally consist of some individuals sensing and acting through a common environment to produce a complex global behavior.

They share many appealing and promising features that can be exploited to solve hard problems. Furthermore, they are particularly well suited for distributed optimization, in which the system can be explicitly formulated in terms of computational agents.

One of the most popular swarm inspired methods in computational intelligence areas is the Ant Colony Optimization (ACO) method. Ants are able to evolve their foraging behavior by changing their environment through the evolving pheromone trails. When an ant follows a shorter path it travels trough it more frequently than the others, building up a higher pheromone count in the process. This attracts more ants to that path, which makes the pheromone level to go up even further and a more number of ants are now drawn into it. Such interactions continue between the ant colony members till an optimum path emerges. The ACO method has become one of the best-known metaheuristic techniques, side to side with tabu search, genetic and evolutionary algorithms, simulated annealing, iterated local search, variable neighborhood search and some other prominent general-purpose search methods. an approach that has originally been developed by Dorigo et al. in the early 1990s, have evolved to a powerful, versatile optimization tool with a still rapidly growing number of publications and numerous applications in diverse areas of operations research, management science and technology.

Genetic algorithms (GA) developed by Holland are heuristic approaches based on evolutionary principles. GA is developed in a way to simulate biological evolutionary process and genetic operations on chromosomes. GA can handle any kind of objective functions and any kind of constraints without much mathematical requirements about the optimization problems. When applying to optimization problems, GA starts with a set of randomly selected chromosomes as the initial population that encodes a set of possible solutions. then the chromosomes are evaluated according to their fitness values using some measures of profit or utility that we want to optimize. Two genetic operators, crossover and mutation, alter the composition of genes to create new chromosomes called offspring. The selection operator is an artificial version of natural selection, a Darwinian survival of the fittest among populations, to create populations from generation to generation, and chromosomes with better fitness values have higher probabilities of being selected in the next generation. After several generations, GA can converge to the best solution. In the past several years, GA has been applied successfully in many fields such as automatic control, programming design, combination optimization, image processing and signal processing.

The population-based approach of the Genetic Algorithms is very efficient for a global search, but they do not use the feedback in the system information enough and the accuracy solution efficiency is low. ACO is a kind of positive feedback mechanism, but it lacks information early, the solution speed is slow. In this chapter, Based on the existed researches of sports competition scheduling (SCS) the author presented a hybrid Ant Colony Optimization and Genetic Algorithms (ACO-GA) to improve the productivity and efficiency of sports competition scheduling (SCS). The ACO-GA procedures of combining ant colony optimization and genetic algorithms were as follows: (1) applying the GA in a specified solution space to generate the activity lists, which provided an initial population for ACO; (2) performing ACO; (3) executing the crossover and mutation operations of GA to generate a new population based on the ACO result; (4) performing ACO and GA alternately and cooperatively in the solution space for n times. In order to test the ACO-GA algorithm, we selected Oliver30 and att48 problems. The results indicated that ACO-GA could find the best solution presented on the TSPLIB95. Finally we converted a sports competition scheduling (SCS) into a TSP model, and then using the ACO-GA algorithm. The result illustrated that the ACO-GA was a good method for solving the SCS. The remaining of this paper is organized as follows. Section 1 introduce the existed researches of sports competition scheduling (SCS), Ant Colony Optimization and Genetic Algorithms. Section 2 converted a sports competition scheduling (SCS) into a TSP model firstly, Secondly we introduce the ACO-GA algorithm, then we selected Oliver30 and att48 problems to test the ACO-GA algorithm. Finally we use the ACO-GA algorithm to solve SCS problem. Sections 3 is conclusion and section 4 is Acknowledgment.

2. A hybrid ACO-GA on Sports Competition Scheduling

In this section we converted a sports competition scheduling (SCS) into a TSP model firstly, Secondly we introduce the ACO-GA algorithm, then we selected Oliver30 and att48 problems to test the ACO-GA algorithm. Finally we use the ACO-GA algorithm to solve SCS problem.

2.1 Modeling of SCS

We consider a situation where there are a number of competitors and sports competitions. Let A_s (s=1,2,…,m) present the competitor and B_t (t=1,2,…,n) present the games. We define C_{ij} as follows:

$$C_{st} = \begin{cases} 1 & \text{competitor } A_s \text{ takes part in sports game } B_t. \\ 0 & \text{otherwise} \end{cases} \quad (1)$$

In this way, we can get a 0-1 matrix C_{st} :

$$(C_{st})_{mn} = \begin{pmatrix} C_{11} & C_{12} & \cdots & C_{1n} \\ C_{21} & C_{22} & \cdots & C_{2n} \\ \vdots & \vdots & & \vdots \\ C_{m1} & C_{m2} & \cdots & C_{mn} \end{pmatrix} \quad (2)$$

For an n -game competition, the complete weighted graph G_n on n vertexes is considered. The vertex i (i = 1, . . . , n) presents the game, and the edge i–j presents the games between games i and j (i,j {1, . . . , n}). The weighted function $D_{ij}(i=1,2,...,n; j=1,2,...,n)$ is the competitors who take part in both games i and j .

The objective of SCS is to design a schedule of sports competitions in which the competitors who take part in two sequential games are minimized. For example, we consider a sports competition with three games B_1, B_2, B_3 and three competitors A_1, A_2, A_3. Matrix C_{st} is $C_{3,3} = \begin{pmatrix} 1 & 0 & 0 \\ 1 & 1 & 0 \\ 0 & 1 & 1 \end{pmatrix}$; the weighted function is $D_{3,3} = \begin{pmatrix} 0 & 1 & 0 \\ 1 & 0 & 1 \\ 0 & 1 & 0 \end{pmatrix}$. Thus the objective is 1, and the games are scheduled to be B_1, B_3, B_2 .

If we combine the first game with the last game, then SCS boils down to a Traveling Salesman Problem (TSP). The TSP is an NP-hard problem in combinatorial optimization studied in operations research and theoretical computer science. Given a list of cities and their pairwise distances, the task is to find a shortest possible tour that visits each city exactly once. Thus, it is likely that the worst case running time for any algorithm for the TSP increases exponentially with the number of cities.

The problem was first formulated as a mathematical problem in 1930 and is one of the most intensively studied problems in optimization. It is used as a benchmark for many optimization methods. Even though the problem is computationally difficult, a large number of heuristics and exact methods are known, so that some instances with tens of thousands of cities can be solved.

The TSP has several applications even in its purest formulation, such as planning, logistics, and the manufacture of microchips. Slightly modified, it appears as a sub-problem in many areas, such as DNA sequencing. In these applications, the concept city represents, for example, customers, soldering points, or DNA fragments, and the concept distance represents travelling times or cost, or a similarity measure between DNA fragments. In many applications, additional constraints such as limited resources or time windows make the problem considerably harder.
TSP can be modeled as an undirected weighted graph, such that cities are the graph's vertices, paths are the graph's edges, and a path's distance is the edge's length. A TSP tour becomes a Hamiltonian cycle, and the optimal TSP tour is the shortest Hamiltonian cycle. Often, the model is a complete graph (i.e., an edge connects each pair of vertices). If no path exists between two cities, adding an arbitrarily long edge will complete the graph without affecting the optimal tour.

2.2 ACO-GA

In this section we introduce the GA algorithm firstly, then we we introduce the ACO algorithm. Finally we introduce the ACO-GA algorithm. The procedures of ACO-GA are as follows. First, GA searches the solution space and generates activity lists to provide the initial population for ACO. Next, ACO is executed, when ACO terminates, the crossover and mutation operations of GA generate new population. ACO and GA search alternately and cooperatively in the solution space and we selected Oliver30 and att48 problems to test the ACO-GA algorithm.

2.2.1 Genetic Algorithm

GA expresses the problem-solving process as the chromosomes' survival of the fittest process. From a population (group of feasible solutions) of the potential solution set of a problem, it is called the original population and is composed of certain individual encoded. In fact, each individual is a chromosome entity with characteristics. The chromosome, namely the gene set is the main carrier of genetic material, whose internal performance (gene) is some kind of gene combination, and it decides the exterior performance (phenotype) of the individual shape.
Therefore, we first need to realize coding—mapping from the phenotype to the gene. After the original population is produced, the "chromosome" generation evolves unceasingly, including selection, crossover and mutation operation. The fine quality is gradually retained and performs to combine, finally restrains to the individual "most adapting to circumstances", thus obtains the problem's the optimal solution or the approximate solution. That GA uses biology evolution and hereditary thought to realize the optimization process distinguishes GA from traditional optimization algorithms. Because it operates on the "chromosome", rather than on problem parameters, GA is not restricted to problem's constraint conditions, like continuity and so on. GA carries on searching only according to the individual's fitness value, no any other information. GA has the ability of global search, connotative parallel search and strong robustness. But its flaw of local search ability is also well-known. GA carries on gradually converging process. In practical application, GA generally converges to a certain feasible solution, which may be not the global optimal point, even not local one. Therefore, it is extremely essential both in theory and practice to introduce other local search algorithm to GA to improve GA's local search ability.
The following algorithm presents the fundamental frame of GA.

```
Begin
    t=0
    Define heredity parameters
    Produce the initial population denoted by X(t)
    Evaluate the individuals X(t)
    While terminal condition does not satisfy do
      Begin
      Select individuals from X(t), crossover and mutation oprations.
      Reorganize (select, crossover and mutate) X(t) to produce population denoted by C(t).
      t=t+1
      End
End
```

2.2.2 Ant Colony Optimization

ACO algorithms are a class of algorithms inspired by the observation of real ants. Ants are capable of exploring and exploiting pheromone information, which have been left on the ground when they traversed. They then can choose routes based on the amount of pheromone. While building the solutions, each artificial ant collects pheromone information on the problem characteristics and uses this information to modify the representation of the problem, as seen by the other artificial ants. The larger amount of pheromone is left on a route, the greater is the probability of selecting the route by artificial ants. In ACO, artificial ants find solutions starting from a start node and moving to feasible neighbor nodes in the process of ants' generation and activity. During the process, information collected by artificial ants is stored in the so-called pheromone trails. In the process, artificial ants can release pheromone while building the solution (online step-by-step) or while the solution is built (online delayed). An ant-decision rule, made up of the pheromone and heuristic information, governs artificial ants to search towards neighbor nodes stochastically. Pheromone evaporation is a process of decreasing the intensities of pheromone trails over time. This process is used to avoid locally convergence and to explore more search space. The following algorithm presents the fundamental frame of ACO.

Step 1. Pheromone initialization. Let the initial pheromone trail $\tau_0 = k$, where k is a parameter,

Step 2. Main loop. In the main loop, each of the m ants constructs a sequence of n nodes. This loop is executed for Itemax = s iterations and each iteration has two steps.

Step 2.1. Constructing a node sequence by each ant. A set of artificial ants is initially created. Each ant starts with an empty sequence and then successively appends an unscheduled node to the partial sequence until a feasible solution is constructed (i.e., all nodes are scheduled). In choosing the next node j to be appended at the current position i is determined by p_{ij}^k which is probability of ant *k* transforming from node *i* to node *j* at time *t*

$$p_{ij}^k = \begin{cases} \dfrac{\tau_{ij}^{\alpha}(t)\eta_{ij}^{\beta}(t)}{\sum\limits_{u \in U} \tau_{iu}^{\alpha}(t)\eta_{iu}^{\beta}(t)} & j \in U \\ o & otherwise \end{cases} \tag{3}$$

Where U is the set of unscheduled jobs and $\tau_{ij}(t)$ is the pheromone trail associated with the assignment node j to position i at time t. The parameter $\eta_{ij}(t)$ is the heuristic desirability of assigning node j to position i at time i. The parameter α is the relative importance of the trace and β is the parameter which determines the relative importance of the heuristic information.

Step 2.2. Update of pheromone trail. The updating rule is applied after each ant has completed a feasible solution (i.e., an iteration). Following the rule, the pheromone trail is added to the path of the incumbent global best solution, i.e., the best solution found so far. If node j is placed at position i in the global best solution during iteration t, then

$$\tau_{ij}(t+1) = p\tau_{ij}(t) + \Delta\tau_{ij} \tag{4}$$

where ρ,(0<ρ<1) is a parameter representing the evaporation of pheromone. The amount $\Delta\tau_{ij} = \frac{1}{wt}$, where wt is the weight tardiness of the global best solution.

2.2.3 ACO-GA

GA and ACO are population-based search algorithms by maintaining a population of structures as key elements in design and implementation of problem solving algorithms. These algorithms are sufficiently complex to provide powerful adaptive search approaches, and usually can be embedded with other approaches to speed up the search performance. GA is very efficient for a global search, but it does not use the feedback in the system information enough and the accuracy solution efficiency is low. ACO is a kind of positive feedback mechanism, but it lacks information early, the solution speed is slow. Combined ant colony optimization (ACO) and genetic algorithm (GA) is an effective method. GA generates the information distributes and ACO seeks the accurate solution. The ACO-GA procedures of combining ant colony optimization and genetic algorithms were as follows: (1) applying the GA in a specified solution space to generate the activity lists, which provided an initial population for ACO; (2) performing ACO; (3) executing the crossover and mutation operations of GA to generate a new population based on the ACO result; (4) performing ACO and GA alternately and cooperatively in the solution space for n times. The ACO-GA is represented by the following steps:

Step 1. GA generates solutions and pheromone is left on the excellent paths.

Step 2. t=0(t is the times of iterative), Each ant starts with an empty sequence and then successively appends an unscheduled node to the partial sequence until a feasible solution is constructed (i.e., all nodes are scheduled). In choosing the next node j to be appended at the current position i is determined by p_{ij}^k (You can see formula 1) .

Step 3. Crossover operation is executed on the solutions and new solutions are generated. If the target of the new solution is better than the old one, we accept the new solution, otherwise refuse.

Step 4. Mutation operation is executed on the solutions and new solutions are generated. If the target of the new solution is better the old one, we accept the new solution, otherwise refuse.

Step 5. calculate the path length L_k, (k=1,2,...,m) of every ant and record the best value.

Step 6. If the path length L_k is less than settle length, update pheromone.

Step 7. t=t+1

Step 8. If t is less than the settle times of iterations and the solution has not improvement, return to step 2.

Step 9. print the best solution.

The mutation operations are as fallowing: Selecting a gene in the gene cluster randomly, this gene is exchanged with his foregoing gene and the other is steadiness. For a example the chromosome is c0=[2,3,4,1,5,7,9,8,6],and the choosing gene is 3. So the mutation chromosome is c=[2,4,3,1,5,7,9,8,6].

The crossover operations are as fallowing: Selecting two chromosomes and crossover area randomly, the gene in the crossover area of the first chromosome replaces the gene in the crossover area of the second chromosome. Then the gene of the first chromosome disappeared in the crossover area of the second chromosome are deleted. For a example the first chromosome is c1=[1,2,3,4,5,6,7,8,9] and the second chromosome is c2=[9,8,7,6,5,4,3,2,1]. The crossover area is [6,5,4,3]. So the crossover chromosome is newc=[1,2,6,5,4,3,7,8,9].

2.2.4 Algorithm testing

In order to test this ACO-GA, we choose Oliver30 (best solution is 423.7406) and att48[20] (best solution is 33522) as examples. We compare the results obtained with that from Ant Colony optimization (ACO), GA, simulated annealing ($T = 100000,\ T_0 = 1,\ \alpha = 0.99$) .The results are reported in Table 1[21]. The best loops of Oliver30 and att48 are in Figure 1 and Figure 2. Every algorithm is tested for 20 times.

Algorithm	Oliver30			Att48		
	mean	best	worst	mean	best	worst
Simulate Anneal	438.522	424.692	478.831	35176	34958	40536
GA	483.457	467.684	502.574	38732	38541	42458
ACO	450.035	441.958	499.933	36532	35876	42234
ACO-GA	431.4987	423.7406	447.6865	33798	33524	36821

Table 1. The results of Oliver30 and Att48 using four algorithms

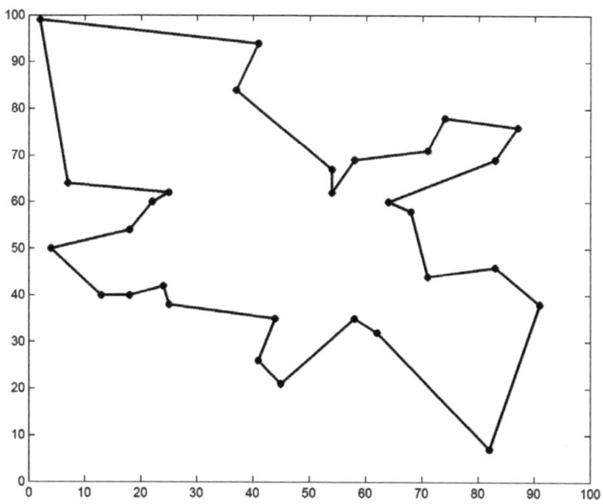

Fig. 1. The best loops of Oliver30 using ACO-GA.

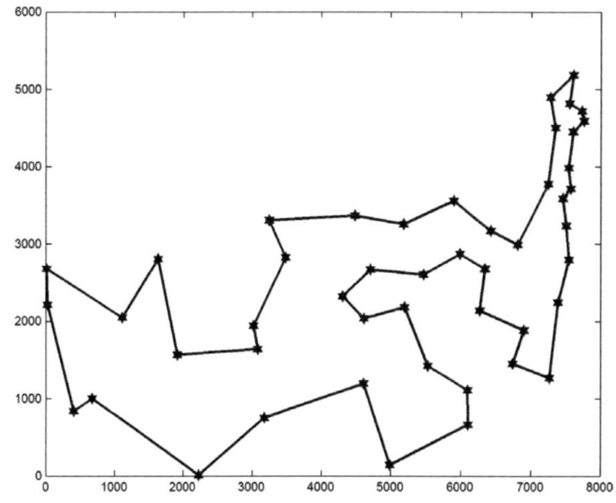

Fig. 2. The best loops of Att48 using ACO-GA.

2.3 Sports competitions scheduling with the ACO-GA

The following gives the explanation of several key operations in the scheduling. The data is in table2 and comes from Chinese Undergraduate Mathematical Contest in Modeling on Electrician of 2005.

2.3.1 Modeling of SCS

Let 1 replace # and 0 replace empty, we can get a 0-1 matrix $C_{14\times 40}$. For a 14-game sports competition, the complete weighted graph G_{14} on 14 vertexes is considered. The vertex i (i = 1, . . . , 14) represents the game, the edge i–j presents the games between i, j {1, . . . , 14}. The weighted function $D_{ij}(i=1,2,...,14; j=1,2,...14.)$ is the competitors who take part in both the games i and j. Summing the competitors who take part in both games i and j, we can get the weighted matrix $D_{14\times 14}$ as following. The objective of SCS is to create a schedule of sports competitions in which the competitors taking part in two sequential games are minimized.

$$D_{14\times 14} = \begin{pmatrix} 0\,2\,1\,2\,0\,0\,1\,0\,1\,2\,1\,1\,1\,1 \\ 2\,0\,1\,4\,1\,0\,1\,1\,1\,3\,1\,0\,2\,1 \\ 1\,1\,0\,1\,0\,0\,0\,3\,1\,1\,0\,2\,2\,1 \\ 2\,4\,1\,0\,1\,1\,2\,1\,0\,2\,1\,0\,1\,1 \\ 0\,1\,0\,1\,0\,2\,0\,1\,1\,1\,0\,1\,1\,2 \\ 0\,0\,0\,1\,2\,0\,1\,2\,1\,1\,1\,2\,1\,2 \\ 1\,1\,0\,2\,0\,1\,0\,1\,1\,1\,0\,2\,2\,1 \\ 0\,1\,3\,1\,1\,2\,1\,0\,1\,2\,1\,4\,2\,2 \\ 1\,1\,1\,0\,1\,1\,1\,1\,0\,1\,1\,1\,3\,1 \\ 2\,3\,1\,2\,1\,1\,1\,2\,1\,0\,1\,0\,0\,3 \\ 1\,1\,0\,1\,0\,1\,0\,1\,1\,1\,0\,3\,1\,1 \\ 1\,0\,2\,0\,1\,2\,2\,4\,1\,0\,3\,0\,1\,0 \\ 1\,2\,2\,1\,1\,1\,2\,2\,3\,0\,1\,1\,0\,4 \\ 1\,1\,1\,1\,2\,2\,1\,2\,1\,3\,1\,0\,4\,0 \end{pmatrix} \quad (5)$$

Competitor \ Game	1	2	3	4	5	6	7	8	9	10	11	12	13	14
1		#	#						#				#	
2								#			#	#		
3		#		#						#				
4			#					#				#		
5											#		#	#
6					#	#								
7												#	#	
8										#				#
9		#		#						#	#			
10	#	#		#			#							
11		#		#									#	#
12								#		#				
13					#					#				#
14			#	#				#						
15			#					#				#		
16									#		#	#		
17						#								#
18							#					#		
19			#							#				
20	#			#										
21									#					#
22		#			#									
23							#					#		
24							#	#					#	#
25	#	#								#				
26					#									#
27						#					#			
28		#						#						
29	#										#	#		
30				#	#									
31						#		#				#		
32							#			#				
33				#		#								
34	#		#										#	#
35					#	#						#		
36				#			#							
37	#								#	#				
38						#		#		#				#
39					#			#	#				#	
40						#	#		#				#	

Table 2. The Registration Form for a Sports Competition

2.3.2 The result of SCS using ACO-GA

First we use GA to generate 100 solutions and select 30 excellent solutions from the 100 solution. Pheromone is left on the excellent solutions. Then ACO is executed, when ACO terminates, the crossover and mutation operations of GA execute on the solutions generated by ACO and generate new solutions. ACO and GA's crossover and mutation operations search alternately and cooperatively in the solution space. Using ACO-GA, we can get a loop of sports competitions, and then we cut the loop at one edge with the biggest weighted function. By this way we can get 3 game schedules using ACO-GA:

(1) 9→4→13→10→12→14→2→6→3→7→11→5→1→8

(2) 13→10→12→14→2→6→3→7→11→5→1→8→9→4

(3) 2→6→3→7→11→5→1→8→9→4→13→10→12→14

Their objective function is two. That is to say, there are two competitors who take part in two successive games.

3. Conclusions

In this chapter, Based on the existed researches of sports competition scheduling (SCS) the author presented a hybrid Ant Colony Optimization and Genetic Algorithms (ACO-GA) to improve the productivity and efficiency of sports competition scheduling (SCS). The ACO-GA procedures of combining ant colony optimization and genetic algorithms were as follows: (1) applying the GA in a specified solution space to generate the activity lists, which provided an initial population for ACO; (2) performing ACO; (3) executing the crossover and mutation operations of GA to generate a new population based on the ACO result; (4) performing ACO and GA alternately and cooperatively in the solution space for n times. In order to test the ACO-GA algorithm, we selected Oliver30 and att48 problems. The results indicated that ACO-GA could find the best solution presented on the TSPLIB95. Finally we converted a sports competition scheduling (SCS) into a TSP model, and then using the ACO-GA algorithm. The result illustrated that the ACO-GA was a good method for solving the SCS. But it is likely that the worst case running time for ACO-GA algorithm for the SCS increases exponentially with the number of sports game.

4. Acknowledgment

This paper would not have been possible without the support of many people. The author wishes to express his gratitude to Prof. Ping Li who was abundantly helpful and offered invaluable assistance, support and guidance. Deepest gratitude are also due to the members of our school workmate, Prof. Dr. Zhaodou Cheng and Prof Dr. Qingxu Yan without whose knowledge and assistance this paper would not have been successful. Special thanks also to all his friends, Zhigang Li Zhengguo Cheng, Linfang Gu, and Xiang Li for sharing the literature and invaluable assistance. Not forgetting to his other friends who always been there. The author would also like to convey thanks to the Ministry and Faculty for providing the financial means and laboratory facilities. The author wishes to express his love and gratitude to his beloved families; for their understanding & endless love.

5. References

Urban TL & Russell RA. Scheduling sports competitions on multiple venues. European Journal of Operational Research 2003; 148(2):302–11.

Russell RA & Leung JMY. Devising a cost-effective schedule for a baseball league. Operations Research 1994; 42(4):614–25.

Kiselyov O. Scheduling algorithms and NP-complete problems. Dr. Dobbs Journal 1997; 22(2):107–9.

Armstrong J & Willis RJ. Scheduling the cricket World Cup—a case study. Journal of the Operational Research Society 1993; 44(11):1067–72.

Willis RJ & Terrill BJ. Scheduling the Australian state cricket season using simulated annealing. Journal of the Operational Research Society 1994; 45(3):276–80.

Wright M. Timetabling county cricket fixtures using a form of tabu search. Journal of the Operational Research Society 1994; 45(7):758–70.

Shirland LE. Computerized dressage scheduling. Interfaces 1983; 13(3):75–81.

Fleurent C & Forland JA. Allocating games for the NHL using integer programming. Operations Research 1993; 41(4):649–54.

Costa D. An evolutionary tabu search algorithm and the NHL scheduling problem. INFOR 1995; 33(3):161–78.

Della Croce F & Tadei R, Asioli PS. Scheduling a round robin tennis tournament under courts and players availability constraints. Annals of Operations Research 1999; 92:349–61.

Corominas A. SUCCESS92—a DSS for scheduling the Olympic Games. Interfaces 1989; 19(5):1–12.

M. Dorigo & G.D. Caro, Ant colony optimization: a new meta-heuristic, Proc. 1999 Congress Evol. Comput. 2 (1999) 1470–1477.

M. Dorigo & T. Stu¨tzle, Ant Colony Optimization, The MIT Press, 2004.

Dorigo M, ManiezzoV & Colorni A. The ant system: an autocatalytic optimization process. Technical Report 91-016, Department of Electronics, Politecnico di Milano, Italy; 1991.

Dorigo M, Maniezzo V & Colorni A. The ant system: optimization by a colony of cooperating agents. IEEE Transactions on Systems, Man, and Cybernetics 1996;26:1–13.

Dorigo M & Di Caro G. The ant colony optimization metaheuristic. In: Corne D, Dorigo M, Glover F, editors. New ideas in optimization. New York: McGraw-Hill; 1999. p. 11–32.

Dorigo M & Blum C. Ant colony optimization theory: a survey. Theoretical Computer Science 2005;344:243–78.

Z.-J. Lee, C.-Y. Lee & S.-F. Su, An immunity based ant colony optimization algorithm for solving weapon-target assignment problem, Appl. Soft Comput. 2 (2002) 39–47.

Holland J. Adaptation in natural and artificial systems: an introductory analysis with applications in biology, control, and artificial intelligence. Ann Arbor, MI: University of Michigan Press; 1975.

Garey M. R & Johnson D. S.. Computers and Intractability: A guide to the Theory of NP-Completeness. San Francisco: W.H. Freeman, 1979.

http://www.iwr.uni-heidelberg.de/groups/comopt/software/TSPLIB95/.

Gao S & Yang J.Y. Swarm Intelligence Algorithms and Applications. China Waterpower Press, 2006.

Ching-Jong Liao & Hsiao-Chien Juan. An ant colony optimization for single-machine tardiness scheduling with sequence-dependent setups. Computers & Operations Research 34 (2007) 1899–1909.

Zne-Jung Lee & Shun-Feng Su, Chen-Chia Chuang, Kuan-Hung Liu. Genetic algorithm with ant colony optimization (GA-ACO) for multiple sequence alignment. Applied Soft Computing (2006)

Issmail Ellabib, Paul Calamai & Otman Basir Exchange strategies for multiple Ant Colony System, Information Sciences 177 (2007) 1248–1264

Walter J. Gutjahr, First steps to the runtime complexity analysis of ant colony optimization, Computers & Operations Research

Robert A. Russell & Timothy L. Urban, A constraint programming approach to the multiple-venue, sport-scheduling problem Computers & Operations Research 33 (2006) 1895-1906

De Werra D. Geography, games and graphs. Discrete Applied Mathematics 1980;2(4):327-37.

De Werra D. Minimizing irregularities in sports schedules using graph theory. Discrete Applied Mathematics 1982;4(3):217-26.

Schreuder JAM. Combinatorial aspects of construction of competition Dutch professional football leagues. Discrete Applied Mathematics 1992;35(3):301-12.

Nemhauser GL & Trick MA. Scheduling a major college basketball conference. Operations Research 1998;46(1):1-8.

Ferland JA & Fleurent C. Computer aided scheduling for a sport league. INFOR 1991;29(1):14 - 25.

Costa D. An evolutionary tabu search algorithm and the NHL scheduling problem. INFOR 1995;33(3):161–78.

Bean JC, Birge JR. Reducing travelling costs and player fatigue in the National Basketball Association. Interfaces 1980;10(3):98-102.

Wright MB. Scheduling fixtures for Basketball New Zealand.Working Paper, Lancaster University Management School, 2003.

Cain WO. The computer-aided heuristic approach used to schedule the major league baseball clubs. In: Ladany SP, MacholRE, editors. Optimal strategies in sports. Amsterdam: North-Holland; 1977. p. 32–41.

Armstrong J & Willis RJ. Scheduling the cricket world cup—a case study. Journal of the Operational Research Society1993;44(11):1067–72.

Willis RJ & Terrill BJ. Scheduling the Australian state cricket season using simulated annealing. Journal of the Operational Research Society 1994;45(3):276 - 80.

Wright M. Timetabling county cricket fixtures using a form of tabu search. Journal of the Operational Research Society1994;45(7):758 - 70.

Della Croce F, Tadei R & Asioli PS. Scheduling a round robin tennis tournament under courts and players availability constraints. Annals of Operations Research 1999; 92:349–61.

http://en.wikipedia.org/wiki/Travelling_salesman_problem

8

Adaptive Sensor-Network Topology Estimating Algorithm Based on the Ant Colony Optimization

Satoshi Kuriharam, Hiroshi Tamaki, Kenichi Fukui and Masayuki Numao
Osaka University
Japan

1. Introduction

Studies on ubiquitous-computing and/or ubiquitous-network systems have recently been very attractive research topics along with interest in rapid developments in information and communications technologies [2]. All kinds of information devices such as computers, cellular phones, electrical appliances, and various sensors will be connected in future ubiquitous-network systems. Consequently, everyone will be able to make use of all kinds of information without stress, anywhere and at any time.

However, we need to bring the idea of "context-awareness" as an essential element into reality to construct ubiquitous-network systems. "Context" refers to the situation in which ubiquitous-network devices are embedded, and "awareness" refers to the recognition of "context" with the ubiquitous network. One goal of context-awareness was to acquire and utilize information about the context to provide services that were appropriate to particular people, places, times, and events. Ubiquitous-network systems were also expected to implement context-awareness by using a sensor network, which was made up of many sensors.

Information about adjacent relationships between sensors is necessary [6] to extract human motion in a sensor-network system. Adjacent relationships indicate the physical connectivity between sensors from the point of view of a person's movement in a sensor network (Fig. 1). This information is usually sent to the system manually [3]. However, investigating and inputting information on the sensor topology becomes much too difficult in proportion to the scale of the sensor-network system. In addition, once the structure of the network changes, e.g., by adding/removing sensor units and by rearranging the network, we have to manually reinvestigate adjacent relationships. Incessantly repetitive investigations and inputs are onerous, and increase the possibility of making mistakes. There is no room for

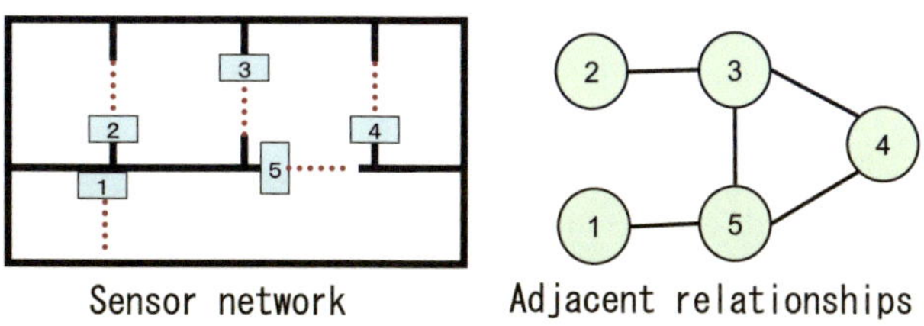

Fig. 1. Adjacent relationships in sensor network

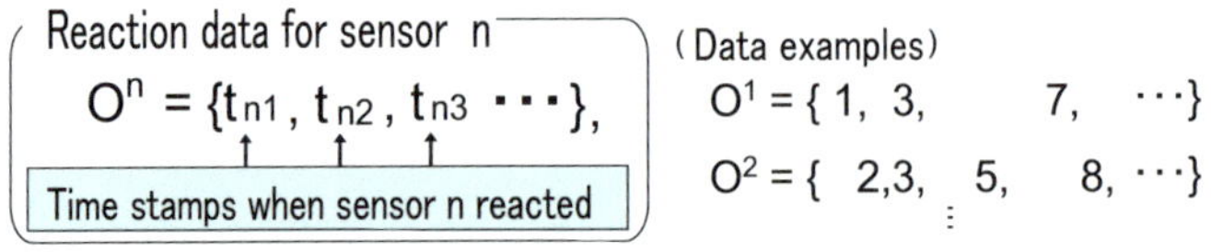

Fig. 2. Format for sensor reaction data

investigating modified topologies, especially in emergency situations. Consequently, it is necessary for sensor-network systems to be able to acquire their own structures automatically without any previous knowledge.

Marinakis and Dudek constructed adjacent relationships in a sensor network and the traffic patterns of people in the network using stochastic expectation maximization [4]. They succeeded in constructing a flexible algorithm independent of any previous knowledge and it was only reliant on information from data observed by all the sensors. However, as the performance of their algorithm strongly depended on the number and traffic patterns of people in the environment, it was based on the assumption that the number of people in the network and their traffic patterns were constant. Moreover, their algorithm required a great deal of analysis with various estimates as to the number of people and traffic patterns to derive the number of persons. It took too much time for it to be of practical use.

This paper proposes an algorithm that could predict sensor relationships by only using real or simulated sensor data. It had to have at least three capabilities: (1) Anytime characteristics - it had be able to output optimal results through analysis over a finite period of time even if the network scale or the frequency of movement increased. (2) Adaptability - the algorithm had to be free of special tuning to accommodate all types of environments. It also had to automatically adapt to changes in network structures. (3) Robustness - it had to maintain extremely accurate analysis results even if the ratio of noise data caused by the simultaneous movements of numerous people or sensing errors increased.

The Ant Colony Optimization (ACO) algorithm is one of the most well known models of pheromone communication derived from the swarming behavior of ants in nature [1]. ACO is recognized as being extremely robust against and adaptable to dynamic changes in the environment, and various kinds of optimization problems have been solved by using ACO-based approaches [5]. As the capabilities of ACO were very appealing to meet our needs, we constructed our algorithm based on this.

The rest of this paper is organized as follows. Section 2 presents an outline of the proposed algorithm. Section 3 describes the details. Sections 4 and 5 describe the experimental results using simulated sensor data and actual data. Section 6 presents the conclusions drawn from this study.

2. Pheromone communication algorithm

2.1 Estimates of standard travel time between sensors

We used the sensor reaction data presented in Fig. 2 in the proposed algorithm, which shows that sensor s_1 reacted at time steps of 1, 3, 7, and 10, and sensor s_2 reacted at time steps of 2, 3, 5, 8, and 13.

If sensors s_i and s_j are adjacent, the travel time between two sensors for any number of people is roughly the same. Consequently, when sensor s_i reacts at $timestep t_1$ and sensor s_j reacts at $timestep t_2$, and $|m_{i,j} - (t_2 - t_1)|$ becomes too small, where $m_{i,j}$ is the average travel time between s_i and s_j, these two sensors are considered to have reacted to one person traveling from s_i to s_j. Conversely, when $|m_{i,j} - (t_2 - t_1)|$ becomes too large, these two sensors are considered to have reacted to two different people. Therefore, if $m_{i,j}$ is calculated from a very long data log of sensor reactions and $|m_{i,j} - (t_2 - t_1)|$ regularly becomes too small, s_i and s_j are considered to be adjacent even if we do not know the relation between both sensors in advance. At this point, we can define $\omega_{i,j} = \frac{1}{|m_{i,j}-(t_2-t_1)|}$ as the likelihood that sensors s_i and s_j will be adjacent to each other.

However, the methodology for estimating the adjacent relation between two sensors by using ω suffers from several weaknesses. For example, even when different people have simultaneous reactions to either sensor and the interval time nears their standard travel time, we mistakenly think both sensors are adjacent. Of course, it is necessary to consider noise such as that from sensor mis-reactions, and it is also important to consider dynamical changes in the adjacent relations of sensors (e.g., when office and room furniture is occasionally re-arranged).

2.2 Necessary functions

Four functions can effectively solve these problems.

1.Positive feedback loop

A positive feedback loop is necessary to accelerate the process by which two such sensors having a higher likelihood of adjacency can be given a higher ω.

2.Avoidance of local solutions

It is necessary to avoid mis-detections where two sensors cannot be considered to be in an adjacent relation, due to the extreme bias of adjacency likelihood. "Item 1" and this item are a trade-off.

3.Using other criteria to calculate the adjacency likelihood

Using other criteria is also necessary to improve accuracy and convergence, and not only using the interval time of sensor reaction, which is the basic methodology used to consider whether two sensors are in an adjacent relation.

4.Deletion of old information

It is necessary to delete relatively old information from the sensor-reaction data log to adapt to dynamic changes in the environment.

Although these items can all effectively be used to solve problems, it is difficult to coordinate them manually, due to the trade-offs between them. As a result, we propose a new methodology in this paper for calculating the adjacency likelihood between sensors based on ACO (Ant Colony Optimization, which is one of the best known pheromone communication models). All four items in the proposed methodology were implemented and adjustments between them were autonomously done.

The adjacency likelihood in our methodology is considered to be the amount of pheromone, and this is accumulated by using both the adjacency likelihood calculated from past sensor reaction data and the presumed distance between sensors derived from the standard travel time. The positive feedback loop where the adjacency likelihood is entirely increased is formed in sensors with adjacent relations by the accumulation mechanism. However, noise due to simultaneous sensor reactions by several persons can be deleted from non-adjacent sensors. Moreover, since pheromones gradually evaporate old information is automatically removed. This means that new information is always given priority. The coordination of items is autonomously and indirectly controlled by the interaction of agents using pheromones.

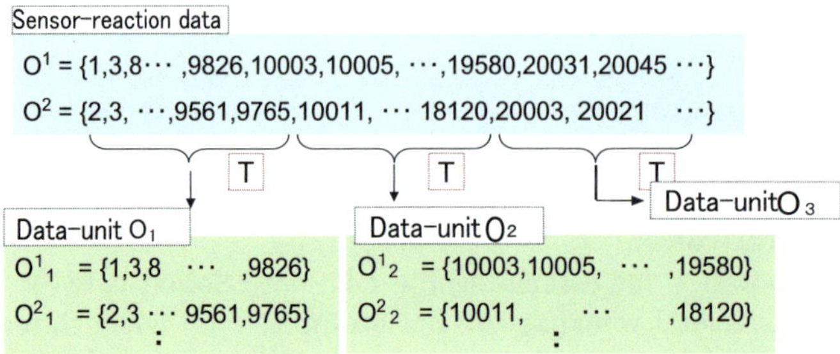

Fig. 3. Example data unit for $T = 10000$.

2.3 Virtual graph

The proposed methodology using the pheromone-communication model is executed on a virtual graph, G, where agents move between sensors and pheromone interactions occur. $G = (V, E)$ is a virtual directed graph and each node $v_i \in V$ corresponds to each sensor $s_i \in S$ in a real environment. Edge $e_{i,j} \in E$ means the edge from node v_i to v_j. As there is no information about adjacent relations, G is initially the complete graph before calculation is started.
Several kinds of pheromones are accumulated and deleted on each $e_{i,j}$, and we propose three kinds: τ, ω, and ϵ.

- Pheromone concerned with adjacency likelihood ω (called "edge pheromone" after this)
  The entire sensor-reaction data in the proposed methodology is divided into several data units (explained in the next section), and calculation is repeatedly done for each unit. ω indicates the adjacency likelihood for each unit and is always initialized before the calculation for each data unit.
- Pheromone being output by agents ϵ (called "agent pheromone" after this)
  Each agent outputs ϵ corresponding to ω on each edge as the evaluated result for the edge. ϵ is also always initialized before each data unit is calculated.
- Pheromone distribution data set τ (called "pheromone distribution" after this)
  τ indicates the accumulation of each ϵ, i.e., τ specifies the total adjacency likelihood of reflecting the calculation results for all units. τ is updated whenever the calculation for a new unit has finished.

Initially, $\tau(0)$ (in this paper, $\tau(0) = 300$) is assigned to whole edges. a agents move on the G and they output pheromones, depending on the number of pheromones on each edge. They are initially placed on the G homogeneously.

2.4 Calculation details

The entire sensor reaction data is divided into several data units O_t containing data on the interval of time T as shown in Fig. 3.
Standard travel time m and pheromone distribution data set τ are updated whenever the calculation for a data unit has finished. Whenever the calculation for a data unit has completed, whether two sensors are adjacent is determined for all the sensors. The locations of all agents, and ω and ϵ are initialized to calculate the next data unit. The next data unit is calculated using m and τ updated in the previous process. Fig. 4 shows the whole sequence for the algorithm.

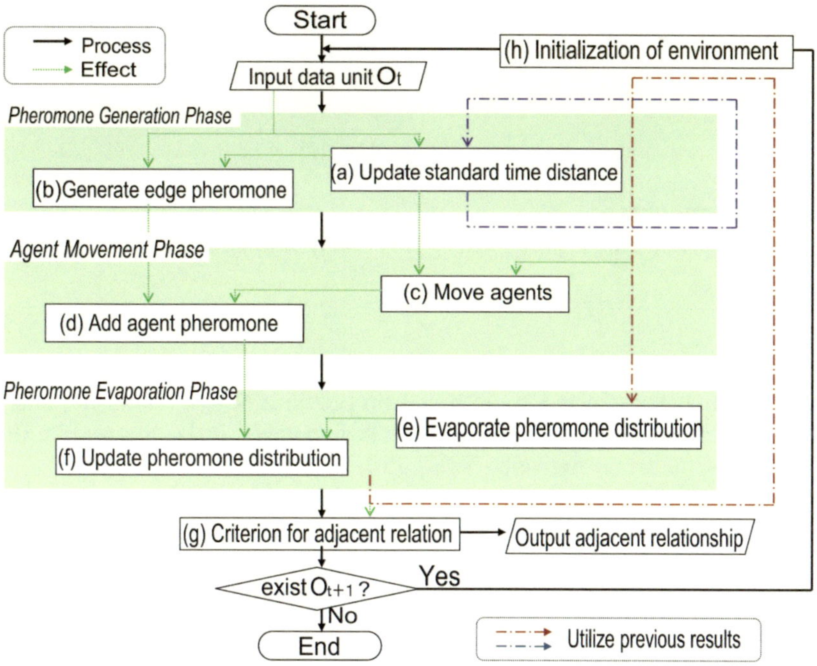

Fig. 4. Overview of proposed algorithm

3. Algorithm for acquisition of adjacent relations

This section describes how the algorithm and adjacent relations are determined in detail.

3.1 Pheromone generation phase

This phase updates $M(t)$ [1] from O_t and generates $\omega(t)$ onto the graph.

(a)Update standard travel time, M

First, a frequency distribution, $d_{i,j}(t)$, for the time distance is created from O_t. $d^c_{i,j}(t)$ represents a frequency where the time interval between two sensors, s_i and s_j, is equal to c within O_t. After an accumulated frequency distribution, $D_{i,j}(t)$, is updated using the current $d_{i,j}(t)$ (Eq. (1)), standard travel time $M(t)$ is updated using $D_{i,j}(t)$ (Eq. (2)). Since $D_{i,j}(t)$ is the accumulated time distance $d_{i,j}(t)$ of each data unit, $M(t)$ is the most frequent time distance up to now.

$$D^c_{i,j}(t) = D^c_{i,j}(t-1) + d^c_{i,j}(t) \tag{1}$$

$$m_{i,j}(t) = \arg\max_{1 \le c \le 50} D^c_{i,j}(t) \tag{2}$$

(b)Generate edge pheromone, ω

$\omega_{i,j}(t)$ is represented by the sum of adjacency likelihoods $\Delta\omega^c_{i,j}(t)$, where each time interval c has

[1] $M(t)$ equals set of standard travel time $m(t)_{i,j}$
$M(t) = \{m(t)_{i,j} | \forall i, j, i \neq j\}$.

$$\Delta\omega^{c}_{i,j}(t) = \frac{d^{c}_{i,j}(t)}{|m_{i,j}(t) - c|} \tag{3}$$

$$\omega_{i,j}(t) = \Sigma_c \Delta\omega^{c}_{i,j}(t) \tag{4}$$

3.2 Agent movement phase

Each agent in this phase moves based on $\tau(t)$ and $M(t)$, and adds $\epsilon(t)$ onto an edge based on $\omega(t)$.

(c)Move agents

Each agent only moves once on an edge within an agent movement phase, and can move to any node. Each agent selects a route based on previous search result $\tau(t)$ and heuristics $\eta(t)$. $\eta_{i,j}(t)$ is the inverse of $m_{i,j}(t)$ on its route. The less $m_{i,j}(t)$ is, i.e., the shorter the distance between sensors is, the larger the value is (Eq. (5)).

$$\eta_{i,j}(t) = \frac{1}{m_{i,j}(t)} \tag{5}$$

All agents are set to prefer an edge where there is a lot of $\tau(t)$ remaining. Therefore, they can focus their search on edges that have a high adjacency likelihood obtained by a previous search. Also, since agents are set up to prefer routes that have high $\eta(t)$, they can conduct more effective searches. It is highly likely that adjacent sensors will be located nearer than non-adjacent sensors. The probability, $p^{k}_{i,j}(t)$, that agent k will moves from v_i to v_j is given by:

$$pa^{k}_{i,j}(t) = \frac{[\tau_{i,j}(t)][\eta_{i,j}(t)]^{\gamma}}{\sum_{j,j\neq i}[\tau_{i,j}(t)][\eta_{i,j}(t)]^{\gamma}} \tag{6}$$

γ is the weight for $\tau(t)$, giving priority to the information for all agents. In addition, all agents are set up to select routes randomly with constant probability r not depending on $\tau(t)$. This prevents the discovered adjacent relation from falling into a local solution. The local solution might be obtained by the effectiveness of the feedback loop of a pheromone increasing. $\gamma = 1$ and $r = 0.1$ are used in this paper.

(d)Add agent pheromone, ϵ

After moving, each agent discharges an agent pheromone, $\Delta\epsilon^{k}_{i,j}(t)$, onto its edge as the evaluation value for the route. The evaluation value reflects information on O_t using $\omega_{i,j}(t)$, which is generated in the pheromone generation phase. Equation (7) represents agent pheromone $\Delta\epsilon^{k}_{i,j}(t)$ that agent k who passed $e_{i,j}$ added onto $e_{i,j}$. Also, Eq. (8) represents the amount of agent pheromone $\epsilon_{i,j}(t)$, where n is the number of agents who moved to $e_{i,j}$.

$$\Delta\epsilon^{k}_{i,j}(t) = \omega_{i,j}(t) \tag{7}$$

$$\epsilon'_{i,j}(t) = \sum_{k=1}^{n} \Delta\epsilon^{k}_{i,j}(t) \tag{8}$$

$$\epsilon_{i,j}(t) = z\left\{1 - \left(1 - \frac{1}{z}\right)^{\epsilon'_{i,j}(t)}\right\} \tag{9}$$

Equation (9) prevents strong bias in the pheromone distribution. When the sum of agent pheromone $\epsilon'_{i,j}(t)$ that the agents discharged who moved to $e_{i,j}$ is low, the amount of pheromone proportional to that value is added. However, the contribution due to the increase in agent pheromone decreases with increasing $\epsilon'_{i,j}(t)$. z was set to 1,000 in this paper.

3.3 Pheromone Evaporation Phase

$\tau(t)$ is evaporated and updated using $\epsilon(t)$ in this phase.

(e)Evaporate pheromone distribution, τ

$\tau_{i,j}(t)$ that is on each edge decreases according to the evaporation rate, ρ, in every evaporation phase. Equation (10) is used to calculate evaporation:

$$\tau'_{i,j}(t) = (1-\rho)\tau_{i,j}(t) \tag{10}$$

(f)Update pheromone distribution, τ

After being evaporated, $\tau'_{i,j}(t)$ is updated by combining it with $\epsilon_{i,j}(t)$, which is generated in the agent movement phase. Equation (11) gives the formula for updating $\tau_{i,j}(t)$ in O_t:

$$\tau_{i,j}(t+1) = \tau'_{i,j}(t) + \epsilon_{i,j}(t) \tag{11}$$

Later searching information is thereby reflected at a constant ratio by discarding old searching information. Evaporation rate ρ affects the update speed. The smaller ρ is, the more weight is given to later information. $\rho = 0.01$ has been used in this paper. When ρ is small, a stable solution can generally be discovered; however, the convergence speed is slow. Whereas, when ρ is large, the convergence speed is fast; however, an unstable solution may be obtained depending on the data unit.

3.4 Determination of adjacent relations

This section describes how adjacent relations are determined after analysis is finished for O_t and G is initialized for O_{t+1}.

(g)Criterion for adjacent relations

$\tau(t)$ represented the adjacency likelihood as the result of total analysis up to now. An edge is determined as an adjacent relation when $\tau(t)$ is greater than a certain threshold. The threshold is given by α times the average of all pheromone distributions $\tau(t)$ as shown in Eq. (12). α has been set to 0.8 in this paper. Here, $|V|$ is the number of nodes.

$$threshold(t) = \alpha \times \frac{\Sigma_{i,j}\tau_{i,j}(t)}{|V|^2} \tag{12}$$

(h)Initialization of environment

If the next data unit, O_{t+1}, exists after the above phases have finished, it restarts analysis from the pheromene generation phase using O_{t+1} after the environment has been initialized.
$\omega(t)$ and $\epsilon(t)$ are discarded for initialization, and agents are also allocated evenly to each node. Only $\tau(t+1)$, $M(t)$, and $D(t)$ are inherited for the next analysis.

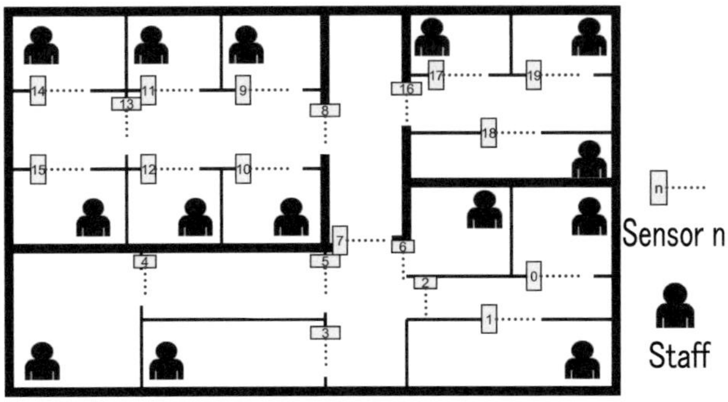

Fig. 5. Virtual environment, E_2.

4. Empirical verification using simulation

We conducted simulation experiments to verify the basic effectiveness of the proposed algorithm. This section presents the results of experiments using simulated sensor data.

4.1 Preparation of data for simulation

We prepared the sensor-reaction data for simulation using a virtual sensor-network environment (Fig. 5). This virtual environment was built with rooms and aisles the sensors were attached to, and in which staff moved around. Each staff member was asked to randomly repeat asynchronously moving from one room to another. In every time step, each decided whether to begin moving or not according to the probability of "movement frequency", which represented how often staff started to move. When a staff member passes in front of a sensor, the sensed data from this sensor was sent and stored with a time stamp. Mis-detection by the sensor also occurred, which depended on the probability of "mis-reaction frequency". Whenever time T passed, data unit O_t was created and analysis was carried out.

We prepared two patterns for a virtual environment in this experiment, E_1 and E_2, which had 10 and 20 sensors, and also 6 and 14 staff members. The movement frequency was also set up for three patterns of F_{Low}, F_{Normal}, and F_{High}, and the mis-reaction frequency was also set up for M_0, M_{20}, and M_{50}[2]. By choosing these elements, we built a variety of virtual sensor networks. We used the following values for the algorithm parameters of a and T, depending on simulation elements E and F, i.e., $\{E,a\} = \{E_1,2{,}000\}, \{E_2,4{,}000\}\}$, $\{F,T\} = \{F_{Low},15{,}000\}$, $\{F_{Normal},8{,}000\}$, and $\{F_{High},1{,}000\}$.

4.2 Verification of robustness

First, we verified the robustness of the algorithm against noise data. We divided the noise data into two types: the first was caused by movements by numerous walkers and the second by mis-reactions by the sensors. We controlled these noise probabilities by selecting simulation elements E, F, and M.

We constructed two more algorithms to calculate adjacency likelihood for comparison, i.e., Test 1 and Test 2. In Test 1, adjacent relations were judged from adjacency likelihood ω without being weighed. Test 2 was based on Test 1 and only adopted the η information to weight ω.

We tested robustness with the noise-production probability related to the ratio of numerous people with simultaneously varying movements. Six kinds of virtual environments were prepared by pairing E with F (M_{20} was used), and for all six we calculated 1,000,000 time

---

[2] M_x means that no sensors detected at a probability of $x\%$

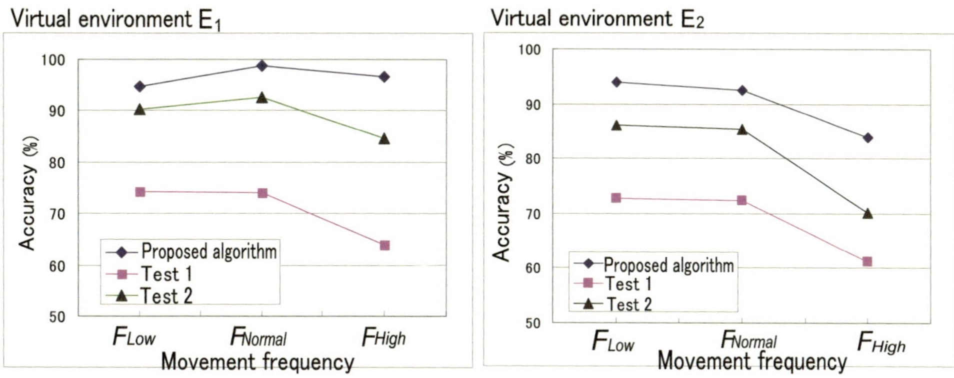

Fig. 6. Relations between F and accuracy.

steps using the proposed algorithm, Test 1, and Test 2. All the calculations were repeated ten times and the average accuracies were calculated (accuracy was the ratio of correct adjacent relationships acquired by calculation). The mean value of accuracies is plotted in Fig. 6 and the process for acquiring adjacent relationships using the proposed algorithm is shown in Fig. 7.

We next verified how robust our algorithm was against mis-reaction noise. We prepared six pattern environments by pairing E with $M(F_{Normal}$ was used), and did experiments in the same way as for the environments using numerous people moving simultaneously. Figure 8 plots the results.

Figures 6 and 8 reveal that the proposed algorithm could analyze more accurately than Tests 1 and 2. In addition, our algorithm always required less sensor data to attain 90% accuracy than the others. Consequently, we concluded that it was more robust against noise data.

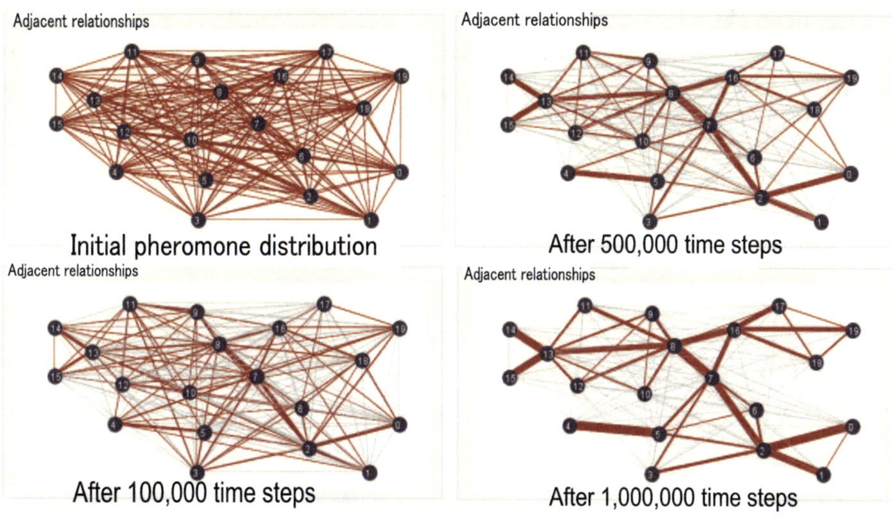

Fig. 7. Transition in acquiring adjacent relationships.

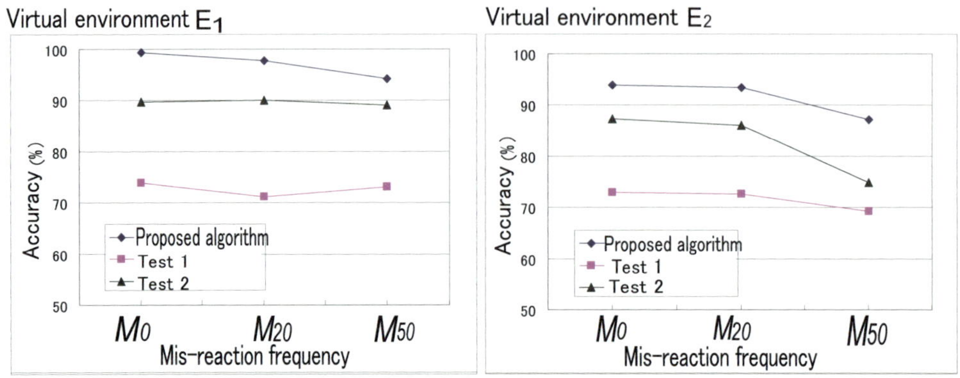

Fig. 8. Relations between M and accuracy.

4.3 Vertification of adaptability

Second, we verified how adaptable our algorithm was against dynamic changes in the topology of sensor-network systems. Structural changes are generated when one sensor fails and is replaced by two others. E_1, F_{Normal} and M_{20} were selected for the simulation elements, and the network structure was shifted after 500,000 time steps had passed. The time to recover accuracy to 90% was taken as the barometer for adaptability to structural change. Figure 9 shows the process of adaptation to dynamic changes in the network structure.

As a result, the proposed algorithm needed about half the time of other algorithms not using the pheromone communication system to recover. Therefore, we concluded that it was basically adaptable to environmental changes.

5. Empirical verification using real-world sensor data

This section describes our empirical verification using real-world sensor data. We used sensor-reaction data that were obtained from an infrared sensor network installed in our laboratory. A person's presence was detected by reading the reflection intensity from a sensor that had beamed an infrared laser from itself. The data were collected over a period of 30 days with 31 infrared sensors that were installed in three rooms. The proposed algorithm was

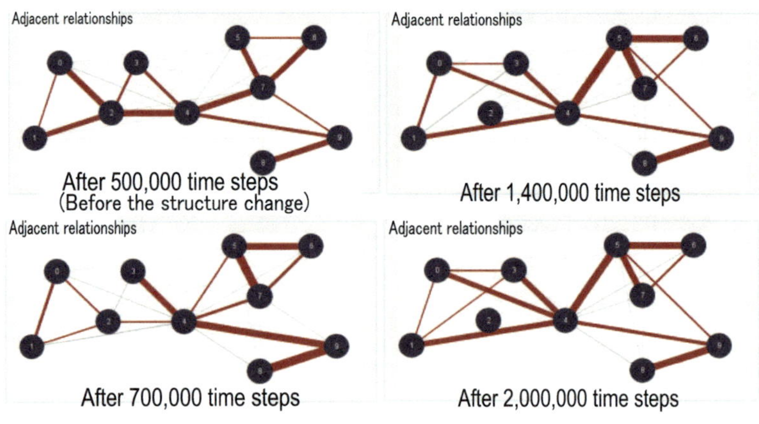

Fig. 9. Process of adaptation.

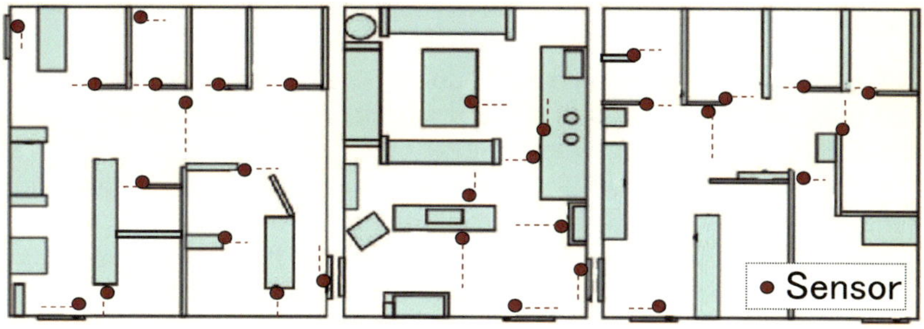

Fig. 10. Actual layout for sensor network.

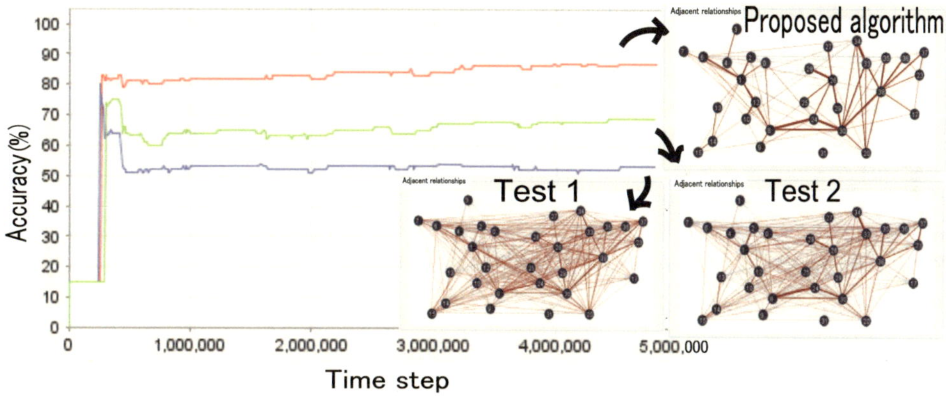

Fig. 11. Accuracy of analysis obtained by algorithms using real-world data and obtained adjacent relationships.

compared with Tests 1 and 2 that were discussed in Section 4. Figure 10 shows the layout for the sensor network.

The sensor data was collected for 24 hours, and each sensor had an average of 2143.2 reactions. The structure of the network also did not change during this period. Parameters $T = 10{,}000$ and $a = 20{,}000$ were used. Figures 11 shows the results discovered with the proposed algorithm, Test 1, and Test 2.

Figure 11 shows that the proposed method is superior to the test algorithms (Accuracies: 87% with proposed, 53% with Test 1, and 64% with Test 2). Note that it continues to remain accurate after approximately 300,000 time steps. Each data unit is created and analyzed every one and a half hours when converted into real-world time. There are large differences in the amount of sensor-reaction information obtained during the day, at night, or on holidays.

Moreover, when someone only makes one sensor react during their one episode of movement, this becomes noise in addition to movements by numerous people and sensor miss-reactions, because it is impossible to extract a sensor-reaction relation when only one sensor reacts. Since the proposed algorithm assumes that sensor-reaction information is the sequence of a person's movements, a single sensor reaction prevents accuracy from being improved. However, the new method also demonstrated greater robustness against this problem than the test algorithms.

6. Conclusion

The basic effectiveness of the proposed methodology could be verified from our evaluations using simulations and experiments in the real world. We used our laboratory as the real environment for the experiments, where a total of 15 persons were working. The actual number of people at work differed depending on the day of the week and the time. The habitual behavior of individuals was of course different as they had their own weekly and daily schedules. The methodology we propose based on the pheromone-communication model could be adapted to the subjects' personal diversity, but unfortunately this might be difficult using the methodology suggested by Marinakis and Dudek. Our methodology has the following features:
(1) A positive feedback loop is used to accelerate the process by which two sensors having a higher adjacent likelihood can be given a higher likelihood autocatalytically.
(2) When an agent selects a node that it wants to move to, random selection is done at a constant rate. This mechanism, which is a heterogeneous factor, is very effective.
(3) Also using other criteria, i.e., the standard traveling time, m, and not only the interval time of sensor reaction, which is the basic methodology that is used to consider whether two sensors are in an adjacent relation, very effectively improves accuracy and convergence.
(4) Since pheromones gradually evaporate, old information is automatically removed, i.e., new information is always given priority. These features support all of the necessary functions discussed in Section 2, and demonstrate the effectiveness of the pheromone-communication model.

7. References

[1] Marco Dorigo and Gianni Di Caro, *The Ant Colony Optimization Meta-Heuristic, New ideas in optimization* (McGraw-Hill), 1999, pp. 11–32.
[2] Satoshi Kurihara, Shigemi Aoyagi, Toshihiro Takada, Toshio Hirotsu, and Toshiharu Sugawara, Agent-Based Human-Environment Interaction Framework for Ubiquitous Environment, INSS2005, pp. 103–108.
[3] Seiichi Honda, Ken-ichi Fukui , Koichi Moriyama, Satoshi Kurihara, and Masayuki Numao. Extracting Human Behaviors with Infrared Sensor Network, INSS 2007, pp. 122–125.
[4] Dimitri Marinakis and Gregory Dudek, Topological Mapping through Distributed Passive Sensors, IJCAI 2007, pp. 2147–2152.
[5] John A. SauterCRobert MatthewsCH. Van Dyke Parunak, and Sven A. Brueckner, Performance of Digital Pheromones for Swarming Vehicle ControlCAAMAS 2005, pp. 903–910.
[6] Taisuke Hosokawa and Mineichi Kubo, Person tracking with infrared sensors, KES 2005, pp. 682–688.

9

Ant Colony Optimization in Green Manufacturing

Cong Lu
School of Mechatronics Engineering,
University of Electronic Science and Technology of China, Chengdu 611731,
China

1. Introduction

In recent years, with more and more requirement on energy sources saving and environmental protection, green manufacturing has become an important approach in production. In green manufacturing, product disassembly process is a key step, by which the parts can be recycled from the outdated or discarded products for reuse, remanufacturing or disposing, thus can save the energy sources and protect the environment efficiently. To find an effective disassembly process, disassembly planning is usually carried out, which aims at a feasible and optimal disassembly sequence with minimal cost or time. An effective disassembly planning approach can not only provide a solution to disassemble the product successfully and economically, it can also help the designer to consider the product life cycle issues by focusing on the product disassembly cost or time in the early design stage. In recent years, with the requirement for green manufacturing technology, investigation on effective disassembly planning approach has attracted much research attention and a variety of approaches have been proposed. Guo et al. [1] proposed a modularization based disassembly sequence planning approach to resolve the problem resulted from a large number of parts in the product, where the Hierarchy Network Graph of product is created, and the precedence constraints related to the hierarchy network graph is used to generate the disassembly sequence. Chung and Peng [2] proposed an integrated approach to selective-disassembly sequence planning, to get a partial disassembly sequence where the parts or components are selected for recycling or reuse. This approach can generate a feasible and practical sequence for selective-disassembly by two matrix- subassembly division precedence matrix and part disassembly route matrix, to ensure both batch disassembly of components and tool accessibility to fasteners. Torres et al. [3] proposed a method to represent the hierarchical relationships among components and/or assemblies of the product. Based on this representation, an algorithm is established to generate a partial non-destructive disassembly sequence of a product. Das and Naik [4] proposed a descriptive model with a structured format for creating, documenting, and evaluating a disassembly process plan. And the model can transmit the product knowledge from the original product manufacturer to the consumer and the end-of-life disassembler via the disassembly bill of materials. Dong et al. [5] proposed an approach to generate the disassembly sequence from a hierarchical attributed liaison graph representation of an assembly automatically, by decomposing the assembly into subassemblies recursively. The graph is built according to the knowledge in engineering, design and demanufacturing, for each layer of the graph, the preferred subassembly is selected in terms of mobility, stability, and parallelism. With the graph, the proposed approach can find the feasible and practical sequence. Veerakamolmal and Gupta [6] proposed a case-based reasoning approach to disassembly process planning, with a method to initialize a case memory and to operate a CBR system. The approach can derive a feasible disassembly process quickly by retrieve, reuse, and revise the product disassembly process plan.

The above works present the different disassembly planning approaches that can provide the feasible and practical disassembly plans with different focus. However, these approaches do not adopt the optimization search algorithm, so they can not easily find the optimal or near optimal solutions.

Besides the above works, the other disassembly planning approaches with some optimization algorithm are discussed as follows. Andres et al. [7] proposed a two-phase approach to determine the optimal disassembly sequence with the goal of minimizing machine acquisition costs. A metaheuristic algorithm named GRASP is used to search for the disassembly sequence for each product that leads to the minimum number of intercellular movements. Rai et al. [8] presented a Petri net model to search a partial reachability graph, with the heuristic function, the proposed approach can generate a feasible and optimal disassembly sequence based on the firing sequence of transitions of the Petri net model. In the above two approaches, only one objective such as the machine acquisition costs was considered, and the other objectives in disassembly process were ignored. Because disassembly planning is a typical multi-objective optimization problem, so the above approaches are not suitable to find the optimal or near optimal solutions considering different objectives in disassembly process.

As an important method, the genetic algorithm (GA) has been widely used in assembly planning [9-12], in the mean time, it is also used in disassembly planning to find the optimal disassembly sequence. Kongar and Gupta [13] proposed a GA approach to disassembly sequence planning, with the objective to minimize the number of direction changes, disassembly method changes, and the group of the identical material components. Because assembly planning or disassembly planning are highly constrained problem, using GA-based approach, sometimes the solution can not be converged to a global optimal or near global optimal solution, or even a feasible solution cannot be found in an evolution trial due to the precedence constraints when a product is complex and composed of many parts.

Recently, a new probabilistic evolutionary optimization algorithm- ant colony optimization (ACO) which simulates the cooperative work of ant colony for searching the shortest path from the nest to the food source, has been given attention and has been used in some engineering optimization problems, such as JIT sequencing problem [14], job-shop scheduling [15], etc. Also, some new research works applying ACO in assembly and disassembly planning have been reported. Wang et al. [16] proposed an ACO approach in assembly sequence planning, in this work, only one objective, the number of orientations during disassembly process is considered as the heuristic information to guide the ants moving to the next node, how the other objectives in assembly planning affect the route selection of the ants was not investigated. For the ACO approach used in assembly or disassembly planning with multiple objectives, Failli and Dini [17] proposed using ACO in assembly planning, in this approach, two heuristic information -number of gripper changes and number of orientation changes which are two objectives considered in assembly planning are used to guide the moving of the ants. The above two heuristic information are given the constant value in ACO according to gripper change and orientation change, thus the directions for guiding the ants moving are fixed. McGovern and Gupta [18] proposed an approach using ACO for disassembly line balancing problem, in this approach, several objectives are considered, but only one objective- the measure of balance is used as the heuristic information for ACO calculations and trail selection, the other objectives are only considered at the end of each cycle to update the best overall solution. In the above mentioned ACO approaches for assembly or disassembly planning with multiple objectives, the ants select the route by evaluating the heuristic value according to the objectives. Although the above ACO approaches have made some success in assembly or disassembly planning, however, these approaches fixed search directions that are used to guide the ants moving, so more trade off solutions for multiple objectives could not be easily found. As disassembly planning is a typical multi-objective optimization problem, how ACO approach can be used in disassembly planning to effectively guide the ants to search and find more trade-off solutions, to provide the decision maker more choice to achieve green manufacturing needs to be further investigated.

2. Principle of ant colony optimization

ACO is the behavior simulation of a colony of ants that are working cooperatively to search and find the shortest path from the nest to the food source. As a key factor in the searching process, pheromone is a chemical substance that is deposited by the ants when they move along the path, and it will be used for the ants to exchange the information. The ants prefer to choose the shorter path, the shorter path will attract more ants to visit, and thereby more pheromone is deposited on the path by the ants. Meanwhile, the pheromone on all paths is decreased through evaporation due to the time past. The probability that the subsequent ants choose the path is based on the amount of the pheromone deposited on the path, so, the shorter path with greater amount of pheromone will get more chance to be selected and thus attract more and more ants to visit later. As a result, the shortest path from the nest to the food source can be found by the ant colony.
In ant colony optimization, the probability that ant z select next node j is given as follows:

$$P_z(i,j)=\begin{cases}\dfrac{\tau(i,j)[\eta(i,j)]^{\lambda}}{\sum\limits_{s\in Allowed_z(i)}\tau(i,s)[\eta(i,s)]^{\lambda}}, & \text{if } j \in \text{Allowed}_z(i)\\ 0, & \text{otherwise}\end{cases} \tag{1}$$

Where, $\tau(i,j)$ is the quantity of pheromone deposited on the edge from node i to node j. $\eta(i,j)$ is the heuristic information corresponding to the edge from node i to node j. λ is the parameter that determine the relative importance of $\tau(i,j)$ versus $\eta(i,j)$. $\text{Allowed}_z(i)$ are the nodes that are allowed to be selected by ant z when choosing next node j. In ACO, the edges with greater $\tau(i,j)$ and $\eta(i,j)$ are the favorable edges for the ants prefer to choose.
During the search process of ACO, there are two important rules for updating the pheromone -Local Updating Rule and Global Updating Rule.

Local Updating Rule:

Local Updating Rule is used for updating the pheromone level of the edge only when the ants visit it, and it can be represented by the Eq. (2)

$$\tau(i,j)=(1-\alpha)\,\tau(i,j)+\alpha\tau_0(i,j) \tag{2}$$

Where, α is a parameter given in the range [0, 1], which determines the pheromone volatility on the edge from node i to node j, and $\tau_0(i,j)$ is the initial pheromone level on the edge. Through local updating, the visited edges will loss some amount of its pheromone, and this can effectively avoid the premature convergence.

Global updating rule:

Global Updating Rule is used for updating the pheromone level of all the edges after the ants have finished the tour, and only the edges belonging to the current global best solution can have extra pheromone added. Meanwhile, the evaporation of the pheromone is performed on all the edges.
The global updating rule can be represented by the Eq. (3)

$$\tau(i,j)=(1-\beta)\,\tau(i,j)+\beta\Delta\tau(i,j) \tag{3}$$

Where, β is the pheromone decay parameter given in the range [0, 1],

$$\Delta\tau(i,j)=\begin{cases} F_{(gb)} & \text{if edge } (i,j)\in \text{globalbest solution} \\ 0 & \text{otherwise} \end{cases}$$

$F_{(gb)}$ is the fitness value of the global best solution found up to now, and the detailed value of $F_{(gb)}$ in disassembly planning will be given in section 5.

3. Multi-objective search directions with uniform design

In order to apply ACO to deal with the multi-objective optimization problem in disassembly planning, this section proposes an algorithm for building the uniformly scattered searching directions towards Pareto frontier, aiming at finding more non-dominated solutions along Pareto frontier.

3.1 Non-dominated solutions in multi-objective optimization problem

For a multi-objective optimization problem, because different objectives are usually conflicting, there exists a set of solutions in the solution space, in which none of them is superior to the others according to each objective. These solutions are usually called non-dominated solutions, which can be regarded as the best trade-off solutions in the multi-objective optimization problem.
The definition of non-dominated solution can be given as follows: Given a multi-objective optimization problem with n objectives to be minimized: minimize $f_1(x)$, $f_2(x)$,……, $f_n(x)$, $X\in\Omega$, where $f_i(x)$ represents the different objectives, $i\in\{1, 2, \ldots\ldots, n\}$, and Ω represents the feasible solution space. For two solutions X_1, X_2, if

$$\begin{cases} f_t(x_1) < f_t(x_2), & \text{for some } t\in\{1,\ 2,\ \ldots\ldots,\ n\} \\ f_t(x_1) \le f_t(x_2), & \text{for all } t\in\{1,\ 2,\ \ldots\ldots,\ n\} \end{cases}$$

then solution X_2 is dominated by solution X_1. In the feasible solution space Ω, if there does not exist any solution which can dominate solution X, then solution X is called as a non-dominated solution.

In the multi-objective optimization problem, a set of non-dominated solutions form the Pareto frontier. An example is shown in Fig. 1 [19], where the solid circles represent the non-dominated solutions which form the Pareto frontier, while the hollow circles represent the dominated solutions. This is a two-objective optimization problem, with the goal to minimize those two objectives, i.e. to search for the non-dominated solutions located along the Pareto frontier.

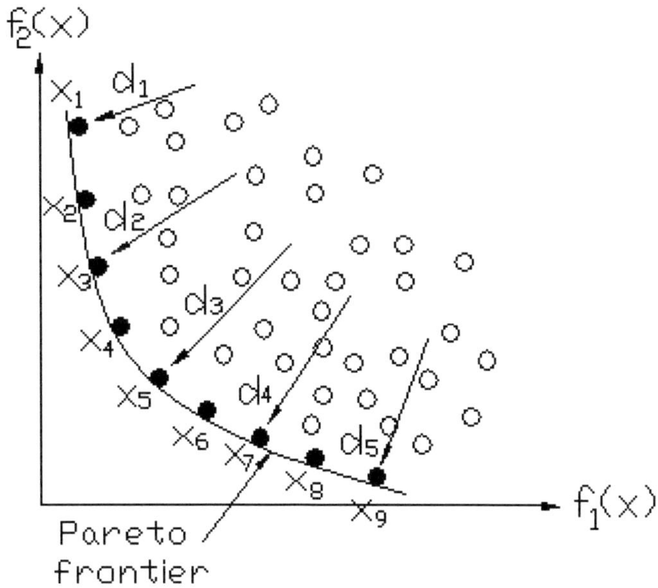

Fig. 1. Non-dominated solutions with multiple search directions

3.2 Uniform design for building multiple search directions

In a multi-objective optimization problem, in order to find more non-dominated solutions for the decision maker to make choice, the search directions towards Pareto frontier need to be expanded effectively. In this work, an experimental design method called uniform design is used to expand the search directions.

Uniform design can be used to sample a small set of points from a given large set of points, so as to make the sampled points uniformly scattered over the space of all the given points. The uniform design method can be described as follows:

Suppose there are n factors, and each factor has k levels, then there are totally k^n combinations. From the above combinations, to select k combinations that are uniformly scattered over the space, a uniform matrix can be given as follows:

$$U(n,k)=[U_{i,j}]_{k\times n}=\begin{bmatrix} U_{11} & U_{12} & \dots\dots & U_{1n} \\ U_{21} & U_{22} & \dots\dots & U_{2n} \\ \dots\dots & \dots\dots & \dots\dots & \dots\dots \\ U_{k1} & U_{k2} & \dots\dots & U_{kn} \end{bmatrix} \tag{4}$$

In Eq. (4), $U_{i,j}$ is the level of the factor j in the ith combination. When k is prime and $k>n$, then $U_{i,j}$ can be concluded as follows [20]:

$$U_{i,j} = (i\sigma^{j-1} \text{mod} k)+1 \tag{5}$$

where, σ is a parameter as shown in Table 1, and it is determined by the number of factors and the number of levels per factor.

No. of levels per factors	5	7	11	13			17	19	
No. of factors	2-4	2-6	2-10	2	3	4-12	2-16	2-3	4-18
σ	2	3	7	5	4	6	10	8	14

Table 1. Values of σ for different No. of levels per factors and different No. of factors

For a multi-objective optimization problem, in order to get a set of search directions that are uniformly scattered toward Pareto frontier in the solution space, Eq.(6) can be used to conclude the weight vectors that determine the above search directions. In Eq. (6), n can be regarded as the number of objective functions, and k as the number of the search directions.

$$W_{ij} = \frac{U_{ij}}{\sum_{j=1}^{j=n} U_{ij}} \quad \text{where, } i \ [1,k], \text{ j } [1,n] \tag{6}$$

Then, the weight matrix

$$[W_{i,j}]_{k\times n} = \begin{bmatrix} W_{11} & W_{12} & \cdots\cdots & W_{1n} \\ W_{21} & W_{22} & \cdots\cdots & W_{2n} \\ \cdots\cdots & \cdots\cdots & \cdots\cdots & \cdots\cdots \\ W_{k1} & W_{k2} & \cdots\cdots & W_{kn} \end{bmatrix} \tag{7}$$

Each row of the above matrix is a weight vector to be used for building the fitness function. There are totally k weight vectors, for each weight vector, the sum of the weights is equal to one. Using the weight vectors concluded from equation (6), the fitness functions with k uniformly scattered search directions can be built.

In this work, uniform design will be used to generate the weight vectors to guide the search directions of the ant colony, which will be discussed in section 5.3.

4. Application of ACO for disassembly planning

In this section, the application of ACO with multiple search directions for disassembly planning is discussed.

4.1 Geometric precedence feasibility in disassembly planning

In disassembly planning, the geometric precedence feasibility is a constraint that the ants must satisfy during the moving process. This means only the parts which can be disassembled without any interference can be chosen by the ants in the next step. To conclude the geometric precedence feasibility, the interference matrix is used in this work.

The interference matrix was first proposed by Dini [21] in assembly planning, and it can also be used for precedence feasibility judgment in disassembly planning. For an assembly consisting of n parts, an interference matrix I_d (d represents the disassembly direction) can be represented as follows:

$$I_d = \begin{array}{c} \\ P_1 \\ P_2 \\ \cdots \\ P_n \end{array} \begin{array}{c} \begin{array}{cccc} P_1 & P_2 & \cdots & P_n \end{array} \\ \begin{bmatrix} P_{11} & P_{12} & \cdots & P_{1n} \\ P_{21} & P_{22} & \cdots & P_{2n} \\ \cdots & \cdots & \cdots & \cdots \\ P_{n1} & P_{n2} & \cdots & P_{nn} \end{bmatrix} \end{array}$$

P_1, ..., P_n are used to represent the n parts in the assembly, let $P_{ij}=1$ ($i\in[1, n], j\in[1, n]$) if part P_i collides with P_j when P_i is disassembled along the direction d from the current assembly position; otherwise, let $P_{ij}=0$. Let $P_{ii}=0$ because the part cannot collide with itself. Because P_{ij} in the $-d$ direction is equal to P_{ji} in the $+d$ direction, three interference matrices I_{+X}, I_{+Y} and I_{+Z} can be used to conclude the precedence feasibility in a disassembly sequence (A Cartesian co-ordinate system whereby the six axes $\pm X$, $\pm Y$, $\pm Z$ are the principal axes along which the components are disassembled is used in this work).

In disassembly process, when part P_i is disassembled before a remaining product assembly S_m consisting of m parts, then the feasible disassembly direction of P_i to S_m can be derived as follows: for disassembly direction d, $d\in\{\pm X, \pm Y, \pm Z\}$, let $P_j\in S_m$, determine $D_d(P_i S_m)=\sum P_{ij}$ (P_{ij} is the element in I_d). If $D_d(P_i S_m)=0$, then direction d is the feasible disassembly direction of P_i to S_m; otherwise, direction d is infeasible. If none of the six directions is feasible, then P_i cannot be disassembled at current stage; otherwise, P_i can be disassembled from the product without collision interference.

4.2 Three objectives in disassembly planning

The purpose of disassembly planning is to derive a feasible disassembly sequence with the minimal disassembly cost or disassembly time. The disassembly cost or time usually can be determined by three objectives: the number of disassembly orientation changes, tool (gripper) changes and changes in disassembly operation types. In the disassembly process, a change of the disassembly orientation or disassembly tool needs time and usually can increase the disassembly cost. Different types of assembly operations are needed to complete the assembly process, such as pressing, screwing, riveting, etc., accordingly, different disassembly operations are needed for different parts in the disassembly process. Changes of the disassembly operations also require tool change, and thus increase the disassembly time and cost. Hence, in disassembly planning, the above three objectives-disassembly orientation changes, tool changes, and changes in disassembly operation types should be minimized to reduce the disassembly time and cost.

4.3 Application of ACO with multiple search directions for disassembly planning

To apply ACO in disassembly planning, the first part in disassembly sequence can be regarded as the nest of ant colony, and the last part in disassembly sequence can be regarded as the food source. The shortest path can be equivalent to the disassembly sequence with the minimal cost or time, thus in this work, the shortest path can be represented by the optimum disassembly sequence considering three objectives: disassembly orientation change, disassembly tool change, and disassembly operation change.

In disassembly planning problem, $P_z(i, j)$ in Eq.(1) can be modified and represented as the probability that ant z select the disassembly sequence step from Part i to Part j in a given search direction t, and it can be represented in Eq.(8):

$$P_{z\,(t)}(i,j)=\begin{cases}\dfrac{\tau_t(i,j)[\eta_t(i,j)]^{\lambda}}{\sum\limits_{s\in Allowed_z(i)}\tau_t(i,s)[\eta_t(i,s)]^{\lambda}}, & \text{if } j\in \text{Allowed}_z(i)\\ 0, & \text{otherwise}\end{cases} \quad (8)$$

Where, $t\in[1, k]$; $\tau_t(i, j)$ is the quantity of pheromone deposited on the disassembly sequence step from Part i to Part j in search direction t; $\eta_t(i, j)$ is the heuristic value corresponding to the disassembly step from Part i to Part j in search direction t, and it can be represented in Eq.(9):

$$\left.\begin{aligned}\eta_1(i,j)&=1.5-\left(W_{11}f_1+W_{12}f_2+W_{13}f_3\right)\\ \eta_2(i,j)&=1.5-\left(W_{21}f_1+W_{22}f_2+W_{23}f_3\right)\\ &\cdots\cdots\cdots\\ \eta_k(i,j)&=1.5-\left(W_{k1}f_1+W_{k2}f_2+W_{k3}f_3\right)\end{aligned}\right\} \quad (9)$$

Where, f_1, f_2 and f_3 are given as follows:

$$f_1=\begin{cases}1, & \text{if need orientation change in disassembly step from Part } i \text{ to Part } j\\ 0, & \text{if no orientation change in disassemblystep from Part } i \text{ to Part } j\end{cases}$$

$$f_2=\begin{cases}1, & \text{if need tool change in disassembly step from Part } i \text{ to Part } j\\ 0, & \text{if no tool change in disassembly step from Part } i \text{ to Part } j\end{cases}$$

$$f_3=\begin{cases}1, & \text{if need operation change in disassembly step from Part } i \text{ to Part } j\\ 0, & \text{if no operation change in disassembly step from Part } i \text{ to Part } j\end{cases}$$

In Eq. (9), $[W_{i,j}]_{k\times 3}$ is the weight matrix derived from Eq. (6), which are used for three objectives: disassembly orientation change, disassembly tool change, and disassembly operation change, respectively. Thus, $\eta_t(i, j)$ ($t\in[1, k]$) can be used for guiding the ants to search the next disassembly sequence step along k different directions which are uniformly scattered toward Pareto frontier, as mentioned in section 4.2.

In disassembly planning, for k different search directions, the local updating function $\tau_t(i, j)$ can be represented as in Eq. (10):

$$\tau_t(i,j)=(1-a)\,\tau_t(i,j)+a\tau_0(i,j),\ t\ \ [1,k] \quad (10)$$

And for k different search directions, the global updating function in ACO can be represented as in Eq. (11):

$$\tau_t(i,j)=(1-\beta)\,\tau_t(i,j)+\beta\Delta\tau_t(i,j),\ t\ \ [1,k], \quad (11)$$

Where,

$$\Delta\tau_t(i,j)=\begin{cases}F_{t\,(\mathrm{gb})}, & \text{if step}(i,j)\in \text{global best disassemblysequence}\\ 0, & \text{otherwise}\end{cases}$$

$F_{t\,(gb)} = Z/(1+W_{t1}N_1+W_{t2}N_2+W_{t3}N_3)$, $t\in[1, k]$, Z is a constant parameter used to adjust the added pheromone level in the step(i, j), and N_1, N_2, N_3 are number of orientation change, number of tool change, and number of disassembly operation change in current global best disassembly sequence, respectively. After local updating and global updating of the pheromone, $\tau_t(i, j)$ is the quantity of pheromone deposited on the disassembly sequence step from Part i to Part j for the search direction t ($t\in[1, k]$).

From the above, it can be seen that for different search directions, the selection probability that ant z select the disassembly sequence step from Part i to Part j could be different due to the quantity of pheromone deposited and the heuristic value.

The overall ACO algorithm with multiple search directions for disassembly planning is proposed as follows:

Algorithm: Overall ACO algorithm for disassembly planning

Step 1. Set the number of factors (objectives) n, and set the number of levels of each factor (search directions) k; derive the parameter σ from Table 1;

Step 2. Conclude the weight matrix using Eq.(4), Eq.(5) and Eq.(6);

Step 3. For the assembly consisting of m parts, place k ants on each of the q parts that can be initially disassembled;

Step 4. Set initial quantity of pheromone on each disassembly step as $\tau_t(i, j)=c$;

Step 5. Set the maximal cycle number Nc(max), and let the cycle number Nc =1;

Step 6. For search direction t ($t\in[1, k]$), let t=1;

Step 7. For the ant Z that is searching the route along the direction t, if the ant z has not completed the visit from the first part to the last one, calculate the selection probability $P_{z(t)}(i, j)$ using Eq.(8), where, Part j belong to the remaining parts in the product that have the feasible disassembly direction at this stage;

Step 8. Select the Part j as the next part to be disassembled using roulette-wheel selection method;

Step 9. Move the ant Z to the new position - Part j;

Step 10. Locally update the pheromone level on the disassembly sequence step from Part i to Part j by Eq. (10);

Step 11. If the ant z has completed the visit from the first part to the last one, go to Step 12; else, go to Step 7;

Step 12. Globally update the pheromone level on the best disassembly sequence found so far by Eq. (11);

Step 13. Let t=t+1, if $t<k$, go to Step 7; else, go to step 14;

Step 14. Let $Nc = Nc$ +1, if $Nc< Nc$(max), go to Step 6; else, go to Step 15;

Step 15. Output the non-dominated solutions found by the ants.

5. Case study and discussion

The proposed disassembly planning approach with ant colony optimization algorithm has been implemented using Visual C++ 6.0. In this section, an assembly product [12] (shown in Fig. 2) is used to validate the proposed approaches.

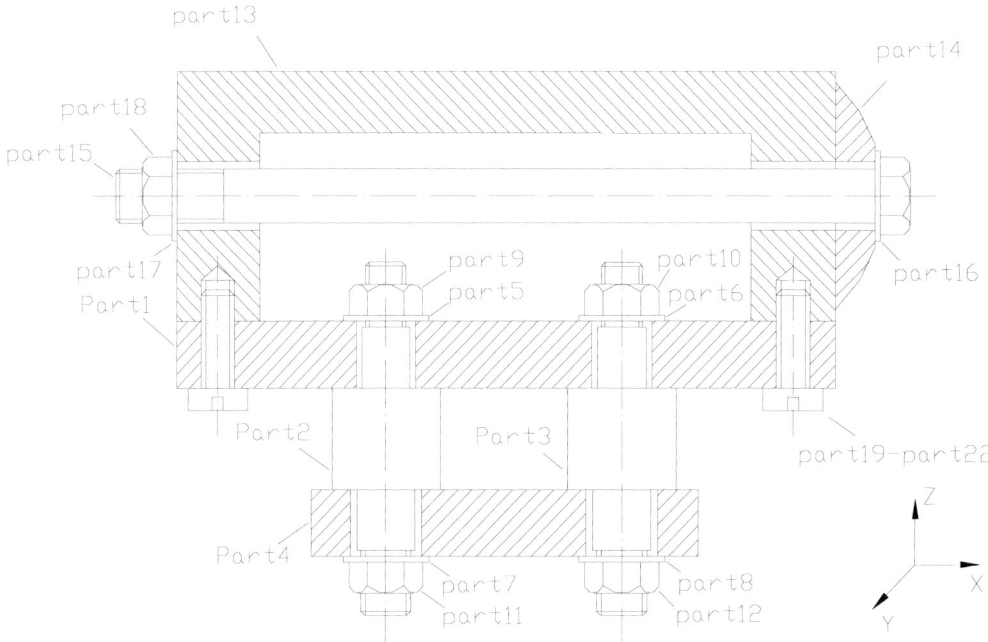

Fig. 2. An assembly consisting of 22 parts

5.1 Case study

In this case, there are 3 objectives to be optimized, and the search directions k is set as 5, then the parameter σ can be derived from Table 1 as: $\sigma = 2$. From Eq. (4) and Eq. (5), the uniform matrix U(3, 5) can be derived as follows:

$$U(3,5)=[U_{i,j}]_{5\times 3} = \begin{bmatrix} 2 & 3 & 5 \\ 3 & 5 & 4 \\ 4 & 2 & 3 \\ 5 & 4 & 2 \\ 1 & 1 & 1 \end{bmatrix}$$

From Eq. (6) and Eq. (7), the weight matrix can be derived as follows:

$$[W_{i,j}]_{5\times 3} = \begin{bmatrix} 1/5 & 3/10 & 1/2 \\ 1/4 & 5/12 & 1/3 \\ 4/9 & 2/9 & 3/9 \\ 5/11 & 4/11 & 2/11 \\ 1/3 & 1/3 & 1/3 \end{bmatrix}$$

For 7 parts that can be initially disassembled in this case, five ants are placed on each part, and each ant will search the route along one of five directions respectively. Based on some reference works [16] [17], some parameters for ACO algorithm are set as follows: The initial quantity of pheromone on each disassembly step is set as $\tau_0 = 0.5$; the pheromone decay parameter a and β are set as 0.1; the parameter λ is set as 0.8. Through the experiment in the case study, the maximal cycle number $Nc(\max)$ is set as 500, and the constant parameter used to adjust the added pheromone level Z is set as 3.

In this case, the part 2, part 3 and part 15 have similar geometric shape and dimension, so they can be grasped with the same tool - chuck in the disassembly process, and this tool is assigned with the number 2 in this case. Similarly, the other parts can be grouped according to their geometric shape, dimension and weight, and can be grasped with different tool with different tool number, as shown in Table 2. For the operation type, part 19, part 20, part 21 and part 22 can be unscrewed with the screw driver in disassembly process, so these four parts are assigned with the same operation type (number 2) in this case, similarly, part 9, part 10, part 11, part 12 and part 18 can be unscrewed with the wrench (operation type number 1) in this case, the other parts do not need any tool to unfasten in disassembly process, so they are assigned with the operation type (number 0) in this case, as shown in Table 2.

Part No.	1	2	3	4	5	6	7	8	9	10	11	12	13	14	15	16	17	18	19	20	21	22
Tool type	1	2	2	1	3	3	3	3	4	4	4	4	1	5	2	3	3	4	6	6	6	6
Operation type	0	0	0	0	0	0	0	0	1	1	1	1	0	0	0	0	0	1	2	2	2	2

Table 2. Tool type and operation type of each part in the assembly

(1) Test 1

In test 1, the evolution test with 5 uniformly scattered search directions is carried out 20 times, and the result is shown in Table 3 [19]. All the 20 trials are converged to the feasible disassembly sequences, during which, 4 trials get 2 non-dominated solution, 8 trials get 3 non-dominated solutions, and 8 trials get 4 non-dominated solutions.

Total trials	**Trials that get 2 non-dominated solutions**	**Trials that get 3 non-dominated solutions**	**Trials that get 4 non-dominated solutions**
20	4	8	8

Table 3. 20 trial results in Test 1

In above test results, 4 non-dominated solutions found in a trial are shown in Table 4 [19].

Non-dominated solution No.	**Orientation changes**	**Tool changes**	**Operation changes**
1	4	7	6
2	3	8	7
3	2	9	5
4	4	8	5

Table 4. Test results of a trial in Test 1

In the above non-dominated solutions, the disassembly sequence of non-dominated solution No.4 is given as follows:

18-20-22-21-19-12-11-15-13-9-10-6-5-1-14-16-17-8-7-4-2-3, the sequence started from the part No.18, with the search direction (W_1=1/4, W_2=5/12, W_3=1/3), and it has 4 orientation changes, 8 tool changes, and 5 operation changes.

For other non-dominated solutions, the non-dominated solution No. 1 has 4 orientation changes, 7 tool changes, and 6 operation changes, with the search direction (W_1=4/9, W_2=2/9, W_3=3/9); the non-dominated solution No. 2 has 3 orientation changes, 8 tool changes, and 7 operation changes, with the search direction (W_1=1/5, W_2=3/10, W_3=1/2); the non-dominated solution No. 3 has 2 orientation changes, 9 tool changes, and 5 operation changes, with the search direction (W_1=5/11, W_2=4/11, W_3=2/11).

To evaluate the evolution performance for 500 generations, in this case, the equation $F= 3/(1+W_1N_1+W_2N_2+W_3N_3)$ is used to record the fitness value of the sequence, where, N_1, N_1, N_3 are the number of orientation changes, number of tool changes, and number of operation changes, respectively, and W_1, W_2, W_3 are the weight for each of above three objectives, respectively. The evolution performance for 500 generations of the sequence in the search direction (W_1=1/4, W_2=5/12, W_3=1/3) is shown as Fig.3 [19].

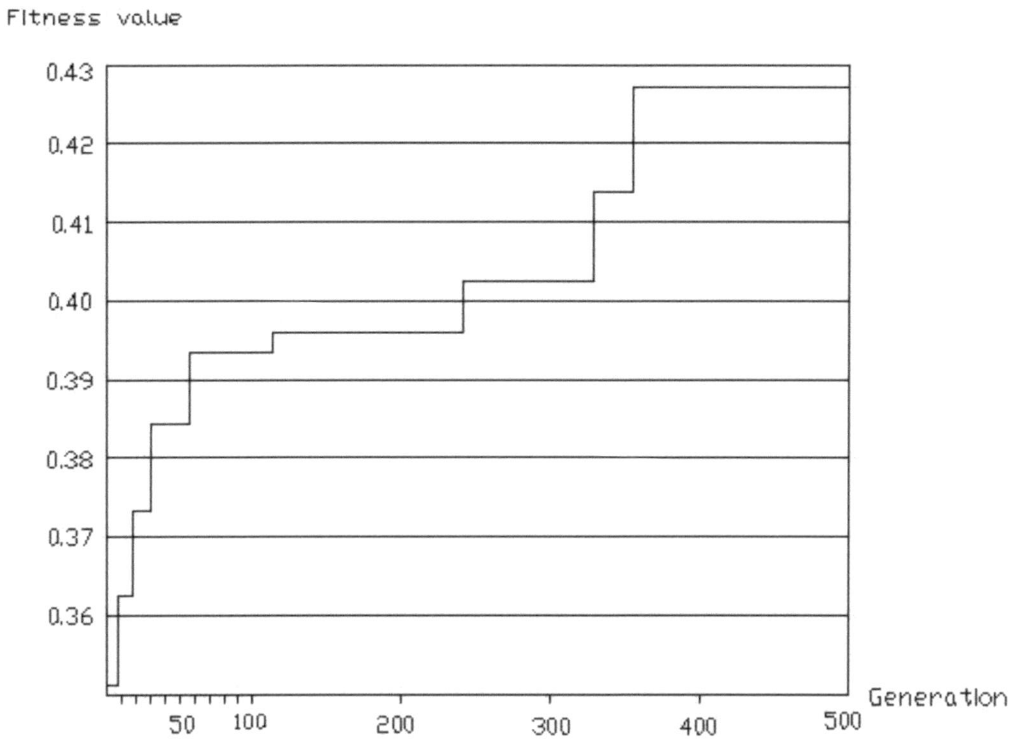

Fig. 3. The evolution performance for 500 generations

(2) Test 2

For comparison with Test 1, only one fixed search direction (W_1=1/4, W_2=5/12, W_3=1/3) is used in Test 2 to guide the ants to search the route. With the same setting of the other parameters, the evolution result is shown in Table 5 [19]. All the 20 trials are converged to the feasible disassembly sequences, during which, 11 trials get 1 non-dominated solution, 8 trials get 2 non-dominated solutions, and 1 trial get 3 non-dominated solutions.

Total trials	Trials that get 1 non-dominated solutions	Trials that get 2 non-dominated solutions	Trials that get 3 non-dominated solutions
20	11	8	1

Table 5. 20 trial results in Test 1

5.2 Discussion

The above two evolution test results show, compared with the ant colony algorithm with only one search direction, the ant colony algorithm with multiple uniformly scattered search directions can be easier to find more non-dominated solutions in one trial, this is probably due to that in the later algorithm, at each step, the ants are guided along the uniformly scattered search directions toward Pareto frontier, so the ants have more chance to find more non-dominated solutions located in the Pareto frontier.

Because the assembly sequence can be concluded by reversing the disassembly sequence, so the proposed approach can be used to derive the assembly sequence in the mean time. Compared with the assembly planning approach with multi-objective genetic algorithm with the same case study [12], the approach with ant colony algorithm is more stable and faster, all of the 20 trials can find the feasible disassembly sequence, and the average run time is 6-8 seconds to converge to a global optimal or near global optimal sequence, however, for the 20 trials using assembly planning approach with multi-objective genetic algorithm, at least 2 trials cannot find the feasible assembly sequence, and the average run time is 20-25 seconds to converge to a global optimal or near-global optimal sequence. This difference could be analyzed as follows: in the disassembly planning approach with ant colony algorithm, the ants search the route step by step, and only the dismountable part can be selected by the ants, so it can avoid the infeasible solution easily, and this can also help find the feasible solution quickly. However, in the assembly planning approach with genetic algorithm, the initial solutions are randomly generated as the whole sequence, there could be much assembly interference due to the precedence constraints, and these solutions are evolved as the whole sequence by genetic operators in the later stage, this could cost much time to repair and evolve the solution to a feasible and optimal solution, and sometimes they can not be evolved to the feasible solutions due to this highly constrained combinatory problem. So, from the above analysis, it can be seen that the disassembly planning approach with ant colony algorithm could be more efficient than the approach with genetic algorithm.

6. Conclusion

In order to achieve green manufacturing effectively, this chapter presents a multi-objective disassembly planning approach with ant colony optimization algorithm. Three objectives in disassembly process are optimized concurrently to get the optimal or near optimal disassembly sequence in this work. In order to guide the ants to search comprehensively and find more feasible non-dominated solutions for decision making, uniform design is used for establishing a multi-objective searching algorithm, and an ant colony optimization algorithm for disassembly planning is developed based on the above searching algorithm. Through the case study and the comparison with the approach using genetic algorithm, it can be verified that the proposed multi-objective disassembly planning approach with ant colony optimization algorithm is more stable, faster and efficient for finding more feasible non-dominated solutions.

7. References

[1] Guo W. X., Liu Z. F., Liu G. F., Pan X. Y., and Huang H. H. Disassembly sequence planning based on modularization. Journal of Computer-Aided Design and Computer Graphics, 2005, vol.17, no.3, pp.498-504.

[2] Chung C, and Peng, Q. J. An integrated approach to selective-disassembly sequence planning. Robotics and Computer-Integrated Manufacturing, 2005, vol.21, no.4-5, pp.475-485.

[3] Torres F., Puente S. T., and Aracil, R. Disassembly planning based on precedence relations among assemblies. International Journal of Advanced Manufacturing Technology, 2003, vol.21, no.5, pp.317-327.

[4] Das S. K., and Naik S. Process planning for product disassembly. International Journal of Production Research, 2002, vol.40, no.6, pp.1335-1355.

[5] Dong T. Y., Zhang L., Tong R. F., and Dong J. X. A hierarchical approach to disassembly sequence planning for mechanical product. International Journal of Advanced Manufacturing Technology, 2006, vol.30, no.5-6, pp.507-520.

[6] Veerakamolmal P., and Gupta S. M. A case-based reasoning approach for automating disassembly process planning. Journal of Intelligent Manufacturing, 2002, vol.13, no.1, pp.47-60.

[7] Andres C., Lozano, S., and Adenso D. B. Disassembly sequence planning in a disassembly cell context. Robotics and Computer-Integrated Manufacturing, 2007, vol.23, no.6, pp.690-695.

[8] Rai R., Rai V., Tiwari M. K., and Allada V. Disassembly sequence generation: a Petri net based heuristic approach. International Journal of Production Research, 2002, vol.40, no.13, pp.3183-3198.

[9] Smith, G. C., and Smith, S. S. F. An enhanced genetic algorithm for automated assembly planning. Robotics and Computer Integrated Manufacturing, 2002, vol.18, no.5-6, pp.355-364.

[10] Lazzerini, B., and Marcelloni, F. A genetic algorithm for generating optimal assembly plans. Artificial Intelligence in Engineering, 2000, vol.14, pp.319-329.

[11] Chen, S. F., and Liu, Y. J. An adaptive genetic assembly-sequence planner. International Journal of Computer Integrated Manufacturing, 2001, vol.14, no.5, pp.489-500.

[12] Lu C., Fuh J. Y. H., and Wong Y. S. An enhanced assembly planning approach using a multi-objective genetic algorithm. Proceedings of the Institution of Mechanical Engineers, Part B: Journal of Engineering Manufacture, 2006, vol.220, no.2, pp.255-272.

[13] Kongar E., and Gupta S. M. Disassembly sequencing using genetic algorithm. International Journal of Advanced Manufacturing Technology, 2006, vol.30, no.5-6, pp.497–506.

[14] McMullen P. R. An ant colony optimization approach to addressing JIT sequencing problem with multiple objectives. Artificial Intelligence in Engineering, 2001, vol.15, pp.309-317.

[15] Rossi A., and Dini G. Flexible job-shop scheduling with routing flexibility and separable setup times using ant colony optimisation method. Robotics and Computer Integrated Manufacturing, 2007, vol. 23, no.5, pp.503-516.

[16] Wang J. F., Liu J. H., and Zhong Y. F. A novel ant colony algorithm for assembly sequence planning. International Journal of Advanced Manufacturing Technology, 2005, vol.25, no.11-12, pp.1137-1143.

[17] Failli F, and Dini G. Ant colony systems in assembly planning: a new approach to sequence detection and optimization. Proceedings of the 2nd CIRP International Seminar on Intelligent Computation in Manufacturing Engineering, 2000, pp.227-232.

[18] McGovern S. M., and Gupta S. M. Ant colony optimization for disassembly sequencing with multiple objectives. International Journal of Advanced Manufacturing Technology, 2006, vol.30, no.5-6, pp.481-496.

[19] Lu C., Huang H. Z., Fuh J.Y.H. and Wong Y.S. A multi-objective disassembly planning approach with ant colony optimization algorithm. Proceedings of the Institution of Mechanical Engineers, Part B: Journal of Engineering Manufacture, 2008, vol. 222, no.11, pp.1465-1474.

[20] Fang K. T., and Wang Y. Number-Theoretic Methods in Statistics, London, U.K.: Chapman & Hall, 1994.

[21] Dini, G., and Santochi, M. Automated sequencing and subassembly detection in assembly planning. Annals of the CIRP, 1992, vol.41, no.1, pp.1-4.

APPENDIX

Notation

$D_d(P_i S_m)$ represented as $\sum P_{ij}$, $P_j \in S_m$

I_d the interference matrix for assembly direction d

N_1 number of orientation change,

N_2 number of tool change,

N_3 number of disassembly operation change

Nc cycle number

Nc(max) maximal cycle number

$P_z(i, j)$ the probability that ant z select next node j

$P_{z(t)}(i, j)$ the probability that ant z select the disassembly sequence step from Part i to Part j in a given search direction t

$U_{i,j}$ the level of the factor j in the ith combination

Z a constant parameter used to adjust the added pheromone level in the step(i, j)

α a parameter which determines the pheromone volatility on the edge from node i to node j

β the pheromone decay parameter

$\tau(i,j)$ the quantity of pheromone deposited on the edge from node i to node j

$\tau_0(i,j)$ the initial pheromone level on the edge

$\tau_t(i, j)$ the quantity of pheromone deposited on the disassembly sequence step from Part i to Part j in search direction t

$\eta(i,j)$ the heuristic information corresponding to the edge from node i to node j
$\eta_t(i, j)$ the heuristic value corresponding to the disassembly step from Part i to Part j in search direction t
λ the parameter that determine the relative importance of $\tau(i,j)$ versus $\eta(i,j)$

Part 2

Applications

10

Optimizing Laminated Composites Using Ant Colony Algorithms

Mahdi Abachizadeh and Masoud Tahani
Department of Mechanical Engineering
Ferdowsi University of Mashhad
Iran, Islamic Republic of

1. Introduction

The high stiffness to weight ratio as well as the possibility of tuning mechanical properties by designing proper fiber orientation and stacking sequence are the key attributes of laminated composites. Hence, they are inevitable candidates against isotropic materials for modern structures especially in aerospace and marine industries. A powerful optimization tool is therefore essential to determine the optimum geometry and lay-up.

1.1 Optimization objectives

Weight, cost, deflection, stress and natural frequencies are general design criteria investigated in laminated structures. Weight and cost minimization, normally being correlated, are the most important design objectives. Decreasing the deflection of structures or maintaining it in safe ranges is also often requested. This goal is generally associated with controlling the maximum amounts of stress or attempting to achieve an optimal pattern of stress distribution. Natural frequency maximization, especially the fundamental one, is of importance in the design of laminates to decrease the risk of resonance caused by external excitations. Frequently, most of the mentioned aspects are tightly connected so multi-objective formulation or considering them as constraints is indispensable.
Besides shape, topology and size optimization applicable to all kinds of structures, number and thickness of layers as well as fiber orientations can be directly considered as design variables to optimize the design objectives in laminated composites. In addition, it is an effective discipline to hybridize the structure by employing high-stiffness and more expensive material in the outer layers and inexpensive low-stiffness material in the inner ones. Hence, Rigidity and material cost remain at reasonable levels. Also, the designer may make use of number of core and surface layers as supplementary optimization variables.

1.2 Optimization levels

Laminated structures optimized in papers are of considerable range of intricacy, nevertheless can be categorized as three main groups. In the first, classical structures such as beams or plates are optimized where generally a closed-form solution to the mechanical analysis is available. As a result, the designer can benefit direct calculation of objective functions. The results reported in these cases are of great value in initial design steps of real-

world applications. Also, when a new optimization method is to be benchmarked, these cases are logically preferred since several iterative evaluations with different parameter settings are necessary. In this group, laminates variables are normally employed and not the geometrical ones.
Structures with average level of complexity are clustered in the second category. Studies on laminated pressure vessels or auto parts such as drive shaft or leaf spring (Shokrieh & Rezaei, 2003) can be referred. The mechanical analysis is regularly performed using FEM packages and the optimization is done using their embedded optimizing tools or independent integrated codes. Both geometrical and laminates variables might be engaged though composites are usually modeled as solid orthotropic structures.
In the final group, assembled systems with multiple design variables are considered. Chassis (Rastogi, 2004), door panels, roof (Botkin, 2000) or hood in automobiles as well as plane wings are typical cases (Venkataraman & Haftka, 2004). Even optimization of fully assembled vehicles or space structures including up to 50000 design variables has been reported (Vanderplaats, 2002). Obviously, analysis in such levels calls for large or very large scale optimization procedures. Additionally, especially developed packages are required to handle the burden of calculations.

1.3 Optimization methods

In the last forty years, nearly all classes of optimization algorithms have been employed for designing laminated composites (Ghiasi et al., 2009). The early attempts have been done using graphical techniques. Gradient-based methods include considerable number of papers mostly earlier ones; while direct methods particularly heuristic algorithms compile the major group of papers. Genetic algorithm (GA) has been the main accepted approach whereas its counterparts such as simulated annealing (SA), Tabu search (TS), scatter search and finally ant colony and bee colony methods have got smaller shares.
In a laminated structure, type and material of each ply are discrete variables while the fiber angles may have any orientations from -90 to 90 degrees. The stacking of plies is also a problem of combinatorial type. In most of papers, fiber angles are considered discrete and hence the whole optimization problem has been tackled using discrete versions of algorithms. It is of course noteworthy to remind that in most real engineering applications, it is reasonable to make use of standard layers with certain thicknesses and limited number of angles. Here, it will be explained later how problems like this with mixed variables can be formulated using ant colony methods. In addition, the results obtained by considering discrete versus mixed variables will be comprehensively discussed for benchmark problems of laminates design.

2. Ant Colony Optimization (ACO)

2.1 Introduction

Inspired by the collective behavior of real ant colonies, Ant System (AS) algorithm was introduced by Marco Dorigo in 1992. The developed metaheuristic named as ant colony system (ACS) was later presented in 1997 by Dorigo and Gambardella for solving the traveling salesman problem (TSP). Up to now, the algorithm has been extensively and successfully applied on many combinatorial problems such as quadratic assignment, vehicle routing and job-shop scheduling (Dorigo & Stutzle, 2004). In the field of structural and mechanical engineering, published papers have been rapidly emerging in the last 5 years.

Trusses (Serra & Venini, 2006), frames (Camp et al., 2005), and manufacturing processes (Vijayakimar et al., 2003) are among the cases optimized using different versions of ant colony algorithms.

Regarding laminated structures, the first study was done by Yang et al (2006). They tried to find optimal orientations of carbon fibers in CFPR composites which were used to reinforce precracked concrete structures. Abachizadeh and Tahani (2007) optimized hybrid laminates for minimum cost and weight using ACS and Pareto techniques. Later, they performed multi-objective optimization of hybrid laminates for maximum fundamental frequency and minimum cost using ACS (2009). Lay-up design of laminated panels for maximization of buckling load with strength constraints was studied by Aymerich and Serra (2008) and the results demonstrated improvement over GA and TS results. A simply supported composite laminate was investigated for optimal stacking sequence under strength and buckling constraints by Bloomfield et al. (2010). They compared the performance of GA, ACS and particle swarm optimization (PSO) methods assuming both discrete and continuous ply orientations. It was claimed that for discrete design spaces, ACS performs better but when it comes to continuous design spaces, PSO outperforms the two other techniques.

For a hybrid laminated plate with mixed domain of solution including fiber angles as continuous and number of surface (or core) layers as integer discrete variables, Abachizadeh et al. (2010) showed that an extension of ACO for continuous domains called ACO_R method proposed by Socha and Dorigo (2008) results in improved designs against GA and ACS. In an industrial application, Hudson et al. (2010) described the appliance of ACO algorithm to the multiple objective optimization of a rail vehicle floor sandwich panel to reduce material as well as cost. A modified ant colony algorithm with novel operators called multi-city-layer ant colony algorithm (MCLACA) is also presented by Wang et al. (2010) exhibiting more robust and efficient comparing with GA for buckling load maximization of a rectangular laminate.

2.2 Solving problems with continuous or mixed design space

While most of the heuristic methods have been initially proposed to tackle combinatorial optimization problems, many real-world engineering problems include either continuous or mixed variables. Hence, there has been a considerable amount of research to suggest new metaheuristics or adapt the existing ones. The same account for ACO, methods were proposed to handle continuous variables. Although taking inspiration from original ACO and expressing relatively acceptable results, they did not follow its original concept exactly (Abachizadeh and Kolahan, 2007). In the original approach of ant algorithms, each ant constructs the solution incrementally using the set of available solution components defined by the problem formulation. This selection is done with help of probabilistic sampling from a discrete probability distribution. For tackling continuous problems using this method, the continuous domain should be discretized into finite ranges. This is not always an appropriate technique especially if the initial range is wide or the resolution required is high. In such cases, methods which can natively handle continuous variables usually perform better.

Besides minor operators which are different in various versions of ant algorithms, there are two distinct differences about ACO_R in comparison with preceding ones. The first is the shift from using a discrete probability distribution to a continuous one called Probability Distribution Function (PDF). Therefore, each ant instead of selecting from available finite sets, samples a PDF biased toward high quality solutions.

The other variation to the original ACO is the revision of the way pheromone information is stored and updated. The continuous nature of design variables prevents a tabular discrete formation and hence, an archive of solutions similar to what is constructed in Tabu search method is employed.
For problems with mixed domain, two common approaches are available. The first is the discretization of continuous variables and as the problem is modified to a totally discrete one; all direct and heuristic methods are applicable with their original procedures. The other approach is relaxation of discrete variables. First, an index is assigned to any element of discrete set of variables. Henceforward, the discrete variable is treated as a continuous variable. Only before evaluation of objective functions, the obtained values for discrete variables are rounded to the nearest index number. It is remarkable that discrete variables are of different types. Integers, zero-one values, ordered standard values (e.g. cross sections of reinforcements round bars) and categorical variables (e.g. different material candidates for a structure) are the major types. Socha (2008) claims that employing relaxation method for mixed problems by ACO_R when no categorical variables exist results in reasonable outcomes. However, facing categorical variables, he expects poor performance and suggests a new method exclusively developed for mixed domains called ACO_{MV} (Socha, 2008).

2.3 ACO_R procedure

Given an n-dimensional continuous problem, an archive of dimension k is constructed. As shown in Fig. 1, s_j^i denotes the value of the ith variable of the jth solution. The two additional columns are considered for the amount of objective function and a weighting parameter associated with each solution.
At the beginning, the rows of this archive are constructed using randomly generated solutions. The solutions in the archive are always sorted according to their quality i.e., the value of the objective function; hence the position of a solution in the archive always corresponds to its rank and the best solution will be on top. At each iteration and with employing m ants, m new solutions are generated and the best k solutions among m+k solutions are kept i.e. the archive is updated with best solutions found so far. For generating new solutions, each ant chooses probabilistically one of the solutions in the archive:

$$p_j = \frac{\omega_j}{\sum_{r=1}^{k} \omega_r} \tag{1}$$

where ω_j is the weight associated with solution j. As proposed by Socha and Dorigo (2008), the flexible and nonlinear Gaussian function is employed to define this weight:

$$\omega_j = \frac{1}{qk\sqrt{2\pi}} e^{\frac{-(j-1)^2}{2q^2k^2}} \tag{2}$$

where q is a parameter of the algorithm. The ant then takes the value s_j^i and samples its neighborhood for a new value for variable i and repeats this procedure for all variables i=1, …, n using the same jth solution. This is done using a probability density function (PDF). There are different choices to be selected for demonstrating this distribution however Gaussian function is again chosen (Socha, 2008):

$$P(x) = \frac{1}{\sigma\sqrt{2\pi}} e^{\frac{-(x-\mu)^2}{2\sigma^2}} \tag{3}$$

where μ and σ are two other algorithm parameters and should be properly defined. For μ, s_j^i is easily assigned. For σ, we have

$$\sigma = \xi \sum_{r=1}^{k} \frac{\left| s_r^i - s_j^i \right|}{k-1} \tag{4}$$

which is the average distance between the ith variable of the solution s_j and the ith variable of the other solution in the archive multiplied by a parameter ξ. This parameter has an effect similar to the evaporation rate in original ACO i.e. with higher values of ξ, the new solutions are positioned closer to existing solutions of higher ranks.

s_1^1	s_1^2	...	s_1^i	...	s_1^n	$f(s_1)$	ω_1
s_2^1	s_2^2	...	s_2^i	...	s_2^n	$f(s_2)$	ω_2
$\vdots$	$\vdots$	$\vdots$	$\vdots$	$\vdots$	$\vdots$	$\vdots$	$\vdots$
s_j^1	s_j^2		s_j^i		s_j^n	$f(s_j)$	ω_j
$\vdots$	$\vdots$	$\vdots$	$\vdots$	$\vdots$	$\vdots$	$\vdots$	$\vdots$
s_k^1	s_k^2	...	s_k^i	...	s_k^n	$f(s_k)$	ω_k

Fig. 1. The structure of solution archive in ACO$_R$ (Socha, 2008)

3. Benchmark problems

A simply supported symmetric hybrid laminated plate with length a, width b and thickness h in the x, y and z direction, respectively, is considered. Each of the material layers is of equal thickness t and idealized as a homogeneous orthotropic material. The total thickness of the laminate is equal to $h = N \times t$ with N being the total number of the layers. In the analysis presented here, the total thickness of the laminate is kept constant which allows for comparing the performance of designs with equal thicknesses.

The optimal design problem involves selection of optimal stacking sequence of hybrid laminated composite plates to obtain maximum fundamental frequency and minimum cost in a multi-objective process. The design variables engaged are the fiber orientation in each layer and the number of core (or surface) layers while the total number of plies is constant in each problem case. Three benchmark problems with different levels of complexity are optimized and the results of ACO_R (Abachizadeh et al., 2010), ACS (Abachizadeh & Tahani, 2009), GA (Tahani et al., 2005) and SA (Kolahan et al.) are reported. It is tried to evaluate the performance of ant algorithms against GA and SA. The improvements obtained by employing continuous operators are also discussed.

3.1 Analysis of vibration in laminates

The hybrid laminate is made up of N_i inner and N_o outer layers so that $N = N_i + N_o$. The governing equation of motion within the classical laminated plate theory for the described symmetric laminate is given below (Reddy, 2004):

$$D_{11}\frac{\partial^4 w}{\partial x^4} + 4D_{16}\frac{\partial^4 w}{\partial x^3 \partial y} + 2(D_{12} + 2D_{66})\frac{\partial^4 w}{\partial x^2 \partial y^2}$$
$$+4D_{26}\frac{\partial^4 w}{\partial x \partial y^3} + D_{22}\frac{\partial^4 w}{\partial y^4} = \rho h \frac{\partial^2 w}{\partial t^2} \quad (5)$$

where w is the deflection in the z direction, h is the total thickness of the laminate and ρ is the mass density averaged in the thickness direction which is given by:

$$\rho = h^{-1}\int_{-h/2}^{h/2} \rho^{(k)} dz = \frac{1}{N}\sum_{k=1}^{N} \rho^{(k)} \quad (6)$$

where $\rho^{(k)}$ represents the mass density of material in the kth layer. The bending stiffnesses D_{ij} in Eq. (5) are defined as:

$$D_{ij} = \sum_{k=1}^{N} \int_{z_k}^{z_{k+1}} \bar{Q}_{ij}^{(k)} z^2 dz \quad (7)$$

where $\bar{Q}_{ij}^{(k)}$ is the transformed reduced stiffness of the kth layer. The boundary conditions are given by:

$$\begin{aligned} w = 0,\ M_x = 0 \quad \text{at} \quad x = 0, a \\ w = 0,\ M_y = 0 \quad \text{at} \quad y = 0, b \end{aligned} \quad (8)$$

where the moment resultants are defined as:

$$(M_x, M_y) = \int_{-h/2}^{h/2} (\sigma_x, \sigma_y)\, dz \quad (9)$$

It is shown by Nemeth (1986) that in buckling problems, the terms D_{16} and D_{26} which demonstrate the bending-twisting interactions in composite laminates, can be safely neglected if the non-dimensional parameters:

$$\gamma = D_{16}(D_{11}^3 D_{22})^{-1/4}, \quad \delta = D_{26}(D_{11} D_{22}^3)^{-1/4} \quad (10)$$

satisfy the constraints:

$$\gamma \le 0.2, \quad \delta \le 0.2 \quad (11)$$

Due to the analogy between buckling and free vibration analysis, the same constraints are used to reduce the complexity of the problem. Taking into account the governing equation and the boundary conditions in Eq. (8), a general form of solution for w in the natural vibration mode (m,n) is presented as:

$$w(x,y,t)=\sum_{m=1}^{\infty}\sum_{n=1}^{\infty}A_{mn}\sin\frac{m\pi x}{a}\sin\frac{n\pi y}{b}e^{i\omega_{mn}t} \tag{12}$$

where ω_{mn} is the natural frequency of the vibration mode (m,n) and $i=\sqrt{-1}$.
Substituting (12) into (5) yields:

$$\omega_{mn}^2=\frac{\pi^4}{\rho h}\left[D_{11}\left(\frac{m}{a}\right)^4+2(D_{12}+2D_{66})\left(\frac{m}{a}\right)^2\left(\frac{n}{b}\right)^2+D_{22}\left(\frac{n}{b}\right)^4\right] \tag{13}$$

Different mode shapes are obtained by inserting different values of m and n. For computing the fundamental frequency, both are obviously put equal to one.

3.2 Problem I

The fundamental frequency for 16-layered glass/epoxy laminates with various aspect ratios is considered to be maximized. The laminate is not hybrid so the problem is single-objective. The benchmark is chosen from Adali and Verijenco (2001) where laminates made up of 0°, $\pm45^\circ$ and 90° plies are optimized by direct enumeration. Here, the fiber angles are allowed to have any value in the range of $[-90^\circ, 90^\circ]$. Hence, the deviation of the fundamental frequency for laminates with the mentioned restricted angles is obtained from the optimal design. Results achieved using ACS is also presented.

3.3 Problem II

The fundamental frequency for 8-layered graphite/epoxy laminates with various aspect ratios is considered to be maximized. The fiber angles are considered continuous in the range of $[-90^\circ, 90^\circ]$ and the results are compared with a solution where the discrete angles have been selected within the same range with 15-degree increments. Although this problem can be considered an independent benchmark, it has been selected so as to be used in the main multi-objective problem.

3.4 Problem III

The fundamental frequencies and material costs of 8-, 16- and 28-layered hybrid laminates with various aspect ratios is considered to be optimized. The fiber angles are continuous as in problems I and II. The results are compared with a solution where discretized fiber angles, the same as problem II, have been employed. The main objective of this reinvestigation is to find the global solution of the problem considering continuous variables in order to verify whether using standard restricted fiber angles is an acceptable approach.
In problems I and II where single-objective optimization is put into operation, the procedure is straightforward. The only point to consider is the penalty added to the solution candidates which violate the constraints in Eq. (11). Obviously, it should be big enough to remove any chance of being selected.

Problem III deals with multi-objective optimization which calls for its own methods. As the objectives in this study are of different dimensions and their relative importance is case-dependent, the Min-Max method is preferred. In this method, the objective functions are normalized and then the deviation from their single-objective optimums is minimized.
The two objective functions engaged here are numbered as 1 for frequency and 2 for material cost. Satisfaction of constraints is imposed by penalty functions just like the first two problems. The general form of the total objective function subjected to minimization is given by:

$$F = k_1 f_1^2 + k_2 f_2^2 + c_1 g_1^2 + c_2 g_2^2 \tag{14}$$

$$f_1 = \left(\frac{\omega_{\max} - \omega}{\omega_{\max}} \right) \tag{15a}$$

$$f_2 = \left(\frac{\text{cost}}{\text{cost}_{\max}} \right) \tag{15b}$$

$$g_1 = \delta - 0.2 \tag{16a}$$

$$g_2 = \gamma - 0.2 \tag{16b}$$

$$k_1 = k_2 = c_1 = c_2 = 1 \tag{16c}$$

In Eqs. (15a,15b), ω and *cost* are the optimization outcomes. The parameter ω_{max} denotes the maximum fundamental frequency and $cost_{max}$ is the cost both obtained by considering all layers being made up of graphite/epoxy. The numerical values of ω_{max} are in fact the results of problem II which can be used for the corresponding aspect ratios in problem III.
In (16 a - 16c), g_1 and g_2 are the penalty terms explained earlier. The other parameters, k_1, k_2, c_1 and c_2 are sensitivity coefficients which are all set to one.
The material cost can be easily calculated as:

$$\text{cost} = ab\frac{h}{N} g\left(\alpha_o \rho_o N_o + \rho_i N_i\right) \tag{17}$$

where ρ_o and ρ_i are the mass densities of the outer and inner layers, respectively. Instead of real material prices, α_o is employed as a cost factor expressing the cost ratio of surface against core material.

4. Numerical results

The three problems defined in the previous section have been optimized using a code written in Matlab®. The laminates geometrical dimensions are $h = 0.002$ m and $b = 0.25$ m. As stated earlier, the total thickness h is considered constant for different number of layers while ply thickness may vary. This is a little far from being practical but necessary for comparing the performance of equal-thickness designs.

In all the three problems, designs with different aspect ratios defined as a/b are investigated varying from 0.2 to 2 with a 0.2 increment. The properties of materials taken from Tsai and Hahn (1980) are as follows:

Graphite/Epoxy (T300/5208):
E_1=181 GPa, E_2=10.3 GPa, G_{12}=7.71 GPa, υ_{12}=0.28, ρ=1600 kgm^{-3}

Glass/Epoxy (Scotchply1002):
E_1=38.6 GPa, E_2=8.27 GPa, G_{12}=4.14 GPa, υ_{12}=0.26, ρ=1800 kgm^{-3}
Although the mechanical properties particularly stiffness to weight ratio are considerably higher in graphite/epoxy layers with respect to glass/epoxy ones, they are about 8 times more expensive; this way $\alpha_0 = 8$ is assigned.
There are several parameters in ACO_R which should be tuned to maximize the efficiency of the algorithm. Here, k=50 is used as proposed by Socha (2008). The other parameters are set based on some trials for these problems:

$$m = 5 \quad , \quad \xi = 0.9 \quad , \quad q = 10^{-5} \tag{18}$$

Table 1 presents the results obtained by solving problem I using ACS, ACO_R and direct enumeration. Clearly, considering continuous fiber angles, stacking sequences with higher fundamental frequencies are achieved using ACO_R. For aspect ratios of 0.6, 0.8, 1.2, 1.4 and 1.6, angles other than standard angles of 0°, $\pm 45^\circ$ and 90° are needed to construct the optimum laminate. However, the greatest difference in frequency (belonging to aspect ratio of 1.4) is equal to 15 rad/s ≡ 2.6%, which is flawlessly negligible and therefore justifies using configurations exclusively made up of either 0°, $\pm 45^\circ$ or 90° plies.
Table 2 with a similar pattern shows that ACO_R has been again successful in improving designs obtained by ACS. From practical point of view, the maximum deviation belonging to aspect ratio of 0.8 is about 19 rad/s ≡ 1%, which is yet again negligible.
Tables 3-5 show the best results found by ACO_R for 8-, 16- and 28-layered laminates. In addition, the related results obtained by ACS, GA and SA are reported. Since Tahani et al. (2005) and Kolahan et al. (2005) have reported nearly identical solutions for GA and SA; the results are presented as only one alternative against ACS and ACO_R. Considering the values of objective functions, it is clear that ACO_R has outperformed both ACS and GA (as well as SA) or in any case equalized in performance. It could be estimated from the results of Table 2 that for aspect ratios in which ACO_R have been able to find designs with higher fundamental frequencies, improvements in the multi-objective problem can be anticipated. This is further verified observing that all three involved methods could find the optimal number of glass and graphite plies i.e. the cost part of the objective function, nearly for all laminates designs.
Regarding the similarity of fiber angles in Tables 3-5 obtained by ACO_R and in single-objective versions of problem reported in Tables 1-2, we can conservatively claim that ACO_R has found global optima for all aspect ratios. The significance is furthermore highlighted if it is reminded that the problem has been tackled considering continuous domain for design variables which is naturally of higher complexity in comparison to the combinatorial problem of constructing laminates from finite available fiber angles.
In analogous to the results of problems I and II, similar deductions can be presented about the reliability of the approach of utilizing standard fiber angles. The optimum designs

obtained by ACO_R do not demonstrate being more than 3% better than the corresponding designs obtained using discretized fiber angles.
Finally, It is noteworthy to mention that for designs with *N*=28 in problem III which are the most complex problem cases in this paper, the results of ACS and ACO_R are considerably better than GA and SA in most cases which can indicate the efficiency and robustness of ant

$\frac{a}{b}$	θ_{best} by ACO_R	ω_{max} by ACO_R (rad/sec)	θ_{best} by ACS	θ_{best} by enum.	ω_{max} by ACS (rad/sec)
0.2	$[0]_{8s}$	10747	$[0]_{8s}$	$[0]_{8s}$	10747
0.4	$[0]_{8s}$	2776	$[0]_{8s}$	$[0]_{8s}$	2776
0.6	$[6.28]_{8s}$	1305.0	$[0]_{8s}$	$[0]_{8s}$	1304.9
0.8	$[\pm 36.85]_{4s}$	852	$[\pm 45]_{4s}$	$[\pm 45]_{4s}$	843
1	$[\pm 45]_{4s}$	663	$[\pm 45]_{4s}$	$[\pm 45]_{4s}$	663
1.2	$[\pm 51.44]_{4s}$	563	$[\pm 45]_{4s}$	$[\pm 45]_{4s}$	559
1.4	$[\pm 59.16]_{4s}$	506	$[\pm 45]_{4s}$	$[\pm 45]_{4s}$	493
1.6	$[\pm 72.64]_{4s}$	475	$[90]_{8s}$	$[90]_{8s}$	474
1.8	$[90]_{8s}$	463	$[90]_{8s}$	$[90]_{8s}$	463
2	$[90]_{8s}$	455	$[90]_{8s}$	$[90]_{8s}$	455

Table 1. Design for maximum fundamental frequency with *N*=16

$\frac{a}{b}$	θ_{best} by ACO_R	ω_{max} by ACO_R (rad/sec)	θ_{best} by ACS	θ_{best} by enum.	ω_{max} by ACS (rad/sec)
0.2	$[0]_{4s}$	24390	$[0]_{4s}$	$[0]_{4s}$	24390
0.4	$[0]_{4s}$	6170	$[0]_{4s}$	$[0]_{4s}$	6170
0.6	$[\pm 11.64]_{2s}$	2802	$[\pm 15]_{2s}$	$[\pm 15]_{2s}$	2801
0.8	$[\pm 37.34]_{2s}$	1816	$[\pm 30]_{2s}$	$[\pm 30]_{2s}$	1797
1	$[\pm 45]_{2s}$	1413	$[\pm 45]_{2s}$	$[\pm 45]_{2s}$	1413
1.2	$[\pm 51.05]_{2s}$	1199	$[\pm 45]_{2s}$	$[\pm 45]_{2s}$	1189
1.4	$[\pm 58.26]_{2s}$	1078.4	$[\pm 60]_{2s}$	$[\pm 60]_{2s}$	1078.2
1.6	$[\pm 70.34]_{2s}$	1017	$[\pm 75]_{2s}$	$[\pm 75]_{2s}$	1016
1.8	$[90]_{4s}$	1003	$[90]_{4s}$	$[90]_{4s}$	1003
2	$[90]_{4s}$	996	$[90]_{4s}$	$[90]_{4s}$	996

Table 2. Design for maximum fundamental frequency with *N*=8

algorithms against these two known methods in engineering optimization. This is of higher value for ACO_R that has been recently developed and for which few benchmark problems has been presented in the literature.

$\frac{a}{b}$	θ_{best} by ACO_R	θ_{best} by ACS	θ_{best} by GA	N_i by ACO_R, ACS & GA
0.2	$[0]_{4s}$	$[0]_{4s}$	$[0]_{4s}$	6
0.4	$[0]_{4s}$	$[0]_{4s}$	$[0]_{4s}$	6
0.6	$[11.64/6.28_3]_s$	$[15/0/0/0]_s$	$[0/30/-30_2]_s$	6
0.8	$[-37.34/36.85_3]_s$	$[\pm 30]_{2s}$	$[\pm 45_2/-45_2]_s$	6
1	$[\pm 45]_{2s}$	$[\pm 45]_{2s}$	$[\pm 45]_{2s}$	6
1.2	$[-51.05/51.44_3]_s$	$[\pm 45]_{2s}$	$[90/45/\pm 45]_s$	6
1.4	$[-58.26/59.16_3]_s$	$[\pm 60]_{2s}$	$[90/60/-60_2]_s$	6
1.6	$[-70.34/72.64_3]_s$	$[\pm 75]_{2s}$	$[90/-75/60_2]_s$	6
1.8	$[90]_{4s}$	$[90]_{4s}$	$[90]_{4s}$	6
2	$[90]_{4s}$	$[90]_{4s}$	$[90]_{4s}$	6

Table 3a. Optimum stacking sequence for maximum frequency and minimum cost with N=8

$\frac{a}{b}$	ω by ACO_R (rad/sec)	ω by ACS (rad/sec)	ω by GA (rad/sec)	Cost by ACO_R, ACS & GA	F by ACO_R	F by ACS	F by GA
0.2	19093	19093	19093	0.1138	0.1735	0.1735	0.1735
0.4	4844	4844	4844	0.2275	0.1725	0.1725	0.1725
0.6	2210.9	2210.4	2208	0.3413	0.17071	0.17076	0.1716
0.8	1435	1421	1306	0.4550	0.1705	0.1708	0.1710
1	1116	1116	1116	0.5687	0.1705	0.1705	0.1705
1.2	947	940	845	0.6825	0.1705	0.1706	0.2103
1.4	851.8	851.4	816	0.7963	0.17051	0.17054	0.1854
1.6	803.2	802.4	799	0.9100	0.17075	0.17086	0.1724
1.8	790	790	790	1.0238	0.1714	0.1714	0.1714
2	784	784	784	1.1375	0.1720	0.1720	0.1720

Table 3b. Optimum stacking sequence for maximum frequency and minimum cost with N=8

$\frac{a}{b}$	θ_{best} by ACO_R	θ_{best} by ACS	θ_{best} by GA	N_i by ACO_R, ACS & GA
0.2	$[0]_{8s}$	$[0]_{8s}$	$[0]_{8s}$	12
0.4	$[0]_{8s}$	$[0]_{8s}$	$[0/0/\pm15/15/0/-15/0]_s$	12
0.6	$[11.64_2/6.28_6]_s$	$[\pm15/0_6]_s$	$[\pm30]_{4s}$	12
0.8	$[-37.34_2/36.85_6]_s$	$[\pm30]_{4s}$	$[-45/30/\pm45_3]_s$	12
1	$[\pm45]_{4s}$	$[\pm45]_{4s}$	$[\pm45]_{4s}$	12
1.2	$[-51.05_2/51.44_6]_s$	$[\pm45]_{4s}$	$[\pm45/-60/-45/-60_2/-45_2]_s$	12
1.4	$[-58.26_2/59.16_6]_s$	$[\pm60]_{4s}$	$[\pm60]_{4s}$	12
1.6	$[-70.34_2/72.64_6]_s$	$[\pm75]_{4s}$	$[\pm60_3/\pm75]_s$	12
1.8	$[90]_{8s}$	$[90]_{8s}$	$[90]_{8s}$	12
2	$[90]_{8s}$	$[90]_{8s}$	$[90]_{8s}$	12

Table 4a. Optimum stacking sequence for maximum frequency and minimum cost with N=16

$\frac{a}{b}$	ω by ACO_R (rad/sec)	ω by ACS (rad/sec)	ω by GA (rad/sec)	Cost by ACO_R, ACS & GA	F by ACO_R	F by ACS	F by GA
0.2	19093	19093	19093	0.1138	0.1735	0.1735	0.1735
0.4	4844	4844	4829	0.2275	0.1725	0.1725	0.1736
0.6	2210.9	2210.4	2171	0.3413	0.17071	0.17076	0.1768
0.8	1435	1421	1418	0.4550	0.1705	0.1708	0.1714
1	1116	1116	1116	0.5687	0.1705	0.1705	0.1705
1.2	947	940	939	0.6825	0.1705	0.1706	0.1707
1.4	851.8	851.4	851.4	0.7963	0.17051	0.17054	0.17054
1.6	803.2	802.4	796	0.9100	0.17056	0.17086	0.1735
1.8	790	790	790	1.0238	0.1714	0.1714	0.1714
2	784	784	784	1.1375	0.1720	0.1720	0.1720

Table 4b. Optimum stacking sequence for maximum frequency and minimum cost with N=16

$\frac{a}{b}$	θ_{best} by ACO$_R$	θ_{best} by ACS	θ_{best} by GA	N_i by ACO$_R$ &ACS	N_i by GA
0.2	$[0]_{14s}$	$[0]_{14s}$	$[0_{12}/15_2]_s$	22	24
0.4	$[0]_{8s}$	$[0]_{14s}$	$[0/\pm15/0/15/0_2/-15/0_3/15/0_2]_s$	22	24
0.6	$[11.64_3/6.28_{11}]_s$	$[15_3/0_{11}]_s$	$[30_5/45/30_3/-45/\pm30]_s$	22	24
0.8	$[-37.34_3/36.85_{11}]_s$	$[\pm30]_{7s}$	$[\pm45_5/45/30/\pm45]_s$	22	24
1	$[\pm45]_{7s}$	$[\pm45]_{7s}$	$[\pm45]_{7s}$	22	24
1.2	$[-51.05_3/51.44_{11}]_s$	$[\pm45]_{7s}$	$[\pm45_3/60/45_7]_s$	22	24
1.4	$[-58.26_3/59.16_{11}]_s$	$[\pm60]_{7s}$	$[\pm60_3/-45/\pm60_2/\pm45/60]_s$	22	22
1.6	$[-70.34_3/72.64_{11}]_s$	$[\pm75]_{7s}$	$[\pm60_2/75/\pm60/75/60_3/75/60/75]_s$	22	22
1.8	$[90]_{14s}$	$[90]_{14s}$	$[90]_{14s}$	22	22
2	$[90]_{14s}$	$[90]_{14s}$	$[90]_{14s}$	22	22

Table 5a. Optimum stacking sequence for maximum frequency and minimum cost with N=28

$\frac{a}{b}$	ω by ACO$_R$ (rad/sec)	ω by ACS	ω by GA	Cost by ACO$_R$ &ACS	Cost by GA	F by ACO$_R$	F by ACS	F by GA
0.2	18339	18339	16518	0.1039	0.0843	0.1670	0.1670	0.1732
0.4	4565	4565	4145	0.2079	0.1686	0.1657	0.1657	0.1771
0.6	2127.7	2127.2	1889	0.3118	0.2529	0.1631	0.1632	0.1768
0.8	1381	1368	1237	0.4157	0.3371	0.1629	0.1631	0.1673
1	1074	1074	974	0.5196	0.4214	0.1629	0.1629	0.1659
1.2	912	905	820	0.6236	0.5057	0.1628	0.1630	0.1660
1.4	819.9	819.6	818.7	0.7275	0.7275	0.1629	0.1630	0.1632
1.6	773	772	767	0.8314	0.8314	0.1630	0.1633	0.1661
1.8	760	760	760	0.9354	0.9354	0.1641	0.1641	0.1641
2	754	754	754	1.0393	1.0393	0.1649	0.1649	0.1649

Table 5b. Optimum stacking sequence for maximum frequency and minimum cost with N=28

5. Conclusion

The results reported here and in many other papers confidently suggest ant colony optimization as a robust and efficient method compared with other known techniques such as genetic algorithm and simulated annealing. Specifically, design and optimization of laminated structures is a field where ant algorithms are expected to outperform other methods. It is also shown here that ACO_R can successfully formulate problems with mixed domains and yield improvements against discretization process. Moreover, it is concluded that using the standard fiber angles which is a practical advantage in laminates production makes negligible variation of optimal designs with respect to the global optima.

6. References

Abachizadeh, M. & Kolahan, F. (2007). Evaluating the discretization of search space in continuous problems for ant colony optimization, *Proceedings of the 37th International Conference on Computers and Industrial Engineering (ICCIE37)*, Alexandria, Egypt

Abachizadeh, M. & Tahani, M. (2007). Ant colony optimization of hybrid laminates for minimum cost and weight, *Proceedings of 6th International Symposium on Advanced Composites (COMP'07)*, Corfu, Greece

Abachizadeh, M. & Tahani, M. (2009). An ant colony optimization approach to multi-objective optimal design of symmetric hybrid laminates for maximum fundamental frequency and minimum cost. *Structural and Multidisciplinary Optimization*, 37, 367-376

Abachizadeh, M.; Shariat Panahi, M.; Yousefi-Koma, A. & Feiz Dizaji, A. (2010). Multi-objective optimal design of hybrid laminates using continuous ant colony method, *Proceeding of 10th ASME Biennial Conference on Engineering Systems Design and Analysis (ESDA 2010)*, Istanbul, Turkey, July 12-14, 2010

Adali, S. & Verijenko, V.E. (2001). Optimum stacking sequence design of symmetric hybrid laminates undergoing free vibrations. *Composite Structures*, 54, 131–138

Aymerich, F. & Serra, M. (2008). Optimization of laminate stacking sequence for maximum buckling load using the ant colony optimization (ACO) metaheuristic. *Composites: Part A*, 39, 262-272

Bloomfield, M.W.; Herencia, J.E. & Weaver, P.M. (2010). Analysis and benchmarking of meta-heuristic techniques for lay-up optimization. *Computers and Structures*, 88, 272-282

Botkin, M.E. (2000). Modeling and optimal design of a fiber reinforced composite automotive roof. *Engineering with Computers*, 16, 16-23

Camp, C.V.; Bichon, B. & Stovall, S.P. (2005). Design of steel frames using ant colony optimization. *Journal of Structural Engineering*, 131, 369-379

Dorigo, M. (1992). *Optimization, Learning and Natural Algorithms*, Ph.D. thesis, DEI, Politecnico di Milano, Italy (In Italian)

Dorigo, M. & Gambardella, L.M. (1997). Ant colony system: a cooperative learning approach to the traveling salesman problem. *IEEE Transactions on Evolutionary Computation*, 1, 1, 53-66

Dorigo, M. & Stutzle, T. (2004). *Ant Colony Optimization*, MIT Press, Cambridge

Ghiasi, H.; Pasini, D. & Lessard, L. (2009). Optimum stacking sequence design of composite materials Part I: Constant stiffness design. *Composite Structures*, 90, 1-11.

Hudson, C.W.; Carruthers, J.J. & Robinson, M. (2010) Multiple objective optimization of composite sandwich structures for rail vehicle floor panels. *Composite Structures*, 92, 9, 2077-2082.

Kolahan, F.; Tahani, M. & Sarhadi, A. (2005). Optimal design of sandwich composite laminates for minimum cost and maximum frequency using simulated annealing, *Proceedings of Tehran International Conference on Manufacturing Engineering (TICME2005)*, Tehran, Iran

Nemeth, M.P. (1986). Importance of anisotropy on buckling of compression-loaded symmetric composite plates. *Journal of AIAA*, 24, 1831-1835

Rastogi, N. (2004). Stress analysis and lay-up optimization of an all-composite pick-up truck chassis structure. *SAE Transactions*, 113, 5, 660-671

Reddy, J.N. (2004). *Mechanics of Laminated Composite Plates and Shells: Theory and Analysis*, 2nd ed., CRC Press, Boca Raton, FL

Serra, M. & Venini, P. (2006). On some applications of ant colony optimization metaheuristic to plane truss optimization. *Structural and Multidisciplinary Optimization*, 32, 6, 499-506.

Shokrieh, M. & Rezaei, D. (2003). Analysis and optimization of a composite leaf spring. *Composite Structures*, 60, 317-325.

Socha, K., (2008). *Ant Colony Optimization for Continuous and Mixed-variable Domains*, Ph.D. thesis, Universite Libre de Bruxelles, Belgium

Socha, K. & Dorigo, M. (2008). Ant colony optimization for continuous domains. *European Journal of Operational Research*, 185, 3, 1155-1173

Tahani, M; Kolahan, F. & Sarhadi, A. (2005). Genetic algorithm for multi-objective optimal design of sandwich composite laminates with minimum cost and maximum frequency, *Proceedings of International Conference on Advances in Materials, Product Design and Manufacturing Systems (ICMPM-2005)*, pp. 741-748, Sathyamangalam, India

Tsai, S.W. & Hahn, H. (1980). *Introduction to Composite Materials*, Wesport Technomic Publishing Company, Connecticut

Wang, W.; Guo, S. & Chang, N. (2010). A modified ant colony algorithm for the stacking sequence optimization of a rectangular laminate. *Structural and Multidisciplinary Optimization*, 41, 711-720

Vanderplaats, G.N. (2002). *Very Large Scale Optimization*, NASA contractor report

Venkataraman, S. & Haftka, R.T. (2004). Structural optimization complexity: What has Moore's law done for us? *Structural and Multidisciplinary Optimization*, 28, 375-387

Vijayakumar, K.; Prabhaharan, G.; Asokan, P. & Saravanan, R. (2003). Optimization of multi-pass turning operations using ant colony system. *International Journal of Machine Tools & Manufacture*, 43, 1633–1639

Yang, X.S.; Lees, J.M. & Morley, C.T. (2006). Application of virtual ant algorithms in the optimization of CFRP shear strengthened precracked structures. *LNCS 3991*, 834-837.

11

Ant Colony Optimization for Water Resources Systems Analysis – Review and Challenges

Avi Ostfeld
Technion-Israel Institute of Technology
Israel

1. Introduction

Water resources systems analysis is the science of developing and applying mathematical operations research methodologies to water resources systems problems comprised of reservoirs, rivers, watersheds, groundwater, distribution systems, and others, as standalone or integrated systems, for single or multiobjective problems, deterministic or stochastic.

The scientific and practical challenge in dealing quantitatively with water resources systems analysis problems is in taking into consideration from a systems perspective, social, economic, environmental, and technical dimensions, and integrating them into a single framework for trading-off in time and in space competitive objectives. Inherently, such problems involve modelling of water quantity and quality for surface water, groundwater, water distribution systems, reservoirs, rivers, lakes, and other systems as stand alone or combined systems.

Numerous models for water resources systems analysis have been proposed during the past four decades. A possible classification for those is into: (1) methods based on decomposition in which an "inner" linear/quadratic problem is solved for a fixed low-dimension decision variables set, while that set is altered at an "outer" problem using a gradient or a sub-gradient technique (e.g., Alperovits and Shamir, 1977; Quindry et al. 1979, 1981; Kessler and Shamir, 1989, 1991; Eiger et al., 1994; Ostfeld and Shamir, 1996), (2) methods which utilize a straightforward non-linear programming formulation (e.g., Watanatada, 1973; Shamir, 1974; Karatzas and Finder, 1996), (3) methods based on linking a simulation program with a general nonlinear optimization code (e.g., Ormsbee and Contractor, 1981; Lansey and Mays, 1989), and (4) more recently, methods which employ evolutionary techniques such as genetic algorithms (e.g., Simpson et. al, 1994; Savic and Walters, 1997; Espinoza et al., 2005; Espinoza and Minsker, 2006), Cross Entropy (e.g., Perelman and Ostfeld, 2008), or the shuffled frog leaping algorithm (e.g., Eusuff and Lansey, 2003).

Among the above classification ant colony optimization (ACO) belongs to category (4) of evolutionary techniques. Although some studies have already been conducted (e.g., Maier et al., 2003, Ostfeld and Tubaltzev, 2008; Christodoulou and Ellinas, 2010) in which ant colony optimization was utilized, the employment of ACO in water resources systems studies is still in its infancy.

This book chapter reviews the current literature of ACO for water resources systems analysis, and suggests future directions and challenges for using ACO for solving water resources systems problems [parts of this Chapter are based on Ostfeld and Tubaltzev (2008), with permission from the American Society of Civil Engineers (ASCE)].

2. Ant Colony Optimization

Proposed by Dorigo (1992), Ant Colony Optimization (ACO) is an evolutionary stochastic combinatorial computational discipline inspired by the behaviour of ant colonies.

One of the problems studied by ethologists is to understand how ants which are almost completely blind could manage to establish shortest paths from their nest to their feeding sources and back. It was found that ants communicate information by leaving pheromone tracks. A moving ant leaves, in varying quantities, some pheromone on the ground to mark its way. While an isolated ant moves essentially at random, an ant encountering a previously laid trail is able to detect it and decide with high probability to follow it, thus reinforcing the track with its own pheromone. The collective behavior that emerges is thus a positive feedback: where the more the ants following a track, the more attractive that track becomes for being followed; thus the probability with which an ant chooses a path increases with the number of ants that previously chose the same path. This elementary behavior inspired the development of ACO (Dorigo, 1992).

ACO has been already successfully applied to a number of NP hard combinatorial optimization problems such as the traveling salesman problem (TSP) or the quadratic assignment problem (QAP), but still to only a limited number of studies in water resources systems analysis.

Consider a colony of ants moving on a graph G (N, E) where N is the set of nodes (decision points) i = 1, ..., N and E is the set of edges (links) e = 1,...E, the basic scheme of ACO (following Dorigo et al., 1996), involves the following steps:

1. The probability of the k-th ant situated at node i at stage t, to choose an outgoing edge e is:

$$P_{e,i}^{k}(t) = \frac{\left[\tau_e(t)\right]^{\alpha} \left[\eta_e\right]^{\beta}}{\sum\limits_{e \in i^{+}(t)} \left[\tau_e(t)\right]^{\alpha} \left[\eta_e\right]^{\beta}} \tag{1}$$

where: $P_{e,i}^{k}(t)$ = the probability of the k-th ant at node i at stage t, to choose edge e; $\tau_e(t)$ = the pheromone intensity (quantity per unit of length) present on edge e at stage t; $i^{+}(t)$ = the set of outgoing edges (i.e., all the outgoing allowable directions) from node i at stage t; η_e, α, and β = parameters (η_e = *visibility*, α, β = parameters that control the relative importance of the pheromone amount present on edge e at stage t, see Dorigo et al., 1996).

2. The pheromone intensity at $\tau_e(t+1)$ is updated using (2) – (4):

$$\tau_e(t+1) = \rho\,\tau_e(t) + \Delta\tau_e(t+1) \tag{2}$$

$$\Delta\tau_e(t+1) = \sum_{k=1}^{A} \Delta\tau_e^{k}(t+1) \tag{3}$$

$$\Delta\tau_e^{k}(t+1) = \begin{bmatrix} \dfrac{R}{C_k(t)} & \text{if the k-th ant used edge e at stage t} \\ 0 & \text{otherwise} \end{bmatrix} \tag{4}$$

where: ρ = a coefficient less than one representing a pheromone *evaporation* intensity between consecutive stages; A = total number of ants; R = a pheromone reward constant;

and $C_k(t)$ = the solution cost generated by ant k during stage t [e.g., the length of a complete k-th ant tour at the traveling salesman problem (TSP) at stage t].
3. Generation of one solution [i.e., $C_k(t)$] by the k-th ant at stage t is termed an *iteration* while the completion of all ants' solutions at stage t denotes a *cycle*. Ants thus complete iterations by generating solutions, and once all ants have produced solutions, a *cycle* (i.e., a stage) has been completed. The algorithm parameters are: α, β, η_e, ρ, R; the number of ants A, and a penalty induced for non-feasible solutions.
A pseudo-code for an ant colony optimization algorithm as described above, can take the following form:

Initialization

- Set: $t = 0; \tau_e(0), \Delta\tau_e(0) = 0 \; \forall \; e \in E$; distribute the A ants (indexed k) on the N nodes (decision points).
- Set the ant colony parameters: α, β, η_e, ρ, and R.
- Compute $P_{e,i}^k(0) \; \forall \; e \in E$ using (1).

Main scheme

REPEAT

Repeat

- For the k-th ant situated at node i generate a solution by performing a random walk on G (N, E) using $P_{e,i}^k(t)$ (e.g., for the TSP visit all towns exactly once).
- Compute $C_k(t)$ - the solution cost produced by the k-th ant.

Until A (total number of ants)

Update the best cost solution found.

Compute $\tau_e(t+1) \; \forall \; e \in E$ using (2) - (4).

Compute $P_{e,i}^k(t+1) \; \forall \; e \in E$ using (1).

Set: $t \leftarrow t+1$

UNTIL T_{max}, where: T_{max} = maximum number of cycles (stages); or until no improvement of the best solution is encountered at some consecutive stages.

3. Literature review

Ant colony optimization is a new evolutionary computational discipline to the water resources systems community. Only few models were developed thus far. Attempts were made to employ ant colony for reservoir operation, groundwater long term monitoring, for some general water resources problems, and in particular for water distribution systems design and operation. This section incorporates a brief description of these efforts.

3.1 Reservoirs optimal operation

Kumar and Reddy (2006) proposed an Ant Colony Optimization algorithm for a multi-purpose reservoir system. To tailor the ACO algorithm for their problem, a finite time series of inflows, classification of the reservoir volume into several class intervals, and defining the reservoir releases for each time period with respect to a predefined optimality criterion, were established. The ACO algorithm was compared to a real coded Genetic Algorithm (GA). It was shown that the ACO algorithm performed better than the GA. Moeini and Afshar (2009) used three max-min ant system formulations for optimal operation of reservoirs using two sets of decision variables – storage and releases, and three graph form representations. The max-min ant system results were compared to each other and to two traditional heuristic evolutionary algorithms: genetic algorithms (GA), and honey bee mating optimization (HBMO). It was shown that the max-min ant system formulation was successful in solving the problem of optimal operation of reservoirs with the releases settings been better than the others. Dariane and Moradi (2009) used ant colony optimization for continuous domains (ACOR) to solve the optimal releases problem of reservoirs. The authors decreased substantially the computational effort required to run an ant colony based optimization problem, and compared their model to a genetic algorithm formulation.

3.2 Groundwater long term (LTM) monitoring

Li et al. (2004) developed a hybrid ant colony genetic algorithm model for groundwater long term monitoring to maximize sampling cost-effectiveness. Groundwater long term monitoring is required to evaluate the in-situ conditions of remedial system performances and for controlling post closure groundwater sites. Their formulation optimizes the groundwater-monitoring network (i.e., location and sampling schedules) as groundwater monitoring resources are expensive and thus limited. Li and Chan Hilton (2005, 2006a, 2006b) extended Li and Chan Hilton (2004) by formulating the LTM optimization for minimizing the number of monitoring wells with constraints on estimation errors and data quality; and for reduction of a monitoring effort plan while minimizing distortions to the information received by the original monitoring set-up. Global optima or near-optimal solutions were received.

3.3 Water resources applications

Ali et al. (2009) used ant colony optimization to accelerate convergence of the differential evolution (DE) technique. Their methodology, entitled ant colony differential evolution (ACDE), initializes the ant population using based learning techniques, utilizes a random localization methodology, and simulates the movement of ants to refine the best solution found in each iteration. The ACDE was applied to different test problems including a simplified water resources system. Abbaspour et al. (2001) utilized ant colony optimization for calibrating an unsaturated soil hydraulic model. The use of ant colony replaced the traditional inverse modelling approach and was found to be successful in overcoming previous parameterization related optimization problems. Li et al. (2006) developed a hybrid ant colony-simulated annealing method for groundwater parameter estimation. The inverse problem of parameter identification was formulated as an optimization problem. Transmissivity and storage coefficients for a two-dimensional unsteady state groundwater flow model were calibrated with the proposed technique.

3.4 Water distribution systems

The first to introduce ant colony optimization for water distribution systems management were Maier et. al. (2003). Maier et al. applied a traditional ant colony settings for optimizing two benchmark gravitational one loading conditions water distribution systems. Zecchin et al. (2005) studied parameterization of ant colony optimization for water distribution systems and suggested guidelines for selecting them. Christodoulou and Ellinas (2010) proposed an ant colony optimization algorithm for efficient routing of piping networks for improving its efficiency and resiliency. López-Ibáñez et al. (2008) used ant colony for optimizing the operation of pumping in water distribution systems.

Ostfeld A. and Tubaltzev A. (2008) generalized the studies of Maier et al. (2003) and López-Ibáñez et al. (2008) for mutually optimizing the design and operation of water distribution systems for extended loading conditions, pumps, and tanks. The algorithm of Ostfeld A. and Tubaltzev A. (2008) is based on Dorigo et al. (1996) and Maier et al. (2003), and is comprised of the following stages:

1. *Representation:* the least cost design problem is discretized and symbolized in the form of a graph with the links representing decision variable values, and the nodes - decision points.
2. *Initialization:* a colony of A ants "starts walking" from node START (see Fig. 1) to node END with each ant having an equal probability to choose a specific link at each node (i.e., each link has an equal initial pheromone intensity of 1 unit). Each ant entire trail (i.e., from START to END) comprises one possible design solution. At the end of this stage a set of random design solutions (i.e., random routes) equal to the number of ants is generated. (2a) Each solution is evaluated using EPANET (USEPA, 2002) with a penalty induced to non-feasible solutions [i.e., solutions violating minimum allowable pressure constraints at consumer nodes are penalized linearly as a function of the pressure head deficiency at the nodes (following Maier et al., 2003)]. (2b) A set (denoted Δ) of the least cost solutions are selected for pheromone updating (e.g., the best twenty ant solutions out of an initial set A of thousand).
3. *Pheromone updating:* each of the links participating at the i-th best solution $(i \in \Delta)$ is added a pheromone amount equal to: $Cost_{max}/Cost_i$ where $Cost_{max}$ is the highest cost among the best set (i.e., Δ) of ants, and $Cost_i$ is the solution cost of the current i-th best solution. Using this mechanism links which participated at lower solutions will receive a higher pheromone quantity (i.e., their likelihood to be chosen at subsequent iterations will increase).
4. *Probability updating:* update the links outgoing probabilities out of node j: $p_i = ph_i \,/\, \sum_{i=1}^{Nj} ph_i$ = where: p_i = the probability of choosing link i; Nj = number of links out of node j; and ph_i = pheromone amount on link i.
5. *Iterate:* go back to stage (2b) with a fraction γ of the initial number of ants A (i.e., γA), while keeping the best solution (i.e., Elitism), if a predefined number of iterations has not yet attained.

A complete formal description of the suggested algorithm is given in Fig. 2. It incorporates the following steps:

Initialization:

1. The ant colony iteration counter t is set to one.
2. The pheromone intensity $\tau_e(1)$ present on each edge $e \in \{1, 2, \ldots, E\}$ at $t = 1$ is set to one.

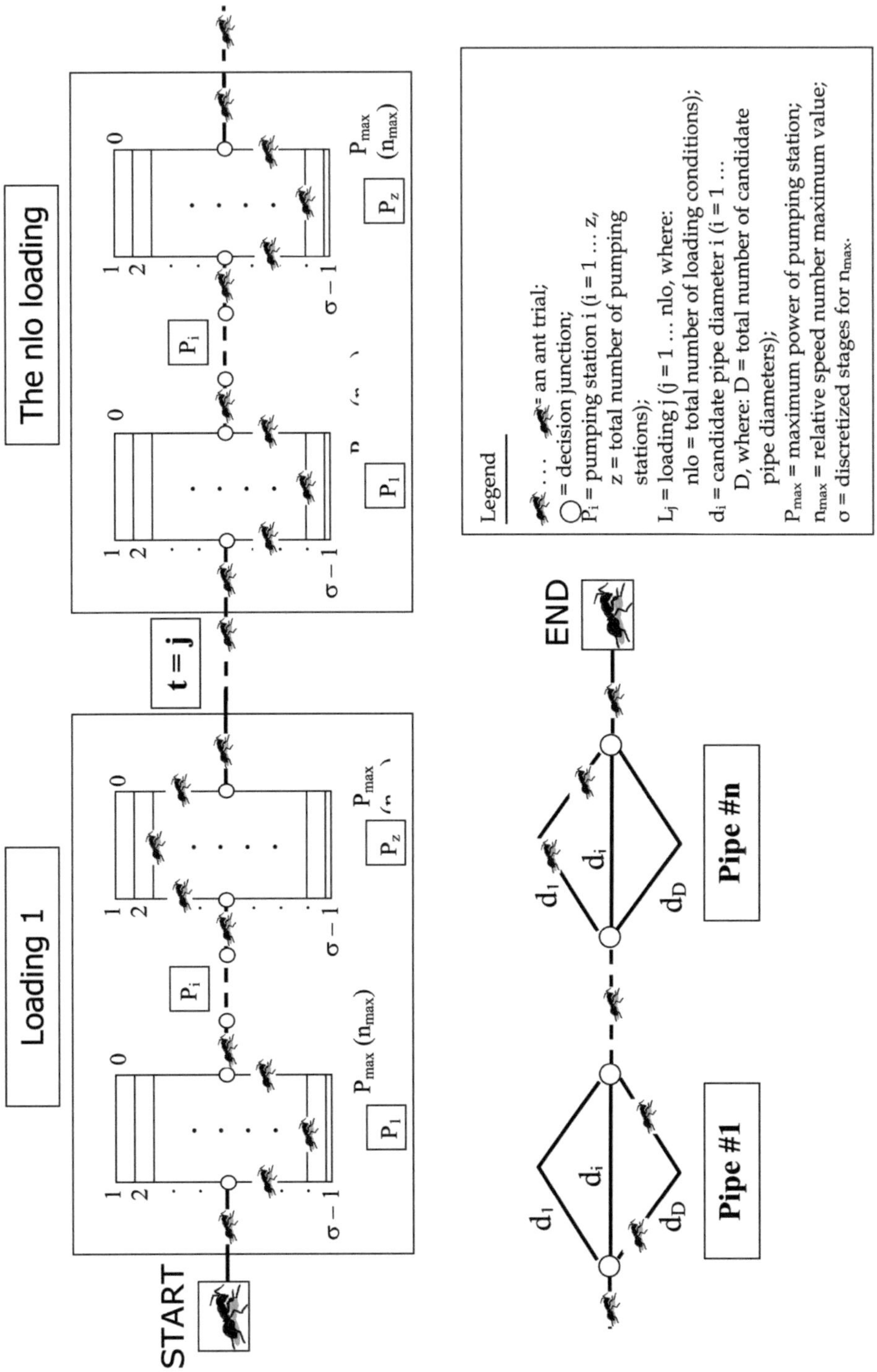

Fig. 1. Water distribution systems representation for Ant Colony Optimization (Ostfeld and Tubaltzev, 2008, with permission from the American Society of Civil Engineers (ASCE))

3. The ant colony parameters are defined: t_{max} = total number of ant colony iterations; α = a parameter controlling the relative importance of pheromone (set to one); β = a parameter controlling the relative importance of local heuristics (set to zero); ρ = a parameter of pheromone persistence (set to one); A = initial number of ants; γ = a fraction of the initial number of ants used for $t > 1$ (i.e., use of γA ants for $t > 1$) ; Δ = number of best ants used for pheromone updating; n_{max} = upper bound of the relative pumping stations speed number; σ = discretized n_{max} number (i.e., the discretization resolution of n_{max}); and PC = linear penalty cost coefficient.
4. The initial number of ants A are placed at node START (see Fig. 1).
5. The probability $P_{e,i}(t)$ to select the outgoing edge e at node i at iteration t (t = 1) is computed:

$$P_{e,i}(t) = \frac{[\tau_e(t)]^{\alpha}\,[\eta_e]^{\beta}}{\sum_{j=1}^{i^+}[\tau_j(t)]^{\alpha}\,[\eta_j]^{\beta}} \quad \forall\, e \in \{1, 2, ..., E\} \tag{5}$$

where: i^+ = the set of outgoing edges out of node i; η_e = visibility of edge e (not used as $\beta = 0$).

6. The ant's trials counter k is set to 1
7. The solution of the first ant (k = 1) trial $\phi_k(1)[P_{e,i}(1)]$ is generated through a random walk to node END (see Fig. 1).
8. The trial solution cost of the first ant (k = 1) $C_k(1)\ [\phi_k(1)]$ is computed;

Stages (9) and (10) guarantee that all ants will perform their trails. The *initialization* stage concludes with keeping the best Δ solutions out of the initial number of ants A.

Main scheme:

11. The pheromone intensity $\tau_e(t+1)$ present on edge e at iteration t + 1 is computed using Eqs. (2) and (3):

$$\tau_e(t+1) = \rho\,\tau_e(t) + \sum_{k=1}^{\Delta}\Delta\tau_e^k(t+1) \quad \forall\, e \in \{1, 2, ..., E\} \tag{6}$$

$$\Delta\tau_e^k(t+1) = \begin{bmatrix} \dfrac{C_{max,\Delta}(t)}{C_k(t)\ [\phi_k(t)]} & \text{if the k-th ant } (k \in \Delta) \text{ used edge e at iteration t} \\ 0 & \text{otherwise} \end{bmatrix} \tag{7}$$

where: $\Delta\tau_e^k(t+1)$ = pheromone intensity addition by the k-th ant on edge e at iteration t + 1; and $C_{max,\Delta}(t)$ = the maximum cost solution out of the best Δ ants at iteration t. At stage (12) the probability $P_{e,i}(t+1)$ to choose the outgoing edge e at node i at iteration t + 1 is computed.

At stage (13) χA ants are placed at node START (see Fig. 1). Stages (14) to (18) correspond to (6) to (10); at stage (19) *Elitism* is invoked (i.e., keeping unchanged the best solution obtained at all iterations); stages (20) and (21) guarantee that all iterations are performed. The algorithm finishes off with the best ant colony solution obtained $\phi^*(t_{max})$, and its corresponding cost $C^*(t_{max})$.

Initial stage

(1) Set: $t = 1$

(2) Set: $\tau_e(1) = 1 \ \forall \ e \in \{1, 2, ..., E\}$

(3) Set the algorithm parameters: t_{max}, $\alpha = 1$, $\beta = 0$, $\rho = 1$, A, γ, Δ, n_{max}, σ, PC

(4) Locate A ants: [1… k … A] at node START (see Fig. 1)

(5) Compute: $$P_{e,i}(1) = \frac{[\tau_e(1)]^{\alpha} [\eta_e]^{\beta}}{\sum_{j=1}^{i^+} [\tau_j(1)]^{\alpha} [\eta_j]^{\beta}} \quad \forall \ e \in \{1, 2, ..., E\}$$

(6) Set: $k = 1$

(7) Generate $\phi_k(1)[P_{e,i}(1)]$ through a random walk to node END (see Fig. 1)

(8) Compute $C_k(1)\ [\phi_k(1)]$

(9) Check if $k = A$

(10) NO – Set: $k \leftarrow k + 1$ and go to step (7)

Iterate

YES – save the least cost set δ (i.e. the best Δ) solutions out of A

The ant colony main algorithm

(11) Compute: $$\tau_e(t+1) = \rho\, \tau_e(t) + \sum_{k=1}^{\Delta} \Delta\tau_e^k(t+1) \quad \forall \ e \in \{1, 2, ..., E\}$$

$$\Delta\tau_e^k(t+1) = \begin{bmatrix} \dfrac{C_{max,\Delta}(t)}{C_k(t)\ [\phi_k(t)]} & \text{if the k-th ant } (k \in \Delta) \text{ used edge e at iteration t} \\ 0 & \text{otherwise} \end{bmatrix}$$

(12) Compute: $$P_{e,i}(t+1) = \frac{[\tau_e(t+1)]^{\alpha} [\eta_e]^{\beta}}{\sum_{j=1}^{i^+} [\tau_j(t+1)]^{\alpha} [\eta_j]^{\beta}} \quad \forall \ e \in \{1, 2, ..., E\}$$

Iterate

(13) Locate γA ants: [1… k … γA] at node START (see Fig. 1)

(14) Set: $k = 1$

(15) Generate $\phi_k(t+1)[P_{e,i}(t+1)]$ through a random walk to node END (see Fig. 1)

(16) Compute $C_k(t+1)\ [\phi_k(t+1)]$

(17) Check if $k = \gamma A$

(18) NO – Set: $k \leftarrow k + 1$ and go to step (15)

Iterate

YES – save the least cost set δ (i.e. the best Δ) solutions out of γA

(19) *Elitism*: if $C^*(t+1) > C^*(t)$ then: $\phi^*(t+1) \leftarrow \phi^*(t)$; $C^*(t+1) \leftarrow C^*(t)$

(20) Check if $t = t_{max}$

(21) NO – Set: $t \leftarrow t + 1$ and go to step (11)

YES – save the least cost ant colony solution $\phi^*(t_{max})$; $C^*(t_{max})$

Fig. 2. Ant Colony Optimization flow chart (Ostfeld and Tubaltzev, 2008, with permission from the American Society of Civil Engineers (ASCE))

4. Future research

Ant colony optimization for water resources systems analysis is in its early stages of exploitation as depicted from the literature review described above.

Applications to optimal reservoir operations, long term monitoring, some general water resources problems, and water distribution systems design and operation were developed.

Still, most of the water resources systems community has not yet utilized the potential of using ant colony optimization, as occurred in other research disciplines such as structural engineering. Research is thus almost completely open for developing and applying ant colony optimization algorithms for water resources systems problems and analysis.

The challenges of using ant colony optimization in water resources systems analysis vary with the specific theme and objective of interest. Yet, commonly to water resources systems analysis is the inherent probabilistic complex nature of the physical systems such as groundwater, watersheds, distribution systems, and others. Those yield non-linearity and non-smoothness in describing the systems physical behavior. As a result, almost any water resources systems model which obviously needs to capture its physics as model constraints, is highly complex. Traditional non-linear algorithms such as gradient type algorithms are thus very much limited.

As every problem has its unique structure and tradeoff among its decision variables and formulations, the challenge of developing ant colony algorithms for water resources systems analysis is mainly in tailoring the specific problems characteristics with an ant colony formulation. This requires the modeler to explore different avenues of formulations such that the resulted model will be computationally feasible. This is a tremendous challenging task which captures most of the innovativeness aspects of new modeling and application.

Below are the major fields of water resources systems analysis for which new ant colony optimization models could be developed and applied:

Climate change: climate variability and change, adaptive management, decision making

Groundwater: parameter estimation, operation, contamination, remediation

Reservoirs: operation, design, inclusion of water quality considerations

Water distribution systems: network models - optimization, calibration and verification, development and application; network hydraulics - steady state, transients; leakage - leak detection, leak management, field studies; water use - monitoring, estimation and simulation, end users; field work - tracer studies, pressure tests, case studies; contaminant intrusion and water security - detection, source identification, response; network vulnerability - security assessments, network reliability, disaster response, emerging issues; network water quality - real-time monitoring and modeling, dose exposure, mixing and dispersion, storage tanks, asset management, Maintenance, system expansion and rehabilitation; sustainable water distribution systems - design and operation, water reuse and supply, dual distribution systems

Water economics: water demand - household, commercial; water supply - cost of production, efficiency studies, technological change, industry studies; valuing water services - ecological services, sanitation navigation, recreation, irrigation, industrial.

Water policy: transboundary, drought, flood, navigation, recreation, irrigation, industrial, climate, energy

Watersheds and river basins: watershed management, water and energy systems, application of hydrologic predictions and forecasts, best management practices, stormwater

5. References

Abbaspour K. C., Schulin R., and van Genuchten M. Th. (2001). "Estimating unsaturated soil hydraulic parameters using ant colony optimization." Advances in Water Resources, Vol. 24, pp. 827-841.

Ali M., Pant M., and Abraham A. (2009). "A hybrid ant colony differential evolution and its application to water resources problems." Proceedings of the 2009 Nature & Biologically Inspired Computing World Congress, pp. 1133 - 1138, doi 10.1109/NABIC.2009.5393816

Alperovits E. and Shamir U. (1977). "Design of optimal water distribution systems." Water Resources Research, Vol. 13, No. 6, pp. 885 - 900.

Christodoulou S. E. and Ellinas G. (2010). "Pipe routing through ant colony optimization." Journal of Infrastructure Systems, Vol. 16, No. 2, pp. 149-159.

Dariane A. B. and Moradi A. M. (2009). "Reservoir operating by ant colony optimization for continuous domains (ACOR) case study: Dez reservoir." International Journal of Mathematical, Physical and Engineering Sciences, Vol. 3, No. 2, 125-129.

Dorigo M. (1992). "Optimization, learning and natural algorithms [in Italian]." PhD thesis, Dipartimento di Electtronica Politecnico di Milano, Milan.

Dorigo M., Maniezzo V., and Colorni A. (1996). "Ant system: optimization by a colony of cooperating agents." IEEE Transactions on Systems, Man, and Cybernetics-Part B, Vol. 26, No. 1, pp. 29-41.

Eiger G., Shamir U., and Ben-Tal A. (1994). "Optimal design of water distribution networks." Water Resources Research, Vol. 30, No. 9, pp. 2637 - 2646.

Espinoza F., Minsker B., and Goldberg D. (2005) "Adaptive hybrid genetic algorithm for groundwater remediation design." Journal of Water Resources Planning and Management Division, ASCE, Vol. 131, No. 1, pp. 14-24.

Espinoza F. and Minsker B. (2006). "Development of the enhanced self-adaptive hybrid genetic algorithm (e-SAHGA)." Water Resources Research, Vol. 42, W08501, doi:10.1029/2005WR004221

Eusuff M. M. and Lansey K. E. (2003). "Optimization of water distribution network design using the shuffled frog leaping algorithm." Journal of Water Resources Planning and Management Division, ASCE, Vol. 129, No. 3, pp. 210–225.

Karatzas G. P. and Finder G. F. (1996). "The solution of groundwater quality management problems with a nonconvex feasible region using a cutting plane optimization technique." Water Resources Research, Vol. 32, No. 4, doi:10.1029/95WR03812.

Kessler A. and Shamir U. (1989). "Analysis of the linear programming gradient method for optimal design of water supply networks." Water Resources Research, Vol. 25, No. 7, pp. 1469–1480.

Kessler A. and Shamir U. (1991). "Decomposition technique for optimal design of water supply networks." Engineering Optimization, Vol. 17, pp. 1–19.

Kumar D. N. and Reddy M. J. (2006). "Ant colony optimization for multi-purpose reservoir operation." Water Resources Management, Vol. 20, pp. 879–898

Lansey K. E. and Mays L. W. (1989). "Optimization models for design of water distribution systems." In, Reliability Analysis of Water Distribution Systems, Mays L. W. Ed., pp. 37–84.

Li S., Liu Y., and Yu H. (2006). "Parameter estimation approach in groundwater hydrology using hybrid ant colony system." In Computational Intelligence and Bioinformatics,

Lecture Notes in Computer Science, 2006, Volume 4115/2006, pp. 182-191, doi 10.1007/11816102_20

Li Y., Chan Hilton A. B., and Tong L. (2004). "Development of ant colony optimization for long-term groundwater monitoring." Proceedings of the 2004 World Water and Environmental Resources Congress, Salt Lake City, UT, pp. 1-10, doi 10.1061/40737(2004)107

Li Y. and Chan Hilton A. B. (2005). "Analysis of the primal and dual problem for long-term groundwater monitoring spatial optimization." Proceedings of the 2005 World Water and Environmental Resources Congress, May 15-19, 2005, Anchorage, Alaska, doi 10.1061/40792(173)355

Li Y. and Chan Hilton A. B. (2006a). "An algorithm for groundwater long-term monitoring spatial optimization by analogy to ant colony optimization for TSP." Proceedings of the 2006 World Environmental and Water Resources Congress, May 21-25, 2006, Omaha, Nebraska, doi 10.1061/40856(200)118

Li Y. and Chan Hilton A. B. (2006b). "Bayesian statistics-based procedure for the groundwater long-term monitoring temporal optimization problem." Proceedings of the 2006 World Environmental and Water Resources Congress, May 21-25, 2006, Omaha, Nebraska, doi 10.1061/40856(200)145

López-Ibáñez M., Prasad T. D, and Paechter B. (2008). "Ant colony optimization for optimal control of pumps in water distribution networks." Journal of Water Resources Planning and Management Division, ASCE, Vol. 134, No. 4, pp. 337-346.

Maier H. R., Simpson A. R., Zecchin A. C., Foong W. K., Phang K. Y., Seah H. Y., and Tan C. L. (2003). "Ant colony optimization for design of water distribution systems." Journal of Water Resources Planning and Management Division, ASCE, Vol. 129, No. 3, pp. 200–209.

Moeini R. and Afshar M. H. (2009). "Application of an ant colony optimization algorithm for optimal operation of reservoirs: a comparative study of three proposed formulations." Transaction A: Civil Engineering, Vol. 16, No. 4, pp. 273-285

Ormsbee L. E. and Contractor D. N. (1981). "Optimization of hydraulic networks." International Symposium on Urban Hydrology, Hydraulics, and Sediment Control, Kentucky, Lexington, KY, pp. 255–261.

Ostfeld A. and Shamir U. (1996). "Design of optimal reliable multiquality water supply systems." Journal of Water Resources Planning and Management Division, ASCE, Vol. 122, No. 5, pp. 322–333.

Ostfeld A. and Tubaltzev A. (2008). "Ant colony optimization for least cost design of water distribution systems." Journal of Water Resources Planning and Management Division, ASCE, Vol. 134, No. 2, pp. 107 - 118.

Perelman L., Ostfeld A., and Salomons E. (2008). "Cross entropy multiobjective optimization for water distribution systems design." Water Resources Research, 44, W09413, doi: 10.1029/2007WR006248.

Quindry G. E., Brill E. D., Liebman J. C., and Robinson A. R. (1979). Comment on "Design of optimal water distribution systems by Alperovits E. and Shamir U." Water Resources Research, Vol. 15, No. 6, pp. 1651–1654.

Quindry G. E., Brill E. D., Liebman J. C. (1981). "Optimization of looped water distribution systems." Journal of Environmental Engineering, ASCE, Vol. 107, No. EE4, pp. 665-679.

Savic D. and Walters G. (1997)."Genetic algorithms for least cost design of water distribution networks." Journal of Water Resources Planning and Management Division, ASCE, Vol. 123, No. 2, pp. 67-77.

Shamir U. (1974). "Optimal design and operation of water distribution systems." Water Resources Research, Vol. 10, No. 1, pp. 27- 36.

Simpson A. R., Dandy G. C., and Murphy L. J. (1994). "Genetic algorithms compared to other techniques for pipe optimization." Journal of Water Resources Planning and Management Division, ASCE, Vol. 120, No. 4, pp. 423–443.

Watanatada T. (1973). "Least-cost design of water distribution systems." Journal of the Hydraulic Division, ASCE, Vol. 99, No. HY9, pp. 1497-1513.

Zecchin, A. C., Simpson, A. R., Maier, H. R., and Nixon, J. B. (2005)."Parametric study for an ant algorithm applied to water distribution system optimization." IEEE Transaction on Evolutionary Computation, Vol. 9, No. 2, pp. 175 - 191.

12

Application of Continuous ACO_R to Neural Network Training: Direction of Arrival Problem

Hamed Movahedipour
Department of Electrical Engineering, Tarbiat Modares University
Iran

1. Introduction

In this chapter, a hybrid ACO_R-based artificial neural network is investigated and applied to solve a Direction of Arrival (DoA) estimation problem. This approach is compared with Radial Basis Function Neural Network (RBFNN) that has been used broadly in the literature for DoA estimation.

The Ant Colony Optimization is a stochastic optimization technique that has attracted much attention towards numerous optimization problems during the past decade. ACO is a subset of swarm intelligence methods in which the collective intelligence emerges in decentralized and self-organized systems with simple individuals.

Social insects are distributed systems that carry out complex tasks, having individuals with very simple and rudimentary cognitive abilities. In many cases, these tasks exceed the capabilities of a single individual. In fact, social insects are self-organized systems and some simple principles and processes such as stigmergy can explain their social behaviour. Stigmergy is an indirect communication among individuals, in which different entities communicate by modifying the environment.

Ants possess very limited visual and vocal perceptive abilities and some types are totally blind. Hence, the only efficient communication channel in these species is various types of chemicals, which are called pheromones. One specific type of pheromone is the trail pheromone that is deposited for instance while searching for food and the other ants smell the pheromone and tend to follow the paths with high pheromone concentration. Therefore, by indirect communication via pheromone and the simple rule of following the higher density of pheromone, one complex colony-level behaviour is emerged which is finding the short paths to the food. This behaviour is quite above the capabilities of each ant. In fact this collective capability emerges out of microscopic simple processes of pheromone laying and pheromone following.

Ant colony optimization is an algorithm, which models foraging behaviour of ants to solve optimization problems and it has inspired many researchers to provide solutions to various combinatorial optimization problems such as travelling salesman problem (Dorigo et al., 1996), routing problem (Schoonderwoerd et al., 1997) and many other NP-hard problems in which the values for discrete variables are found to optimize an objective function. In fact ACO, models ant agents walking on a graph that implies typical discrete problems or structures. Since ACO was originally proposed for discrete optimization problems, its application to continuous domain was not straightforward. Among various adaptations of

ACO algorithm for continuous optimization problems, the approach of Socha tries to avoid conceptual changes to principles of ACO by introducing ACO_R algorithm (Socha, 2004; Socha & Blum, 2007; Socha & Dorigo, 2008). Socha's approach to adapt ACO to continuous domain is utilized in this work to optimize the numerical weights of a Multi-Layer Perceptron (MLP) network for interpolation of the nonlinear relation of antenna array outputs and Angle of Arrival (AoA). In other words, ACO_R is used to minimize Mean Square Error (MSE) of the output layer of the neural network by adjusting continuous variables of weights during training phase.

Direction of arrival estimation has turned out to be a substantial part of many applications like channel characterization, car tracking (Danneville et al., 2005), source localization in radar and sonar (Godara, 2002), receiver algorithm design and co-channel interference reduction (Christodoulou, 2001). Spectral-based algorithmic solutions like Multiple Signal Classification (MUSIC) and parametric methods such as Maximum Likelihood (ML) have been the major methods to tackle DoA problem for a long period. The foremost drawback of these techniques is that they are computationally expensive and do not perform quite efficiently in real time operation. Artificial neural networks have been also utilized to estimate DoA, often using RBF networks due to its acceptable estimation error, capability of inexpensive implementation and fast performance (Zooghby et al., 2000; Titus et al., 1994).

In this chapter, after a general introduction to ant colony optimization, ACO_R adaptation to continuous domain is explained. ACO_R has been applied to train a classifier neural network (Socha & Blum, 2007) and in this work, its application to an interpolator neural network is investigated. The possibilities to enhance the performance of ACO_R are studied as well.

2. Ant Colony Optimization

2.1 Combinatorial Optimization

Combinatorial optimization (CO) problem $P = (S,f)$ is an optimization problem in which $f:S \rightarrow R^+$ is an objective function that assigns a positive value, called cost to each solution $s \in S$ in the finite search space S which encompasses feasible solutions. The goal of this kind of problem is to find a solution in the search space with the lowest cost (Papadimitriou & Steiglitz, 1982). The search space in combinatorial problems includes variables X_i, $i=1, \ldots, n$ in discrete domains, therefore combinatorial problems are in fact discrete optimization problems. CO problems are arisen in industry and in applied sciences such as statistics, physics and chemistry. Some instances in industry are manufacturing and distribution, telecommunication network design and routing, airline crew scheduling, etc. Meanwhile this field is connected to various areas of mathematics such as algebra, analysis and continuous optimization, geometry, numerical analysis, topology, graph theory and enumerative combinations (Lee, 2004). Therefore, due to the wide range of important applications of CO problems, various algorithms and methods have been developed to attack them.

2.1 ACO algorithm

ACO is an algorithm which finds an approximate optimal solution in a reduced amount of time for NP-hard problems and it was introduced by Dorigo and colleagues (Dorrigo et al., 1991 and 1996) in the early 1990's. ACO simulates the foraging behavior of ants, which communicate using pheromone trails and manage to find the shortest path from their nest to feeding source. The significant features of this model are positive feedback, distributed computation and incremental construction of solutions.

Double bridge experiment was a practice designed by Deneubourg and colleagues (Deneubourg et al., 1990) in which the ability of real ant colonies in finding shorter paths to food was investigated. In this experiment a bridge with two branches l_i $(i=1, 2)$ was used to connect a nest of real ants to a food source. In the first phase of the experiment equal branches were used and the behavior of ants regarding choosing branches was studied. The observations showed that at the beginning, ants had random choices but after a while they were converged to one of the branches. In fact at the start of the experiment, there was no pheromone on the bridge so the ants chose different branches randomly, but after awhile due to random fluctuations more pheromone was accumulated in one of the branches and after a short time all other ants converged to that branch. This positive feedback process is one of the main characteristics of the foraging ant behavior and consequently ACO algorithm. In the second phase of the experiment, branches with different lengths were used and it was observed that in most of the trials ants were converged to the shorter branch. In fact again at the start, ants chose branches randomly but the ants that opted the short branch reached the food sooner and also started their return to the nest sooner than the ants which selected the long branch. In this way, more pheromone was accumulated in the shorter path and consequently biased decision of the other ants in its favor. It is noteworthy that in the second phase of the experiment, the effect of the random fluctuations was overcame by the difference in the path length and the ants converged to the shorter path.

This experiment showed optimization capability of ant colonies and inspired researchers to design artificial ants and exploit the same principles utilized by ants to solve combinatorial optimization problems. Double bridge is modeled by a graph, passing the nodes constructs the solution and finally the length of the chosen path can be considered as the cost. By considering a static, connected graph and the described mechanism to solve a combinatorial optimization problem, the ants may generate loops while solution construction and this will prevent them from finding the short paths between source and destination. By extending the capabilities of artificial ants like a limited form of memory, getting trapped in the loops can be avoided. Besides if each arc in the graph has a cost, artificial ants can not deposit pheromone before reaching to the destination because first they need to construct the solution and then evaluate the solution according to the objective function.

In one of the double bridge experiments, ants were faced with one long branch for 30 minutes and then one short bridge was added. In this experiment ants were trapped in the suboptimal path, because once they were converged to the long branch and it was difficult for them to reinforce the pheromone concentration in the shorter path. In fact the evaporation rate of pheromone was too slow and ants couldn't forget the converged solution, or in other words the lifetime of pheromone was comparable to the duration of trial. Therefore enhanced evaporation mechanism is utilized in artificial ants to avoid being trapped in suboptimal solutions. In fact evaporation can favor exploration of more possible solutions and paths. Therefore to tackle the inefficiencies of real ant colonies, the capabilities of artificial ants are extended in a way that the main principles of real ants are not violated. The major differences of real ants and the algorithm of ACO are as follows:

- Ants deposit pheromone while they move but artificial ants just leave pheromone on their path back to the nest which is called backward path pheromone update.
- Real ants do not evaluate the quality of their solution explicitly. It means naturally shorter paths are traversed earlier and consequently pheromone is accumulated more quickly in the shorter paths. In this way without any need of explicit calculation, the

quality of solution is evaluated. In contrast, the artificial ants calculate the objective function and perform pheromone update with respect to the quality of constructed solution.
- Artificial ants hold a memory and store the partial paths they have traversed as well as the costs of the paths. Therefore they can avoid loops and also evaluate the solution according to the objective function.
- After pheromone update, a portion of the accumulated pheromone is evaporated to enhance exploration.

Considering above extensions, ant colony optimization algorithms encompasses following basic steps:
- Probabilistic solution construction in forward mode is biased by pheromone concentration, without pheromone updating.
- Deterministic backward path pheromone update is done with loop elimination.
- Evaluation of the constructed solution and pheromone update is carried out based on the quality of solution. Note that this behavior is also visited in some types of real ants that deposit higher densities of pheromone when they return from a rich food source.
- Evaporation mechanism is used to enable the artificial ants to forget the suboptimal solutions that they have found at the early stages of the search.

4. Continuous ACO

Ant colony optimization was initially developed for combinatorial optimization problems and due to the concept and structure of the algorithm, it was difficult to apply it to continuous optimization problems.

Some methods have been developed to apply ACO to continuous optimization problems but some basic principles of ACO have been deviated in these methods. Generic principles behind ACO can be categorized in following key characteristics:
- Data source is distributed.
- Incremental construction of solutions is performed by a population of individuals.
- No direct communication is present among ants and stigmergy is utilized as the indirect communication.

ACO is a constructive algorithm in which solutions are constructed incrementally. It means ants add solution components in each step until a complete solution is developed. Contrary to various proposed methods to adapt ACO to tackle continuous optimization problems, Socha (Socha, 2004) proposed an extension of ACO to continuous domain called ACO_R without any change in basic characteristics of original ACO method. ACO_R algorithm is described in this section.

In ACO algorithm for combinatorial problems, probabilistic decision is made among different choices for certain solution component and the probability is calculated according to the amount of pheromone in available choices. In combinatorial optimization problems, available choices are discrete; therefore, each probabilistic decision is made according to a discrete probability distribution. In case of continuous ACO, solution components may assume any real value in a defined range. Therefore, in ACO_R it is proposed to use Probability Density Function (PDF) instead of discrete probability distribution and PDF is sampled by ants to model pheromone effect in probabilistic selection of solution components. In regular ACO, while pheromone update, ants add a certain amount of pheromone to each solution component with respect to the quality of solution and in this way, each possible value of solution components gets a pheromone value which reflects the search experience of the ants. In case of combinatorial optimization problems, this is possible since the set of possible values for solution components is finite. In case of continuous optimization problem, the set of possible values is not finite and to store the search experience of the algorithm, a limited number of recent found solutions are stored in an explicit memory called solution archive (Socha & Dorigo, 2008).

$$Solution\ Archive = \begin{bmatrix} s_1^1 & s_1^2 & \cdots & s_1^n \\ s_2^1 & s_2^2 & \cdots & s_2^n \\ . & . & & . \\ . & . & & . \\ s_k^1 & s_k^2 & \cdots & s_k^n \end{bmatrix}_{k\times n} \quad (1)$$

where n is the number of variables or solution components, k is the number of solutions that are stored in the archive and s^i_j is the i-th solution component of j-th solution. It is noteworthy that in ACO for combinatorial optimization problems, the whole history of search is stored but in ACO$_R$ the limited number of solutions k represent the history of search. For instance if k=30 it means in each stage of the algorithm the solutions of 30 ants are utilized to make probabilistic solutions. Each row in the solution archive corresponds to a found solution, and by calculation of the objective function, the quality of each solution is measured. In fact, guidance towards better solutions and promising areas of search space in ACO$_R$ is accomplished by formation of w_j, which is associated with solution j and is attained with respect to the value of objective function.

$$w = \begin{bmatrix} w_1 \\ w_2 \\ . \\ . \\ w_k \end{bmatrix}_{k\times 1} \quad (2)$$

4.1 Pheromone initialization

Initialization of solution archive is performed in a way that a uniform distribution over the search domain *(a,b)* is generated. This is accomplished by defining k normal distributions with uniformly distributed means.

$$P^i(x^i) = \sum_{j=1}^{k} \frac{1}{k} \cdot g\left(x^i, a + (2j-1)\frac{b-a}{2k}, \frac{b-a}{2k}\right) \quad (3)$$

4.2 Solution construction

In solution construction phase of ACO$_R$, each ant chooses probabilistically one of the solutions in the archive according to its corresponding weight.

$$p_j = \frac{w_j}{\sum_{i=1}^{k} w_i} \tag{4}$$

After the j-th solution is selected, an ant starts constructing the solution incrementally and assigning value to each solution component $i = 1, \ldots, n$ separately. Starting with the first variable, the ant generates a random number by sampling a Gaussian function centered by the value of first variable of the chosen solution s^1_j and assigns the sampled value to the first variable of the solution under construction. Same process is performed for each solution component until the whole solution is constructed. In the above process the Gaussian function is utilized to sample the neighborhood of s^i_j (Socha, 2004).

$$P(x) = g(x,\mu,\sigma) = \frac{1}{\sigma\sqrt{2\pi}} e^{\frac{-(x-\mu)^2}{2\sigma^2}} \tag{5}$$

where μ is the mean of the normal distribution and equals the value of s^i_j for i-th variable of j-th solution. In this way, the value of s^i_j has the highest probability of being chosen while sampling. σ is the standard deviation of normal distribution.

After each solution construction, pheromone update is performed to modify the probability distributions and to provide guidance for ants to discover better solutions in the next iterations. Pheromone update is carried out in two forms of positive update and negative update.

4.3 Positive update

In positive update, the solutions with good quality are stored in the solution archive to bias the probabilistic decision of ants in favor of promising areas of the search space.

After solution construction phase, the performance of solutions is measured using objective function and the weight of each solution is determined. Then a number of high performing solutions are added to the solution archive:

$$k \leftarrow k + nos \tag{6}$$

nos is the number of solutions added to solution archive. After positive update, the size of stored solutions is increased to $k+nos$.

4.4 Negative update

In ACO algorithms, negative update is performed to forget the old solutions, avoid being stuck in local optimum solutions and in general enhance exploration. Pheromone evaporation is the traditional method to perform negative update in ACO for combinatorial optimization problems. In ACO_R, there are different ways to accomplish negative update (Socha, 2004).

- One of the methods for negative update in ACO_R is removing some old or low performing solutions from solution archive. To keep the size of solution archive constant, same number of solutions that were added in positive update phase can be removed.

$$k \leftarrow k - nos \tag{7}$$

- Another method for negative update is similar to pheromone evaporation in generic ACO. In case of ACO_R the vector of weight is evaporated:

$$w^i_j \leftarrow (1-\rho).w^i_j \tag{8}$$

- Last method utilizes normal distribution property to implement negative update. In this method after each iteration, standard deviation of normal distributions are increased:

$$\sigma^i_j \leftarrow \gamma.\sigma^i_j \tag{9}$$

where γ is the rate of dissolving. By increasing the standard deviation of normal distributions, the random numbers generated based on normal PDFs will be more spread and it implies the decrease of impact of old solutions. This type of negative update is called dissolving.

Depending to various applications, different methods for negative update may be used. In our application, all methods of negative update are combined.

5. Direction of arrival estimation

Rapid development of high-speed data services and increasing demand for coverage and capacity in new wireless systems has caused a substantial need for more effective solutions. For instance in cellular communications, frequency reuse is utilized to fulfill capacity requirements. In these networks, increasing the capacity is possible by allowing closer co-frequency cells that on the other hand will increase the risk of interference. Therefore, interference cancelation gives us the freedom of using additional frequency reuse. The most effective way of interference reduction is to make use of direction of arrival estimation to locate the users and then exploit an adaptive array antenna to steer its main lobe toward the subscribers of interest and nulls toward the co-frequency cells. On the other hand, as mobile satellite communication systems and global positioning systems (GPS) grow, smart antennas can enhance the performance of those systems. Therefore, direction estimation is a major concern of any spatial division multiple access (SDMA) system. Besides, due to various applications of DoA in car tracking, channel characterization and source localization, it has received substantial attention for several decades. Neural network is one of the methods that has been used to model DoA estimators and it has shown an efficient performance. Neural networks approach for handling computational task of DoA estimation has following advantages:

- Fast execution, which facilitates real-time operation
- Acceptable estimation error
- Possibility of inexpensive manufacturing

Radial basis function neural network has been presented as a successful candidate among various neural structures (Christodoulou, 2001; zooghby et al., 2000). In this chapter ACO_R method is used to train a feed forward neural network and it is compared to RBFNN method. The improvements in estimation error are discussed.

5.1 DoA problem formulation

In this section, the DoA is formulated and the training set of neural network that is applied to the input layer is attained.

For DoA estimation, the phase shift between the received signals in different array elements can be used to find the direction of signals.

$$e^{-jw_c t_d} = e^{-j\frac{2\pi d \sin(\theta)}{\lambda}} = e^{-jk} \tag{10}$$

where d is the element spacing of the antenna array and λ is the wavelength of incoming waves. Consider a linear array antenna with M elements exposed to K $(K<M)$ narrowband plane waves impinging on the antenna from directions $\{\theta_1 \ \theta_2 \ \ldots \ \theta_K\}$. Using wave propagation relations and complex signal notation, the received signal of the i-th array element can be shown as

$$x_i(t) = \sum_{m=1}^{K} s_m(t) e^{-j(i-1)k_m} + n_i(t) \qquad i = 1,2,\ldots M \tag{11}$$

$s_m(t)$ is the signal of m-th wave, $n_i(t)$ is the noise signal which i-th element receives and

$$k_m = \frac{w_0 d}{c} \sin(\theta_m) \tag{12}$$

where w_0 is the center frequency and c is the speed of light. We can convert the summation to vector notation and then express the output of the array in matrix form (Christodoulou, 2001).

$$X(t) = AS(t) + N(t) \tag{13}$$

where $X(t)$, $S(t)$, A and $N(t)$ are defined as follows

$$X(t) = [x_1(t) \ x_2(t) \ \ldots \ x_M(t)]^T \tag{14}$$

$$N(t) = [n_1(t) \ n_2(t) \ \ldots \ n_M(t)]^T \tag{15}$$

$$S(t) = [s_1(t) \ s_2(t) \ \ldots \ s_K(t)]^T \tag{16}$$

$$A = [a(\theta_1) \ \ldots \ a(\theta_m) \ \ldots \ a(\theta_K)] \tag{17}$$

$$a(\theta_m) = [1 \ e^{-jk_m} \ e^{-j2k_m} \ \ldots \ e^{-j(M-1)k_m}]^T \tag{18}$$

Assuming noise signals as statistically independent white noise with zero mean and independent of $S(t)$, we can form the spatial correlation matrix R which is used to provide the input data for neural network (Christodoulou, 2001).

$$R = E\{X(T)X^H(t)\} = AE\{S(t)S^H(t)\}A^H + E\{N(t)N^H(t)\} \tag{19}$$

where H represents the conjugate transpose. The antenna array receives signals in different directions and forms the matrix $X(t)$ which is the output of array elements. According to the fact that receiver noise is the dominating noise source, *n(t)* is assumed to be white and Gaussian distributed:

$$E\{n(t)\} = 0,\ E\{n(t)n^H(s)\} = \sigma^2 I\delta_{ts},\ E\{n(t)n^T(s)\} = 0 \tag{20}$$

The signal is also assumed to be Gaussian distributed.

$$E\{s(t)\} = 0,\ E\{s(t)s^H(s)\} = P\delta_{ts},\ E\{s(t)s^T(s)\} = 0 \tag{21}$$

$E\{S(t)S^H(t)\}$ can be considered as a diagonal matrix P for uncorrelated signals. Note that A has $M{\times}K$ dimension and P is a $K{\times}K$ matrix, consequently R is an $M{\times}M$ matrix. Hence, the spatial correlation matrix is presented as:

$$\begin{aligned} R &= E\{X(T)X^H(t)\} \\ &= AE\{S(t)S^H(t)\}A^H + E\{N(t)N^H(t)\} \\ &= APA^H + \sigma^2 I \end{aligned} \tag{22}$$

By exploiting the symmetry in *R*, either the upper or the lower triangular of the matrix is required (Christodoulou, 2001). As a result, the input data of neural network is decreased. Notice that *R* contains complex values and regular neural networks do not support complex values. Hence, the real and imaginary parts in the correlation matrix should be separated and all presented in a vector, termed *b* (Christodoulou, 2001; zooghby et al., 2000; Movahedipour et al., 2006). Matrix *b* with scaled values is applied to the neural network as a training set and known directions are considered as target values. Therefore, by considering just one triangular part of the matrix and real and image separation, *b* will include *M (M+1)* elements (Christodoulou, 2001). Normalized *b* is applied to the input layer of neural network.

6. ACO$_R$-based neural network for DoA estimation

In the simulations, two *S*=2 uncorrelated signals impinge on array antenna with five *M*=5 elements. These assumptions are made based on the literature to facilitate the comparison (Titus et al., 1994; Zooghby, 1997).

The neural network contains five neurons in its hidden layer. Array elements receive two uncorrelated narrow band signals in training mode with angular separations of 15° and 20° with the assumption that DoA is uniformly distributed from -90° to +90°. Therefore the first source is set at θ = -90° and the second source at θ = -75° (15° separation). Next, we set the first source at -89° and the second source at -74° and so on until the interval -90° to 90° is covered. Same method is used for 20° angular separation. For validation phase, separation angles of 15°, 16°, 17°, 18°, 19° and 20° are used to investigate the generalization capability of the neural network. All of the results are compared with RBF, which has been found as a substantially powerful solution to DoA estimation problem (Zooghby, 1997).

6.1 Application of ACO$_R$ to train feed forward neural network

In this work, ACO$_R$ is utilized to train a feed forward neural network, therefore numerical weights of neuron connections represent the solution components of the optimization problem and minimizing the MSE of output neurons is the performance criterion or

objective function. Search domain is (-1, 1), i.e. solution components may assume any real value in this range.
The solution archive and its correspondent normal distributions are implemented in a three dimensional matrix.

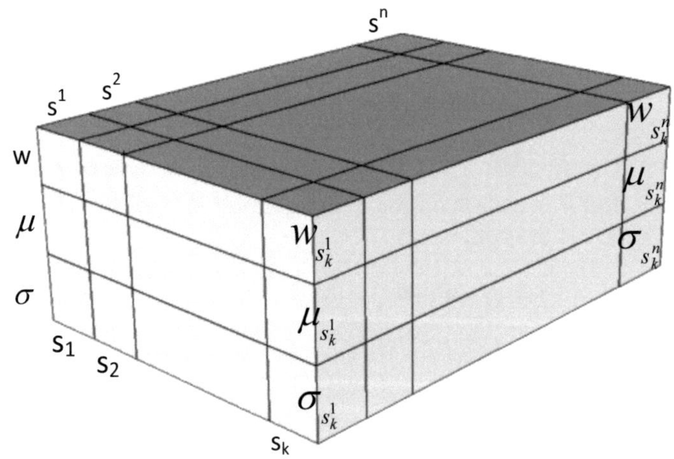

Fig. 1. The mixture $3\times k\times n$ matrix to store k solutions with their corresponding normal distributions.

Figure 1 demonstrates the mixture matrix and the way solutions and their corresponding normal distributions are stored. Mixture is a $3\times k\times n$ matrix in which the first row, represents the weight $w_{s_j^i}$ assigned to each variable of solutions. The second row holds the mean of the normal distribution which equals the value x^i of i-th variable of j-th solution s^i_j. The standard deviations of solutions are stored in the third row. In this way, for each variable of each solution, three values of w_j^i, μ_j^i and σ_j^i are assigned and ants can find probabilistic solutions referring to the mixture matrix. In fact, pheromone maintenance is performed by updating this matrix. In the simulations positive and negative update are carried out so that k is constant. n is the number of variables that is the number of weights of the neural network in this application.
In positive update phase, weights of the solutions stored in solution archive are calculated according to the MSE of the output layer. In this work, two approaches are utilized to calculate the weight of probability distributions. In the first attempt w_j is assigned in inverse relation to MSE as the objective function and it is termed *MSE-function* method.

$$w_j = \frac{t}{MSE_j} \quad j = 1,\dots,K \tag{23}$$

where t is a constant.
The second approach is sorting the solutions according to their performance and assigning them a *"rank"* value. Then the weight of each solution is calculated according to below *Rank-function* (Socha & Blum, 2007).

$$w_j = \frac{1}{\sqrt{2\pi}qk} e^{\frac{-(r_j-1)^2}{2q^2k^2}} \tag{24}$$

where q is a parameter and r represents the rank of corresponding solution. The mean of the above Gaussian function is set to 1, therefore the best solution with r=1 has the highest value.

The mean μ of normal PDFs are equal to the solution component values. The standard deviation of normal PDFs is calculated as

$$\sigma_j^i = \max\left\{\frac{\max(x^i_{1..m}) - \min(x^i_{1..m})}{\sqrt{c}}, \varepsilon\right\} \tag{25}$$

where c represents the iteration and m is the number of ants. Standard deviation is inversely proportional to the iteration number and it implies that solutions found in the first iterations are less useful than the outputs of the final iterations. Note that less standard deviation leads to the higher probability for selection of values around x^i. In this work, following equation for standard deviation is proposed to enhance the performance of algorithm.

$$\sigma_j^i = \max\left\{\frac{\max(x^i_{1..m}) - \min(x^i_{1..m})}{u.w_j.\sqrt{c}}, \varepsilon\right\} \tag{26}$$

where u is a parameter and standard deviation of each normal PDF is inversely proportional to its weight, therefore superior solutions with higher weights, lead to smaller standard deviations and higher probability of selection. Low rank and larger standard deviation is almost equivalent to uniform distribution and it results in decreasing the effect of bad solutions. The performance of proposed equation is evaluated in section 7.3.

6.2 Parameter setting for weight assignment

As shown in the equations (6) and (7), *nos* is the number of solutions used to update solution archive which is equivalent to pheromone update in regular ACO. After each iteration, all ants are sorted with respect to their solution quality and then the normal distribution correspondent to the *nos* best solutions are added to the mixture matrix. As shown in figure 1, the first row of the mixture matrix is the weight of each distribution and it is attained by *MSE-function* or *Rank-function* using equations (23) or (24). *Rank-function* is a normal distribution with qk as the standard deviation. Considering nos=10 and K=40, we need to calculate *Rank-function* for r=1, …, 10. r=10 gives the weight w_{10} to the solution of 10th ant. Depending on the value of qK as the σ of the *Rank-function*, the weight of last ants may get values quite close to zero. To avoid assignment of weights close to zero to the last solutions of the sorted ants, we can determine a limit C for the last $r=nos$ solution and find its correspondent standard deviation:

$$\frac{1}{\sigma\sqrt{2\pi}} e^{\frac{-(nos-1)^2}{2\sigma^2}} = C \tag{27}$$

$$nos = 1 + \sigma\sqrt{-2(Ln(C) + Ln(\sigma) + 0.9189)} \tag{28}$$

Assuming C=0.01, K=40 and nos=10, the standard deviation and consequently q is achieved ($\sigma = qK = 4.254$, $q = 0.1063$). By calculating q using above relation, no solution of *nos* ants will get a weight under the limit C, and in fact, one parameter is reduced in parameter setting of the algorithm.

7. Simulation results

In the literature, RBFNN method is utilized for DoA problem and its performance in terms of its feasibility to handle real time computation is investigated (Titus et al., 1994; Zooghby et al., 1997i; Kuwahara & Matsumoto, 2005). In this section, result of applying ACO_R-based neural network to DoA problem is presented and estimation errors are compared with RBFNN method. Besides possible ways to enhance the performance of ACO_R are investigated. The achieved results using *Rank-function* and *MSE-function* are compared to RBFNN method in figure 2. The separation angles of 3° to 7° are used and the generalization capability of the neural network is verified with 4°, 5° and 6° separation angles that were not part of the training set.

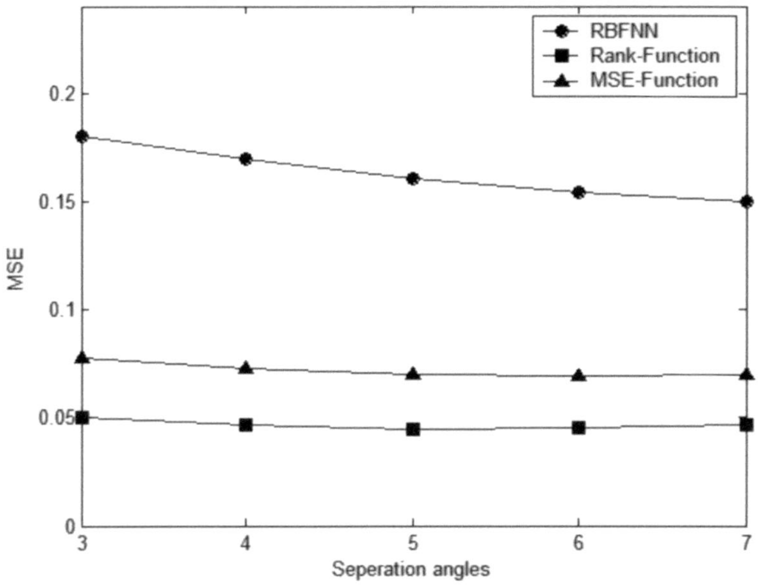

Fig. 2. The neural network is trained with 3° and 7° separation angles and its generalization capability is verified in 4°, 5°, 6° separation angles. *Rank-function* and *MSE-function* based weight assignments are compared as well.

Figure 3 demonstrates MSE for one more set of separation angles of 15° to 20° and it indicates that *Rank-function* method attains 3.12 to 5.9 times less MSE in comparison with RBFNN. Therefore, in DoA applications that high resolution is needed, ACO_R can be utilized to achieve lower and more uniform estimation errors.

As it is shown in figures 2 and 3, *Rank-function* approach for pheromone update generates better solutions but it takes three times longer than *MSE-function* approach to converge. This is reasonable because ranking function normalizes weight assignments for achieved MSE and this leads to uniform effect of performance in different stages of the simulation. Hence, stagnation is avoided and consequently search time is extended (Movahedipour et al., 2008). The ACO_R parameters used in above simulations are presented in table 1.

To study the behaviour of ACO_R algorithm, we investigated the role of various parameters on the performance of ACO_R and presented the results in the following sections.

Parameter	*Description*	*Value*
k	Number of solutions in mixture matrix	15
nos	Number of solutions used for pheromone update	8
m	Number of ants	85
ρ	Evaporation rate	0.2
γ	Dissolving rate	1.1
q	Ranking function parameter	0.2

Table 1. ACO_R Parameters

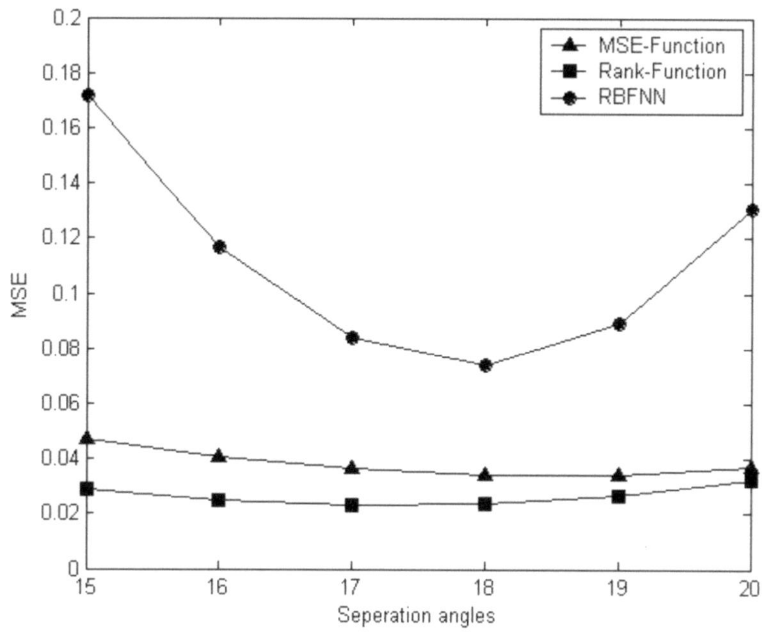

Fig. 3. The neural network is trained with 15° to 20° separation angles and its generalization capability is verified in 16°, 17°, 18° and 19° separation angles.

7.1 Number of solutions (*k*, *nos*, *q*)

We ran ACO_R using parameter settings of $k \in \{10, 15, 20, 25, 30, 35, 40, 45, 50\}$. We repeated the execution three times for each parameter setting, selected the best performing one for each k, and presented them in figure 4. nos was set to $k/3$ and $k/2$, q was achieved using equation (28) and all other choices were left the same. The parameter k represents the stored history of the algorithm and it guides ants to the promising areas of the search space. The algorithm does not show acceptable performance for k=10 because in this configuration very few number of found solutions are stored in the solution archive and consequently the experience of other ants cannot be utilized in a proper way to generate better solutions (see figure 4). On the other hand assigning values larger than 40, increases simulation time and decreases the quality of found solutions because a big solution archive keeps a larger amount of solutions with less quality. The numbers from one to nine and letters from *a* to *i*, indicate various parameter settings presented in table 2.

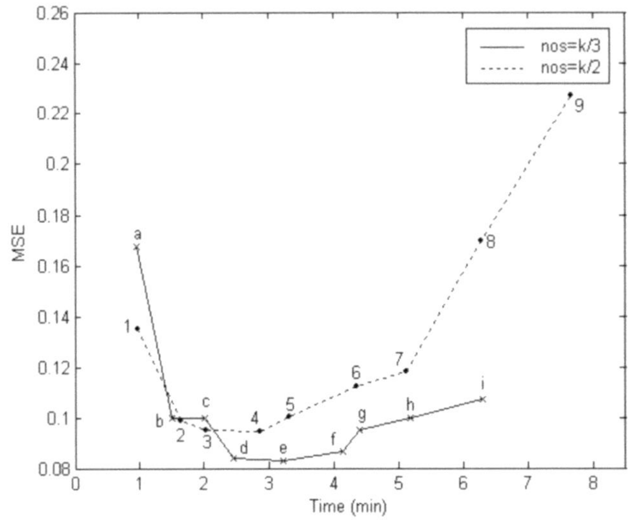

Fig. 4. ACO_R is executed for $k \in \{10, 15, 20, 25, 30, 35, 40, 45, 50\}$, *nos*={k/3, k/2} and *q* is achieved according to equation (28).

	k	*nos*	*q*
a	10	3	0.07
b	15	5	0.1
c	20	7	0.13
d	25	8	0.13
e	30	10	0.14
f	35	12	0.16
g	40	13	0.16
h	45	15	0.17
i	50	17	0.19
1	10	5	0.16
2	15	8	0.21
3	20	10	0.21
4	25	13	0.25
5	30	15	0.26
6	35	18	0.3
7	40	20	0.3
8	45	23	0.37
9	50	25	0.44

Table 2. ACO_R parameter settings for different *k*, *nos* and *q*. Other parameters are *m*=30, ρ =0.2 and γ =1.1.

7.2 Number of ants (*m*)

The results presented in figure 5 are based on the parameter settings of $m \in \{20, 35, 40, 50, 60, 70, 80, 90, 100\}$ leaving all other parameters the same. Increasing the number of ants improves the final solution but the computation time increases as well. We ran three times the ACO_R algorithm for each m, chose the best execution and plotted in figure 5.

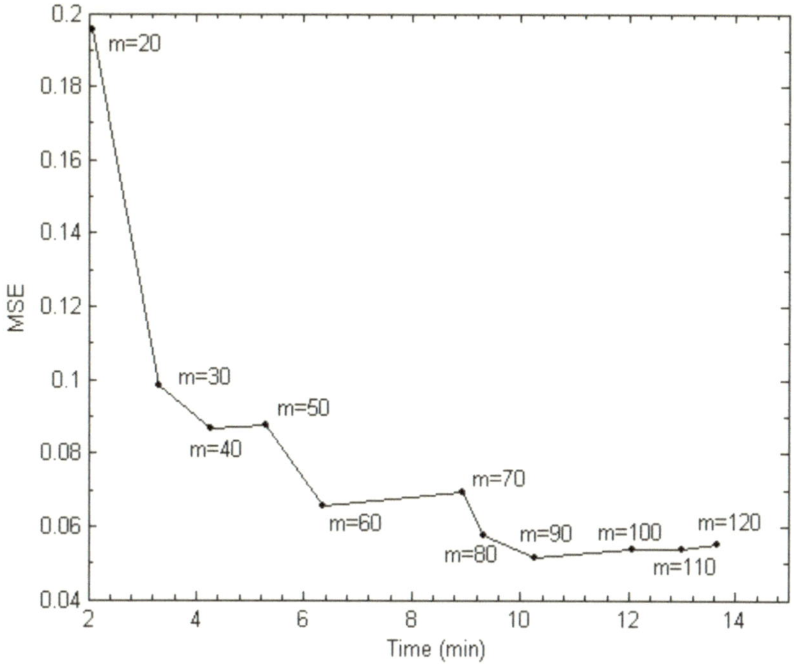

Fig. 5. ACO_R is executed for different numbers of ants. The other parameters are left same. (k=15, nos=8, ρ =0.2, γ =1.1, q=0.21)

7.3 Standard deviation

In this section, two methods of standard deviation assignment to PDFs are evaluated (see equations 25 and 26). The ACO_R algorithm was executed ten times for each method. The results illustrated in figure 6, indicate that the proposed equation (26) can decrease the found minimum for 29% but the convergence happens later and the computation time increases. The parameter u is set to 1 and 2 and the experiments suggest ACO_R is converged earlier if u is set to a large value and this results in lower quality solutions. Therefore, the parameter u can be used to compromise computation time with solution quality.

7.4 Exploration and exploitation

The experimental results summarized in previous sections, indicate ACO_R usually suffers from lack of simultaneous exploitation and exploration strategies. For instance, when the number of ants m is set to high values in comparison with k, exploitation is accomplished since the solution archive is fed with high quality solutions but the lack of enough exploration in this strategy results in fast convergence and suboptimal solutions. On the other hand, when k, ρ and γ are set to high values, exploration is achieved but the

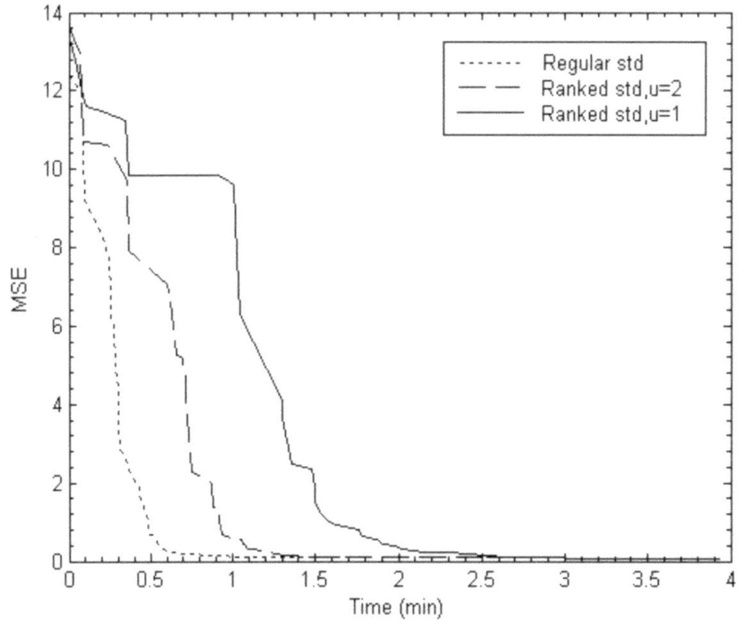

Fig. 6a. Different methods for standard deviation calculation are investigated. "Regular std" denotes equation (25) and "Ranked std" refers to equation (26). The other parameters are left same. (k=15, nos=8, ρ =0.2, γ =1.1, q=0.21)

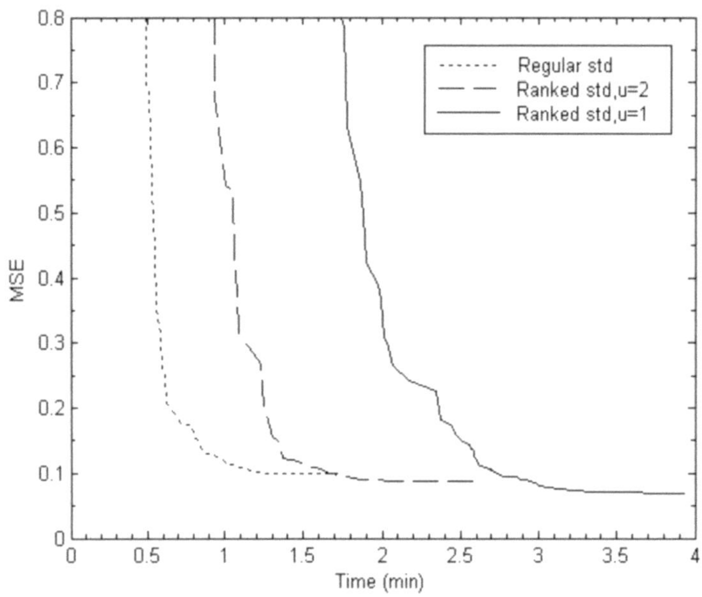

Fig. 6b. The convergence behaviour of algorithm in figure 6a is magnified.

algorithm suffers from lack of exploitation to take advantage of explored areas and construct high quality solutions. Starting the algorithm with dominant exploration strategy, provides a substantial information about the search space and then if it enters exploitation phase, this information will guide the ants to promising areas of search space and better solutions. Hence, it is proposed to implement two phases of exploration and exploitation in ACO_R and apply two different sets of parameter settings to implement each phase. This approach was experimented and best solutions were achieved among all different parameter settings with slight increased computation time (see figures 7a and 7b).
Different parameter sets used in this experiment are summarized in Table 3.

	k	nos	m	ρ	γ	q
Exploration set	30	10	35	0.25	1.15	0.2
Exploitation set	15	8	85	0.2	1.1	0.2
Exploration-Exploitation (Phase I)	30	10	35	0.25	1.15	0.2
Exploration-Exploitation (Phase II)	15	8	85	0.2	1.1	0.2

Table 3. The "Exploration", "Exploitation" and "Exploration-Exploitation" configuration.

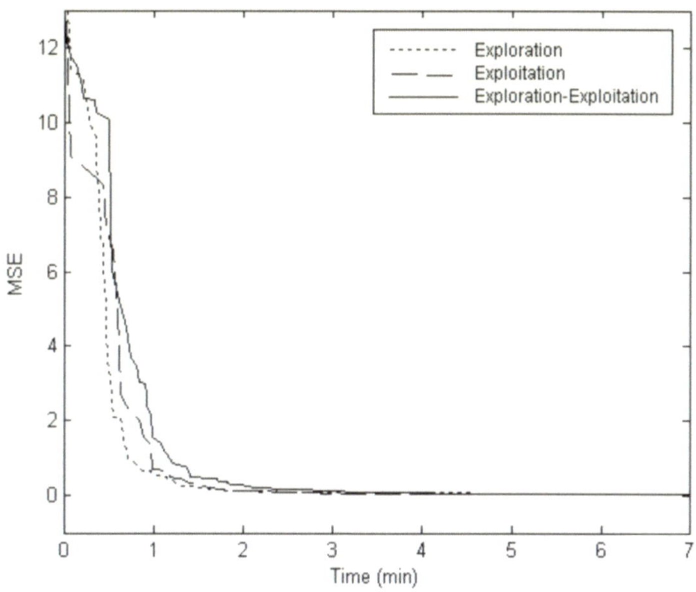

Fig. 7a. Two different parameter sets are defined for exploration and exploitation phases and three configurations of these parameter sets are tested. ACO_R with "Exploration", Exploitation" and "Exploration-Exploitation" parameters are executed for 10 times and the best run of each configuration is presented for comparison. In "Exploration-Exploitation", first ACO_R is executed with "Exploration" parameter set and then after 400 iterations, algorithm enters a new phase and uses "Exploitation" parameter set.

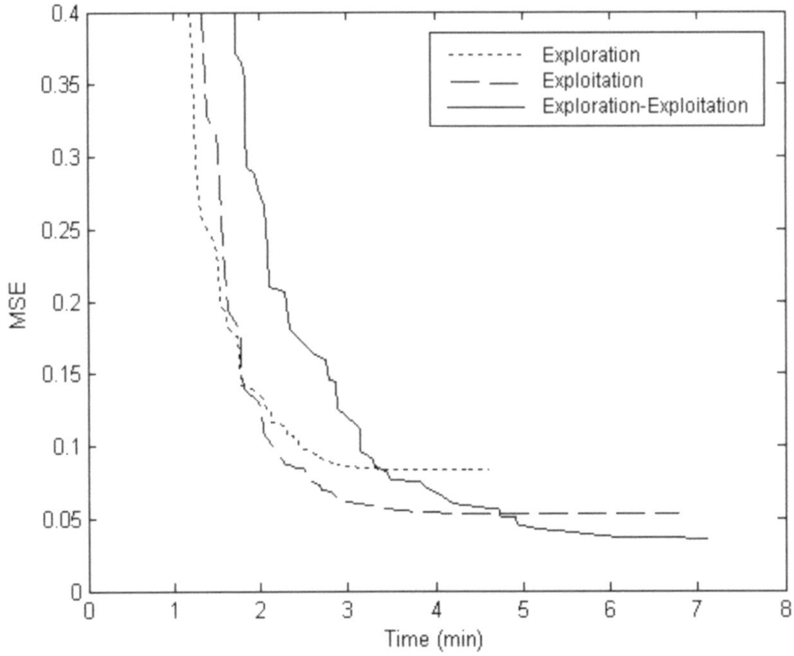

Fig. 7b. The convergence behaviour of algorithm in figure 7a is magnified.

In the exploration set, *k* is set to a higher value with comparison to exploitation set, so that the algorithm keeps a larger amount of information about the history of search. However, *m* is set to smaller value and *nos* is almost one third of *m*, implying that the most solutions found by ants are stored in the solution archive. In the exploitation phase, *nos*=0.09*m* and that points out just a small number of very high performing solutions (8 out of 85) are stored in the solution archive. In this way, high-quality solution archive guides the ants to explore more deeply, the areas that were found to be promising in the exploration phase.
We ran ACO_R algorithm with "Exploration", Exploitation" and "Exploration-Exploitation" parameters for 10 times and the result of each execution is summarized in Table 4.

	MSE of the converged solution in each execution									
Exploration	0.1085	0.0953	0.1088	0.1084	0.1308	**0.0836**	0.1062	0.1107	0.4797	0.0960
Exploitation	0.0636	0.0691	0.0578	0.0628	0.0573	0.0665	0.0777	0.0599	**0.0534**	0.0603
Exploration-Exploitation	**0.0362**	0.0629	0.0516	0.0524	0.0515	0.0549	0.0511	0.0526	0.0657	0.0641

Table 4. MSE per execution for each configuration

The bold numbers in Table 4 are related to the executions with lowest MSE and their computation time are summarized in Table 5. The complete iterations of these executions are illustrated in figure 7a and 7b. This approach resulted in the lowest MSE of 0.0362 that was the best-found solution in all of our experiments with various parameter settings.

	Min	*Time*
Exploration	0.0836	3.76
Exploitation	0.0534	4.52
Exploration-Exploitation	0.0362	6.88

Table 5. Minimum MSE and the computation time for best executions of each configuration

8. Conclusion

The application of ACO_R algorithm to train an interpolator feed-forward neural network and perform DoA estimation have been studied in this chapter. The ACO_R based neural network has been used to model DoA estimation and it demonstrated superior performance in comparison with RBFNN as the known approach for DoA problem.

Various parameter settings in ACO_R were investigated and the behaviour of algorithm was discussed accordingly. The possibilities to enhance ACO_R behaviour were examined. Standard deviation calculation in positive update phase is proposed to be inversely proportional to the rank function. In addition, it was investigated how the algorithm performance is improved by guiding the algorithm through exploration and exploitation phases by different parameter sets during execution.

9. References

Christodoulou, C. (2001). Applications of Neural Network in Electromagnetics, Artech House.

Danneville, E; Brault, J & Laurin, J. (2005). Implementation of an MLP-based DOA System Using a Reduced Number of MM-wave Antenna Elements, Proceedings of International Joint Conference on Neural Networks, Montreal, Canada, July 31-August 4, 2005.

Deneubourg, J.-L; Aron, S.; Goss, S. & Pasteels, J.-M. (1990). The self-organizing exploratory pattern of the Argentine ant. Journal of insect behavior, 3, 159-168.

Dorigo, M.; Maniezzo, V. & Colorni, A. (1991). Positive feedback as a search strategy, Technical Report 91-016, Dipartimento di Elettronica, Politecnico di Milano, Italy, 1991.

Dorigo, M.; Maniezzo, V. & Colorni, A. (1996). The Ant System: Optimization by a colony of cooperating agents, IEEE Trans SMC Part B, 1996.

Dorigo, M. & Stutzle, T. (2004). Ant Colony Optimization, MIT Press, Cambridge, MA.

Godara, L. (2002). Handbook of antennas in wireless communications, CRC Press.

Kuwahara; Matsumoto (2005). Experiments of direction finder by RBF neural network with post processing, IEEE Electronic Letters, Volume 41, Issue 10, May 2005.

Lee, J. (2004). A first course in combinatorial optimization, Cambridge texts in mathematics.

Movahedipour, H.; Atlasbaf, Z. & Hakkak, M. (2006). Performance of Neural Network Trained with Genetic Algorithm for Direction of Arrival Estimation, IEEE MCWC Conference, 2006.

Movahedipour, H; Atlasbaf, Z; Mirzaee, A & Hakkak, M. (2008). A Hybrid Approach Involving Artificial Neural Network and Ant Colony Optimization for Direction of Arrival Estimation, IEEE CCECE Conference, Canada, 2008.

Papadimitriou, CH & Steiglitz, K. (1982) Combinatorial optimization—Algorithms and complexity, Dover.

Schoonderwoerd, R.; Holland, O. & Bruten, J. (1997). Ant-based Load Balancing in Telecommunications Networks", Adaptive behaviors, 1997.

Socha, K. (2004). ACO for continuous and mixed-variable optimization, in M. Dorigo, M. Birattari, C. Blum, L. M. Gambardella, F. Mondada and T. Stutzle (eds), Ant Colony Optimization and Swarm Intelligence, 4th International Workshop, ANTS 2004, Vol. 3172 of LNCS, Springer-Verlag, Berlin, Germany, pp. 25–36.

Socha, K. & Blum, C. (2007). Hybrid ant algorithms applied to feed-forward neural network training: An application to medical pattern classification, Neural Computing and Applications, 16(3): 235–248, 2007.

Socha, K. & Dorigo, M. (2008). Ant colony optimization for continuous domains, European Journal of Operations Research 185(3): 1155–1173.

Titus, K ; Leung, H. & Litva, J. (1994). Radial Basis Function Neural Network for Direction-of-Arrival Estimation, IEEE Signal Processing Letters, vol. 1, No. 2, February 1994.

Titus, K ; Leung, H. & Litva, J. (1994). Artificial neural network for AOA estimation in a multipath environment over the sea, IEEE Journal of Oceanic Engineering, vol. 19, (Oct. 1994), pp 555-562.

Zooghby, A.; Christodoulou, C. & Georgiopoulos, M. (1997). Performance of Radial-Basis Function Networks for Direction of Arrival Estimation with Antenna Arrays, IEEE Transactions on Antenna and Propagation, Vol. 45, No. 11, November 1997.

Zooghby, A.; Christodoulou, C. & Georgiopoulos, M. (1997i). Antenna array signal processing with neural networks for direction of arrival estimation", IEEE Antennas and Propagation Society International Symposium, Volume 4, Issue 13, July 1997.

Zooghby, A.; Christodoulou, C. & Georgiopoulos, M. (2000). A neural network-based smart antenna for multiple source tracking, IEEE Trans. Antennas Propagation, pp. 768-776, May 2000.

13

Ant Colony Optimization for Coherent Synthesis of Computer System

Mieczysław Drabowski
Cracow University of Technology
Poland

1. Introduction

The goal of high-level synthesis of computer systems is to find an optimum solution satisfying the requirements and constraints enforced by the given specification of the system. The following criteria of optimality are usually considered: costs of system implementation, its operating speed, power consumption and dependability. A specification describing a computer system may be provided as a set of interactive tasks (processes, functions).

The partition of the functions between hardware and software is the basic problem of synthesis. Such partition is significant, because every computer system must be realized as result of hardware implementation for its certain tasks. In the synthesis methods so far, the software and hardware parts were developed separately and then connected in process the co-called co-synthesis, which increased the costs and decreased the quality and reliability of the final product. The resources distribution is to specify, what hardware and software are in system and to allocate theirs to specific tasks, before designing execution details.

The problems of tasks scheduling are one of the most significant issues occurring at the procedure synthesis of operating systems responsible for controlling the distribution of tasks and resources in computer systems.

The objective of this research is to present the concept of coherent approach to the problem of system synthesis, i.e. a combined solution to task scheduling and resource partition problems. The model and approach are new and original proposals allowing synergic design of hardware and software for performing operations of the computer system. This is approach, which we called a par-synthesis (coherent co-synthesis). This research shows the results selected of computational experiments for different instances of system par-synthesis problems proving the correctness of the coherent synthesis concept and shows the methods solving these problems. Due to the fact that synthesis problems and their optimizations are NP-complete we suggest meta-heuristic approach: **Ant Colony Optimization**.

Coherent co-synthesis of computer systems, as well as synergic design methodology their structures and scheduling procedures may have practical application in developing the tools for automatic aided for rapid prototyping of such systems.

2. General model and synthesis of computer system

2.1 The classical process of computer system synthesis

The classical process co-synthesis (D'Ambrioso & Hu, 1994) – hardware and software – for computer system consists of the following stages (Fig. 2.1):

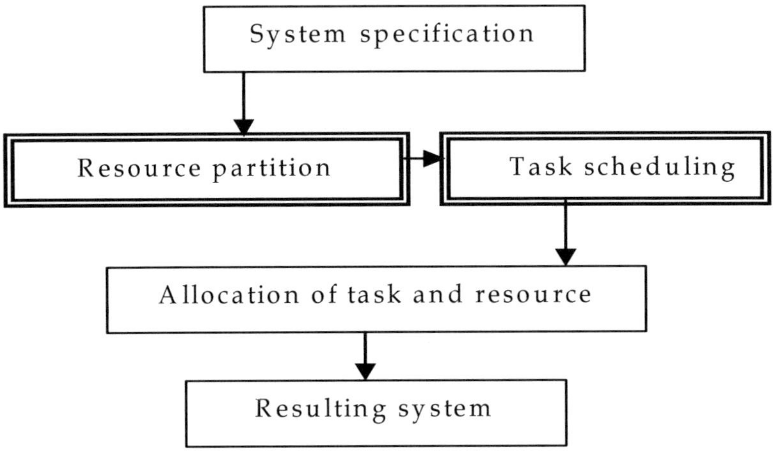

Fig. 2.1. The process co-synthesis

1. Specification of the designed system in terms functional and behavioural – requirements and constraints analysis. The system description in a high-level language, abstracting from the physical implementation.
2. Resource partition – architecture development.
3. Task scheduling – system control development.
4. Allocation the system functions to the architecture elements – generating the system modular architecture, control adaptation and the whole system integration.

The system being constructed consists of hardware elements and software components performed by selected hardware modules (Gajski, 1997) . The system is specified by a set of requirements to be met. In general, each requirement may be satisfied by hardware elements or software components executed by universal processors and memories. Obviously, at this stage of design, one must take into account appropriate system constraints and criteria of optimal system operation. Accordingly, the key issue in the synthesis is efficient partitioning of system resources due to their hardware and software implementation, providing fulfilment of all requirements and the minimum implementation cost (Sgroi et al., 2000).

Such partitioning methodology (Gupta & De Micheli, 1993) may accept, as a starting point, assignment of the hardware implementation to all system functions and further optimization of project costs, search for possibilities of replacing certain tasks realized by hardware with their software equivalents. Other methods (De Micheli, 1994) of the resources partitioning start with an exclusive software implementation and further search for implementation of certain tasks by hardware. In both approaches the objective is optimization of the implementation cost of the same tasks, i.e. in particular minimization of the execution time by specialized hardware (Axelson, 1997). Obviously the requirements and constraints, especially those regarding time and power consumption, have decisive influence upon selection of necessary hardware components.

The measure for an efficient implementation of a computer system is the degree of its modules utilization, minimized idle-time of its elements and maximized parallel operation of its elements (Schulz et al., 1998).
A non-optimum system contains redundant modules or modules that are excessively efficient in comparison to the needs defined by the tasks what, consequently, increases the system cost. In high-level synthesis, the optimization of the designed system costs, speed and power consumption is usually an iterative process, requiring both changes in the architecture and task scheduling (Steinhausen, 1993). That is, why an optimum system may be created as a compromise between the system control algorithm and its hardware organization.

2.2 The general model for the problem of system synthesis

System synthesis is a multi-criteria optimization problem. The starting point for constructing our approach to the issues of hardware and software synthesis is the deterministic theory of task scheduling (Błażewicz et al., 2007). The theory may serve as a methodological basis for multiprocessor systems synthesis.
Accordingly, decomposition of the general task scheduling model is suggested, adequate to the problems of computer system synthesis. From the control point of view such a model should take into account the tasks, which may be either preemptable or nonpreemptable Coffman, 1976). These characteristics are defined according to the scheduling theory. Tasks are preemptable when each task can be interrupted and restarted later without incurring additional costs. In such a case the schedules are called to be preemptive. Otherwise, tasks are nonpreemptable and schedules nonpreemptive .
Preemptability of tasks in our approach cannot be a feature of the searched schedule - as in the task scheduling model so far. The schedule contains all assigned tasks with individual attributes: preemptive, nonpreemptive. From the point of view of the system synthesis, the implementation of certain tasks from the given set must be nonpreemptible, for the other may be preemptible (what, in turn, influences significantly selection of an appropriate scheduling algorithm) (Węglarz, 1999). Moreover, we wish to specify the model of task scheduling in a way suitable for finding optimum control methods (in terms of certain criteria) as well as optimum assignment of tasks to universal and specialised hardware components. Accordingly, we shall discuss the system of type the complex of resources and operations (Błażewicz et al., 2000):

$$\sum = \{ \mathbf{R}, \mathbf{T}, \mathbf{C} \} \quad (1)$$

Where:
R - is the set of resources (hardware and software),
T - is the set of the system's tasks (operations),
C - is the set of optimization criteria for the system's behaviour and structure.
Resources. We assume that processor set $P = \{P_1, P_2,..., P_m\}$ consists of m elements and additional resources $A = \{ A_1, A_2,..., A_p\}$ consist of p elements.
Tasks. We consider a set of n tasks to be processed with a set of resources. The set of tasks consists of n elements $T = \{T_1, T_2,..., T_n\}$. A feasible schedule is optimal, if its length is minimal and it is implemented using minimum resource cost.

Each task is defined by a set of parameters: resource requirements, execution time, ready time and deadline, attribute - preemptable or nonpreemptable. The tasks set may contain defined precedence constraints represented by a digraph with nodes representing tasks, and directed edges representing precedence constraints. If there is at least one precedence constraint in a task set, we shall refer it to as a set of dependent tasks; otherwise they are a set of independent tasks.

Optimality criteria. As for the optimality criteria for the system being designed, we shall assume its minimum cost, maximum operating speed and minimum power consumption.

The proposed model may be used for defining various synthesis problems for optimum computer systems.

The model of a system in our approach, (Drabowski et al., 2002) typical for the theory of task scheduling, consists of a set of requirements (operations, tasks) and existing relationships between them (related to their order, required resources, time, readiness and completion deadlines, preemptability/nonpreemptability, priority etc.). The synthesis procedure contains the following phases: identification of hardware and software resources for task implementation, defining the processing time, defining the conflict-free task schedule and defining the level of resource co-sharing and the degree of concurrency in task performance (Drabowski, 2008).

The synthesis has to perform the task partitioning into hardware and software resources. After performing the partition, the system shall be implemented partially by specialized hardware in the form of integrated circuits (readily available on the resources pools or designed in accordance to the suggested characteristics) (Harel, 1987). Software modules of the system are generated with the use of software engineering tools. Appropriate processors shall be taken from the resource pool. Synthesis of a system may also provide a system control, create an interface and provide synchronization and communication between the tasks implemented by software and hardware.

The system synthesis, i.e. defining system functions, identifying resources, defining control should be implemented in synergy and be subject to multi-criteria optimization and verification during implementation.

2.3 The coherent process of system synthesis

Modeling the joint search for the optimum task schedule and resource partition of the designed system into hardware and software parts is fully justified. Simultaneous consideration of these problems may be useful in implementing optimum solutions, e.g. the cheapest hardware structures. Synergic approach enables also performing of all assigned tasks with the minimum schedule length. With such approach, the optimum task distribution is possible on the universal and specialized hardware and defining resources with maximum efficiency.

We propose the following schematic diagram of a coherent process of systems synthesis (Drabowski & Czajkowski, 2005), (Fig. 2.2).

The suggested coherent synthesis consists of the following steps:

1. specification of requirements for the system to be designed and its interactions with the environment,
2. specification of tasks, including evaluation of task executive parameters using available resources (e.g. execution times),
3. assuming the initial values of resource set and task scheduling – initial resource set and task schedule should be admissible, i.e. should satisfy all requirements in a non-optimum way,

4. task scheduling and resource partitioning,
5. evaluating the operating speed and system cost, multi-criteria optimization,
6. the evaluation should be followed by a modification of the resource set, a new system partitioning into hardware and software parts (step 4).

Iterative calculations are executed till satisfactory design results are obtained - i.e. optimal (or sub-optimal) system structure and schedule. The designed system should be fast, cheap and small of power consumption.

3. Ant Colony and Branch & Bound methods in coherent synthesis of computer systems

The synthesis based on two algorithms behaving in totally different ways lets you not only find the (sub-)optimal solution, but also verify this solution by algorithm searching through all possible solutions.

Presented algorithms let us find the solution, but at the same time they let us evaluate the algorithms themselves. This way we can tell which of the algorithms is faster in finding better and better solutions, which algorithm is more tolerant to modifications of system parameters, and also which of them enables fast adaptation to new parameters, while the system changes dynamically.

If we assume that solution is changing dynamically, it would be a big obstacle for greedy algorithms, because modification of single parameter (giving eventually better parameters) forces another verification of the full set of solutions.

In our approach, the obtained solutions are considered allowing for the following parameters:

- size and cost of operational memory,
- size and cost of mass storage,
- number of processors and the cost of computing power,
- the time needed for scheduling the tasks.

To evaluate obtained solution, we use the method of weighted average: evaluated are all parameters considered during the analysis with appropriate weights; if the final grade of the new solution is better than the grade of the previous one, the new solution is being saved.

3.1 Adaptation of ACO to solve the problems of synthesis

The Ant Colony Optimization (ACO) algorithm is a heuristics using the idea of agents (here: ants) imitating their real behavior (Blum, 2005). Basing on specific information (distance, amount of pheromone on the paths, etc.) ants evaluate the quality of paths and choose between them with some random probability (the better path quality, the higher probability it represents). Having walked the whole path from the source to destination, ants learn from each other by leaving a layer of pheromone on the path. Its amount depends on the quality of solution chosen by agent: the better solution, the bigger amount of pheromone is being left. The pheromone is then "vapouring" to enable the change of path chosen by ants and let them ignore the worse (more distant from targets) paths, which they were walking earlier (Fig. 3.1).

The result of such algorithm functioning is not only finding the solution. Very often it is the trace, which led us to this solution. It lets us analyze not only a single solution, but also permutations generating different solutions, but for our problems basing on the same

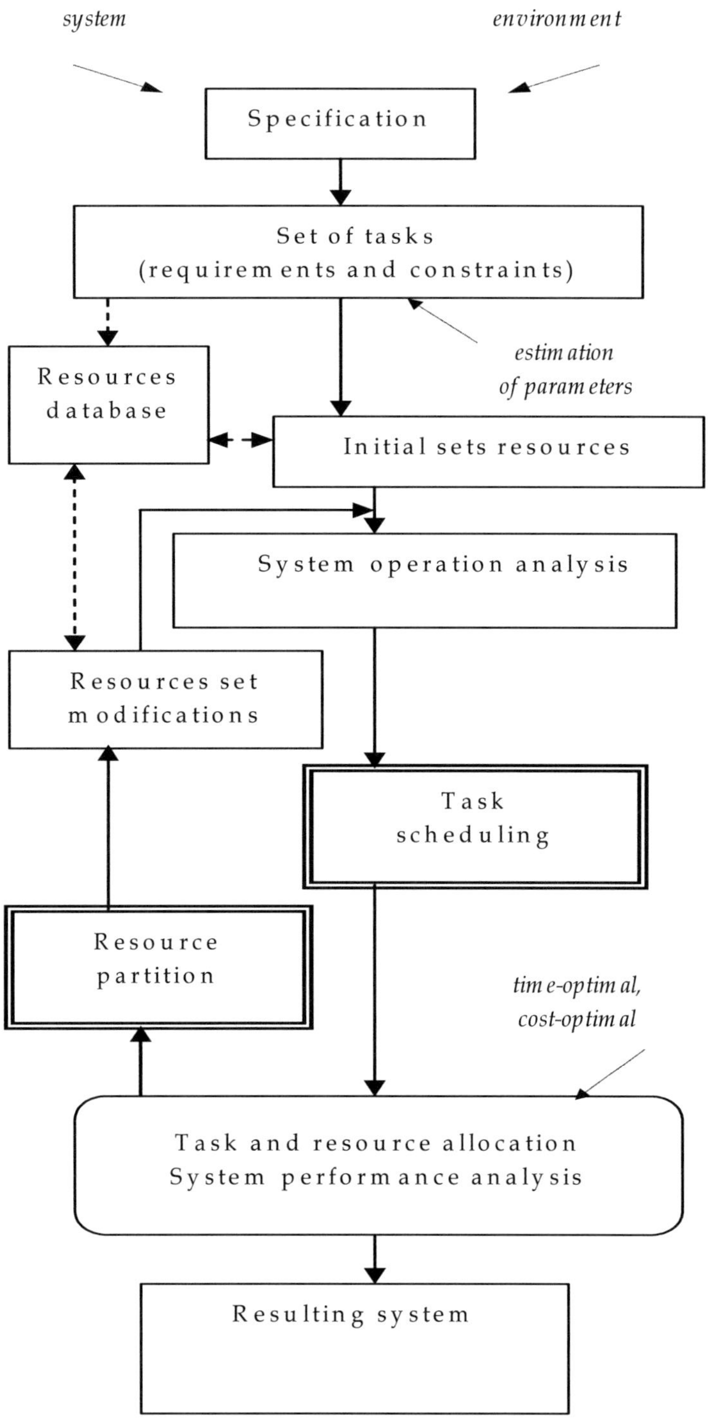

Fig. 2.2. The coherent process of computer system synthesis

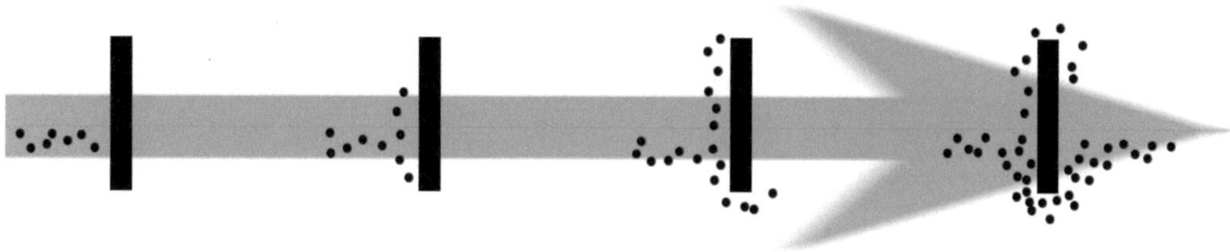

Fig. 3.1. The idea of algorithm - overcoming the obstacle by ants

division (i.e. tasks are scheduled in different order, although they are still allocated to the same processors). This kind of approach is used for solving the problems of synthesis, where not only the division of tasks is important, but also their sequence (Montgomery et al., 2006). To adapt the ACO algorithm to synthesis problems, the following parameters have been defined:

- Number of agents (ants) in the colony,
- Vapouring factor of pheromone (from the range (0; 1)).

The process of choosing these parameters is important and should consider that:

- For too big number of agents, the individual cycle of algorithm can last quite long, and the values saved in the table ("levels of pheromone") as a result of addition will determine relatively weak solutions.
- On the other hand, when the number of agents is too small, most of paths will not be covered and as a result, the best solution can long be uncovered.

The situation is similar for the vapouring factor:

- Too small value will cause that ants will quickly "forget" good solutions and as a result it can quickly come to so called *stagnation* (the algorithm will stop at one solution, which doesn't have to be the best one).
- Too big value of this factor will make ants don't stop analyze "weak" solutions; furthermore, the new solutions may not be pushed, if time, which has passed since the last solution found will be long enough (it is the values of pheromone saved in the table will be too big).

The ACO algorithm defines two more parameters, which let you balance between:

- α - the amount of pheromone on the path, and
- β - "quality" of the next step.

These parameters are chosen for specific task. This way, for parameters:

- $\alpha > \beta$ there is bigger influence on the choice of path, which is more often exploited,
- $\alpha < \beta$ there is bigger influence on the choice of path, which offers better solution,
- $\alpha = \beta$ there is balanced dependency between quality of the path and degree of its exploitation,
- $\alpha = 0$ there is a heuristics based only on the quality of passage between consecutive points (ignorance of the level of pheromone on the path),
- $\beta = 0$ there is a heuristics based only on the amount of pheromone (it is the factor of path attendance),
- $\alpha = \beta = 0$ we'll get the algorithm making division evenly and independently of the amount of pheromone or the quality of solution.

Having given the set of neighborhood N of the given point i, amount of pheromone on the path τ and the quality of passage from point i to point j as an element of the table η you can present the probability of passage from point i to j as:

$$p_{ij}^k = \begin{cases} \dfrac{[\tau_{ij}]^{\alpha}[\eta_{ij}]^{\beta}}{\sum\limits_{l \in N_i^k} [\tau_{il}]^{\alpha}[\eta_{il}]^{\beta}} & \text{when } j \in N_i^k \\ 0 & \text{else} \end{cases} \tag{3.1}$$

Formula 3.1. Evaluation of the quality of the next step in the ACO algorithm

In the approach presented here, the ACO algorithm uses agents to find three pieces of information:

- the best / the most beneficial division of tasks between processors,
- the best sequence of tasks,
- searching for the best possible solution for the given distribution.

Agents (ants) are searching for the solutions which are the collection resulting from the first two targets (they give the unique solution as a result). After scheduling, agents fill in two tables:

- two-dimensional table representing allocation of task to the given processor,
- one-dimensional table representing the sequence of running the tasks.

The job of agent involves (Fig. 3.2):

- collecting information (from the tables of allocation) concerning allocation of tasks to resources and running the tasks
- drawing the next available task with the probability specified in the table of task running sequence
- drawing resources (processor) with the probability specified in the table of allocation the tasks to resources
- is it the last task?

To evaluate the quality of allocation the task to processor, the following method is being used (Fig. 3.3):

- evaluation of current (incomplete) scheduling
- allocation of task to the next of available resources
- evaluation of the sequence obtained
- release the task
- was it the last of available resources?

The calculative complexity of single agent is polynomial and depends on the number of tasks, resources and times of tasks beginning.

After initiating the tables (of allocation and sequence) for each agent, the algorithm starts the above cycle, after which the evaluation of solutions takes place. Having completed the particular number of cycles, the parameters are being updated and algorithm continues working (Fig. 3.4):

- initiation of tables of tasks running sequence and allocation of tasks to resources
- completing the cycle of analysis for each agent
- evaluation of the best solution found in current cycle
- for each agent – basing on the best solution – updating the tables of tasks running sequence and allocation of tasks to resources
- is it the last cycle?
- Optimization/customization of system parameters.

3.2 Customization of B&B to synthesis problems solving

Branch & Bound (B & B) algorithm is a greedy algorithm browsing the set of solutions and "pruning" these branches, which give worse solutions than the best solution already found (Mitten, 1970). This kind of approach often significantly reduces the number of solutions, which must be considered. However in the worst case scenario, "pruning" the branches is impossible and as a result, the B & B algorithm analyzes the complete search-tree.

Both forms (DFS and BFS) of B & B algorithm were used for synthesis. It let us comprehend the problem of analysis of three different kinds of optimization (cost, power, time) without discrediting any of the problems.

B&B algorithm investigates the problem by:

- choice of the task,
- definition of initial time to which you can schedule the task,
- choice of processor on which the task will be allocated.

Because allocating the chosen task in the first available time unit or on the first available processor is not always the best idea, all available time units and processors are being considered. As a result, calculative complexity of algorithm changes exponentially when new tasks are added or polynomial after addition of new processors. Although B&B algorithm operation process is relatively simple, the number of solutions, which must be examined, is huge.

Example

In scheduling of ten independent tasks on 4 different processors and on 2 additional resources is the full tree which included more than 10^{18} potential solutions!

3.3 Calculative experiments

Because one algorithm creates unlimited cycle and the other one takes a very long time to finish in many cases, the results given in the tables' present state of the system after not more than given time limit of analysis (Drabowski, 2007). Depending on the solution criterion, there were used both forms of B&B – DFS and BFS – for the algorithm to be able to find a good solution in time. Each solution given by Ant Colony algorithm will be graded on the basis of solutions found by Branch & Bound algorithm.

Formula for the assessment of obtained solution is following:

$$assessment = ASS = 100\% \cdot \frac{1}{criterions} \cdot \sum_{criterion=1}^{criterions} \frac{result_{B\&B}}{result_{ACO}} \tag{3.2}$$

Formula 3.2. Assessment of solutions

The final grade is influenced only by these parameters, which were being optimized by algorithms: cost, power and time of scheduling (Drabowski, 2009).

The assessment of proposed system includes all three parameters (scheduling time, cost and power consumed by the system):

- the assessment higher than 100% means that ACO algorithm has found better solution than B&B,
- the assessment equal 100% means that both algorithms have found equally good solutions,
- the assessment less than 100% means that B&B algorithm has found better solution.

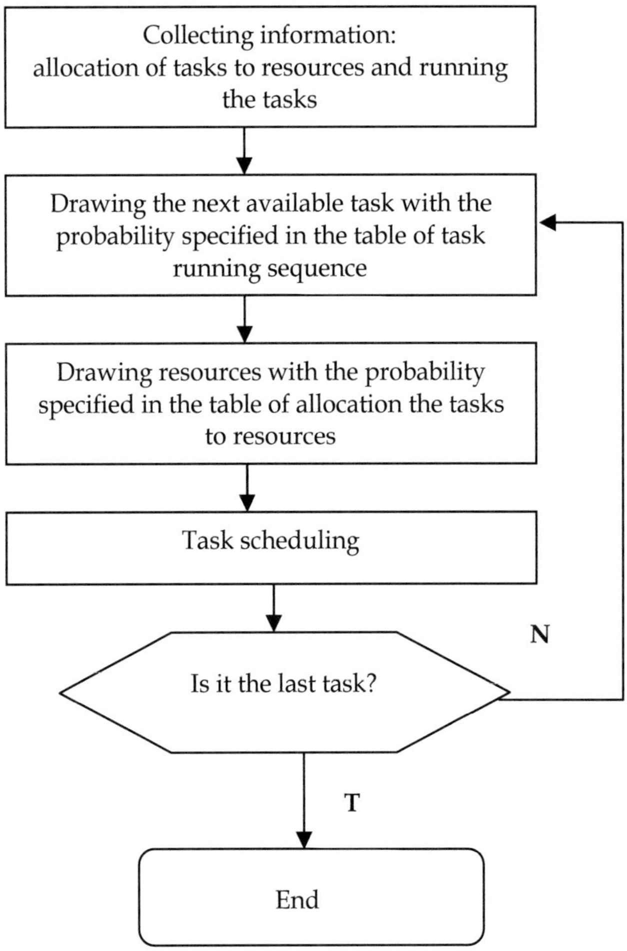

Fig. 3.2. Agent operation scheme

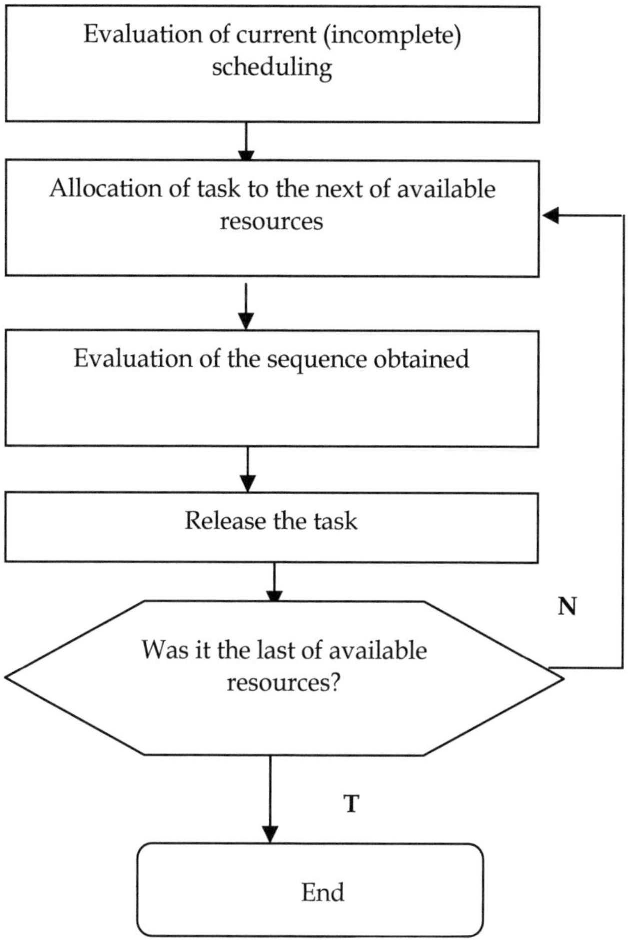

Fig. 3.3. The principle of path evaluation

3.3.1 Verification of tasks schedule

Task schedule proposed by ACO and B&B algorithms was verified on the basis of the following examples.

For the simplicity of tasks descriptions, the *(n: i, j)* scheme was adopted, where *n* - name of the task, *i* - constant time (independent of the speed of processor), *j* - time dependent on the speed of processor.

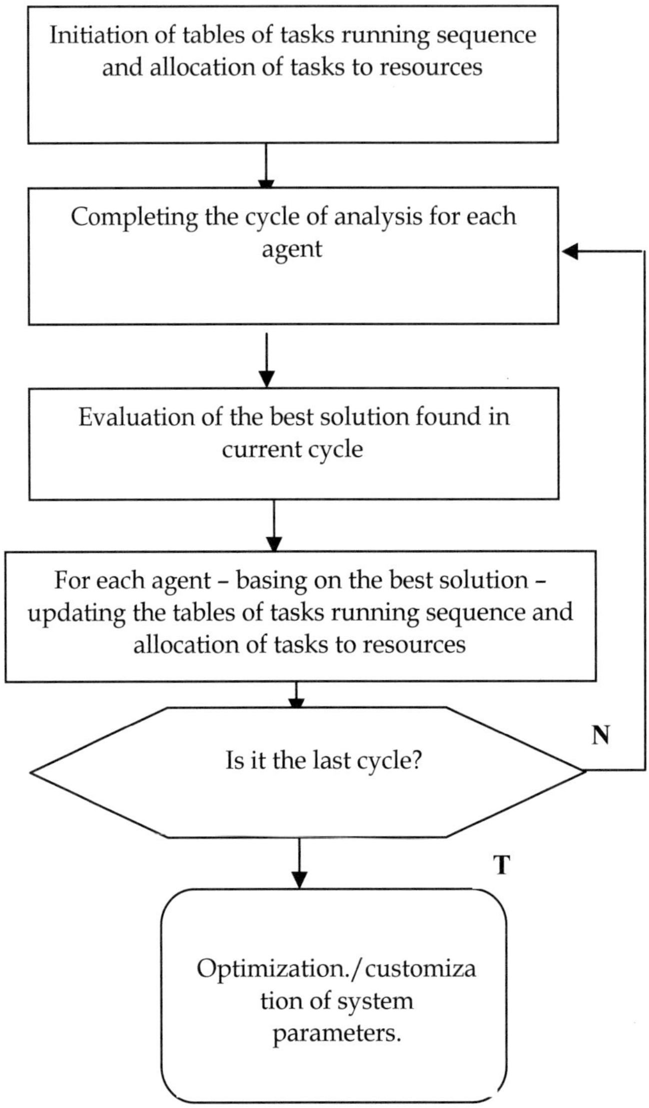

Fig. 3.4. The principle of ACO algorithm operation

Example 1

Parameters of the problem:

- 5 tasks.
- 2 identical, universal processors.
- Additional resources (memory, storage): without of constraints.
- Parameters of tasks:

Tasks	Time	memory	storage
Task1	1	2	1
Task2	1	2	1
Task3	2	1	1
Task4	1	1	1
Task5	1	2	1

- Relations between tasks are shown on the figure:

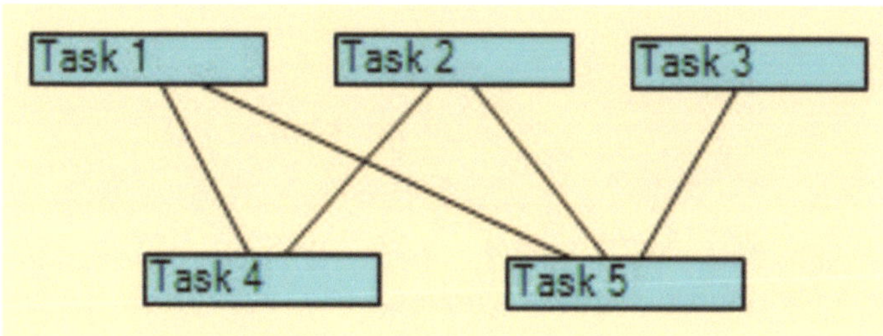

Scheduling obtained by both algorithms is identical.

- Total time of scheduling: 3 units,
- Use of resources: 2 units.

The algorithms have found solutions immediately after their activation. Obtained scheduling is presented on the figure (Fig. 3.5):

Fig. 3.5. Schedules - results of operations of algorithms

Example 2

Parameters of the problem:

- 12 identical tasks UET (time equal 1); Unit Execution Tasks.
- 2 identical, universal processors.
- Relations between tasks are shown on the figure:

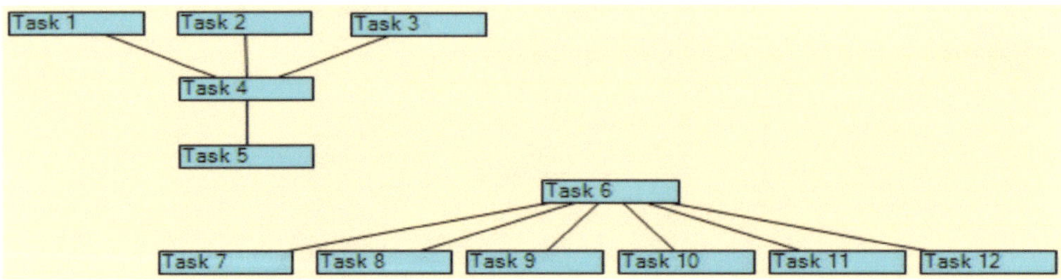

Scheduling obtained by both algorithms is identical: 6 total time of scheduling.
The algorithms have found solutions immediately after their activation. Obtained scheduling is presented on the figure (Fig. 3.6):

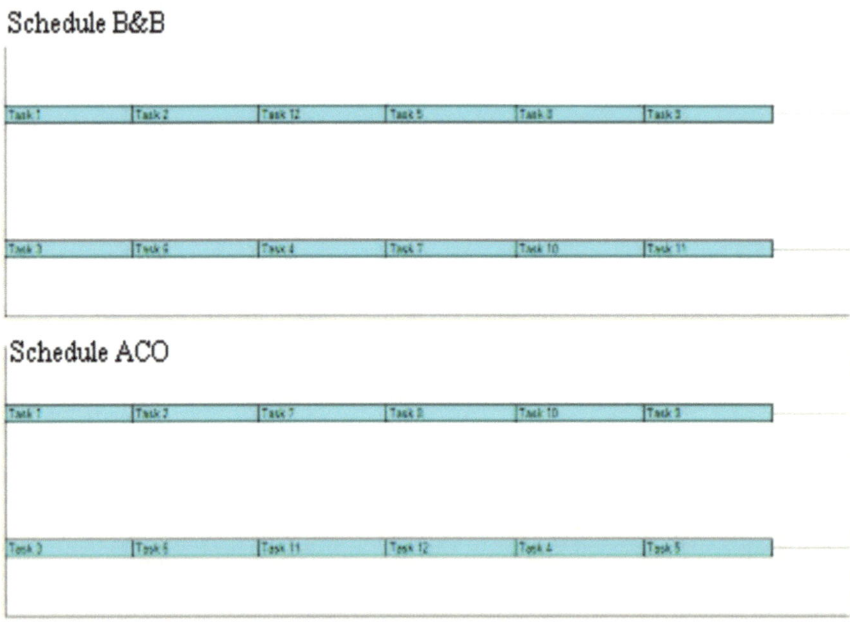

Fig. 3.6. Schedules - results of operations of algorithms

Example 3

Example from link STG (*Standard Graph Set:* task 000 with packet RNC50), [<http://www.kasahara.elec.waseda.ac.jp/schedule/index.html>].
Parameters of the problem:

- 50 dependent tasks about difference parameters.
- 2 identical, universal processors.
- Additional resources (memory, storage): without of constraints.

The algorithms have found solutions 15 minutes after their activation. Scheduling obtained by both algorithms is identical: schedule length: 131 units (optimum by STG, too).
Scheduling obtained by both algorithms is identical: 131 total time of scheduling, are presented on the figure (Fig. 3.7):

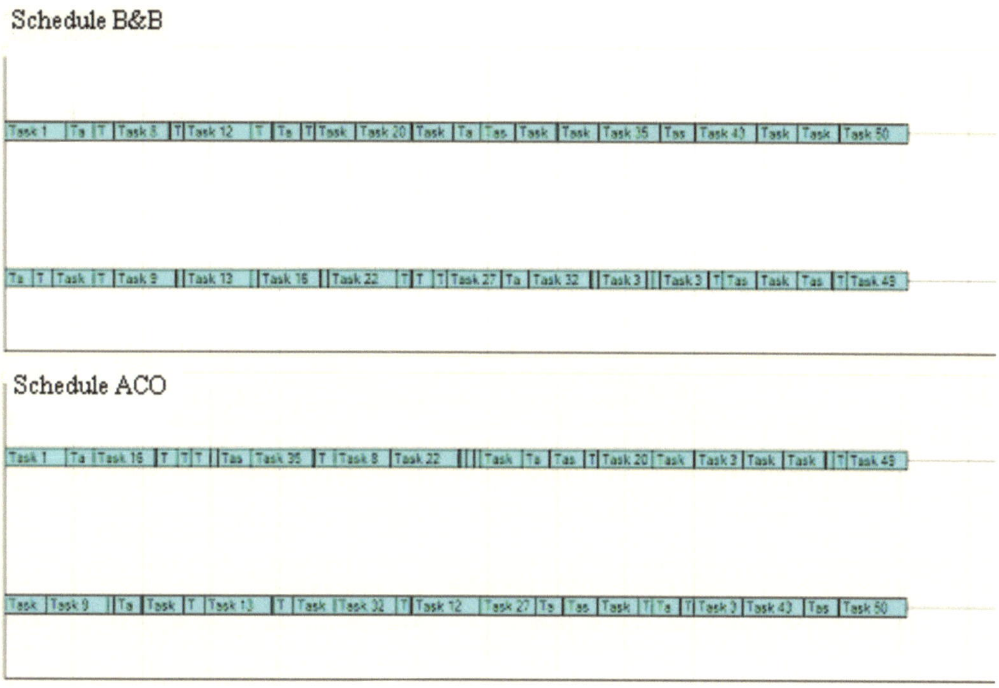

Fig. 3.7. Schedules - results of operations of algorithms

3.3.2 Verification of resources partition

Resources partition proposed by ACO and B & B algorithms were verified on the basis of the following examples.

Example 1

Parameters of the problem:

- 5 tasks.
- 2 identical, universal processors.
- Additional resources: 3 units of memory, 3 units' storage.
- Parameters of tasks:

Tasks	Time	Memory	Storage
Task1	1	2	1
Task2	3	2	1
Task3	2	1	1
Task4	1	1	1
Task5	1	2	1

- Relations between tasks are shown on the figure:

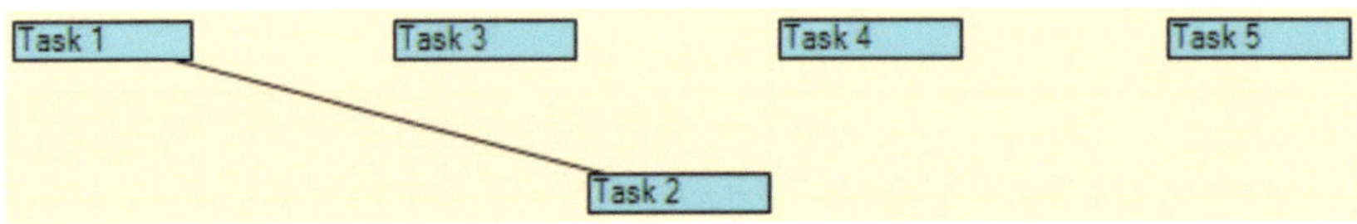

The algorithms have found solutions immediately after their activation.
Scheduling obtained by both algorithms is identical: 5 total time of scheduling.
Obtained scheduling is presented on the figure (Fig. 3.8):

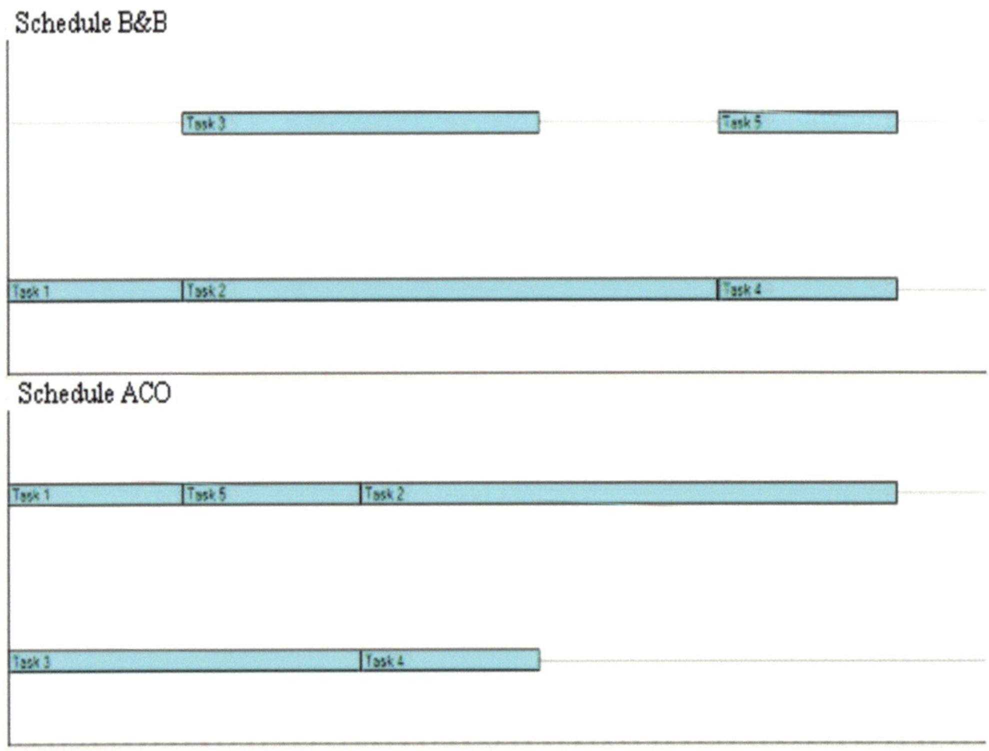

Fig. 3.8. Schedules - results of operations of algorithms

Example 2

Parameters of the problem:

- 10 tasks.
- 2 identical, universal processors.
- Additional resources: 3 units of memory, 3 units of storage.
- Parameters of tasks:

Tasks	Time constants	Memory	Storage
Task1	1	2	1
Task2	3	2	1
Task3	2	1	1
Task4	1	1	1
Task5	1	2	1
Task6	1	2	3
Task7	3	2	2
Task8	2	1	1
Task9	1	3	1
Task10	1	1	1

- Relations between tasks are shown on the figure:

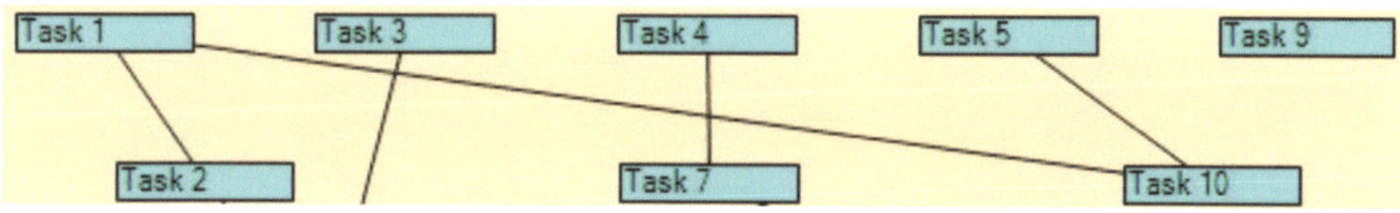

The algorithms have found solutions immediately after their activation.
Scheduling obtained by both algorithms is identical: 10 total time of scheduling.
Obtained scheduling is presented on the figure (Fig 3.9):

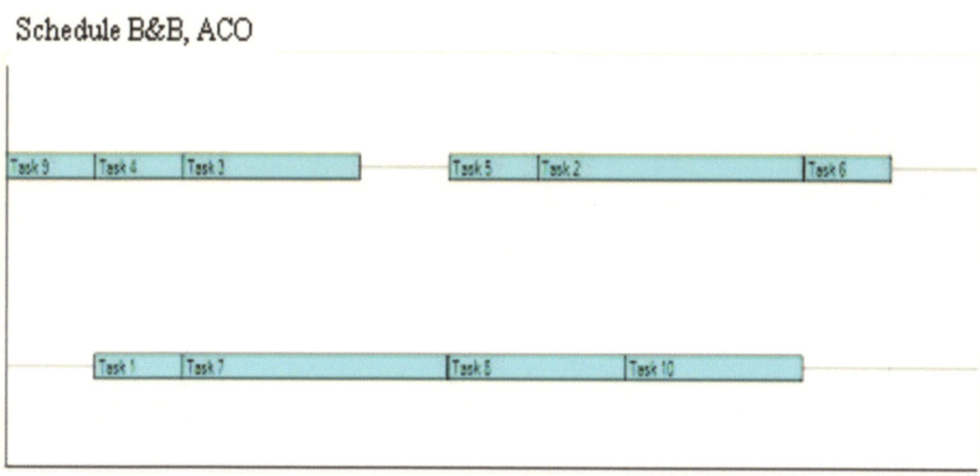

Fig. 3.9. Schedules - results of operations of algorithms

Example 3

Parameters of the problem:

- 10 tasks.
- 2 identical, universal processors.
- Additional resources: 3 units memory, 3 units storage.
- Parameters of tasks:

Tasks	Time constants	Memory	Storage
Task1	1	2	1
Task2	3	2	1
Task3	2	1	1
Task4	1	1	1
Task5	1	2	1
Task6	1	2	3
Task7	3	2	2
Task8	2	1	1
Task9	1	3	1
Task10	1	1	1

- Relations between tasks are shown on the figure:

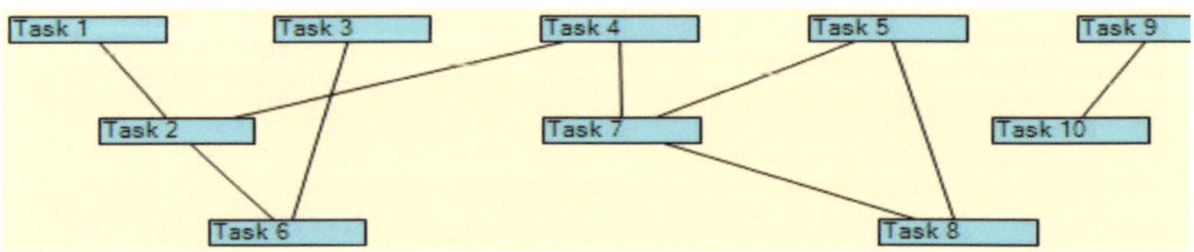

The algorithms have found solutions immediately after their activation.
Scheduling obtained by both algorithms is identical: 10 total time of scheduling
Obtained scheduling is presented on the figure (Fig. 3.10):

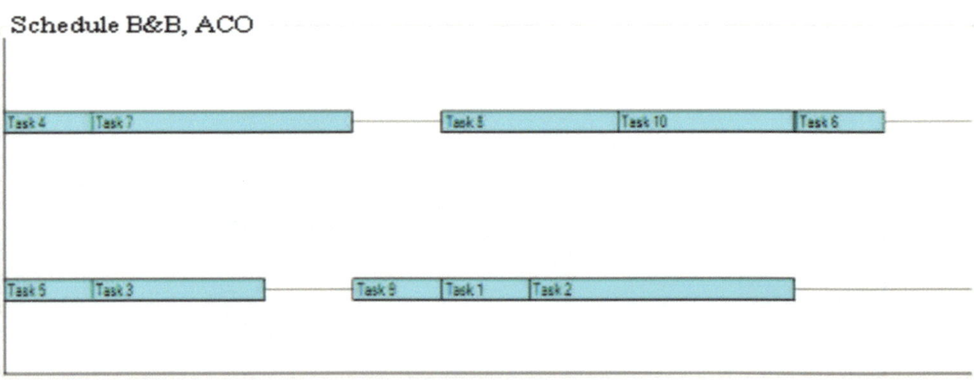

Fig. 3.10. Schedules - results of operations of algorithms

3.3.3 Comparison of coherent and non-coherent synthesis

Coherent synthesis is based on recurring division and scheduling tasks, in order to define the best set of hardware and scheduling for the system. As a result, the systems proposed by coherent synthesis may be better than the ones obtained as a result of incoherent synthesis (which makes division at the beginning of synthesis process) not only in relation to optimized parameters, but also in general (eventually, the system can enable much faster tasks completion at the same or even lower energy consumption, etc.). The results obtained by coherent and incoherent synthesis will be presented on the basis of the following examples.

Example 1

- 25 independent tasks with different completion times.
- 3 identical processors.
- Criterion of optimization: power.

The time of algorithm operation until finding the solution, length of scheduling, cost and power consumption of the system as well as the quality of solution obtained as a result of coherent synthesis are presented in the table (Tab. 3.1).

Algorithm	Coherent				Non-coherent				ASS (%)
	Time	Length	Cost	Power	Time	Length	Cost	Power	
ACO	45.0	42.0	7.00	691.5	12.0	32.0	8.00	692.7	100.2
B&B	45.0	69.0	6.00	690.0	12.0	63.0	8.00	702.0	101.7

Table 3.1. Results of coherent and non-coherent synthesis - Example 1

Systems obtained as a result of coherent synthesis consume less energy and are cheaper. In the case of B&B algorithm, system obtained as a result of coherent synthesis is generally better than the one obtained by incoherent synthesis (assessment = 108.8%).

Example 2

- 25 independent tasks with different completion times.
- 3 identical processors.
- Criterion of optimization: cost.

The time of algorithm operation until finding the solution, length of scheduling, cost and power consumption of the system as well as the quality of solution obtained as a result of coherent synthesis are presented in the table (Tab. 3.2).

Algorithm	Coherent				Non-coherent				ASS (%)
	Time	Length	Cost	Power	Time	Length	Cost	Power	
ACO	2.0	45.0	7.00	692.1	3.0	38.0	8.00	694.5	114.3
B&B	2.0	69	6.00	690.0	3.0	65	8.00	702.6	133.3

Table 3.2. Results of coherent and non-coherent synthesis - Example 2

Similarly how in previous case, systems for coherent synthesis are clearly cheaper and quicker.

Example 3

- 25 identical, independent tasks.
- 5 identical processors.
- Criterion of optimization: cost.

The time of algorithm operation until finding the solution, length of scheduling, cost and power consumption of the system as well as the quality of solution obtained as a result of coherent synthesis are presented in the table (Tab. 3.3).

Algorithm	Coherent				Non-coherent				ASS (%)
	Time	Length	Cost	Power	Time	Length	Cost	Power	
ACO	12.5	28.0	4.00	500.6	4.5	20.0	8.00	505.0	200.0
B&B	12.5	50.0	2.00	500.0	4.5	50.0	6.00	520.0	300.0

Table 3.3. Results of coherent and non-coherent synthesis - Example 3

In presented examples is visible the considerable superiority of coherent synthesis with non-coherent. Except improvement of the costs, the power consumption improved also. The larger number of processors was eliminated as well as the demand lowered of memory and storage too. In result of the assessment of system for algorithm the ACO is equal 124.1 % and for algorithm B & B is equal 168.0 %.

Example 4

- 25 identical, independent tasks.
- 5 identical processors.
- Criterion of optimization: power consumption.

The time of algorithm operation until finding the solution, length of scheduling, cost and power consumption of the system as well as the quality of solution obtained as a result of coherent synthesis are presented in the table (Tab. 3.4).

Algorithm	Coherent				Non-coherent				ASS (%)
	Time	Length	Cost	Power	Time	Length	Cost	Power	
ACO	8.5	10.0	10.00	500.0	29.5	10.0	10.00	500.0	100.0
B&B	8.5	50.0	2.00	500.0	29.5	44.0	7.00	517.0	103.4

Table 3.4. Results of coherent and non-coherent synthesis - Example 4

Systems for coherent synthesis are clearly cheaper and quicker. The difference is visible in case of algorithm B&B: the assessment of solution for coherent synthesis is higher though the assessment of proposed solutions in both cases is considerably worse than in case of solutions proposed by algorithm the ACO (206.7 %).

Example 5

- 25 identical, independent tasks.
- 5 unrelated processors.
- Criterion of optimization: power consumption.

The time of algorithm operation until finding the solution, length of scheduling, cost and power consumption of the system as well as the quality of solution obtained as a result of coherent synthesis are presented in the table (Tab. 3.5).

Algorithm	Coherent				Non-coherent				ASS
	Time	Length	Cost	Power	Time	Length	Cost	Power	(%)
ACO	87.5	50.0	2.00	500.0	14.0	48.0	7.00	539.0	107.8
B&B	87.5	50.0	2.00	500.0	14.0	50.0	6.00	520.0	104.0

Table 3.5. Results of coherent and non-coherent synthesis - Example 5

Algorithm ACO for coherent synthesis finds good solution, better than solution for non-coherent. We have again the superiority of coherent synthesis. Solutions for non - coherent synthesis are weak, assessment 75% for ACO as well as 76% for B & B.

3.3.4 Optimization of scheduling length and cost

Optimizing two aspects of system is much more difficult for the algorithms than minimizing a single parameter. As a condition of the choice we can take the assessment of obtained solution. The set of resources used for the optimization of the time and cost of system

- Memory (max. 100, cost 1mpower/unit).
- Storage (max. 100, cost 1spower[/unit).
- Processors, cost 1ppower/unit.

Type	Speed	Power consumption (action)	Power consumption (idle)
Processor 1	1	100	10
Processor 2	2	120	12
Processor 3	4	150	15
Processor 4	8	200	20
ASIC 1	1	80	8
ASIC 2	2	110	11
ASIC 3	4	150	15
ASIC 4	8	180	18

Time, which has passed until solution was found and the parameters of the target system are presented in the table (Tab. 3.6).

Number of tasks	Ant Colony				Branch & Bound				ASS (%)
	Time	Length	Cost	Power	Time	Length	Cost	Power	
20	59.0	10.0	15.00	4007	≥ 59.0	6.0	30.50	4173	131.7
25	60.0	9.0	20.50	5054	≥ 60.0	7.9	30.51	5281	118.3
30	12.5	11.3	19.00	6057	≥ 12.5	10	30.51	6394	124.5
35	16.0	12.5	19.00	7004	≥ 16.0	11.3	30.51	7448	125.4
40	15.5	15.0	19.00	8010	≥ 15.5	13.5	30.51	8568	125.3
45	42.5	16.5	19.00	9011	≥ 42.5	15	30.51	9654	125.7
50	26.5	18.0	19.00	10024	≥ 26.5	16.5	30.51	10693	126.1
55	34.5	20.0	19.00	11009	≥ 34.5	18	30.51	11772	125.3
60	44.0	21.4	19.00	12003	≥ 44.0	20	30.51	12872	127.0

Table 3.6. The results of schedule length of tasks and cost optimization

In the multi-objective optimization it is clear that ACO algorithm exceeds the greedy algorithm B & B in relation to the quality of solutions: solutions proposed by ACO algorithm are better than the ones proposed by B & B algorithm even by 31.7%. Interesting are the graphs presenting solutions, which were found by ACO algorithm before the final result was obtained (Chart 3.1). As a result of such operation of algorithm, the quality (comparing to the first solution found) was changing as follows (Chart 3.2).
Apart from better quality of the solution it proposed by ACO algorithm, we should notice that the total quality of the system is also very high (Chart 3.3).

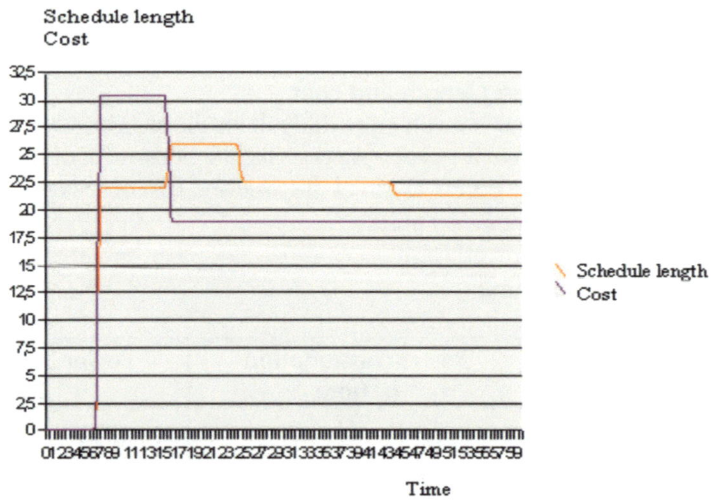

Chart 3.1. The change of cost and scheduling length in time

3.3.5 Optimization of power consumption and cost

The set of resources used for the optimization of the time and cost of system

- Memory (max. 100, cost 1 mpower/unit).
- Storage (max. 100, cost 1 spower/unit).

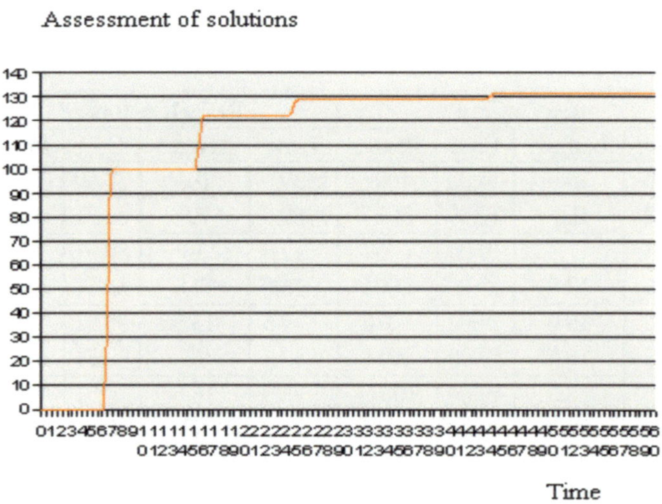

Chart 3.2. Improvement of the assessment of consecutive solutions in time function

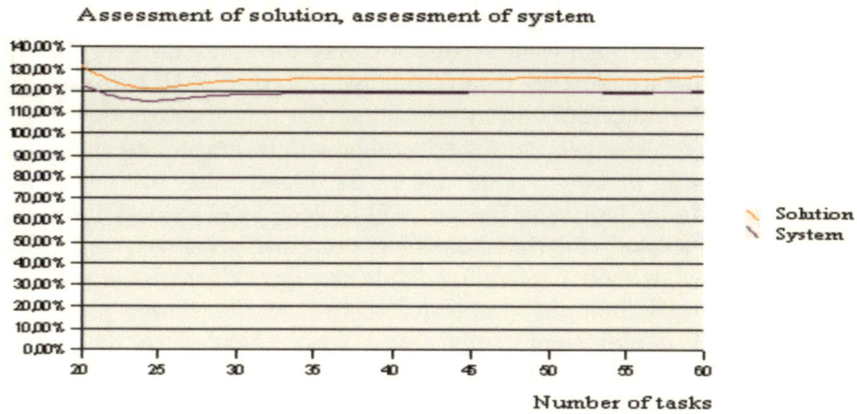

Chart 3.3. The assessment of proposed solutions and systems in relation to the number of tasks

- Processors, cost 1 ppower/unit.

Type	Speed	Power consumption (action)	Power consumption (idle)
Processor 1	1	100	10
Processor 2	2	120	12
Processor 3	4	150	15
Processor 4	8	200	20
ASIC 1	1	80	8
ASIC 2	2	110	11
ASIC 3	4	150	15
ASIC 4	8	180	18

Time, which has passed until solution was found and the parameters of the target system are presented in the table (Tab. 3.7).

Number of tasks	Ant Colony				Branch & Bound				ASS (%)
	Time	Length	Cost	Power	Time	Length	Cost	Power	
10	0.5	20.0	2.00	2000	≥ 0.5	20.0	2.00	2000	100.0
15	3.5	30.0	2.00	3000	≥ 3.5	30.0	2.00	3000	100.0
20	4.5	18.0	5.00	3780	≥ 4.5	40.0	2.00	4000	72.9
25	10.0	22.0	5.00	4732	≥ 10.0	50.0	2.00	5000	72.8
30	12.5	27.0	5.00	5670	≥ 12.5	60.0	2.00	6000	72.9
35	12.0	20.0	10.00	6677	≥ 12.0	70.0	2.00	7000	62.4
40	27.0	28.0	10.00	7869	≥ 27.0	80.0	2.00	8000	60.8
45	16.5	33.0	10.00	8835	≥ 16.5	90.0	2.00	9000	60.9
50	57.5	32.0	10.00	9673	≥ 57.5	100.0	2.00	10000	61.7
55	43.5	38.0	10.00	10766	≥ 43.5	110.0	2.00	11000	61.1
60	55.5	37.5	11.50	11822	≥ 55.5	120.0	2.00	12000	59.4

Table 3.7. The results of power consumption and system cost optimization

This example illustrates that ACO algorithm isn't better than greedy algorithms for all kinds of problems. The reason of such weak results is a very difficult choice for the algorithm between power and cost. To illustrate the problem we will try to analyze the scheduling of three first tasks (Drabowski, 2007). Even scheduling the first task causes some kind of dilemma: you can do this cheaper, but the scheduling will be longer and at the same time more power consuming, or you can do this at the higher cost, but with less power consumption (on the faster processor, the task will be completed sooner). If the algorithm chooses the second processor – the choice of slower processor in the next step will turn out more expensive as well as more demanding, while staying with the faster one will let us keep the same cost and limit the power (comparing to the slower processor). Also scheduling time will reduce significantly (what was presented in the table above) (Drabowski & Wantuch, 2006). The final quality of the system is then difficult to determine during the whole cycle – it is possible to determine only when you know the total scheduling length (and thus the power consumed by system, in other words – after the end of the whole cycle).

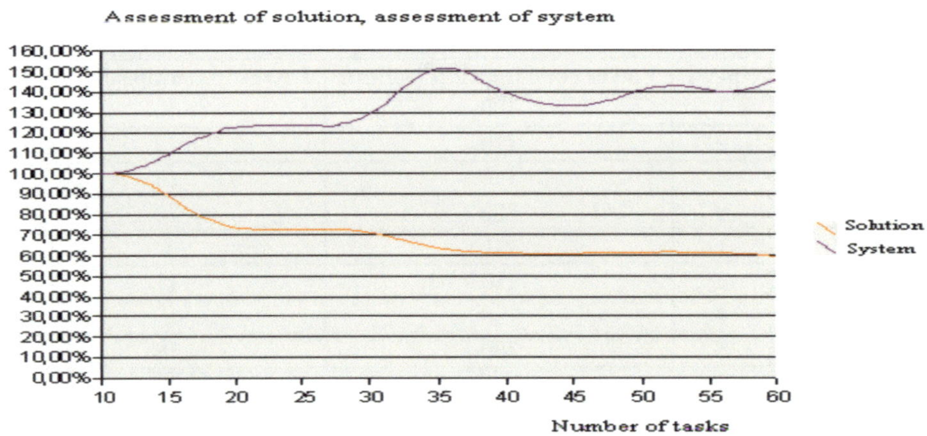

Chart 3.4.The assessment of solution and the systems proposed in relation to the number of tasks

When the number of tasks grows, the quality of solution decreases more and more, but you cannot say the same about the quality of system; the ACO algorithm shows, that at the higher expenditure you can obtain solution which is economical and fast at the same time (Drabowski, 2009). The graphs illustrating the quality of solution and system are presented on the chart (Chart 3.4).

4. Conclusions

We may say, basing on the above research, that the ACO algorithm is better suitable for both one- and multi-objective analyses of optimization of computer systems. Furthermore, the use of coherent analysis significantly improved the quality of obtained solutions. In the case of multi-objective synthesis, heuristic algorithm gave comparable results for optimized parameters and at the same time, the final grade of the systems it proposed was much better. The computational experiments prove the superiority of coherent synthesis over the incoherent synthesis and heuristic algorithms over the greedy ones.

Solutions of this method are better both, for their cost, as and of time of executing the tasks and of optimization of multi-criterions.

5. References

D'Ambrioso J., Hu X., (1994), *Configuration Level Hardware/Software Partitioning for Real-Time Systems,* Proc. of the Int. Workshop on Hardware/Software Codesign, Vol. 14, 34-41.

Gajski D., (1997), *Principles of Digital Design,* Prentice Hall, Upper Saddle River, NJ.

Sgroi M., Lavagno L., Sangiovanni-Vincentelli A., (2000), *Formal Models for Embedded System Design, IEEE Design&Test of Computers,* Vol. 17, No. 2, 14-27.

Gupta R.K., De Micheli G., (1993), *Hardware-Software Co-synthesis for Digital Systems,* IEEE Design&Test of Computers, Vol. 10, No. 3, 29-41.

De Micheli G., (1994), *Computer-Aided hardware-Software Codesign,* IEEE Micro, Vol. 14, No. 4, pp. 10-24.

Axelson J., (1997), *Architecture Synthesis and Partitioning of Real-Time Systems: A Comparison of Three Heuristic Search Strategies,* Proc. of the Int. Workshop on Hardware/Software Codesign, 161-165.

Schulz S., Rozenbilt J.W., Mrva M., Buchenrieder K., (1998), *Model-Based Codesign,* IEEE Computer, Vol. 31, No. 8, 60-67.

Steinhausen U., (1993), *System Synthesis Using Hardware/Software Codesign,* Proc. of the Int. Workshop on Hardware-Software Co-Design.

Błażewicz J., Ecker K., Pesch E., Schmidt G., Węglarz J., (2007), *Handbook on Scheduling, From Theory to Applications,* Springer-Verlag Berlin Heidelberg.

Coffman E. G., Jr., (1976), *Computer and Job-shop scheduling theory,* John Wiley&Sons, Inc. New York.

Węglarz J., (1999), *Project Scheduling – Recent Models, Algorithms and Applications,* Kluwer Academic Publ.

Błażewicz J., Ecker K., Plateau B., Trystram D., (2000), *Handbook on Parallel and Distributed Processing,* Spinger-Verlag, Berlin – Heidelberg.

Drabowski M., M., Rola M, Roślicki A., (2002), Algorithm in control of allocation tasks and resources in frameworks, 2rd International Congress of Intelligent Building Systems, INBus2002, Kraków, 45-52.

Drabowski M., (2008), *Par-synthesis of multiprocessors parallel systems,* International Journal of Computer Science and Network Security, Vol. 8, No. 10, 90-96.

Harel D., (1987), *Statecharts: A Visual Formalism for Complex Systems,* Science of Computer Programming, Vol. 8, No. 3, 231-274.

Drabowski M., Czajkowski K., (2005), *Task scheduling in coherent, co-synthesis of computer system,* Advanced Computer Systems - Computer Information Systems and Industrial Management Application (ACS-CISIM 2005), in. Image Analysis, Computer Graphics, Security Systems and Artificial Intelligence Applications, vol. 1, 53-60.

Blum C., (2005), *Beam-ACO – Hybridizing ant colony optimization with bean search: An application to open shop schedling,* Comput. Oper. Res. 32, 1565-1591.

Montgomery J., Fayad C., Petrovic S., (2006), *Solution representation for job shop scheduling problems in ant colony optimization,* LNCS 4150, 484-491.

Mitten L.G., (1970), Branch-and-bound methods: general formulation and properties, Oper. Res. 18, 24-34.

Drabowski M., (2007), *Coherent synthesis of heterogeneous system – an ant colony optimization approach,* Studia Informatica, vol. 2/9, 9-18.

Drabowski M., (2009), *Ant Colony and Neural method for scheduling of complex of operations and resources frameworks – comparative remarks,* in: Proceedings of the IASTED International Conference on Computational Intelligence, Honolulu, USA, ACTA Press, Anaheim, USA, 91-97.

Drabowski M., (2007), *An Ant Colony Optimization to scheduling tasks on a grid,* Polish Journal of Environmental Studies, vol. 16, No. 5B, 16-21.

Drabowski M., Wantuch E., (2006), *Coherent Concurrent Task Scheduling and Resource Assignment in Dependable Computer Systems Design,* International Journal of Reliability, Quality and Safety Engineering, vol. 13, no. 1. World Scientific Publishing, 15-24.

Drabowski M., (2009), *High-level synthesis of self-testing parallel multiprocessors computer systems,* in: Proceedings of the IASTED International Conference on Computational Intelligence, Honolulu, USA, ACTA Press, Anaheim, USA, 127-133.

14

Ant Colony Optimization Approach for Optimizing Traffic Signal Timings

Ozgur Baskan and Soner Haldenbilen
Pamukkale University
Engineering Faculty
Department of Civil Engineering
Transportation Division
Denizli,
Turkey

1. Introduction

In urban networks, traffic signals are used to control vehicle movements so as to reduce congestion, improve safety, and enable specific strategies such as minimizing delays, improving environmental pollution, etc (Teklu et al., 2007). Due to the increasing in the number of cars and developing industry, finding optimal traffic signal parameters has been an important task in order to use the network capacity optimally. Through the last decade, developments in communications and information technologies have improved the classical methods for optimising the traffic signal timings toward the intelligent ones.

There is an important interaction between the signal timings and the routes chosen by individual road users in road networks controlled by fixed time signals. The mutual interaction leads to the framework of a leader-follower or Stackelberg game, where the supplier is the leader and the user is the follower (Fisk, 1984). Network design problem (NDP) that it may contain the signal setting problem is characterized by the so called bi-level structure. Bi-level programming problems generally are difficult to solve, because the evaluation of the upper-level objective involves solving the lower level problem for every feasible set of upper level decisions (Sun et al., 2006). On the upper level, a transport planner designs the network. Road users respond to that design in the lower level. This problem is known to be one of the most attractive mathematical problems in the optimization field because of non-convexity of feasible region that it has multiple local optima (Baskan, 2009).

Moreover, the driver's behaviours on the network should be taken into account when the traffic signal timings are optimised. When drivers follow the Wardrop's (1952) first principle, the problem is called the "user equilibrium" (UE). On the other hand, it turns to the stochastic user equilibrium (SUE) in the case that the users' face with the decision of route choice between the each Origin-Destination (O-D) pair for a given road network according to perceived travel time. The difference between SUE and UE approaches is that in SUE models each driver is meant to define 'travel costs' individually instead of using a single definition of costs applicable to all drivers. SUE traffic assignment takes into account the variability in driver's perception of cost. This is done by treating the perceived cost on particular path as a random variable distributed across the population of users, and so a different cost for each driver can be modelled. Using the probabilistic choice models, the O-D demand is assigned to paths, where the cheapest path attracts the most flow. Road users generally use a variety of routes between their origins and destinations in urban networks based on their perception of travel time. Hence, the SUE is more appropriate than the DUE assignment (Ceylan, 2002).

A wide range of solution methods to the signal setting problem have been discussed in the literature. Allsop & Charlesworth (1977) found mutually consistent (MC) traffic signal settings and traffic assignment for a medium size road network. In their study, the signal setting and link flows were calculated alternatively by solving the signal setting problem for assumed link flows and carrying out the user equilibrium assignment for the resulting signal settings until convergence was achieved. The obtained mutually consistent signal settings and equilibrium link flows, will, however, in general be non-optimal as has been discussed by Gershwin & Tan (1979) and Dickson (1981). Abdullaal & LeBlanc (1979) reported the formulation and solution by means of the Hooke-Jeeves' method for an equilibrium network design problem with continuous variables. An unconstraint optimisation problem in which the dependence of equilibrium flows on decision variables was dealt with as one of the decision variables is solved directly by means of the convex-combination method. Suwansirikul et al. (1987) solved equilibrium network design problem that using a direct search based on the Hooke-Jeeves' method for a small test network. The direct search method, however, is computationally intensive, because frequent evaluations of deterministic (or stochastic) user equilibrium traffic assignment are required. Hence, it was emphasized that the proposed method is only suitable for small example road networks. Heydecker & Khoo (1990) proposed a linear constraint approximation to the equilibrium flows with respect to signal setting variables and solved the bi-level problem as a constraint optimisation problem. Using the linear constraint approximation method to solve the bi level problem can be carried out in a number of iterations by which the resulting equilibrium flows are regressed as the signal setting variable changes in a simple linear form.

Canteralla et al. (1991) proposed an iterative approach to solve the equilibrium network design problem, in which traffic signal settings are performed in two successive steps; green timing at each junction, and signal co-ordination on the network. Green timing calculation at each junction was based on a mixed binary linear program. Signal coordination for the whole network was performed by solving a discrete programming model with a total delay minimisation objective function. Yang & Yagar (1995) used derivatives of equilibrium flows and of the corresponding travel times to solve a bi-level program for the equilibrium network design problem for a signal control optimisation. Lee & Machemehl (1998) applied Genetic Algorithm (GA) to individual signalized intersection. Their objective function was a function of green split and the UE links flows. For stage length and cycle time optimization without considering offsets to minimise total travel time, Lee (1998) presented a comparison of GA and simulated annealing with iterative and local search algorithms and showed that different algorithms perform better for different network supply and demand scenarios. Chiou (1999) explored a mixed search procedure to solve an area traffic control optimization problem confined to equilibrium network flows, where good local optima can be effectively found via the gradient projection method. Ceylan & Bell (2004) is proposed GA approach to solve traffic signal control and traffic assignment problem is used to tackle the optimization of signal timings with SUE link flows. The system performance index is defined as the sum of a weighted linear combination of delay and number of stops per unit time for all traffic streams. It is found that the GA method is effective and simple to solve equilibrium network design problem.

The optimization methods developed so far to solve signal setting problem are either calculus and mathematically lengthy or are based on the heuristic approaches. Although proposed algorithms are capable of solving signal setting problem for a road network, an efficient algorithm, which is capable of finding the global or near global optima of the upper level signal timing variables considering the equilibrium link flows under SUE conditions, is still needed. This chapter deals with the problem of optimising traffic signal timings without considering offset term taking stochastic user equilibrium (SUE) conditions into account. A bi-level technique and MC approach have been proposed and compared, in which signal setting problem is dealt with as upper level problem whilst the SUE traffic assignment is dealt with as lower level problem. In this chapter, Ant Colony Optimization (ACO) approach which is arisen from the behaviours of real ant colonies is introduced to solve the upper level problem in which traffic signal timings are optimised. Although ACO algorithms are capable of finding global or near global optimum, it may be further improved to locate better global optima for any given problem. In this study, ACO Reduced Search Space (ACORSES) algorithm is used for finding better signal timings. It differs from other approaches in that its feasible search space (FSS) is reduced with best solution obtained so far using the previous information at the each iteration (Baskan et al., 2009). At the core of ACORSES, ants search randomly the solution within the FSS to reach global optimum by jumping on each direction. At the end of the each iteration, only one ant is near to global optimum. After the first iteration, when global optimum is searched around the best solution of the previous iteration using reduced search space, the ACORSES will reach to the global optimum quickly without being trapped in bad local optimum.

In this chapter, signal timings are defined as cycle time and green time for each junction and stage, respectively. The objective function is adopted to minimise the total system cost of network as the system optimum formulation. In order to represent the route choice behaviours of drivers, the probit route choice model is used whilst SUE traffic assignment problem is solved by the method that proposed Sheffi (1985). The effectiveness of the proposed ACORSES algorithm is demonstrated through a numerical experiment. The results showed that the bi-level approach based on ACORSES is considerably effective according to MC approach in terms of the signal timings and the final values of degree of saturation to solve the problem of optimising traffic signal timings under SUE conditions.

This chapter is organized as follows. The basic notations are defined in the next section. Section 3 is about the problem formulation. The solution methods for optimising signal timings under SUE conditions are given in Section 4. Numerical experiment is carried out in Section 5. Last section is about the conclusions.

2. Notations

$\mathbf{A}$	matrix of signal timings
c	cycle time for each junction of a given road network
$\mathbf{c}(\mathbf{q},\boldsymbol{\psi}) = [c_a(q_a,\boldsymbol{\psi})]$	the vector of all link travel times, where element $c_a(q_a,\boldsymbol{\psi})$ is travel time on link a as a function of flow on the link itself and the signal setting variables, $\boldsymbol{\psi} = (c,\boldsymbol{\varphi})$.
C_a	perceived travel time on link a

c_a	measured travel time on link a
$\mathrm{h}=[h_p;\forall p\in \boldsymbol{P}_w,\forall w\in \boldsymbol{W}]$	vector of all path flows
I_i	intergreen time between signal stages
J	number of junctions
K	threshold value
L	number of links
M	numbers of signal stages at a signalised road network
m	numbers of signal stages for a signalised junction, $\forall m\in M$
R	colony size
s_a	degree of saturation on link a
$\mathbf{q}=[q_a;\forall a\in \boldsymbol{L}]$	vector of flow q_a on link a
$\mathbf{q}^*(\psi)$	vector of equilibrium link flows subject to signal parameters
TC	total cost of a given road network
$\mathbf{t}=[t_w;\forall w\in \boldsymbol{W}]$	vector of origin destination flows
ψ	signal setting variables
$\boldsymbol{\varphi}$	vector of duration of green times
Ω	feasible set of signal setting variables
δ	link-path incidence matrix
Λ	OD-path incidence matrix
$\boldsymbol{\beta}$	vector of search space constraints at ACO
β	variance of the perceived travel time
σ_a	standard error for each link a
$\boldsymbol{\alpha}$	random generated vector as initial solution for ACO

3. Formulation

The problem of optimising of signal setting variables $\psi=(c,\varphi)$ without considering offset term on a road network is defined as bi-level structure. The planners aim to minimise the total cost (*TC*) of a given road network on the upper level whilst the SUE link flows $\mathbf{q}^*(\psi)$ on the lower level are dealt with altering signal timings. The objective function is therefore to minimise *TC* with respect to equilibrium link flows $\mathbf{q}^*(\psi)$ subject to signal setting constraints $\psi=(c,\varphi)$. Mathematically the problem is defined as:

$$\underset{\psi\in\Omega_0}{Min}\ TC(\psi,q^*(\psi))=\sum_a^L q_a t_a(\psi,q^*(\psi)) \tag{1}$$

$$\text{subject to } \psi=(c,\varphi)\in\Omega\ ;\ \left\{\begin{array}{ll} c_{\min}\le c\le c_{\max} & \text{cycle time constraints for each junction}\\ \varphi_{\min}\le\varphi\le\varphi_{\max} & \text{green time constraints for each stage}\\ \sum_{i=1}^{m}(\varphi_i+I_i)=c\quad \forall m\in M & \end{array}\right\}$$

where $\mathbf{q}^*(\psi)$ is implicitly defined by

$$\underset{q}{\text{Minimise}}\ Z(\psi,\mathbf{q})$$

$$\text{subject to}\ \ \mathbf{t}=\Lambda\mathbf{h}\ ,\ \mathbf{q}=\delta\mathbf{h}\ ,\ \mathbf{h}\geq 0$$

3.1 ACORSES algorithm for optimising of signal timings (upper-level problem)

Ant algorithms were inspired by the observation of real ant colonies. Ants are social insects, that is, insects that live in colonies and whose behaviour is directed more to the survival of the colony as a whole than to that of a single individual component of the colony. Social insects have captured the attention of many scientists because of the high structuration level their colonies can achieve, especially when compared to the relative simplicity of the colony's individuals. An important and interesting behaviour of ant colonies is their foraging behaviour, and, in particular, how ants can find shortest paths between food sources and their nest (Dorigo et al., 1999). Ants are capable of finding the shortest path from food source to their nest or vice versa by smelling pheromones which are chemical substances they leave on the ground while walking. Each ant probabilistically prefers to follow a direction rich in pheromone. This behaviour of real ants can be used to explain how they can find a shortest path (Eshghi & Kasemi, 2006).

The ACO is the one of the most recent techniques for approximate optimization methods. The main idea is that it is indirect local communication among the individuals of a population of artificial ants. The core of ant's behavior is the communication between the ants by means of chemical pheromone trails, which enables them to find shortest paths between their nest and food sources. This behaviour of real ant colonies is exploited to solve optimization problems. The general ACO algorithm is illustrated in Fig. 1. The first step consists mainly on the initialization of the pheromone trail. At beginning, each ant builds a complete solution to the problem according to a probabilistic state transition rules. They depend mainly on the state of the pheromone.

Step 1:	Initialize Pheromone trail

Step 2:	Iteration
	Repeat for each ant
	  Solution construction using pheromone trail
	  Update the pheromone trail
	Until stopping criteria

Fig. 1. A generic ant algorithm

Once all ants generate a solution, then global pheromone updating rule is applied in two phases; an evaporation phase, where a fraction of the pheromone evaporates, and a reinforcement phase, where each ant deposits an amount of pheromone which is proportional to the fitness. This process is repeated until stopping criteria is met. In this study, ACORSES algorithm proposed by Baskan et al. (2009) to solve upper-level problem is used to tackle the optimization of signal timings with stochastic equilibrium link flows. The ACORSES algorithm is based on each ant searches only around the best solution of the previous iteration with reduced search space. It is proposed for improving ACO's solution performance to reach global optimum fairly quickly. The ACORSES is consisted of three main phases; Initialization, pheromone update and solution phase. All of these phases build a complete search to the global optimum. At the beginning of the first iteration, all ants search randomly to the best solution of a given problem within the Feasible Search Space (FSS), and old ant colony is created at initialization phase. After that, quantity of pheromone is updated. In the solution phase, new ant colony is created based on the best solution from the old ant colony. Then, the best solutions of two colonies are compared. At the end of the first iteration, FSS is reduced by **β** and best solution obtained from the previous iteration is kept. **β** guides the bounds of search space during the ACORSES application, where **β** is a vector, βj (j=1,2,....n), and n is the number of variables. The range of the **β** may be chosen between minimum and maximum bounds of any given problem. Optimum solution is then searched in the reduced search space during the algorithm progress. The ACORSES reaches to the global optimum as ants find their routes in the limited space.

Let the objective function given in Eq. (1) take a set of ψ signal timing variables, $\psi = (c_1, \varphi_1, ..., c_n, \varphi_n)$. On the assumption that each decision variable ψ can take values from a domain $\mathbf{\Omega} = [\psi_{\min}, \psi_{\max}]$ for all $\psi \in \Omega$. The presentation of signal timing variables, $\psi = (c, \varphi)$, based on ACO approach is given in Eq. (2).

$$A = \begin{bmatrix} c_{11}\, c_{12}\, c_{13} .... c_{1J}\, ; \varphi_{11}\, \varphi_{12}\, \varphi_{13} .... \varphi_{1M} \\ c_{21}\, c_{22}\, c_{23} .... c_{2J}\, ; \varphi_{21}\, \varphi_{22}\, \varphi_{23} .... \varphi_{2M} \\ .. \quad .. \quad .. \quad .. \qquad\qquad\qquad .. \\ .. \quad .. \quad .. \quad .. \quad .. \quad .. \qquad .. \\ .. \quad .. \quad .. \quad .. \quad .. \quad .. \quad .. \quad .. \quad .. \\ c_{R1}\, c_{R2}\, c_{R3} .... c_{RJ}\, ; \varphi_{R1}\, \varphi_{R2}\, \varphi_{R3} .... \varphi_{RM} \end{bmatrix} \tag{2}$$

where *M*, *J* and *R* are the number of signal stages, the number of junctions at a signalised road network and the value of colony size, respectively. In order to optimise the objective function in ACO real numbers of decision variables are used instead of coding them as in GA. This is one of the main advantage of ACO approach that it provides to optimise the signal timings at a road network with less mathematically lengthy. Moreover, ACORSES algorithm has ability to reach to the global optimum quickly without being trapped in bad local optimum because it uses the reduced search space and the values of optimum signal timings are then searched in the reduced search space during the algorithm progress. The ACORSES reaches to the global optimum or near global optimum as ants find their routes in the limited space. In that algorithm, **A** consists of the cycle and green timings for each junction and stage at a given road network. In order to provide the constraint of cycle time for each junction, the green timings can be distributed to the all signal stages in a road network as follows (Ceylan & Bell, 2004):

$$\varphi_i = \varphi_{\min,i} + \frac{\varphi_i}{\sum_{k=1}^{m} \varphi_i} \left(c_i - \sum_{k=1}^{m} I_k - \sum_{k=1}^{m} \varphi_{\min,k} \right) \quad i = 1,2,....,m \tag{3}$$

3.2 The solution method for the lower level problem

In this study, probit stochastic user equilibrium (PSUE) model is used to solve lower level problem. Probit model has the advantage of being able to represent perceptual differences in utility of alternatives on a road network. Although it behaves like the logit model for statistically independent paths, it has many advantages in the case of existing correlated paths at a network. For example, two paths that overlap for virtually their whole length are likely to be perceived very similarly by an individual since they have many links in common, but this cannot be captured by a logit model. This can lead to unrealistically high flows being assigned to the common parts of these paths of a given road network. The PSUE model is able to overcome these drawbacks, by supposing path costs are formed from a sum of link costs, with the error distribution (Clark & Watling, 2002). Therefore, PSUE model proposed by Sheffi (1985) is used to find path choice probabilities in order to overcome this drawback. To the best of our knowledge, this is the first time to date that the PSUE model is used to solve SUE traffic assignment problem at the lower level whilst the optimization of signal timings is dealt with upper level problem.

Monte-Carlo simulation method is adopted to obtain probit choice probabilities so as to none of the analytical approximation methods can be practically applied to medium or large scale networks due to probit choice probabilities cannot be written in closed form. The advantage of the simulation method is that it does not require the sampling of perceived path travel times only perceived link travel times are sampled at every iteration thus avoiding path enumeration. The underlying assumption of probit model, the random error term of each alternative is assumed normally distributed. The notation $\xi \sim \text{MVN}(\mu,\Sigma)$ indicates that the vector of error terms ξ is multivariate normal (MVN) distributed with mean vector μ and covariance matrix Σ. The algorithm to solve PSUE is given as follows (Sheffi, 1985):

Step 0. Initialization. Set n=1

Step 1. Sampling phase. Sample $C_a^{(n)}$ from $C_a \sim N(c_a, \beta c_a)$ for each link a.

Step 2. Based on $C_a^{(n)}$, assign t_w to the shortest path connecting each O-D pair w. Obtain the set of link flows, $q_a^{(n)}$

Step 3. Link flow averaging. Let $q_a^{(n)} = \left[(n-1)q_a^{(n-1)} + q_a^{(n)}\right]/n \quad \forall a$

Step 4. Stopping criterion (standard error). Let $\sigma_a^{(n)} = \sqrt{\frac{1}{n(n-1)}\sum_{m=1}^{n}(q_a^{(m)} - q_a^{(n)})^2} \qquad \forall a$

If $\max_a \left\{\frac{\sigma_a^{(n)}}{q_a^{(n)}}\right\} \le K$, stop. The solution is $q_a^{(n)}$. Otherwise, set n=n+1 and go to step 1.

where K is the predetermined threshold value. In PSUE algorithm, perceived link travel time for each link is random variable that is assumed to be normally distributed with mean equal to the measured link travel time and with variance of related link. According to this assumption, perceived link travel times for each link are sampled. Then, demand between each O-D pair $w \in \mathbf{W}$ assigned to the shortest path to obtain set of link flows, $a \in \mathbf{L}$. The link flows have to be averaged at every iteration in order to compute the standard error to test for convergence of algorithm. The PSUE algorithm is terminated when the stopping criterion is met.

4. Solution methods

4.1 The Mutually Consistent (MC) solution for optimising signal timings

The MC solution process was proposed by Allsop (1974) and Gartner (1974). It is an iterative optimisation and assignment procedure that is very similar in nature to other iterative procedures in the literature. In this method, the upper level problem is solved by keeping the flows fixed, and then the traffic assignment problem is solved by keeping the signal timings fixed. MC calculation of signal timings and the corresponding equilibrium flows for bi-level problem starts with an initial assignment and tries to reach a MC solution by solving sequentially an equilibrium assignment problem and a traffic signal setting problem until two successive flow patterns or signal timings are close enough within a specified tolerance. If convergence is reached in a finite number of iterations, the solution is considered to be mutually consistent. This means that the signal settings generate a set of link costs which determine flow pattern such that these settings are optimal for it (Ceylan, 2002). The MC calculation is performed in the following steps.

Step 0. Set k=0 for given signal timings $\boldsymbol{\psi}^{(k)}$, find the corresponding equilibrium flows $\mathbf{q}^*(\boldsymbol{\psi}^{(k)})$ by solving the problem of PSUE at the lower level.

Step 1. Solve the upper level problem to obtain the optimal signal timings $\boldsymbol{\psi}^{(k+1)}$ for the flows $\mathbf{q}^*(\boldsymbol{\psi}^{(k)})$.

Step 2. Update the travel time function of all links according to obtained signal timings $\boldsymbol{\psi}^{(k+1)}$.

Step 3. Calculate the corresponding equilibrium flows $\mathbf{q}^*(\boldsymbol{\psi}^{(k+1)})$ by solving the PSUE problem.
At Step 3, method of successive averages (MSA) (Sheffi, 1985) smoothing is applied to the equilibrium link flows in the iterative process in order to overcome fluctuations on equilibrium link flows. The MSA smoothing approach is carried out using the following relationship.

$$q_a^{(k+1)} = \frac{1}{k} q_a^{(k-1)} + (1 - \frac{1}{k}) q_a^{(k)}$$

where k is the iteration number and a is a set of links in $\boldsymbol{L}$

Step 4. Solve the upper level problem again to obtain the optimal signal timings $\boldsymbol{\psi}^{(k+2)}$ given by the $\mathbf{q}^*(\boldsymbol{\psi}^{(k+1)})$.

Step 5. Compare the values of $\boldsymbol{\psi}^{(k+2)}$ and $\boldsymbol{\psi}^{(k+1)}$, if there is no change between $\boldsymbol{\psi}^{(k+1)}$ and $\boldsymbol{\psi}^{(k+2)}$ then go to Step 6; otherwise, k=k+1 and go to Step 2.

Step 6. Stop: $\boldsymbol{\psi}^{(k+1)}$ and $\mathbf{q}^*(\boldsymbol{\psi}^{(k+1)})$ are the mutually consistent signal timings and equilibrium flows.

The MC calculation process is terminated when the difference in values of signal timings or of PSUE flows between successive iterations is smaller than a predetermined threshold value.

4.2 The bi-level solution for optimising signal timings

The problem of optimizing signal timings can be seen as a particular case of the NDP in which the signal timings play a critical role to optimize the performance of the network while the network topological characteristics are fixed. It is also a difficult problem because the evaluation of the upper level objective involves solving the lower level problem for every feasible set of upper level decisions. The complexity of the problem comes from the non-convexity of objective functions and constraints at both levels. In this chapter, the ACORSES algorithm is used to overcome this drawback. Although ACO algorithms are similar to other stochastic optimization techniques, the ACORSES differs from that it uses reduced search space technique to prevent being trapped in bad local optimum (Baskan et al., 2009). The solution steps for the bi-level solution are:

Step 0. *Initialisation*, k=1. Set the user-specified ACO parameters ($\boldsymbol{\beta}$, R, $\boldsymbol{\alpha}$); represent the decision variables $\boldsymbol{\psi}$ within the range $\boldsymbol{\psi}_{\min}$ and $\boldsymbol{\psi}_{\max}$.

Step 1. If k=1 generate the initial random population of signal timings $\boldsymbol{\psi}_k$ as shown in (2). Else generate random population of signal timings according to best signal timings obtained in Step 8 and $\boldsymbol{\beta}$ vector of search space constraints.
This step plays a critical role because the ACORSES uses the random generated population within the reduced search space at each iteration to prevent being trapped in bad local optimum.

Step 2. Solve the lower level problem by solving the PSUE. This gives an equilibrium link flows for each link a in $\boldsymbol{L}$.

Step 3. Calculate the value of objective function using Eq. (1) in order to obtain old ant colony ($\mathbf{A}_{\text{old}}$) in which signal timings are presented, for resulting signal timings at Step 1 and the equilibrium link flows resulting in Step 2.

Step 4. Carry out the pheromone evaporation and updating phases.

Step 5. Determine the search direction and generate the matrix of length of jump.

Step 6. According to search direction and generated matrix of length of jump, produce the new ant colony ($\mathbf{A}_{\text{new}}$).

Step 7. Calculate the new values of objective function using produced new ant colony.

Step 8. Compare the values of objective functions relating to the old and new ant colonies, then we have best decision variables, $\boldsymbol{\psi}_{\text{best}}$.

Step 9. If the difference between the values of $\boldsymbol{\psi}_k$ and $\boldsymbol{\psi}_{k+1}$ is less than predetermined threshold value, the algorithm is terminated. Else go to Step 1.

5. Numerical example

The test network is chosen that is used by Allsop & Charlesworth (1977) in order to show the performance of the ACORSES to optimise signal setting variables. The network topology and stage configurations are given in Fig. 2a and 2b, where figures are adapted from Ceylan & Bell (2004). Travel demands for each O-D are given in Table 1. This network has 20 O-D pairs and 20 signal setting variables at six signal-controlled junctions. The signal timing constraints are given as follows:

$c_{\min}$, $c_{\max}$ = 60, 100 sec cycle time for each junction

$\phi_{\min}$ = 7 sec minimum green time for signal stages

Origin/Destination	A	B	D	E	F	Origin totals
A	--	250	700	30	200	1180
C	40	20	200	130	900	1290
D	400	250	--	50*	100	800
E	300	130	30*	--	20	480
G	550	450	170	60	20	1250
Destination totals	1290	1100	1100	270	1240	5000
* where the travel demand between O-D pair D and E are not included in this numerical test which can be allocated directly via links 12 and 13						

Table 1. Travel demands for the test network

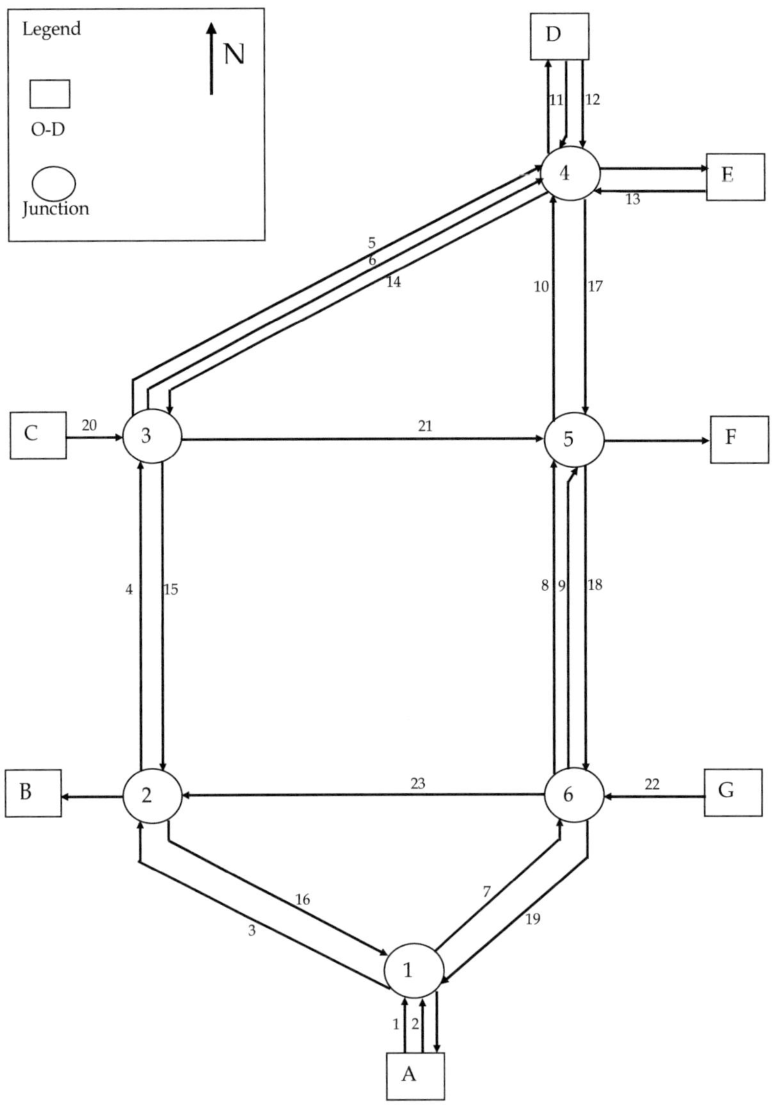

Fig. 2. (a) Layout for the test network (Ceylan & Bell, 2004)

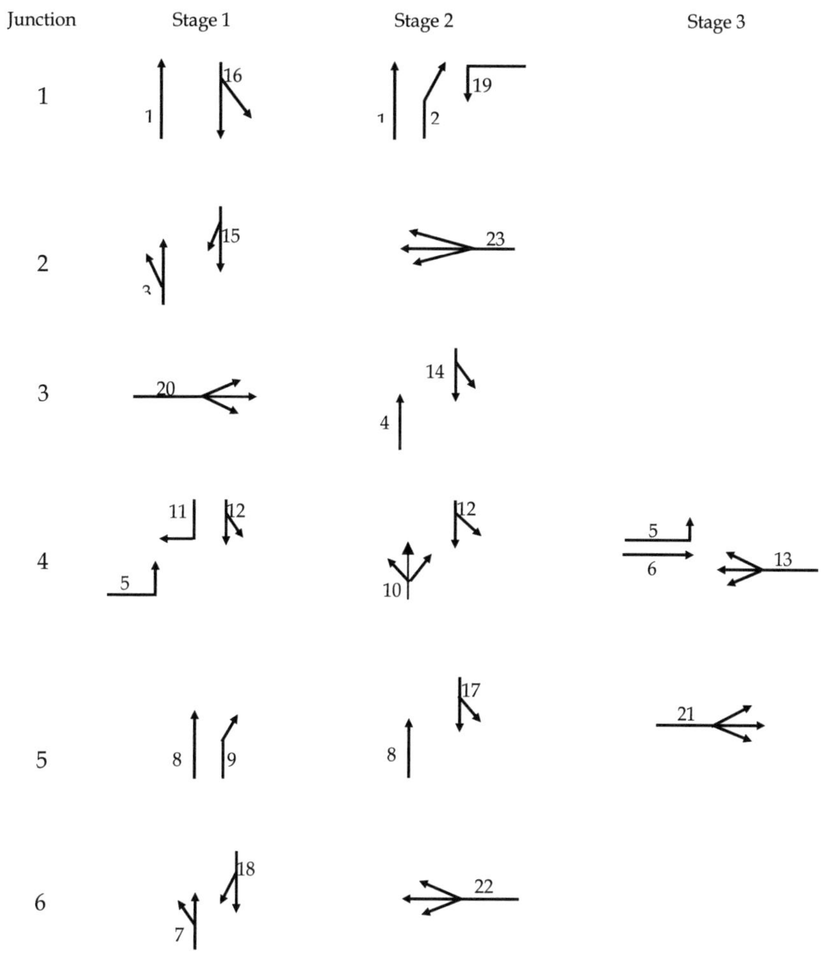

Fig. 2 (b) Stage configurations for the test network (Ceylan & Bell, 2004)

The ACORSES is performed with the following user-specified parameters. **β** vector should be chosen according to constraints of cycle time as proposed by Baskan et al. (2009).

Colony size (R) is 50.

Search space constraint for ACORSES is chosen as **β**= [100,100,....100].

The length of jump is chosen as α=1/random(10).

5.1 The bi-level solution for the test network

This numerical test attempted to show that the ACORSES is able to prevent being trapped in bad local optimum although the bi-level programming is non-convex. In order to overcome this non-convexity, the ACORSES starts with a large base of solutions, each of which provided that the solution converges to the optimum and it also uses the reduced search space technique. In ACORSES, new ant colony is created according to randomly generated α value. In this reason, any of the newly created solution vectors may be outside the reduced search space. Therefore, created new ant colony prevents being trapped in bad local optimum. The ACORSES is able to achieve global optimum or near global optimum to optimise signal timings because it uses concurrently the reduce search technique and the orientation of all ants to the global optimum.

The application of the ACORSES to the test network can be seen in Fig. 3, where the convergence of the algorithm and the evaluation of the objective function are shown. As shown Fig. 3, the ACORSES starts the solution process according to signal timing constraints. It was found that the value of objective function is 133854 veh-sec at first iteration. The ACORSES keeps the best solution and then it uses the best solution to the optimum in the reduced search space. Optimum solution is then searched in the reduced search space during the algorithm progress. The significant improvement on the objective function takes place in the first few iteration because the ACORSES starts with randomly generated ants in a large colony size. After that, small improvements to the objective function takes place since the pheromone updating rule and new created ant colony provide new solution vectors on the different search directions. Finally, the number of objective function reached to the value of 124587 veh-sec.

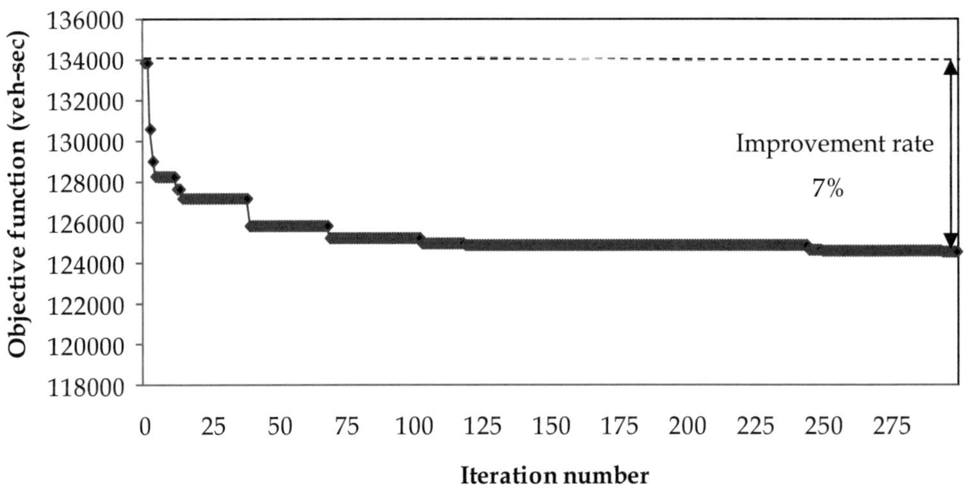

Fig. 3. Convergence behaviour of the bi-level solution

The ACORSES is performed for the 297th iteration, where the difference between the values of ψ_k and ψ_{k+1} is less than 1%, and the number of objective function is obtained for that is 124587 veh-sec. The improvement rate is 7% according to the initial solution of objective function. Table 2 shows the signal timings and final value of objective function.

Objective function (veh-sec)	Junction number	Cycle time c (sec)	Green timings in seconds		
			Stage 1	Stage 2	Stage 3
124587	1	86	7	79	-
	2	76	32	44	-
	3	69	38	31	-
	4	62	11	30	21
	5	74	11	35	28
	6	80	50	30	-

Table 2. The final values of signal timing derived from the bi-level solution

The degrees of saturation are given in Table 3. No links are over-saturated and the final values of degree of saturation of them are not greater than 95%.

s_1	s_2	s_3	s_4	s_5	s_6	s_7	s_8	s_9	s_{10}	s_{11}	s_{12}
30	39	45	25	57	23	51	52	84	58	76	40
s_{13}	s_{14}	s_{15}	s_{16}	s_{17}	s_{18}	s_{19}	s_{20}	s_{21}	s_{22}	s_{23}	
60	25	38	74	93	68	81	84	76	93	33	

Table 3. The final values of degree of saturation (%) obtained from the bi-level solution

5.2 MC solution for the test network

The MC calculations were carried out with random generated initial set of signal timings for first iteration. It was found that the value of objective function is 129500 veh-sec at first iteration. The value of objective function decreases steadily as from the second iteration. As can be seen in Figure 4, after MC solution process, the value of objective function decreased to 125216 veh-sec from 129500 veh-sec. The improvement rate was also found 3% according to initial value of objective function.

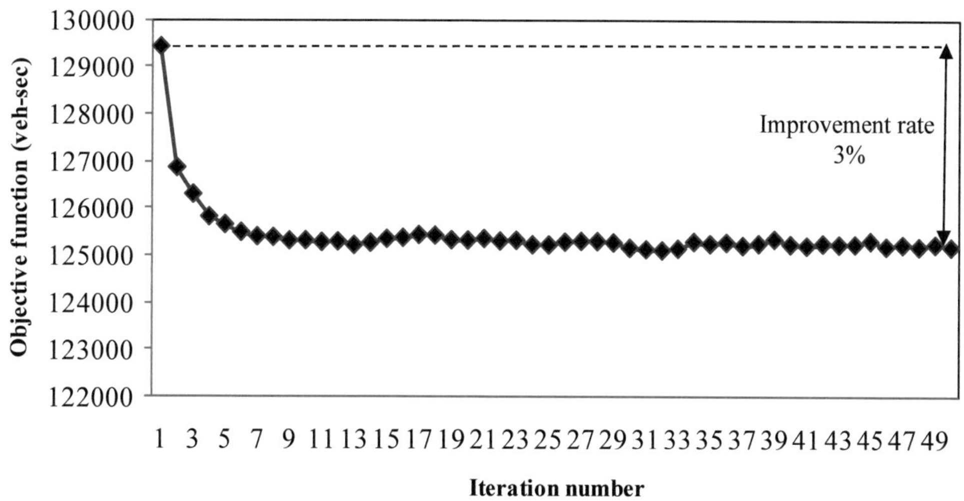

Fig. 4. Convergence behaviour of the MC solution

The final value of objective function and corresponding signal timings for the MC solution are given in Table 4. As can be seen in Table, the MC solution for optimize signal timings produces greater cycle times for each junction compared with the bi-level approach.

Objective function (veh-sec)	Junction number	Cycle time c (sec)	Green timings in seconds		
			Stage 1	Stage 2	Stage 3
125216	1	89	8	81	-
	2	100	50	50	-
	3	74	47	27	-
	4	81	17	41	23
	5	100	14	50	36
	6	91	58	33	-

Table 4. The final values of signal timing derived from the MC solution

Table 5 shows the degree of saturation for the MC solution. No links are over-saturated but some of them approach the critical degree of saturation (i.e. 100%).

s_1	s_2	s_3	s_4	s_5	s_6	s_7	s_8	s_9	s_{10}	s_{11}	s_{12}
28	43	35	27	54	26	54	56	95	60	65	37
s_{13}	s_{14}	s_{15}	s_{16}	s_{17}	s_{18}	s_{19}	s_{20}	s_{21}	s_{22}	s_{23}	
72	32	33	70	87	65	81	73	81	96	39	

Table 5. The final values of degree of saturation (%) obtained from the MC solution

6. Conclusions

In this chapter, ACORSES algorithm was used to optimize signal timings on a given road network without considering offset term using bi-level approach and MC solution procedures. The Allsop & Charlesworth's test network was used to denote the performance of the ACORSES in terms of the value of objective function and the degree of saturation on links. According to the results, the final values of degree of saturation from the bi-level solution were not greater than 95% while no links are over-saturated but some of them approach the critical degree of saturation (i.e. 100%) for the MC solution. The ACORSES algorithm is performed on PC Core2 Toshiba machine and each iteration for this test network was not greater than 12.3 sec of CPU time in Visual Basic code. On the other hand, the computation effort for the MC solution on the same machine was carried out for each iteration in less than 15.4 sec of CPU time.

The ACORSES algorithm was found considerably successful in terms of the signal timings and the final values of degree of saturation. Although the MC solution gives the similar results in terms of the value of objective function, it produces greater cycle times than the bi-level solution. Moreover, the MC solution was also dependent on the initial set of signal timings and its solution was sensitive to the initial assignment.

7. References

Allsop, R. E. (1974). Some possibilities of using traffic control to influence trip distribution and route choice. in: Transportation and Traffic Theory. *Proceedings of the 6th*

International Symposium on Transportation and Traffic Theory, Elsevier, 345-374, Amsterdam.

Abdulaal, M. & LeBlanc, L. J. (1979). Continuous equilibrium network design models. *Transportation Research*, 13B(1), 19-32.

Allsop, R. E. & Charlesworth J. A. (1977). Traffic in a signal-controlled road network: an example of different signal timings including different routings. *Traffic Engineering Control*, 18(5), 262-264.

Baskan, O. (2009) *Network design using ant colony optimization*. PhD Thesis, the Graduate School of Natural and Applied Sciences, Pamukkale University, Turkey, (in Turkish).

Baskan, O., Haldenbilen, S., Ceylan, H. & Ceylan, H. (2009). A new solution algorithm for improving performance of ant colony optimization. *Applied Mathematics and Computation*, 211(1), 75-84.

Cantarella, G. E., Improta,G. & Sforza, A. (1991) Iterative procedure for equilibrium network traffic signal setting. *Transportation Research*, 25A(5), 241-249.

Ceylan, H. (2002). *A Genetic Algorithm Approach to the Equilibrium Network Design Problem*. PhD Thesis, University of Newcastle upon Tyne.

Ceylan, H. & Bell, M. G. H. (2004). Traffic signal timing optimisation based on genetic algorithm approach, including drivers' routing. *Transportation Research*, 38B (4), 329–342.

Chiou, S. W. (1999). Optimizaton of area traffic control for equilibrium network flows. *Transportation Science*, 33(3), 279-289.

Clark, S. D. & Watling, D. P. (2002). Sensitivity analysis of the probit-based stochastic user equilibrium assignment model. *Transportation Research*, 36B, 617–635.

Dickson, T. J. (1981). A note on traffic assignment and signal timings in a signal-controlled road network. *Transportation Research*, 15B(4), 267-271.

Dorigo, M., Di Caro, G. & Gambardella, L. M. (1999). Ant Algorithms for Discrete Optimization. *Artificial Life*, MIT press.

Eshghi, K. & Kazemi, M. (1999). Ant colony algorithm for the shortest loop design problem. *Computers & Industrial Engineering*, 50, 358-366.

Fisk, C. (1984). Optimal signal controls on congested networks, *In: 9th International Symposium on Transportation and Traffic Theory*, VNU Science Press., 197-216.

Gartner, N. H. (1974). Area traffic control and network equilibrium methods, *In: Traffic Equilibrium Methods, (M. Floran, Ed.)*, 274-297, Springer-Verlag, Berlin.

Gershwin, S. B. & Tan, H. N (1979). Hybrid optimisation: optimal static traffic control constrained by drivers' route choice behaviour, *Laboratory for Information and Decision System Report LIDS-p-870*, Massachusetts Institute of Technology.

Heydecker, B. G. & T.K. Khoo (1990). The equilibrium network design problem, *Proceedings of AIRO'90 conference on Models and methods for Decision Support*, Sorrento, 587-602.

Lee, C. (1998). *Combined traffic signal control and traffic assignment: Algorithms, implementation and numerical results*. Ph.D. dissertation, the University of Texas at Austin, Texas.

Lee, C. & Machemehl, R. B. (1998). Genetic algorithm, local and iterative searches for combining traffic assignment and signal control, *Traffic and Transportation Studies: In: Proceedings of ICTTS 98*, 489-497.

Sheffi, Y. (1985). *Urban Transportation networks: Equilibrium Analysis with Mathematical Programming Methods*. MIT Prentice-Hall, Inc. New Jersey.

Sun, D., Benekohal, R. F. & Waller, S. T. (2006). Bi-level programming formulation and heuristic solution approach for dynamic traffic signal optimization. *Computer-Aided Civil and Infrastructure Engineering*, 21, 321-333.

Suwansirikul, C., Friesz, T. L. & Tobin, R. L. (1987). Equilibrium decomposed optimisation: a heuristic for the continuous equilibrium network design problem. *Transportation Science*, 21(4), 254-263.

Teklu, F., Sumalee, A. & Watling, D. (2007). A genetic algorithm approach for optimizing traffic control signals considering routing. *Computer-Aided Civil and Infrastructure Engineering*, 22, 31-43.

Wardrop, J. G. (1952). Some theoretical aspects of road research, *Proc. Inst. Civ. Engineers (Part II)*, 1(2), 325-362.

Yang, H. & Yagar, S. (1995). Traffic assignment and signal control in saturated road networks. *Transportation Research*, 29A(2), 125-139.

15

Forest Transportation Planning Under Multiple Goals Using Ant Colony Optimization

Woodam Chung and Marco Contreras
The University of Montana
USA

1. Introduction

For more than a century, forestry practitioners and decision makers have given significant attention to forest transportation planning because transportation is one of the most expensive activities in timber harvesting (Greulich, 2003). The traditional goal of forest transportation planning has been to develop road networks that minimize costs of log hauling and road construction. However, modern forest transportation planning problems (FTPP) are not driven only by the financial aspects of timber management, but also by the multiple uses of roads as well as their social and environmental impacts such as recreation, soil erosion, and stream water quality. These additional considerations and requirements introduce multiple objectives into transportation planning problems, increasing their size and complexity.

Two different problem-solving approaches have been applied to solve FTPP; exact algorithms such as mixed-integer programming (MIP) and approximation algorithms generally called heuristics (Falcao & Borges, 2001; Weintraub et al., 1995). MIP has been used to optimally solve these complex FTPP, but its application has been limited by the difficulty of solving large, real world problems within a reasonable amount of computation time (Gottlieb & Paulmann, 1998; Sun et al., 1998). On the other hand, heuristic algorithms, although might not always provide optimal solutions, have been the focus of a large number of researchers because of their high efficiency and problem solving capability especially for large and complex optimization problems (Olsson & Lohmander, 2005; Bettinger and Chung, 2004; Sessions et al., 2003; Zeki 2001; Falcao & Borges, 2001; Martell et al., 1998; Weintraub et al., 1995; Jones et al., 1991).

FTPP considering fixed and variable costs form complex optimization problems that to date have only been solved efficiently using heuristic approaches (Kowalski, 2005; Adlakha & Kowalski, 2003). NETWORK II (Sessions, 1985) and NETWORK 2000 (Chung & Sessions, 2003), which use a heuristic network algorithm combined with the shortest path algorithm (Dijkstra, 1959), have been widely used for over twenty years to solve such FTPP. NETWORK 2000 can solve multi-period, multi-product, multi-origin and -destination transportation planning problems. However, it used a single objective function for either profit maximization or cost minimization without taking into account other attributes of road segments modeled as side constraints. A recently developed approach used the ant colony optimization (ACO) to solve FTPP considering fixed and variable costs as well as side constraints (Contreras et al., 2008). This approach provided near-optimal solutions for small to medium scale FTPP including road construction and hauling costs as well as total sediment yields from the road network as a side constraint.

In this paper, we investigated two different problem formulation and solution approaches to handle multiple goals in large scale, real world FTPP. One is the single objective function approach where multiple goals are incorporated into one objective function (Rackley & Chung 2008). The other approach is to formulate transportation problems using side constraints (Contreras et al., 2008). We applied the two approaches to the Mica Creek watershed in northern Idaho in the United States where reducing environmental impacts of forest roads is considered as an additional goal and incorporated into a cost minimization FTPP. In this study, sediment delivery estimated by the USDA Forest Service WEPP: Road is used to represent the environmental impact of forest roads. A heuristic network algorithm implemented in NETWORK 2000 (Chung & Sessions, 2003), and an Ant Colony Optimization algorithm (Contreras et al., 2008; Dorigo et al., 1999) were used to solve the two differently formulated FTPP. The results indicate that solving transportation problems with multiple goals enables us to analyze trade-offs between goals and generate alternative road networks that can reduce both transportation costs and negative environmental impacts.

2. Methods

2.1 Problem formulations

The specific FTPP we address in this paper is to find the set of least-cost routes from multiple timber sale locations to selected destination mills on multiple planning periods, while considering environmental impacts of forest roads represented by sediment yields. As with most transportation problems, these FTPP can be modeled as network problems. The transportation network is represented by a graph, where vertices represent mill locations, timber sale locations, and intersections of road segments, and edges represent the road segments connecting these vertices.

Three attributes are associated with every edge in the network: fixed cost, variable cost, and amount of sediment delivery. A fixed cost is a one-time cost which occurs if the road segment is used regardless of traffic volume, whereas a variable cost is typically proportional to traffic or timber volume transported over the road segment. The sediment associated with each edge, expressed in tons per year per edge, represents the amount of sediment eroding from the road segment due to the traffic of heavy log trucks. Similar to fixed cost, we assumed sediment is produced when roads are open regardless of traffic volume.

2.1.1 Single objective function approach

The problem of finding the transportation routes that minimize both the total costs and sediment delivery can be formulated into one objective function as follows:

$$\text{Minimize} \sum_{p\in P}\sum_{ab\in E}\left[\left(vc_{ab,p}\times\left[vol_{ab,p}+vol_{ba,p}\right]\right)+\left(fc_{ab,p}\times B_{ab,p}\right)+\left(M\times sed_{ab,p}\times B_{ab,p}\right)\right] \quad (1)$$

Subject to

$$vol\_sale_{b,p}+\sum_{ab\in L} vol_{ab,p}-\sum_{ba\in L} vol_{ba,p}=0 \quad \forall b\in S,\ \forall p\in P \quad (2.1)$$

$$\sum_{ab\in L} vol_{ab,p} - \sum_{ba\in L} vol_{ba,p} = 0 \quad \forall b \in T, \forall p \in P \tag{2.2}$$

$$\sum_{ac\in L} vol_{ac,p} - \sum_{b\in S} vol\_sale_{b,p} = 0 \quad \forall c \in D, \forall p \in P \tag{2.3}$$

$$M * B_{ab,p} - \left(vol_{ab,p} + vol_{ba,p}\right) \geq 0 \quad \forall ab \in E, \forall p \in P \tag{3}$$

$$vol_{ab,p}, vol_{ba,p} \geq 0 \quad \forall ab \in E, \forall p \in P \tag{4}$$

$$B_{ab,p} \in \{0,1\} \quad \forall ab \in E, \forall p \in P \tag{5}$$

where;

$vol_{ab,p}$ = timber volume transported over the edge ab (connecting vertices a and b) in period p

$vol_{ba,p}$ = timber volume transported over the edge ba (connecting vertices b and a) in period p

$B_{ab,p}$ = $\begin{cases} 1 & \text{if timber is transported over edge ab or ba (either direction) for the first time in period p} \\ 0 & \text{otherwise} \end{cases}$

$vc_{ab,p}$ = discounted variable cost ($ per unit of timber volume) for edge ab in period p

$fc_{ab,p}$ = discounted fixed cost ($) for edge ab in period p

$sed_{ab,p}$ = sediment (kg) expected to erode from edge ab in period p

M = multiplier converting the amount of sediment into a one-time environmental cost ($)

$[M\times sed_{ab,p}]$ = discounted environmental cost ($) associated with sediment amount eroded from edge ab (kg) in period p

$vol\_sale_{b,p}$ = timber volume entering origin vertex b in period p

E = number of edges in the road network

V = number of vertices in the road network

P = number of periods in the planning horizon

L = set of edges adjacent to vertex b

S = set of origin vertices (timber sale locations)

T = set of intermediate vertices

D = set of destination vertices (mill locations)

C = constant greater than or equal to the total amount of timber volume to be transported over the entire road network

Equation 1 specifies the objective function which is set to minimize variable and fixed transportation costs as well as the costs associated with sediment yields. The first three sets of constraints (Eqs. 2.1 through 2.3) are the conservation of flow constraints which ensure that all volume entering the road network is channeled through the network to the destination vertices (mill locations). Constraint set 2.1 applies to the set of origin vertices (timber sale locations), S, and ensures the sum of timber volume entering the network at vertex b plus the sum of volume transported to b from other vertices equals the sum of volume leaving vertex b. Constraint set 2.2 applies to the set of intermediate vertices (that are neither origin nor destination vertices), T, and ensures the sum of volume entering vertex b equals the sum of volume leaving that vertex. Constraint 2.3 applies to the destination vertices (mill locations), D, and specifies the sum of volume arriving at destination vertices equals the sum of the timber volume loaded onto the origin vertices, thus ensuring all volume that enters the road network is routed to the destination vertices. The fourth set of constraints (Eqs. 3) represents the road-trigger constraints which makes sure that if there is volume transported over edge ab, the edge must be constructed and open for traffic and thus the sediment amount is counted. Lastly, the fifth and sixth sets of constraints (Eqs. 4 and 5) represent the non-negativity and binary value constraints of our problem formulation, respectively.

2.1.2 Side constraint approach

The transportation problem mentioned above can be also formulated into the following objective function and side constraint.

$$\text{Minimize} \sum_{p \in P} \sum_{ab \in E} \left[\left(vc_{ab,p} \times \left[vol_{ab,p} + vol_{ba,p} \right] \right) + \left(fc_{ab,p} \times B_{ab,p} \right) \right] \tag{6}$$

Subject to

$$\sum_{p \in P} \sum_{ab \in E} \left(sed_{ab,p} \times I_{ab,p} \right) \leq allowable\_sed \quad \forall p \in P \tag{7}$$

$$\sum_{i \in p} B_{ab,i} - I_{ab,p} \geq 0 \quad \forall ab \in E, \forall p \in P \tag{8}$$

$$I_{ab,p} \in \{0,1\} \quad \forall ab \in E, \forall p \in P \tag{9}$$

Equation 6 represents the objective function set to minimize total variable and fixed transportation costs. In addition to the sets of constraints described above (Eqs. 2 through 5), equation 7 represents an additional constraint added to limit the maximum allowable sediment amount (allowable_sed) to be delivered from the entire road network in tons. The ninth set of constraints (Eqs. 8) represents the fixed cost-trigger constraints that ensure that if there is sediment being counted from edge ab (thus volume is being transported over edge ab) in one or more periods, the associated fixed cost is counted only the first time the edge is used. The last set of constraints represents the additional binary value constraints for this formulation.

2.2 Solution techniques

2.2.1 A heuristic network algorithm

NETWORK 2000 (Chung & Sessions, 2003) is used to solve the FTPP with the single objective function approach. NETWORK 2000 uses a heuristic network algorithm for optimizing transportation problems, which takes into account both fixed costs (road construction) and variable costs (timber hauling). Although the problem solving technique is based on a shortest path algorithm similar to that proposed by Dijkstra (1959), it is

different from the regular shortest path algorithm in that it iteratively applies the algorithm and at each iteration variable costs are recalculated based on fixed costs and estimated traffic volume over each edge.
The process begins with sorting timber sales by time period and volume, then solving the shortest path problem and "tracking" on the fixed costs for each edge associated with the best variable cost solution. Timber volumes transported over each edge (vol_{ab}) are accumulated so at the end of the first iteration the sum of timber volumes (Σvol_{ab}) over each edge are available. Timber volumes for sales entering in the future are "discounted" to account for the discount rate. The variable cost for each edge (vc_{ab}) is then recalculated using Equation 9. The volume over all edges is then reset to zero and the next iteration starts. This process continues until the same or very similar solution is repeated for two consecutive iterations. To diversify the search, a negative value is substituted for each positive variable cost on edges not in the solution, such that $vc_{ab} < 0$ for all edges with $vol_{ab} = 0$. The solution procedure is then repeated until the solution re-stabilizes with each time an edge with a negative value (variable cost) is used, and its value returns to the original value. This process rapidly eliminates the substituted negative values while providing an additional opportunity to consider alternative edges.

$$rvc_{ab,p,i} = vc_{ab,p} + \frac{fc_{ab,p}}{\sum vol_{ab,p}} \tag{10}$$

where;

$rcv_{ab,p,i}$ = recalculated discounted variable cost ($ per unit of timber volume) for edge ab in period p at iteration i

2.2.2 An Ant Colony Optimization (ACO) algorithm

The ACO is a metaheuristic approach for solving difficult combinatorial optimization problems (Dorigo & Stützle, 2003). ACO algorithms are inspired by the observation of the foraging behavior of real ant colonies, and more specifically, by their ability to find shortest paths between food sources and the nest. When walking, ants deposit a chemical substance on the ground called pheromone, ultimately forming a pheromone trail. While an isolated ant moves essentially at random, an ant that encounters a previously laid pheromone trail can detect it and decide with a high probability to follow it, therefore reinforcing the trail with its own pheromone. This indirect form of communication is called autocatalytic behavior, which is characterized by a positive feedback, where the more ants following a trail, the more attractive that trail becomes for being followed (Maniezzo et al., 2005; Dorigo & Di Caro, 1999).
In this study, we used an ACO algorithm similar to that developed by Contreras et al. (2008) to solve FTPP considering a single planning period. The ACO algorithm uses a finite colony of artificial ants that concurrently move through adjacent vertices in a given road network, starting from each timber sale location until reaching the destination mills. Artificial ants selects where to move applying a stochastic transition policy that considers two parameters called trail intensity and visibility. Trail intensity refers to the amount of pheromone in the path, which indicates how proficient the move has been in the past, representing an a posteriori indication of the desirability of the move. Visibility is computed as a heuristic value indicating an a priori desirability of the move (Maniezzo et al., 2004), such as costs

and sediment amount associated with each edge. Therefore, moving through adjacent vertices, ants incrementally build a feasible solution to the optimization problem. Once an ant has found a solution, the algorithm evaluates the solution and deposits pheromone on the edges/vertices it used, proportionally to the goodness of the solution (Contreras et al., 2008).
In our ACO algorithm, once an ant is located on a given vertex, it decides what vertex to go next based on a transition probability for each adjacent edge calculated as follows:

$$\rho_{ab}(c) = \frac{(\tau_{ab})^{\alpha} * (\eta_{ab})^{\beta}}{\sum_{d \in N} (\tau_{ad})^{\alpha} * (\eta_{ad})^{\beta}} \tag{11}$$

where, $\rho_{ab}(c)$ indicates the transition probability with which an ant chooses the edge ab in iteration c; N is the set of edges sharing the same from-vertex a; α and β are the parameters that control the relative importance of the pheromone trail intensity (τ_{ab}) and the visibility (η_{ab}) values on edge ab. The visibility value is calculated according to the following equation (Eq. 12).

$$\eta_{ab} = (vc_{ab} * vol_{ab})^{-1} * fc_{ab}^{-1} * sed_{ab}^{-1} \tag{12}$$

Consequently, by combining equations 10 and 11, the resulting transition probability formula for a given edge is determined as follows:

$$\rho_{ab}(c) = \frac{(\tau_{ab})^{\alpha} * \left[(vc_{ab} * vol_{ab})^{-1} * fc_{ab}^{-1} * sed_{ab}^{-1}\right]^{\beta}}{\sum_{d \in N} (\tau_{ad})^{\alpha} * \left[(vc_{ad} * vol_{ad})^{-1} * fc_{ad}^{-1} * sed_{ad}^{-1}\right]^{\beta}} \tag{13}$$

Based on the transition probability values of all edges in N, accumulated transition probabilities for each of these edges are computed. Then, a random number between zero and one is selected using a random number generator. If this random number is smaller than the accumulated transition probability of edge ab and larger than the accumulated transition probability of previous edge on the N list, then edge ab is selected.
Starting with the first planning period, ants are located at a randomly selected timber sale. The ants incrementally build a route, from the timber sale until reaching the mill destination, moving through adjacent edges based on their transition probability (Eq. 13).
When each ant has found a route for a given timber sale/mill destination, the route yielding the lowest fixed and variable costs is selected as the least-cost path. Thereafter, ants move to the next randomly selected timber sale to find the least-cost path. When all timber sales have been routed to their destination mills for the first period, ants move to randomly selected timber sales for the second period. When all second period timber sales have been routed, ants move to third period timber sales and so on. Once all timber sales for all planning periods have been routed, an iteration is completed and all the edges forming all least-cost paths (one for every timber sale-destination pair for each period) are identified, the objective function value is computed and the solution feasibility is evaluated. If the current solution is not better than the best found so far or is infeasible, the current solution is ignored, the pheromone trail intensities remain the same, and another iteration starts.

However, if the current solution is better than the best solution found so far, the current solution becomes the new best solution and the pheromone trail intensity of the edges forming all least-cost paths is updated. At the same time, pheromone intensity on all edges decreases (evaporates) in order to avoid unlimited accumulation of pheromone. Also pheromone evaporation avoids a too-rapid convergence of the algorithm towards a sub-optimal solution, allowing the exploration of the solution space. Pheromone trail intensity is updated using the following equation (Eq. 14):

$$\tau_{ab}(c+1) = \lambda * \tau_{ab}(c) + \Delta\tau_{ab} \tag{14}$$

where two components are considered; the current pheromone trail intensity on edge ab at iteration c, indicated by $\tau_{ab}(c)$, multiplied by $0 < \lambda < 1$ which is a coefficient such that $(1 - \lambda)$ represents the pheromone evaporation rate between iteration c and c + 1; and $\Delta\tau_{ab}$ which represents the newly added pheromone amount to edge ab, calculated as follows:

$$\Delta\tau_{ab} = \sum_{k=1}^{s} \Delta\tau_{ab}^{k} \tag{15}$$

where, s is total number of timber sales, and $\Delta\tau_{ab}^{k}$ is the quantity of pheromone laid on edge ab by the ants in iteration c; which is given by:

$$\Delta\tau_{ab}^{k} = \begin{cases} Q / L_k & \text{if the ants used edge ab in the } k_{th} \text{ least-cost path} \\ 0 & \text{otherwise} \end{cases} \tag{16}$$

where, Q is a constant and L_k is the total transportation cost over the selected least-cost path. The value of Q has to be chosen so the amount of pheromone added to edge ab by a given ant slightly increases the probability of that edge during the following iterations.

3. Application

3.1 Study area

The study area is located within the Mica Creek watershed, which is part of the St. Joe River basin in Idaho, USA (Fig. 1). Potlatch Forest Holdings, Inc. (Potlatch), a private timber company, owns and manages most of the watershed. The entire watershed is about 13,000 ha in size with 760 km of roads. The study area is situated in the upper part of the Mica Creek watershed and is 7,070 ha in size, which is about 54% of the entire watershed.

There are 261 harvest units ranging from 1.4 ha to 182.3 ha in size, and approximately 407 log landings predetermined for timber harvesting (Fig. 2). Landing locations were designated for each stand considering different logging methods (i.e., ground-based vs. cable logging) based on average ground slopes within stands. The total road length inside the study area is 342 km (Fig. 3). Of these roads, 271 km is existing roads, while 71 km is proposed roads analyzed in this study for the future access to timber sale locations. Existing roads were classified into primary, secondary, and primitive roads by Potlatch based on road standards such as width, maximum grades, and design vehicle.

The harvest schedule provided by Potlatch consisted of expected harvestable timber volume per product in each harvest unit, year of harvest, and destination mill. The harvest schedule from Potlatch for the Mica Creek watershed included 5-year plans for the next 30 years and 10-year plans afterward up to 70 years, resulting in a total of 10 planning periods. The total timber production from the 261 harvest units over the 70-year planning horizon is approximately 2 million cubic meters. In our analysis, we only considered two products, logs and pulp. St. Maries and Lewiston in Idaho, located about 45 and 100 km away from the study area were selected as the product destinations for logs and pulp respectively (See Fig. 1).

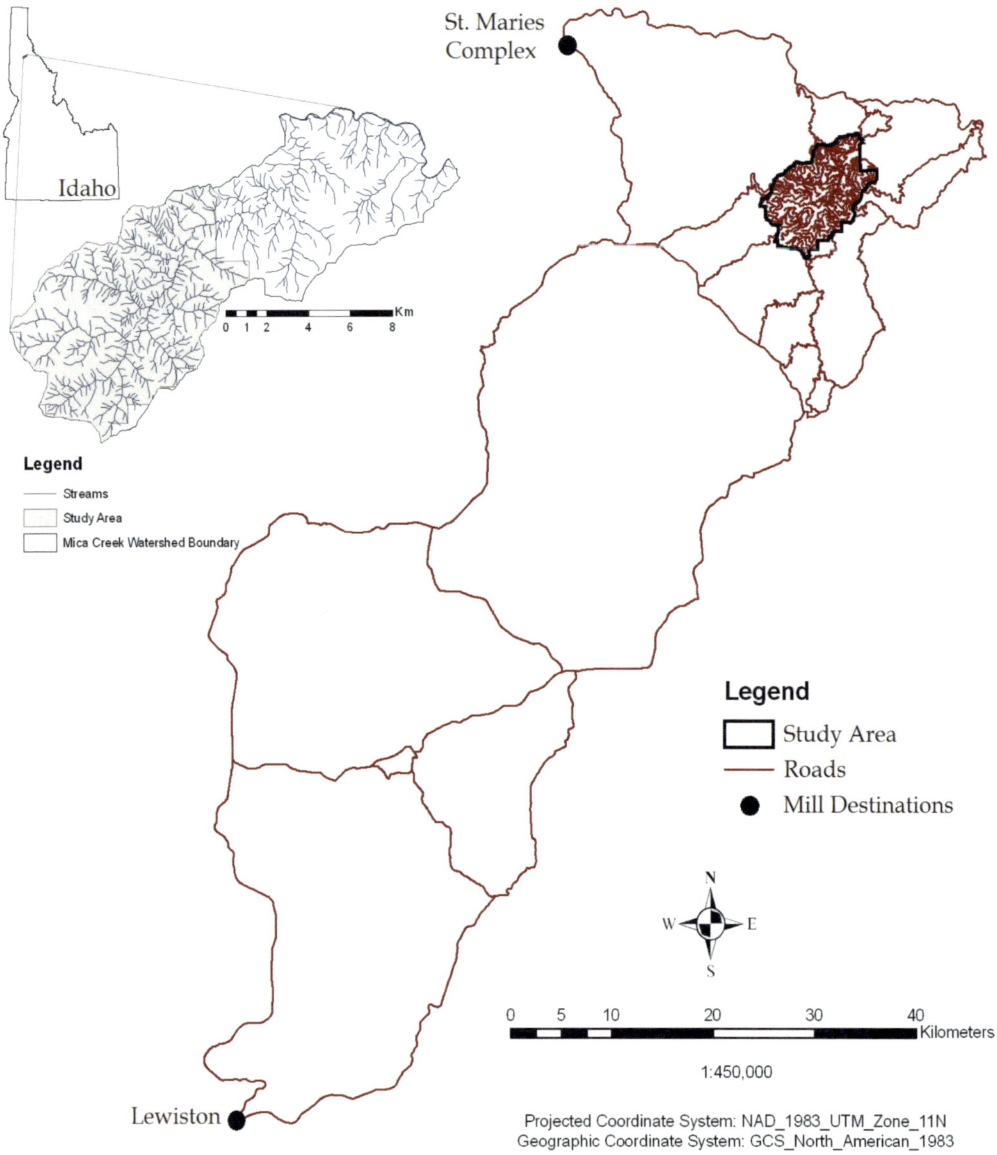

Fig. 1. Study area located in the upper part of the Mica Creek watershed in Idaho, USA.

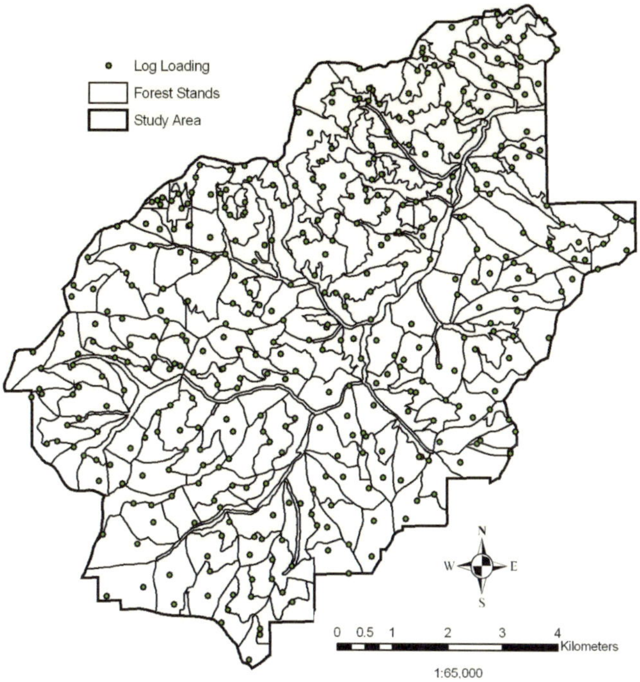

Fig. 2. Harvest units and log landing locations in the study area.

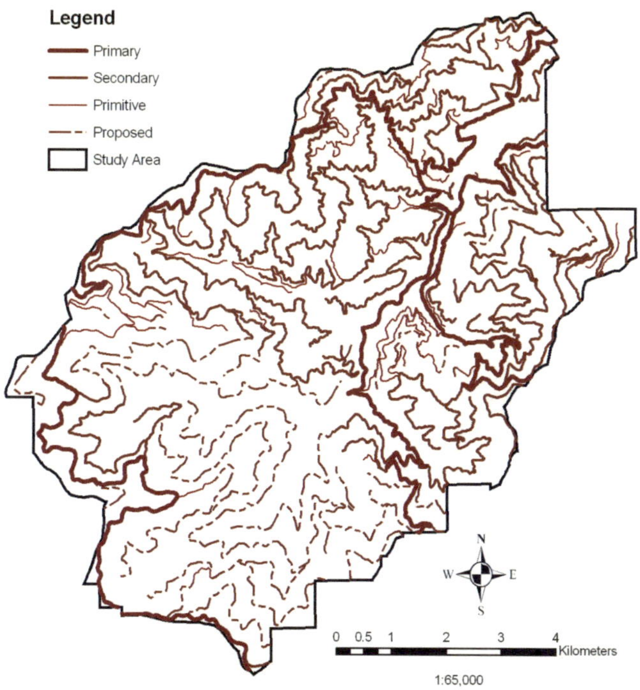

Fig. 3. Forest road classes and locations in the study area.

3.2 Estimating sediment yields using WEPP:ROAD

Developed by the USDA Forest Service, the WEPP:Road erosion model (Elliot et al., 1999) predicts runoff and surface erosion from a road segment, and the sediment yield to an adjacent stream channel. We used WEPP:Road to predict the mean annual sediment yield from the road surface per year (referred to as "road sediment").

WEPP:Road requires the following input data to predict road erosion: road segment length, width and gradient, surface soil texture, road design, road surface material including percent rock content, fill slope and length, buffer slope and length, and traffic level. To obtain road segment length and gradient from the GIS layers, we manually digitized the existing roads in the study area using a 1x1 meter LiDAR (Light Detection and Ranging)-derived intensity layer and a DEM (digital elevation model), while ensuring road features in a GIS map correctly represent actual road surface. The DEM was then used to estimate road gradients and identify high and low elevation points which are used along with road junctions to split roads into multiple road segments and locate sediment delivery points. A total of 5,906 delivery points were identified, of which 4,643 points were on existing roads, and 1,263 points were on proposed roads. After being split into multiple road segments by delivery points and road junctions, both existing and proposed roads in the study area were analyzed using WEPP to estimate the amount of sediment coming from each road segment. Road inventory data from Potlatch was used to obtain road width, surface (i.e., native, gravel, paved), design (i.e., in-sloped, out-sloped), and fill gradient (%). Fill length was estimated by computing the horizontal distance from road edge to the intersection point between the fill gradient line and the average cross-section slope obtained from the DEM. For buffer length, we used the Flow Direction function in the Spatial Analysis Tools in ArcMap to obtain the flow direction for each delivery point and then calculate the horizontal distance along the flow path from the delivery point to the nearest stream. A buffer slope was estimated using the elevation difference between the delivery point and the nearest stream. A soil map of the study area was used to identify three soil types in the study area: loam, silt load, and sandy loam. Rock fragment percentage was estimated as a function of road surface and ranged from 10 to 65%. A high traffic level was assumed for the primary roads, while a low traffic level was assumed for all the other road classes (i.e., secondary, primitive, and proposed).

3.3 Optimizing road networks using NETWORK 2000

All of the predicted amounts of road sediment produced from WEPP:Road were incorporated into environmental costs, which were further combined with actual transportation costs using the single objective function approach and analyzed in NETWORK 2000. NETWORK 2000 inputs require two data sets: link and sale data. Link data are arranged by road segments (edges). These segments are identified by a beginning and ending vertex, which in our study represents a high, delivery, or intersection point. Each edge in the road network has a variable cost (hauling cost), which is defined by a road class factor (ranging from \$0.075 $km^{-1}\cdot m^{-3}$ to \$0.373 $km^{-1}\cdot m^{-3}$) multiplied by the length of road segment. The variable cost units are set as dollar per unit volume in m^3 or thousand board feet (MBF) in this study. For proposed roads, a fixed cost is calculated and assigned using a construction cost of an assumed \$15,500 km^{-1} multiplied by the road segment length, whereas zero construction cost is assigned to existing road segments. In addition, in order to include the environmental impact of each road segment in the model, the environmental cost was added to the fixed cost for each road segment as sediment yield (kg) from the road segment predicted by WEPP:Road multiplied by a cost factor. Two different cost factors ($2.2 and $55 per kilogram of sediment) were used in this study to analyze the effects of different weights on the optimal road network. The total road network consists of over 6,000 vertices and almost 10,000 road segments connecting all 407 log landing to the two selected mill destinations.

Sale data were developed using the harvest schedules provided by Potlatch. Based on the 407 log landing located on the 261 harvest units and the 10 planning period, a total of 1,043 sales were generated. Sale data consists of timber sale id, destination mill, volume, and year of harvest for each timber sale. NETWORK 2000 was then run for the same harvest schedule for four different alternatives with the following objectives: minimizing transportation costs only without considering environmental costs, minimizing total costs including environmental costs as additional fixed costs (estimated $2.2 or $55 per kilogram of road sediment), and minimizing total road sediments without considering transportation costs.

3.4 Optimizing road networks using the ACO algorithm

The network problem described above was re-formulated using the side constraint approach. The ACO algorithm was then employed to solve four different alternative road networks with different sediment constraint levels. The following objectives were used to generate four alternative transportation problems: minimizing transportation costs only without any side constraints for road sediments, minimizing transportation costs with two increasing levels of sediment constraints, and minimizing total road sediments without considering transportation costs.

For this application, we used similar ACO parameter values as those used in Contreras et al. (2008). Due to the difference in problem size, we changed beta (importance of costs and sediment relative to pheromone amount) and lambda (pheromone persistence rate), and used a larger number of iterations (I_{max}). Alpha (relative importance of pheromone), Q (constant that controls the additional amount of pheromone) and q (initial amount of pheromone) remained the same (Table 1; For more descriptions of each parameter, see Contreras et al. 2008).

Parameter	Description	Parameter value
α	Relative importance of the pheromone amount to other attribute values on a given link	1.5
β	Relative importance of attribute values to the pheromone amount on a given link	0.35
λ	Pheromone persistence rate	0.95
Q	Constant controlling the additional amount of pheromone added on selected links between consecutive iterations	0.001
q	Initial amount of pheromone assigned to each link	0.001
M	Number of ants	100
I_{max}	Number of iterations	150

Table 1. ACO parameters used in this study.

4. Results

The results of WEPP:Road show that the mean annual road sediment from the road segments within the study area is 336 tons per year. With an average road width of 3.6 m, the mean annual road erosion rate is calculated to be 2.73 tons per ha of road surface. Predicted road sediment is attributed to each road segment and plotted in Figure 4.

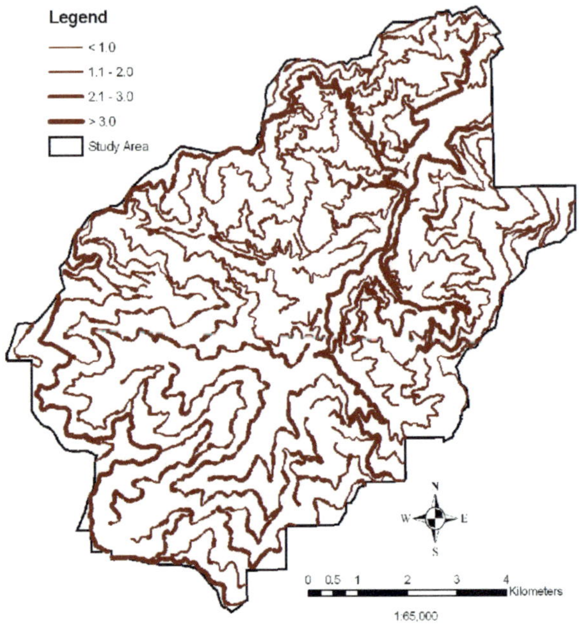

Fig. 4. Annual sediment leaving roads in tons per hectare of road surface estimated by WEPP:Road.

Table 2 summarizes the results of NETWORK 2000 and the ACO algorithm for the eight FTPP analyzed in this study. The four transportation problems formulated using the single objective function approach and solved using NETWORK 2000 show that the total amount of sediment decreases and the total transportation costs increase as the sediment goal is more heavily weighed. Compared with the cost minimization problem, the sediment minimization problem has a 40% cost increase, but the total sediment decreases by 34%. Similar results are found in the solution of the four transportation problems formulated using the side constraint approach and solved by the ACO algorithm. Transportation costs range from \$15.8 to \$25.5 per MBF in the cost and sediment minimization solutions, respectively, while the amount of sediment ranges between 306 and 445 tons. Total transportation costs increase and total sediment amounts decrease as the restriction level of sediment constraint increases (Table 2).

The most cost-efficient transportation solution was found by NETWORK 2000, where the total transportation cost is \$6,654,716. The ACO solution for the same problem (cost minimization) has a slightly higher total transportation cost of about 0.07%. In addition, the solutions from NETWORK 2000 and the ACO algorithm have the similar amount of total road sediments. For the sediment minimization problem, NETWORK 2000 also found a slightly better solution than the ACO algorithm. By producing only 294.5 tons of sediment,

Problem Formulation Approach	Solution Method	Problem Objective	Transportation Cost ($)	Sediment Amount (tons)	Road Length (km)
Single objective function	NETWORK 2000	Cost minimization	6,654,716 15.8 ($/mbf)	444.6	270.0
		Cost minimization with environmental cost ($2.2/kg or $1/lb)	6,668,568 15.8 ($/mbf)	392.9	258.5
		Cost minimization with environmental cost ($55/kg or $25/lb)	7,668,862 18.2 ($/mbf)	333.9	248.2
		Sediment minimization	9,285,180 22.7 ($/mbf)	294.5	247.3
Side constraint	ACO	Cost minimization	6,659,164 15.8 ($/mbf)	445.1	270.2
		Cost minimization with sediment constraint (400 tons)	6,666,625 15.8 ($/mbf)	397.8	259.1
		Cost minimization with sediment constraint (350 tons)	7,164,888 17.0 ($/mbf)	347.7	258.5
		Sediment minimization	10,778,539 25.5 ($/mbf)	305.9	248.9

Table 2. Results of the eight transportation problems analyzed in this study.

the NETWORK 2000 solution becomes the least road sediment solution among the eight network alternatives. Direct comparisons between solutions from the transportation problems with environmental costs (single objective function) and the cost minimization problems with sediment constraints are not appropriate. However, their results are consistent with the trend of higher transportation costs associated with solutions yielding lower sediments amounts.

5. Concluding remarks

Negative impacts of forest roads on the environment are often recognized, but these impacts are rarely incorporated into the economic analyses of forest transportation planning. This is partially due to lack of analytical methods and tools that are able to directly integrate environmental impacts into decision making for road and transportation networks. In this study, we investigated two problem formulation and solution approaches to incorporate road sediment into the economics of forest transportation planning.

The single objective function approach is relatively simple, and the existing transportation planning tools that were developed to minimize transportation costs, such as NETWORK 2000, can be used without modifications. However, it is a challenge to put a price on environmental impacts and select an appropriate environmental cost factor for predicted sediment yields. The second approach with side constraints can avoid this problem, but it may require more complex problem formulation and solution techniques, as well as a large solution time, to provide good quality solutions.

Both NETWORK2000 and the ACO algorithm are based on heuristic solution techniques. Unlike MIP, such heuristic techniques do not guarantee the solution optimality, but they can be applied to large, real world transportation planning problems and provide feasible solutions in a reasonable amount of solution time. In addition, the problem formulation approaches and solution tools used in this study can be easily expanded to incorporate other environmental impacts into forest transportation planning. These tools can provide forest managers with environment-friendly road network alternatives that help them make informed decisions for their road management and planning.

Further development of the ACO algorithm is suggested to enhance its performance and applicability as a generalized approach for solving large scale, real world FTPP with side constraints. First, the road attributes used to evaluate the transition probability associated with each edge could be standardized to a mean of zero and a variance of one. This would avoid the differences in magnitude of the attribute values affecting the evaluation of transition probability. Consequently a more homogenous weight can be given to each road attribute when predicting the goodness of a road segment in the solution. Lastly, as the solution quality is heavily dependent on the fine tuning of the algorithm parameter values, the incorporation of a sub-routine that dynamically determines the best parameter values during running time based on the problem size and range of road attribute values may be essential for facilitating the use of the ACO algorithm.

6. References

Adlakha, V. & Kowalski, K. (2003). A simple heuristic for solving small fixed-charge transportation problems. *OMEGA: International Journal of Management Science*, 31,3,205-211.

Bettinger, P. & Chung W. (2004). The key literature of, and trends in, forest-level management planning in North America, 1950-2001. *International Forestry Review* 6,1,40-50.

Contreras, M.; Chung, W. & Jones, G. (2008). Applying ant colony optimization metaheuristics to solve forest transportation planning problems with side constraints. *Canadian Journal of Forest Research*, 38,11,2896-2910.

Chung, W. & Sessions, J. (2003). NETWORK 2000: A Program for Optimizing Large Fixed and Variable Cost Transportation Problems. *Proceedings of the 2003 Symposium on Systems Analysis in Forest Resources,* Arthaud, G.J., & Barrett, T.M. (Eds), pp 109-120, Kluwer Academic Publishers.

Dijkstra, E. (1959). A note on two problems in connection with graphs. *Numerische Mathematik*, 1,269-271.

Dorigo, M.; Di Caro, G. & Gambardella, M. (1999). Ant algorithms for discrete optimization. *Artificial Life*, 5,2,137-172.

Dorigo, M. & Di Caro, G. (1999). The ant colony optimization meta-heuristic. *Proceeding on New Ideas in Optimization*, Corne, D.; Dorigo, M. & Glover, F. (Eds), pp 11-31, McGraw-Hill, London, UK.

Dorigo, M. & Stützle, T. (2003). The ant colony optimization metaheuristic: Algorithms, applications, and advances. *Handbook of Metaheuristics*, Glover, F. & Kochenberger, G. (Eds.), pp 251-285, Kluwer Academic Publishers, Norwell, MA.

Elliot, W.J.; Hall, D.E. & Scheele, D.L. (1999). WEPP interface for predicting forest road runoff, erosion and sediment delivery. *Technical Documentation WEPP: Road (Draft 12/1999)*. USDA Forest Service, Rocky Mountain Research Station and San Dimas Technology and Development Center [online]. Available from http://forest.moscowfsl.wsu.edu/fswepp/docs/wepproaddoc.html, Accessed 20 January 2008.

Falcao, A. & Borges, J. (2001). Designing an evolution program for solving integer forest management scheduling models: An application in Portugal. *Forest Science*, 47,2,158-168.

Greulich, F. (2003). Transportation networks in forest harvesting: early development of the theory [online]. *In Proceedings International Seminar on New Roles of Plantation Forestry Requiring Appropriate Tending and Harvesting Operations*, S3.04/3.06/3.07 Subject Area, IUFRO 2–5 October 2002, Tokyo, Japan. IUFRO, Vienna. Available from faculty.washington.edu/greulich/ Documents/IUFRO2002Paper.pdf [accessed August 20 2010].

Gottlieb, J. & Paulmann, L. (1998). Genetic algorithms for the fixed charge transportation problem. *Proceedings of the 1998 IEEE International Conference on Evolutionary Computation*, pp 330-335, IEEE Press.

Jones, G.; Weintraub, A.; Meacham, M. & Megendzo, A. (1991). A heuristic process for solving mixed-integer land management and transportation problems planning models. *USDA Forest Service, Intermountain Research Station*. Research Paper INT-447.

Kowalski, K. (2005). On the structure of the fixed charge transportation problem. *International Journal of Mathematical Education in Science and Technology*, 36,8,879-888.

Maniezzo, V.; Gambardella, M. & de Luigi, F. (2004). Ant colony optimization. *New Techniques in Engineering*, Onwubolor, G. & Babu, V. (Eds.), pp 101-117, Springer-Verlog, Berlin Heidelberg.

Martell, D.; Gunn, E. & Weintraub, A. (1998). Forest management challenges for operational researchers. *European Journal of Operational Research*, 104,1,1-17.

Olsson, L. & Lohmander, P. (2005). Optimal forest transportation with respect to road investments. *Forest Policy and Economics*, 7,3,369-379.

Rackely J. & Chung, W. (2008). Incorporating forest road erosion into forest resource transportation planning: a case study in the Mica Creek Watershed in northern Idaho. *Transaction of the ASABE*, 51,1,115-127.

Sessions, J.; Chung, W. & Heinimann, H. (2003). New algorithms for solving large-scale transportation planning problems. *Workshop Proceedings: New Trends in Wood Harvesting with Cable Systems for Sustainable Forest Management in the Mountains*, pp 253-258, Ossiach, Austria, June 2001.

Sessions, J. (1985). A heuristic algorithm for the solution of the fixed and variable cost transportation problems. *In Proceedings of the 1985 Symposium on Systems Analysis in*

Forest Resources, 9–11 December 1985, Athens, Georgia. P.E. Dress & R.C. Field (Eds), pp 324-336. University of Georgia, Athens, Ga.

Sun, M.; Aronson, J.; McKeown, P. & Drinka, D. (1998). A tabu search heuristic procedure for the fixed charge transportation problem. *European Journal of Operational Research*, 106,2-3,441-456.

Weintraub, A.; Jones, G.; Meacham, M.; Magendzo, A.; Magendzo, A. & Malchauk, D. (1995). Heuristic procedures for solving mixed-integer harvest scheduling-transportation planning models. *Canadian Journal of Forest Research*, 25,10,1618-1626.

Zeki, E. (2001). Combinatorial optimization in forest ecosystem management modeling. *Turk Journal of Agriculture and Forestry*, 25,187-194.

16

Ant Colony System-based Applications to Electrical Distribution System Optimization

Gianfranco Chicco
Politecnico di Torino
Italy

1. Introduction

Electrical distribution networks are structurally weakly meshed, but are typically operated in radial configurations to simplify the network protection schemes. This implies the need to carry out suitable selection of the redundant network branches to open in normal conditions, as well as to define the control variables to set up in order to guarantee effective system operation and voltage quality. Furthermore, the structure of the distribution networks has to be upgraded to meet future needs, according to economic objective functions defined for distribution system planning. Finally, distribution systems need to face possible interruptions through the formulation of appropriate service restoration strategies, based on switching on and off a number of branches, reducing the effects of faults occurring in the networks by defining a time-dependent path to restore electricity supply to all consumers. All these aspects can be addressed by formulating and solving suitable optimization problems for distribution network operation and planning. Typically these problems are defined within discrete domains for the decision variables. However, for large real distribution systems the highly-dimensional and/or combinatorial nature of the optimization problems make it impracticable to resort to exhaustive search, since the number of combinations would be excessively high to be processed in reasonable computation times. Global optimizations can then be solved in terms of adopting suitable meta-heuristics.

In this context, ant colony optimization (ACO) provides viable solutions to the various distribution system optimization problems. Key features of ACO, such as parallel search, shortest path finding, adaptability to changes in the search space, long-term memory and information sharing, have been fully exploited in their classical formulations, in advanced versions such as the hyper-cube ACO framework, as well as in hybrid formulations combining the ACO properties with those of other meta-heuristics.

This chapter summarizes the formulation and use of ACO algorithms and variants to solve different types of electrical distribution system optimization problems, namely:

- *Distribution system optimal reconfiguration and voltage support.* Various objective functions to minimize can be set up in the presence of a set of structural and operational constraints. The objectives include total distribution system losses, voltage deviations with respect to their reference values, maximum load on system components, load balancing, and capacitor placement. Performing network configuration changes and setting up the level of insertion of compensating devices or distributed generation and resources connected to the network nodes are the main actions needed, according to which the decision variables are defined.

- *Optimal planning of distribution networks and resources*. The classical objective function is composed of the total (fixed and variable) costs for network reinforcement, taking into account structural network components, as well as possible introduction of distributed energy resources. For the purpose of application of an ACO algorithm to a minimization problem, the inverse of the total costs can be considered as objective function.
- *Optimization of service restoration and reliability*. The typical objective in this case is maximization of distribution network reliability under specific constraints. For this purpose, composite reliability indices are formulated by taking into account frequency and duration of the interruptions. Multi-objective formulations with reliability and economic terms have also been adopted. The decision variables for distribution system upgrade are defined with the purpose of increasing the level of automation or exploiting the potential of distributed generation and resources to assist service restoration.

The specific aspects concerning the implementation of ACO algorithms are illustrated and discussed in the next sections, taking into account the representation of the search space with definition of the variables, the parameters and their initialization, the formulation of global and local heuristic rules for pheromone update, and finally the stop criterion. The dedicated solutions adopted to take into account the nature of the distribution system optimization problems addressed are highlighted, as well as the role of ACO parameters within hybrid formulations of the solution algorithms.

Dedicated reference is made to literature papers, mainly to those appeared in scientific journals. Uniform notation and symbols are used throughout this chapter. As a consequence, the symbols may differ with respect to the ones included in the original referenced papers.

2. Ant colony optimization characteristics and general framework

2.1 Basic features of the ant colony optimization algorithms

ACO algorithms are stochastic search procedures based on a parametrized probabilistic model called *pheromone model* (Dorigo & Blum, 2005). ACO algorithms adopt an iterative solution process in which each iteration corresponds to the parallel search operated by M ants. The pheromone quantity is typically initialized to a constant positive value and is updated during the solution process, enhancing its relative concentration in the most promising regions of the search space, in such a way to increase the probability of accessing these regions during the successive phases of the stochastic search.

Dorigo et al., 2006, indicate that the most widely adopted ACO algorithms in general applications are the ant system (Dorigo et al., 1996), the max-min ant system (Stützle & Hoos, 2000), and the ant colony system (Dorigo et al., 1996). The latter is the most widely used for solving electrical distribution system optimization problems. The general scheme of ACO algorithms adopted for these problems is summarized in the flow-chart shown in Fig. 1. Besides the user-defined number of ants M, the general parameters include a number of specific parameters that are introduced in the following subsections. At the beginning of the solution process, the ants are placed in locations randomly selected or defined with specific criteria. At each iteration, the ants move within the search space on the basis of a state transition rule. The ant movement and the objective functions corresponding to the solution points reached during the search determine the pheromone update according to a global heuristic rule. An optional local heuristic rule can be introduced to further impact on the search process.

As for any stochastic search process, the solutions reached depend on the extraction of random numbers, typically from a uniform probability distribution in the range [0, 1]. When repeatability of the results under the same conditions is needed, the seed for random number extraction is set to a fixed value at the beginning of the execution of the algorithm.

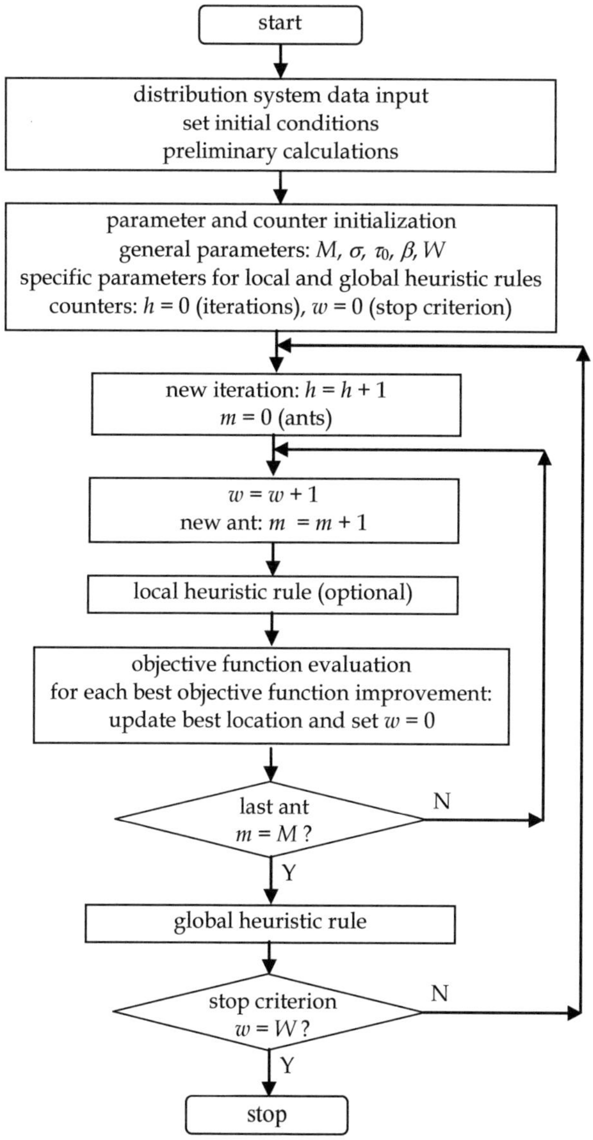

Fig. 1. General flow-chart for ant-colony optimization application to electrical distribution systems.

2.2. Weighted probabilistic selection mechanism

At each iteration, each ant $m = 1,..., M$ moves along a path selecting the new locations according to a *state transition rule*: for ant m, the probability $p_{(i,j)}^{(m)}$ of moving from location i to a location j (belonging to the set $\mathbf{S}_i^{(m)}$ of the locations that can be visited by ant m starting from location i) is expressed as

$$p_{(i,j)}^{(m)} = \frac{\tau_{(i,j)} \left(d_{(i,j)}\right)^{-\beta}}{\sum_{\nu \in \mathbf{S}_i^{(m)}} \tau_{(i,\nu)} \left(d_{(i,\nu)}\right)^{-\beta}} \tag{1}$$

where $\tau_{(i,j)}$ is the amount of pheromone existing in the connection between the locations i and j, the term $d_{(i,j)}$ represents the *distance* between the locations i and j, and the exponent $\beta > 0$ quantifies the relative importance of the pheromone and distance entries[1]. In practice, a transition from i to j becomes most probable when the distance between the locations is relatively low and there is a relatively high amount of pheromone deposed on the connection between the locations i and j.

On the practical point of view, after calculating the probabilities $p_{(i,j)}^{(m)}$, the transition of ant m from location i to a location belonging to the set $\mathbf{S}_i^{(m)}$ is identified by using a *weighted probabilistic selection* mechanism based on the construction of the cumulative distribution function (CDF) (Carpaneto & Chicco, 2008), analogous with a biased roulette wheel mechanism. In fact, since the sum of the probabilities satisfies the basic probability law $\sum_{\nu \in \mathbf{S}_i^{(m)}} p_{(i,\nu)}^{(m)} = 1$, it is possible to construct the CDF of the probabilities associated to the state transition rule. An example in which ant m starts from location i and can reach four possible destinations (numbered as 1, 2, 3 and 4) with corresponding probabilities equal to 0.2, 0.3, 0.4 and 0.1, respectively, is shown in Fig. 2. Then, taking a random number r extracted from a uniform probability distribution in [0, 1] and entering it onto the vertical axis, it is possible to identify the destination to reach by determining the corresponding step on the CDF. In the example of Fig. 2, if the random number $r = 0.35$ is extracted the destination is $j = 2$.

2.3 Local heuristic rule

This rule is optional and can be formulated in different ways. A typical formulation is the one of the ant colony system (Dorigo et al., 1996), that considers a small positive constant τ_c not lower than the initial pheromone τ_0 and not higher than a quantity depending on the objective function values. The amount of pheromone existing in the connection between the

[1] In some applications the pheromone terms indicated in (1) are associated to a further exponent. However, for the sake of reducing the overall parameters, a single exponent can be sufficient for tuning the relative importance of the pheromone quantity and distance terms. In the applications shown in this chapter, the double exponent representation used in some papers is reported to the single-exponent scheme.

locations i and j is changed from $\tau_{(i,j)}^{previous}$ to $\tau_{(i,j)} = \rho\tau_c + (1-\rho)\tau_{(i,j)}^{previous}$, where ρ is a user-defined parameter. This rule changes dynamically the characteristics of the path from i to j, thus modifying the extent to which this path is likely to be successively visited by the ants.

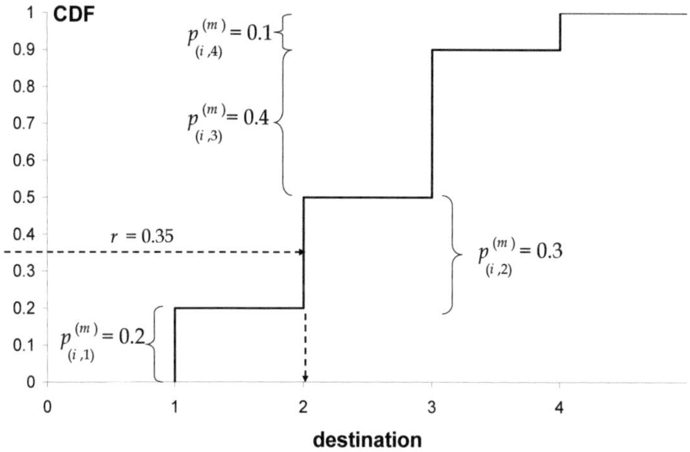

Fig. 2. Selection of the destination based on the construction of the CDF.

2.4 Global heuristic rule

This rule is applied at the end of each iteration h. During the iteration, the path followed by one of the ants exhibited the best performance. The global heuristic rule is implemented by considering two terms: (i) pheromone *evaporation* applied to all connections, driven by the parameter $\sigma \in [0, 1]$; (ii) pheromone *reinforcement* limited to the connections among the locations reached by the best path, depending on a specifically defined function $\psi^{(h)}$:

$$\tau_{(i,j)}^{(h)} = (1-\sigma)\tau_{(i,j)}^{(h-1)} + \sigma\psi^{(h)} \tag{2}$$

Generally, the function $\psi^{(h)}$ is inversely proportional to the distance covered by the best path. According to Dorigo & Blum, 2005, in the *iteration-best update rule* the best path can be the one found at iteration h, that is, $\psi^{(h)} = \kappa_\tau / d_{best}^{(h)}$, where $d_{best}^{(h)}$ represents the distance and κ_τ is a user-defined factor. Alternatively, in the *best-so-far update rule* the best distance $\hat{d}_{best}^{(h)}$ found so far is used, thus obtaining $\psi^{(h)} = \kappa_\tau / \hat{d}_{best}^{(h)}$. The update rule could also change during the iteration process, for instance using the iteration-best update rule in the first iterations and best-so-far update rule in the successive iterations.

2.5 Pheromone bounds and hypercube framework

Successful rules for driving the pheromone update have been set up by limiting the minimum and maximum amounts of pheromone. The ant colony system algorithm (Dorigo et al., 1996) applies to all pheromone values a non-fixed lower bound, possibly depending on the objective function values. The max-min ant system (Stützle & Hoos, 2000) applies to all pheromone values an explicit lower bound and a non-fixed upper bound depending on the objective function values. The hypercube framework (Blum & Dorigo, 2004) provides an automatic scaling of the objective function values used in the search process, and results in a more robust and easier way to implement computational procedure. The initial pheromone quantity $\tau_0 \in [0, 1]$, and the pheromone values are always limited within the interval [0, 1] by properly formulating the pheromone update rules.

2.6 Elitism

In the basic version of the heuristic, each iteration starts with a set of locations, and these locations are then changed during the iteration according to the rules applied. As such, there is no certainty that the best solution found at a given point is maintained for the whole iterative process. In the *elitistic* version of the heuristic, the best solution found in the previous iteration is maintained without being subject to any change during the current iteration. In this case, a monotonically increasing path for the objective function to be maximized (e.g, fitness), or, correspondingly, a monotonically decreasing path for the objective function to be minimized, is generated in the successive iterations. The elitistic version of a heuristic is generally convenient to apply in terms of effectiveness of the solution process (Reeves, 1993).

In ACO, a specific technique is used to implement elitistic considerations. Considering the set $\mathbf{S}_i^{(m)}$ of locations that can be visited by ant m starting from location i, the selection process of the destination is driven by a user-defined parameter $q_0 \in [0,1]$. After extracting a random number $r \in [0,1]$, if $r > q_0$ the selection is made by using the weighted probabilistic selection mechanism (Section 2.2) with probabilities defined as in (1), obtaining the destination $\hat{j}$. Conversely, for $r \le q_0$ the destination with relatively high pheromone and relatively low distance in the connection is sought. In summary, the destination $j \in \mathbf{S}_i^{(m)}$ to be reached by ant m is selected by applying the following rule:

$$j = \begin{cases} \arg\max\limits_{u \in \mathbf{S}_i^{(m)}} \left\{ \tau_{(i,u)} d_{(i,u)}^{-\beta} \right\} & \text{if } r \le q_0 \\ \hat{j} & \text{otherwise} \end{cases} \tag{3}$$

The more the parameter q_0 is close to unity, the more the selection becomes driven by elitistic considerations.

2.7 Stop criterion

The most convenient stop criterion for a heuristic refers to conclude the iterative process when no objective function improvement occurs after a predefined number W of successive iterations. This criterion is by far more effective than the simple use of a maximum number of iterations H. In fact, setting up a maximum number of iterations could result either in premature stop of the solution process when substantial improvements are still occurring, or in unnecessary computational overburden when no change in the best solution is found for a large number of the last successive iterations. The maximum number of iterations H can be used as a last-resource option, mainly for algorithm testing. However, many references still adopt the simple stop criterion based on the maximum number of iterations.

2.8 Parameter values

The choice of the ACO parameters is made by the user, who can conduct dedicated parameter analyses for assessing the most suitable parameter values to be used to solve the specific problem on the specific system under analysis. In order to summarize the parameters used in various applications to distribution system optimization, Table 1 shows the numerical values of the parameters adopted in the reference papers recalled in this chapter. Multiple indications are included to represent ranges of values used for parametric analysis.

Reference	Parameters					
	M	σ	τ_0	β	W	H
Ahuja et al., 2007	-	0.05	100	-	-	100
Carpaneto et al., 2004	20	0.02	10	1	10	-
Carpaneto & Chicco, 2004	100	0.1	10	1	5	-
Carpaneto & Chicco, 2005	10÷600	0.01÷0.2	10	1	10	-
Carpaneto & Chicco, 2008	10	0.04	1	1	5	-
Chang, 2008	5	0.05÷0.2	0.1	0.1, 0.15	-	450
Chiou et al., 2004	5	]0, 1[	(*)	1	-	500
Falaghi et al., 2009	50	0.1	0.1 (lower bound)	(-)	-	100
Favuzza et al., 2006	50	0.00001	0.2	2	20	-
Favuzza et al., 2007	50	0.00001	0.2	2	20	-
Gomez et al., 2004	4÷50	0.2÷1	random	1÷4	-	30
Niknam, 2008	10÷200	(*)	(*)	0.01÷0.1	-	100
Su et al., 2005	5	0.1÷0.5	(*)	0.1÷0.25	-	30
Teng & Liu, 2003	50÷250	0.1÷0.6	> 0 (small)	1	-	100
Tippachon & Rerkpreedapong, 2009	(*)	0.2	not fixed	2	-	(*)
Wang & Singh, 2008	200	0.27	> 0 (small)	1	-	200
Zamboni & Monteiro, 2009	5	-	0.01	0.15	-	200

Table 1. Numerical values of the parameters used in reference papers. A dash indicates that the parameter is not used. An asterisk (*) indicates that a numerical value is not available.

3. Optimal reconfiguration and voltage support

3.1 Distribution system topology and network calculations

In the weakly-meshed distribution system structure, the network topology typically lacks of regularity. As such, it is not possible to exploit concepts like network symmetry or uniformly distributed connection among the network nodes to simplify the computational procedures for network topology analysis.

For a generic weakly-meshed distribution system structure, let us assume the following notation: the set of nodes $\mathbf{N}$ contains $i = 1,\ldots, N$ nodes, the subset of supply nodes $\mathbf{S} \subset \mathbf{N}$ contains $s = 1,\ldots, S$ supply nodes, and the set of branches $\mathbf{B}$ contains $b = 1,\ldots, B$ branches.

Furthermore, the set $\boldsymbol{T} \subset \boldsymbol{B}$ contains the transformers located in the distribution network, and the set $\boldsymbol{X}$ contains all the possible radial configurations of the distribution system.
A general property is that each radial network obtained from the weakly-meshed network structure has the same number $\Lambda = B\text{-}N\text{+}S$ of open branches. However, opening Λ branches is a necessary but not a sufficient condition for obtaining a radial network, since by arbitrarily opening Λ branches it could be possible to isolate one or more network nodes and to maintain loops in the network. As such, the identification of the radial structures is not straightforward. Even the enumeration and generation of all radial configurations that can be obtained for a given weakly meshed structure is a difficult task, that can be addressed by using specific algorithms (Andrei & Chicco, 2008). However, the size of the real distribution systems is typically large, and the corresponding number of possible radial configurations is high enough to make exhaustive search practically intractable in terms of computational burden.
For a radial configuration $X \in \boldsymbol{X}$, the distribution network calculations are carried out by solving the power flow with a specific iterative method like the backward-forward sweep (Shirmohammadi et al., 1988; Baran & Wu, 1989; Andrei et al., 2008). The power flow results provide the complex voltages at every distribution system node. The branch currents and losses in the distribution system are then computed on the basis of the power flow results. In specific cases approximate solutions for loss calculation (Baran & Wu, 1989b) are adopted (for instance in Chiou et al., 2004; Su et al., 2005; Chang, 2008).

3.2 Objective functions and constraints

3.2.1 Optimization problem formulations

The optimal reconfiguration of the distribution system is a *discrete* problem, consisting of the search of the radial configuration that minimizes (or maximizes) a specified objective function $f(X)$ under various operational constraints. The general formulation for a minimization problem is $\min_{X \in \boldsymbol{X}} \{f(X)\}$, subject to a set of equality and inequality constraints.
The *equality constraints* are the power flow or approximate loss calculation equations.
Concerning the *inequality constraints*, the constrained variables are the voltage magnitude at each node (a bilateral constraint with maximum and minimum limits implemented independently of each other), the phase-to-ground current at each node (with maximum limit), the three-phase short circuit current at each node (with maximum limit), the thermal current at each branch (with maximum limit). Other operational constraints (Carpaneto et al., 2003) may reflect the need to avoid the presence of multiple cascade circuit breakers in any path of the radial network (being the circuit breakers non-selective), the need to avoid simultaneous interruption of two (or more) supply points for the customers requiring enhanced supply availability in their contractual provision (according to which independent supply points have to be maintained, that is, connected to radial networks starting from different substations), and, in case, a constraint on the maximum number of switching operations occurring to move from the standard distribution system configuration to the new configuration found in the solution process.
There are two ways to introduce the inequality constraints in the optimization problem:

1. checking the constraints for each solution and *discarding* any solution that does not satisfy *all* constraints;
2. embedding the inequality constraints into a *penalized* objective function, by adding penalty terms to the specific objective function.

The use of the penalized objective function is commonplace for heuristic methods. In this way, it is possible to obtain a numerical value of the objective function in any condition, provided that the network structure is acceptable (in our case, the network is radial), without the need of detecting and eliminating infeasible solutions that do not meet the operational constraints. This allows for reducing the limits on the size of the search space. Using the penalized objective function together with a dedicated mechanism to avoid the generation of non-radial networks (Section 3.3), the check for the existence of valid solutions indicated in the framework of a basic ACO algorithm in Dorigo & Blum, 2005, is not necessary, and thus it is not represented in the flow-chart of Fig. 1.

Let us consider an objective function composed of a specific term $f'(X)$ based on the objective to be assessed. Let us further assume that the objective function has to be *minimized*. In this case, positive penalty terms are added to $f'(X)$ in case of violations, obtaining the *penalized* objective function expressed for instance in the form:

$$\min_{X \in \mathbf{X}} \left\{ f(X) = f'(X) + \mathbf{w}^{\mathrm{T}} \Delta\mathbf{u}(X) \right\} \tag{4}$$

where:

- $\mathbf{u}(X)$ is a column vector containing the variables subject to constraints, and $\Delta\mathbf{u}(X)$ is a column vector whose components are positive in case of violations and zero elsewhere; these components can be the absolute deviations with respect the corresponding constraints, in case elevated to an user-defined exponent (e.g., squared);
- $\mathbf{w}$ is a column vector containing positive user-defined weights for the variables belonging to $\mathbf{u}(X)$ for which a violation occurs, and null values for the components without violation;
- the superscript T denotes transposition.

3.2.2 Specific objective functions

The specific objective function $f'(X)$ can be written as follows:

- For *total distribution system losses*, considering the branch series resistance R_b and the branch current I_b:

$$f'(X) = P_{\mathrm{L}}^{tot}(X) = \sum_{b \in \boldsymbol{B}} R_b I_b^2 \tag{5}$$

- For *voltage deviations* with respect to the rated value, considering the voltage magnitude V_k at node k and the rated voltage $V^{(r)}$:

$$f'(X) = \Delta V^{\max}(X) = \max\left\{ \left| V^{(r)} - \max_{k \in \boldsymbol{K}} \{V_k\} \right|, \left| V^{(r)} - \min_{k \in \boldsymbol{K}} \{V_k\} \right| \right\} \tag{6}$$

- For *maximum load* on branches (feeders or transformers), the objective function is the maximum ratio between the branch current I_b and the corresponding current rating $I_b^{(r)}$:

$$f'(X) = L^{\max}(X) = \max_{b \in B} \left\{ \frac{I_b}{I_b^{(r)}} \right\} \tag{7}$$

- For *transformer load balancing*, the rationale of this objective is to make the load sharing of each transformer (expressed in relative values with respect to the transformer capacity) proportional to the capacity of that transformer. The objective function is the total unbalance, expressed in terms of the total network apparent power load A_{LL}^{tot} (including losses), of the apparent power $A_b(X)$ of each transformer $b \in \boldsymbol{T}$ in the configuration X under study, and the ratio $\ell_b = A_b^{(r)} \Big/ \sum_{v \in \boldsymbol{T}} A_v^{(r)}$ between the transformer capacity and the sum of capacities of all network transformers:

$$f'(X) = \Delta U_T^{tot}(X) = \sum_{b \in \boldsymbol{T}} \frac{A_b(X) - \ell_b A_{LL}^{tot}}{\ell_b A_{LL}^{tot}} \tag{8}$$

  Alternatively, it is possible to define a transformer load balancing index (Wu et al., 2010).
- For *feeder load balancing*, the objective is to make the branch loading as uniform as possible throughout the network, comparing the apparent power of each branch $b \in \boldsymbol{B}$ to the corresponding MVA limit $A_b^{\max}$:

$$f'(X) = \Delta B^{tot}(X) = \sum_{b \in \boldsymbol{B}} \left(\frac{A_b(X)}{A_b^{\max}} \right)^2 \tag{9}$$

- For *capacitor placement*, the objective function can be set up as the sum of the total system losses and of the annual cost of the capacitors installed, in order to highlight the convenient solutions in which the loss reduction makes it possible at least to compensate the capacitor costs. Considering the specific cost ρ_c in monetary units per kvar, and the rated power $Q_{C_k}^{(r)}$ of the capacitor to be installed at node $k \in \boldsymbol{K}$:

$$f'(X) = P_L^{tot}(X) + \sum_{k \in \boldsymbol{K}} \rho_c Q_{C_k}^{(r)} \tag{10}$$

  In the capacitor placement problem, an additional constraint is set up in order to limit the size of the capacitor to be installed at each node to the reactive power load Q_{L_k} at that node, i.e., $Q_{C_k}^{(r)} \le Q_{L_k}$ for $k = 1, \ldots, \boldsymbol{K}$.

A specific aspect adopted in the optimal reconfiguration problem formulation in Carpaneto & Chicco, 2008, refers to the consideration that each branch has two switches, one at each terminal, and for any open branch it is possible to choose which switch has to be maintained open. If the switches have different levels of automation, the switch-on/switch-off operations are convenient to be done only at the terminal with higher level of automation, because of easier manoeuvrability. The on/off position of the switches is then specified in detail in the problem formulation for each open branch.

The above objective functions are expressed in terms of *power* quantities, that is, they are valid for a single snapshot in time. However, with the progressive introduction of distributed resources in the energy networks, the focus is now shifted to distribution system operation in a given time interval. For this purpose, the distribution network objectives have to be reformulated by explicitly considering the dependence on time of the relevant variables.

Let us represent the time domain with a set of regularly spaced discrete points $j = 1,\ldots, J$, as in Carpaneto & Chicco, 2010. Without taking into account the possibility of making configuration changes in the time interval of analysis, the general form of the objective function is expressed as:

$$\min_{X \in \mathbf{X}} \left\{ f(X) = f'(X) + \sum_{j=1}^{J} \mathbf{w}^{\mathrm{T}} \Delta \mathbf{u}_j(X) \right\} \tag{11}$$

and the specific objective functions are written taking into account the results of the power flow calculations at the various points in time. As an example, the voltage deviations with respect to the reference value can be assessed by considering, for $j = 1,\ldots, J$, the voltage magnitude V_{kj} at node $k \in \mathbf{K}$, the rated voltage $V^{(r)}$, the consumer damage constant C_k (Strezoski et al., 2001), and the consumer energy E_{kj} introduced as a weighting factor to enhance the importance of nodes and time intervals with relatively high energy consumption (Carpaneto et al., 2004; Carpaneto & Chicco, 2010):

$$f'(X) = \sum_{j=1}^{J} \sum_{k \in \mathbf{K}} \left(C_k E_{kj} \left(V_{kj} - V^{(r)} \right)^2 \right) \tag{12}$$

Similar formulations can be obtained by considering, instead of a regular discretizazion in time, a reduced number of load variation steps, as in the minimum electrical energy generation cost problem defined in Niknam, 2008, applied to a fixed radial network configuration in which the decision variables refer to capacitors, transformer tap changers, distributed generators and voltage regulators.

Multi-objective functions can be formulated as well, by simultaneously considering two or more objectives (Ahuja et al., 2007).

3.3 Approaches for ant colony optimization applications

3.3.1 Classification of the alternative approaches

For the purpose of constructing *radial* system configurations, alternative approaches can be exploited. A first classification can be made on the basis of the starting conditions used:

1. *constructive* approach: the initial network is only composed of the supply points, and the network branches are successively added until a radial network is formed;
2. *loop-based* approach: all branches are initially considered in their closed state, and the Λ branches to open are determined in such a way to open Λ loops identified in the network;
3. *variation-based* approach: the initial network is radial and a new configuration is obtained by closing and opening some branches according to a specific branch-exchange rule formulated to preserve radial configurations after each variation.

The details of these approaches and the corresponding ACO algorithms used are illustrated in the sequel.

3.3.2 Constructive approach

The constructive approach uses a pheromone-driven application of the Prim-Jarník algorithm (Prim, 1957) to form the radial network by successively adding edges that do not form any loop. In the presence of multiple supply (root) points, with $S > 1$, there are S radial networks simultaneously growing by adding one branch at a time to one of these networks. A key aspect is the selection of the next branch to be added.

In the constructive scheme illustrated in Carpaneto & Chicco, 2004, the initial network is composed of the only substation nodes. The specific objective function (5) is used. The pheromone is applied to all the branches of the weakly-meshed distribution system structure. The initial pheromone is set to $\tau_b^{(0)} = \tau_0$ for any branch $b \in \mathbf{B}$. An additional parameter $\xi > 1$ is used to represent the pheromone reinforcement factor and is set to $\xi_b^{(h)} = 1$ at the beginning of each iteration for any branch $b \in \mathbf{B}$. At each iteration, each ant $m = 1,\ldots, M$ builds a radial system by adding K-S branches to the initial network. At each step of the branch addition, a list of candidate nodes is formed, containing all the nodes to which it is possible to connect a further open branch without closing a loop (at the beginning, this list contains only the substation nodes). Then, one of the open branches converging to a node included in the list has to be added to the radial network under formation. For this purpose, a branch selection mechanism is applied. The selection is driven by the definition of a suitable distance in the state transition rule (1). For instance, branch resistance (or impedance) can be used as distance. In the version illustrated in Carpaneto & Chicco, 2004, a specific selection mechanism is implemented, in order to enable a relatively balanced growth of the radial networks supplied by different substations. The series resistance of the branches already belonging to the path from each node contained in the list and the corresponding supply substation is used as the distance related to that node[2]. Then, the state transition rule based on the weighted probabilistic selection mechanism (Section 2.2) is applied to extract the node belonging to the list formed to which an open branch has to be connected. Once the node has been selected, if there are multiple open branches that can be connected to its terminals without forming any loop, another extraction is carried out by using again the weighted probabilistic selection mechanism, in which the distances now consist of the resistances of the branches that can be connected. At the end of the radial network construction for the current iteration h, the pheromone reinforcement factor is set to $\xi_b^{(h)} = \xi$ at each branch belonging to the radial network formed, and to zero at every other branch.

The global heuristic rule is applied to each branch by using an expression similar to (2), in which the function $\psi^{(h)}$ multiplied by the evaporation factor σ contains the pheromone reinforcement factor, as well as a further component given by the ratio between the best solution $f(X_{best})$ found so far and the best solution $f\left(X_{best}^{(h)}\right)$ found at the current iteration (excluding the best solution found in previous iterations and reproduced in the current iteration according to the application of the elitism principle):

---

[2] For the substation nodes not yet connected to any other node, the distance is set to a very low default value (e.g., 10^{-8}), thus increasing at these nodes the probability of being extracted by the weighted probabilistic selection mechanism with respect to other nodes already connected to the corresponding supply substations through a series of branches.

$$\tau_b^{(h)} = \sigma\,\xi_b^{(h)} \frac{f\left(X_{best}\right)}{f\left(X_{best}^{(h)}\right)} + (1-\sigma)\,\tau_b^{(h-1)} \tag{13}$$

The ratio between the two best solutions is equal to unity if the best solution found so far has been obtained in the current iteration, otherwise is lower than unity, being the objective function to be minimized. In the latter case, the pheromone reinforcement at the current iteration h is in some way mitigated with respect to the case in which the best solution was updated during the iteration.

3.3.3 Variation-based approach

The initial distribution system configuration $X^{(0)} \in \mathbf{X}$ is chosen as a radial network, typically corresponding to the standard configuration adopted by the distribution company. The solution algorithm proceeds by progressively introducing *variations* in the configuration according to specific local and global heuristic rules. Each variation is constrained by the need of forming a radial structure, thus adopting the branch-exchange mechanism (Civanlar et al., 1988; Baran & Wu, 1989b) to maintain network radiality.

Two types of branch-exchange mechanisms can be defined, based on inverse strategies:

a. *close-open branch exchange*: consists of closing an open branch, detecting the *loop* formed in the system, and restoring the radial configuration by opening a branch inside the loop;
b. *open-close branch exchange*: consists of opening a closed branch, detecting the *island* formed in the system and all the possible connections among any node of the island and the remaining part of the network, and restoring the radial configuration by closing one of these connections.

In both mechanisms, the way in which the branches to open and close are selected depend on the characteristics of the solution strategy. For this purpose, it is possible to make a distinction between *deterministic* methods (in which specific rules are set up to apply the branch-exchange mechanism, with the possibility of trapping into local optima, Carpaneto et al., 2003) and *probability-based* methods (in which the selection is performed on the basis of random number extractions dependent on probability values, such as in the weighted probabilistic selection mechanism described in Section 2.2). ACO algorithms belong to the latter type of methods.

In the approach presented in Carpaneto & Chicco, 2008, the pheromone is associated to each branch (more specifically, to each switch, but general reference will be made here to branches, for the sake of comparison with the other methods). The rationale is to enhance the pheromone at the branches that have to remain open in the configuration corresponding to the best objective function. This approach operates in the hyper-cube ACO framework (Blum & Dorigo, 2004), so that the pheromone has to be initialized and vary in the [0,1] range. The objective function (5) is used. Two additional parameters are introduced to be used in the local heuristic rule: the reduced neighbourhood size A and the number ζ of successive configuration changes produced by each ant. The value ζ cannot be too low, in order to allow for exploring the solution space by introducing relatively large variations, but at the same time it cannot be too high, to avoid the introduction of many changes to the reference configuration used.

At each iteration h, the reference configuration is set to the one corresponding to the best solution obtained so far. The M ants are initially located on randomly selected branches.

Each ant $m = 1,..., M$ introduces a number of successive configuration changes $\zeta_m^{(h)}$ randomly selected from 1 to ζ by applying the local heuristic rule. The changes are operated by applying $\zeta_m^{(h)}$ times the close-open branch-exchange mechanism. A further variant embedded in the local heuristic is the identification of a reduced neighbourhood of size A, such that the choice of the branch to open after closing a selected branch is limited to the A branches adjacent to the closed branch in the loop formed. Within the neighbourhood formed, the branch to open is chosen by applying the weighted probabilistic selection mechanism (Section 2.2) by using as weight the pheromone associated to each branch. After $\zeta_m^{(h)}$ successive configuration changes have been introduced, the objective function is computed. The best configuration $X_{best}^{(h)}$ of the current iteration h and the best configuration X_{best} found so far are updated in case new best solutions are found during the calculations. In the global heuristic rule, the pheromone is updated according to the following relation:

$$\tau_b^{(h)} = \sigma \upsilon_b^{(h)} \frac{f\left(X_{best}\right)}{f\left(X_{best}^{(h)}\right)} + \left(1-\sigma\right)\tau_b^{(h-1)} \tag{14}$$

where $\upsilon_b^{(h)} = 1$ if branch b is open in the best configuration found at iteration h, otherwise $\upsilon_b^{(h)} = 0$. The considerations on the ratio between the two best solutions, corresponding to the function $\psi^{(h)}$ in (2) are the same as the ones discussed in (13). Since the first addend in (14) cannot be higher than unity, and the initial pheromone cannot exceed unity by definition of the hyper-cube framework, the pheromone updated by the global heuristic rule always remains in the range [0, 1], thus maintaining full consistency with the hypotheses of the hyper-cube ACO framework.

The multi-objective optimization presented in Ahuja et al., 2007, considers a set $\boldsymbol{\Omega}$ of objectives, such as total loss minimization (5), voltage deviations with respect to the rated value (6) and transformer load balancing (8), and searches for the best-known Pareto front, composed of the non-dominated solutions for which it is not possible to found other solutions with better values of all individual objective functions (Shukla & Deb, 2007). The initial solutions are generated through the Prim-Jarník constructive algorithm (Prim, 1957), then configuration changes are determined by exploiting cloning principles and pheromone-based hypermutation. Pheromone is used to store information on the solution effectiveness, in order to use this information during the solution process. A separate pheromone table is initialized (with equal values τ_0) and used for each individual objective. Each pheromone element is denoted as $\tau_{b,\omega}^{(h)}$, with reference to iteration h, branch b and objective function $\omega \in \boldsymbol{\Omega}$. Each non-dominated solution is subject to cloning to obtain a number of copies of it. Each clone is then subject to hypermutation on the basis of the pheromone values. To do that, the open-close branch-exchange mechanism is used, driven by weighted probabilistic selection (Section 2.2) to select the branch to open (using the pheromone weights) and to further select the branch to close among the remaining open branches (using equal weights). The pheromone update is performed by considering pheromone evaporation at all branches according to the second addend of (2), then including an addend providing pheromone reinforcement only on the branches corresponding to non-dominated solutions. This addend contains a constant χ and the ratio between two terms: the upper-side term is the minimum value of the objective function for objective ω in the set $\boldsymbol{X}^{(h)}$ of configurations providing non-dominated solutions at the current iteration, and the lower-side value is the objective function for objective ω in the current non-dominated solution:

$$\tau_{b,\omega}^{(h)} = \chi \frac{\min\limits_{X \in \mathbf{X}^{(h)}} \{f_\omega(X)\}}{f_\omega(X)} + (1-\sigma)\tau_{b,\omega}^{(h-1)} \tag{15}$$

The update formula (15) is applied at each iteration to each branch and to each objective function.

3.3.4 Loop-based approach

The loop-based approach exploits a *loop-opening* principle. The weakly-meshed distribution system structure is initially considered with all branches closed, thus containing a number of loops. The ants are initially located at random positions in the network. The search space contains a number of loops $\Lambda = B\text{-}N\text{+}S$ equal to the number of branches to be open (Section 3.1). Each ant selects one switch to be opened for each loop. The loops are processed one at a time, by listing for each loop the branches it contains and selecting among them the branch to open with a probabilistic transition rule based on the pheromone located on these branches.

Minimum loss reconfiguration is addressed from the loop-based viewpoint in Su et al., 2005, Chang, 2008, and Wu et al., 2010. The approximate solution for loss calculation introduced in Baran & Wu, 1989b, is used in Su et al., 2005, and in Chang, 2008, on any radial network constructed during the solution process, while Wu et al., 2010, includes as objectives both total losses and load balancing, performing full power flow calculation. The iterative process follows standard ACO concepts. Pheromone is located on the system branches and is initialized to the value τ_0. Pheromone update is made according to the local heuristic rule (Section 2.3). The initial ants are located on the distribution system nodes. Each ants selects the next node in which it has to move on the basis of the state transition rule (1). Elitism is introduced by saving the best configuration found during the process, or by applying the concepts indicated in Section 2.6. In addition to the maximum number of iterations, in some cases the stop criterion includes as a rule the fact that all ants selected the same tour.

In Chang, 2008, the optimal reconfiguration is addressed by taking into account capacitor placement, either as a single solution and combined with loop-based open branch selection. In this case, the search space is extended to include, for each node, different capacitor sizes. Each ant operates in this extended search space, by including in a single tour both the loops and the set of nodes containing the capacitors. The addition of capacitor placement to open branch selection gives the possibility to set up additional problem variables and to enhance the performance of the optimal reconfiguration process.

Chiou et al., 2004, address the optimal capacitor placement problem by using an ant direction hybrid differential evolution method. The objective function to be minimized is the overall cost of power losses and capacitor placement (10). In this method, different mutation operators are available, and ACO is used to select the most convenient mutation operator to be used during the solution process. Each ant selects a mutation operator on the basis of a transition rule of the type (1) driven by a distance calculated on the diversity among the individuals (genes) generated with respect to the best individual found at the previous generation. A mutation operator is considered to be proper if the objective function of the current generation is better than the best objective function of the previous generation:

$$\ell^{(h,m)} = \left| \frac{f'\left(X^{(h,m)}\right)}{f'\left(X_{best}^{(h-1)}\right) - f'\left(X^{(h,m)}\right)} \right| \tag{16}$$

For ant m, the pheromone update is performed by summing up a term containing the remaining pheromone after evaporation and a *fluctuant* pheromone quantity added if the proper mutation operator has been chosen by the ant:

$$\tau^{(h,m)} = \Delta\tau^{(h,m)} + (1-\sigma)\tau_b^{(h-1,m)} \tag{17}$$

where, considering the user-defined constant value κ:

$$\Delta\tau^{(h,m)} = \begin{cases} \kappa / \ell^{(h,m)} & \text{if the mutation operator is proper} \\ 0 & \text{otherwise} \end{cases} \tag{18}$$

Zamboni & Monteiro, 2009, start with the weakly meshed structure with all branches closed, and adopt the classical weighted probabilistic selection mechanism as in (1), in which the branch resistance is considered as distance. The pheromone is associated to the branches, and all branches are assigned the same initial pheromone quantity τ_0.
The local pheromone update at iteration h is driven by the square of the current required to transfer the active power P_i and reactive power Q_i from node i to node j, being i and j the terminals of branch b:

$$\Delta\tau_b^{(h)} = \sqrt{\left(\frac{P_i}{R_b}\right)^2 + \left(\frac{Q_i}{X_b}\right)^2} \tag{19}$$

The additional parameter q_0 is introduced to further bias the selection mechanism by applying the elitistic criterion indicated in Section 2.6, allowing an ant located in a given node to move with probability q_0 to the node with highest pheromone among the ones reachable, and partitioning the remaining 1-q_0 probability of selection by using the selection mechanism (1). The authors indicate to set $q_0 \leq 0.5$ in order to avoid giving excessive weight to the local information.
Ants are initially located in some nodes, and each ant tends to move to a neighbouring node. The paths already visited are stored in order to avoid visiting them again. The ant transition from one node to another is repeated for a specified number p of steps. If the ant selects visiting an already visited path, it remains at the initial location. Any ant reaching a substation node remains in that node for the following steps. In this way, each ant collects the contributions of the loads served along the path from a node to a substation.
The solution method exploits the concept of *élite ants*, as the ones that cover the lowest distance paths. A maximum number $M^{(e)}$ of élite ants (set up as a parameter) is considered in the global pheromone update at iteration h, where pheromone reinforcement is done in each branch belonging to the corresponding paths $\mathbf{B}^{(e)} \subset \mathbf{B}$ containing the subset of nodes $\mathbf{K}^{(e)} \subset \mathbf{K}$, by introducing an extra pheromone quantity expressed as:

$$\Delta\tau_b^{(h)} = \sqrt{\left(\frac{R_b \sum\limits_{k \in \mathbf{K}^{(e)}} P_k}{\sum\limits_{v \in \mathbf{B}^{(e)}} R_v}\right)^2 + \left(\frac{X_b \sum\limits_{k \in \mathbf{K}^{(e)}} Q_k}{\sum\limits_{v \in \mathbf{B}^{(e)}} X_v}\right)^2} \tag{20}$$

where the active power P_k and reactive power Q_k refer to the nodes encountered in the path. In this way, the extra pheromone in somehow proportional to the total load encountered in the path traced by each élite ant. When at a given iteration no élite ant is formed, the procedure moves to the next iteration.

The stop criterion is based on reaching a predefined maximum number of iterations. At the end of the iterative process, the pheromone matrix contains different values, characterizing each branch. Considering the initial weakly-meshed structure, in order to decide which branches to open to form the best radial network, an algorithm is used which starts from a substation and proceeds until forming a mesh. Then, the branch belonging to that mesh having the least amount of pheromone is open. This procedure is run for $\Lambda = B\text{-}N\text{+}S$ times, then the final radial configuration is found.

Voltage control optimization is addressed in Carpaneto et al., 2004, for distribution systems with distributed generation, by using the objective function (12) formulated for time-varying loads and generations. The control variables are partitioned into time-independent and time-dependent, and are all expressed through discrete values. The solution is carried out by using nested heuristics, with a primary loop solved with a genetic algorithm to find pseudo-optimal combinations of the time-independent variables, and a secondary loop solved with ACO to find the best path for the time-dependent variables corresponding to the assigned values of the time-independent ones. In the secondary loop, the limits of the path are represented by a rectangle, with time and voltage magnitude as coordinates. Within this rectangle, a number of discrete points are identified, and these points are assigned an initially equal pheromone quantity. An iterative process is then started, in which M ants are sent at each iteration to generate a path. The transition from a given point to the successive one (in time) is driven by a local heuristic rule, based on the weighted probabilistic selection mechanism (Fig. 2) applied to a neighbourhood of the current voltage magnitude, using the pheromone of the candidate points as weights. Once an ant has constructed an entire path, the objective function (12) is evaluated. After M ants have been sent, the global heuristic rule is applied by evaporating part of the current pheromone at every point, and by reinforcing the pheromone in the points belonging to the path producing the best objective function at that iteration through the use of a pheromone amplification factor. If the path is also the best one found so far, an higher value of the pheromone amplification factor is used. The secondary loop is concluded when the objective function exhibits no improvement after a predefined number of successive iterations.

For the distribution system optimal reconfiguration problem, ACO algorithms showing better performance than other heuristics are indicated in some references, for instance in comparison with the simulated annealing algorithm (Su et al., 2005; Carpaneto & Chicco, 2008; Chang, 2008) and with genetic algorithms (Su et al., 2005; Chang, 2008).

4. Distribution system optimal planning

4.1 Formulation of the optimal planning problems

In a planning problem, the objective function is generally set up in *economic* terms. A basic distinction occurs between *operational* planning (carried out at constant load) and *expansion* planning (carried out at variable load).

A predefined set $\boldsymbol{J}$ of alternative planning actions (e.g., addition/removal of branches, distribution automation enhancement, addition of local generation units), each of which has to maintain a radial distribution network configuration after its activation, is chosen by the decision maker, in order to assess the most effective solution among the possible combinations of these alternatives. Since in real systems the number of possible combinations can be so high to make exhaustive search intractable, the use of heuristics like ACO can conveniently assist the decision-making process.
Starting from the current state of operation of the distribution system, it is possible to formulate the problem by considering the variations that can be introduced in the systems, thus calculating the corresponding effects. Considering a combination $\boldsymbol{R} \subseteq \boldsymbol{J}$ of planning actions activated at the stage of the solution process under analysis, in Carpaneto & Chicco, 2005, the objective function for the operational planning problem is formulated as:

$$f(\boldsymbol{R}) = C_A(\boldsymbol{R}) + \Delta C_R(\boldsymbol{R}) + \Delta C_M(\boldsymbol{R}) + \Delta C_V(\boldsymbol{R}) \tag{21}$$

where $C_A(\boldsymbol{R})$ is the cost of activation of the combination $\boldsymbol{R}$ of planning actions, and the terms $\Delta C_R(\boldsymbol{R})$, $\Delta C_M(\boldsymbol{R})$ and $\Delta C_V(\boldsymbol{R})$ are the *variations* of the cost components referred to reliability (power and energy not served), maintenance and annual investment, respectively, with respect to the present system operation. The cost component $\Delta C_V(\boldsymbol{R})$ can also be constrained by a budget limit.
Favuzza et al., 2006, address the distribution system reinforcement with distributed generation, using the annual cost of distribution systems reinforcement strategy as objective function in a multi-year planning approach. The objective function is expressed as:

$$f(\boldsymbol{R}) = C_L(\boldsymbol{R}) + C_M(\boldsymbol{R}) + C_V(\boldsymbol{R}) - R_D(\boldsymbol{R}) - R_I(\boldsymbol{R}) \tag{22}$$

where, in addition to the previously defined terms, $C_L(\boldsymbol{R})$ is the cost of losses, $R_D(\boldsymbol{R})$ is the saving referring to the energy not bought from the transmission system because of distributed generation exploitation, and $R_I(\boldsymbol{R})$ is the revenue resulting from incentives (e.g., for production from renewable sources).
In Favuzza et al., 2007, the objective function for distribution system reinforcement with gas microturbines is formulated by taking into account also the costs $C_E(\boldsymbol{R})$ of the electrical energy bought and the revenues $R_E(\boldsymbol{R})$ from selling electricity and heat:

$$f(\boldsymbol{R}) = C_L(\boldsymbol{R}) + C_M(\boldsymbol{R}) + C_V(\boldsymbol{R}) + C_E(\boldsymbol{R}) - R_E(\boldsymbol{R}) \tag{23}$$

Gomez et al., 2004, formulate expansion planning as a mixed nonlinear integer optimization problem by considering the total (fixed and variable) costs and partitioning these costs among existing and proposed distribution system circuits and substations, with a given maximum load condition. The same partitioning is used to express the capacity constraints. Bi-directional voltage magnitude constraints are introduced as well. Other constraints refer to the energy balance and to consider only radial networks. A maximization problem is solved, in which the objective function is the inverse of the previously mentioned total costs.

4.2 Ant colony optimization applications

In the ACO application presented in Carpaneto & Chicco, 2005, the pheromone is associated to the individual planning actions. Initially, all planning actions $j \in \boldsymbol{J}$ are associated to the same quantity of pheromone τ_0. During the iterative process, each ant $m = 1,\ldots, M$ activates a number of planning actions chosen at random by applying the weighted probabilistic selection mechanism (Fig. 2) according to the probabilities (1), depending on the distance formulated for the specific problem. For instance, the application presented in Carpaneto & Chicco, 2005, deals with the placement of remote controllers in the distribution system nodes, considering as planning action the placement of an individual remote controller in a node belonging to a set of candidate nodes. In this case, the distance referring to a given node is the inverse of the product of the power not served times the equivalent failure rates in the upstream and downstream portions of the network with respect to that node. At the end of each iteration, the global heuristic rule is applied by evaporating part of the pheromone and increasing the pheromone quantity for the planning actions providing the best objective function during the iteration (if the solution is the best one found so far the amplification factor is higher than the one used for the best solution at the current iteration).

In Favuzza et al., 2006, and Favuzza et al., 2007, the problem is represented as a graph, in which the (reinforced) distribution system configurations at the different years are the nodes, and the distances between the nodes are the actualized transition costs (including investment and operation) from the reference configuration to the new one. In this application, the set of nodes to be visited is not unique, but it is in principle infinite. The solution algorithm is then set up as a dynamic ant colony search, in which the algorithm creates at each year a finite number of candidate solutions, forming a dynamic tree structure. Basically, a parameter N_s is introduced to set up the number of candidate solutions generated (corresponding for instance to different sizes of the local generation units), and a mechanism to replace the worst search directions with most convenient ones (in terms of pheromone value and distance) is included to avoid excessive expansion of the dynamic tree during the solution process. Each resulting multi-year path is associated to a cost determined as the sum of the actualized transition costs.

For a given ant m, starting from the configuration $X_i^{(m,y)}$ at a given year y, the configuration $X_j^{(m,y+1)}$ reached at the successive year is selected among the set $S_i^{(m,y+1)}$ of the configurations generated dynamically. The selection is carried out by using elitistic considerations as in Section 2.6. The user-defined parameter q_0 is adapted during the solution process, decreasing it when the number of successive solutions without improvement increases, thus reducing the importance of elitistic choice in favour of the weighted probabilistic selection. The pheromone is updated according to the standard local heuristic rule (Section 2.3), and to the global heuristic rule (2) applied at the end of each iteration, in which the function $\psi^{(h)}$ is the inverse of the cost of the best path found during the iteration.

In Gomez et al. 2004, initially a random pheromone quantity is associated to each branch of the network. Then, each ant explores the network to reach all its nodes with a radial network, with a search guided by the weighted probabilistic selection mechanism illustrated in Section 2.2. The selection is carried out by using elitistic considerations as in Section 2.6. Classical local and global heuristic rules are used for pheromone update. In the global heuristic rule (2), the function $\psi^{(h)} = \kappa_\tau / C_{\min}^{(h)}$ is given by the ratio between the user-defined factor κ_τ and the minimum cost of the best path found during the iteration. The distance used for pheromone update takes into account the branch length, the magnitude of the load at the end of the path, and the incremental cost of the network.

5. Optimization of service restoration and reliability

5.1 Formulation of the service restoration and reliability optimization problems

Faults in a distribution system are generally classified as *temporary* (when the protection trip is followed by successful reclosure and final normal operation) and *permanent* (requiring successive restoration phases after the protection trip, with remote-controlled operations, additional manual operations, on-site repair and eventual service restoration (Carpaneto & Chicco, 2004b).
Distribution system reliability is represented by using *local* indices (referring to a single load point) and *global* indices (characterizing the overall distribution system). The relevant quantities are frequency and duration of the interruptions, and the corresponding global indices (Billinton & Allan, 1984) are the system average interruption frequency index (*SAIFI*) and the system average interruption duration index (*SAIDI*).
The relevant functions of the devices installed in distribution systems for reliability and service restoration purposes are switch and protection. The switch function refers to isolate a fault occurring downstream with respect to the switching device location, and can be operated by reclosers (with protection capability) or switches (with no protection capability). The protection function can be performed by circuit breakers, fuses and reclosers. The reclose function reduces the interruption duration after a temporary fault.
Different objective functions have been formulated for the optimization problems involving service restoration and reliability. In Teng & Liu, 2003, the objective function consists of the customer interruption costs (*CIC*) per year, taking into account voltage drop and feeder load transfer capability constraints. In Ahuja et al., 2007, service restoration is addressed starting from the solutions obtained for the multi-objective optimal reconfiguration problem (Section 3.3.3), considering only the voltage deviation objective as relevant for restoration purposes.
Wang & Singh, 2008, address the location of reclosers and distributed generation units for improving distribution system reliability. The objective function to minimize is written as:

$$f = w_1 \frac{SAIFI}{SAIFI^{(T)}} + w_2 \frac{SAIDI}{SAIDI^{(T)}} \tag{24}$$

where w_1 and w_2 represent the weights associated with the interruption frequency and duration terms, respectively. $SAIFI^{(T)}$ and $SAIDI^{(T)}$ are the target values for SAIFI and SAIDI.
Falaghi et al., 2009, formulate a fuzzy optimization procedure to solve the multiobjective optimization with the two conflicting objectives of improving service reliability (assessed through the calculation of the annual expected energy not supplied) and minimizing the cost of sectionalizing switches. The objective function is composed of the weighted sum of the two objectives, $\tau'_0 = w_1 \bar{\mu}_R + w_2 \bar{\mu}_C$, where $\bar{\mu}_R$ and $\bar{\mu}_C$ are the fuzzy membership function used for reliability improvement and cost of sectionalizing switches, respectively, and the coefficients w_1 and w_2 satisfy the condition $w_1 + w_2 = 1$. This function is used as a quality function in the heuristic rules for pheromone addition to the best paths.
Tippachon & Rerkpreedapong, 2009, address the multi-objective optimization problem concerning the optimal placement of reclosers and fuses. The objectives considered are SAIFI, SAIDI, and the total cost C^{tot}, and are addressed with the aim of searching for the non-dominated solutions belonging to a Pareto front (Shukla & Deb, 2007). The latter includes the average cost of temporary and permanent interruptions, and the fixed cost for investment and installation of switches and protective devices. The constraints refer to the

possibility of installing only reclosers and switches on the main distribution system feeders, the avoidance of fuse location upstream of a recloser, and the maximum number of fuses to be placed in a series path. The max-min operator is applied to select the best multiobjective solution.

5.2 Ant colony optimization schemes and solutions

In Ahuja et al., 2007, the pheromone table corresponding to the voltage deviation objective is used in order to obtain a feasible configuration for the service restoration problem after a contingency. The distribution network is progressively constructed starting from scratch by using the Kruskal's algorithm (Kruskal, 1956) to connect branches not forming any loop until all nodes are reached. As relatively high pheromone values indicate the quality of a branch to remain open, the inverse of the pheromone values (added to a user-defined constant to avoid biasing the search towards the solution found in normal conditions) are used in the weighted probabilistic selection mechanism (Section 2.2) in order to extract the branch to be connected to the network. Falaghi et al., 2009, apply a classical version of ACO.
An efficient scheme for addressing reliability optimization through ant ACO algorithms is illustrated and used in some references (Teng & Liu, 2003; Wang & Singh, 2008; Tippachon & Rerkpreedapong, 2009). This scheme adopts a multi-stage representation of the search space, in which the number of stages D is equal to the number of devices to be located in the distribution system (Fig. 3). Furthermore, at each stage the information dimension includes the candidate locations $\xi = 1,\ldots, \Xi$. In a given stage $\delta = 1,\ldots, D$, a state γ_δ in the search space is defined by the pair (location ξ, device type).
Each ant starts from the nest and proceeds on the various stages until reaching the destination. At each stage, an ant selects one state to go in the next stage, on the basis of a function of the pheromone and of the distance $d_{(i,j)}$ of the connection from the present state $\gamma_\xi^{(\delta)}$ to a state $\gamma_{\xi'}^{(\delta+1)}$ in the following stage.

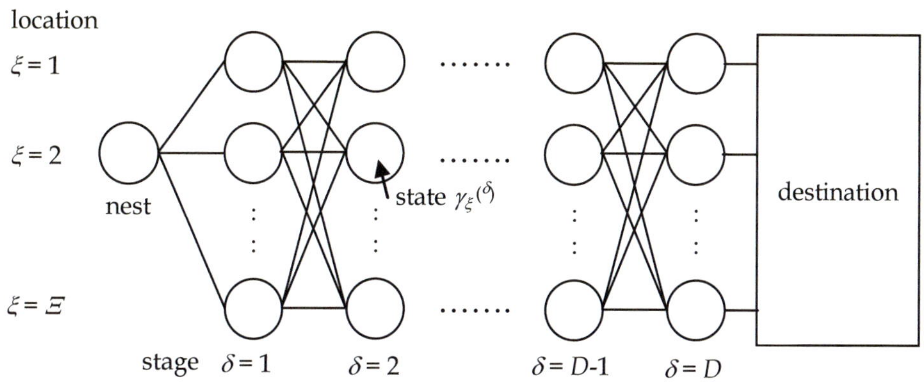

Fig. 3. Multi-stage representation of the search space.

In Teng & Liu, 2003, the max-min ant colony system (Stützle & Hoos, 2000) is used to address the switch relocation problem. For an ant m moving from the state $i = \gamma_\xi^{(\delta)}$ at stage δ to the point $j = \gamma_{\xi'}^{(\delta+1)}$ at stage δ+1, the transition probability is expressed by considering as distance $d_{(i,j)}$ the inverse of the *CIC* reduction between stage δ and δ+1, using the set $S_i^{(m,\delta)}$ of the states that can be reached at the successive stage to obtain:

$$p_{(i,j)}^{(m,\delta)} = \frac{\tau_{(i,j)}^{(m,\delta)} d_{(i,j)}^{-\beta}}{\sum_{u \in \mathbf{S}_i^{(m,\delta)}} \tau_{(i,u)}^{(m,\delta)} d_{(i,u)}^{-\beta}} \tag{25}$$

Alternatively, equation (25) can be rewritten by avoiding the use of the distance information to make calculations faster.

In Wang & Singh, 2008, ACO is applied by initially positioning the ants in randomly selected starting nodes. The pheromone is associated to the connections among the nodes, with equal initial values τ_0. The multi-stage scheme of Fig. 3 is used. The distance is proportional to the inverse of the improvement of the objective function in two successive stages. Classical local and global heuristic rules are used. Elitism is applied as in Section 2.6.

In Tippachon & Rerkpreedapong, 2009, the multi-stage representation of Fig. 3 is extended to solve a multi-objective optimization problem through the multiple ant colony system (MACS) (Gambardella et al., 1999). MACS uses a single pheromone matrix and several heuristic information functions. The pheromone matrix values are initialized by using as initial estimation the value $\tau_0 = \left(SAIFI_0 \cdot SAIDI_0 \cdot C_0^{tot}\right)^{-1}$.

Starting from the state i on a given stage, let us consider the set S_i of the states that can be reached at the successive stage, the distances $d_{(i,j)} = \left\{SAIFI_{(i,j)}, SAIDI_{(i,j)}, C_{(i,j)}^{tot}\right\}$ when an ant m reaches the state $j \in S_i^{(m)}$, the user-defined parameter $q_0 \in [0, 1]$ to introduce elitism (Section 2.6), and a random number $r \in [0, 1]$ extracted each time a selection has to be made. The state j to be reached is then selected by applying the following rule:

$$j = \begin{cases} \arg\max_{u \in S_i^{(m)}} \left\{ \tau_{(i,u)} \prod_{v=1,2,3} \left(d_{(i,u)}^{(v)}\right)^{-\lambda_v \beta} \right\} & \text{if } r \le q_0 \\ \hat{j} & \text{otherwise} \end{cases} \tag{26}$$

where the term $\lambda_v = \mathrm{mod}\left(m / M + \lambda_v - 1, 1\right)$ is introduced to force the ants $m = 1,\ldots, M$ to search in different directions of the Pareto front, and the state $\hat{j}$ is chosen by applying the weighted probabilistic selection mechanism by computing the probabilities in a way similar to (1) for $j \in S_i^{(m)}$, namely:

$$p_{(i,j)}^{(m)} = \frac{\tau_{(i,j)} \prod_{v=1,2,3} \left(d_{(i,j)}^{(v)}\right)^{-\lambda_v \beta}}{\sum_{u \in \mathbf{S}_i^{(m)}} \tau_{(i,u)} \prod_{v=1,2,3} \left(d_{(i,u)}^{(v)}\right)^{-\lambda_v \beta}} \tag{27}$$

After each ant movement from i to j, the local heuristic rule (Section 2.3) is applied to update the pheromone $\tau_{(i,j)}$.

The pheromone τ_0 may be changed during the solution process. After the generation of new solutions, it is verified which solutions are non-dominated (i.e., belong to the set $\boldsymbol{P}'$, and are potential solutions to belong to the Pareto front $\boldsymbol{P}$). For each solution $p \in \boldsymbol{P}'$, the value τ_0'

is calculated as $\tau_0' = (SAIFI_p \cdot SAIDI_p \cdot C_p^{tot})^{-1}$. If $\tau_0' > \tau_0$ the pheromone is reinitialized to τ_0', otherwise the global update rule is applied to all connections (i,j) of each solution $p \in \mathbf{P}'$:

$$\tau_{(i,j)} = \frac{\sigma}{SAIFI_p \cdot SAIDI_p \cdot C_p^{tot}} + (1-\sigma)\tau_{(i,j)}^{previous} \tag{28}$$

6. Conclusions

This chapter has summarized the framework of application referring to some typical distribution system optimization problems. While some applications use classical versions of the ACO algorithms, specific adaptations of the algorithms to specific problems led to customized versions with ACO variants or hybridizations with other heuristics.

Future work can be developed to improve the effectiveness of the solutions of the ACO algorithms, also benefiting from recent theoretical findings, such as the ones concerning the choice of an appropriate pheromone model to avoid the so-called second-order deception with decreased algorithm performance over time (Blum & Dorigo, 2005; Dorigo & Blum, 2005), the development of ACO algorithms functionally equivalent to the original ones, with pheromone independent of the scale of the problem instance considered (Birattari et al., 2007), the possible ACO application to continuous optimization problems (Blum, 2005), and the analysis of the convergence time of the ACO algorithms (Huang et al., 2009).

7. References

Ahuja, A.; Das, S. & Pahwa, A. (2007). An AIS-ACO hybrid approach for multi-objective distribution system reconfiguration. *IEEE Trans. on Power Systems*, Vol. 22, No. 3, (August 2007) 1101–1111, ISSN 0885-8950.

Andrei, H.; Caciula, I. & Chicco, G. (2008). A comprehensive assessment of the solutions of the distribution system minimum loss reconfiguration problem. *Proc. 7th World Energy System Conference*, ISSN 1198-0729, Iaşi, Romania, 30 June - 2 July 2008.

Andrei, H. & Chicco, G. (2008). Identification of the radial configurations extracted from the weakly meshed structures of electrical distribution systems. *IEEE Trans. on Circuits and Systems. Part I: Regular Papers*, Vol. 55, No. 4, (May 2008) 1149-1158, ISSN 1549-8328.

Baran, M.E. & Wu, F.F. (1989). Optimal capacitor placement on radial distribution systems. *IEEE Trans. on Power Delivery*, Vol. 4, No. 1, (January 1989) 725-732, ISSN 0885-8977.

Baran, M.E. & Wu, F.F. (1989b). Network reconfiguration in distribution systems for loss reduction and load balancing. *IEEE Trans. on Power Delivery*, Vol. 4, No. 2, (April 1989) 1401–1407, ISSN 0885-8977.

Billinton, R. & Allan, R.N. (1984). *Reliability Evaluation of Power Systems*. Plenum, New York, 1984, ISBN 978-0306452598.

Birattari, M.; Pellegrini, P. & Dorigo, M. (2007). On the Invariance of Ant Colony Optimization. *IEEE Trans. on Evolutionary Computation*, Vol. 11, No. 6, (December 2007) 732-741, ISSN 1089-778X.

Blum, C. (2005). Ant colony optimization: Introduction and recent trends. *Physics of Life Reviews*, Vol. 2, No. 4, (December 2005) 353-373, ISSN 1571-0645.

Blum, C. & Dorigo, M. (2004). The hyper-cube framework for ant colony optimization. *IEEE Trans. on Systems, Man and Cybernetics: Part B*, Vol. 34, No. 3, (April 2004) 1161–1172, ISSN 1083-4419.

Blum, C. & Dorigo, M. (2005). Search bias in ant colony optimization: on the role of competition-balanced systems. *IEEE Trans. on Evolutionary Computation*, Vol. 9 , No. 2, (April 2005) 159-174, ISSN 1089-778X.

Carpaneto, E.; Chicco, G. & Roggero, E. (2003). Comparing deterministic and simulated annealing-based algorithms for minimum losses reconfiguration of large distribution systems. *Proc. IEEE Bologna PowerTech*, Vol. 2, ISBN 0-7803-7967-5, Bologna, Italy, 23-26 June 2003.

Carpaneto, E.; Chicco, G.; De Donno, M. & Napoli, R. (2004). Voltage controllability of distribution systems with local generation sources. *Proc. Bulk Power System Dynamics and Control* – VI, pp. 261-273, ISBN 88-87380-47-3, Cortina d'Ampezzo, Italy, August 22-27, 2004.

Carpaneto, E. & Chicco, G. (2004). Ant-colony search-based minimum losses reconfiguration of distribution systems. *Proc. IEEE Mediterranean Electrotechnical Conference (Melecon 2004)*, Vol. 3, ISBN 0-7803-8271-4, Dubrovnik, Croatia, 971–974, 12–15 May 2004.

Carpaneto, E. & Chicco, G. (2004b). Evaluation of the probability density functions of distribution system reliability indices with a characteristic functions-based approach, *IEEE Trans. on Power Systems*, Vol. 19, No. 2, (May 2004) 724-734, ISSN 0885-8950.

Carpaneto, E. & Chicco, G. (2005). Optimal operational planning of large distribution systems with Ant Colony Search, *Proc. 15th Power System Computational Conference (PSCC 2005)*, Liège, Belgium, 22-26 August 2005.

Carpaneto, E. & Chicco, G. (2008). Distribution system minimum loss reconfiguration in the hyper-cube ant colony optimization framework. *Electric Power Systems Research*, Vol. 78, No. 12, (December 2008) 2037–2045, ISSN 0378-7796.

Carpaneto, E. & Chicco, G. (2010). Steady-state assessment of the DG impact on voltage control and loss allocation. Chapter 3 in Gaonkar, N.D. (ed.), *Distributed generation*, In-Teh, Vukovar, Croatia, February 2010, 51-76, ISBN 978-953-307-046-9.

Chang, C.-F. (2008). Reconfiguration and capacitor placement for loss reduction of distribution systems by ant colony search algorithm. *IEEE Trans. on Power Systems*, Vol. 23, No. 4, (November 2008) 1747-1755, ISSN 0885-8950.

Chiou, J.-P.; Chang, C.-F. & Su, C.-T. (2004). Ant direction hybrid differential evolution for solving large capacitor placement problems. *IEEE Trans. on Power Systems*, Vol. 19, No. 4, (November 2004) 1794-1800, ISSN 0885-8950.

Civanlar, S.; Grainger, J.; Yin, H. & Lee, S. (1988). Distribution feeder reconfiguration for loss reduction. *IEEE Trans. on Power Delivery*, Vol. 3, No. 3, (July 1988) 1217–1223, ISSN 0885-8977.

Dorigo, M.; Maniezzo, V. & Colorni, A. (1996). Ant system: optimization by a colony of cooperating agents. *IEEE Trans. on Systems, Man and Cybernetics: Part B*, Vol. 26 (February 1996) 29–41, ISSN 1083-4419.

Dorigo, M. & Gambardella, L.M. (1997). Ant colony system, a cooperative learning approach to the traveling salesman problem. *IEEE Trans. on Evolutionary Computation*, vol. 1, no. 1, (April 1997) 53–66, ISSN 1089-778X.

Dorigo, M. & Blum, C. (2005). Ant colony optimization theory: A survey. *Theoretical Computer Science*, Vol. 344, No. 2-3, (November 2005) 243-278, ISSN 0304-3975.

Dorigo, M.; Birattari, M. & Stützle, T. (2006). Ant colony optimization. *IEEE Computational Intelligence Magazine*, Vol. 1, No. 4, (November 2006) 28-39, ISSN 1556-603X.

Falaghi, H.; Haghifam, M.-R. & Singh, C. (2009). Ant Colony Optimization-Based Method for Placement of Sectionalizing Switches in Distribution Networks Using a Fuzzy Multiobjective Approach. *IEEE Trans. on Power Delivery*, Vol. 24 , No. 1, (January 2009) 268-276, ISSN 0885-8977.

Favuzza, S.; Graditi, G. & Riva Sanseverino, E. (2006). Adaptive and Dynamic Ant Colony Search Algorithm for Optimal Distribution Systems Reinforcement Strategy. *Applied Intelligence*, Vol. 24, No. 1, (February 2006) 31-42, ISSN 1573-7497.

Favuzza, S.; Graditi, G.; Ippolito, M.G. & Sanseverino, E.R. (2007). Optimal Electrical Distribution Systems Reinforcement Planning Using Gas Micro Turbines by Dynamic Ant Colony Search Algorithm. *IEEE Trans. on Power Systems*, Vol. 22, No. 2, (May 2007) 580-587, ISSN 0885-8950.

Gambardella, L.M.; Taillard, E. & Agazzi, G. (1999). MACS-VRPTW: A Multiple Ant Colony System for Vehicle Routing Problems with Time Windows. In: Corne, D.; Dorigo, M. & Glover, F. (ed.), *New Ideas in Optimization*. McGraw-Hill, UK, 1999, 63-76, ISBN 978-0077095062.

Gomez, J.F.; Khodr, H.M.; De Oliveira, P.M.; Ocque, L.; Yusta, J.M.; Villasana, R. & Urdaneta, A.J. (2004). Ant colony system algorithm for the planning of primary distribution circuits. *IEEE Trans. on Power Systems*, Vol. 19, No. 2, (May 2004) 996-1004, ISSN 0885-8950.

Huang H.; Wu, C.-G. & Hao, Z.-F. (2009). A Pheromone-Rate-Based Analysis on the Convergence Time of ACO Algorithm. *IEEE Trans. on Systems, Man, and Cybernetics, Part B: Cybernetics*, Vol. 39, No. 4, (August 2009) 910-923, ISSN 1083-4419.

Kruskal, J.B. (1956). On the shortest spanning subtree of a graph and the traveling salesman problem. *Proceedings of the American Mathematical Society*, Vol. 7, No. 1, (February 1956) 48–50, ISSN 0002-9939.

Niknam, T. (2008). A new approach based on ant colony optimization for daily volt/var control in distribution networks considering distributed generators. *Energy Conversion and Management*, Vol. 49, No. 12, (December 2008) 3417-3424, ISSN 0196-8904.

Prim, R.C. (1957). Shortest connection networks and some generalizations. *Bell System Technical Journal*, Vol. 36, No. 6, (1957) 1389-1401, ISSN 0005-8580.

Reeves, C.R. (Ed.) (1993). *Modern heuristic techniques for combinatorial problems*. Blackwell Scientific Publications, Oxford, UK, 1993, ISBN 0-470-22079-1.

Shirmohammadi, D.; Hong, H.W.; Semlyen, A. & Luo, G.X. (1988). A compensation-based power flow method for weakly meshed distribution and transmission networks. *IEEE Trans. on Power Systems*, Vol. 3, No. 2, (May 1988) 753–762, ISSN 0885-8950.

Shukla, P.K. & Deb, K. (2007). On finding multiple Pareto-optimal solutions using classical and evolutionary generating methods. *European Journal of Operational Research*, Vol. 181, No. 3, (September 2007) 1630-1652, ISSN 0377-2217.

Strezoski, V.C.; Katic, N.A. & Janjic, D.S. (2001). Voltage control integrated in distribution management system. *Electric Power Systems Research*, Vol. 60, No. 2, (December 2001) 85-97, ISSN 0378-7796.

Stützle, T. & Hoos, H.H. (2000). Max–min ant system. *Future Generation Computer Systems*, Vol. 16, No. 8, (June 2000) 889-914, ISSN 0167-739X.

Su, C.-T.; Chang, C.-F. & Chiou, J.-P. (2005). Distribution network reconfiguration for loss reduction by ant colony search algorithm. *Electric Power Systems Research*, Vol. 75, (August 2005) 190–199, ISSN 0378-7796.

Teng, J.-H. & Liu, Y.-H. (2003). A novel ACS-based optimum switch relocation method. *IEEE Trans. on Power Systems*, Vol. 18, No. 1, (February 2003) 113-120, ISSN 0885-8950.

Tippachon, W. & Rerkpreedapong, D. (2009). Multiobjective optimal placement of switches and protective devices in electric power distribution systems using ant colony optimization. *Electric Power Systems Research*, Vol. 79, No. 7, (July 2009) 1171-1178, ISSN 0378-7796.

Wang, L. & Singh, C. (2008). Reliability-Constrained Optimum Placement of Reclosers and Distributed Generators in Distribution Networks Using an Ant Colony System Algorithm. *IEEE Trans. on Systems, Man, and Cybernetics, Part C: Applications and Reviews*, Vol. 38, No. 6, (November 2008) 757-764, ISSN 1094-6977.

Wu, Y.-K.; Lee, C.-Y.; Liu, L.-C. & Tsai, S.-H. (2010). Study of reconfiguration for the distribution system with distributed generators. *IEEE Trans. on Power Delivery*, Vol. 25, No. 3, (July 2010) 1678-1685, ISSN 0885-8977.

Zamboni, L. & Monteiro, L.H.A. (2009). Optimization of the topology of electric energy distribution networks by using algorithm inspired on ant behavior. *IEEE Latin America Transactions*, Vol. 7, No. 1, (March 2009) 85-91, ISSN 1548-0992.

17

Ant Colony Optimization for Image Segmentation

Yuanjing Feng and Zhejin Wang
Zhejiang University of Technology
China

1. Introduction

Image segmentation is a complex visual computation problem, which refers to the process of distinguishing objects from background. Ant colony optimization (ACO) is a cooperative search algorithm inspired by the behavior of real ants. In order to achieve an approving performance, we use ACO global optimization algorithm to solve image segmentation problems.

1.1 Related literature

A variety of approaches have been developed for solving image segmentation problems. In these approaches, different methods have defined various cost functions for the task of image segmentation. A popular tool for minimization of these cost functions is the curve evolution framework and active contour model (ACM). ACMs have been proposed by Kass et al. (1987) which converts the segmentation to a functional extremum problem. Within ACM framework, evolution of the curves can be controlled by segmentation cost functions, external force fields, and geometric forces such as curvature flow and constant expansion forces (e.g., balloons, see Cohen, 1991). Many approaches have been proposed to solve this model, such as, greedy algorithm, dynamic programming method, directional image force method, genetic algorithm(GA) snakes method and so on (Amini et al., 1990; Williams & Shah, 1990; MacEachern & Manku, 1998; Gunn & Nixon, 1996; Xu & Prince, 1998; Hsien-Hsun et al., 2000; Lam & Yan, 1994; Mishraa et al., 2003). However, these methods still cannot perform very well. For example, the greedy algorithm has a high efficiency, but it cannot guarantee the global convergence (Lam & Yan, 1994). GA and SA are proved to be convergent with probability one, nonetheless the procedure is time-consuming (Mishraa et al., 2003).
ACO is first introduced by M. Dorigo (Dorigo et al., 1996). One basic idea of the ACO approach is to use the counterpart of the pheromone trail used by real ants as a medium for communication and as an indirect form of memory of previously found solutions. The artificial ants are simple agents that have some basic capabilities, e.g., the case of the traveling salesman problem (TSP). They may use some heuristic information like the distance between cities to construct tours and maintain a tabu list in which they store the partial tour constructed so far. The ants build solutions constructively guided by heuristic information and the pheromone trails left by ants in previous iterations. ACO has been applied successfully to numerous combinatorial optimization problems including in TSP (Dorigo & Ganbardella, 1997), vehicle routing problem (Bullnheimer et al., 1998), flow shop

problem (Stutzle, 1998) and others. The successful applications of ACO attract image processing researchers' attention. Quadfel et al. proposed an algorithm for image segmentation based on the Markov Random Field (MRF) and ACO (Ouadfel & Batouche, 2003). S.Meshoul cast the point matching problem in point-based image registration method as combinatorial optimization task and solved by ACO (Meshoul & Batouche, 2003). In our previous work, an ACO algorithm similar to MAX-MIN ant system for image segmentation based on ACM was developed (Feng, 2005). This method is usually more effective than the other global optimization algorithms such as GA and SA.

In recent years, more and more novel ACO algorithms are advanced by researchers. An improved ACO for fuzzy clustering in image segmentation has been proposed by Han et al.(Han & Shi, 2006). In their paper, three features such as gray value, gradient and neighborhood of the pixels, are extracted for the searching and clustering process. They make improvements by initializing the clustering centers and enhancing the heuristic function to accelerate the searching process. Tests show ACO is successfully applied in image segmentation combined with fuzzy clustering. Then, Tao et al. present an object segmentation method using ACO algorithm and fuzzy entropy (Tao et al., 2007). They have investigated the infrared object segmentation performance of the fuzzy entropy principle and additionally, designed an ACO strategy to find the optimal combination of all the parameters.

Moreover, a new approach that concerns ACO for image regularization based on a nonstationary markov modelling was proposed by Le Hegarat-Mascle et al. (Hegarat-Mascle et al., 2007). They show that this corresponds to an automatic adaptation of the neighborhood to the segment form, and that it outperforms the fixed-form neighborhood used in classical Markov random field regularization techniques. The performance of this new approach is illustrated on a simulated image and on actual remote sensing images. Two years later, Ma et al. put forward a universal texture segmentation and representation scheme based on ACO for iris image processing (Ma et al, 2009). They propose a framework for ACO based image processing methods and create the flexibility of defining different mechanisms for an ant's behaviour according to various problems, which turned out competitive and quite promising, with excellent effectiveness and practicability especially for images with complex local texture situations. Besides, in terms of the pheromone, someone has proposed a new algorithm for image segmentation based on the concept of aggregation pheromone density, which is inspired by the ants' property to accumulate around points with higher pheromone density (Susmita et al., 2009).

1.2 Contributions

This chapter introduces two ant colony algorithms for image segmentation in ACM framework. We first present a new ant colony algorithm based on boundary searching process of ACM, which uses ACO to search for the best path in a constrained region. We describe how the image edge detection problem can be transferred to the ant colony searching process by means of constructing cost function, solution space, pheromone model, and heuristic information. However, the previous work of ACO on ACM shows that this algorithm is also time-consuming. One of the main causes is the updating method of the pheromone in general ACO. Experimental results show general ACO algorithms try to update the pheromone values in such a way that the probability to generate high-quality solutions increases over time. Second, in consideration of the computation burden, a modified ACO called finite grade ACO (FGACO) is proposed. It classifies pheromone into finite grades, the higher the grade, the more the pheromone. Moreover, updating of the pheromone is achieved by changing the grades. The updated quantity of pheromone is independent from the objective function, and the grade is changed by addition and subtraction operations. The algorithm is proved to converge to the global optimal solutions linearly by means of finite Markov chains. Finally, the proposed algorithm is applied in phase change line detection of complex phase change thermography. In this part we apply ACM based ACO algorithm to sub-image segmentation, which converts image segmentation to a problem of searching for the best path in a constrained region. The experimental results show that the algorithm extracts the phase change active contour well.

2. Ant colony optimization for active contour model based image segmentation

2.1 Active contour model in image segmentation

As formulated above, ACM is a popular tool for the minimization of cost functions. The original ACM described by Kass et al. (1987) refers to a set of points, $v(s)=(x(s),y(s))$, on an image parameterized with respect to the contour length, s. Each possible configuration of the contour has an energy associated with it, which is a combination of internal and external energies. The energy function can be written as:

$$E_{snake}=\int_0^1 E_{snake}(v(s))ds=\int_0^1 [E_{\text{in}}(v(s))+E_{image}(v(s))+E_{con}(v(s))]ds \tag{1}$$

where E_{in} represents the internal energy of the active contour, E_{image} represents the image forces, and E_{con} represents the external constraint forces. The internal energy is composed of a first order and a second order term forcing the active contour to act like a membrane of a thin plate.

$$E_{\text{in}}=(\alpha(s)|v_s(s)|^2+\beta(s)|v_{ss}(s)|^2)/2 \tag{2}$$

Let $E_{ext}=E_{image}+E_{con}$, with

$$E_{image}=w_{line}E_{line}+w_{edge}E_{edge}+w_{cur}E_{cur} \tag{3}$$

The energy term due to image forces is a linear combination of line, edge and termination energy terms, all computed from an image, $I(x,y)$. $E_{line}=I(x,y)$, $E_{edge}=-|\nabla I(x,y)|^2$ and E_{cur} is the curvature of the level contours in a Gaussian smoothed image.

The energy integral becomes

$$\int_0^1 E_{ext}(v(s))+\frac{1}{2}(\alpha(s)|v_s(s)|^2+\beta(s)|v_{ss}(s)|^2)ds \tag{4}$$

According to the lemma of necessary condition for functional extremum (Lao, 2004) to minimize (4), a pair of independent Euler equations is obtained (Amini & Jain, 1990),

$$-\alpha x_{ss}+\beta x_{ssss}+\frac{\partial E_{ext}}{\partial x}=0 \tag{5}$$

$$-\alpha y_{ss}+\beta y_{ssss}+\frac{\partial E_{ext}}{\partial y}=0 \tag{6}$$

Discretizing the above equation with $f_x(i)=\frac{\partial E_{ext}}{\partial x_i}$ and $f_y(i)=\frac{\partial E_{ext}}{\partial y_i}$, we get

$$\begin{aligned}\alpha_i(v_i-v_{i-1})-\alpha_{i+1}(v_{i+1}-v_i)+\beta_{i-1}(v_{i-2}-2v_{i-1}+v_i)\\ -2\beta_i(v_{i-1}-2v_i+v_{i+1})+\beta_{i+1}(v_i-2v_{i+1}+v_{i+2})+(f_x(i),f_y(i))=0\end{aligned} \tag{7}$$

with $v(0)=v(n)$ .Writing (7) in matrix forms, it has

$$Ax+f_x(x,y)=0 \tag{8}$$

$$Ay+f_y(x,y)=0 \tag{9}$$

Discretizing the energy term in (2), it has the form

$$\begin{aligned}E_{snake}&=\sum_{i-0}^{n-1}E_{\text{int}}(i)+E_{ext}(i)\\ &=\sum_{i=0}^{n-1}E_{\text{int}}(i)+E_{ext}(i)\sum_{i=0}^{n-1}(\alpha_i|v_i-v_{i-1}|^2+\beta_i|v_{i-1}-2v_i+v_{i+1}|^2)/2+E_{ext}(i)\end{aligned} \tag{10}$$

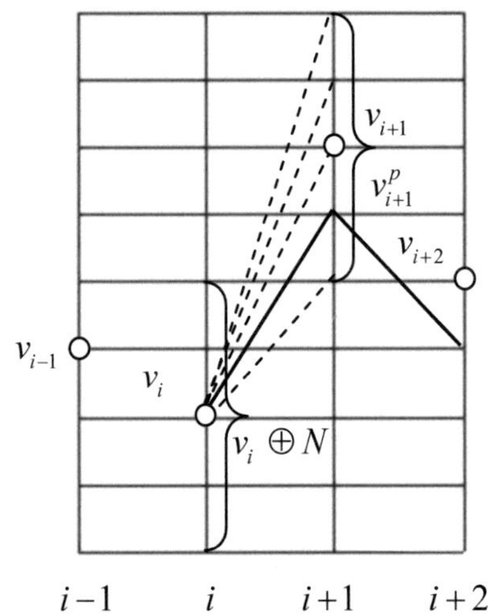

Fig. 1. Searching graph

The problem of energy minimization can be viewed as a discrete multistage decision process. At each stage, only a local neighborhood of a point on the active contour is considered. This characterizes the set of admissible paths in each iteration. For convenience, let us first consider only the first order term of the internal energy measure. With i representing the stage and k the possible choices at each stage, the multistage decision problem of (10) can be computed to be:

$$E_t(i+1,k)=E_t(i,k)+\frac{1}{2}\alpha_i(v_{i+1}\oplus k-v_i\oplus j)^2+E_{ext}(v_{i+1}\oplus k) \tag{11}$$

where, $0 \le k \le N$ (N being the number of possible directions at each stage), v_m is the mth point on the active contour, and $\oplus$ is an operation by which all the points in a local neighborhood of a given point on the lattice are generated.
The image can be represented as the grid shown in Fig.1. The connection of nodes $\{v_1, v_2, \cdots, v_n\}$, is the initial contour. Supposing that $v_i^l \in v_i \oplus N$ is the current edge point, then the next point is the choice point or not depends on whether it makes the energy function (10) decrease.
Let us now consider the case where the second order term is also included in the internal energy measure. When including this in the computation of $E_{\min}(t)$, at stage $i+1$ one should consider all the possible points at stage i. However, it would be a pitfall to consider only the (i,k) entry of the position matrix for the point at stage $i-1$. We need to consider all the possible combinations for the i and $i-1$ stages once at stage $i+1$.
The energy for each sub-cell is computed to be:

$$E_t(i+1,j,k) = E_t(i,k,m) + E_{ext}(v_i \oplus k) + \frac{1}{2}\alpha_i(v_i \oplus k - v_{i-1} \oplus m)^2 + \beta_i(v_{i+1} \oplus j - 2v_i \oplus k + v_{i-1} \oplus m)^2 \quad (12)$$

2.2 Graph based ant colony optimization

Consider a minimization problem (S, f, Ω) where S is the set of (candidate) solutions, f is the objective function, which assigns to each candidate solution max($\bullet$) an objective function (cost) value $f(s)$, and Ω is a set of constraints, which defines the set of feasible candidate solutions. The goal of the minimization (S, f, Ω) problem is to find an optimal solution, i.e., a feasible candidate solution of minimum cost. The combinatorial optimization problem (S, f, Ω) is mapped on a problem that can be characterized by the following.

1. A finite set $\varsigma = \{c_1, c_2, \cdots, c_{NC}\}$ of components.
2. A finite set χ of states of the problem, defined in terms of all possible sequences $x = < c_i, c_j, \cdots, c_k, \cdots >$ over the elements of ς.
3. The set of (candidate) solutions S is a subset of χ (i.e., $S \subseteq \chi$).
4. A set of feasible states $\tilde{\chi}$, with $\tilde{\chi} \subseteq \chi$, defined via a problem-dependent test that verifies that it is not impossible to complete a sequence $x \in \tilde{\chi}$ into a solution satisfying the constraints Ω.
5. A nonempty set S^* of optimal solutions, with $S^* \subseteq \tilde{\chi}$ and $S^* \subseteq S$.

In the given above formulation, the combinatorial optimization problem (S, f, Ω) can be expressed as the graph $G = (\varsigma, \Lambda)$ called construction graph, where the vertices are the components ς, the set Λ fully connects the components ς. The vector $\tau(n)$ is pheromone values on the arcs of ς at iteration n, and the vector $\hat{s}(n)$ is the current optimal path at iteration n with corresponding cost function values $\hat{f}(n)$.
In the ACO algorithm, ants start from an initial node, perform repetitive stochastic transitions form one node to another node and find feasible routes that correspond to the feasible solutions of the optimization problem. The optimization process can be represented as:

1. Ant solution construction

While ($H(\bullet)$ and $x_k \notin S$) do:

At each step k after building the sequence $x_k =< c_1, c_2, \cdots, c_k >$, select the next vertex l randomly following

$$p_{kl} = \begin{cases} \dfrac{(\tau_{kl})^{\alpha}(\eta_{kl})^{\beta}}{\sum\limits_{(c_k, y) \in J_{ck}} (\tau_{ky})^{\alpha}(\eta_{kl})^{\beta}} & if (c_k, c) \in J_{ck} \\ 0 & otherwise \end{cases} \tag{13}$$

where η_{kl} is heuristic information value corresponding to the cost function. α, β are the weight parameters respectively for pheromone and heuristic information value in p_{kl}. And a connection $(c_k, y) \in J_{ck}$ if the sequence $x_{k+1} =< c_1, c_2, \cdots, c_k, y >$ is such that $x_{k+1} \in \tilde{\chi}$. If J_{ck} is empty, the solution construction is finished.

2. Pheromone update

Once all the ants have terminated their local searches, a pheromone update phase is started in which pheromone trails are modified. Let $\hat{s}$ be the best feasible solution found so far and s_t be the best feasible solution in the current algorithm iteration t; $f(\hat{s})$ and $f(s_t)$ are the corresponding objective function values. The pheromone update procedure decreases by a small factor ρ, called the evaporation rate, the value of the pheromone trails on all the connections in Λ and then increases the value of the pheromone trails on the connections belonging to $\hat{s}$. The pheromone update procedure is described as follows.

(u1) $\forall (i,j)$: $\tau_{ij} \leftarrow (1-\rho) \cdot \tau_{ij}$

(u2) if $f(s_t) < f(\hat{s})$, then $\hat{s} \leftarrow s_t$

(u3) $\forall (i,j) \in \hat{s} : \tau_{ij} \leftarrow \tau_{ij} + \rho \cdot g(\hat{s})$

(u4) $\forall (i,j)$: $\tau_{ij} \leftarrow \max\{\tau_{\min}, \tau_{ij}\}$ (14)

where $0 < \rho < 1$ is the evaporation rate, $\tau_{\min} > 0$ is a parameter, and $g(s)$ is a function of s with: $f(s) < f(s') \Rightarrow g(s) \geq g(s')$.

2.3 Algorithm ingredients

To apply the ACO algorithm to the ACM based image segmentation problems, we must convert the ACM solving process to the searching graph. From the describing of above sections, the ACO can also be illustrated under the guidance of Fig.1. Supposing that theoretical contour has the minimal energy. Set an ant at $v_i^j \in v_i \oplus N$, it selects the next point $v_{i+1}^p \in v_{i+1} \oplus N$ under the influence of pheromone. With the cooperation of the ant colony, the path of final minimal energy is acquired.

Therefore, the solving process of ACM is quite similar to ACO. On the basis of our previous research (Feng, 2005), a kind of ACO that used to solve ACM is proposed, which provides a new efficient way for image segmentation.

2.3.1 Definition of pheromone

Set the ant at any position $v_i^j \in v_i \oplus N$ (there exists N choices), it will select any element from set $v_{i+1} \oplus N$ (there also exists N choices). That is, there are $N * N$ compages between the two sets. If the contour is discretized into M points then the pheromone matrix τ_{ijk} is obtained, which consists of all adjacent connections. Where $i=(1,2,...M)$, $j,k=(1,2,...N)$.

2.3.2 Probability decision

Set the ant at the position of $v_i^j \in v_i \oplus N$, and the ant selects the next node $v_{i+1}^p \in v_{i+1} \oplus N$ according to the following probability,

$$P\left(v_{i+1}^p \in v_{i+1} \oplus N \,\middle|\, v_i^j \in v_i \oplus N, \tau\right) = \begin{cases} \dfrac{\tau(i, v_i^j, v_{i+1}^p)^\alpha \cdot \eta(v_{i+1}^p)^\beta}{\sum\limits_{l \in v_{i+1} \oplus N} \tau(i, v_i^j, v_{i+1}^l)^\alpha \cdot \eta(v_{i+1}^l)^\beta}, & l \in v_{i+1} \oplus N \\ 0, & others \end{cases} \tag{15}$$

where $i=(1,2,...M)$, $j,k=(1,2,...N)$, α,β are the weight parameters for pheromone and heuristic information value, respectively. $\tau(i,v_i^j,v_i^p)$ is the pheromone value on the arc (i,v_i^j,v_i^p). $\eta(v_{i+1}^p)$ is the heuristic information represented as

$$\eta(v_{i+1}^p) = 1/[f(\nabla I)_{v_{i+1}^p}] \tag{16}$$

2.3.3 Pheromone update

(u5) $\forall(i,j,k)$: $\tau_{ijk} \leftarrow (1-\rho)\cdot\tau_{ijk}$

(u6) If $E_{snake}(t_{ai}) < E_{snake}(\hat{t}_{ai})$, then $t_{ai} \leftarrow \hat{t}_{ai}$

(u7) $\forall(i,j,k) \in \hat{t}$, $\tau_{ijk} \leftarrow \tau_{ijk} + \rho \cdot g(\hat{t})$ (17)

where $0<\rho<1$ is the evaporation rate, $g(t)$ is the function of path t, which satisfies: $E_{snake}(t) < E_{snake}(\hat{t}) \Rightarrow g(t) \geq g(\hat{t})$.

2.3.4 Solving process

The algorithm is described as follows：

Step 1. Given: Initial value $\forall(i,j,k)$, $\tau_{ijk}=\tau_0$, $\tau_0 \geq 0$; path t (decided by the initial contour).

Step 2. Calculate: For each dimension of search space, for each ant, select the next position v_{i+1}^p according to equation (15), until it satisfies the termination-criterion.

Step 3. Calculate: Energy E_{snake} of every path the ant passed, according to equation (10).

Step 4. Calculate: The minimized energy path $\hat{t}$ and update τ according to equation ((u5)~(u7)).

Step 5. Restoring: $\hat{t}$ is the best path of search space, so the best segmentation is obtained.

3. Finite grade pheromone ant colony optimization for image segmentation

3.1 Finite grade pheromone ant colony optimization

For the multistage decision of ACM based image segmentation problems, whose feasible decision set at each stage increases exponentially with the dimension of the decision variable. The previous work of ACO on ACM shows that the algorithm is also time-consuming. One of the main reasons is the updating method of the pheromone in general

ACO. From Eqs. (15) and (17), at run-time, ACO algorithms try to update the pheromone values in such a way that the probability to generate high-quality solutions increases over time. The pheromone values are updated using previously generated solutions. The update aims to concentrate the search in regions of the search space containing high-quality solutions. In particular, the reinforcement of solution components depending on the solution quality is an important ingredient of ACO algorithms. It implicitly assumes that good solutions consist of good solution components. To learn which components contribute to good solutions can help to assemble them into better solutions. Based on the experimental observation, during the run time of standard ACO, there are many arcs which have similar pheromone, and similar pheromone has almost the same effect on solution construction, this inspires us to classify pheromone into finite grades, and this motivates the FGACO for image segmentation. In the new framework, we classify pheromone into finite grades, the higher the grade, the more the pheromone. If an arc belongs to the best solution found so far, the grade of this arc would be increased, vice versa. Let $\tau_{\min}$ and $\tau_{\max}$ be the minimal and maximal pheromone trail, $h(i,j,k)$ be the grade of arc (i,j,k), $g(x)$ be a real positive increasing function , it maps grade to pheromone, let $g(1)=\tau_{\min}$ and $g(M)=\tau_{\max}$, r_1 is penalty number, r_2 is encouragement number, M is maximal grade, here r_1, r_2 and M are integers, $\tilde{w}$ is the best feasible solution found so far, w_t is the best feasible solution found in current iteration, in our numerical calculations, we always fix $r_1=1$ and $\tau_{\min}=1$. Employing these symbols, we define the updating rules as follows:

(u8) $\forall(i,j,k)$: $h(i,j,k)\leftarrow h(i,j,k)-r_1$.

(u9) if $f(\tilde{w})>f(w_t)$, then $\tilde{w}=w_t$.

(u10) for $\tilde{w}$, $\forall(i,j,k)\in\tilde{w}$, $h(i,j,k)\leftarrow h(i,j,k)+r_2$.

(u11) $\forall(i,j,k)$: $h(i,j,k)\leftarrow \max(1,h(i,j,k))$.

(u12) $\forall(i,j,k)$: $h(i,j,k)\leftarrow \min(M,h(i,j,k))$.

(u13) $\forall(i,j,k)$: $\tau(i,j,k)=g(h(i,j,k))$.

where $\max(\bullet,\bullet)$ is maximum function, $\min(\bullet,\bullet)$ is minimum function.

For each ant, the transition probability from node i to j obeys solution construction rules

$$\mathrm{P}_{ij}=\begin{cases}\dfrac{\tau_{ij}{}^{\alpha}\cdot\eta_{ij}{}^{\beta}}{\sum\limits_{r\in C_i}\tau_{ir}{}^{\alpha}\cdot\eta_{ir}{}^{\beta}}, & if \quad j\in C_i\\ 0, & otherwise\end{cases} \tag{18}$$

where C_i is the set of nodes that can be selected from node i, τ_{ir} is the pheromone of arc (i,r), η_{ir} is heuristic information of arc (i,r), α and β are parameters. And we choose

$$g(x)=\sqrt[m]{\frac{\tau_{\max}{}^{m}-1}{M-1}(x-1)+1}\,,\ 1\le m \tag{19}$$

If $m=1$, $g(x)$ is a linear function, it changes equally, if $m>1$, $g(x)$ is a concave function, it changes fast at the beginning, and slowly later. Without speaking, we always let $m=2$.
FGACO uses maximal grade, encouragement number, penalty number and $g(x)$ to control the changing of pheromone. FGACO has three main features as follows:

1. The differentia between FGACO and standard ACO mainly lies in the rules of pheromone updating.
2. It classifies pheromone into finite grades, and pheromone updating is realized by changing the grades.
3. The updated quantity of a pheromone is independent of the objective function value, and the grade is changed by addition and subtraction operations.

3.2 Convergence analysis

In this subsection, FGACO is described as a finite Markov chain based on the properties of Markov chain. It will be shown that FGACO converges with probability 1 to the global optimum. The reader could see (Xu & Prince, 1998) for more details about Markov chains. An important property of finite Markov chains is given in the Lemma below (Xu & Prince, 1998).

Lemma 1

In any finite Markov chain, no matter where the process starts, the probability after n steps, that the process is in an ergodic state, tends to 1 as n tends to infinity.
The iterative process of FGACO is a discrete stochastic process. The states of this process are $s_n=(\tau(n),w(n))(n=1,2,\ldots)$, all the states form the state space S, where $\tau(n)$ is the matrix of the pheromone values at the nth cycle, $w(n)$ is the best solution found so far until the nth cycle is a discrete vector. s_n can only take one of the finite values, therefore S has finite states.
On account of the solution construction rules, we have Proposition 1 for FGACO, S is a finite Markov chain. Due to the pheromone updating rules (u8), (u9) and (u10), we have Proposition 2 for FGACO, if $s_n,s_m\in S$, let $P_{s_ns_m}$ be the transitive probability from s_n to s_m, $P_{s_ns_m}$ has following results:

- if $f(H(s_n))<f(H(s_m))$, then $P_{s_ns_m}=0$
- if $H(s_n)=H(s_m)$, and exist the arc $(i,j)\in H(s_n)$, $G_{(i,j)}(s_n)>G_{(i,j)}(s_m)$, then $P_{s_ns_m}=0$

where $f(\bullet)$ is the objective function, here, we only discuss minimal optimization problem, $H(\bullet)$ is the vector function, it maps state space into feasible solution space, $G_{(i,j)}(\bullet)$ is the real function, it maps the state space into grade, here (i,j) is the arc. Therefore, two cases will occur if the state changes, the one is that the best solution, found so far changes, and the objective function value decreases, the other is that the objective function value holds the same, and the pheromone of arcs corresponding to the best solution increases. For the latter case, on account of (u1) and (u3), the pheromone of all the arcs converges after finite cycles, all the pheromone keeps changeless and the pheromone of the arcs corresponding to the best solution is $\tau_{\max}$, the pheromone of the other arcs is 1. The state space can be partitioned into three sorts.

Definition 1 (stagnant state, optimal state and normal state)

For $s\in S$, pheromone of the arcs corresponding to the best solution is $\tau_{\max}$, the pheromone of the other arcs is 1, then s is called a stagnant state. Furthermore, if $H(s)$ is the global optimal solution, then s is an optimal state. The other states are called normal states. For an optimal state s^*, due to (u8), (u9) and (u10), we know that $P_{s^*s^*} = 1$, so an optimal state is an absorbing state. Based on Proposition 2 and the definition of transient state, it is convenient to show that the other states are transient states.

Theorem 1

For FGACO, $s_n = (\tau(n), w(n))$ is the finite Markov chain, every state is either transient or absorbing and all optimal states are absorbing states. As a result of theorem above, we have the following convergent property of FGACO.

Theorem 2

For FGACO, the probability of finding optimal solutions at least once is one as the cycle n tends to infinite.

3.3 FGACO for image segmentation

3.3.1 Energy function

For convenience, in Eq. (10), the external energy $E_{ext}(v)$ is defined in Eq. (20)

$$\int E_{ext}(v)ds = -\gamma \int \|f(\nabla I)\|^2 ds \tag{20}$$

In discrete form, $E_{ext}(v)$ can be defined as

$$E_{ext}(i) = -\gamma |f(g_i)|^2 \tag{21}$$

where g_i , the normalized value of the gradient $\nabla I(v_i)$ is expressed in Eq. (22)

$$g_i = \frac{\nabla I(v_i)}{g_{\max}} \tag{22}$$

where $g_{\max}$ is the maximum gradient on the individual search grids.

A nonlinear mapping function is incorporated to transform the normalized gradient so that it discourages the contour to adhere to low gradient region (Mishraa et al., 2003).

$$f(g_i) = \frac{1}{1 + \exp(0.7 - c \times g_i)} \tag{23}$$

Therefore, the final energy function of Eq. (10) can be written in the form

$$E_{snake} = \sum_{i=0}^{n-1} (\omega_1 |v_i - v_{i-1}|^2 + \omega_2 |v_{i-1} - 2v_i + v_{i+1}|^2) / 2 - \omega_3 |f(g_i)|^2 \tag{24}$$

where ω_1, ω_2, ω_3 are assumed to be constants over the whole boundary. The boundary is detected by minimizing the energy function defined in Eq. (24).

3.3.2 Algorithm for image segmentation

The algorithm is described as follows:

Step 1. Given: Initial value $\forall(i, j, k)$, $\tau_{ijk} = \tau_0$, $\tau_0 \geq 0$; path t (decided by the initial contour).

Step 2. Calculate: For each dimension of search space, for each ant, select the next position v_{i+1}^{p} according to equation (18), until it satisfies the termination-criterion.

Step 3. Calculate: Energy E_{snake} of every path the ant passed, according to equation (20).

Step 4. Calculate: The minimized energy path $\hat{t}$ and update τ according to equation (u(8)~u(13)).

Step 5. Restoring: $\hat{t}$ is the best path of search space, so the best segmentation is obtained.

4. Experimental results

In order to illustrate our proposed algorithms, we have done two experiments separately for ACM based ACO and FGACO. They are in the same experimental environment.

4.1 Simulation and analysis for ACM based ACO

Taking the segment of the heart image and left ventricle (LV) as examples to illustrate the resolving process of ACO. The result is compared with other algorithms in the end.

4.1.1 Image preprocessing

In most of the cases, the initial solution to the contour detection algorithm in medical ultra sound transducers images is provided by manually outlined contours. However, we have implanted a preprocessing technique (Mishraa et al., 2003), such as, Gaussian and morphological, to detect an initial boundary followed by our ACO optimization procedure. A potentially good image is selected as Fig. 2(a), which is filtered by convolving with a 3 × 3 Gaussian low pass filter with variance σ = 3. To eliminate the noise in the image, two successive stages of morphological filtration, i.e., dilation and erosion have been applied. The rough initial contour is extract as Fig. 2(b).

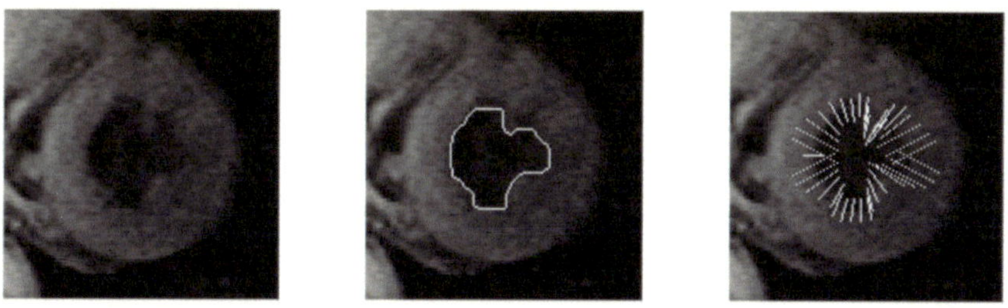

(a) (b) (c)

Fig. 2. (a) Origin picture of heart. (b) Initial contour of heart image. (c) Search space.

4.1.2 Construction of search space

From Fig. 2(b), we find the initial contour is a closed-ring. In order to apply the algorithm proposed above, the search space is constructed as follows:

Discretiaing the contour, we will get M differently equidistant points, those are P_i. Set the center of contour as C, a line is formed through C and P_i, so M lines are obtained, which is shown in Fig.2(c). We choose $2*N+1$ points along each line, of which P_i is the center. Get the average grey of every point in line section, the search space Ω is formed.

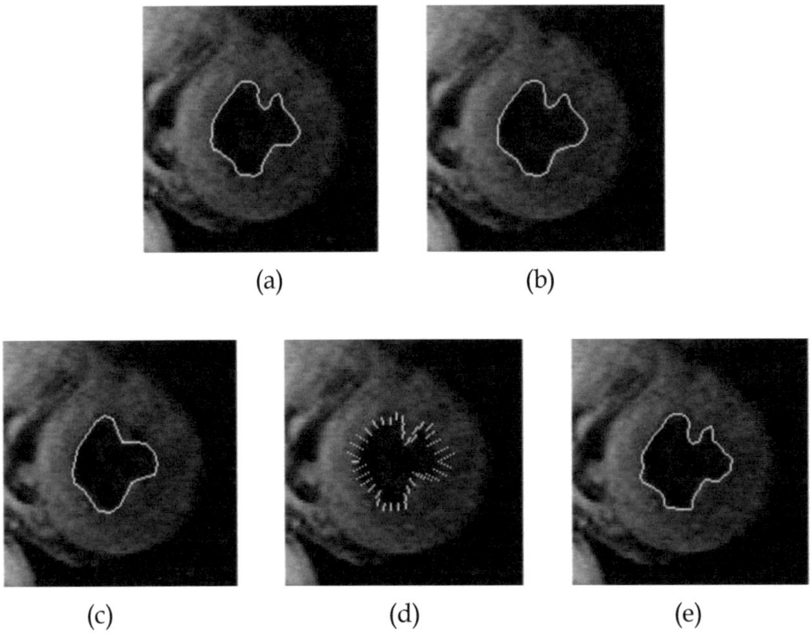

Fig. 3. (a) Final contour. (b) Contour of the 2nd group of parameters. (c) Contour of the 3rd group of parameters. (d) Search space construction of $N = 5$. (e) Contour of $N = 5$.

4.1.3 Experimental results

Set parameters $N = 11, M = 100, A = 10$ (10 ants), the value w_1, w_2, w_3 refer to the 1st line in Table 1. And we always firmly use these parameters in our experiments unless we explain. The final result is shown in Fig. 3(a). It is obvious that the contour is more rational than that in Fig. 2(b).
Keep the parameters *N, M, A* unchangeable. The results of parameters of the 2nd and the 3rd group in Table 1 are illustrated in Fig. 3(b) and Fig. 3(c).
When the search space is shrunk, that is, $N = 5$, shown in Fig.3(d), the energy no longer decreases after 28 iterations, and the contour is displayed in Fig. 3(e).

Parameters / Energy*	ω_1	ω_2	ω_3	Iterations
13.0663	0.06	0.03	1	44
1.0309	0.6	0.6	0.1	50
72.6886	0.01	0.01	10	47

The mark * denotes the average of 10 times tests.

Table 1. Three groups of parameters and their results.

Furthermore, we test the performance with left ventricle shown in Fig. 4(a). The construction of search space is the same as what mentioned above. The initial contour is shown in Fig. 4(b), the final result with the parameters in 1st line in Table 1 is displayed in Fig. 4(c). The energy no longer decreases after 48 iterations.

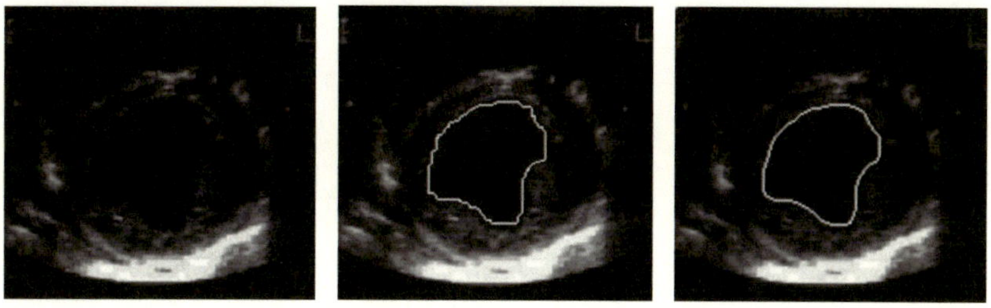

(a) (b) (c)

Fig. 4. (a) left ventricle. (b) Initial Contour of LV. (c) Result with 48 iterations.

4.2 Experiment and analysis for FGACO

Here, we use the same example images of the heart image and left ventricle (LV) in Sect. 4.1. The method of preprocessing and construction of search space is the same as general ACO. Firstly, the boundary detection of heart image provides the detail process of FGACO image segmentation algorithm. Experiments with different parameters are done for performance evaluation. Secondly, we compare the results of FGACO with general ACO and GA with left ventricle (Mishraa et al., 2003).

4.2.1 Experimental results and performance evaluation with the heart image

Set $N = 11$, $M = 100$, $A = 10$ (10 ants), $a = 100$, $\tau_{max} = 50$, $r_2 = 3$, the value $\omega_1, \omega_2, \omega_3$ refer to the 1st line in Table 1. The final result is shown in Fig. 5(a). We can easily find that the contour is more rational than that in Fig. 2(b). Fix N, M, A, the results of parameters of the second and the third group in Table 1 are illustrated in Figs. 5(b) and 5(c).

To test the influence of the parameters maximal grade and the maximal pheromone value τ_{max} on the optimization results, we set $N = 11$, $M = 100$, $A = 10$, $r_2 = 3$ and take the parameters $\omega_1, \omega_2, \omega_3$ referring to the first line in Table 1. The compared results, with the difference a, is shown in Table 2. The compared results, with the difference τ_{max}, is shown in Table 3. From Table 2, we can see that if take the maximal grade a with small value $(a = 10)$, the algorithm reaches a premature solution with fewer iterations, while if take large value $(a = 100)$, the algorithm is with more iterations. The compared results of Table 3 suggest that the τ_{max} should be limited in a suitable region.

Maximal grade a	10	50	100	1000
Energy*	14.067	12.0663	12.0663	12.0663
Iteration Number*	18	20	24	42

Table 2. Influence of parameter maximal grade a with $\tau_{max} = 50$.

Maximal pheromone τ_{max}	10	50	100	1000
Energy*	18.067	12.0663	12.0663	24.0663

Table 3. Influence of parameter maximal pheromone τ_{max} with $a = 100$.

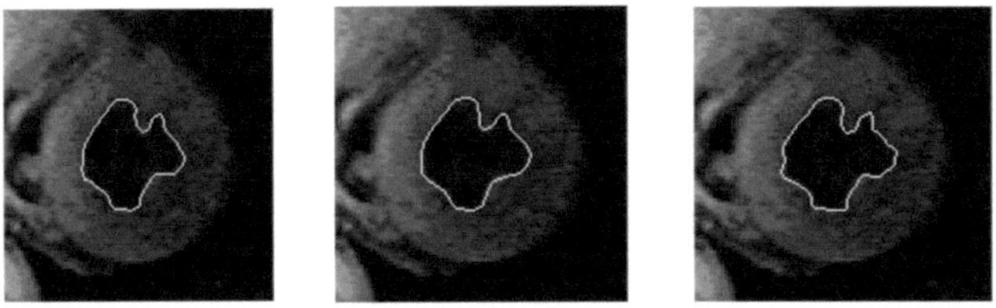

(a) (b) (c)

Fig. 5. (a) Optimized contour with the first parameters in Table 1. (b) Optimized contour with the second parameters in Table 1. (c) Optimized contour with the third parameters in Table 1.

4.2.2 Compared results with general ACO and GA for left ventricle

In order to compare FGACO algorithm with others and test the influence of the new finite grade pheromone updating rule on optimization process, we select the boundary detection of left ventricle which is also considered in literature (Mishraa et al., 2003). A potentially good left ventricle image is selected as Fig. 6(a). We take the same preprocessing in Sect.4.1.1, and obtain the initial contour as Fig. 6(b). The construction of a search space is the same as in Sect. 4.1.2. Firstly, we detect the boundary with a general ACO, the result of which is shown as Fig. 6(d). The result with FGACO is shown in Fig. 6(e). Conveniently, we place the segment results by GA of (Mishraa et al., 2003) in Fig. 6(f). Also, the fitness curves by iterations (or generations) are showed in Fig. 8.

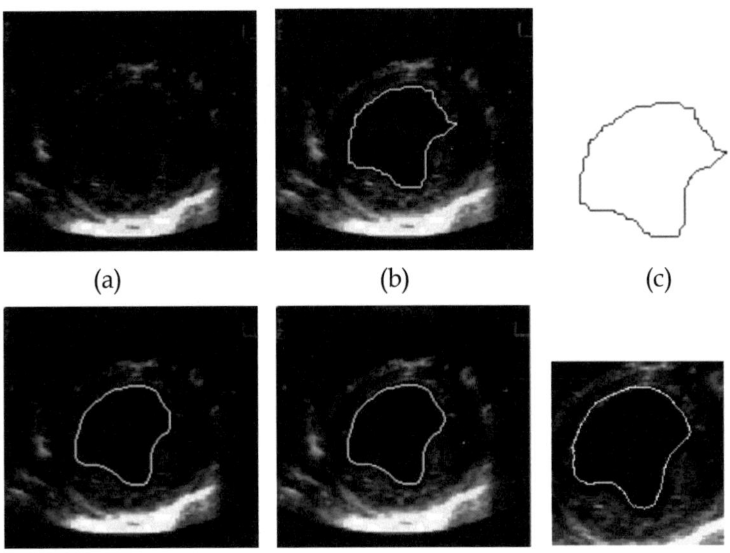

(a) (b) (c)

(d) (e) (f)

Fig. 6. (a) Original ultrasound image of left ventricle. (b) Rough boundary of the endocardial boarder on original image. (c) Rough boundary of the endocardial boarder on original image. (d)Optimized contour by general ACO. (e) Optimized contour by FGACO. (f) Optimized contour by GA of reference (Mishraa et al., 2003).

By observing the images from Figs. 6(d) to 6(f), it is obvious that the three optimization algorithms can successfully extract the boundary. But ACO based algorithms detect with fine boundary and FGACO algorithm is more effective. Furthermore, the extracted boundaries agree with the human visual judgment and are exactly consistent with the true ones in the original grey level images. From Fig. 7, we can note that the computational times required for each generation are different for different algorithms. Evidently, in our experiment, the computing efficiency of the FGACO is the best which shows the effectiveness of finite grade pheromone updating rules.

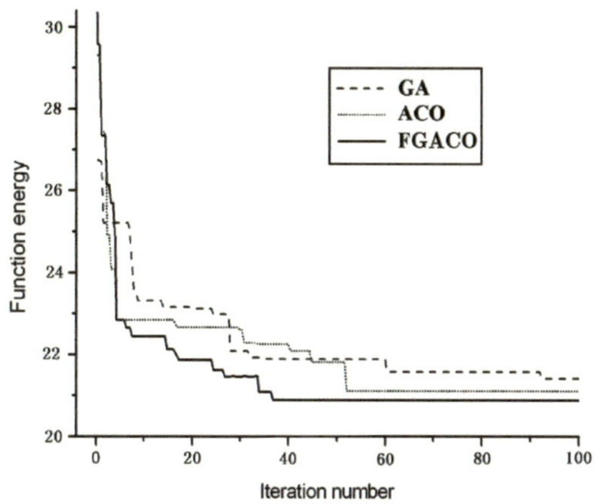

Fig. 7. Function energy comparison of FGACO with ACO and GA

5. Algorithm in phase change line detection of thermography

5.1 Phase change thermography sequence

During the research and development of aerocraft, we always need to obtain the heat distribution on the aerocraft surface. The phase change thermography is a test technique in wind tunnel for measuring thermal flow in a large area(Tang & Huang, 2003; Zhang & Fang, 1995), which becomes an effective way to get the thermography map. Theoretically, the color of the phase change material will change with a given temperature of the test object from white to black, which gradually form the boundary between two parts on the surface, called phase change line(PCL) (Tang & Huang, 2003). The key of this technique is to extract the PCL from phase change thermography sequence (PCTS). However, owing to the bad condition in wind tunnel and the complexity of aero-craft surface, sequence images are noisy(see in Fig. 8), which contributes to the difficulty of sequence image analysis, and that's why common segmentation methods does not work well. Fig. 8 gives out some frames in PCTS, and in order to clearly capture the phase change process, we install lights in the corner of the room, which leads to reflection on the surface, as showed in Fig. 8(d).

In order to address problems mentioned above, a new dynamic programming method has been proposed by Wang et al., which works well on the models with simple surface. In his method, the initial PCTS is transformed into a series of synthesized images by compression and conversion, then, a virtual illumination model is formulated to eliminate the influence of specular reflection, and finally, the approving isotherm is gained after the glisten is removed (Wang & Feng, 2007). Here, we replace the dynamic programming method described above by our ACO algorithm. We first divide PCTS into multiple associated sub-images, then, we use ACO algorithm to extract PCL for each sub-image, so finally we can obtain the target PCL after combining all the sub-image PCLs.

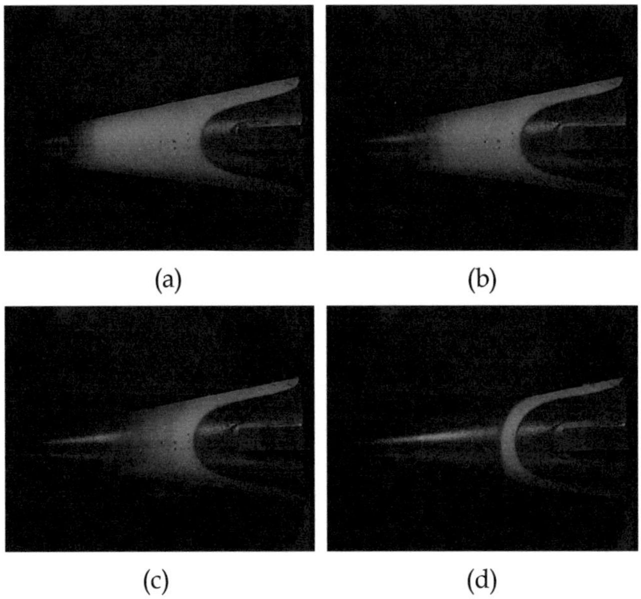

Fig. 8. Some frames in PCTS. (a) the 96th frame. (b) the 180th frame. (c) the 237th frame. (d) the 364th frame.

5.2 Ant colony optimization for phase change line detection

5.2.1 Image segmentation algorithm for PCTS

From Fig. 8, we can see that PCL is a fuzzy band so that it is difficult to segment every frame individually using traditional methods. Therefore, using the information of target motion and solving the image segmentation problem concerning the whole sequence is a quite large challenge. We propose an image segmentation algorithm for PCTS based on region-division, and we will realize image segmentation under ACO. The process of segmentation is showed in Fig.9.

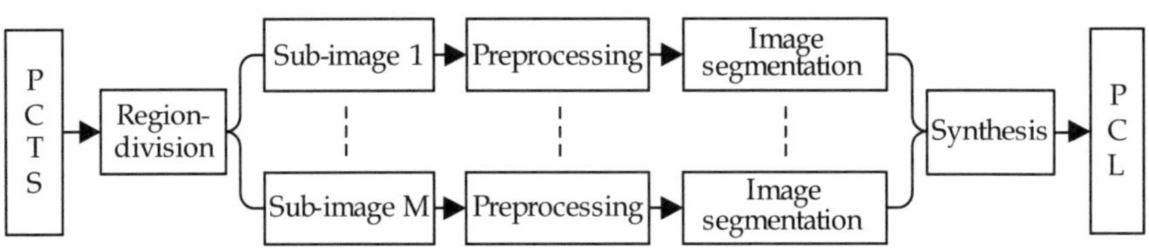

Fig. 9. Segmentation process in PCTS

5.2.1.1 Region-division

Sequence image can be expressed as $\Phi = \{\psi_1(x,y), \psi_2(x,y), \cdots, \psi_N(x,y)\}$, where $\psi_i(x,y)$, (x,y) is the image coordinate, and $i = 1,2,\cdots,N$ is one domain in image sequence, also be called frame. Each frame $\psi_i(x,y)$ is divided into M sub-regions $\psi_{ij}(j=1,2,\cdots,M)$ and a background sub-region ψ_{ib}, that is, $\psi_i=\sum_{j=1}^{M}\psi_{ij}+\psi_{ib}$. Here the sub-regions and the back ground satisfy $\psi_{iS}\cap\psi_{ij}=\phi(s\neq j)$, $\psi_{ib}\cap\psi_{ij}=\phi(j=1,2,\cdots,M)$, separately. Therefore, we divide image sequence Φ into M sub-sequence, namely, $\Phi_j=\{\psi_{1j},\psi_{2j},\cdots,\psi_{Nj}\}$, $j=1,\cdots,M$. Based on the characteristics of PCTS, we can easily separate the object region from background. To take advantage of the correlation among image sequence, we split each segmented object into M sub-regions. The split steps are as follows:

1. Separate the needed region from target image.
2. Divide the left part of needed region into M copies, and so does the right part.
3. Each frame forms M sub-regions.

Fig.10 shows the division results of some region in a PCTS example, where $M=9$.

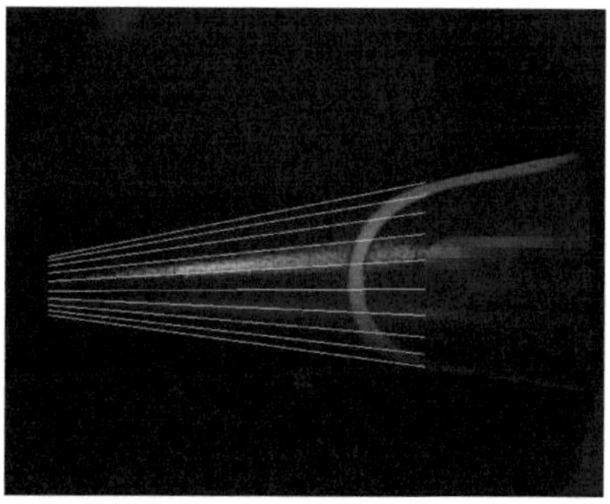

Fig.10. An example of region-division $(M=9)$

5.2.1.2 Region-space conversion

For each sub-region ψ_{ij}, we take the longitudinal axis as main direction, compute the sum of grey value of all pixels, and then divide it by the number of pixels, i.e.

$$c(j,k)=\frac{1}{n_k}\sum_{s=y_k}^{y_k+n_k}\psi_{ij}(k,s),\ i=1,\cdots,N;j=1,\cdots,M \tag{25}$$

where n_k is the number of pixels on the horizontal axis k in sub-sequence image, $\psi_{ij}(k,s)$ represents the grey value of j th region coordinate (k,s) in i th image, y_k is the minimum vertical axis on the horizontal axis k in sub-sequence image, and $k=1,2,\cdots,H$ is the length of image domain.

In this way, each original phase-change image is transformed into a $M\times H$ grey scale matrix. Thus, the whole image sequence is transformed into N matrixs with $M\times H$. Take the same line of each matrix in turn, so the whole image sequence Φ comes into being M images with $N\times H$. Fig. 11 shows the conversion process where $M=9,N=600,H=500$ and conversion results are given out in Fig. 12. From Fig. 12, it is apparent that we have transformed the original PCTS to M segmented images. Here, the transformed image is called sub-image, and then we will introduce the segmentation of sub-image.

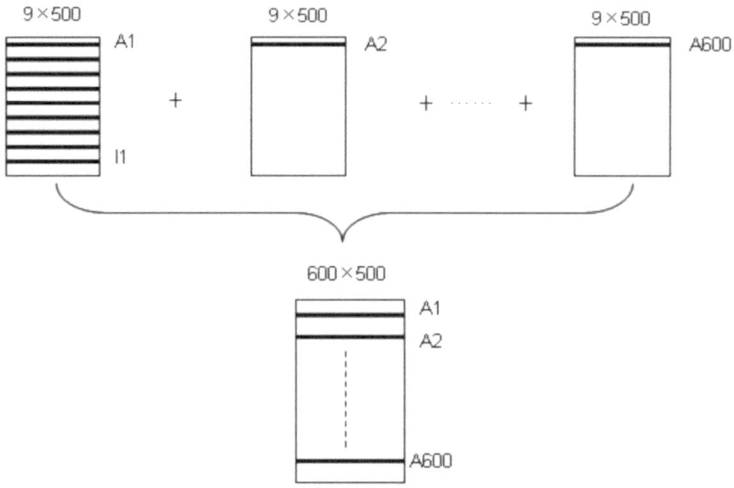

Fig. 11. Conversion process

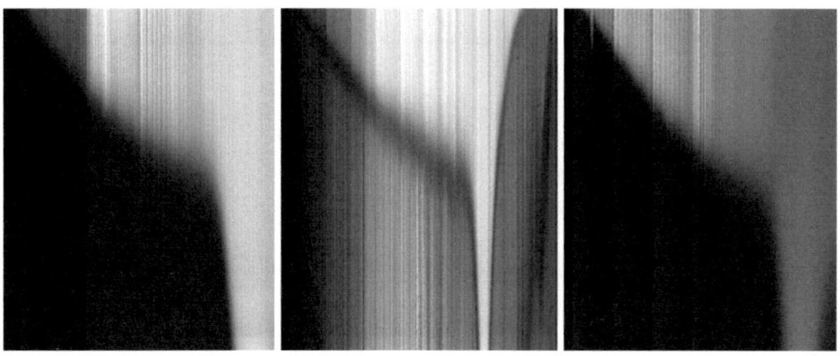

Fig. 12. Some sub-images

5.2.1.3 The preprocessing of sub-image

From Fig.12, we can see that the sub-images are noisy because of the illumination and reflection . The preprocessing including three steps is performed to improve the sub-image. First, smoothing technique is used to eliminate image noise with a mean filter. Second, in order to eliminate the influence of specular reflection, we do the following processing for image data in each column: if $f(i,j) > f(i,j-1)$, then $f(i,j) = f(i,j-1)$. Third, a normalizeation step is carried out with the image from left to right in each column, that is, for every pixel (m,n) in a given image $f(i,j)$, the grey value is calculated according to

$$f'(i,j) = \frac{f(i,j) - f_i^{\min}}{f_i^{\max} - f_i^{\min}} \tag{26}$$

where $f_i^{\min}$ and $f_i^{\max}$ is the minimum and maximum grey value in i th column, separately.

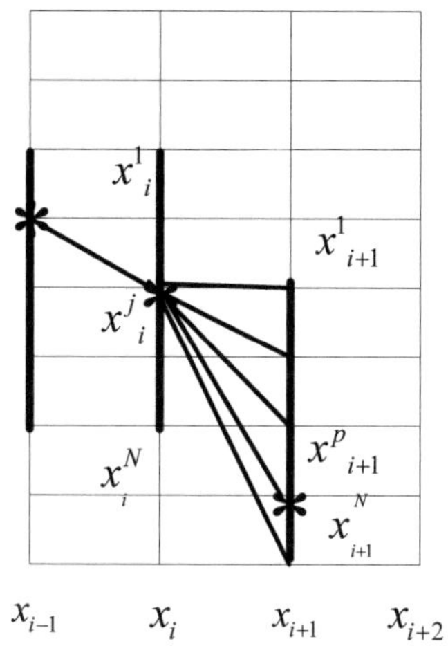

Fig. 13. Example of search

5.2.2 ACM based ACO image segmentation algorithm

ACM based ACO image segmentation algorithm has already been proposed in Sect.2. Here, we will apply the algorithm to realize the sub-image segmentation.

5.2.2.1 Construction of search space

After the normalization, we must choose an initial segmentation line in order to construct the search space of our ACO algorithm. The detail is stated as follows:

Step 1. Draw a grey value changes curve from left to right under a column unit and determine the upper edge and lower edge of the grey value, respectively denoted as MAX and MIN.

Step 2. For MAX and MIN in every column, we do: $mean = \alpha \cdot MAX + (1-\alpha) \cdot MIN$, where α is the coefficient to be determined.

Step 3. In terms of the grey value changes curve, the pixel value of middle point corresponds to its vertical axis. Therefore, for each $mean$ in every column, we can find a point corresponds to it until every point is determined. These points form an initial segmentation line, according to which we draw a segmentation band with bandwidth δ.

From the phase change process, we know that the PCL in present image must have shifted back from the previous one, that is, the present coordinate value of segmentation line is greater than the previous one(coordinate value is shown in Fig. 13). We suppose the present coordinate value is x_i^j, so the feasible zone of next point is $\vartheta = \{x_{i+1}^k \mid j \le k \le j+\delta \;\&\; k \in \Psi\}$, where δ is the search space given out.

5.2.2.2 Algorithm description

The energy function is defined as:

$$E_{snake} = \sum_{i=1}^{n} \{\alpha[|x_i - x_{i-1}| + |y_i - y_{i-1}|] + \beta[|x_{i-1} - 2x_i + x_{i+1}| + |y_{i-1} - 2y_i + y_{i+1}|] + wf(\nabla I)\} \quad (26)$$

where x_i, y_i is the coordinate value of present segmentation line, $f(\nabla I)$ is the edge energy in image force, and ∇I represents the first order difference of grey value I . α, β, w are the coefficients given out.

The target of our algorithm is to find an optimal path t^* in search space Ψ , which contributes to the minimum of energy function. Our algorithm includes definition of pheromone, probability decision, and pheromone update, which have already been introduced in Sect.2.3. Furthermore, the description of our algorithm is the same as Sect.2.3.4.

5.2.2.3 Segmentation results

Set $N = 10, M = 60, A = 10$, $\alpha = 5, \beta = 0.1, w = 2$ and the final results is shown in Fig. 14.

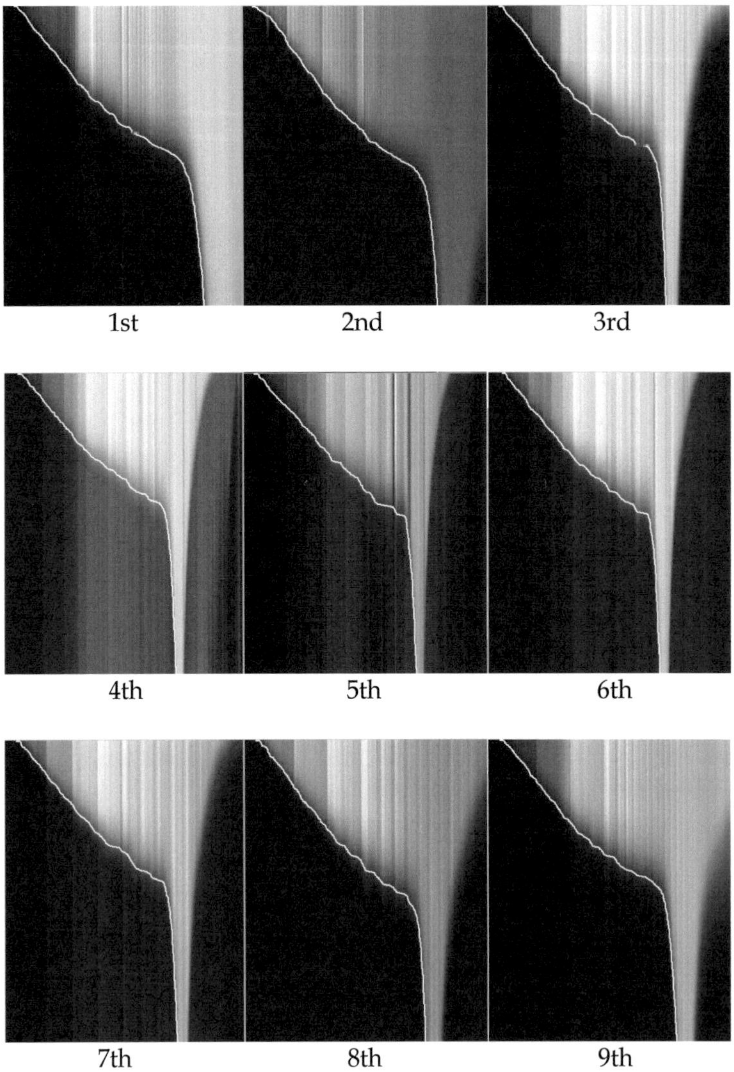

Fig. 14. Results of sub-image segmentation

After obtaining the PCL of sub-image, we can return it to original image sequence. As we divide the segmented object into M sub-regions, the points that return from PCL to original image sequence locate in the middle of M sub-regions. Then we use quadratic spline to fit these points so that we acquire the final PCL, shown in Fig. 15.

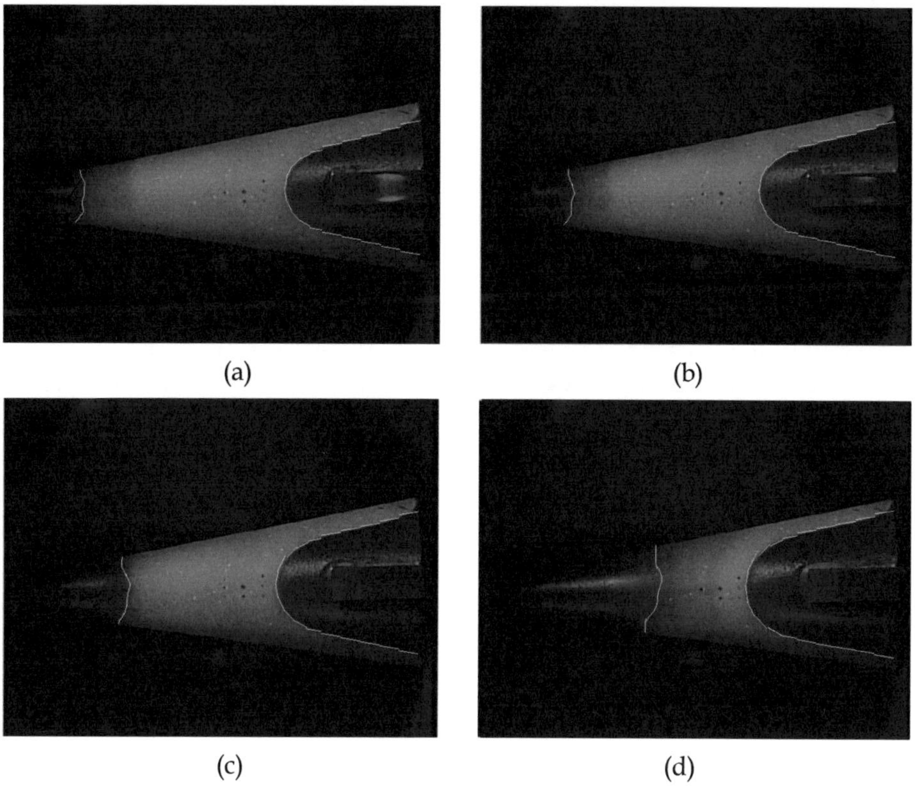

Fig. 15. Some results of PCTS segmentation. (a) 100th frame (b) 120th frame (c) 180th frame (d) 284th frame

6. Discussion and conclusion

This chapter describes application of the ACO algorithm to the image segmentation problems. First, based on the similarity between the solving process of ACM and ACO, the ACO algorithm for image segmentation is proposed. Taking medical image segmentation as examples, the result indicates that the contour is continuous, and more smooth and rational than the raw contour (shown in Figs. 3,4). This algorithm provides a new approach to obtain precise contour. It is proved to be convergent with probability one, and will reach the best feasible boundary with minimum energy function value. Moreover, this algorithm can also be used to solve other revised ACM problems.

In addition, a new pheromone updating rule is designed for improving the time performance of the algorithm. The convergence prosperities are given by finite Markov chain. The proposed algorithm has been tested for automatic boundary detection of the endocardial border in a set of ecdocardio graphic images.

Finally, we have introduced the application of the proposed algorithm in phase change line detection of complex phase change thermography. In the algorithm, phase change sequence is changed into multiple associated sub-images by region division which includes the moving information of the moving contour.
The main contribution of this paper is to apply ACO in optimum contour extraction for noisy images. Even though implementation of ACO in discrete combinational optimization problems is successful, the results of the general ACO found to be time-consuming because feasible decision set increases exponentially with the dimension of the decision variable. By introducing the finite grade pheromone updating rules, the contour extraction is reasonably insensitive to the initial approximation in the search space. The experimental results show that our general ACO algorithm for image segmentation is more effective than the genetic algorithm in related literature, and our FGACO algorithm works quite satisfactorily, and ultimately reduces computational time compared to general ACO (shown in Figs. 6,7).
The experimental results with the PCTS show that the algorithm extracts the phase change active contour well. But as the relationship between multi-regions is not taken into account by us, the segmentation results cannot reach perfect accuracy. Therefore, our future work will focus on how to use the coordinate characteristics between the individuals of ant colony to solve the problem mentioned above.

7. Acknowledgements

This work is partially supported by the Natural Science Foundation Fund of China Grant #60475023 and the Natural Science Fundation Fund of Zhejiang Province Grant #Y106660. In addition, we are also thankful to Liangjun Ke, Zuren Feng from Xi'an Jiaotong University for their stimulating comments and useful supports, which helped to improve the quality of the manuscript.

8. References

Kass, M.; Witkin, A. & TeizoPoulos, D. (1987). Snakes: active contour models[J]. *International Journal of Computer Vision*, 1(4): 321 - 331

Cohen, L.D. (1991).On active contour models and balloons, *Computer Vision Graph.* 53, 211–218.

Amini, A.A.; Weymouth T.E. & Jain, C.R. (1990). Using dynamic programming for solving variational problems in vision, *IEEE T. Pattern Anal.* 12, 855–867.

Williams, D.J. & Shah M. (1990). A fast algorithm for active contours, *Proc. 3rd Int. Conf. on Computer Vision*, 592–595.

MacEachern, L.A. & Manku, T. (1998). Genetic algorithms for active contour optimization, *Proceedings - IEEE International Symposium on Circuits and Systems 4*, 229–232.

Gunn, S.R. & Nixon, M.S. (1996). Snake head boundary extraction using global and local energy minimization, *Proc. 13th Int. Conf. on Pattern Recognition*, 581–585.

Xu, C. & Prince, J.L. (1998). Snake shape and gradient vector flow, *IEEE T. Pattern Anal.* 7, 359–369.

Hsien-Hsun, W.; Jyh-Charn, L. & Chui, C. (2000). A wavelet-frame based image force model for active contouring algorithms, *IEEE T. Image Process.* 9, 1983–1988.

Lam, K.M. & Yan, H(1994). Fast greedy algorithm for active contours, *Electronics Letters*, v 30, p 21-23.

Dorigo, M; Manjezzo, V. & Colorni, A. (1996). The ant system: Optimization by a colony of cooperating agents. *IEEE Transaction on Systems, Man& Cybernetics B*, 2692: 29-41.

Dorigo, M. & Ganbardella, L.M. (1997). Ant colony system: A cooperating learning approach to the traveling salesman problem. *IEEE Transactions on Evolutionary* Computation. 1997, 1(1), 53-66.

Bullnheimer, B.; Hartl, R. & Strauss, C. (1998). Applying the ant system to the vehicle routing problem. Meta-Heuristics: Advances and Trends in Local Search Paradigms for Optimization [M], *Kluwer Academics*, pp. 285-296.

Stutzle, T. (1998) An ant approach to the flow shop problem[C]. *Proceedings of European Congress on Intelligent Techniques and Soft Computing.* Aachen, Germany, 1560-1564.

Ouadfel, S. & Batouche, M. (2003). Ant colony system with local search for Markov random field image segmentation [C], *International Conference on Image Processing*, 1:133-136

Meshoul, S. & Batouche, M. (2002). Ant colony system with external dynamics for point matching and pose estimation [J]. *Pattern Recognition*, 2002. 3 :823 - 826.

Feng, Y.J. (2005). Ant colony cooperative optimization and Its Application in image segmentation. Dissertation of Ph.D. Xi'an Jiaotong University. China.

Han, Y. F. & Shi, P. F. (2006). An improved ant colony algorithm for fuzzy clustering in image segmentation. *Neurocomputing*, 70 (2007) 665-671.

Tao, W.B.; Jin, H. & Liu, L.M. (2007). Object segmentation using ant colony optimization algorithm and fuzzy entropy. *Pattern Recognition Letters* 28 788-796.

Hegarat-Mascle, L.; Kallel, S. & Velizy, A. etc. (2007). Ant Colony Optimization for image regularization based on a nonstationary markov modeling, *IEEE Transactions on Image Processing*, 16(3): 865-878.

Ma, L.; Wang, K.Q. & Zhang, D. (2009). A universal texture segmentation and representation scheme based on ant colony optimization for iris image processing. *Computers and Mathematics with Applications* 57 (2009) 1862_1868.

Susmita, G.; Megha, K.; Anindya, H. & Ashish, G. (2009). Use of aggregation pheromone density for image segmentation. *Pattern Recognition Letters* 30 (2009) 939-949.

Lao, D.Z. (2004) Foundation of variational methods. *National Defense Industry Press.* p.85-88

Mishraa, A.; Duttab, P.K. & Ghoshc, M.K. (2003). A GA based approach for boundary detection of left ventricle with echocardio graphic image sequences. *Image and Vision Computing* 21 (2003) 967–976.

Tang, Q. & Huang, G. (2003). The reaserch and application of phase change thermograghy technique, *Experiments and Measurements in Fluid Mechanics*, 17(1):15-17(in Chinese).

Zhang, J. & Fang, D. (1995). The application of the phase change thermo-graghy technology in measurement of surface heat transfer rate, *Aerodynamic Experiment and Measurement Control*, 1995, 9(1):67-72(in Chinese).

Wang, X. & Feng, Z. (2007). The automatic extraction of isothermal line in phase-change thermograthy sequence, *Pattern Recognition and Artificial Intelligence*, 20(4):469-477(in Chinese).

18

SoC Test Applications Using ACO Meta-heuristic

Hong-Sik Kim[1], Jin-Ho An[2] and Sungho Kang[1]
[1]Department of Electrical and Electronic Engineering, Yonsei University
[2]Department of Electronic Engineering, Hoseo University
Korea

1. Introduction

As the integrity of VLSI (very large scale integration) circuits increases, their test has become more complex and time consuming task so that test cost has been significantly increased. Recent SoC (system on chip) design and test environments have deteriorated this trend more significantly. For example, the traditional scan cell ordering problem for low power testing is a well known NP-complete problem and has become more time consuming job as circuit density increases. In addition, as the SoC design environment takes root in the semiconductor industry, the test sequence for each IP (intellectual property) core comes to influence the total test time and the total power consumption of the system chip under test. Recently hot spot induced by scan testing also should be considered during SoC testing in order to improve circuit reliability and reduce unexpected yield loss. Test scheduling, therefore, became more important in order to meet the design specifications, such as the test time constraint, the power consumption limitation, the thermal constraint, and so on. Finally, SoC design methodology requires more test storage since more IP cores are integrated in a SoC product so that the test compression techniques are widely used to reduce both the test time and the external ATE (automatic test equipment) memory/channel requirements. In many cases, the test compression efficiency depends on the given test cube set and as the size of test cube set increases in SoC test environment, it will take too much time to calculate the optimal seed set for the given test cube set in case of arithmetic built-in self test (ABIST) scheme.

ACO (ant colony optimization) meta-heuristic is an algorithm inspired by the real ant system in order to find the optimal solutions for TSP (travel salesman problem) which is well known to be an NP-complete problem and has been successfully applied to lots of NP-complete problems in various fields. In this chapter, we try to transform several important problems in the field of SoC testing into ACO applicable ones, which are solved by the ACO meta-heuristic. For the ACO-based test applications, three important test problems such as test scheduling, scan cell ordering, and test seed calculation for ABIST, are selected. Each problem has unique characteristics in order to be transformed into ACO applicable one, so that bundles of techniques have been devised and will be described in this chapter. According to the experimental results, the ACO meta-heuristic could considerably improve the quality and cost efficiency of SoC test methodologies such as test scheduling, scan cell ordering, and test seed calculation.

2. SoC test scheduling using ACO heuristic

The number of cores embedded in an SoC is increasing rapidly, and cores are more deeply embedded. Therefore, testing the cores by means of direct access through the SoC's I/O pins is almost impossible. In order to solve this problem, methods like the IEEE 1500 standard and Test Access Mechanism(TAM) have been proposed. An SoC test scheduling is a process to minimize the test application time of all built-in cores in the SoC under given constraints like TAM bandwidth and power budget. It includes the optimization of the test wrapper design, the assignment of TAM width to each core, and the determination of test start and finish time for each core.

In this section, we introduce an ant colony optimization (ACO)-based SoC test scheduling method including power and layout information. The proposed method efficiently combines the rectangle packing method with ACO and improves the scheduling results by dynamically choosing the TAM widths for cores and changing the testing orders. The power dissipation and adjacency of cores are incorporated for actual testing conditions.

2.1 ACO-based rectangle packing [Ahn, J.-H. & Kang, S., 2008]

An SoC test scheduling problem can be formulated in terms of a 2-dimensional bin packing problem [Huang, Y. et al, 2001; Iyengar, V. et al, 2002]. The test time varies with TAM width in a staircase pattern, and the testing of a core is represented as a rectangle whose height indicates the TAM width assigned to that core and whose width denotes the test time of the core for the corresponding value of the TAM width. Thus, we can obtain a number of TAM width and test time combinations for the same core. Taken as a whole, a test scheduler chooses just one rectangle from the candidate rectangle set of each core and then packs it into a bin of a fixed height and an unlimited width until the bin is filled with rectangles of all cores embedded in SoC, while minimizing the overall width of the bin without overflowing the bin's height.

Now, we describe how the ACO algorithm can be implemented for a rectangle packing solution. A rectangle packing problem consists of two sub-parts: rectangle selection and rectangle packing. The ACO algorithm can be applied to part rectangle selection and/or rectangle packing. Through some experiments, we determined that ACO should be used only to select rectangles due to the computation time. Therefore, the rectangle packing method is based on the procedure used in [Ahn, J.-H. & Kang, S., 2006]. Before describing the implementation of ACO for the rectangle packing solution, some features related to ACO need to be clarified.

a. *Definition of Pheromone Trail $\tau_i(k)$*

We define the pheromone trail, $\tau_i(k)$, as the favorability of choosing k as the TAM width assigned to core i and calculate it as

$$\tau_i(k) = \sum\nolimits_{j \in S} \tau(k_i, g_j), \quad 1 \le i,\ j \le m, \quad 1 \le 2^k, 2^g \le W, \tag{1}$$

where S denotes the cores already visited by the current ant, g_j is the TAM width selected for core j, m is the number of embedded cores, and W is the channel width of TAM. Consequently, (k_i, g_j) is the favorability of choosing k as the TAM width for core i when the TAM width assigned to core j is g.

b. *Heuristic Variable η_i*

The ACO algorithm combines pheromone information with heuristic values to find solutions, since heuristic parameters can help ACO be applicable to various conditions.

Here, we use a preferred TAM width for core i, $w_{prefer}(i)$, as the heuristic favorability, η_i. The calculation flow to seek $w_{prefer}(i)$ is shown in [Ahn, J.-H. & Kang, S., 2006].

c. *Stochastic Decision with $\tau_i(k)$ and η_i*

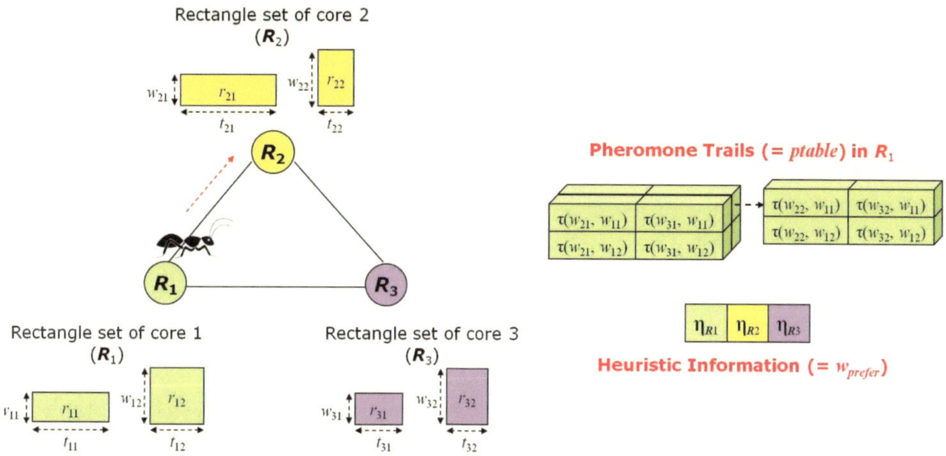

Fig. 1. ACO-based rectangle selection

The probability pi(k) that an ant will choose k for core i is given by

$$p_i(k) = \frac{\tau_i(k) \cdot \beta}{\sum_{x=1}^{W} (\tau_i(x) \cdot \beta)}, \tag{2}$$

where $\beta \geq 1$ if $w_{prefer}(i)=k$ and 1 otherwise.

d. *Policy for Pheromone Updating*

According to test scheduling results, pheromone trails are updated as follows:

$$\tau(k_i, g_j) = \rho \cdot \tau(k_i, g_j) + \Delta\tau(k_i, g_j), \tag{3}$$

where ρ is the evaporation parameter, which determines the speed of decay of pheromone; Δτ is the amount of pheromone deposited by the ant on the basis of the quality of the scheduling result and is defined as

$$\Delta\tau(k_i, g_j) = N_{k_i g_j} \cdot \lambda, \tag{4}$$

where $N_{k_i g_j}$ indicates how many times k of core i and g of core j go together in the best scheduling result S_{best}, and λ is the constant value to weigh.

The method of rectangle selection using ACO is explained in the following example. As shown in Fig. 1, let an SoC include three cores. The rectangle sets of cores, R_i ($1 \leq i \leq 3$), can be represented as nodes linked with one another in the graph. At first, an ant randomly selects a starting node and a rectangle in that node. In Fig. 1, we assume that the ant chooses R_1 as a starting node and rectangle r_{11}. Then, the ant can select R_2 or R_3 as a next node. After arbitrarily selecting a next node, according to pheromone trails (ptable in the figure) stored in R_1 and heuristic information, w_{prefer}, the ant chooses a rectangle in that node. For example, if R_2 becomes the next node, two pheromone trails, $\tau(w_{21}, w_{11})$ and $\tau(w_{22}, w_{11})$, and one heuristic value, ηR_2, are used to choose a rectangle in R_2 by (5). As previously mentioned, $\tau(w_{21}$(or w_{22}), $w_{11})$ is the favorability of choosing w_{21}(or w_{22}) as the TAM width for core 2 when the TAM width assigned to core 1 is w_{11}, and ηR_2 is the preferred TAM width of core 2. In this example, we assumed that r_{21} in R_2 is selected by (2). The ant continues this process until all nodes are visited just once. After choosing all rectangles in R_i, the ant packs them using the method used in [Ahn, J.-H. & Kang, S., 2006] and gets a scheduling result. Figure 1 illustrates a scheduling result with three rectangles, r_{11}, r_{21}, and r_{32}. Finally, the result is based on updating pheromone values. If the result is better than the current best result, pheromone values, such as $\tau(w_{21}, w_{11})$ in R_1 and $\tau(w_{32}, w_{21})$ in R_2, can be reinforced.

In addition to basic ACO methods, we adopt several heuristic tips, such as iteration-best ant (S_{ib}), global-best ant (S_{gb}), and lower limit of the pheromone values (τ_{min}) [Glover, F. et al, 2003; Stutzle, T. et al, 2000]. These methods are efficient means to balance exploitation of the best solution found and exploration of the solution space. Furthermore, we assume that just one ant per colony can form a pheromone trail.

2.2 Thermal distribution consideration

During testing, the peak power cannot be over the power limit of the system [Cota, E. et al, 2003]. In addition, thermal management is also considered to reduce hot spots for the purpose of minimizing the local heating. In order to make thermal-aware scheduling, we added a thermal constraint by the analysis of geometrical adjacency of cores. It is for this reason that cooling effect diminishes when cores tested concurrently are geometrically close to each other. In [Liu, C. et al, 2005], the corresponding distance matrix is used to measure the adjacency of cores. However, as the matrix only represents the relative position within chip layout, the amount of adjacent area cannot be identified. Thus, we calculate the adjacency value as follows.

$$ADJ_{ij} = \sum \sqrt{(c_i(x) - c_j(x))^2 + (c_i(y) - c_j(y))^2}, \quad 1 \le i,\ j \le m, \tag{5}$$

where c_i denotes the unit cell of core i and $c_i(x)$ is the x-axis position of core i. c_j, $c_i(y)$, $c_j(x)$, and $c_j(y)$ can be defined in similar way. Position in X/Y-axis is normalized, and ranges from 0 to 99. In order to get the effective adjacency value, the value can increase iff the distance between two cells is less than 10% of the longest distance. Since we normalize the chip size as (100, 100), the longest distance is 140 or so.

a. Overall Test Scheduling Procedure

```
Compute R from wrapper design of cores;
Compute heuristic information (= w_prefer) ;
Set ACO parameters;
Initialize pheromone trails (= ptable);
While (result is unsatisfactory) {
  While (N_ib < γ) {
    While (i < N_colony) { ant_exploration; }
  Find S^ib;  pheromone_update(S^ib); }
Find S^gb;  pheromone_update(S^gb); }
```

Fig. 2. ACO-based test scheduling procedure

```
Select a TAM width, w_selected, using ACO-based rectangle selection procedure
Initialize data structure of all cores;
While (there exist untested cores) {
   Select TAM position, p, that has the lowest current time;
   // Start of rectangle packing heuristics
   If (there remains TAM available) {
      If core i satisfies the next conditions:
         - power budget and adjacency limit
         - largest test time among remained cores
         - smaller TAM width than currently available,
        Rectangle packing process with w_assigned(i) = w_selected(i);
    Else
         If core i satisfies the next conditions:
            - power budget and adjacency limit
            - largest test time among remained cores which are not over
                                  the smallest time among cores tested currently,
           Find w(i), where w(i) is the highest Pareto-optimal width,
                such that requires smaller TAM width than currently available;
           Rectangle packing process with rectangle insertion in idle time;
           Set w_assigned(i) = w(i);
         Else
            If core i satisfies the next conditions:
               - scheduled at current time
               - largest test time with extended TAM width,
              Find w(i), where w(i) is the highest Pareto-optimal width,
                   such that extended TAM is smaller than TAM currently available;
              Rectangle packing process with increasing TAM widths to fill idle time;
              Set w_assigned(i) = w(i);
   }
   Else  { Move to next time and update information; }
} // End of rectangle packing heuristics
Update the best test time;
```

Fig. 3. Ant exploration process

The ACO-based test scheduling procedure is given in Fig. 2. In Fig. 2, Ncolony denotes the number of ants in one colony, N_{ib} is the iteration-best ant number, γ is the waiting number until S_{gb} is used again, and ant_exploration means an ant's action. The ACO parameters include the variables previously mentioned, such as N_{colony}, γ, λ, β, ρ, τ_{min}, and so on. R in Fig. 2 (line 1) indicates the test wrapper set for embedded cores and wprefer is the preferred TAM width.

In the ant exploration procedure as shown in Fig. 3, an ant will search the solution space continuously with new r_i combinations. After choosing r_i for all cores, Each ant packs them while minimizing the idle space. As in [Ahn, J.-H. & Kang, S., 2006], we use the packing method, which is based on TAM_optimizer [Iyengar, V. et al. 2002] for its simplicity and feasibility. Finally, if the packing result of the ant is better than the current best result, the scheduler updates the best test time. $w_{selected}$ is the TAM width from the ACO-based rectangle selection process and $w_{assigned}$ is the TAM width assigned at the end. If a core doesn't satisfy the power budget, the acceptable maximum power consumption in a whole chip level, and the adjacent limit, the acceptable adjacency value of cores tested concurrently, the core will not be selected by the ant. $w_{assigned}$ will be reinforced at the end of the ant exploration process, if the packing result is excellent.

3. Experimental results

We simulated three ITC'02 benchmark circuits to evaluate the proposed scheduling algorithm. The final results reported in this section are based on the following ACO parameter values:

N_{colony}: 10, γ: 10, ρ: 0.9~0.96, τ_{min}: 2.0, $\tau(0)$: 20.0, β : 10~20, λ: 0.2,

where $\tau(0)$ is an initial value of a pheromone trail. To obtain parameter values that achieve good performance, tests using circuits with different sizes and structures are required. The parameter values used here are chosen for balancing the test application times with the calculation times through some experiments.

SoC Name	Power Constrants	TAM Width					
		W=32			W=16		
		[Iyengar, V. et al. 2002]	[Huang, Y. et al 2002]	Proposed	[Iyengar, V. et al. 2002]	[Huang, Y. et al 2002]	Proposed
p22810	No Power Constraint	**246150**	**223462**	**238109**	**452639**	**446684**	**441408**
P9379	No Power Constraint	**975016**	**900798**	**896835**	**1851135**	**1791860**	**1783397**
d695	No Power Constraint	**23021**	**21389**	**21429**	**43723**	**42716**	**42315**
	Pmax=2000	NA	**24171**	**21437**	NA	**43221**	**42351**
	Pmax=1500	NA	**27573**	**23097**	NA	**45560**	**42587**

Table 1. Scheduling Results with Various Power Constraints

Table 1 displays the results of an experiment in which various power constraints were used for the core test. The given TAM width is either 32 or 16 bits. First, in the experimental results without power budgets, we compare the test times of the proposed method with those of the method presented in [Iyengar, V. et al. 2002] and [Huang, Y. et al 2002] using the bin packing algorithm for test scheduling. As a result, compared with [Iyengar, V. et al. 2002], the test time reduction ratio increases by up to 8% at W=32 and 3% at W=16 on average. However, our results are almost similar to [Huang, Y. et al 2002]. Next, we show the experimental results incorporating power constraints on the power consumption model in [Huang, Y. et al 2002]. As the results demonstrate, though the reduction ratio is somewhat variable on a case-by-case, the proposed algorithm shows good performance in the main. When P_{max} is set to 2000, the test time reduction ratio goes up to 16% at W=32 and 6% at W=16.

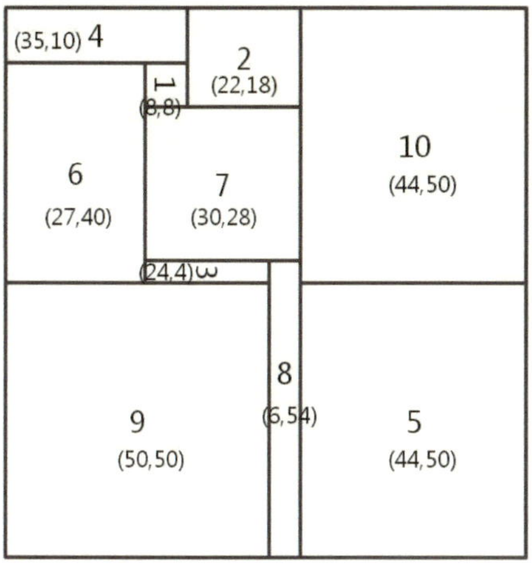

(a)

SoC Name	W=32				
	100%	80%	60%	50%	30%
d695	**21437**	**22350**	**22403**	**22571**	**23121**
	W=16				
	100%	80%	60%	50%	30%
	42351	**42481**	**42481**	**42786**	**43456**

(b)

Table 2. Scheduling Results with Thermal Management

Finally, we introduce the scheduling results using thermal management in Table 2. As layout information on benchmark circuits is not available, we make it freely in terms of the numbers of scan flip-flops, inputs, outputs, and bidirectional ports of cores. The example floorplan of d695 is shown in Table 2 (a). Each rectangle denotes a core and center number in a rectangle is the core ID. Numbers in parentheses mean the scaling size of a core, (X-axis size, Y-axis size). The results are shown in Table 2 (b). To evaluate the scheduling results considering the core adjacency, we set the adjacency limit, ADJmax, to 30~100% of the maximum adjacency value among cores.

Experimental results show that the adjacency constraint partly influences the scheduling results as we expected. When the adjacency limit goes down to 30 %, the scheduling time extends by up to 7%. The proposed algorithm can be utilized to estimate the overall test application time just with the number and size of flip-flops, memory and rough floorplan information.

3. Scan cell ordering using ACO heuristic

The scan-based test structure is widely used for its high controllability and observability, which is obtained by direct access to the memory elements in the circuit. Power consumption during a scan test is much greater than that of normal operation, because all scan flip-flops are clocked during shift operations, and a much larger percentage of the flip-flops will change values in each clock cycle. Excessive power consumption during a test can cause several problems: circuit damage, yield loss, decreased system reliability, and increased product costs. Since the switching activities in scan flip-flops are the dominant source of test power consumption, the number of transitions during a scan test should be minimized to prevent these problems. Scan cell ordering methods have been proposed to reduce the switching activity in a scan-chain during scan test. Genetic algorithm (GA) is used to determine an optimized scan cell order [Jelodar, M. S. et al, 2006; Giri, C. et al, 2005]. However, the power reduction rate of these methods decreases as the number of scan-cells increases.

We propose an efficient scan-cell ordering method using an ACO meta-heuristic [Dorigo, M. et al, 1999] to reduce the transition count during scan testing. The ACO decision-making-based experiential probability can provide a scan-cell order optimized with respect to both the sum of the Hamming distances between successive test vector columns and the total transition count during a scan test. According to the experimental results based on ISCAS 89 benchmark circuits, the proposed scan cell ordering methodology could reduce considerable power consumption compared to the previous works.

3.1 Proposed scan cell ordering methodology

The basic idea of the proposed method is to arrange scan-cells to minimize the sum of Hamming distances between successive test vector columns. The total transition count can be decreased as the sum of Hamming distances between test vector columns decreases, because Hamming distances between test vector columns represent the number of transitions caused by shift operations during a scan test. As shown in Fig. 4, however, minimizing the sum of Hamming distances does not always result in minimum total transition count. Therefore, the order of scan-cells must be optimized with respect to both the sum of the Hamming distances and the total transition count. We use an ACO meta-heuristic to find an optimal scan-cell order by formulating the ordering problem as a travelling-salesman problem (TSP). ACO is an algorithm inspired by the behaviour of real ants using pheromone trails to communicate. The pheromone trails are distributive and contain numerical information which the ants use to find solutions probabilistically.

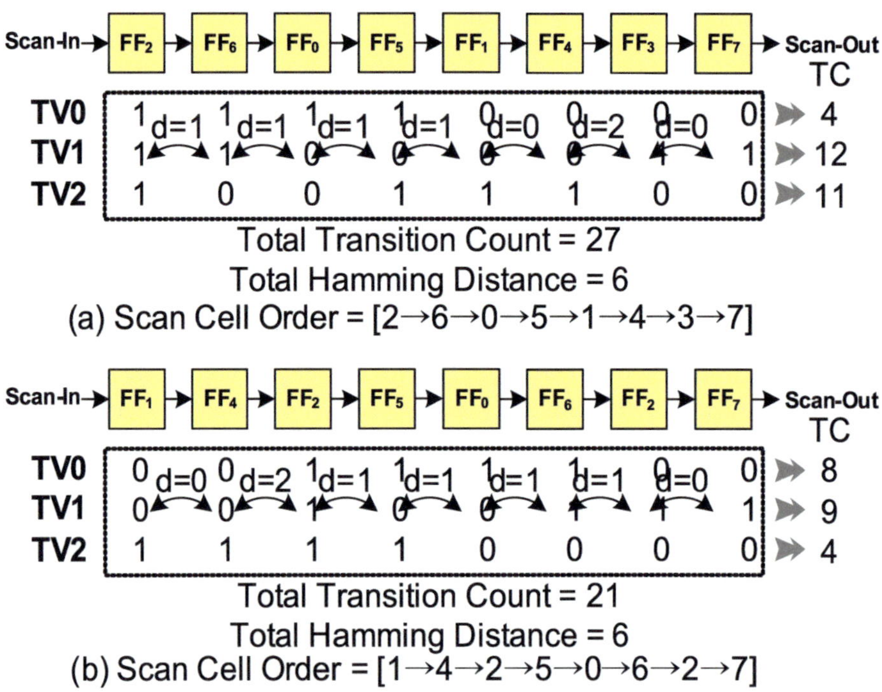

Fig. 4. Total transition count and hamming distance during scan shift

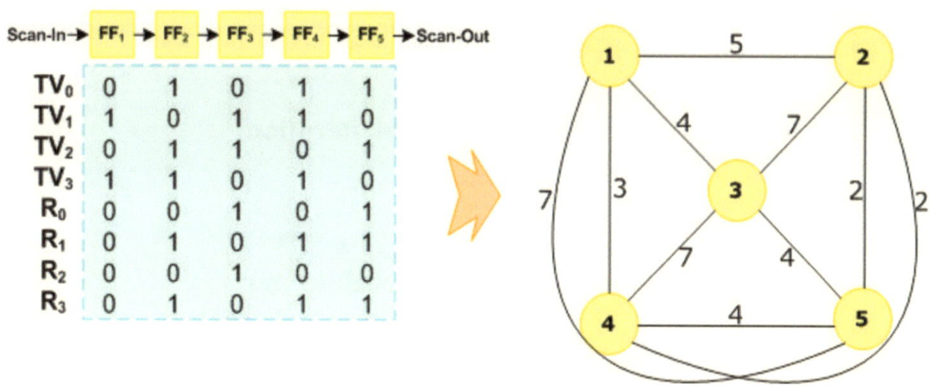

Fig. 5. An example of constructing a graph based on hamming distance

The probability that a solution candidate is chosen to construct a solution is analogous to the amount of pheromone in trails formerly laid by the ants. The objective of scan-cell ordering using ACO is to find the minimum transition Hamiltonian cycle on the graph $G=(C, L)$ where $C=\{c_1, c_2, \dots, c_{Nc}, N_c=$the size of scan chain$\}$ is a set of scan-cell bit positions in a target scan chain and $L=\{l_{ij} \mid (c_i, c_j) \in C'$, C'=subset of a Cartesian product $C \times C\}$, $[L] \leq N_c^2$ represents the Hamming distance between test vector column i and j corresponding to scan-cell bit positions i and j, respectively. Fig. 5 shows an example of constructing a graph using a set of test vectors and responses.

Scan-cell ordering problems can be characterized as follows using ACO:

- J_{cicj} is a Hamming distance between scan-cell bit positions i and j.
- $A=\{a_{ij} \mid (c_i, c_j)\ C'\}$, $[A] \leq N_c^2$ is a local information table between each scan-cell bit position. a_{ij} can be calculated as $1/J_{cicj}$. So this value becomes larger as the Hamming distance decreases.
- J_k is a total transition count estimated using the order constructed by an artificial ant k.
- τ_k is a pheromone trail stored by an ant k. It can be calculated as $1/J_k$. When the solution is constructed more efficiently, larger pheromone trails can be stored.
- $\tau=\{\tau_{ij} \mid (c_i, c_j) \in C'\}$, $[\tau] \leq N_c^2$ represents pheromone trails stored on the arc between scan-cell bit positions i and j. It can be calculated as follows: $\tau_{ij}=(1-\rho)\cdot\tau_{ij}+\rho\cdot\tau_k$. The variable $\rho \in (0, 1]$ is the pheromone trail evaporation coefficient. The evaporation of pheromone trails takes place to avoid overly-rapid convergence of the algorithm toward a sub-optimal solution.
- $p_{ijk} = [\tau_{ij}]a \cdot [a_{ij}]\beta$ is the probability with which an ant k positioned in bit position i chooses the bit position j. The parameters a and β determine the relative weight of the total transition count and the sum of Hamming distances, respectively.

According to these definitions, the proposed scan-cell ordering proceeds as shown in Fig. 6. Once the test vector columns are ordered by the proposed scan-cell ordering method, the rows of the test vectors are ordered again. A transition occurs when the MSB (most significant bit) of a test response to be scanned-out is different from the LSB (least significant bit) of the next test vector to be scanned-in. Since this transition is propagated throughout the whole scan chain, the number of transitions caused by this difference is equal to the length of a scan chain. To reduce these transitions, the consecutive test vectors are, therefore, arranged by the simple condition of whether the LSB of one vector is equal to the MSB of its predecessor's response.

```
Procedure ScanCellReordering()
  ants_generation();
  while (current iteration != target_iteration)
    initialize_ants();
    while (available_ants)
      while (current_state != target_state)
        P = compute_transition_probabilities();
        next_state = apply_ant_decision_policy(P);
        move_to_next_state(next_state);
      end while
    end while
    pheromone_update_on_the_visited_arc();
  end while
End procedure
```

Fig. 6. Proposed scan cell ordering heuristic

3.2 Experimental results

Experiments were performed to compute scan test power reduction rates on the ISCAS'89 benchmark circuits. Test vectors were generated from the full-scan versions of the circuits using the Synopsys Design Analyzer with two vector filling methods (random-fill (R-fill) and minimum-transition fill (MT-fill)) and two compaction types (high compaction and no compaction). The heuristic parameters of ACO were set to α=1, β=5 and ρ=0.5. All the experiments were carried out for 100 ant-cycles and averaged over 10 trials.

Circuits	No. of scan cells	Total Transition Reduction Rate					
		R-fill & Compaction high			R-fill & No-Compaction		
		[Jelodar, M. S. et al, 2006]	[Giri, C. et al 2005]	Proposed	[Jelodar, M. S. et al, 2006]	[Giri, C. et al 2005]	Proposed
s298	14	11.51%	11.81%	16.30%	7.65%	13.07%	15.02%
s1423	74	17.01%	18.92%	24.19%	9.74%	11.39%	15.46%
s5378	179	12.41%	13.53%	25.66%	6.73%	13.53%	18.34%
s9234	211	10.41%	11.34%	29.19%	7.66%	8.19%	20.40%
s13207	638	4.02%	4.25%	27.34%	3.12%	3.34%	20.02%
s15850	534	5.15%	5.83%	26.84%	3.58%	4.03%	19.06%
s35932	1728	2.87%	3.14%	42.95%	2.33%	2.69%	27.13%
s38417	1636	1.76%	2.41%	18.44%	1.04%	1.03%	10.79%
s38584	1426	2.58%	2.98%	24.14%	1.46%	1.55%	14.68%

Table 3. Comparison using random-filled test vectors

Circuits	No. of scan cells	Total Transition Reduction Rate					
		MT-fill & Compaction high			MT-fill & No-Compaction		
		[Jelodar, M. S. et al, 2006]	[Giri, C. et al 2005]	Proposed	[Jelodar, M. S. et al, 2006]	[Giri, C. et al 2005]	Proposed
s298	14	17.80%	16.98%	26.78%	9.42%	10.57%	19.22%
s1423	74	16.18%	19.16%	19.22%	27.28%	28.58%	41.59%
s5378	179	11.35%	19.61%	25.20%	20.75%	18.11%	41.10%
s9234	211	4.63%	9.43%	21.01%	10.15%	13.81%	31.48%
s13207	638	2.60%	3.78%	19.79%	6.38%	7.86%	48.67%
s15850	534	2.27%	4.81%	17.52%	8.53%	10.65%	42.41%
s35932	1728	0.22%	6.00%	26.72%	3.47%	29.43%	82.50%
s38417	1636	8.79%	15.67%	38.86%	21.78%	29.82%	84.19%
s38584	1426	4.40%	4.30%	29.07%	2.36%	6.23%	51.55%

Table 4. Comparison using minimum transition-filled test vectors

Tables 3 and 4 include the comparison of the proposed method with previous works [Jelodar, M. S. et al, 2006; Giri, C. et al 2005] using R-filled and MT-filled test vectors, respectively, in terms of the transition reduction rates during scan testing. As can be seen in Table 3 and 4, the proposed method gave 14% to 42% power reduction for R-filled test vectors and 19% to 84% power reduction for MT-filled test vectors. The maintenance of the high reduction rates for the circuits that have a large number of scan-cells demonstrates that the proposed method can efficiently find an optimized scan-cell order regardless of circuit size. It shows, too, that power reduction rates obtained by the proposed method are superior to those of the previous works in all cases.

4. ABIST triplet calculation using ACO heuristic

In arithmetic built-in self test scheme [Gupta, S. et al, 1999; Chiusano, S. et al, 2000; Manich, S. et al 2007], the accumulator with an n-bit adder is used to generate a sequence of binary patterns by continuously accumulating a constant as shown in Figure 4-1. First, the initial vector is loaded into the accumulator register, and new test patterns are generated as a result of the iterative addition of the incremental value to the initial vector. Consecutive test patterns are described by the following equation: $T_0 = S_j$, $T_i = T_{i-1} + I_j$, $(i = 1, 2, \ldots, L_j)$, where S_j is the j-th initial vector, I_j is the increment value, T_i is the test pattern by j-th initial vector at the i-th cycle, and L_j is the total number of cycles. The combination of values (S_j, I_j, L_j), called as a triplet, will generate $L_j + 1$ test patterns. If n triplets are used to achieve target fault coverage, then random patterns will be applied to the CUT (circuit under test). Without a loss of generality, the number of the triplets, n, should be decreased without any loss of target fault coverage to reduce the test application time.

The proposed methodology finds an optimal triplet by selecting the best solution in terms of fault coverage among the solutions of the ant agents generated by the ACO heuristic and by a local search algorithm. Once ants have completed their solution construction, the solutions are taken to their local optimum by the application of a local search routine. Then pheromones are updated on the arcs of the locally optimized solutions. The local search procedure to send local solutions into the regions of the global ants is performed. The local search starts by generating a new triplet by cross-mutating two solutions that have been randomly selected from the global ants. Then the fault coverage of the random test patterns generated by the new triplet is calculated by fault simulation. If the fault coverage of the new triplet is higher than the minimum fault coverage of the global ant set, then the new triplet is sent to the region of the global ants, and the ant of which the fault coverage was the minimum is dropped from the global ant set. This process is repeated until a predefined number of successive iterations with no improvement in fitness values have been reached. Elitist ant system was used for the best ant selection.

ACO based heuristic and local search method were implemented by C language, and Hope fault simulator [Lee, H. K. & Ha, D. S., 1991] was used for the fault simulation of the test patterns generated by each ant agent. Experiments were performed on both largest ISCAS 85 and ISCAS 89 benchmark circuits in terms of the fault coverage, the total test length, and the number of triplets. In most of the benchmark circuits, the proposed scheme showed the highest fault coverage, fewest triplets, and shortest test lengths. Since the memory and test channel bandwidth requirements of ATE directly depend on the number of triplets, even though the proposed scheme requires slightly longer test time in some benchmark circuits, the proposed scheme could reduce the test cost significantly. On average, the number of triplets of the proposed scheme was smaller than the previous schemes by about 0.8~63.0% for all the benchmark circuits. Reduced number of triplets can decrease the memory requirements of external ATE so that the proposed methodology can guarantee a considerable reduction of test costs. In addition, the proposed methodology reduced the average test length considerably compared to two previous schemes, respectively. The proposed scheme, therefore, can shorten the test application times significantly.

4.1 Proposed triplet calculation methodology for ABIST

The proposed methodology finds an optimal triplet by selecting the best solution in terms of fault coverage among the solutions of the ant agents generated by the ACO heuristic and by a local search algorithm. Once ants have completed their solution construction, the solutions are taken to their local optimum by the application of a local search routine. Then pheromones are updated on the arcs of the locally optimized solutions. In case of triplet calculation application, fault coverage is not available for heuristic information since new fault simulation is required for each generated ant so that the number of fault simulation increases impractically. Therefore, in the proposed methodology, instead of using heuristic information, a new local search method is applied to prevent local minimum problem.

Procedural steps of the proposed scheme are summarized Fig. 7. First, an initial solution is created, and the values of pheromones and other variables are initialized. The initial solution consists of an initial vector, increment data, and test length, and is used as a seed to generate ant agents in the next processes. First, an initial vector, $S_j = (s_1, s_2, s_3, \ldots, s_n)$, where n is the total number of primary inputs of a CUT, is randomly generated. If the initial value is odd, then S_j is used for the increment data, I_j. If the initial value is even, $S_j + 1$ is used for I_j to ensure the generation of the maximum number of random test patterns. Random test patterns are generated by iteratively accumulating the initial vector, S_j, with the increment data, I_j, and are fault simulated until a predefined number of successive test patterns with no improvement in fault coverage have been reached. Then the final number of random test patterns will be the value for L_j.

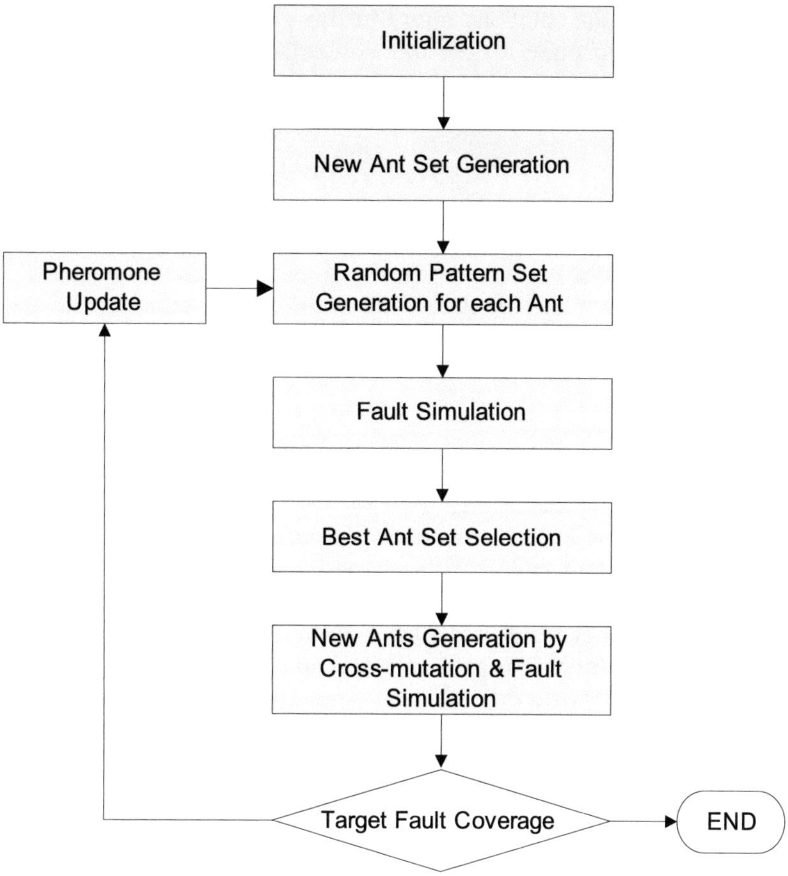

Fig. 7. Proposed Triplet Calculation Flow

New ants are created according to the fitness function, and then fault simulation is performed for random test patterns generated by each ant to achieve its fault coverage. The purpose of Step 2 is to create N new global ants using a Roulette wheel selection scheme by the following fitness function,

$$p_i(k) = \tau_i(k) / \sum_{k=1}^{N} \tau_i(k), \qquad (1)$$

where $1 \le i \le n$, $\tau_i(k)$ is the pheromone value in the i-th primary input of ant k. $p_i(k)$ denotes the probability that the k-th ant lets the i-th primary input of CUT have a logic value of 1.

After best ant set is selected, new ant agents are generated by cross-mutating randomly selected ants from the best ant set. Then the fault coverage of the random test patterns generated by the new ant is calculated by fault simulation. If the fault coverage of the new ant is higher than the minimum fault coverage of the best ant set, then the new ant is sent to the region of the best ants, and the ant of which the fault coverage was the minimum is dropped from the best ant set. If the fault coverage of the ant set meets the target fault coverage, the process stops. Otherwise, the trails of the best solution found in the present cycle are reinforced and the process repeats. At the end of every local search cycle, the pheromone trails laid on the solutions found in this cycle are reinforced to facilitate the search around the specified point for the best solutions. The pheromone value in the i-th primary input of an ant k is calculated by the following equation,

$$\tau_i(k) = \tau_i(k) + \sum_{k}^{N} \Delta\tau_i(k), \tag{2}$$

where $\Delta\tau_j(k) = 1/FC_k$. FC_k means the fault coverage of an ant k. For this process, Elitist ant system has been used. In our previous work [Kang, S. et al, 2008], the normal ant system was used for the pheromone update. According to the experimental results, with the new ant system, the proposed system could considerably improve the memory requirement and test application time reduction, which will be discussed in the following sub-section.

4.2 Experimental results

The ACO based heuristic and GA-based local search method were implemented by C language, and Hope fault simulator was used for the fault simulation of the test patterns generated by each ant agent. Experiments were performed on both ISCAS 85 and ISCAS 89 benchmark circuits. In case of ISCAS 89 benchmark circuits, scanned versions have been used. Table 5 shows the comparison between the proposed scheme and other arithmetic BIST schemes [Chiusano, S. et al, 2000; Manich, S. et al, 2007; Kang, S. et al, 2008] in terms of fault coverage (FC), the number of triplets (M), and total test length (L). In case of [Kang, S. et al, 2008] and the proposed method, the same test patterns were used so that the fault coverage results of the two schemes were the same. In most of the benchmark, the proposed scheme showed the highest fault coverage, fewest triplets, and shortest test lengths. On

Circuit	[Chiusano, S. et al 2000]			[Manich, S. et al, 2007]			[Kang, S. et al 2008]			Proposed		
	FC	M	L	FC	M	L	FC	M	L	FC	M	L
c432	99.0	2	243	99.2	2	**111**	**100**	**1**	194	**100**	2	102
c499	98.8	2	369	**100.0**	2	361	**100.0**	**1**	**319**	**100.0**	2	**323**
c880	**100.0**	**2**	2104	**100.0**	**2**	1112	**100.0**	**2**	504	**100.0**	**2**	**472**
c1355	99.4	2	1151	**100.0**	2	1409	**100.0**	**1**	827	**100.0**	**1**	**801**
c1908	99.6	**2**	3773	99.9	**2**	3198	**100.0**	**2**	1819	**100.0**	**2**	**1724**
c2670	95.6	66	10179	97.6	33	2016	**100.0**	28	**1474**	**100.0**	**25**	1483
c3540	96.0	2	3467	97.1	2	2167	**99.8**	**2**	1696	**99.8**	**2**	**1521**
c5315	98.8	2	1324	99.9	2	1453	**100.0**	**1**	925	**100.0**	**1**	**824**
c6288	99.6	2	56	99.7	2	66	**100.0**	**1**	48	**100.0**	**1**	**43**
c7552	96.0	128	4000	**98.9**	**20**	2918	98.7	**20**	2748	98.7	**20**	**2654**
s1196	**100.0**	**8**	10000	**100.0**	**8**	2086	99.0	8	**1731**	99.0	**7**	1821
s1238	94.7	8	7256	98.9	8	4977	**99.0**	**6**	2622	**99.0**	**6**	**2211**
s1423	99.0	**6**	3100	99.5	**6**	**630**	**100.0**	**6**	921	**100.0**	6	879
s5378	**99.0**	14	5000	98.9	14	2078	**99.0**	**3**	3568	**99.0**	5	**2021**
s9234	NA	NA	NA	91.4	73	14803	**93.5**	**5**	**5826**	**93.5**	6	6712
s13207	NA	NA	NA	97.2	42	14476	**98.5**	**9**	8248	**98.5**	**9**	**8123**
s15850	NA	NA	NA	96.7	118	14902	**96.6**	**8**	5239	**96.6**	**8**	**5039**
s38417	NA	NA	NA	99.5	224	10665	**99.5**	87	22021	**99.5**	**86**	**22010**
s38584	NA	NA	NA	95.9	71	8449	**97.4**	43	**4228**	**97.4**	**41**	4321

Table 5. Comparison of the proposed methodology with other arithmetic BIST schemes

average, the number of triplets of the proposed scheme was smaller than the previous schemes by about 0.8% ~ 63.0%. Fewer triplets entail reduced memory requirements and IO channel bandwidth of the external ATE so that the proposed methodology can guarantee a considerable reduction of test costs. In addition, the proposed methodology reduced the average test length by about 2.0% ~ 28.2%. The test length determines the total test time so that the proposed scheme can shorten the test application times significantly in arithmetic BIST based SoC testing.

5. Concluding remarks

In this chapter, three SoC test issues such as the low power test scheduling, the low power scan cell ordering, and the seed calculation for arithmetic BIST, are considered for ACO applications. Unique techniques and problem transformation to apply ACO meta-heuristic to each test issue are described and the experimental results are provided. According to the experimental results, ACO meta-heuristic based test methodologies for SoC test scheduling, scan cell ordering and test seed calculation could improve test efficiency and reduce the test cost significantly compared to the previous methodologies.

6. References

Ahn, J.-H. & Kang, S. (2006). Test Scheduling of NoC-based SoCs Using Multiple Test Clocks, *ETRI Journal*, vol. 28, no. 4, Aug. pp. 475-485.

Ahn, J.-H & Kang, S. (2008). NoC-Based SoC Test Scheduling Using Ant Colony Optimization, *ETRI Journal*, vol. 30, no. 1, pp. 129-140.

Chiusano, S.; Prinetto, P. & Wunderlich, H. J. (2000). Non-intrusive BIST for system-on-a-chip, *Proc. of International Test Conference*, pp. 644-651.

Cota, E.; Carro, L. Wagner, F. & Lubaszewski, M. (2003). Power-Aware NoC Reuse on the Testing of Core-Based Systems, *Proc. of International Test Conference*, vol. 1, pp. 612-621.

Giri, C.; Kumar, B.N. & Chattopadhyay, S. (2005). Scan flip-flop ordering with delay and power minimization during testing, *Proc. of IEEE Indicon 2005 Conference*, pp. 467-471.

Dorigo, M.; Caro, G. (1999). Ant colony optimization: a new meta-heuristic, *Proc. of Evolutionary Computation*, Vol 2, pp. 1470-1477.

Glover, F.; Kochenberger, G. (2003). *Handbook of Metaheuristics*, Kluwer Academic Publishers.

Gupta, S.; Rajski, J. & Tyszer, J. (1996). Arithmetic additive generators of pseudo-exhaustive test patterns, *IEEE Trans. on Computers*, vol. 45, no. 8, pp. 939-949.

Huang, Y.; Cheng, W.-T. Tsai, C.-C. Mukherjee, N. Samman, O. Zaidan, Y. & Reddy, S.M. (2001). Resource Allocation and Test Scheduling for Concurrent Test of Core-Based SOC Design, *Proc. of Asian Test Symposium*, pp. 265-270.

Huang, Y.; Reddy, S.M. Cheng, W.-T. Reuter, P. Mukherjee, N. Tsai, C.-C. Samman, O. & Zaidan, Y. (2002) Optimal Core Wrapper Width Selection and SOC Test Scheduling Based on 3-D Bin Packing Algorithm, *Proc. of International Test Conference*, pp. 74-82.

Iyengar, V; Chakrabarty, K. & Marinissen, E.J. (2002). On Using Rectangle Packing for SOC Wrapper/TAM Co-Optimization, *Proc. of VLSI Test Symposium*, pp. 253-258.

Jelodar, M.S.; Mizanian, K. (2006). Power aware scan-based testing using genetic algorithm, *Proc. of IEEE CCECE/CCGEI*, pp. 1905-1908.

Kang, S.; Kim, H. -S. & Kim, H. (2008). Ant Colony Based Efficient Triplet Calculation Methodology for Arithmetic Built-in Self Test, *ELEX*, Vol. 5, No. 20, pp. 877-881.

Lee, H. K. & Ha, D. S. (1991). An Efficient Forward Fault Simulation Algorithm Based on the Parallel Pattern Single Fault Propagation, *Proc of International Test Conference*, pp. 946-955.

Liu, C.; Veeraraghavan, K. & Iyengar, V. (2005). Thermal-Aware Test Scheduling and Hot Spot Temperature Minimization for Core-Based Systems. *Proc. of the 20th IEEE International Symposium on Defect and Fault-Tolerance in VLSI Systems*, pp. 552-560.

Manich, S.; Garcia-Deiros, L. & Figueras, J. (2007). Minimizing test time in arithmetic test-pattern generators with constrained memory resources, *IEEE Trans. On Computer-Aided Design of Integrated Circuits and Systems*, Vol. 26, No. 11, pp. 2046-2058.

Stutzle, T.; Hoos, H. (2000). MAX-MIN Ant System, *Future Generation Computer Systems*, Vol. 16, No. 8, pp. 889-914.

19

Ant Colony Optimization for Multiobjective Buffers Sizing Problems

Hicham Chehade, Lionel Amodeo and Farouk Yalaoui
Université de Technologie de Troyes, Institut Charles Delaunay, Laboratoire d'Optimisation des Systèmes Industriels
France

1. Introduction

The optimization of production lines relies on many parameters such as the equipment selection, the buffers sizing, the line balancing or others. This is done in order to get high performed lines with the lowest costs so that line manufacturers remain competitive in the markets.

In this work, we are interested in the buffers sizing problem on assembly lines (figure 1). It is widely studied in the literature. However, few works are focused on solving multiobjective buffers sizing problems. Indeed, despite the large number of papers in the literature dealing with the buffers sizing problem, one can feel the lack in the works dealing with the multiobjective problems. In fact, we may notice that almost the total number of papers dealing with the buffers sizing problem takes in consideration one criterion at once (Altiparmak et al., 2002), (D'Souza & Khator, 1997), (Hamada et al., 2006). Some other works take in consideration more than one criterion but they use weighted sums in the fitness function (Abdul-Kader, 2006), (Dolgui et al., 2002). In 2007 and later in 2009, Chehade et al. have applied the multiobjective optimization using multiobjective ant colony optimization algorithms (Chehade et al., 2007), (Chehade et al., 2009).

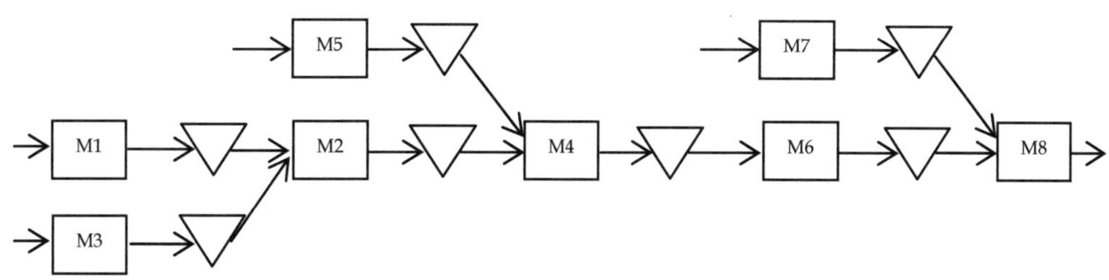

Fig. 1. An example of an assembly line with 8 machines (Mi) and 7 intermediate buffers

The lack of studies dealing with multiobjective buffers sizing problems is probably due to the complexity of the problem (Harris & Powell, 1999) and the difficulty to develop the suitable tool to optimize it efficiently. However, dealing with a single objective may lead to sidestep the problem (Collette & Siarry, 2002). Moreover, a multiobjective optimization allows some freedom degrees that do not appear in the single objective optimization. Based on that, we have decided to continue studying this problem with its multiobjective type. The performances evaluations of the different configurations are done using the ARENA simulation software. Indeed, analytical methods seem to be inappropriate to solve hard and complex computational problems (Han & Park, 2002).

In this work, and similarly to our previous works, the problem consists of sizing the buffers of different stations in an assembly line taking in consideration that the size of each buffer is bounded by a lower and an upper value. Two objectives are taken in consideration: the maximization of the throughput rate and the minimization of the buffers total size. Our contribution in this work is to present two new multiobjective resolution methods for the studied problem. These two methods are first a multiobjective ant colony algorithm with a guided local search and then a Lorenz multiobjective ant colony algorithm.

In the literature and among the methods applied to solve the buffers sizing problems, the most efficient ones are metaheuristics for their ability to solve complex operations research problems. Indeed, the stochastic nature of these methods allows affording the combinatorial explosion in the number of possible solutions (Dréo et al., 2003). Genetic algorithms belong for example to metaheuristics which can be applied to solve buffers sizing problems (Dolgui et al., 2002), (Hamada et al., 2006). Simulated Annealing is another method applied in many works (Spinellis et al., 2000), (Papadopoulos & Vidalis, 2001). The literature presents also other methods such as neural networks (Altiparmak et al., 2002) or Tabu search (Lutz et al., 1998).

In this work, the different resolution methods are therefore based on ant colony optimization. The first one, initially presented in a previous work (Chehade et al., 2009) is a multiobjective ant colony optimization algorithm (MOACS). Ant colony optimization algorithms have been, until a recent period, applied on single objective problems. Initially developed to solve the travelling salesman problem (Dorigo & Gambardella, 1997), they have been later applied efficiently in different other fields such as scheduling or line balancing. Recently, we have noticed the development of the first algorithms based on ant colony optimization to solve multiobjective optimization problems (Benlian & Zhiquan, 2007), (Pellegrini et al., 2007).

Afterthat, a guided local search is coupled to the MOACS algorithm (MOACS-GLS) in order to enhance the performances of the latter. Indeed, the guided local search is used to avoid the occurrence of local optimum solutions. Voudouris and Tsang (Voudouris & Tsang, 1996) were the first to introduce a general optimization technique suitable for a wide range of combinatorial optimization problems which is the guided local search. This metaheuristic is used to guide the search out of a local optimum and it was successfully applied to many practical problems such as frequency applications (Voudouris & Tsang, 1996), vehicle routing problems (Kilby et al., 1999) and the quadratic assignment problem (Hani et al., 2007).

The last algorithm is a multiobjective ant colony algorithm but using the Lorenz dominance (L-MOACS). The Lorenz dominance relationship, as shown below, allows retaining the solutions which better fit the objectives of the problem. This is done by providing a better domination area by rejecting the solutions founded on the extreme sides of the Pareto front. The Lorenz dominance relationship also called equitable dominance relationship was defined in 1999 (Kostreva & Ogryczak, 1999) and extended in 2004 (Kostreva et al., 2004). This relationship, which is considered as equitable and rational, has been applied efficiently in many works (Perny et al., 2004), (Dugardin et al., 2009a), (Dugardin et al., 2009b).

The remainder of this work is organized as follows. The problem description is in section 2. Section 3 presents the resolution methods. Computational experiments are presented in section 4 and we finish by a conclusion and perspectives in section 5.

2. Problem description

In this work, we are interested in sizing the buffers of assembly lines. The structures of the lines are formed by unreliable machines with exponential distribution and finite buffers. The lines have N machines and N-1 intermediate buffers taking in consideration that each two workstations are separated by one buffer. The goal of our study is therefore to identify the best size for each intermediate buffer taking in consideration the characteristics of the machines. We assume here that the size of each buffer is bounded by a lower (l) and an upper value (u).

The objectives of this problem are as follows. For the first objective, we aim to maximize the throughput rate of the lines. As for the second objective, we look at minimizing the total size of the buffers. Therefore, the optimal configurations of the multiobjective problem are the lines configurations that give the highest throughput rates with the lowest buffers sizes.

The mathematical formulation of this multiobjective buffers sizing problem can be stated as follows. The objective function Z to be optimized (see (1)) depends on the two studied objectives: the maximization of the throughput rate E (see (2)) and the minimization of the total size of the buffers in the line (see (3)). The decision variable is Y_{ij} (size i of buffer j).

$$Z = (O1, O2) \tag{1}$$

$$O1 : Maximize(E) \tag{2}$$

$$O2 : Minimize(\sum_{j=1}^{N-1} \sum_{i=1}^{B} Y_{ij}.b_{ij}) \tag{3}$$

Subject to:

$$E = f(Y_{ij}) \tag{4}$$

$$E_{lj}^{B} \leq E_{ij}^{B} \leq E_{uj}^{B}; \forall i = 1,...B; \forall j = 1,...,N-1 \tag{5}$$

$$\sum_{j=1}^{N-1} \sum_{i=1}^{B} Y_{ij}.b_{ij} \leq S_{\max} \tag{6}$$

$$\sum_{i=1}^{B} Y_{ij} = 1; \forall j = 1,...,N-1 \tag{7}$$

$$Y_{ij} \in \{0,1\}; \forall i = 1,...,B; \forall j = 1,...,N-1 \tag{8}$$

Notation:

N: the number of machines in the line.

N-1: the number of intermediate buffers in the line.
B: the number of the possible sizes of a buffer.
S_{max}: the total available space for the buffers of the line.
Y_{ij}: a binary variable equals 1 if buffer size *i* is assigned to buffer *j* and 0 otherwise.
b_{ij}: the size *i* of buffer *j*.
E: the throughput rate of the line
E_{ij}^{B} : the throughput rate of a buffer *j* while having a size *i*.
E_{lj}^{B} : the lower bound for the throughput rate of a buffer *j*.
E_{uj}^{B} : the upper bound for the throughput rate of a buffer *j*.

Constraint (4) indicates that the throughput rate *E* of the line is a function of the sizes of the buffers. Constraint (5) shows that the size of each buffer is bounded by a lower (*l*) and an upper value (*u*). Constraint (6) means that the total space of the buffers must not exceed the total available space for the buffers of the line. Constraint (7) imposes that a unique size must be assigned to each buffer. Constraint (8) defines the binary decision variables.
For the performances evaluations of the different tested configurations, we have used the discrete event simulation through the ARENA simulation software.

3. Resolution methods

In this section, we discuss the resolution methods that we have developed for our multiobjective problem. First, we present the multiobjective ant colony optimization algorithm (MOACS) and then we present the Lorenz dominance relationship. Finally, we present the overall algorithm that we call L-MOACS (Lorenz Multiobjective Ant Colony Algorithm).

3.1 Multiobjective Ant Colony Algorithm

In this section, we present the multiobjective ant colony system algorithm (MOACS) that we have applied in this work. It is based on the general structure of a classical ant colony optimization algorithm by being based on four main steps: the solutions encoding, the ants tours construction, the local pheromone updates and the global pheromone updates. The only difference is related to the number of the pheromone matrices. In fact, knowing that the multi objective optimization takes in consideration different criterion simultaneously, we consider that the total number of pheromone matrices should be equal to the number of objectives to be optimized. Therefore, we have in this work two pheromone matrices.

Solutions encoding

This encoding is presented in figure 2 where we consider that we have *N* stations and *N*-1 intermediate buffers. A lower (l_j) and an upper (u_j) value bound the capacity of each buffer *j*.

Buffer *1*	l_1	$l_1 + 1$	…	$u_1 - 1$	u_1
Buffer *2*	l_2	$l_2 + 1$	…	$u_2 - 1$	u_2
⋮			⋮		
Buffer *N-1*	l_n	$l_n + 1$	…	$u_n - 1$	u_n

Fig. 2. Solutions encoding

Tours construction

First, each ant is deposited randomly on a starting point which represents the size that has to be assigned to the first buffer. After that, an ant k chooses to move from a point r to another point s based on (9).

$$s = \begin{cases} \arg\max_{u \in J_k(r)} \left\{ \left[\sum_{o=1}^{O} w_o.\tau_{r,u}^{o} \right]^{\alpha} .\eta_{r,u}^{\beta} \right\} & if\ q \leq q_0 \\ S^{*} & otherwise \end{cases} \tag{9}$$

Where:
O : the number of the considered objectives.
$\tau_{r,s}^{o}$: the quantity of pheromone between the points r and s based on objective o.
w_o : the coefficient of importance granted to each objective (we consider that $w_1 = w_2 = 0.5$).
q : is a random number generated between 0 and 1.
q_0 : is a parameter ($0 \leq q_0 \leq 1$) which determines the relative importance of exploitation against exploration.
S^* : is a random variable chosen based on a probability given by (10).
$\eta_{r,s}$: is a static value used as a heuristic of innate desirability to choose s starting from r and is also called the ant visibility to choose a point starting from another point.
α and β are used to determine the relative importance of pheromones versus the visibility.
$J_k(r)$: is the set of points not yet visited by ant k.

$$S^{*} = \begin{cases} \dfrac{\left[\sum_{o=1}^{O} w_o \tau_{r,s}^{o}\right]^{\alpha} \left[\eta_{r,s}\right]^{\beta}}{\sum_{u \in J_k(r)} \left[\sum_{o=1}^{O} w_o \tau_{r,u}^{o}\right]^{\alpha} \left[\eta_{r,u}\right]^{\beta}} & if\ s \in J_k(r) \\ 0 & otherwise \end{cases} \tag{10}$$

Local pheromone updates

The local pheromone update is applied once all ants have finished their tours. It is computed based on (11) where τ_0 is the initial quantity of pheromone.

$$\tau_{r,s}^{o} = (1-\rho).\tau_{r,s}^{o} + \rho.\tau_0 \tag{11}$$

Global pheromone updates

The global pheromone update is realized according to (12) while being based on the non dominated solutions obtained at each generation.

$$\tau_{r,s}^{o} = (1-\rho).\tau_{r,s}^{o} + \rho.\Delta\tau_{r,s}^{o} \tag{12}$$

$\Delta\tau_{r,s}^{o}$ consists on supporting the non dominated solutions found so far. It is computed based on (13) and (14) where C_{gb} and E_{gb} represent, respectively, the lowest total size of buffers and the highest throughput rate found so far by ants.

$$\Delta\tau^1_{r,s} = \begin{cases} (C_{gb})^{-1} & if\ r,s \in non-dominated-solutions \\ 0 & otherwise \end{cases} \tag{13}$$

$$\Delta\tau^2_{r,s} = \begin{cases} E_{gb} & if\ r,s \in non-dominated-solutions \\ 0 & otherwise \end{cases} \tag{14}$$

3.2 Guided local search

In order to adapt the guided local search and to couple it with the MOACS algorithm, a local search procedure based on the neighborhood search is first applied. This local search is applied on the first optimal front obtained after the ants tours and before discarding the non feasible solutions. Afterthat, we will now be able to check if the space constraint is satisfied or not.

In fact, if the total space of the buffers according to a given solution in the optimal front is higher than the allowed one (S_{max}), then we try to minimize it by decreasing the capacity of each buffer by one. This is done on all the buffers. Note that as we are limited by a lower and an upper bound for buffers, we are not able, all the times, to apply this procedure. For example, we may not be able to decrease the size of a given buffer (if its size is equal to the lower value l).

In the other side, if the total covered space is smaller than the allowed one, we try to look for a neighborhood solution which can decrease the total size of the buffers and increase the throughput rate. We increase then at each time the size of the buffers by one.

At the end of the local search, we take in consideration the non dominated solutions according to the Pareto dominance rule. As using only the local search may lead to local optimum cases and not necessarily to global ones, we have seen that the best way to overcome this lack is by applying the guided local search metaheuristic as explained below.

The purpose of making a local search procedure getting out of a local optimum is satisfied by adapting the guided local search metaheuristic to our problem. That is based on using augmented objective functions by adding penalties to the initial objective functions. Therefore, we associate features to the objective functions taking in consideration that those features are in the local optimum. The features are selected based on the type of the problem to be optimized. However, each feature f_i must have the following components:

- An indicator function $I_i(s)$ indicating whether the feature is present in the current solution s ($I_i(s) = 1$) or not ($I_i(s) = 0$).
- A cost function $c_i(s)$ giving the cost of having f_i in s.
- A penalty factor p_i (initially set to 0) to penalize the occurrence of f_i in local optimum.

We are using here one feature (f_1) in our case as we have one element which is the buffers sizing. Based on the local search procedure, the indicator function I_1 of feature f_1 is equal to 1 if we are able to modify the size of a given buffer and 0 otherwise (if the size of the buffer is equal to the lower l or the upper u value). The occurrence of a local optimum allows the manipulation of the augmented cost function by applying a penalty modification procedure. The penalty parameters p_i are incremented by one for all features f_1 that maximize an expression called utility as shown in (15) where $c_1(s)$ is computed according to (16) and $c_2(s)$ according to (17).

$$util(s, f_1) = I_1(s).c_1(s) / (1 + p_1) \tag{15}$$

$$c_1(s) = \sum_{j=1}^{N-1} \sum_{i=1}^{B} Y_{ij}.b_{ij} \tag{16}$$

$$c_2(s) = 1 / E \tag{17}$$

The augmented cost function is present in (18) for the space objective and in equation (19) for the throughput rate objective. It is used to make the local optimum more costly than other solutions in the surrounding search space in order to avoid it.

$$h_1(s) = c_1(s) + \lambda_1.I_1(s).p_1 \tag{18}$$

$$h_2(s) = c_2(s) + \lambda_2.I_1(s).p_1 \tag{19}$$

Where λ is a parameter for controlling the constraints strength with respect to the solution objective. λ_1 is computed based on the total space of the buffers of the line and the different possibilities of the sizes of the buffers as shown in (20) where B is the number of possible sizes for each buffer. λ_2 is computed as illustrated in (21).

$$\lambda_1 = (\sum_{j=1}^{N-1} \sum_{i=1}^{B} Y_{ij}.b_{ij}) / (2.B) \tag{20}$$

$$\lambda_2 = (1 / E) / (2.B) \tag{21}$$

To resume the adaptation of the guided local search metaheuristic to our problem, starting from the set of the non dominated solutions obtained by the MOACS algorithm, a local search procedure is applied to find local minima with respect to the augmented cost function. If those minima have objective functions (not augmented) better (smaller for the space objective and greater for the throughput objective) than the best objective functions ever found, they are saved as non dominated solutions. Finally, the configurations having the maximum utilities would have their penalties increased. The process is repeated until a stopping criterion. At this step, we are able to identify the feasible non dominated solutions.

3.3 Multiobjective Ant Colony algorithm with a Guided Local Search

The structure of the multiobjective ant colony algorithm with the guided local search (MOACS-GLS) is presented by algorithm 1.

Algorithm 1: MOACS-GLS algorithm

Step 1: Parameters initialization
Step 2: For the k ants

> *Compute the desirability factors associated with each objective, so as to select the successive nodes according to the visibility factor and the pheromone trails*
> *Apply a local update of the pheromone trails*
> *Apply the guided local search procedures*
> *Apply a global update of the pheromone trails while being based on the non dominated solutions*

End For

Step 3: Iterate from Step 2 until a stopping criterion

3.4 The Lorenz dominance relationship

The Lorenz dominance relationship restricts the Lorenz searching space to a subset of the Pareto searching space. Thus, the Lorenz dominance increases the speed of the algorithm by focusing on the promising solution set 0. It provides then a larger domination area to each solution which implies the rejection of the solutions that are at the furthest end of a Pareto front.

Indeed, let us take in consideration, for example, two criterion f_1 and f_2 to be minimized. Figure 2 describes the Pareto dominance area of a solution X. With the Pareto dominance, the solution X dominates any other solution X′ that has either f_1(X′) or f_2(X′) higher than f_1(X) or f_2(X). However, for the same point X, the Lorenz dominance area is shown in figure 3. It is clear that the Lorenz dominance area is larger than the Pareto dominance area.

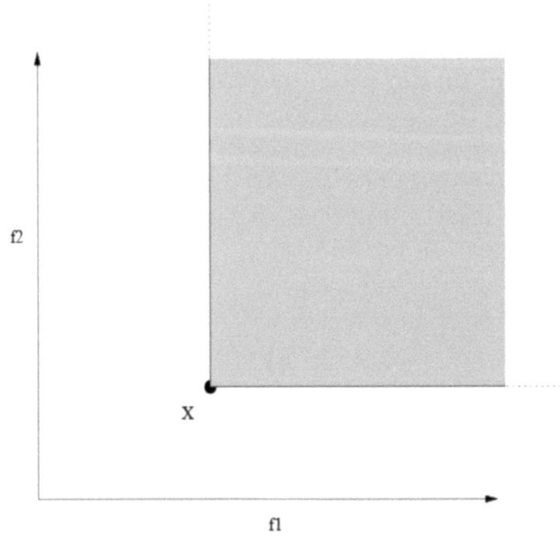

Fig. 2. Pareto dominance area (Dugardin et al. 2009a)

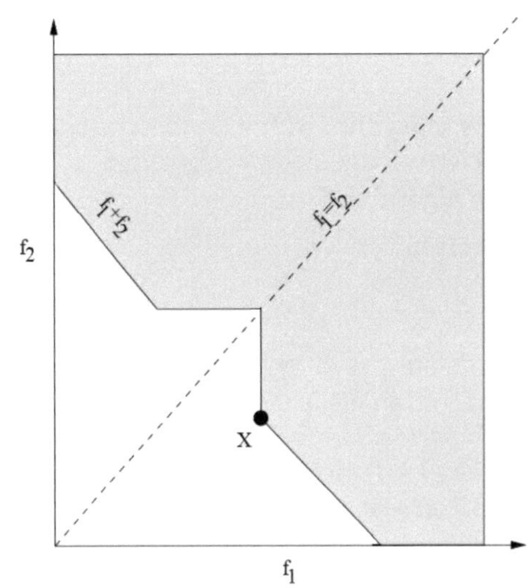

Fig. 3. Lorenz dominance area (Dugardin et al. 2009a)

Using the Lorenz dominance, denoted by $\prec_L$, we can consider that X is Lorenz-optimal if, and only if, no solution X′ exists so that $f(X') \prec_L f(X)$. Given a vector $y(y_1, y_2)$ with two components, the corresponding Lorenz generalized vector is $y_L(\max(y_1, y_2), y_1+y_2)$. For more details about the Lorenz dominance relationship and its different characteristics and principles, reader is referred to the work of Dugardin et al. (Dugardin et al., 2009a) where a deep explanation about the Lorenz dominance is presented.

3.5 Lorenz Multiobjective Ant Colony algorithm

As mentioned before, the Lorenz Multiobjective Ant Colony algorithm (L-MOACS) is based on a multiobjective ant colony system algorithm using the Lorenz dominance relationship. Therefore, once all ants have constructed their tours and that local pheromone updates are applied, we identify the non dominated solutions based on the Lorenz dominance. The set of the Lorenz non dominated solutions, on which we should be based to globally update the pheromone matrices, constitute the optimal front of the problem. The overall L-MOACS algorithm is shown in algorithm 2.

Algorithm 2: L-MOACS algorithm

Step 1: Initialization of parameters
Step 2: For all ants:

- *Assign sizes to buffers*
- *Local pheromone updates*
- *Identification of the non dominated solutions based on the Lorenz dominance*
- *Global pheromone updates*

Step 3: Return to step 2 until a stopping criterion is satisfied

3.6 Comparison criteria

In this section, we describe the methods used to compare two optimal fronts (*F1* and *F2*) obtained by the different algorithms (MOACS, MOACS-GLS and L-MOACS) in order to get an idea and to evaluate the performances of the solutions of each algorithm. Three comparison criteria are used: the number of solutions N_i in an optimal front i, the distance proposed by Riise μ (Riise, 2002), the Zitlzler measure C_i (Zitzler & Thiele, 1999).
The distance of Riise, μ, is computed as the sum of the distances d_x between a solution x belonging to front *F1* and its orthogonal projection on front *F2* ($\mu = \sum_{x=1}^{N} d_x$). μ is negative if *F1* is under *F2* and positive otherwise. As the value of μ depends on the number of solutions N_i in each front, a normalized value ($\mu^* = \mu / N_i$) is generally taken in consideration.
The Zitzler measure C_1 represents the percentage of solutions in *F1* dominated by at least one solution in *F2*. Taking in consideration that the measure is not symmetric, it is advised to compute C_2 as well. In conclusion, a front *F1* is better than another front *F2* if C_1 is smaller than C_2.

4. Computational experiments

Computational experiments are realized on assembly lines with finite buffers and where the machines time between failures, the times to repair and the processing times are exponentially distributed.

In order to compare the three algorithms, MOACS, MOACS-GLS and L-MOACS, several tests have been first realized so that we can set efficiently the different parameters of the algorithms. Final values are determined as a compromise between the quality of the final solutions and the convergence time needed. Those final values are as follows: $k = 20$, $\rho = 0.7$, $q_0 = 0.7$, $a = 0.7$, $\beta = 0.3$, $\tau_0 = 2$. The stopping criterion for the ant colony algorithms is a given number of generations and is fixed at 100. The stopping criterion for the guided local search is a number of iterations which is fixed at 50.
Once the parameters values have been set, we apply the three algorithms on different instances. Two assembly lines are tested. The first is a non balanced assembly line where the machines have different processing times (T_i). This is the first problem P1. The second concerns a balanced assembly line where the different machines have the same processing time (T_i). This is then the second problem P2.
For the input data of the machines characteristics, we have adopted those used by Nahas et al. (Nahas et al., 2006). Those characteristics are the processing times (T_i), the mean times to repair (*MTTR*) and the mean times to failure (*MTTF*). The values of these parameters are presented in tables 1 and 2.

Machine	MTTR	MTTF	T_i
1	450	820	40
2	760	5700	34
3	460	870	39
4	270	830	38
5	270	970	37
6	650	1900	40
7	320	1100	43
8	480	910	39
9	340	1050	41

Table 1. Input data for problem P1 (Nahas et al., 2006)

Machine	MTTR	MTTF	T_i
1	7	20	1
2	7	30	1
3	5	22	1
4	10	22	1
5	9	25	1
6	14	40	1
7	5	23	1
8	8	30	1
9	10	45	1

Table 2. Input data for problem P2 (Nahas et al., 2006)

Each buffer may have a size that is bounded between the lower value (l) which is equal to 1 and the upper value (u) which is equal to 20. Three different assembly line structures are tested for the two problems. Each structure is different from the other one by the number of machines N and thus the number of buffers N-1. N is equal to 3, 7 and 9 for the first (S1), second (S2) and third (S3) structures respectively.

We have realized three comparisons. The first one is between the MOACS-GLS and the MOACS algorithms and is presented in table 3. Table 4 shows the second comparison which is between the L-MOACS and the MOACS algorithms. The last comparison is between the L-MOACS and the MOACS-GLS algorithms and it is presented in table 5.
The results of the generated instances for the comparison between the MOACS-GLS and the MOACS algorithms are compared in table 3. It shows a comparison between the best fronts with the non dominated solutions obtained for each algorithm. N_1 stands for the number of solutions in the optimal front obtained by the MOACS-GLS algorithm and N_2 for the MOACS algorithm. The distance of Riise is presented under the μ^* column. C_1 and C_2 stand for the Zitzler measure. C_1 is a measure for front *F1* of the MOACS-GLS algorithm and C_2 for that of front *F2* of the MOACS algorithm.
The comparisons are done on all of the 6 different tests realized for the two problems. To better explain table 3 for the reader, let us take the first line as an example. It shows a comparison between the two algorithms (MOACS-GLS and MOACS) applied on problem P1 and on an assembly line with 3 machines and 2 buffers (structure S1). The number of non dominated solutions (N_1) in the MOACS-GLS best front is 15 and is equal to that of the MOACS Pareto front. The negative value of the μ^* column (-0.01) shows that *F1* is under *F2*. Columns 6 and 7 show that 6.67% of solutions in the MOACS-GLS best front are dominated by at least one solution in the MOACS front while 13.33% of solutions in the MOACS front are dominated by at least one solution in the MOACS-GLS front. The same logic is followed to read the comparison parameters in the rest of the table.

		N_1	N_2	μ^*	C_1	C_2
P1	S1	15	15	-0.01	6.67	13.33
	S2	16	16	-0.02	6.25	18.75
	S3	17	16	-0.03	5.88	37.50
P2	S1	16	16	-0.04	6.25	43.75
	S2	19	18	-0.05	0.00	44.44
	S3	19	18	-0.06	0.00	50.00
Mean		17	16.5	-0.03	4.175	34.62

Table 3. Comparison between MOACS-GLS (F1) and MOACS (F2) algorithms

Based on all the tested configurations, we may conclude that on the majority of the generated instances, the MOACS-GLS performs more efficiently than the MOACS algorithm. Indeed, we have noticed that as the size of the problem increases, the advantages of the MOACS-GLS algorithm get more obvious. In general, the mean value of the number of non dominated solutions for the MOACS-GLS is 17 against 16.5 for the MOACS. The mean value of the Riise distances is -0.03 which means that the optimal front of the MOACS-GLS (*F1*) is under that of the MOACS algorithm (*F2*). That means that we are maximizing the throughput rate of the line and at the same time minimizing the total size of the buffers when we apply the MOACS-GLS algorithm compared to the application of the MOACS algorithm. Finally, there is a general mean of 4.175% of solutions in the *F1* fronts that are dominated by at least one solution from the *F2* fronts against 34.62% of the *F2* solutions that are dominated by at least one solution from the *F1* fronts.
Once the first comparison is done, we have realized the second one between the L-MOACS algorithm based on the Lorenz dominance relationship and the MOACS algorithm using the Pareto dominance relationship. Table 4 shows the comparison between fronts *F1* (L-MOACS) and *F2* (MOACS). The same interpretation used to analyze table 3 is applied for table 4 with the three comparison criteria: N_1 and N_2, μ^*, C_1 and C_2.

The first criterion which is the number of non dominated solutions shows that there are less non dominated solutions in the L-MOACS optimal front (N_1) than in the MOACS optimal front (N_2). On all the tested structures, the mean number of solutions with the Lorenz dominance is equal to 13.5 against 16.5 with the Pareto dominance. This is due to the fact that, with the Lorenz dominance, we can get fewer solutions compared to the Pareto dominance. The second criterion (μ^*) shows the clear advantage of the L-MOACS algorithm compared to the MOACS algorithm. The value of μ^* is always negative for all the tested instances which means that the optimal front of the L-MOACS algorithm fits better the two objectives of the problem (maximization of the throughput rate and minimization of the total size of the buffers). The same conclusion may be deduced based on the third criterion when one can notice that the mean percentage of solutions in the L-MOACS front that are dominated by at least one solution in the MOACS front (3.86%) is largely smaller than that of the MOACS front (43.84%).

		N_1	N_2	μ^*	C_1	C_2
P1	S1	13	15	-0.03	7.69	20.00
	S2	12	16	-0.03	8.33	31.25
	S3	13	16	-0.05	0.00	56.25
P2	S1	14	16	-0.04	7.14	50.00
	S2	14	18	-0.07	0.00	44.44
	S3	15	18	-0.08	0.00	61.11
Mean		13.5	16.5	-0.05	3.86	43.84

Table 4. Comparison between L-MOACS (F1) and MOACS (F2) algorithms

The third comparison is between the L-MOACS algorithm and the MOACS-GLS algorithms. Table 4 presents first the number of non dominated solutions N_1 and N_2 in fronts *F1* (for the L-MOACS) and *F2* (for the MOACS-GLS) respectively. As in the comparison between L-MOACS and MOACS, the number of non dominated solutions with the Lorenz dominance relationship is fewer than that with the Pareto dominance relationship. For the two other criteria, we may notice a small advantage for the L-MOACS algorithm compared to the MOACS-GLS algorithm. Indeed, taking in consideration the Riise distance, the two algorithms have the same performances for 2 instances over 6 tested ones. In general, the mean value of μ^* is only equal to -0.01. That small advantage may be confirmed while being based on the Zitzler measure. Here also, for two tested instances the two algorithms have the same performances. For the four other instances, the mean percentage of L-MOACS solutions that are dominated by at least one MOACS-GLS solution (C_1) is equal to 2.67% against 5.63% for C_2.

		N_1	N_2	μ^*	C_1	C_2
P1	S1	13	15	-0.00	0.00	0.00
	S2	12	16	+0.01	8.33	6.25
	S3	13	17	-0.02	7.69	11.76
P2	S1	14	16	-0.00	0.00	0.00
	S2	14	19	-0.01	0.00	0.00
	S3	15	19	-0.03	0.00	15.79
Mean		13.5	17	-0.01	2.67	5.63

Table 5. Comparison between L-MOACS (F1) and MOACS-GLS (F2) algorithms

In conclusion, and taking in consideration the three comparisons between the three applied algorithms, we may deduce that while applying the Pareto dominance relationship, hybrid algorithms perform better than classic ones. That was obvious while comparing the classical multiobjective ant colony algorithm (MOACS) and the hybrid algorithm which is a multiobjective ant colony algorithm with a guided local search (MOACS-GLS). In addition to that, we may notice the advantages of the Lorenz dominance relationship over the Pareto dominance relationship. For the comparison between L-MOACS and MOACS and that between L-MOACS and MOACS-GLS, the Lorenz dominance relationship presents more advantages compared with the Pareto dominance.

5. Conclusion

In this paper, we have studied a multiobjective buffers sizing problem using ant colony optimization. The two objectives of our study are the maximization of the throughput rate and the minimization of the total size of the buffers. To solve the problem, three multiobjective metaheuristics have been developed: a multiobjective ant colony optimization algorithm, a multiobjective ant colony algorithm with a guided local search and a Lorenz multiobjective ant colony optimization algorithm. Computational experiments have been realized on different assembly lines configurations and we have compared our three methods to each others. We have noticed that the L-MOACS performances are better than those of the MOACS and slightly better than those of the MOACS-GLS algorithm. Regarding the perspectives of this work, other methods based on the Pareto or the Lorenz dominance may be tested such as genetic algorithms or particle swarm optimization algorithms. Other hybridization techniques may also be tested in order to see the impact on the achieved solutions. Finally, exact methods may be developed to compare the optimal solutions with those of the applied metaheuristics.

6. References

Abdul-Kader, W. (2006). Capacity improvement of an unreliable production line - an analytical approach. *Computers & Operations Research*, 33, 1695 - 1712.

Altiparmak, A.; Bugak, A. & Dengiz, B. (2002). Optimization of buffer sizes in assembly systems using intelligent techniques. *In Proceedings of the 2002 Winter Simulation Conference*, pp. 1157–1162, December 2002, San Diego, USA.

Benlian, X. & Zhiquan, W. (2007). A multi-objective-ACO-based data association method for bearings-only multi-target tracking. *Communications in Nonlinear Science and Numerical Simulation*, 12, 1360 - 1369.

Chehade, H.; Amodeo, L.; Yalaoui, F. & De Guglielmo, P. (2007). Optimisation multiobjectif appliquée au problème de dimensionnement de buffers. *In Proceedings of the International Workshop on Logistic and Transport*, November 2007, Sousse, Tunisia.

Chehade, H. ; Yalaoui, F.; Amodeo, L. & De Guglielmo, P. (2009). Optimisation multi-objectif pour le problème de dimensionnement de buffers. *Journal of Decision Systems*, 18, 2, 257–287.

Collette, Y. & Siarry, P. (2002). *Optimisation multiobjectif*, Eyrolles, ISBN 2-212-11168-1, Paris.

D'Souza, K. & Khator, S. (1997). System reconfiguration to avoid deadlocks in automated manufacturing systems. *Computers & Industrial Engineering*, 32, 2, 445 - 465.

Dolgui, A.; Eremeev, A.; Kolokolov, A. & Sigaev, V. (2002). A Genetic Algorithm for Allocation of Buffer Storage Capacities in a Production Line with Unreliable Machines. *Journal of Mathematical Modelling and Algorithms*, 1, 89 - 104.

Dréo, J.; Pétrowski, A.; Siarry, P. & Taillard, E. (2003). *Métaheuristiques pour l'optimisation difficile*, Eyrolles, ISBN 2-212-11368-4, Paris.

Dugardin, F.; Yalaoui, F. & Amodeo, L. (2009a). New multi-objective method to solve reentrant hybrid flow shop scheduling problem. *European Journal of Operational Research*, 203, 1, 22 - 31.

Dugardin, F.; Amodeo, L. & Yalaoui, F. (2009b). Multiobjective scheduling of a reentrant hybrid flowshop. *In Proceedings of CIE'39*, pp. 193 - 198, July 2009, Troyes, France.

Hamada, M.; Martz, H.; Berg, E. & Koehler, A. (2006). Optimizing the product-based avaibility of a buffered industrial process. *Reliability Engineering and System Safety*, 91, 1039 - 1048.

Han, M.S. & Park, D.J. (2002). Optimal buffer allocation of serial production lines with quality inspection machines. *Computers & Industrial Engineering*, 42, 75 - 89.

Hani, Y.; Amodeo, L; Yalaoui, F. & Chen, H. (2007). Ant colony optimization for solving an industrial layout problem. *European Journal of Operational Research*, 183, 633 - 642.

Harris, J. & Powell, S. (1999). An algorithm for optimal buffer placement in reliable serial lines. *IIE Transactions*, 31, 287 - 302.

Kilby, P.; Prosser, P. & Shaw, P. (1999). Guided local search for the vehicle routing problem with time windows. In: Voss S, Martello S, Osman IH, Roucairol C, editors. *Meta-heuristics advances and trends in local search paradigms for optimization*. Boston: Kluwer; 473 - 86.

Kostreva, M. & Ogryczack, W. (1999). Linear optimization with multiple equitable criteria. *RAIRO Operations Research*, 33, 275 - 297.

Kostreva, M.; Ogryczack, W. & Wierzbicki, A. (2004). Equitable aggregation and multiple criteria analysis. *European Journal of Operational Research*, 158, 2, 362 - 377.

Lutz, C.; Roscoe Davis, K. & Sun, M. (1998). Determining buffer location and size in production lines using tabu search. *European Journal of Operational Research*, 106, 301 - 316.

Nahas, N.; Ait-Kadi, D. & Nourelfath, M. (2006). A new approach for buffer allocation in unreliable production lines. *International Journal of Production Economics*, 103, 873 - 881.

Papadopoulos, H.T. & Vidalis, M. (2001). Minimizing WIP inventory in reliable production lines. *International Journal Production Economics*, 70, 185 - 197.

Pellegrini, P.; Favaretto, D. & Moretti, E. (2007). Multiple Ant Colony Optimization for a Rich Vehicle Routing Problem: A Case Study. *Knowledge-Based Intelligent Information and Engineering Systems, Lecture Notes In Computer Science*, 4693, 627 - 634.

Perny, P.; Spanjaard, O. & Storme, L.X. (2006). A decision-theoretic approach to robust optimization in multivalued graphs. *Annals of Operations Research*, 147, 317 - 341.

Riise, A. (2002). Comparing genetic algorithms and tabu search for multiobjective optimization. In Proceedings of the IFORS conference, July 2002, Edinburgh, UK.

Spinellis, D.; Papadopoulos, C. & MacGregor Smith, J. (2000). Large production line optimisation using simulated annealing. *International Journal of Production Research*, 38, 3, 509 - 541.

Voudouris, C. & Tsang, E. (1996). Partial constraint satisfaction problems and guided local search. *In proceedings of the second international conference on practical application of constraint technology (PACT'96)*, pp. 337 - 356, London.

Zitzler, E. & Thiele, L.(1999). Multiobjective evolutionary algorithms: a comparative case study and the strength pareto approach. *IEEE Transactions on evolutionary computation*, 3, 4, 257 - 271.

20

On the Use of ACO Algorithm for Electromagnetic Designs

Eva Rajo-Iglesias, Óscar Quevedo-Teruel and Luis Inclán-Sánchez
University Carlos III of Madrid
Spain

1. Introduction

The use of Global Search Optimization Methods to solve electromagnetic problems has been widely extended. Among these methods the most popular ones for the antenna and electromagnetism communities are Genetic Algorithms (GA) and recently Particle Swarm Optimization (PSO). Algorithms based on these methods have been used to face the design of arrays and other types of antennas (Ares-Pena et al. (1999); Yan & Lu (1997); Tennant et al. (1994); Robinson & Rahmat-Samii (2004); Khodier & Christodoulou (2005)). It is always a matter of discussion which algorithm to use for a given problem, being this topic considered as an *art* as discussed in (Quevedo-Teruel et al. (2007)). In this sense we propose in this chapter the application of an algorithm based on ACO (using real numbers) to solve several electromagnetic problems. The algorithm is implemented in such a way that fits well to problems where the desired solution is not far away from the initial one but where the evaluation of solutions is time demanding.

2. Algorithm description

The Ant Colony Optimization was developed by Dorigo in 1996 (Dorigo et al. (1996), Dorigo et al. (1999), Dorigo & Stutzle (2004)) and it has been used to solve a different type of problems (Hoshyar et al. (2000), Wang et al. (2005), Bullnheimer et al. (1999)) by employing different realizations of the algorithm. The usefulness of this optimization technique is especially powerful in distributed problems like (Sim & Sun (2003), Ahuja & Pahwa (2005), Premprayoon & Wardkein (2005)) and (Liang & Smith (2004)). This algorithm is based on the behavior of ant colonies when they are looking for food and storing it in their nests.
ACO has been very rarely used to solve electromagnetic problems (Coleman et al. (2004), Quevedo-Teruel & Rajo-Iglesias (2006), Rajo-Iglesias & Quevedo-Teruel (2007)), however its characteristics could be interesting for this purpose in some situations as it will be shown along this chapter.

2.1 Basis of the algorithm

For many authors, Ant Colony Optimization is a particular case of PSO, since biologically a colony of ants is a particular case of swarm (Dorigo et al. (2004)), however ACO uses some bases of operation that makes it clearly different from PSO. ACO means algorithms based on the ant behavior in the searching for food and posterior transportation to the nest to be stored. These insects have the ability of finding the "shortest path" in this task by using pheromones.

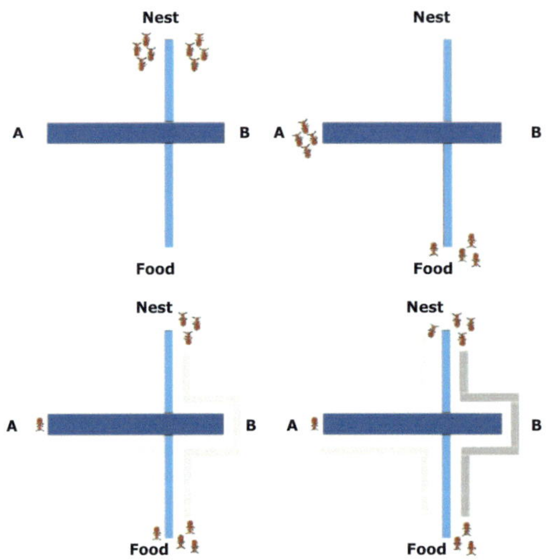

Fig. 1. Diagram of pheromone operation in Ant Colony

Some ant species use pheromones for making paths on the ground, in their way from food to the nest. This helps other ants, by pheromones sensing, to follow the path towards food discovered by other ants. Because ants deposit pheromones while walking, a larger number of ants on a path results in a larger amount of pheromones, this larger amount of pheromones stimulates more ants to choose that path and so on until the ants finally converge to one single (short) path. These pheromones also evaporate with time to "delete" the path to an exhausted food source.

Figure 1 shows a graphical example of ant behavior. The ant nest, a food source and two possible paths are depicted. These two paths are of unequal lengths, and it is assumed that the longest path (path A) takes two time steps to cover, whilst the shortest one (path B) takes only a single time step. At $t = 0$, eight ants are introduced into the system with the objective of getting food and bringing it back to the nest. The initial selection of the path is random, then it is assumed that four ants select each one of the two possible paths. At $t = 1$, the ants that have chosen the shortest path B have acquired the food and begin to travel back home. As there is existing pheromone on path B the ants have a higher probability of using this path, consequently three ants select path B and one ant selects path A. The ants that had chosen path A are only half way along this path. At $t = 2$, the three ants that traversed path B are at home again whilst the ant that embarked on path A only half way along this path. The four ants that were traversing A have made it to food and embark on their journey back home via either path A or B. Path B has a larger amount of pheromone on it (the pheromone intensity is represented by the darkness of the path) as it has been traversed seven times, whereas path A has only been traversed five times. Consequently, by probability, three ants select path B and one ant selects A.

Finally, at $t = 3$, three ants have returned to the nest along path B except the one that is still in the middle of path A, being also three more ants that decided to take path B, and they have found the food. At that time, path B has a greater amount of pheromone on it as it has been traversed thirteen times in total, while the longer path A has been traversed only five times. Future ants entering the system will have a higher probability of selecting path

B. The diagram in Figure 1 illustrated how the swarm intelligence operates to determine the shortest path. The pheromone trails also decay with time. This means that in paths that are not regularly used, pheromone concentration will eventually decay to zero intensity. This decaying quality of pheromone also helps in the ability of the Ant Colony to find the shorter paths. The longer paths, which receive less pheromone, will decay more rapidly enabling shorter paths to have a higher probability of being selected.
Although most of the ant population use paths with high pheromone concentration, there is always some ant exploring new paths. This avoids the algorithm stagnation. Further details of the implementation of this algorithm will be discussed in Section 3.1.

3. Examples

We will present along this chapter some of the examples which show how useful this algorithm can be for electromagnetic designs.

3.1 Implementation of the Algorithm

In our implementation of the algorithm, an ant means a solution of the problem, and the main steps are the ones shown in the flowchart of Figure 2. Besides, we have to point out that there are two main states of operation, in the first one (*forward*) the ant is looking for food whilst in the second one (*backward*) the ant has to look for the path to come back home.
Paths are divided into nodes and, to decide the next node the ant is going to move towards, typically, the most extended decision criterium is the one proposed by Dorigo et al. (1996) and described as:

$$p_{i,j}(t) = \frac{[\tau_j(t)]^{\alpha} \cdot [\eta_j]^{\beta}}{\sum_{l \in \theta_i} [\tau_l(t)]^{\alpha} \cdot [\eta_l]^{\beta}} \tag{1}$$

Where $p_{i,j}$ is the probability of node j to be chosen at iteration t being at node i, $\tau_j(t)$ represents the pheromone concentration associated with node j at iteration t, α establishes the importance of pheromone concentration in the decision process whilst β does the same with the desirability, η_j is the desirability of node j, and θ_i is the set of nodes l available at decision point i.
The desirability η_j is a function that depends on the optimization goal. This function has to be evaluated at every node j for every ant. Its role is equivalent to the one of the fitness function in other algorithms. When the algorithm is developed, the definition of this function is one of the critical issues, as in many other algorithms.
The function τ_j can be implemented in different ways. In our case, we will use the expression:

$$\tau_j(t+1) = \tau_j(t) + \Delta\tau_j(t) - d(t) \tag{2}$$

Where $\Delta\tau_j(t)$ is the pheromone addition on node j, and $d(t)$ is the pheromone persistence:

$$d(t) = \begin{cases} \rho & \text{if } \mathrm{mod}\left(\frac{t}{\gamma}\right) = 0 \\ 0 & \text{if } \mathrm{mod}\left(\frac{t}{\gamma}\right) \neq 0 \end{cases} \tag{3}$$

Where γ is the period of pheromone elimination, and ρ is the coefficient of pheromone elimination by period.
The choice of the values of γ and ρ parameters is critical to achieve good results. For the particular examples that will be studied along the following pages, these values have been empirically selected as $\gamma = 20$, $\rho = 1$. The pheromone addition has been defined as $\Delta\tau_{i,j}(t) = 1$

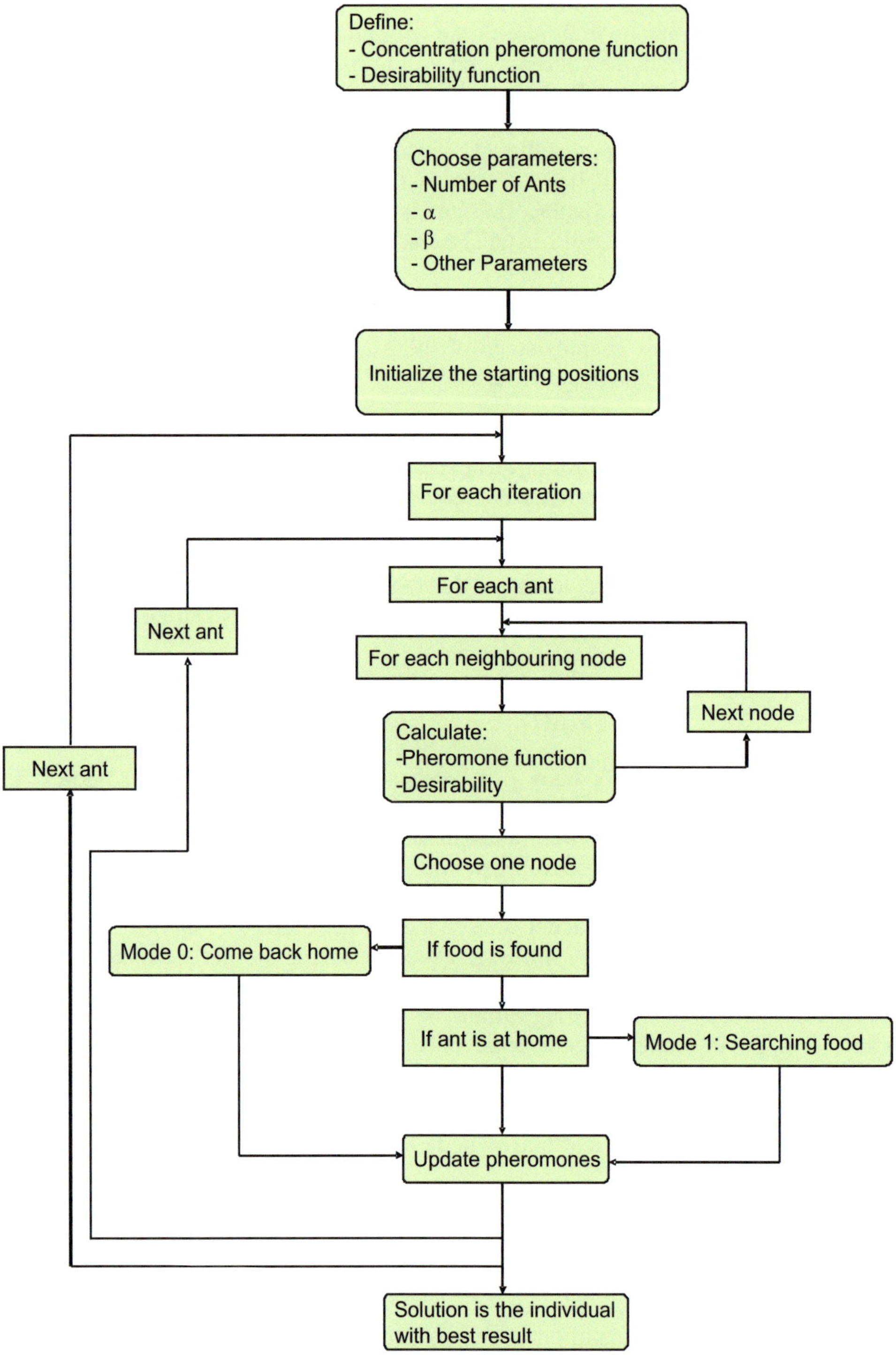

Fig. 2. Flowchart of the principal steps in the proposed Ant Algorithm

when an ant goes to the node j from any node i. On the other hand, the parameters α and β have been set differently for each example depending on the optimization goal.
Obviously, the value of $\Delta\tau_{i,j}(t)$ and the parameters γ and ρ are related to α, because they give the magnitude of the element $(\tau_j(t))$ that is raised to the power of α (Equations 1, 2 and 3).
As β is related to the importance of the desirability in the decision process whilst α does the same but with the pheromone concentration effect, for every example β has been chosen much larger than α in order to increase the effect of the better solutions on the pheromone concentration (that would fix strict ant trails and therefore, slow evolution of the algorithm or even, algorithm stagnation). The empirical selection of these parameters is a common issue in most optimization algorithms. However, some guidelines can be found in the theoretical basis of this method as well as some range of variation of the parameters (Dorigo & Stutzle (2004)).
The number of ants and/or iterations in the algorithm can be decided based on the computational capacity. The food is defined as the desired condition, i.e, for example in array synthesis, can be the Side Lobe Level (SLL), the null in given directions or a specific Beam Width (BW).

3.2 Array synthesis

The initial example of application of the algorithm is considered as a "classical" problem of optimization among the electromagnetic community. We are talking about the *array synthesis* where many other algorithms have been previously applied (Haupt & Werner (2007), Khodier & Christodoulou (2005),Robinson & Rahmat-Samii (2004)). Along this section we will show some examples of synthesis carried out by using an ACO algorithm (Quevedo-Teruel & Rajo-Iglesias (2006), Rajo-Iglesias & Quevedo-Teruel (2007)).

3.2.1 Linear array synthesis

We initially propose to deal with a simple case of synthesis: a linear array of $2N$ elements, all of them with uniform amplitude and phase. The optimization will be performed changing the element positions (becoming a non-equally spaced array, but keeping symmetry) as in (Khodier & Christodoulou (2005), Jin & Rahmat-Samii (2007)).
The initial array is composed of $2N$ elements uniformly distributed along the $\hat{z}$ axis. The Array Factor (AF) in this case can be written as

$$AF(\theta) = 2\sum_{n=1}^{N} I_n cos[k \cdot z_n \cdot \cos(\theta) + \varphi_n] \tag{4}$$

If the amplitude and phase are uniform ($I_n = I_0, \phi_n = \phi_0$), the AF can be simplified as

$$AF(\theta) = 2\sum_{n=1}^{N} cos[k \cdot z_n \cdot \cos(\theta)] \tag{5}$$

Our goal will be to find out the positions $\{z_1, z_2, ..., z_N\}$ of the elements that accomplish the design requirements using an algorithm based on Ant Colony Optimization.
This example of synthesis is directly based on the work presented in (Khodier & Christodoulou (2005)) where Particle Swarm was used for this type of array synthesis. Here, we will present similar examples to the ones included in that paper.
ACO is discrete in nature, hence, a discretization of the variables that we use in the optimization process is needed. Consequently, the positions of the array elements will be

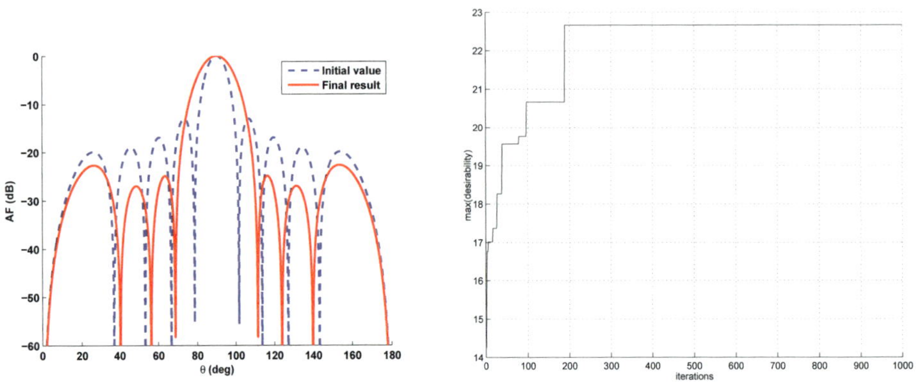

(a) Radiation pattern (b) Convergence

Fig. 3. Normalized radiation pattern of *10*-element linear array obtained by the ant algorithm (solid line) compared to the initial value (dotted line) and convergence of the algorithm

discretized. A step of 0.1λ has been considered in all the examples. In addition, the initial array element positions (*home*) have been chosen as the ones with an inter-element separation of 0.5λ. Moreover, when the ants have found the food, they have to come back to *home*, i.e. to these initial positions.

Next, we will show three particular examples having each one different design criteria: to minimize the SLL level, obtaining three null directions, and to minimize the SLL keeping the BW narrow and obtaining a null in a given direction. In all cases, the algorithm convergence as well as the defined desirability function will be shown. The values of α and β are respectively 1 and 5 for all the following cases.

A: SLL level

As a first example, the typical case of SLL minimization will be synthesized. The desirability will be defined as the absolute value of the SLL including all directions (in dB and normalized). This can be written as

$$\eta_j = |SLL|_{dB} \tag{6}$$

Figure 3 shows the achieved result after 1000 iterations when 20 ants are used, for the synthesis of a 10 element array. The food is defined as a SLL of -20 dB level. In the same Figure, the initial AF (with equally spaced elements) is plotted. The achieved solution has a SLL of -22.66 dB.

Figure 3.b includes a representation of the algorithm convergence. The plotted line corresponds to the node with best desirability found in every iteration. The algorithm converges in approximately 200 iterations.

The obtained solution (the one illustrated in Figure 3) has the following element positions:

$z_1 = 0.15\lambda$	$z_2 = 0.35\lambda$	$z_3 = 0.75\lambda$	$z_4 = 0.95\lambda$	$z_5 = 1.55\lambda$

B: three null directions

The second example is an array synthesis with three desired null directions in the radiation pattern (θ_1, θ_2 and θ_3). Actually, the three directions will be spatially closed in order to produce a null in an angular range. The definition of desirability function is especially critical in this case. Empirically it has been chosen the following

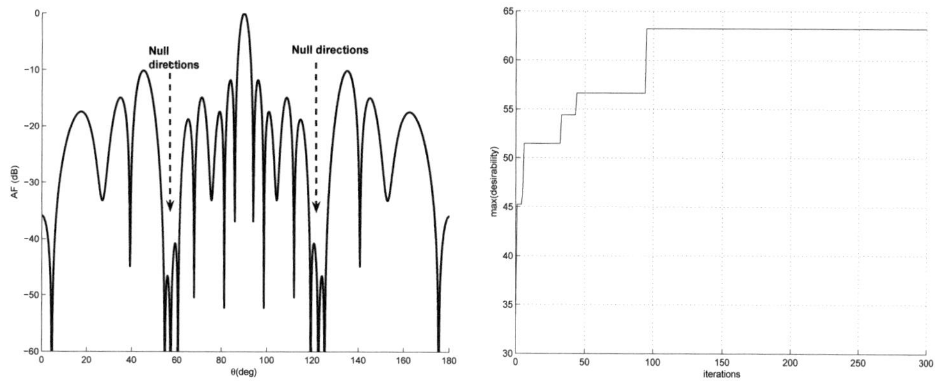

(a) Radiation pattern (b) Convergence

Fig. 4. Normalized radiation pattern of *28*-element linear array obtained by the ant algorithm and its convergence. Getting the three null directions at $\{55°, 57.5°, 60°\}$ and $\{120°, 122.5°, 125°\}$

$$\eta_j = \sqrt[3]{(|FA(\theta_1)|_{dB}) \cdot (|FA(\theta_2)|_{dB}) \cdot (|FA(\theta_3)|_{dB})} \quad (7)$$

Figure 4 shows an example of synthesis using 20 ants and 300 iterations. The number of array elements has been chosen to be 28 (N=14) and we have considered food when the normalized AF in directions $\{55°, 57.5°, 60°\}$ is -60dB. Obviously, in the symmetrical directions $\{120°, 122.5°, 125°\}$ we have nulls too. The algorithm converges very fast, in approximately 100 iterations.
In this case, the solution for the array geometry is

z_1=0.15λ	z_2=0.55λ	z_3=1.25λ	z_4=1.65λ	z_5=2.75λ
z_6=2.95λ	z_7=3.25λ	z_8=3.75λ	z_9=4.15λ	z_{10}=4.45λ
z_{11}=5.15λ	z_{12}=5.75λ	z_{13}=5.85λ	z_{14}=6.65λ	

This array accomplishes with the required null radiation in the three directions as Figure 4 shows.

3.2.1.1 C: SLL, BW and null in a given direction

As a last example, three conditions will be imposed concerning SLL, BW and a null in a defined direction. Particularly a null will be required at θ=81°, a SLL below -15dB and a BW of 7.7°. The array will have 32 elements.
To this aim 20 ants and 500 iterations have been used. As previously, the desirability function has to be carefully selected including now two modulating parameters $\beta_2 = 20$ and $\beta_3 = 6$. This can be expressed as

$$\eta_j = |FA(\theta_1)|^{\frac{1}{\beta_3}} \left(\frac{1}{BW(°) - \theta_f}\right)^{\frac{1}{\beta_2}} \cdot |SLL|_{dB} \quad (8)$$

A $\theta_f = 7°$ was used due to the minimum value of BW (with equally spaced elements) of 7.2°. After using this desirability function, the algorithm finds a solution that fulfills the required conditions. In this case, the array has a BW of 7.66° and a SLL of -17.85dB, as well as the null

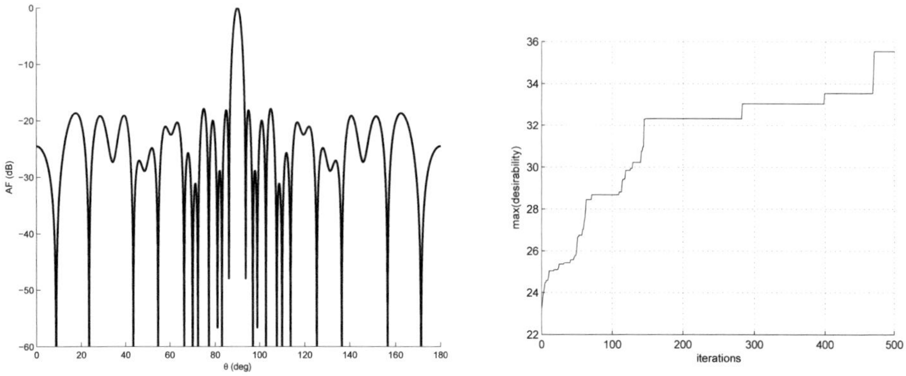

(a) Radiation pattern (b) Convergence

Fig. 5. Normalized radiation pattern and convergence of *32*-element linear array obtained by the ant algorithm. ($SLL < -15$dB, BW <7.7°, and a null at 81°)

in the specified direction (see Figure 5). A zoom of the central area is illustrated in Figure 6 in order to show the performances with detail.
The array with these characteristics has the elements distributed as follows,

z_1=0.35λ	z_2=0.65λ	z_3=1.15λ	z_4=1.55λ	z_5=2.15λ	z_6=2.75λ
z_7=3.15λ	z_8=3.25λ	z_9=3.85λ	z_{10}=4.35λ	z_{11}=4.85λ	z_{12}=5.45λ
z_{13}=6.25λ	z_{14}=7.05λ	z_{15}=7.65λ	z_{16}=8.35λ		

3.2.2 Thinned array

A second set of examples is devoted to synthesize thinned arrays which is another method of designing aperiodic arrays especially when the number of array elements is large (Schwartzman (1967), Haupt (1994), Haupt (2005)). We will now employ this method with the ACO algorithm, where the positions of the elements will be fixed but each element is able

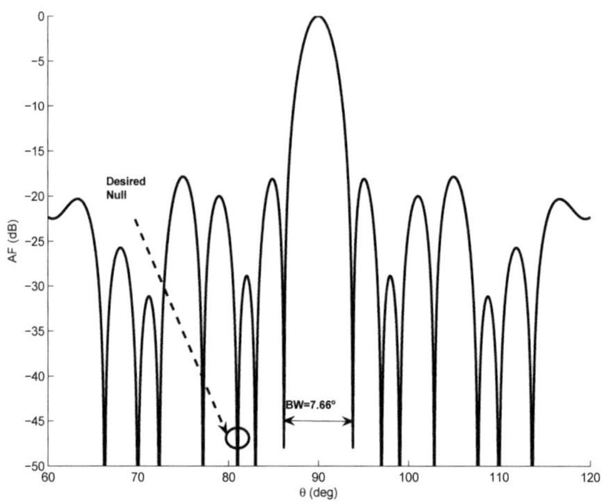

Fig. 6. Detail of the AF shown in Figure 5.a

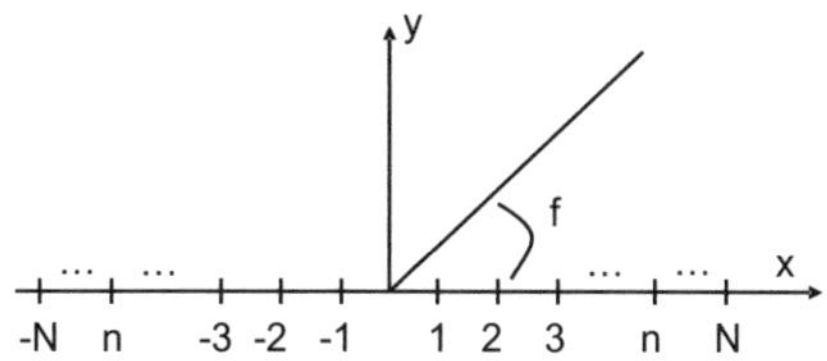

Fig. 7. Geometry of a $2N$-element symmetric linear array along x-axis

to present two states: "on" (when the element is fed) and "off" (when the element is passively terminated by an impedance equal to the source impedance of the fed elements).
According to the structure shown in Figure 7, where there are $2N$ elements symmetrically distributed along the x-axis, the array factor in the azimuth plane (XY plane) can be written as

$$AF(\phi) = 2\sum_{n=1}^{N} I_n cos[\frac{\pi}{2} \cdot (2n-1) \cdot \cos(\phi)] \tag{9}$$

where I_n is the excitation amplitude of the nth element. In our case, I_n is 0 if the state of the nth element is "off" and 1 if it is "on". The distance between elements is 0.5λ and all of them have identical phases.
Figure 8 shows a planar array structure of $2N \times 2M$ elements. The array factor for this structure is given by (assuming the same considerations as in the linear array case):

$$\begin{aligned} AF(\theta,\phi) = 4\sum_{n=1}^{N}\sum_{m=1}^{M} I_{nm} cos[\pi \cdot (2n-1) \cdot \sin(\theta)\cos(\phi)] \cdot \\ cos[\pi \cdot (2m-1) \cdot \sin(\theta)\sin(\phi)] \end{aligned} \tag{10}$$

Therefore, we need to find out which array elements should be enabled or disabled ($I_{nm} = 1$ or $I_{nm} = 0$) to get the desired radiation pattern characteristics.
For the thinned array optimization we will have N bits, thus corresponding to an N-dimensional space of solutions. In this case, every ant means an array solution, i.e., a vector with N bits. Ants describe paths that are divided into nodes. They move from one node to another through the N-dimensional space of solutions by checking the desirability and the pheromone concentration level of their neighboring nodes before making a probabilistic decision among all of them. A neighboring node is calculated by toggling the state of only one element of the array. This means that every ant has N neighboring nodes and has to decide which one among them to move towards, in a probabilistic manner.

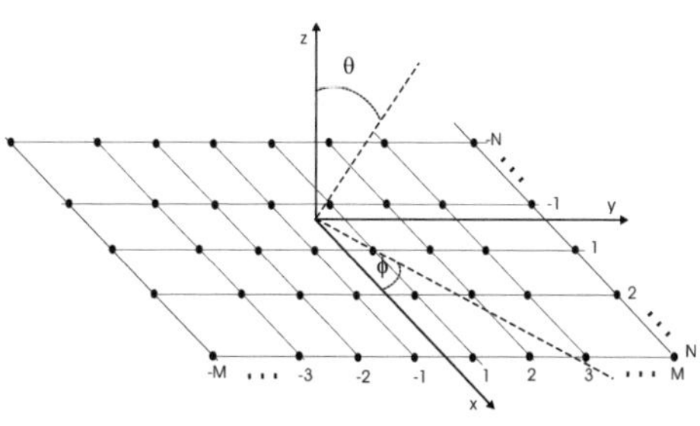

Fig. 8. Geometry of a $2N \times 2M$-element symmetric planar array in XY plane

We present now several examples to show how our ACO based algorithm performs in thinned array synthesis. In all the examples, we use as initial value the array with all elements "on" to take advantage of the entire structure that can be used.
In all the following examples we have set the parameter values as: $\alpha = 5$ and $\beta = 30$. The food is defined as a particular SLL value which changes depending on the example. However as our stopping criterion is to complete a number of iterations, the algorithm assigns better desirability values to solutions with lower SLL. Thus, even if the food is found, better solutions can be achieved and this often happens in the way back to the nest.

3.2.2.1 Linear array with a specific SLL

In this first example we search the lowest value of SLL with isotropic elements. The desirability is defined as the absolute value of the normalized SLL (in dBs).

$$\eta_j = |SLL(dB)| \tag{11}$$

Figures 9 and 10 show the result obtained with 10 ants, 100 iterations and 100 elements. Food was defined as -20 dB of SLL. In the same figure the initial case where all the elements were "on" has been plotted. The synthesized array accomplish the design goal. Besides we can see how the algorithm converges in approximately 70 iterations.
The best array obtained (SLL = -20.52 dB) is given below as a status table ($on = 1$, $off = 0$) for half of the elements (as the array is symmetric):

1 1 1 1 1 1 1 1 1 1 1 1 1 1 1 1 1 1 1 1 1 1 1 1 1
1 0 1 1 1 1 0 0 1 0 1 0 0 1 1 1 1 1 0 0 1 0 0 1 1

3.2.2.2 Planar array

As a final example, we will now deal with the design of a thinned planar array. The SLL level will be checked in the two main planes of the array. To this aim, we have used the desirability function given below:

$$\eta_j = min(|SLL_{\phi=0}(dB)|, |SLL_{\phi=90}(dB)|) \tag{12}$$

Figure 11 shows the result obtained with 10 ants, 100 iterations and 20×10 elements. The food is considered to be -24 dB of SLL in each plane ($\phi = 0°$ and $\phi = 90°$). The algorithm has a fast convergence (in approximately 40 iterations).
The achieved solution is given below as a status table for one quadrant (x-positive in horizontal and y-positive in vertical) of the elements (the obtained SLLs are -25.76 dB and -25.67 dB for planes $\phi = 0°$ and $\phi = 90°$, respectively):

1 1 1 1 1 1 1 1 1 1
1 1 1 1 1 1 1 1 1 0
1 1 1 1 1 1 1 0 0 0
1 1 1 1 1 0 0 0 0 0
1 1 1 0 0 0 0 0 0 0

After all the presented examples we can stand that ACO has demonstrated to be an useful optimization tool for array design, but also, since it can provide a good solution with low number of iterations and a low population, it could be a good candidate for solving more complex electromagnetic problems where the evaluation of the fitness function has a high computational cost (since a full wave simulation is typically required) as it will be shown in the following Sections.

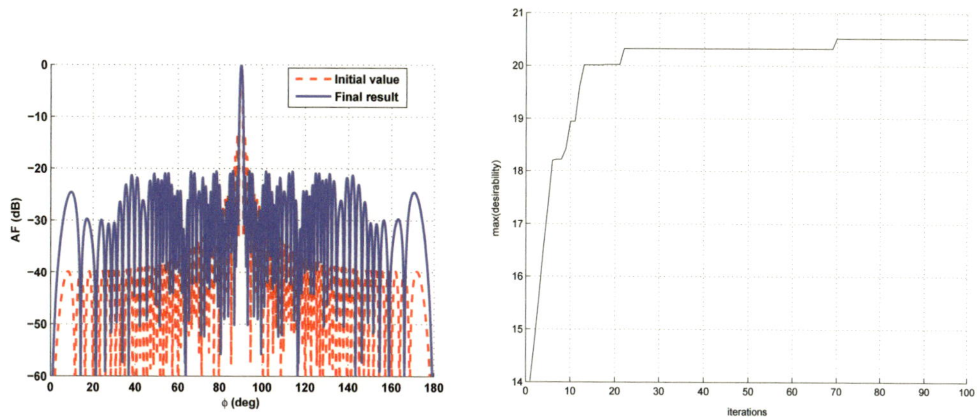

(a) Radiation pattern (b) Convergence

Fig. 9. Radiation pattern and convergence of a *100*-element array obtained by the ant algorithm (dashed line) compared to the initial value (solid line). ($SLL < -20\,\text{dB}$)

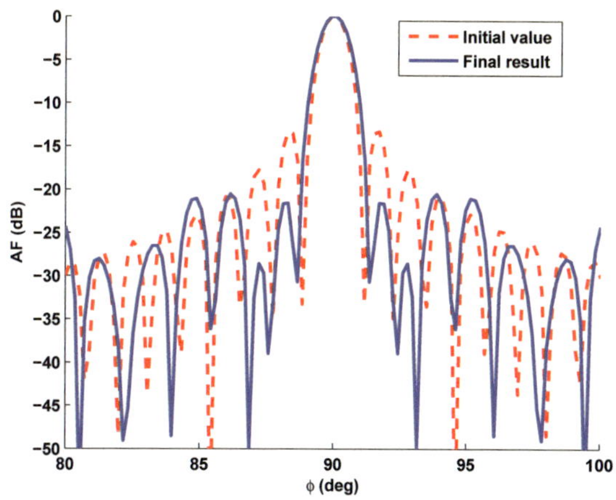

Fig. 10. Detail of the Array Factor (AF) shown in Figure 9.a.

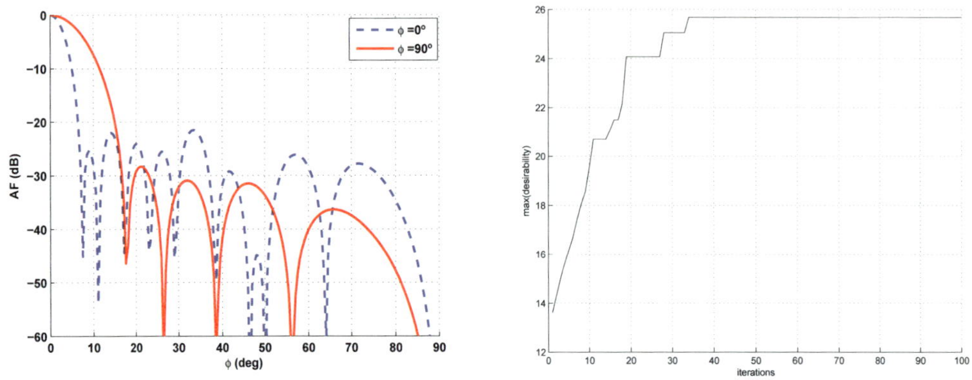

(a) Radiation pattern (b) Convergence

Fig. 11. Radiation pattern and convergence of 10×20-element planar array in the planes $\phi = 0°$ and $\phi = 90°$. ($SLL < -24\,\text{dB}$ in both planes)

3.3 Mutual coupling reduction in patch antenna arrays by using a planar EBG

The first problem in which we are going to use the ACO algorithm combined with a commercial full wave simulator is the reduction of mutual coupling between patch antennas by using a periodic structure (Electromagnetic Band Gap (EBG) type).

Mutual coupling reduction in arrays has deserved much attention from antenna designers. This coupling becomes especially critical in arrays of patch antennas where coupling comes from two sources (Pozar (1987), Bamford et al. (1997)). The first one is due to the free space radiation which is present in all types of array antennas. The second path arises from surface waves and it constitutes a very important factor in patch antennas (James & Hall (1997), Pozar & Schaubert (1995)). Moreover, the use of thick or high permittivity substrates increases the coupling.

Periodic structures such as EBGs have the ability of suppressing surface waves propagation in a frequency band. Consequently, their use in mutual coupling reduction for printed antennas can be of interest. For the particular case of patch antennas, the reduction of mutual coupling by using a periodic structure becomes particularly challenging when grating lobes must be avoided, since the distance between the edges of two neighboring patches is very small under this no grating lobes constraint.

For this reason, most of the proposals in the literature to reduce the coupling use a high permittivity dielectric and a modest number of periods of the structure in between the array elements. This means that this is a very challenging problem and the use of an optimization tool could be very helpful. In (Yang & Rahmat-Samii (2009)), the authors recognize this difficulty, and they made use of PSO to carry out the optimization of the periodic structure. In this section we will employ ACO for the same purpose.

Most of the previous works related to mutual coupling reduction for printed antennas are aimed at EBGs non completely planar, as it is the case of (Yang & Rahmat-Samii (2003), Yang et al. (2005), Fu & Yuan (2004), Zheng et al. (2008) and Caminita et al. (2009)). Besides, all of them use thin high permittivity substrates and both the periodic structure and the patch antenna are printed on the same layer. Our purpose is to provide another approach in the mutual coupling reduction for patch antennas by using completely planar EBGs.

One of the key aspects for this design is the use of a multilayer dielectric substrate (Chiau et al.

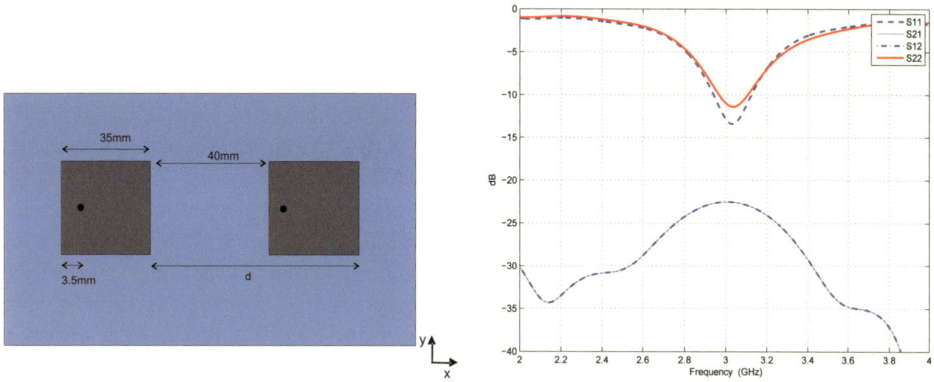

(a) Antenna top view (b) S parameters

Fig. 12. Simulated mutual coupling between antennas and input impedance of both antennas.

(2003), Inclán-Sánchez et al. (2005), Rajo-Iglesias et al. (2008)). With the combination of high permittivity and low permittivity dielectric layers, we can print the patch antenna and the EBG in different substrates (the EBG on the high permittivity material for the sake of compactness and the antenna on the low permittivity one for increasing the radiation efficiency). The advantages of this configuration will be further discussed.

A basic type of planar EBG, made of metallic patches printed on a grounded dielectric substrate, is the proposed periodic structure to be used for mutual coupling reduction (Yang et al. (2000), Goussetis et al. (2006)).

3.3.1 Initial design

In this section, we define a starting point for the subsequent optimization. The chosen EBG (Goussetis et al. (2006)) is not so compact and consequently most of the authors employ a high permittivity substrate. Here, we will use a material with $\epsilon_r \simeq 10$ and a 2.54mm thickness.

Unfortunately, this substrate will produce an antenna with a low bandwidth as well as a moderate directivity (James & Hall (1997)). Consequently, we propose a multilayer dielectric structure. The EBG will be placed above the high permittivity lower layer, obtaining a structure with a reduced size. Over the latter, the second layer with a low permittivity and thick thickness will be located for achieving an equivalent low permittivity to the patches, which will be placed above this upper substrate. This multilayer configuration is inspired in the work presented in (Inclán-Sánchez et al. (2005)). The chosen upper layer will have an $\epsilon_r \simeq 1$ and 6mm thickness.

To study the mutual coupling between array elements, we will employ a basic configuration with two patch antennas. The antennas will be designed to work at 3GHz. The dimensions of the patches and the distances between them are illustrated in Figure 12.a. For this structure, the simulated mutual coupling (S_{12}) is represented in the same Figure, with the input impedance as a reference for the operating frequency. Both antennas are well matched (with a S_{11} and S_{22} smaller than -10dB), and the maximum mutual coupling is approximately -23dB.

The EBG unit cell is illustrated in Figure 13.a. The initial chosen dimensions for the EBG following (Goussetis et al. (2006)) are $d_x = d_y = 15$mm and $p_x = p_y = 25$mm. Considering this structure infinite we can obtain its associated dispersion diagram represented in Figure 13.b. The two blue lines correspond to the two first modes propagating in the structure, and

the dashed red line represents the light line. We can conclude that there is a band around 3GHz where the propagation in x direction is not allowed.
This is however a theoretical study, assuming infinite number of cells in the EBG. For the proposed application it is necessary to truncate the EBG and only two lines of elements will fit between the patches in the E-plane, whilst in the H-plane, in principle, there is no constraint. This fact limits the characteristics of our filtering structure.
After these previous considerations, we are able to define the complete antenna with the EBG for the mutual coupling reduction. The scheme of this design is shown in Figure 14.a with the side and top views of an array of two elements. We have initially considered four elements in the H-plane for the compactness of the design. Figure 14.b shows the S parameters for the complete structure. A considerable reduction of the mutual coupling has been achieved, with a maximum of -29dB, that is 6dB less than in the previous case without the EBG (Figure 12.b). Moreover, the antennas are even better matched than in the case without EBG, having a higher total antenna efficiency.

3.3.2 Definition of the ant colony algorithm parameters

Although we have obtained a considerable reduction of the mutual coupling (approximately 6dB), an optimization with an ACO algorithm is now carried out to further improve these results. As previously mentioned, this algorithm fits properly with this problem where a good initial solution has already been obtained. The parameters to be optimized are the dimensions of the cells and the distance between them: d_x, d_y, p_x and p_y. These parameters have as constraint the space between the patches, not being allowed to overlap the volume defined by the patches. The goal for the optimization will be the maximum reduction of the mutual coupling.
The chosen parameters for this optimization problem, have been the following: $\gamma = 20$, $\rho = 1$, $\alpha = 30$, $\beta = 2$. These parameters have been selected heuristically. The chosen desirability was the module of S_{21} at the operation frequency of patches (at the lowest value of S_{11}).
The algorithm was developed in *MATLAB*© and employed *CST*© commercial software as analysis tool (in transient solver) to calculate the mutual coupling between the patches. Each ant must calculate the desirability of all the neighboring nodes (defined by increasing and decreasing one step each of the 4 parameters to optimize). With this value of desirability as

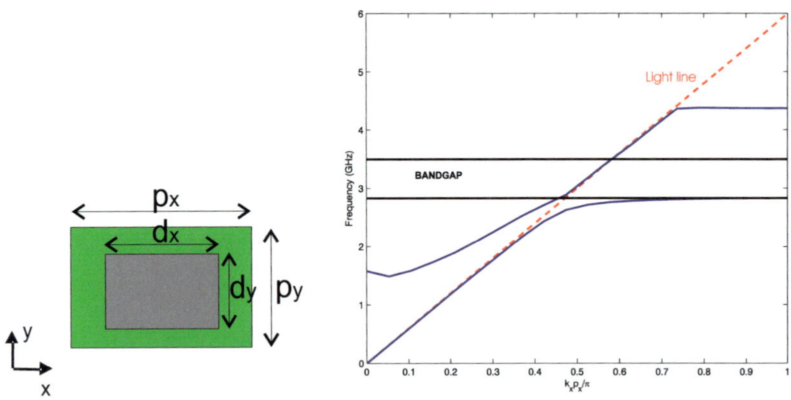

(a) EBG unit cell (b) Dispersion diagram

Fig. 13. Dispersion diagram of the EBG (represented in E-plane direction).

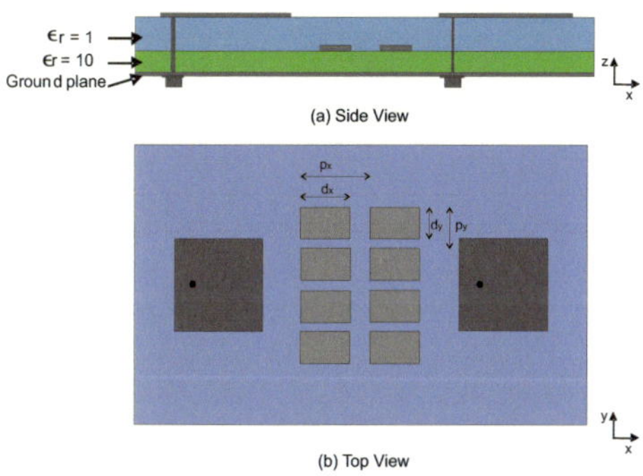

(a) Description of the geometry

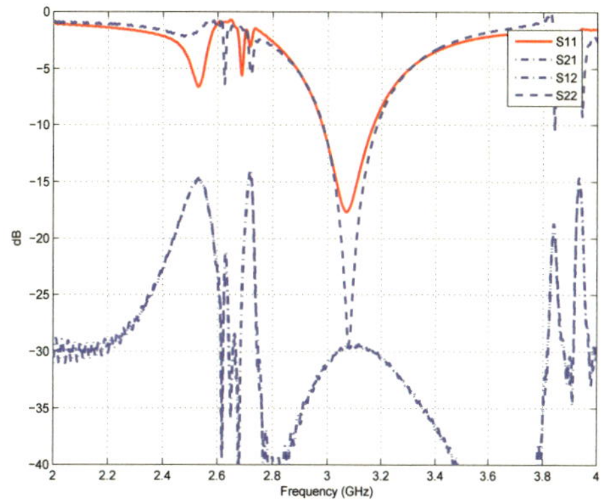

(b) S parameters

Fig. 14. Simulated mutual coupling and matching for the array with EBG.

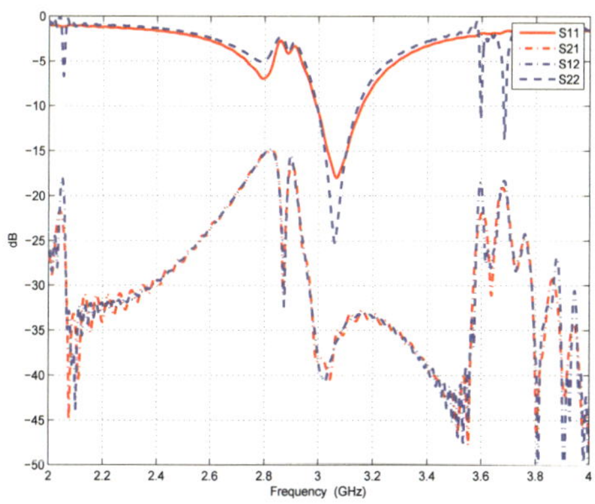

(a) 8 element EBG.

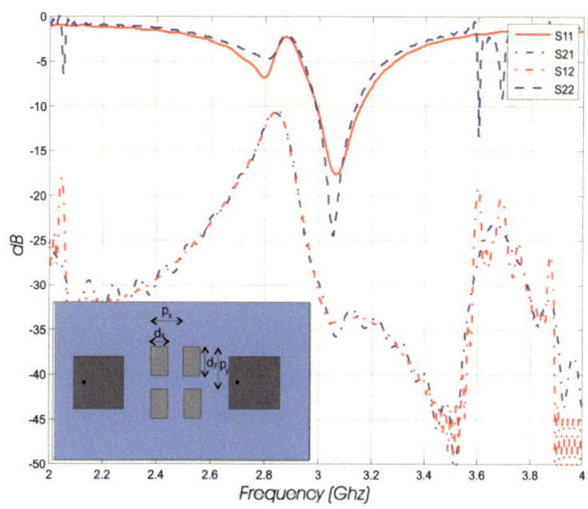

(b) 4 element EBG.

Fig. 15. Simulated mutual coupling for the array with optimized EBG.

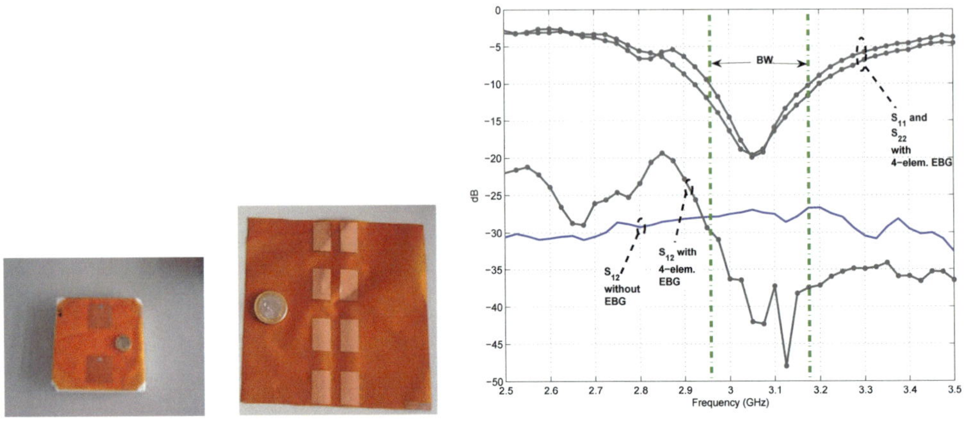

(a) Manufactured *two*-element multilayer array (b) Planar periodic 8-element EBG (c) Measured S parameters: with and without EBG

Fig. 16. Experimental mutual coupling for the array with optimized EBG.

well as with the pheromone concentration, each ant makes the decision of moving to a new position with the probability expression defined in Equation 1.

3.3.3 Optimized results

After several iterations, the obtained dimensions were $d_x = 13\text{mm}$, $d_y = 22\text{mm}$, $p_x = 20\text{mm}$ and $p_y = 35\text{mm}$. Figure 15(a) shows the simulated result obtained for these dimensions. The mutual coupling is below -35dB. This means that the mutual coupling reduction is approximately 6dB if we compare with the case before optimization, and 12dB with the structure without EBG. Looking for the most compact design in H-plane, in Figure 15(b), we illustrate the simulated results for a structure with only 4 elements as the inset of this Figure shows.

3.3.4 Experimental results

In order to validate the results obtained by the previous simulations, some prototypes were manufactured. In Figure 16, we show a photograph of the structure with the patches including a multilayer substrate and the EBG, as well as the picture of the layer with the eight printed metallic elements.

In Figure 16.c, the measured parameter S_{12} is illustrated for the case of 4-elements with the band within which S_{11} is below -10dB defined by the two vertical dashed lines. In most parts of the band, a reduction of the mutual coupling by more than 10dB is achieved and the EBG does not affect the matching of the antennas.

3.4 Split ring resonators loaded on the sidewalls of rectangular waveguides

The next example will deal with how to operate ordinary waveguides below its cutoff frequency to get miniaturized structures (Hrabar et al. (2005), Kehn et al. (2006)). We show now a possible solution based on Split Ring Resonators (SRR) (Quevedo-Teruel et al. (2009)) that has been designed by using an ACO algorithm. This is a problem where the proposed ACO algorithm is especially convenient as the computational cost of the evaluation of each solution is very high.

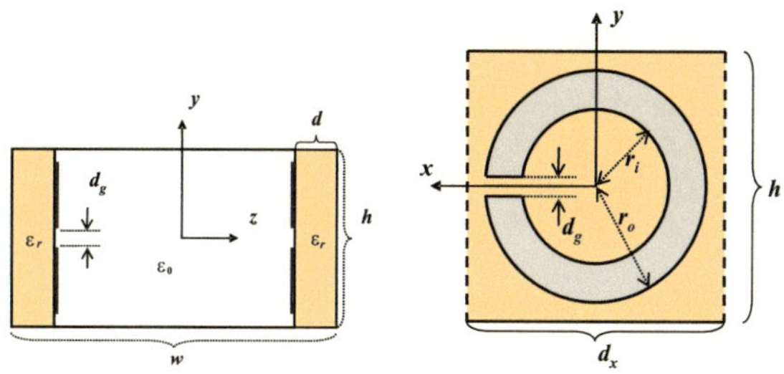

(a) Waveguide cross section (b) SRR dimensions

Fig. 17. Geometry of the analyzed waveguide.

The possibility of operating the waveguide below its usual fundamental modal cutoff frequency provides miniaturization of the structure (Falcone et al. (2004), Marqués et al. (2002), Burokur et al. (2007), Esteban et al. (2005), Quevedo-Teruel et al. (2009)). To this aim, in the work of (Hrabar et al. (2005)), the waveguide was loaded with arrays of SRR printed on both sides of a centrally located dielectric slab. Instead, in this work we propose to place these SRRs on the lateral sidewalls as Figure 17 shows. This structure is inspired in the one investigated in (Kehn et al. (2006)), in which an array of rectangular patches is printed on the surface of each sidewall dielectric of a rectangular waveguide for obtaining a TEM behavior. This unusual effect of propagation below cutoff will be only produced in a narrow band where the SRRs resonate, being possible to tune that resonant frequency below or above the cutoff frequency of the dominant ordinary waveguide mode of the structure. Below, backward passband will be achieved, whereas above the cutoff frequency, these waveguides will exhibit stopbands (Shelkovnikov & Budimir (2006), Jitha et al. (2006), Rajo-Iglesias et al. (2009), Kehn et al. (2008)).

In this section we study the case of SRR loadings in the waveguide sidewalls using again an Ant Colony Optimization algorithm to optimize the SRR parameters for achieving the lowest operation frequency of the backward travelling modal passband that is significantly below the cutoff frequency of the dominant mode. The schematic of this SRR-loaded rectangular waveguide is shown in Figure 17.

3.4.1 Dispersion diagrams

Before the optimization, numerical studies of the proposed waveguide were developed in (Quevedo-Teruel et al. (2009)). To this aim, different values of the main parameters of the structure shown in Figure 17 were analyzed by making use of dispersion diagrams obtained with the eigenvalue analyzer of *CST Microwave Studio*© which requires a high computational cost.

An example of the dispersion curves obtained from simulations is shown in Figure 18. With reference to Figure 17, the example is for a configuration with a waveguide width w of 20 mm, height h of 10 mm and a period d_x of 10 mm along $\hat{x}$. The thickness d of the dielectric slab is 2 mm, and its relative permittivity $\epsilon_r = 3.2$. For the SRR, which is geometrically centered within the unit cell, its outer radius r_o is 4 mm, inner radius r_i is 3.2 mm, and the gap distance d_g is 1 mm.

Two narrow backward-modal passbands appear around 4.2 GHz as Figure 18 shows. This is then followed by a stopband from around 4.5 GHz to 7.5 GHz, beyond which the dominant mode appears. The second mode also re-emerges at a higher frequency. Hence, each of the

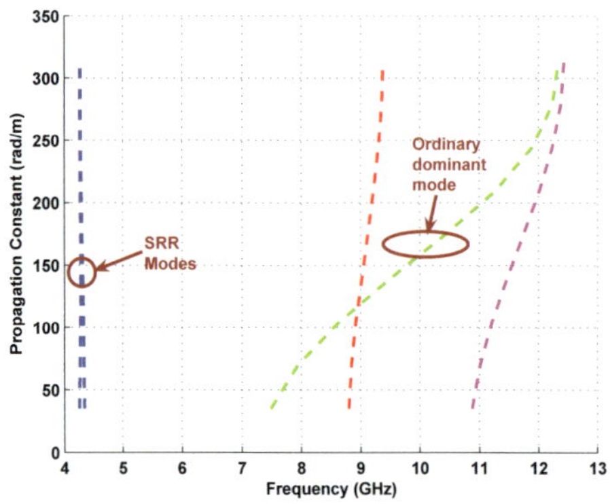

Fig. 18. Dispersion diagram of SRR-waveguide, loaded with a dielectric material of $\epsilon_r = 3.2$, with dimensions: $w = 20$mm, $h = 10$mm, $d_x = 10$mm, $d = 2$mm, $r_o = 4$mm, $r_i = 3.2$mm, and $d_g = 1$mm.

two dominant modes first appears as a backward travelling mode within a low and narrow passband, goes to cutoff, and then reappears as ordinary modes in the higher band.

3.4.2 Optimized design

After this previous example, we now deal with a real design where the dimensions of the supporting waveguide are established to be the standard C-band type whose cross-sectional dimensions are 3.5cm×1.6cm. The material on which the SRR array is printed has been selected to be conventional fiber glass with $\epsilon_r = 4.5$, loss tangent 0.012 and with 1.55mm thickness.

The proposed optimization goal is to achieve the new passband below ordinary waveguide cutoff at the lowest possible frequency. This is intended for possible miniaturization purposes. Therefore, we employed an ACO algorithm, making use of the following parameters for the optimization: the SRR dimensions, i.e. inner and outer radii, gap of the SRR and period of the unit cell. The desirability function employed for this optimization was the following:

$$\eta_j = (10 - median(\{f_i\}/10^9)) \tag{13}$$

in which $\{f_i\}$ represents the set of frequencies that allows the propagation of the mode that is being targeted for minimization of its passband frequency. For each frequency in this set, there is an associated propagation constant of that considered mode. The aim of the algorithm is to maximize this function, and hence, to minimize the frequency of the backward mode. The index j of η denotes the case index, where each case pertains to a certain set of optimization parameters.

In this case, the eigenmode solver of *CST©* is used as the analysis tool to compute the dispersion diagrams for solution evaluation; and as previously, ACO was implemented in *MATLAB©* which uses *CST©* to evaluate the goodness of the solutions. As a consequence, this process will be computationally heavy. Therefore, both a moderate number of ants and iterations have been used. As mentioned before, this fact provides a lower computational time than other global search algorithms (for example genetics) where the number of individuals must be much higher to achieve good results. In order to decide the movement of each ant, the algorithm has to compute the dispersion diagrams of all the neighboring nodes. As 4

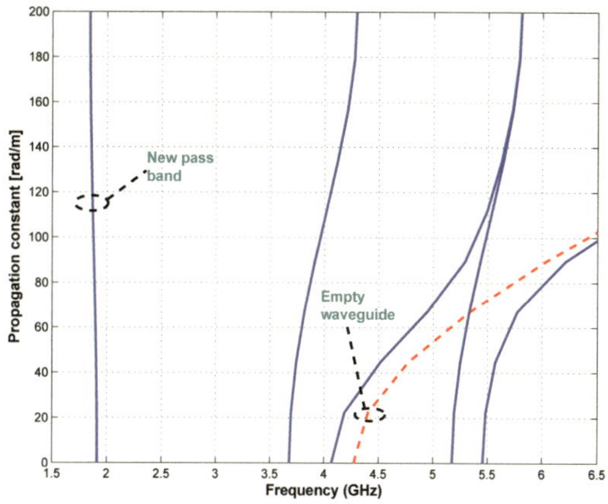

Fig. 19. Dispersion diagram of the optimized waveguide and comparison with the waveguide without SRR (red dashed line).

parameters are used for optimization, each ant movement requires the evaluation of 8 possible solutions.
After several iterations of the optimization algorithm, the final optimized SRR dimensions are r_i: 6.4mm, r_o: 7.6mm, d_g: 1.4mm and unit cell period: 15.6mm. With these dimensions the dispersion diagram is the one shown in Figure 19. There is a backward mode at a low frequency of approximately 1.8GHz. For the sake of comparison, the dispersion diagram of the same waveguide with the dielectric loaded walls but without the SRR loading is shown in the same Figure 19, in which a total absence of propagating modal passbands below the waveguide cutoff is clear. In the presented frequency range, three additional modes appear as a consequence of the SRR loading.
The dispersion diagram for the SRR loaded waveguide with the optimized SRR dimensions shows a narrow passband near 2GHz, whilst the original waveguide cutoff is slightly over 4GHz. Thus a significant degree of miniaturization has been achieved.

3.4.3 Experimental results

A demonstrator has been manufactured whose dimensions correspond to the ones described in the previous section for the optimized case. Figure 20.a shows a picture of the manufactured waveguide with the top wall open in order to show the SRR array of 12 elements which is placed on each wall. As the field of the SRR-attributed modes is weak in the center of the waveguide, the feeding system consists of two vertical probes allocated close to the lateral walls, i.e., close to the SRR. These two probes for each port, were excited with a rat-race that was designed at the operation frequency (Quevedo-Teruel et al. (2009)).
At the operation frequency, both even and odd modes are, in principle, possible. The rat-race is used to divide the signal in two ports with the same phase or a 180° difference, obtaining an even or odd mode, respectively. The two rat-races were placed at each end of the waveguide and the transmission coefficient between them (S_{12}) was measured. The measurement results are presented in Figure 20.b for the frequency range in which the new passband is created. The odd mode presents a higher level of transmission when compared to the even one. In the figure, the results for the same waveguide but without the SRR loadings are included for comparison purposes. Although the transmission is low, it is still 30dB higher than the levels outside the new SRR-attributed passband. Hence, this new transmission band which would

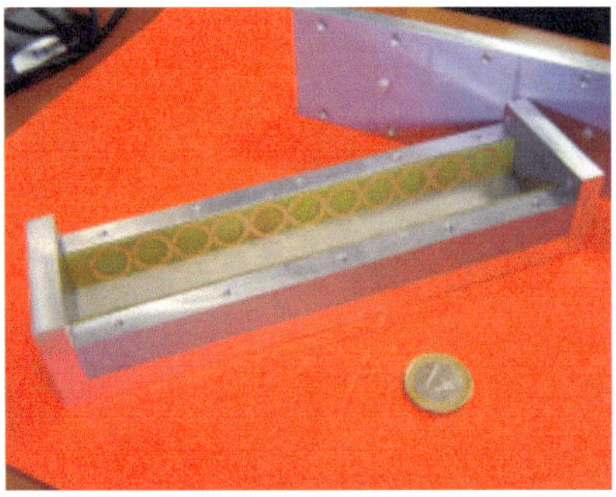

(a) Manufactured waveguide

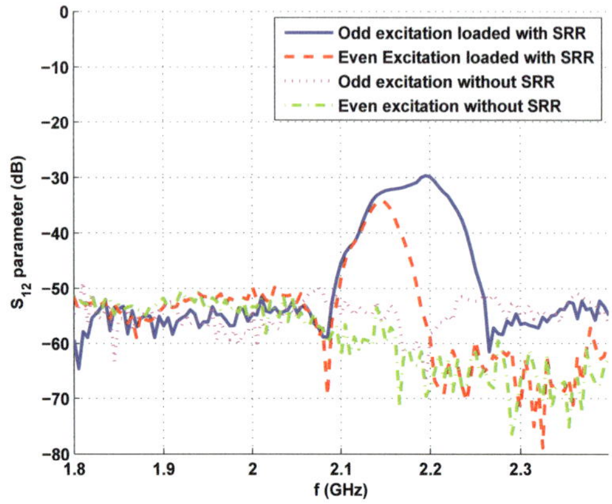

(b) S_{21}

Fig. 20. Measured transmission coefficient with and without SRR loading.

otherwise be absent in the empty waveguide, is clearly verified in these experimental results. The main reason for the low transmission is the mismatch due to the difference between the impedance of the experimental waveguide and the port impedance of the employed feeding probe.

3.5 Monopolar ultra wide band (UWB) microstrip antenna

As a last example of application of the ACO algorithm, an optimization of a monopolar UWB microstrip antenna is presented. Printed monopolar-type UWB antennas are becoming more and more popular. They can have many different shapes, as for instance the PICA (Planar Inverted Cone Antenna, Suh et al. (2004)), rectangular (Choi et al. (2004)), or circular disc. This type of antennas (in its both feeding versions: microstrip and co-planar) have been extensively studied (Liang et al. (2004), Lin & Huang (2005), Ren & Chang (2006), Suh et al. (2005)), due to their broadband and planar nature and hence, a low cost of manufacturing and low weight. However, the design of these antennas is not trivial, and a parametric study is not always enough since their parameters do not scale linearly in different frequency bands. Consequently, an optimization process is often convenient to obtain a design that fulfills given requirements.

As an example, a particular microstrip monopolar antenna has been optimized. The antenna is represented in Figure 21.a. The optimization goal is to get S_{11} below -10 dB in the largest possible band. To achieve this aim an ACO algorithm is employed together with the transient solver of $CST^{©}$ for obtaining the S_{11} of the antenna. A possible desirability function, for the design of such an antenna in a certain band is the one shown in Equation 14 where N represents the number of frequency points obtained by the simulation tool whose S_{11} values are above -10 dB in the band under study.

$$\eta_j = \frac{1}{N} \cdot \sum_{n=1}^{N} (10 - |S_{11}(f_n)|) \tag{14}$$

In this case, the following variables are chosen for optimization: the radii (r and R), the length of the ground plane (L), the width of the feeding line (W) and the distance between the circle

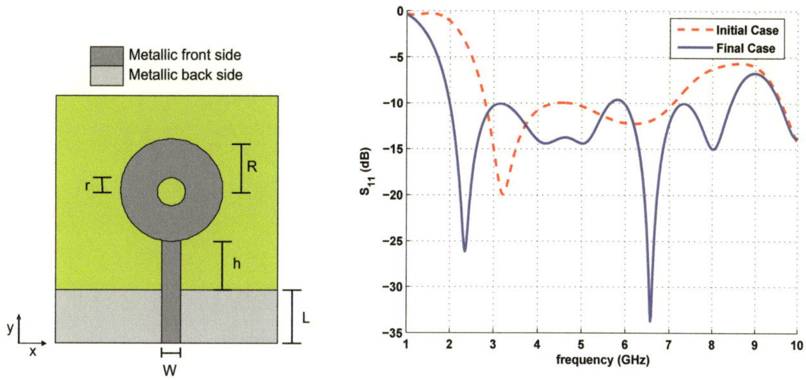

(a) Antenna geometry (b) S_{11}

Fig. 21. Monopolar UWB microstrip antenna and simulated return losses before and after optimization.

and the ground plane (h). The food has been established to be 11, in order to be all the time in the *forward way* of the ACO algorithm. The number of ants was 10 and the optimization parameters were: $\alpha = 1$ and $\beta = 30$. The discrete step of variation was 0.5 mm. Figure 21.b shows the initial and optimized S_{11} for the studied antenna for a band between 2 and 8 GHz with fiber glass as dielectric ($\epsilon_r = 4.5$ with 1.55 mm thickness).
The best obtained result has the following parameters: $R = 14.5$ mm, $r = 2.5$ mm, $h = 0.5$ mm, $L = 20$ mm and $W = 2.6$ mm. Figure 22 shows a photograph of the manufactured prototype and a comparison between simulations and measurements associated to this prototype. This antenna fulfills the S_{11} requirements in the frequency band between 2 and 8 GHz. The simulated radiation patterns for this antenna at different frequencies are plotted in Figure 23. The radiation patterns have some variations when the frequency increases, since the optimization was developed only in terms of return losses.

4. Conclusion

In this chapter we have shown the possibilities of ACO algorithm for solving electromagnetic problems. Several examples illustrate the advantages of using this algorithm. Initially we have explored the possibilities of the algorithm for a classical optimization problem in electromagnetism: the array synthesis. We have shown through different examples how the ACO algorithm is as useful as other types of algorithms such as Genetics or Particle Swarm to be applied in this type of problems.
However the interesting performance of this algorithm for electromagnetic designs is shown with examples where the evaluation of the goodness of a potential solution is computationally very costly. Three examples of such type of problems have been as well studied along this chapter. In all of them the implemented algorithm was able of outperform an initial good solution obtained after parametric studies. This demonstrates the enormous potential of the algorithm in this field of application.

(a) Manufactured prototype

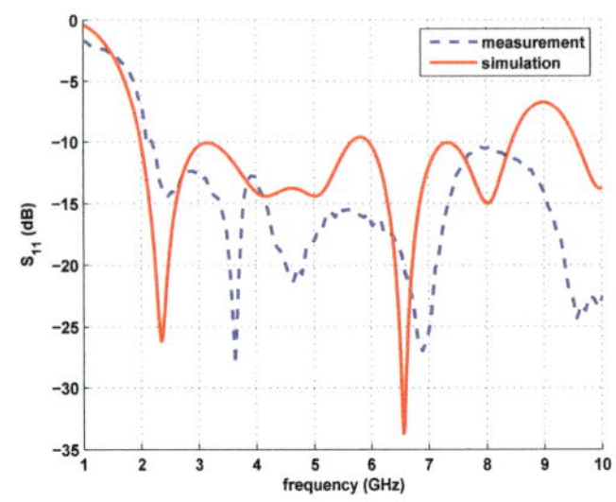

(b) S_{11}

Fig. 22. Measured S_{11} parameter after optimization for the monopolar UWB microstrip antenna

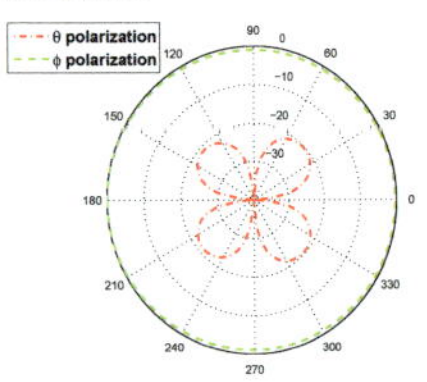

(a) $\phi = 0°$ (2GHz)

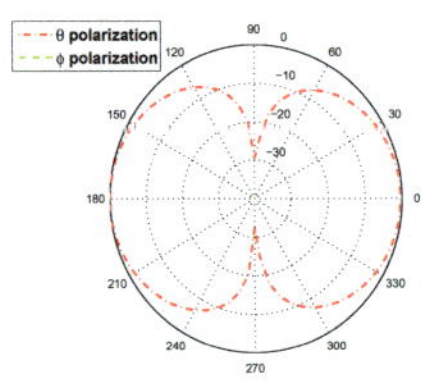

(b) $\phi = 90°$ (2GHz)

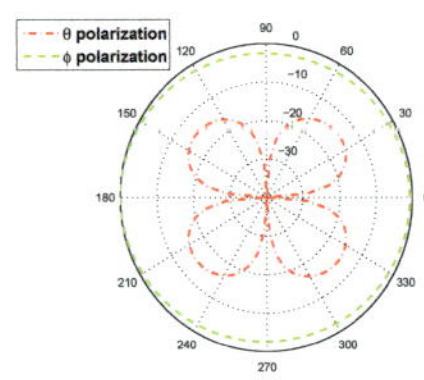

(c) $\phi = 0°$ (3GHz)

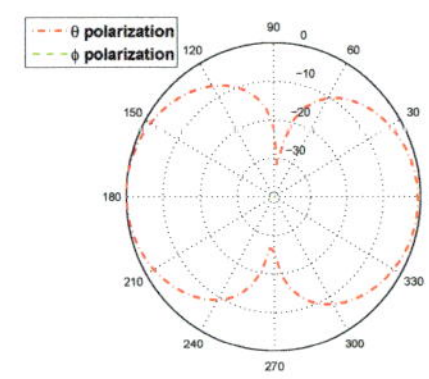

(d) $\phi = 90°$ (3GHz)

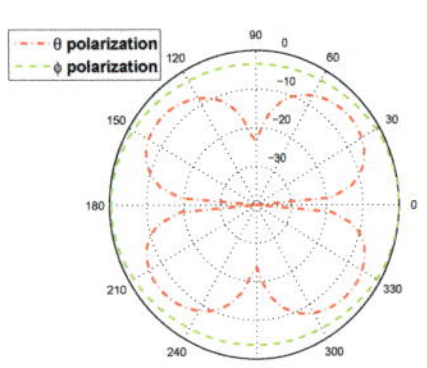

(e) $\phi = 0°$ (4GHz)

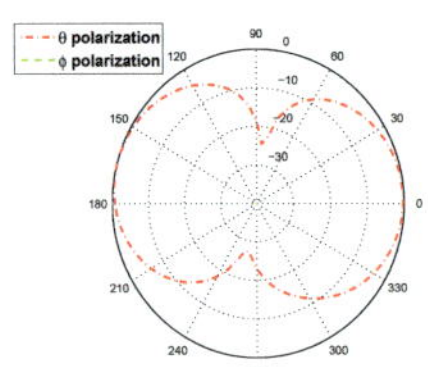

(f) $\phi = 90°$ (4GHz)

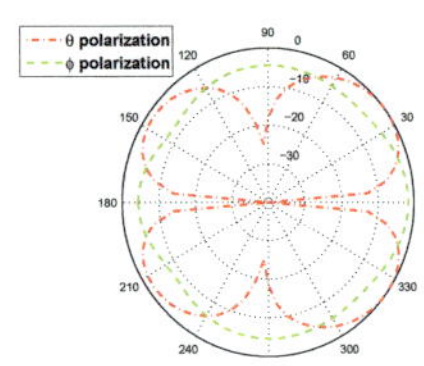

(g) $\phi = 0°$ (5GHz)

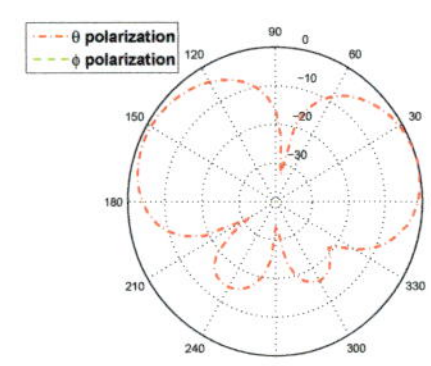

(h) $\phi = 90°$ (5GHz)

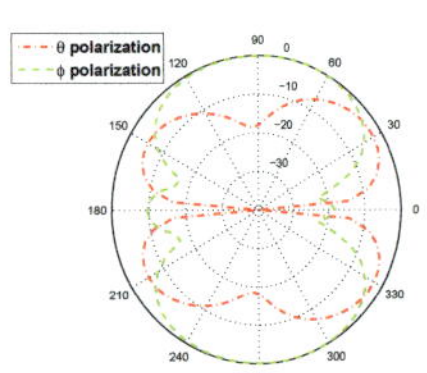

(i) $\phi = 0°$ (6GHz)

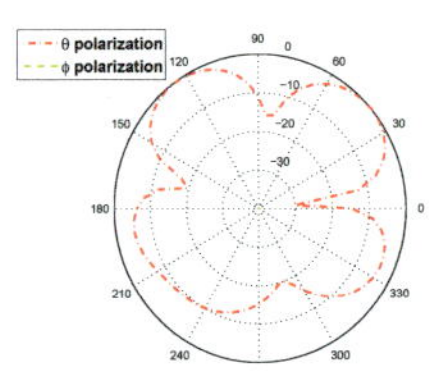

(j) $\phi = 90°$ (6GHz)

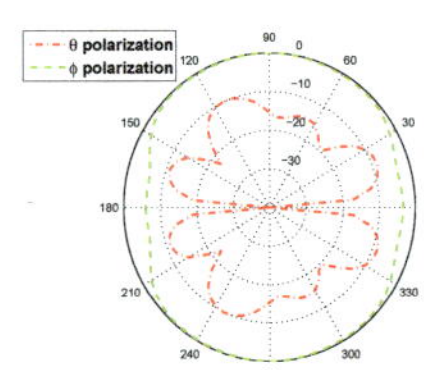

(k) $\phi = 0°$ (7GHz)

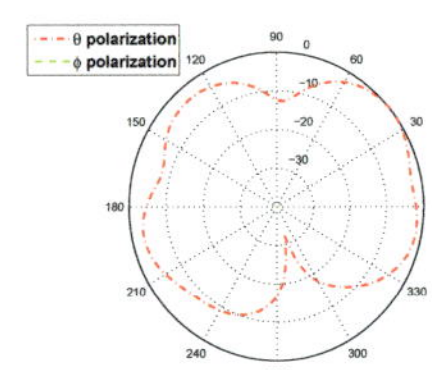

(l) $\phi = 90°$ (7GHz)

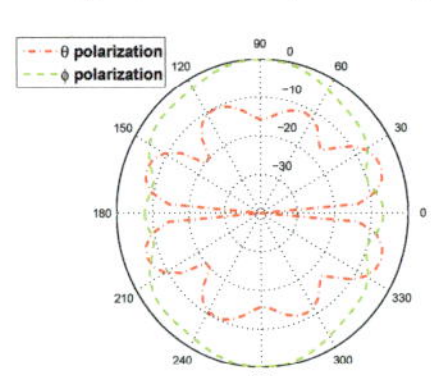

(m) $\phi = 0°$ (8GHz)

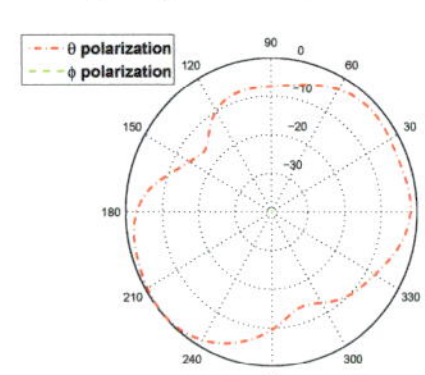

(n) $\phi = 90°$ (8GHz)

Fig. 23. Simulated radiation patterns of the optimized monopolar UWB Microstrip Antenna.

5. References

Ahuja, A. & Pahwa, A. (2005). Using ant colony optimization for loss minimization in distribution networks, *Proceedings of the 37th Annual North American Power Symposium*, pp. 470–474.

Ares-Pena, F. J., Rodriguez-Gonzalez, J. A., Villanueva-Lopez, E. & Rengarajan, S. R. (1999). Genetic algorithms in the design and optimization of antenna array patterns, *IEEE Transactions on Antennas and Propagation* 47(3): 506–510.

Bamford, L. D., James, J. R. & Fray, A. F. (1997). Minimising mutual coupling in thick substrate microstrip antenna arrays, *Electronics Letter* 33(8): 648–650.

Bullnheimer, B., Hartl, R. & Strauss, C. (1999). A new rank based version of the ant system - a computational study, *Central Eur. J. Oper. Res. Econ.* 7(1).

Burokur, S. N., Latrach, M. & Toutain, S. (2007). Influence of split ring resonators on the properties of propagating structures, *IET Microwaves, Antennas and Propagation* 1(1): 94–99.

Caminita, F., Costanzo, S., Di Massa, G., Guarnieri, G., Maci, S., Mauriello, G. & Venneri, I. (2009). Reduction of patch antenna coupling by using a compact EBG formed by shorted strips with interlocked branch-stubs, *IEEE Antennas and Wireless Propagation Letters* 8: 811–814.

Chiau, C., Chen, X. & Parini, C. (2003). A microstrip patch antenna on the embedded multi-period EBG structure, *Proceedings of 6th International Symposium on Antennas, Propagation and EM Theory, 2003.*, pp. 96–99.

Choi, S. H., Park, J. K., Kim, S. K. & Park, J. Y. (2004). A new ultra-wideband antenna for UWB applications, *Microwave and Optical Technology Letters* 40: 339–401.

Coleman, C. M., Rothwell, E. J. & Ross, J. E. (2004). Investigation of simulated annealing, ant-colony optimization, and genetic algorithms for self-structuring antennas, *IEEE Transactions on Antennas and Propagation* 52(4): 1007–1014.

Dorigo, M., Birattari, M., Blum, C., Gambardella, L. M., Mondada, F. & Sttzle, T. (2004). *Ant Colony Optimization and Swarm Intelligence*, Springer.

Dorigo, M., Caro, G. D. & Gambardella, L. M. (1999). Ant algorithms for discrete optimization, *Artificial Life* 5(2): 137–172.

Dorigo, M., Maniezzo, V. & Colorni, A. (1996). Ant system: Optimization by a colony of cooperating agents, *IEEE Transactions on Systems, MAN, and Cybernetics-Part B* 26(1): 29–41.

Dorigo, M. & Stutzle, T. (2004). *Ant Colony Optimization*, The MIT Press.

Esteban, J., Camacho-Penalosa, C., Page, J., Martin-Guerrero, T. & Marquez-Segura, E. (2005). Simulation of negative permittivity and negative permeability by means of evanescent waveguide modes-theory and experiment, *IEEE Transactions on Microwave Theory and Techniques* 53(4): 1506–1514.

Falcone, F., Martin, F., Bonache, J., Marqués, R., Lopetegi, T. & Sorolla, M. (2004). Left handed coplanar waveguide band pass filters based on bi-layer split ring resonators, *IEEE Microwave and Wireless Component Letters* 14(1): 10–12.

Fu, Y. & Yuan, N. (2004). Elimination of scan blindness in phased array of microstrip patches using electromagnetic bandgap materials, *IEEE Antennas and Wireless Propagation Letters* 3: 64–65.

Goussetis, G., Feresidis, A. & Vardaxoglou, J. (2006). Tailoring the AMC and EBG characteristics of periodic metallic arrays printed on grounded dielectric substrate, *IEEE Transactions on Antennas and Propagation* 54(1): 82–89.

Haupt, R. L. (1994). Thinned arrays using genetic algorithms, *IEEE Transactions on Antennas and Propagation* 42(7): 993–999.

Haupt, R. L. (2005). Interleaved thinned linear arrays, *IEEE Transactions on Antennas and Propagation* 53(9): 2858–2864.

Haupt, R. L. & Werner, D. H. (2007). *Genetic Algorithms in Electromagnetics*, Wiley.

Hoshyar, R., Jamali, S. H. & Locus, C. (2000). Ant colony algorithm for finding good interleaving pattern in turbo codes, *IEE Proceedings on Communications* 147(5): 257–262.

Hrabar, S., Bartolic, J. & Sipus, Z. (2005). Waveguide miniaturization using uniaxial negative permeability metamaterial, *IEEE Transactions on Antennas and Propagation* 53(1): 110–119.

Inclán-Sánchez, L., Rajo-Iglesias, E., González-Posadas, V. & Vázquez-Roy, J. (2005). Design of periodic metallo-dielectric structure for broadband multilayer patch antenna, *Microwave and Optical Technology Letters* 44(5): 418–421.

James, J. R. & Hall, P. S. (1997). *Handbook of Microstrip and Printed Antennas*, New York: Wiley.

Jin, N. & Rahmat-Samii, Y. (2007). Advances in particle swarm optimization for antenna designs: Real-number, binary, single-objective and multiobjective implementations, *IEEE Transactions on Antennas and Propagation* 55(3): 556–567.

Jitha, B., Nimisha, C. S., Aanandan, C. K., Mohanan, P. & Vasudevan, K. (2006). SRR loaded waveguide band rejection filter with adjustable bandwidth, *Microwave and Optical Technology Letters* 48(7): 1427–1429.

Kehn, M. N. M., Nannetti, M., Cucini, A., Maci, S. & Kildal, P.-S. (2006). Analysis of dispersion in dipole-FSS loaded hard rectangular waveguide, *IEEE Transactions on Antennas and Propagation* 54(8): 2275–2282.

Kehn, M., Quevedo-Teruel, O. & Rajo-Iglesias, E. (2008). Split-ring resonator loaded waveguides with multiple stopbands, *Electronics Letters* 44(12): 714–716.

Khodier, M. M. & Christodoulou, C. G. (2005). Linear array geometry synthesis with minimun sidelobe level and null control using particle swarm optimization, *IEEE Transactions on Antennas and Propagation* 53(8): 2674–2679.

Liang, J., Chiau, C. C., Chen, X. & Parini, C. G. (2004). Printed circular disc monopole antenna for ultra-wideband applications, *Electronic Letters* 40(20): 1246–1247.

Liang, Y.-C. & Smith, A. E. (2004). An ant colony optimization algorithm for the redundancy allocation problem (RAP), *IEEE Transactions on Reliability* 53(3): 417–423.

Lin, S.-Y. & Huang, K.-C. (2005). A compact microstrip antenna for GPS and DCS application, *IEEE Transactions on Antennas and Propagation* 53(3): 1227–1229.

Marqués, R., Martel, J., Mesa, F. & Medina, F. (2002). Left-handed media simulation and transmission of EM waves in sub-wavelength SRR-loaded metallic waveguides, *Physical Review Letters* 89(18): 183901/1–4.

Pozar, D. M. (1987). Radiation and scattering from a microstrip patch on a uniaxial substrate, *IEEE Transactions on Antennas and Propagation* 35(6): 613–621.

Pozar, D. M. & Schaubert, D. H. (1995). *Microstrip Antennas: The Analysis and Design of Microstrip Antennas and Arrays*, Wiley-IEEE Press.

Premprayoon, P. & Wardkein, P. (2005). Topological communication network design using ant colony optimization, *The 7th International Conference on Advanced Communication Technology*, Vol. 2, pp. 1147–1151.

Quevedo-Teruel, O. & Rajo-Iglesias, E. (2006). Ant colony optimization in thinned array synthesis with minimum sidelobe level, *IEEE Antennas and Wireless Propagation*

Letters 5: 349–352.

Quevedo-Teruel, O., Rajo-Iglesias, E. & Kehn, M. N. M. (2009). Numerical and experimental studies of split ring resonators loaded on the sidewalls of rectangular waveguides, *IET Microwaves, Antennas and Propagation* 3(8): 1262–1270.

Quevedo-Teruel, O., Rajo-Iglesias, E. & Oropesa-Garcia, A. (2007). Hybrid algorithms for electromagnetic problems and the no-free-lunch framework, *IEEE Transactions on Antennas and Propagation* 55(3): 742–749.

Rajo-Iglesias, E. & Quevedo-Teruel, O. (2007). Linear array synthesis using an ant colony optimization based algorithm, *IEEE Antennas and Propagation Magazine* 49(2): 70–79.

Rajo-Iglesias, E., Quevedo-Teruel, O. & Inclán-Sánchez, L. (2008). Mutual coupling reduction in patch antenna arrays by using a planar EBG structure and a multilayer dielectric substrate, *IEEE Transactions on Antennas and Propagation* 56(6): 1648–1655.

Rajo-Iglesias, E., Quevedo-Teruel, O. & Kehn, M. (2009). Multiband SRR loaded rectangular waveguide, *IEEE Transactions on Antennas and Propagation* 57(5): 1571–1575.

Ren, Y.-J. & Chang, K. (2006). An annular ring antenna for UWB communications, *IEEE Antennas and Wireless Propagation Letters* 5: 274–276.

Robinson, J. & Rahmat-Samii, Y. (2004). Particle swarm optimization in electromagnetics, *IEEE Transactions on Antennas and Propagation* 52(2): 397–407.

Schwartzman, L. (1967). Element behavior in a thinned array, *IEEE Transaction on Antennas and Propagation* 15(4): 571–572.

Shelkovnikov, A. & Budimir, D. (2006). Left-handed rectangular waveguide bandstop filters, *Microwave and Optical Technology Letters* 48(5): 846–848.

Sim, K. M. & Sun, W. H. (2003). Ant colony optimization for routing and load-balancing: Survey and new directions, *IEEE Transactions on Systems, Man and Cybernetics, Part A* 33(5): 560–572.

Suh, S.-Y., Stutzman, W. & Davis, W. (2004). A new ultrawideband printed monopole antenna: The planar inverted cone antenna (PICA), *IEEE Transactions on Antennas and Propagation* 52(5): 1361–1364.

Suh, S.-Y., Stutzman, W. L., Davis, W. A., Waltho, A. E., Skeba, K. W. & Schiffer, J. L. (2005). A UWB antenna with a stop-band notch in the 5-ghz WLAN band, *IEEE/ACES International Conference on Wireless Communications and Applied Computational Electromagnetics*, pp. 203–207.

Tennant, A., Dawoud, M. & Anderson, A. (1994). Array pattern nulling by element position perturbations using a genetic algorithm, *Electronic Letters* 30(3): 174–176.

Wang, X.-N., Feng, Y.-J. & Feng, Z.-R. (2005). Ant colony optimization for image segmentation, *Proceedings of 2005 International Conference on Machine Learning and Cybernetics*, Vol. 9, pp. 5355–5360.

Yan, K. & Lu, Y. (1997). Sidelobe reduction in array-pattern synthesis using genetic algorithm, *IEEE Transactions on Antennas and Propagation* 45(7): 1117–1122.

Yang, F. & Rahmat-Samii, Y. (2003). Microstrip antennas integrated with electromagnetic band-gap (EBG) structures: A low mutual coupling design for array applications, *IEEE Transaction on Antennas and Propagation* 51(10): 2936 – 2946.

Yang, F. & Rahmat-Samii, Y. (2009). *Electromagnetic Band Gap Structures in Antenna Engineering*, Cambridge University Press.

Yang, H.-Y. D., Kim, R. & Jackson, D. R. (2000). Design consideration for modeless integrated circuit substrates using planar periodic patches, *IEEE Transactions on Microwave Theory and Techniques* 48(12): 2233–2239.

Yang, L., Fan, M., Chen, F., She, J. & Feng;, Z. (2005). A novel compact electromagnetic-bandgap EBG structure and its applications for microwave circuits, *IEEE Transactions on Microwave Theory and Techniques* 53(1): 183–190.

Zheng, Q.-R., Fu, Y.-Q. & Yuan, N.-C. (2008). A novel compact spiral electromagnetic band-gap (EBG) structure, *IEEE Transactions on Antennas and Propagation* 56(6): 1656–1660.